PRAISE FOR THE GRAND SLAM

"FROST IDENTIFIES WHAT MAKES JONES CONTINUALLY INTERESTING AND STARTLINGLY CONTEMPORARY."
—SPORTS ILLUSTRATED

"IF YOU THOUGHT YOU KNEW THE STORY OF BOBBY JONES AND THE GRAND SLAM, THEN THINK AGAIN: THIS BOOK IS THE ENGROSSINGLY DEFINITIVE ACCOUNT."
—SCOTTISH GOLF MAGAZINE

"VERY WELL DONE. HIGHLY RECOMMENDED FOR ALL SPORTS COLLECTIONS." —LIBRARY JOURNAL

"FROST UNDERSTANDS PACE AND STRUCTURE, AND HE HAS A GIFT FOR DRAMATIZING HISTORIC GOLF MATCHES AND MAKING THEM SEEM SUSPENSEFUL ALL OVER AGAIN."
—THE NEW YORK TIMES BOOK REVIEW

THE
GRAND SLAM

ALSO BY MARK FROST

The Greatest Game Ever Played

THE
GRAND SLAM

BOBBY JONES, AMERICA,
AND THE STORY OF GOLF

MARK FROST

HYPERION

NEW YORK

Library of Congress Cataloging-in-Publication Data

Frost, Mark
    The grand slam : Bobby Jones, America, and the story of golf / Mark Frost.—1st ed.
        p. cm.
    ISBN 1-4013-0108-8
    1. Jones, Bobby, 1902–1971.   2. Golfers—United States—Biography.
I. Title.
GV964.J6F76 2004
796.352'092—dc22
[B]

                                                                                    2004052353

PAPERBACK ISBN 1-4013-0751-5

Hyperion books are available for special promotions and premiums. For details contact Michael Rentas, Assistant Director, Inventory Operations, Hyperion, 77 West 66th Street, 11th floor, New York, New York 10023 or call 212-456-0133.

FIRST PAPERBACK EDITION

Designed by Lorelle Graffeo

10   9   8   7   6   5   4   3   2   1

For my father, Warren,

and my son, Travis

CONTENTS

PART THREE THE GRAND SLAM

THE PLAYERS

BRITISH PROFESSIONALS

JAMES BRAID, Earlsferry, Scotland, 1870–1950

ARCHIE COMPSTON, Wolverhampton, England, 1893–1962

GEORGE DUNCAN, Methlick, Scotland, 1883–1964

ABE MITCHELL, East Grinstead, England, 1887–1947

TED RAY, Jersey, England, 1877–1943

JOHN HENRY TAYLOR, Northam, England, 1871–1963

HARRY VARDON, Jersey, England, 1870–1937

TOM VARDON, Jersey, England, 1872–1942

BRITISH AMATEURS

JOHN BALL, Hoylake, England, 1861–1940

BERNARD DARWIN, Kent, England, 1876–1961

HAROLD HILTON, West Kirby, England, 1869–1942

CYRIL JAMES HASTINGS TOLLEY, London, England, 1895–1978

JOYCE WETHERED, Maldon, England, 1901–1997
ROGER WETHERED, Maldon, England, 1899–1983

AMERICAN EXPATRIATE PROFESSIONALS

THOMAS DICKSON ARMOUR, Edinburgh, Scotland, 1895–1968
JAMES BARNES, Lelant, England, 1887–1966
"LIGHTHORSE" HARRY COOPER, Leatherhead, England, 1904–2000
ROBERT CRUICKSHANK, Granton-on-Spey, Scotland, 1894–1975
JOCK HUTCHISON, St. Andrews, Scotland, 1884–1977
WILLIE MACFARLANE, Aberdeen, Scotland, 1890–1961
STEWART "KILTIE" MAIDEN, Carnoustie, Scotland, 1886–1948
MACDONALD SMITH, Carnoustie, Scotland, 1890–1949
CYRIL WALKER, Manchester, England, 1892–1948

AMERICAN PROFESSIONALS

MIKE BRADY, Brighton, Massachusetts, 1887–1972
LEO DIEGEL, Detroit, Michigan, 1899–1951
AL ESPINOSA, Monterey, California, 1894–1957
JOHN J. FARRELL, White Plains, New York, 1901–1988
WALTER HAGEN, Rochester, New York, 1892–1969
WILLIAM MEHLHORN, Elgin, Illinois, 1898–1989
EUGENE SARAZEN, Harrison, New York, 1902–1999
HORTON SMITH, Springfield, Missouri, 1908–1963
JOE TURNESA, Elmsford, New York, 1901–1991
ANDREW ALBERT WATROUS, Yonkers, New York, 1899–1984

AMERICAN AMATEURS

PERRY ADAIR, Atlanta, Georgia, 1900–1953
CHARLES "CHICK" EVANS JR., Indianapolis, Indiana, 1890–1979
ALEXA STIRLING FRASER, Atlanta, Georgia, 1897–1977

ROBERT GARDNER, Hinsdale, Illinois, 1890–1956

JOHN GOODMAN, Omaha, Nebraska, 1910–1970

WATTS GUNN, Macon, Georgia, 1905–1994

S. DAVIDSON HERRON, Pittsburgh, Pennsylvania, 1897–1956

HARRISON "JIMMY" JOHNSTON, St. Paul, Minnesota, 1896–1969

ROBERT TYRE JONES, Atlanta, Georgia, 1902–1971

CHARLES BLAIR MACDONALD, Niagara Falls, New York, 1856–1939

FRANCIS OUIMET, Brookline, Massachusetts, 1893–1967

JESS SWEETSER, St. Louis, Missouri, 1902–1989

WALTER TRAVIS, Maldon, Australia, 1862–1927

GEORGE VOIGT, Buffalo, New York, 1894–1985

GEORGE VON ELM, Salt Lake City, Utah, 1901–1960

AMERICAN JOURNALISTS

OSCAR BANE "POP" KEELER, Chicago, Illinois, 1881–1950

AL LANEY, Pensacola, Florida, 1896–1988

GRANTLAND RICE, Murfreesboro, Tennessee, 1880–1954

PROLOGUE

In an average year lightning strikes the United States over 22 million times. Your chance of being hit by one of those strikes is 1 in 300,000: 7.7 casualties per million people per million lightning strikes. Lightning kills a hundred people a year in the United States alone, and critically injures over a thousand. An average bolt carries the power of 30 million volts, and somewhere between 10,000 and 200,000 amps, enough electricity to illuminate a hundred-watt bulb for six months. On July 10, 1926, lightning strikes detonated a naval ammunition depot in Mount Hope, New Jersey, killing nineteen people and injuring thirty-eight others.

On July 29, 1929, a young Atlanta lawyer named Bobby Jones and the members of his regular Monday afternoon foursome were making the turn onto the back nine at East Lake Country Club when they noticed a bank of towering thunderclouds building to the southeast. Bobby had grown up on the East Lake course, dodged a hundred storms during his life there, and decided they would have time to finish their round before the body of the storm threatened them. The first drops of rain began to fall as they putted out on the twelfth green, set near the right arm of the horseshoe-shaped lake that curves around the stately Tudor clubhouse and gives the course its name. As they made their way to the thirteenth tee, a bolt of lightning struck the tenth fairway less than forty yards to their right. Jones felt an ominous tingle surge through his metal spikes. He yelled to his buddies to make a run for the clubhouse, and they had no sooner changed direction than a second bolt hit a small tree at the back of the thirteenth tee, not twenty yards away, exactly where they'd been standing moments earlier. They sprinted across the small bridge that spans the northeast corner of the lake, leading back to the eighteenth green and clubhouse. Huddled under their umbrellas, Jones and his friends lost count of the lightning strikes hammering down on the course around them, a ferocious concentration of energy unlike any storm they'd ever seen.

As they hustled across the broad gravel drive, the last stretch of open ground before the safety of the portico sheltering the locker-room entrance, a monstrous bolt blasted the high double chimney on top of the clubhouse. The chimney exploded in a shower of bricks and mortar. Jones felt his umbrella collapse around his head and he blindly staggered the last few steps to the protection of the door. Safely inside, the men shared a nervous, gasping laugh of relief. When Jones discarded his umbrella and turned around, his friends gasped again: the back of his shirt had been ripped from collar to waist, and he was bleeding from a six-inch gash that ran from his right shoulder to the middle of his spine. A heavy fragment of the chimney had punched through his umbrella, struck him a glancing blow, and torn the shirt from his back. He hadn't felt a thing. Only now, as the adrenaline began to burn off, did he even realize he'd been injured. The men shared a moment of silent wonder at how close — inches — their great friend had come to certain death. Bobby was the first to break the tension with a joke — the golf gods were obviously displeased with him, but at least he knew where to send the bill for a new shirt. The luck of the Irish again: What else would you expect from a man born on St. Paddy's Day? Drinks flowed from the jug of bootlegged corn liquor Jones stored in his locker, the worst-kept secret at the club; a survivor's warmth rekindled in them, and the shadow passed.

When the storm moved through they walked outside and stared again in wonder: the driveway was littered, a debris field of bricks and mortar, some fragments scattered as far as the eighteenth tee box, three hundred yards away. Any one of those objects, thought Jones, could have killed him had it struck him on the head. He took it in stride, fully aware that no matter how much good fortune came your way, one day the final bill comes due. The gods get the last laugh. Time is on their side. A fatal blow had been struck, but no one would know it for twenty-five years.

The myth that lightning never strikes twice in the same place is exactly that; the mast atop the Empire State Building, for example, attracts on average a hundred bolts a year. Lightning of an equally powerful but more metaphysical variety had also centered Robert Tyre Jones Jr. in its sights on the old twelfth hole at East Lake, striking him square sixteen years earlier. Its impact changed the course of his life, propelling him forward to the abundant promise of this moment in 1929, already one of the celebrated names of his age and on the cusp of immortality, as surely as this second strike would lead to his ruin.

THE

GRAND SLAM

PART ONE

EVOLUTION OF A GENIUS

No matter what happens, keep on hitting the ball.

— HARRY VARDON

Bobby Jones, age six.

CHAPTER ONE

East Lake

On September 20, 1913, America welcomed a new hero into its sporting pantheon and for the first time the broad middle of the country embraced with curiosity and enthusiasm the exotic game he'd mastered. Playing alone on rain-soaked fairways at The Country Club in Brookline, Massachusetts, against the two greatest golfers in the world, Francis Ouimet defeated Harry Vardon and Ted Ray in an eighteen-hole play-off to win the United States Open Championship. The twenty-year-old former caddie personified a cherished American ideal: that anyone with perseverance, modesty, and backbone could rise above the limits imposed by humble beginnings to achieve greatness. Seldom discussed is how often a person's real problems begin with that success. Lesser men might have failed a hundred ways under the pressures of Ouimet's sudden fame, but Francis stood up to that challenge and every other that life subsequently put in his path. You could find in him no trace of destructive pride, ego, false humility, or spite, and he stayed true to the best in himself until the day he died. He never turned professional, choosing instead to focus on a business career and raising a family. In spite of this he remained a first-rate player for nearly twenty years and would go on to win two National Amateur Championships, but in the long run his sterling character contributed even more to the development of the game than his accomplishments as a player. Golf could not have built a better ambassador in God's own laboratory.

Vardon and Ray had toured America for months leading up to the 1913 Open, facing every one of the country's finest players without suffering a loss. Victory by one or the other of them had all but been conceded before the national championship; instead, Ouimet's shocking defeat of the two British immortals made banner headlines across America and around the world. Teenaged boys in particular embraced Francis as a role model and, for once, even their parents approved. Caddie shacks and clubhouses swarmed with new recruits, professionals and amateurs alike, eager to follow Francis into the game. Many would go on to memorable careers, a select few earning the credentials to land them in a Hall of Fame that hadn't yet been dreamt of. Only one of them would exceed the impact of Francis's historic breakthrough, relegate the memory of an entire generation of greats to also-ran status, and give rise to a legend that casts shadows over the American sporting landscape to this day.

While his improbable championship spread the gospel of the game and heralded a bright future for native-born players, Francis Ouimet unknowingly served as a kind of secular stand-in for John the Baptist. The game's messiah was coming, and he was a lot closer at hand than anybody realized. He would emerge from the unlikeliest ground, and only after a cast of extraordinary characters necessary to shape his formative years had assembled around him. Call it destiny or coincidence, but by October of 1913 all the elements necessary for the creation of a sporting miracle had aligned, and they required just one last spark to ignite the subsequent chain of events. As fate, or chance, would have it, the same two players who had precipitated Francis Ouimet's triumph were about to provide that charge.

Harry Vardon and Ted Ray sailed into New York and embarked on their barnstorming exhibition tour of America in early August 1913. Designed to climax at Brookline in September with a Vardon or Ray victory at the Open, their grand scheme unraveled on that soggy Saturday when Ouimet seized the cup for the United States. The architect of that scheme, their robber baron patron, megalomaniacal Fleet Street mogul Lord Northcliffe, sailed back to Britain bitter and empty-handed. The two defeated sportsmen, professionals to the end, declined Northcliffe's offer to join his early exit and vowed to complete an additional month of appearances, originally conceived as an extended victory march after their anticipated Open triumph. To their credit they honored their commitments, and, to their surprise, Harry and Ted enjoyed their time after the Open more than the hectic weeks leading up to it.

Harry in particular relished the country's relaxed, class-free openness, and ever since his earlier exhibition tour in 1900 first introduced golf to much of the country, Americans had returned that affection with compound interest. Ted observed that the fierce, joyful excitement Ouimet brought to their show-down restored Harry's passion for the game. After years of frustration as a cele-brated hero denied entry into English society's upper ranks because of his low birth, Harry viewed the sport as a job, a grind, and by his own admission had for some time been going through the motions. It was Ted's opinion that as a result of the affectionate respect paid to him by Francis and his fellow Ameri-cans, Harry Vardon found a lasting peace inside his own skin.

A vibrant Indian summer had settled over Georgia when Harry and Ted rolled into Atlanta during the second week of October 1913. A two-day, seventy-two-hole match had been arranged with the best two local pros the New Center of the South had to offer: Willie Mann from Druid Hills and Stewart Maiden of East Lake Country Club. On Saturday, October 11, the four men teed it up at East Lake, a sprawling entertainment complex built on the site of a turn-of-the-century amusement park. National sports headlines the next day would feature the Philadelphia Athletics' dismantling of the New York Giants in the World Series, their third championship in the last four years. Reporters down south, where no professional baseball team would put down roots for nearly half a century, knew their lead story was taking shape on the fairways five miles east of downtown Atlanta.

Atlanta had come back from the dead in the fifty years since Sherman's devastating March to the Sea had razed it to the ground. Beginning life as an obscure railway crossroads called Terminus, the city had become a crucial strategic target for Union forces seeking to decimate Southern resistance. The pain and suffering of what is to this day still referred to by some there as the "War of Northern Aggression" was for thousands of Atlantans in 1913 still a liv-ing memory. Two industries drove its rapid recovery: the fifteen railroad lines that made Atlanta the South's hub for transportation and trade, and a fizzy, bottled refreshment that began to be mass manufactured in 1892 called Coca-Cola. Originally marketed as a health tonic, America's first soft drink's rise in popularity coincided with the ascendance of the soda fountain as a social gathering place. Because they were introduced to dispense a variety of drinks with therapeutic properties—many of them marketed as "patent medicines"—soda fountains were attached to drugstores or pharmacies, a puzzling proximity that lingered far into the next century, long after "fountains" had stopped serving anything stronger than phosphates and milk shakes. Atlanta was chosen as the state's capital in 1877, and by 1900 its population had reached ninety thousand. Most residents viewed the city's rise from the ashes as the region's most important resurrection; they called it "the phoenix city," a modern capitalist center built along Yankee corporate lines, without relinquishing the style and social graces that characterized the traditional Southern way of life. Hope and pride, in short supply during the lean decades of Reconstruction, found new life in a city that appeared ready to put the bitterness of the Civil War behind it and shoulder a significant role in forging the young American century.

Private downtown athletic clubs served as vital gathering places for the business elites of early-century American cities. In 1898 the New South's first such club, the Atlanta Athletic Club, opened for business in a three-story brownstone on Auburn Avenue, featuring a gym, courts for racquet sports, and a grand dining room. The club was such a success that the original sixty-seven members began looking to expand their facilities. One charter member, banker Henry Atkinson, happened to be a close friend of Chicago business tycoon Charles Blair Macdonald, a crucial figure in golf's American development. A Niagara Falls native, Macdonald picked up the game while studying at the University of St. Andrews in Scotland, where his grandfather was a member of the Royal and Ancient Golfing Society. In need of an outlet for his new passion after returning home, Macdonald founded the Chicago Golf Club, the first eighteen-hole course in the United States, in 1892. A tireless advocate of the sport, Macdonald infected thousands of others with his incurable Scottish affliction. One of those men was Henry Atkinson, who happened to own a parcel of prime country real estate just beyond the Atlanta city limits that included the old East Lake amusement park. When the Athletic Club's vice president, Atlanta real estate mogul George Adair, approached him about acquiring the 187-acre property with the idea of creating a golf course on it, Atkinson replied, "Name your price."

The club's board of directors convinced the Atlanta Rapid Transit Company to extend an electric streetcar line out to the shores of East Lake in early 1904, and that July the Atlanta Athletic Club took possession of Atkinson's property. The line terminated a few steps outside the club entrance. Swimming and boating became the club's first official activities, a welcome respite from the brutal Southern heat, and four clay tennis courts were laid in that first summer. Telephone service took a year to organize, a single line at the exorbitant rate of three dollars a month. More than a few backs got scratched along the way: George Adair owned a substantial tract of undeveloped land adjacent to Atlanta's first country club—as did Asa Candler, another AAC member and owner of the Coca-Cola Company—and the area was soon crawling with exclusive summer homes. In 1905 a primitive seven-hole golf course appeared, a stopgap effort to satisfy early enthusiasts. The next year new club president George Adair imported an architect from Chicago named Tom Bendelow to expand the layout to a full eighteen. Ambitions for the project ran high; Henry Atkinson, who had played the original with C. B. Macdonald overseas, later remarked: "I could at times even visualize the birth of another St. Andrews."

Tom Bendelow was a native Scotsman, the son of a couple who owned a pie shop in Aberdeen. He immigrated to New York in 1892 and took a job as a typesetter at the New York Herald. Although he'd played golf as a youth, Bendelow stumbled into a career in the game almost entirely by accident. While setting the classifieds one day he spotted a want ad placed by a man looking for an instructor to teach the game of golf to his family on Long Island. The man turned out to be a Mr. Pratt, senior vice president of Standard Oil of New Jersey. During their interview, while struggling to decipher Bendelow's thick Scottish brogue, Pratt decided that since this confident young man spoke with the proper accent, the game must flow in his blood like single-malt whiskey. Before teaching the Pratts how to play, Bendelow laid out a short course on the grounds of their Oyster Harbor estate. He parlayed the presence of the Pratts on his resume into a stint as greenkeeper of New York City's municipal course at Van Cortlandt Park in the Bronx. When he remodeled the original nine-hole course and added a second nine, Tom Bendelow became the architect of America's first public eighteen-hole track. In the summer of 1900, Bendelow received an invitation to play in an exhibition in Connecticut with Harry Vardon, who had professed admiration for Bendelow's Bronx layout during a swing through New York. When Vardon moved on to Chicago and won the U.S. Open at Charles Blair Macdonald's Chicago Golf Club, Harry mentioned to Albert Spalding, who'd sponsored his tour, that he'd made the acquaintance of a talented new course designer.

A former star pitcher for the Boston Red Stockings, Albert Spalding had already made his fortune as America's first mass producer of sporting goods. He was convinced there was pure gold to be mined in the manufacture and sale of golf equipment and in 1900 hired three-time British Open champion Harry Vardon to tour the country and publicize a new Spalding golf ball called the "Vardon Flyer." The ball failed to catch on, not on its own merits but because the solid rubber "Haskell" ball was soon introduced, rendering Harry's old gutta-percha ball obsolete; but the widespread display of Harry's Olympian skills encouraged thousands to take an interest in the sport. That inspired Spalding to pursue another audacious marketing angle. If this strategy was going to work, however, he needed a man who could build golf courses in a hurry. Hundreds of them.

Spalding hired Tom Bendelow as the company's first official golf course consultant. Bendelow traveled relentlessly back and forth across the country, by rail and later in a custom touring car. He would arrive at dawn in the town engaging his services and walk the proposed golf course site, followed by a flock of anxious local dignitaries. After Bendelow picked an appropriate spot for the first tee, his assistant hammered the first of a color-coordinated series of stakes into the ground. Bendelow laid out the rest of the tees and greens on the fly, stakes going in every hundred yards, wending his way back to their starting place, eighteen holes later. Leaving behind standardized instructions for local contractors who would do the building—and an address where they could direct queries about construction—Bendelow was back on the road by sundown, moving on to his next appointment. The resulting courses universally featured flat, square greens and tee boxes, oblong cross-bunkers that split nearly every fairway, and strange triangular mounds called "chocolate drops" for their resemblance to the iconic Hershey's Kisses. These were more the product of utility than whimsy: instead of hauling away the tons of rocks turned up during construction, builders sorted them into piles and covered them with topsoil and sod, often in the middle of bunkers. A few survive today, odd as gnomes' hats.

For his traveling expert's sought-after services Spalding charged not a penny; his interest was in selling clubs and balls to the courses' new golfers, but the program proved such a success that within a few years Spalding tacked on a nominal fee of twenty-five dollars. After World War I, when golf course construction exploded, Bendelow went into business for himself, and made his first real money. In the first thirty years of the twentieth century Bendelow designed between seven hundred and a thousand golf courses. Only a few survive that in any way resemble his original designs; hundreds have vanished altogether. The majority were reworked within a few years by the next generation of architects, adding layers of sophistication not available when Bendelow first hit the road. A few gems squeaked through; he was not without talent, and while introducing the game to countless thousands of players his work did improve over time.

A strictly religious teetotaler and a devoted member of a nondenominational Christian sect called "the Brethren," Bendelow incorporated their stark beliefs about right and wrong into his work. He was an early adherent of what has since been identified as the penal school of course design: commit the sin of a bad shot and players pay for their transgression with a lost stroke. Bendelow's courses offered no hope of redemption, as the later, more progressive and forgiving, strategic school of course design would encourage. The harshly difficult Number Three course at Medinah Country Club, built outside Chicago in 1928—host to multiple Western and U.S. Opens—stands as a prime example of this species, and as the best Tom Bendelow eventually had to offer.

The same cannot be said, when it first came into existence, of his design at East Lake Country Club. The clubhouse and eighteen-hole golf course opened for business on the Fourth of July, 1908. Regardless of how rudimentary Bendelow's plans appeared, it took over two years of hard manual labor to carve its bones out of the rolling, heavily forested terrain. East Lake's list of playing members initially numbered less than twenty-five, ranging in age from six to forty. That original roster includes two names—one boy, one girl, both then under the age of ten—who would not only reach golf's Hall of Fame but be considered by many as the finest players America has ever produced. Without knowing it, East Lake was already a nursery for genius.

. . .

Harry Vardon and Ted Ray arrived for their match at East Lake on Saturday morning, July 11, 1913. They enjoyed a hot breakfast from the club's kitchen, served on outdoor tables; despite their celebrity, as working-class pros they were not allowed—here or at any other private club in the world—to set foot in the clubhouse. First to welcome them was one of their opponents that day, East Lake's resident professional, Stewart Maiden, a small, unassuming man from Carnoustie, Scotland. Carnoustie contributed a disproportionate number of recruits to the upstart American golf industry. The Smith brothers, Willie and Alex—the latter a past and future U.S. Open Champion—had hailed from there, and their younger brother, Macdonald, had recently joined them. Alex briefly worked as East Lake's first professional before turning over the reins to his young assistant and brother-in-law, Jimmy Maiden, a man more committed to servicing the members' needs than the ambitious Mr. Smith. For his troubles Jimmy pulled down sixty dollars a month and collected one dollar for every forty-five-minute lesson. He supplemented his guaranteed income with a pro's bread and butter: exclusive license to make, repair, and sell golf clubs in his shop to the members. In 1910 Jimmy moved on to the Nassau Country Club, in New York. East Lake's golfers voted to promote Stewart Maiden to replace his departing brother as their head professional.

The members at East Lake called him "Kiltie," which today might be considered a demeaning cultural stereotype, but the intent seemed born from affection. A compact, flat-faced, perpetually sunburned man, Stewart Maiden embodied the stereotype of the dour, laconic Scot. He possessed an uncanny ability to pinpoint and correct swing faults with a minimum of words, doling advice out with the inscrutable precision of a Zen master. Kiltie almost never addressed his students' problems verbally; for those who worked with him on a regular basis expressions or small gestures spoke volumes. He appears to have genuinely resented the emotional exertion required by speech. Never an easy man to know, he took scant interest in players without talent, with whom he was obligated to spend most of his time—the bane of the teaching pro—and he didn't suffer fools gladly. After one utterly hopeless longtime student hit his first six shots of a lesson dead sideways, Stewart asked: "Damn it, man, do you *have* to play golf?" He spoke these final words to another pathetic hacker: "The only thing for you to do is lay off for two weeks, then quit altogether."

By 1913 Stewart had also developed a serious dependence on strong drink, which did nothing to soften his sharp tongue. But during his first ten years at East Lake, blessed with students of rare ability, he offered instruction of magnificent value and inspired in them undying loyalty. A gifted player, Stewart lacked the temperament for a sustained competitive career—too demanding of his talent, too unforgiving of his faults—but his swing was a thing of beauty; balanced, rhythmic, and deceptively powerful. He had enormously strong hands that drove down and delivered crushing force to the ball at the conclusion of an indolent windup. When he got it going, and wasn't nursing a beady-eyed hangover, Stewart could hold his own with any pro in the world. That October he'd spent a week brushing up his game and had gone to bed without taking a single nip the night before his match against Vardon and Ray.

No players with their international pedigrees had ever ventured as far south as Atlanta before; this was golf's equivalent of Siberia, a million miles from the game's dominant Philadelphia–New York–Boston corridor, or its Midwestern stronghold in Chicago. As was often the case in the city's early bumptious years, when called upon to measure itself against the best of anything somewhere else had to offer, the local papers decided that Atlanta's pride was on trial. The little Scottish pro's professional pride was on the line as well, and in Stewart Maiden's universe, nothing counted for more.

Among the reporters roaming East Lake's grounds to follow their match that day was Oscar Bane Keeler, O.B. to his colleagues, better known as "Pop" to his friends. He was thirty-one years old and until this moment a man singularly devoted to making as little as possible out of a classical education. As a student he'd fallen in love with words and letters, but to date his affections had gone unrequited. He'd boxed some in his youth and could shoot skeet with passable skill, but by now Keeler appeared a thoroughly unpromising specimen; a tall, ungainly stork of a man, burdened with bad eyesight, declining motor skills, a weak constitution, and rapidly thinning hair. Not to suggest Keeler possessed no exceptional native gifts—charm, first and foremost; he could talk the birds out of the trees. Pop also possessed a photographic memory: he could recite volumes of verse like a babbling brook and turned out serviceable poems of his own by the dozen. He adored people of every stripe, male and female companionship—for vastly different reasons—and corn liquor, not necessarily in that order. Keeler also possessed a gregarious talent for collecting friendships that he faithfully maintained with bonds of trust and loyalty built to last a lifetime.

From the start of his career Keeler exhibited a gift for distilling unruly chunks of reality into sharply turned phrases, and he could type ten pages an hour without a single error; clearly Pop was born to be a newspaperman, but he had only recently arrived at that conclusion after a long, eventful detour. The son of a hard-driving businessman, during the first decade of his own career Keeler had been fired from a bank, two railroad offices, an iron foundry, a marble finishing mill, a fertilizer manufacturing outfit, and a Mexican silver mine. His last job as cashier for an insurance company ended abruptly in 1908 when a new accounting system he installed proved utterly indecipherable to anyone but himself.

A flirtation with suicide followed, one lonely afternoon on a railroad bridge over the Chattahoochee River. Although his account of this incident, written decades later, skates on a veneer of gallows humor, his despair seeps through; this brush with self-destruction was a close call. Pop had a wife and two kids at the time and had married well, on paper at least. His wife was the daughter of the owner of the Georgia Marble Company, where Keeler's father worked as general manager. Irreconcilable differences between the newlyweds arose immediately; Keeler was an untidy whirlwind who thrived on thrill and novelty. His wife had been in the market for a husband much more dull and conventional, and harbored ambitions of turning Pop in that direction. After a decade of misery, the Keelers were divorced in 1915. His wife vanishes afterward from Pop's every accounting of his life; she retired to a sprawling family estate in Marietta, Georgia, called Tranquilla, where she raised their children and never remarried. Whatever darkness drove him onto that bridge, Keeler never gave it full voice. One suspects the disintegration of his young family played the leading role, but self-confession wasn't the style of the age. Writers hadn't yet discovered, or readers developed, a voyeuristic hunger for guided tours of personal hells. Throughout his early years Keeler appeared heavily burdened by his successful father's disappointment in him. His flirtation with death ended with an epiphany that he was living the wrong life; Keeler came down off the bridge and shortly thereafter volunteered his services as a reporter to the managing editor of the *Atlanta Georgian*.

At this crossroads in his life Pop Keeler gave off an air of the grifter, the wised-up protagonist from a noir novel, drifting from job to job, living below his station and education, working on his advanced degree from the school of hard knocks. A few more bad breaks might've put him right back up on that bridge. Keeler knew how narrow his margin for error had become, because before the editor at the *Georgian* could turn him down, Keeler made him an offer he couldn't refuse. He would work for free, until such time as his new boss decided he was worth what he was being paid. After tracking down leads like a bloodhound and producing useful items for two weeks, Pop nailed down a real job on the payroll, at eighteen dollars a week—more than he had ever taken home in, as he put it, "ten and a half years of miscellaneous guerilla warfare about the outskirts of the world of business and finance."

Pop followed his year on the *Georgian* with three with the *Kansas City Star,* learning his trade from the ground up and making the acquaintance of a young fellow reporter named Ernest Hemingway. Pop cut his teeth on every kind of story: "hotels, zoos, personals, street-walkers, theaters, baseball, boxing." In 1912 he returned to the *Georgian* and the next year chanced upon the subject that would occupy him as a journalist for the next thirty-seven years. Keeler had begun playing golf during a boyhood summer in Lake Geneva, Wisconsin, in 1897; Southerners of means often traveled to the upper Midwest to escape the blistering seasonal heat. He spotted a story about the new sport in a magazine, and golf got its hooks into him the moment he picked up a club. When he moved back to Atlanta his interest flowered into an obsession, even though as a player he would only get steadily worse. Twelve years later Pop published a book entitled *The Autobiography of an Average Golfer,* a charitable assessment of the talents he describes in this account of his amateur career. Suffice it to say Keeler never once in his life broke 90, which makes *Average Golfer* a long two hundred fifty pages.

Fortunately, Pop also found substantially more skilled golfers to write about, beginning on that same October afternoon at East Lake Country Club.

Keeler could barely contain his excitement when he got off the streetcar at East Lake that morning. Pop connected with readers because he had such easy access to his own emotions. He picked up feelings in the air at sporting events as if they were radio waves and boiled them down into strong, declarative sentences, letting you experience whatever he witnessed as clearly as if he'd let you borrow his nervous system. And it was the nervous system of a big, excitable shaggy dog, chasing after every new enthusiasm like a passing car. Like most everyone else in Atlanta who followed the game, Keeler had never seen immortals like Vardon and Ray play golf before, and his experience of seeing them stride out to the first tee was overpowering.

I had heard so much about Vardon's style and the beauty of his play, and the Brobdingnagian walloping of Ted Ray, that I had difficulty in realizing that these wonders were about to be enacted before my very eyes. I was, in fact, so nearly hypnotized by the event that I followed the whole morning round pop-eyed and palpitating.

Pop's wonder increased when he saw Ted Ray put the wood to a golf ball for the first time.

He teed the ball and took his stance—pipe in mouth; that was another wonder—and caught with a photographic sort of mental impression that has not faded to this day the heave and lunge with which he tore into the ball, coat tails snapped out like the crackling silk of a jockey's blouse.

I switched my gaze to the hillside across the lake, well beyond where I was accustomed to see the drives of the club's experts alight. I didn't see anything. Horrors—had he hooked out of bounds? No. Up toward the top of the hill, far beyond what seemed human range, I saw a spurt of yellow dust fly as if from a rifle bullet, and in my ears was the prolonged "Ah-h-h-h!" the gallery pronounces on such occasions. I believe I helped pronounce it.

Ted had spanked one of his patented, eye-popping three-hundred-yard drives, and with the benefit of a hard fairway relocated his ball within thirty yards of a green that sat over four hundred ten yards away. While Ted wowed the crowd all morning, firing like a howitzer, making birdies and bogies with equal abandon, Vardon quietly went about hitting fairways and greens and recording pars with machinelike regularity. When his putter cooperated—

putting being the only weakness in his game; a nerve in his right hand had been damaged by a bout with tuberculosis—Harry dropped his share of birds as well. Opponents often felt as if Harry wasn't even aware of their presence, and they weren't wrong; experience had taught him his opponent was the golf course, not the other guy. He played against par, an elusive concept for the casual viewer. Not as spectacular a style in the heat of battle, Harry's economical method was even deadlier than Ted's showy fireworks. This was the partnership they'd formed during their tour, reflecting their different temperaments, and it was the reason they were nearly impossible to beat in a best-ball match. In their morning round at East Lake Ted turned in a par 75, and Harry shot 72.

Stewart Maiden and his partner, Willie Mann, looked intimidated by their famous competition and the size of the crowd that morning; both scored 78 and were three holes down at intermission, with eighteen left to play. Although all was convivial on the surface among the four men, Stewart Maiden was determined to put up a stiffer fight that afternoon; he worshipped Harry Vardon like every other pro his age did, but that didn't mean he couldn't beat him. Kiltie birdied three of the first eight holes to square the match. When he stuck his approach at the ninth within three feet of the pin and made his fourth birdie of the round, the home team went one up on Vardon and Ray, and the crowd cheered the local boys as if they were the Georgia Tech football team. They halved the first two holes after the turn and came to the twelfth tee with the famous visitors still trailing.

Someone else was following the action at East Lake that day.

A more plainly American name would be hard to conjure: Bobby Jones. Eleven years old. Towheaded, hair still worn in a no-nonsense bowl cut. Knock-kneed, a touch short for his age and a little chubby, baked dark brown with a spray of freckles sprinkled across his face. Knickers, a white shirt, a jaunty little cap; from a distance he looked like a hundred other kids running around in that crowd. You had to get up close to spot the watchful intelligence in his slate-blue eyes, and the crooked right corner of his ready smile, shaded by a sense of irony. That face already owned a degree of self-possession that was almost spooky; an old soul, you might have thought. He'd ridden out from town that day on the streetcar with his best friend, Perry Adair, son of the East Lake Country Club's current president. A year older, taller and leaner than his little sidekick, Perry enjoyed a growing reputation as the best junior player at East Lake, the city of Atlanta, and the state of Georgia. His younger friend and playing partner was a good golfer, too, but at this stage, when mentioned in the same breath as Perry or paired against him on the course, Bobby Jones always came in second.

Both families had taken summer homes in East Lake the year the country club first opened. The Adairs—wealthier by far, on their way to becoming one of the richest families in the South; they also owned the huge spread of land where Hartsfield Airport would eventually rise—soon built a grand house with all the amenities. The Joneses lived a much more modest existence: still apartment dwellers in Atlanta, albeit in the better part of town. They spent their first two summers at East Lake in rented rooms at a boardinghouse before moving into a ramshackle cottage on the edge of the second fairway called "the mule house." Local lore on the origin of that name is muddled, but it may at one point have been a stable for a Civil War–era farm that once occupied the grounds. A skirmish during Sherman's maneuvers around Atlanta in 1864 had raged right across where the golf course stood now, then part of the main highway to Fayetteville. The faint outlines of a trench where Confederate troops dug in and put up a fight still crease the third fairway. Colonel Robert Alston, second in command to a fabled brigade of Kentucky cavalry known as Morgan's Raiders, lived in the first farmhouse built across the way on what is now called Alston Street. Union army officers commandeered his home during that fight and hoofprints of the mounts they stabled inside are still visible, stamped into its old hardwood floors. In 1878 Colonel Alston founded the *Atlanta Herald*, which grew into the respected *Journal-Constitution*, the paper known as "the Voice of the New South," which would employ Pop Keeler. Alston survived all of the above only to be gunned down in a scandalous shoot-out inside the old State House, in downtown Atlanta.

The myth has persisted that Bobby's father, Robert Purmedus Jones, was a wealthy man, but during Bobby's childhood he worked as a corporate lawyer in Atlanta, under his own shingle, and was bringing home a middle-class income at best. Robert Purmedus was himself the son of an extremely successful man, Robert Tyre Jones. Folks called the Jones family patriarch R.T., out of respect more than affection. At a ramrod six feet five, two hundred thirty-five pounds, R.T. commanded attention. A stern, fervently religious character without an ounce of frivolity, he parlayed a small general store into a thriving cotton mill—one of the first blue-denim factories in the country—the leading industry around which the small town of Canton, Georgia, organized during Reconstruction.

The son of a struggling hardscrabble farmer, R.T. had lived through the horrors of the Civil War, and it informed every inch of his character. Life on earth was not for the faint of heart; you wrestled for every advantage, buried your dead, feared God, and gave Him all credit on those rare occasions when any was due. Fear and awe tended to be the reactions R.T. inspired in others. Finding even the harsh determinism of his parents' Presbyterian faith too liberal for his tastes, at twenty-one he had himself initiated as a strict Southern Baptist. He didn't drink, smoke, cuss, work on Sunday, or even break down and enjoy a refreshing Coca-Cola. He might indulge in a few hands of Rook every once in a while, but he played no game that required the pagan idolatry of face cards. His instinctual search for a strong faith to sustain him proved sound, because that faith would be sorely tested; his father was later robbed and murdered on the family farm, and his first wife died suddenly at the age of forty-two. While raising seven children on his own, R.T. took the entire extended family under the shelter of his formidable arms. Building his legacy according to dynastic English traditions, R.T. selected a revealing motto for the rising Jones clan: *Coelitis Mihi Vires.* My Strength Is from Heaven.

Born in 1879, R.T.'s oldest child, Robert Purmedus Jones—he always preferred Bob—grew up enjoying the advantages of his father's prodigious energies, but his temperament could not have taken a more radically different turn. Lighthearted, fun-loving, athletically inclined, Bob left Canton for the brighter lights of a bigger city at the earliest opportunity. A gifted baseball player, Bob attracted the attention of some local scouts bird-dogging for big-league northern franchises. R.T. never once went to see his son play in a game. Bob was offered a minor league deal by the National League's Brooklyn Superbas— forerunner of the Brooklyn Dodgers—but R.T. put the kibosh on his dreams of glory; sign that contract, he was told, and I'll disown you. Bob stayed in school at the University of Georgia, went on to attend law school at Mercer University in Macon, and passed the Georgia state bar exam. Having paid for his son's education, R.T. made it clear he expected Bob to come back to Canton and practice his profession for the benefit of the family concern.

But his experience of the world out from under his father's shadow had taught Bob a few crucial facts about himself; he liked to drink, smoke, cuss, tell off-color jokes, hang out with the boys and play poker, and do all of the above on Sunday if he felt like it. Father and son were destined to butt heads, but Bob might never have broken away without an ally to help him resist the pull of R.T.'s gravity. From the town of Auburn and another family whose Georgia roots ran six generations deep, Clara Thomas stood barely five feet tall, weighed ninety pounds, and was physically frail, but she possessed the classic resolve of the Southern belle in the cast-iron petticoat. Bob and Clara met and married immediately in 1900. When their first child, William, died after three agonizing months of illness, the tragedy devastated them. Clara turned the page first, with shocking finality, and never again referred to William by name; from that point on he was only "that baby who died." In August of 1901, realizing she was pregnant again, Clara insisted they move fifty miles south to Atlanta, to be closer to better medical care. In the diminutive Clara, R.T. had met his match in willpower; not even he could argue with that logic. She also insisted, and Bob agreed, that they would accept no money from his father in order to establish themselves in the big city. Strings came attached to such generosity; R.T. couldn't help but see it that way. Bob and Clara were determined to build their own life from scratch.

Bob opened a small law office and within a few months picked up enough freelance contract work inside the burgeoning Coca-Cola empire to support his family, maintaining patents and drafting boilerplate bottling and distribution contracts. Networking with his fellow Georgia alums, he joined the downtown Atlanta Athletic Club and befriended charter member George Adair. Clara took to her bed for the last few months of her second pregnancy, taking every precaution to avoid a repeat of their earlier heartbreak. When their son arrived on St. Patrick's Day, March 17, 1902, the young couple paid homage to R.T. by naming him Robert Tyre Jones. Bobby himself added the "junior" years later, to complete the tribute. But at first, and for some time to come, the boy's prospects appeared every bit as bleak as those of his late, lamented brother.

Weighing just over five pounds at birth, the baby struggled to maintain his weight, went through operatic fits of colic for weeks at a time, and couldn't keep solid food in his system long enough to do him much good until he was nearly five years old. Six doctors they consulted were baffled by the boy's infirmities, offering no treatment more useful than a strict diet of boiled egg whites. At the age of five Bobby still weighed less than forty pounds. Clara's heightened anxiety about her lost first child played a major part in shaping and disrupting the nervous system of her second; his elusive and fragile "condition" might have been a self-fulfilling projection of his mother's hyperactive concern for him. The experience of raising a second frail young boy convinced both parents that Bobby should grow up an only child. Terrified of infection from other children, in this era before routine vaccinations when childhood diseases were a deadly threat, Clara kept the boy cloistered in their home, a virtual prisoner to her fears. Aside from the family's African-American live-in maid, Camilla, and her on-again, off-again boyfriend—who took glee in first teaching him how to cuss—young Bobby could count his circle of friends on the knuckles of his thumb.

Frustrated by his son's fitful development and hailing from a long line of strapping alpha males, Bob found the prospect of his sickly son wasting away like a hothouse flower distasteful in the extreme. Had Bobby inherited his wife's delicate constitution, or was Clara raising the child in her own neurasthenic image? It was time to find out. Big Bob, as friends and family had now begun to call him, decided to move the family out to East Lake for the summer to see if clean air and exercise would do for Little Bob what the advice of six doctors had failed to. The Joneses rented rooms in the middle-class home of Mrs. Frank Meador, whose seven-year-old son Frank was conscripted as Little Bob's friend and guardian. Big Bob and Clara began enjoying the facilities at East Lake, taking lessons in golf—a new game that they both enjoyed—with resident pro Jimmy Maiden. Although this was country living, they weren't exactly roughing it: Mrs. Meador's butler used a megaphone to summon boarders on the golf course to dinner.

Big Bob's gamble paid off: given a chance to run around in the open air for the first time like a normal kid, Little Bob thrived. He spent a Huck Finn summer. When they could find enough players, the local boys played baseball, the first group activity Bobby had ever been allowed to join. He and Frank Meador discovered a creek they could dam up for fishing and didn't mind that they never caught anything. Bobby adopted an old broken-down pony at a nearby stable, naming it Clara, an honor his mother seemed reluctant to appreciate. The boys were delighted to find that their hunting ground provided "a reasonable supply of snakes to kill." Most exotic of all was the discovery of a "gypsy camp" across the creek in a small park; whether these were genuine descendants of Romany or itinerant migrant workers made little difference to their excited imaginations.

On a fateful afternoon, one of their fellow boarders, an earnest young man named Fulton Colville, noticed Bobby watching him practice chip shots on the front lawn. He asked the little boy if he wanted to try his hand at a few swings. The club was an old iron cleek, too oversized for Bobby to master. Fed up with how the damn thing was behaving, Colville sawed off the shaft below the grip and offered it as a gift to Bobby after dinner. Bobby and Frank were too young to be allowed on the East Lake course, so they fashioned one of their own on a dirt lane beside the Meador house. There were two fairways identical in length fashioned from the Georgia clay—one no more than an extended ditch—precious little grass, and long stretches of wagon ruts as constant hazards. It's an overstatement to say the game possessed Bobby from the start. It was just another activity in a rich and varied repertoire of fun, but one detail stood out: Little Bob hated making a bad shot. When he knocked his ball into a briar patch under the bridge that crossed the ditch, it made him mad enough to dance in the road. While such displays looked amusing in a five-year-old, a hunger for perfection and his furious inability to accept anything less from himself already loomed as the biggest mountain he'd have to climb in the first half of his life.

The family moved back to the city in the fall with a healthy son. Little Bob started school and Clara stopped fussing over him. Big Bob's practice advanced. He took a partner into his firm, and in deference to his warm and courtly Southern manners, friends and colleagues around town began affectionately referring to him as "the Colonel." The family headed out to East Lake again for the summer of 1908. One evening at twilight Clara took Bobby with her to meet Big Bob as he returned from his Atlanta office on the streetcar, the Suburban Express. On their way to East Lake for dinner they ran into their pro, Jimmy Maiden, about to move on to Long Island and in the process of saying his good-byes to the members. He introduced them to his younger brother, Stewart, not long off the boat from Carnoustie. In many ways a perfectly ordinary moment, it was nevertheless one that six-year-old Bobby would remember vividly.

There was nothing sensational about Stewart. He said very little and I couldn't understand a single word of what he did say. Jimmy and Dad and Mother did all the talking, and at first I wondered if Stewart could talk at all. Jimmy was going away and Stewart was taking his place. There wasn't any sensation, any more than when I swung the first time at a golf ball. Stewart was just another little Scot, like Jimmy, only Scotcher. But it wasn't long before I was following him about the East Lake course and watching him.

Stewart never appeared to notice his little shadow, and if he did he never seemed to mind. Upon arrival Stewart instantly became the best player at the club anyone there had ever seen. He had a classic swing built to the old Carnoustie form: flat, round, and fluid, guided by an even, leisurely tempo to keep the hickory shafts from torquing the head off target as it squared to the ball. Kiltie was all business on the course; hit the ball, find it, hit it again. Bobby couldn't then identify exactly what it was about the little Scot's game that so fascinated him, but it was no mystery: this was his first glimpse of perfection—consistent biomechanical precision, lit with a touch of poetry— and he drank it deep down into his unconscious. Bobby never carried a club when he tagged after the little pro; all his focus was on watching. After four or five holes, he would break off to return home, grab a hatful of balls and his three-club kit—his parents had given him a cut-down two wood and a short iron to go with his old cleek—head out to the thirteenth green, and hit balls at the flag until the sun went down. Without any thought to technique, without a single formal lesson from Kiltie, he mimicked that perfect swing and absorbed it into muscle memory until he made it his own. His interests still roamed over the full range of an active boy's life, but slowly golf staked a greater claim in his sleeping and waking mind.

The game gradually became the center of the Jones family's social life. Reg-

ular Sunday dinners—fried chicken, mashed potatoes, biscuits, and gravy—
were followed by informal tournaments played by Big Bob, Clara, and their
friends.

Big Bob often led the group in sing-alongs, the era's most popular form of
home entertainment, exercising a pleasant, rumbling baritone. Bobby's talent
for mimicry also became a favorite feature during cocktail hour on the
veranda, when his father would call on him to imitate the swings of the regu-
lars in attendance. Bobby enjoyed the attention of his well-lubricated audience; his impressions punctured the deluded self-image of more than a few
hackers. (At least one victim, a no-nonsense judge with a torturous preshot
routine, was livid over this blow to his dignity. He wasn't invited back.) The
Adair family had moved into the Joneses' social orbit during this summer and
their son Perry joined the kids' table. Two years older than Bobby, a tall and
handsome blond, Perry had been taking regular lessons from Kiltie for over a
year and was much further along in his game. The boys quickly became best
friends. Bobby now enjoyed the benefit of regularly playing with, and competing against, a better player. A third player soon joined their regular outings,
and she was better than both of them.

Alexa Stirling was the second of three daughters of a Scottish-born ear,
nose, and throat specialist, who'd brought his lifelong love for golf when he
moved to Atlanta near the turn of the century. By the time his daughters were
of school age, Dr. Stirling had been named British consul in the city. Alexa
played every weekend with her father and began taking formal lessons from
Jimmy and then Kiltie Maiden. A redheaded tomboy, five years older than
Bobby, willowy, beautiful, and spirited, she loved to hunt and fish as much as
Bobby and Perry did, adding a well-turned third leg to the triangle. Her father
taught her how to repair automobiles, a skill Alexa retained her entire life. She
studied the violin and later performed in professional concerts. She would also
become a furniture maker, an accomplished cook, and one of the first female
securities traders on Wall Street. With her athletic, economical swing, at a
hundred and ten pounds she could drive the ball over two hundred thirty
yards. Add to this a personality of charm and winsome modesty, and you realize that Alexa Stirling was one of the remarkable young women of her day.
(She was an early classmate of another of those women, Margaret Mitchell;
during her twenty years as an Atlanta housewife she wrote a novel called *Gone*

With the Wind.) Every boy she met fell under Alexa's spell and Bobby was no exception, even if he didn't yet know the word for it. Another extraordinary role model had found her way into Bobby's life, and the supporting cast around him was now complete, their impact began to affect his development like tumblers falling into place on a complicated lock.

Later that summer in 1908 someone suggested a tournament for the kids might make an amusing addition to the grown-ups' regular games. A foursome of Bobby, Perry, Alexa, and Frank Meador were sent out to play a six-hole stroke-play match, a gallery of parents and friends in attendance. Bobby later admitted that Alexa won the contest, but her generosity of spirit changed the outcome. Sensing how much more it would mean to him, she suggested they award the three-inch-tall cup to six-year-old Bobby. Bobby liked winning; he found that out right from the start. He slept with his little silver prize that night and hung on to it for as long as he lived, always polished, in place of pride alongside some of the greatest trophies in the world. Bobby seemed to have an inkling of how important this game might become to him. As an adult he wrote of his peculiar awareness of the simultaneity of time, the dreamlike merging of past and present in the pool of memory. Although these swirling recollections often came unstuck from a strict chronology, he vividly recalled these early days of playing around East Lake with Alexa and Perry as the happiest and most carefree of his life, when golf was still only a game.

This established the enduring rhythm of his boyhood: school years spent at home in Atlanta, where he was always a good, if not exceptional, student; idyllic summers at East Lake, where golf gradually overtook tennis, baseball, fishing, boating, and swimming. His temper continued to flare up hot and ready. During a round with Dr. Stirling and Alexa, Bobby hit a less than perfect shot, tossed his club, and let fly a shocking string of expletives. A proper Englishman, Dr. Stirling forbade him to play with Alexa for the rest of the summer and complained to the Colonel about his outburst. Bobby said he was glad, he didn't like playing with a girl anyway, which sounds like a ten-year-old's sour grapes. Two years later Bobby met Perry in the finals of a match-play tournament for kids and beat him for the first time, 2 and 1. Because they were competing in a match, adult golfers stood aside to let them play through, which gave both boys a kick of self-importance. This time Bobby took home a small vase.

In 1911 nine-year-old Bobby entered his first formal tournament, the junior championship of the Atlanta Athletic Club. His first experience with brackets and starting times, pairings and handicaps didn't daunt him for a second. Playing his way into the finals, Bobby faced a big sixteen-year-old named Howard Thorne and beat him 5 and 4 over thirty-six holes. That win earned Bobby his first mention and a small photograph in *American Golfer*, the game's monthly bible. No one was prouder of Bobby's win than Big Bob; he carried Bobby and the trophy home on his broad shoulders, shouting out the news to Clara. Unlike so many kids of his generation, Bobby never had to walk the extra mile to earn his father's approval, and the bighearted Colonel gave him no reason to doubt how much he was loved. The harder-edged Clara played the bad cop when Bobby needed discipline. The only spanking he ever remembered getting from his dad came when Bobby nearly drowned after falling into East Lake while trying to land a big fish; even then the Colonel seemed more frightened about losing his only son than angry at him. Scarred by R.T.'s scathing indifference to his once promising baseball career, Big Bob never missed one of Bobby's important matches and was always first to greet him with a hug when he came off the final green. If there was any trace in Big Bob of the frustrated athlete living out his fantasies through the exploits of a gifted son, Bobby never voiced one word of complaint, and once they moved past childhood's dynamics they remained devoted friends. There's an argument to be made that his father's unwavering support provided the bedrock for every good thing Bobby Jones ever accomplished.

By 1913 the little golf academy that Kiltie Maiden had quietly gone about building at East Lake was about to yield a bountiful harvest. Forty-one-year-old club president George Adair won the first of two city amateur championships. His son Perry captured East Lake's junior crown for the second year in a row. Alexa Stirling played her first USGA event and established herself as a presence to reckon with in the future. With the membership at East Lake expanding, George Adair contacted renowned Boston-based golf architect Donald Ross about adding a second course and redesigning their original layout. Typical of George Adair's adroit business transactions, this was the only occasion in his fabled career where Ross ever delivered two courses for the price of one. George bankrolled a trip to Scotland that summer for himself, Perry, and

Kiltie to scout the classic links courses for inspiration. They returned full of suggestions and philosophies that Ross embraced in his East Lake designs. Perry's stories about their adventures on the courses of the faraway land where the game was born thrilled Bobby and created in him a hunger to see it for himself.

Back in school that September, Bobby followed the exploits of Francis Ouimet at the 1913 Open, waiting eagerly on the front steps for his dad to return home with the afternoon papers. When Ouimet pulled off his improbable victory, the story landed on the front pages and suddenly the quaint little game Bobby had grown up playing took on mythic dimensions. The news that the two British giants who had battled Ouimet were coming to the only course he'd ever known stirred up sensational excitement in Bobby, as if gods from another planet had announced a visitation. That he was far from alone in this feeling speaks to the subtle but profound sense of inferiority the South still suffered as a region, a culture, and a tribe of people. The South's collective psyche had been battered in the Civil War, nowhere more decisively than in Georgia, where Union general William Tecumseh Sherman had systematically crushed their way of life.

The re-creation of a vital, assimilated Southern culture needed new role models around which its people could rally. The region's leaders had traditionally come from politics or the military, but their devastating defeat had disabled those breeding grounds for greatness since the Civil War. A new industry that would revolutionize the experience of self-perception was about to take up the slack. During the early twentieth century motion pictures made possible the first national popular culture. Theatrical movies, popular serials, and newsreels of sporting events distributed from coast to coast created a whole new class of demigods. America's population had exploded in a flood of European immigration, many not yet fluent in English. Silent pictures arrived at this precise moment, the perfect medium to entertain illiterate masses. These new Americans discovered their heroes could for the first time be admired for politically neutral talents, such as throwing a baseball, performing goofball slapstick comedy, or rescuing a girl tied to phony railroad tracks. Old World class issues that sorted out who reached the top rungs of society's ladder were made irrelevant by the screen's two-dimensional immortality. Even without the aid of movie cameras—although they would show up for every subsequent U.S. Open—Francis Ouimet had just proved that a golfer, of all people, could stand up there on Mount Olympus.

Eleven-year-old Bobby Jones inhaled the news from Brookline. All he glimpsed in that breakthrough was a small ray of hope for himself; if this twenty-year-old caddie could win the U.S. Open, anything was possible. While watching Vardon and Ray play the game in person, Bobby's young dreams for glory of his own took their first steps.

When Vardon and Ray played exhibitions against local professionals, one of two things happened: the pros would either collapse under pressure or play the game of their lives. Stewart Maiden and Willie Mann had mounted a comeback that put them in the second category; the two British greats knew they were now in a match. Kiltie had already played his second shot onto the twelfth green. Harry followed, landing even closer to the pin. Ted, as usual, had hit the longest drive, but pushed it right. He found his ball in the rough, a hundred sixty yards out and twenty yards behind a forty-foot-tall pine that stood directly between him and the green.

Bobby and Perry were in the gallery that scrambled around to watch Ted play his shot. So was Pop Keeler, although he didn't yet know either of the boys; they might have been standing right beside each other. As Ray walked to his ball, puffing on his pipe, wise veterans in his gallery—Keeler among them—speculated that he would have to punch back to the fairway around the tree and take his medicine.

"He'll lose a shot here for sure," Bobby remembered saying to Perry. "He's dead behind that tree."

Ted took one look at his ball, one at the tree, and a quick glance at the green. Without hesitation he pulled his favorite club—a one-of-a-kind hand-crafted thing he called a "Snieler," the rough equivalent of a nine iron—from his bag, planted his feet, and swung down at the ball as if he meant to kill it.

"He hit that ball harder than I ever have seen a ball hit since, as if he would drive it through to China," Bobby later wrote. "Up flew a divot the size of Ted's foot. Up also came the ball, buzzing like a partridge from the prodigious spin imparted by that tremendous wallop—almost straight up it got, cleared that tree by several yards, and sailed on at the height of an office building, to drop on the green not far from the hole. The gallery was in paroxysms. I remember how men pounded each other on the backs, and crowed and cackled and shouted and clapped their hands. As for me, I didn't really believe it. A sort of wonder persists in my memory to this day. It was the greatest shot I ever saw."

Keeler picks up the action from there: "And Ted Ray, his pipe in his mouth, the club tucked under his arm, was striding on toward the green long before the ball had come down, as if nothing at all had happened. He did not ever look after it."

Just another day at the office for Ted.

Bobby watched the last six holes of the match in a state of wonder as the drama shifted into high gear and held that crowd in thrall. Harry made his birdie at twelve. He and Ray went on to birdie the next three holes, but Kiltie birdied fifteen as well, and then got another at sixteen to cut the Englishmen's lead back down to one. After halving the seventeenth, Stewart dropped a twelve-footer for his third birdie in the last four holes on the eighteenth. That left Ted Ray with an eight-foot putt for birdie to secure the victory and avoid a sudden-death play-off. He studied the line from both sides for the first time that day, stepped up, and slapped it into the back of the cup to win the match. All four men had played their second round in at least two strokes under par and received a sustained ovation. After witnessing such an amazing exhibition, the home crowd didn't seem to mind that their favorites had been nosed out at the wire. Pop Keeler waited his turn on the club's single telephone as reporters lined up to call in their headlines, while club members repaired to the bar and relived the great day long into the night.

Young Bobby could hardly sleep that night, lying in bed replaying every shot over and over. He had witnessed a display of astonishing skill, but beneath the placid surface of their polished play he had sensed a fierce struggle, capable of producing moments of rare wonder, delicacy, and power. Not so much man against man, but each man against himself, testing his limits and his capacity for rising to meet the test. Everything about it appealed to him; he wanted to be in that place, try to hit those shots under pressure, feel what those men felt. Lightning had struck Little Bob, and it ricocheted over to hit Pop Keeler square as well. Both their attitudes about the game of golf had been transformed in that instant, forever. They spent the following day at another Atlanta country club, Brookhaven, watching Vardon and Ray play two flawless rounds on yet another course they'd never seen before against another pair of local pros, the Mackenzie brothers. The English visitors played with equal brilliance and won handily. Ted thrilled the crowd again by hitting his drive on the ninth across a swamp, a forced carry of over two hundred eighty yards, a shot no man had ever pulled off before. All Harry did in Atlanta was play for par, and average 72 over his four rounds, on bumpy, unfamiliar Bermuda greens he later likened to "putting on grapevines." Ray's monstrous power shots had seized center stage in Bobby and Pop's memories, but in the days and weeks to come, something about Vardon's quiet persistence loomed larger.

Bob later wrote: "Harry seemed to be playing something beside Stewart and Willie or the Mackenzies; something I couldn't see, which kept him serious and sort of far away from the gallery and his opponents and even from his big partner; he seemed to be playing against something or someone not in the match at all. I couldn't understand it at the time; but it seemed that way."

A few weeks later that October Bobby experienced a milestone of his own, and he raced across four fairways to share it with his dad, near the end of his Saturday game at East Lake. Bobby waited for his father to walk off the eighteenth green. The Colonel was puzzled when he saw the look on Bobby's face; the boy's hand trembled as he solemnly held out the scorecard. Big Bob read the card carefully.

"I made sure Perry attested to it," said Bobby. "He signed it, right there."

Bobby had shot his first 80 and made sure Perry signed the card so there'd be no question about its legitimacy. The Colonel smiled, held out his arms, and wrapped his only son in a bear hug, blinking back some tears. There would be a lot of whooping and hollering for the Jones boys on their walk home that evening. To put this eleven-year-old's achievement in perspective, only 3 percent of the people who take up the game ever break 80 in their lives.

The lessons Bobby had learned in golf were clear: the game was played for pleasure, but when you excelled in competition other people admired you, and your dad lavished you with praise, sometimes to an extravagant degree. By acquiring value in the eyes of others you could begin to believe you possessed it yourself, which in turn helped generate the self-confidence necessary to play this fiendishly difficult game at increasingly higher levels. A shortcut forward into the wider world had opened for the young lawyer's son like an enchanted passage, a priceless opportunity for anyone, particularly a bright, precocious kid with such abundant natural gifts.

Harry Vardon's method had quietly seeped into Bobby. He had been playing a match against Perry Adair in his record-breaking round, but for once he never gave a thought to what his opponent was doing, or who was winning. It was the first round he had ever played against the only opponent that mattered, the invisible one he hadn't yet given a name to, the toughest of them all.

Pop Keeler called him Old Man Par.

Bobby, twelve, winning at Roebuck.

CHAPTER TWO

One Wrong Turn

THE YEAR 1914 IS best remembered as a hinge on which the modern world swung into the open jaws of hell. As the twentieth century began, developing technologies had created an unprecedented period of sustained prosperity. Mass manufacturing and new systems of distribution made possible by the car, railroad, and steamship had created the first global economy. Banking, industry, education, psychology, the arts and sciences took profound leaps toward what appeared to be the dawn of a golden age. Political efforts on behalf of the poor led to the organized labor movement, easing the suffering of the lower classes. Borders opened across Europe and the emergence of travel as a leisure activity among their upper classes created mutual appreciation and empathy between once avowed enemies. International commissions working to standardize means of commerce like Weights and Measures spoke to this spirit of cooperation. Similar efforts led to the abolition of the African slave trade, the outlawing of child prostitution, and the first treaty to halt the trafficking of opium. The Hague Conference of 1899 even established benchmarks for the humane conduct of war, an unthinkable development only scant years before. By the spring of 1914, the continent had been free of bloodshed for forty-four years, since the end of the Franco-Prussian War. All these developments contributed to a growing perception that Europe embodied mankind's potential as a morally progressive, self-improving species. Schoolchildren of Bobby Jones's age were being taught that hope for the future had never been brighter.

Only these nations' rulers stood in the way of achieving that dream. With the exception of democratic France and Switzerland, Europe was ruled by an inbred nest of corrupt nineteenth-century monarchies. Centuries of politically motivated marriages between these ruling families meant the inhabitants of every palace were related by blood; the grandchildren of Queen Victoria alone occupied key positions in the royal households of seven different countries. Simmering with ruling-class intrigues, the self-absorbed imperial courts of these otherwise modern nations were about to allow their petulant family squabbles to escalate into an apocalypse.

An arms race between the French and Germans began in earnest with the advent of the twentieth century. France's principal ally, Great Britain, whose navy had ruled the seas for a hundred years, felt threatened by Germany's decision to create a militant fleet and filled their own shipyards with steel-clad destroyers. Germany's chief ally, the Austro-Hungarian court of the ancient Hapsburg Dynasty, fearing attack from czarist Russia, maintained a huge standing army. A mare's nest of shifting alliances and mutual defense treaties among these five major powers locked their fates together. To protect those obligations, the armies of Europe's five empires grew by over 600 percent between 1900 and 1914, and armed with increasingly powerful weapons of destruction, their generals felt an increasing obligation to put them to use. Battle was part of life's natural rhythm, a time-honored method of letting off steam. It became a common belief among senior military staffs that a war should be waged because it could be. They developed elaborate contingencies in the event trouble arose, pairing with each imaginable ally against every conceivable enemy. They expected the worst of their neighbors—the lesson of a thousand years of European history—and the sound of rattling sabers filled the air. Europe had entered a labyrinth honeycombed with trip wires; any act of aggression would trigger an escalating string of retaliations.

Although each nation had an able corps of statesmen, the ability of their kings and kaisers and czars to negotiate with each other lagged far behind the drumbeat of these preparations for war. There were no "hotlines." The telegraph was too impersonal to be an effective diplomatic tool. These nineteenth-century heads of state refused to conduct state business over the newfangled telephone, and two-way radio had not evolved enough to be of any practical use. During the summer in which this was about to come to a head, instead of meeting face-to-face as common sense demanded, the leaders all left for their traditional summer retreats. Viewed from the perspective of a future century, what happened next seems nothing less than a willful act of collective insanity.

The impending European crisis could not have been further from the mind of America's champion golfer when he set sail for England from Boston in the middle of May 1914. Francis Ouimet had just turned twenty-one, and a generous offer from the members of his home club allowed him to accept an invitation to play in Britain's Amateur Championship. After making landfall, Francis sat down for his first English breakfast in a London hotel and found himself under surveillance by a nearby table full of reporters, whose stories in the evening papers reported that the young giant-killer ate grapefruit, eggs, dry toast, and coffee. Reporters dogged his every step for the next six weeks, on and off the course, looking for faults. England's sporting establishment felt they had a score to settle with Ouimet; most refused to accept that his win over Vardon and Ray could have been anything other than a fluke. On the train to London, concealed behind a sports page splashed with photographs of his arrival, Francis overheard a conversation between two proper gents who took seats in his compartment. After spotting the photos of Francis on his raised newspaper they launched into a diatribe.

"Obviously he knows precious little about the game," one of them complained.

"Yes. Very poor indeed compared to our better English players."

Francis had to pinch himself to stop from laughing out loud from behind his paper.

As much as he enjoyed the sightseeing and hospitality, Francis didn't play well in England. Like hundreds of American golfers before him, and hundreds of thousands afterward, he was baffled by his first exposure to Britain's seaside links. The keys to conquering their subtle topography and quirky, treeless layouts eluded him, and when the winds kicked up, his game was defenseless; he could barely break 80. By the time he'd figured out how to play an effective knockdown shot with his irons—from watching the great English champion Harold Hilton—it was too late to perfect it for the Amateur. The British Amateur is the greatest endurance test in championship golf, requiring seven match-play victories of its winner in five days. Held on the links at Royal St. George's, in Sandwich, Kent, the prevailing winds blew in relentlessly over Pegwell Bay. After eking out a first-round win, Francis went down without putting up a fight in the second, 2 and 1. He endured an even worse beating afterward in the British press, who seized on this as confirmation that the "Boy Wonder" possessed more luck than skill. They hardly seemed to notice that one of Francis's traveling companions, American champion Jerry Travers, played far worse; he was eliminated in the first round by a middle-aged Englishman suffering from lumbago who limped in with 88. The only American who managed to hold his own was Charles "Chick" Evans Jr., the gifted, persnickety Chicagoan, who had arrived in Sandwich with only three days to prepare.

Chick Evans was twenty-four years old in 1914, and his best golf was still ahead of him, although he had already reached the semifinals of the U.S. Amateur three times, losing in the finals to Jerry Travers in 1912. The child of a librarian father and a doting mother, he had a sunny, toothy, extroverted public persona that concealed an insecure underdog's psyche. Chick liked to portray himself as an up-from-nothing kid, a former caddie who'd never been handed a break, but his childhood had been solidly middle class. Although he presented a pleasing face to the world, Chick fueled his competitive fires with a get-even edge that bordered on spite. He had worked his way to the top of the game around Chicago while still a happy, carefree personality. He laughed and joked constantly with his gallery, remembering hundreds of people by name, and this created a warm atmosphere of support that Chick needed to play his best golf. Herbert Warren Wind, the great American golf writer, noted that there was something "pleasingly rural" about him. Chick won so many tournaments so easily that his series of meltdowns on the national stage of the Amateur began to look like either cruel fate or the fatal symptoms of a man who choked under pressure. As one defeat followed another, darkness dragged down Chick's buoyant confidence; he began to refer to himself as the "uncrowned champion," and reports surfaced of his simmering resentment over Ouimet's victory at the 1913 Open. He told friends that this breakthrough moment that galvanized American interest in the sport was supposed to have been his; he was the better player and had been for years, everyone said so. He referred to Ouimet in print as "a young boy," even though Chick was only three years older. He even seized on a quote of Vardon's that Chick was the best amateur he had faced during his American tour. Chick neglected to add that Harry made that statement weeks before meeting Francis in the Open at Brookline.

Although he was the most gifted amateur the Midwest had ever produced, Chick frequently bumped heads with the game's Eastern establishment. He felt, not without justification, that players associated with the Western Golf Association—who governed the game in Illinois and points west—were often treated as the USGA's poor relations. Now struggling to make ends meet as a young Chicago stockbroker, Chick made it a point of pride when entering any competition to always pay his own expenses, refusing all patronage. He tended to resent any amateur who had the means to do so with less strain, which set him on an inevitable collision course with Francis and later on with young Bobby Jones.

Although the underlying reasons were more complicated—psychologists might have a field day exploring the fact that he never married, coupled with an intense, lifelong attachment to his mother—there was a simpler physical explanation for Chick's difficulties than paranoid favoritism or ill fortune. He was always a superb tee-to-green player, a master shot maker whose career spanned half a century; he would play in his last U.S. Amateur, incredibly, in 1961. As a testament to his shot-shaping skill, he seldom carried more than seven clubs in his bag, but Chick suffered from a nasty case of the yips, and down the stretch of every major he'd played in—and lost—he came unraveled with a putter in his hands. This was Chick's second trip to England—he bowed out early in the 1911 British Amateur to a left-handed Tasmanian—so he already had experience with links play under his belt, and his craftsman's talents carried him further than any other American at Royal St. George's; Evans reached the fifth round before losing when he missed a three-foot putt.

Francis redeemed himself the following week, when he accepted a last-minute invitation to travel across the channel to La Boulie, the premier Parisian country club, to compete in the French Amateur Championship. Although not considered a major on the scale of its British and American counterparts, the French Amateur still attracted a strong competitive field from throughout Europe. Playing on a more familiar American-style parkland course, Francis found his form again and captured the trophy. The French, predictably, hailed him as the "great French-American golfer." He sailed back to America in the first week of June with his confidence renewed and a second national title. He also had time while stopping in London to share a dinner with his friends Harry Vardon and Ted Ray.

Harry Vardon was forty-four and in fitful health, the legacy of an eight-year battle with tuberculosis that cut the heart out of what otherwise might have become the greatest professional record in the game's history. In the two decades since 1894, three men had dominated British golf: Harry; his fellow Englishman John Henry Taylor; and a tall, angular Scotsman, James Braid. Each had stamped his name on the Claret Jug five times—only five other men during their era even won it once—and a debate still raged about which of the Great Triumvirate was greatest. By 1914 these friends and rivals were running out of chances to settle the issue. The arena couldn't have been more appropriate; Prestwick, on Scotland's Ayrshire coast, had been home to Old Tom Morris, the game's patriarch professional. It had played host to the first twelve Opens and twenty-three to date. Harry had notched two of his Opens there, most recently in 1903, just before his illness; Braid had won the fourth of his five titles the last time they'd played Prestwick in 1908, and Taylor was the event's defending champion, having edged out Harry the year before.

When by the end of the first day at Prestwick Vardon and Taylor had turned this Open into a two-man race, interest in the tournament hit an all-time high; hourly special trains were added from Glasgow and Edinburgh, bringing hundreds who'd never seen competitive golf before. The two men were paired together for the final thirty-six holes. Seven thousand people teemed around them as they began that morning; Harry estimated that number doubled for their final round that afternoon. Unlike the polite, appreciative fans who typically patronized the Open, this crowd was out of control; people surged and swarmed around them, fighting to establish a view for the next shots as they raced down the fairway. The players were pushed, elbowed, and kicked by the stampede, and their clubs nearly snapped in two when they tried to exchange them with their caddies. Stewards trying to control the crowd finally just gave up, but the two men in the fight never did. Vardon held a two-shot lead as they left the course for their lunch break. Alone in the pro shop, the two men compared injuries. Both their shins and ankles were black and blue from the beatings they'd taken.

A solid wall of people lined three hundred fifty yards of fairway from tee to green when they began their final round. Harry lost a stroke on the first hole but sensed their running battle with the gallery was wearing down his old friend. Both men were so exhausted by the grueling ordeal each later confessed they were afraid they might pass out. Harry had lived through this sort of hysteria at Brookline the year before, but it was an unwelcome new experience for the highly strung Taylor. From the second to the ninth Harry ran off seven consecutive pars; his lead grew to five as they reached the back stretch, and he closed Taylor out with two tough pars at the finish, winning his sixth Open by three strokes. When the crowd danced around them after his last putt fell, all Harry wanted to do was sit down and rest. He later considered this the greatest of all his victories.

The verdict was in: Harry had edged ahead of Taylor and Braid at the finish line. The Great Triumvirate they would always remain, but from that day forward no one ever questioned who was the greatest among those extraordinary equals. Harry's sentimental victory at Prestwick would prove as important to his legacy as Jack Nicklaus's 1986 Masters win later was for his. It was the last major championship any of the three would ever win, although Harry had one last hurrah in him and would emerge as a surprising mentor to a promising young golfer from Atlanta, Georgia.

It was June 19, 1914. Not a single person in the crowd that mobbed Prestwick that afternoon suspected they had just witnessed the last sporting championship Great Britain would hold for the next six years.

Nine days later, the world exploded.

Archduke Franz Ferdinand, nephew of Emperor Franz Josef of Austria, was heir to the Hapsburg throne. He was fifty-one, a dull, prideful, and humorless royal who was intensely unpopular at home. Other than waiting for his uncle to die, his primary governmental responsibility was the ceremonial post of inspector general to the Austrian army. In June 1914, Ferdinand arrived in Bosnia to observe their annual maneuvers.

After four decades of occupation Bosnia had been annexed by the Austrian empire in a blatant land grab only six years before. Serbia, a quarrelsome republic to the south of Bosnia, had won its independence from the Ottoman Turks after centuries of resistance in 1878. Borders in the tempestuous Balkans—the Turkish word for mountains—have always been slippery, usually with blood. As a result tens of thousands of Serbs still lived in Bosnia. When Serbia's diplomatic attempts to unite those Serbian regions of Bosnia into a Greater Serbia failed, Serbs in both countries transferred their hatred of the Turks to the occupying Austrians. The Balkans had already become a stone in Austria's shoe, but the Hapsburgs decided that allowing geopolitical lines in this treacherous little corner of the world to be redrawn according to ethnic allegiance invited wide-scale disaster. Serbian resistance to Austria's occupation hardened. A few desperate men, members of a secret Serbian nationalist group called the Black Hand, decided that the only way to force Austria out of Bosnia was through an act of terror.

At the conclusion of maneuvers, Franz Ferdinand and his wife, Sophie, traveled to the Bosnian capital of Sarajevo on June 28. Theirs was a union unique to European royalty; they married for love. Sophie was a lady-in-waiting from an upper-class family, but miles too far down the royal food chain to satisfy the Hapsburgs. Franz Josef enlisted three heads of state and even the Pope to persuade Ferdinand to give her up. He refused, more determined to marry her than ever. The emperor finally granted approval on the condition their children be removed from the line of succession. Not a single member of the royal family attended their wedding. Ferdinand's devotion to his mate emerges as the most admirable part of his character.

June 28 happened to be their fourteenth wedding anniversary, and Sophie was expecting their fourth child. Ferdinand decided to take his beloved into Sarajevo so she could ride in a royal procession, a right denied her in Vienna. By dread coincidence, June 28 also happened to be a day of dark import on the Serbian calendar; it marked the anniversary of their defeat at the hand of the Turks in 1389, the dawn of their enslavement under the Ottomans. As far as the radicals of the Black Hand were concerned, it was the perfect day to ruin everyone else's history. Expressions of alarm poured into Vienna from all over Europe: keep the archduke out of Sarajevo. Serbia's ambassador to Austria delivered an explicit warning: if Ferdinand entered the capital there would be an attempt on his life. Tipped off by an informant within the Black Hand, they even knew the names and whereabouts of the assassins; arrest orders were issued to every border crossing, but the assassins entered undetected and the warnings never reached the archduke. Not only did Ferdinand make the trip to the Bosnian capital, he dismissed his Austrian army escort beforehand in order to avoid irritating the locals with a show of foreign military force.

It was an uncommonly hot summer day in Sarajevo. Ferdinand and Sophie rode in the second car of their motorcade, with the top down so they could wave to the crowds. Seven Black Hand assassins had distributed them-selves along the parade route, all poor young working-class Serbs, every one of them suffering from terminal tuberculosis, the definition of nothing left to lose. As the motorcade passed, one of them threw a hand grenade at the arch-duke's car. Ferdinand saw something fly toward his wife, reached up and deflected it into the street, where it exploded, resulting in minor injuries to spectators and members of the royal party in the car behind them. Their assailant swallowed a cyanide pill—which he vomited up—then threw himself in the river. Authorities beat him half to death and took him into custody. The motorcade sped on to city hall where, after calming the furious Ferdinand, dig-nitaries gave their scheduled speeches to the crowd thanking the archduke for his visit, at the conclusion of which he stood up and thanked them for their hospitality.

Convinced they should now leave the city, Ferdinand insisted they first visit the hospital where an injured member of his staff was being treated. The royal party jumped back into their cars and departed city hall. The driver of the car in front of Ferdinand's had not heard the change of plans and took a wrong turn, following the route that would have taken them to a museum, the next scheduled stop in their original itinerary. After they made the turn, Ferdinand's chief of staff, riding in the car with him, shouted at their driver to halt at once and turn around. The driver hit the brakes.

They came to a dead stop outside a sandwich shop on Franz Josef Street, six feet away from Gavrilo Princip, the Black Hand's lead assassin. Believing they'd missed their chance, Princip had just finished his lunch. When he looked up and saw the royal couple in front of him, Princip pulled a gun from his pocket, stepped next to the car, and fired twice. The shots sounded muted; the chief of staff assumed they had missed, since both Ferdinand and Sophie seemed uninjured. He screamed at their driver to move. As their car sped away

Princip tried to turn the gun on himself, but witnesses wrested it from his hands and threw him to the ground.

As they crossed the river, Ferdinand gestured frantically and a jet of blood streamed from his mouth; he'd been shot in the neck, severing an artery. Sophie screamed, then collapsed at her husband's feet in shock; the second shot had hit her in the stomach. Only the archduke realized they'd both been shot; he pleaded with Sophie to stay alive for the sake of their children, then tried to comfort her, whispering: "It is nothing . . . it is nothing . . ." until he lost consciousness. Both died before their car reached the hospital.

The remaining conspirators were captured within days. One cracked under interrogation and named three senior Serbian military officers as the masterminds. Austria demanded they be turned over for prosecution. Serbia refused. Three days later, on July 28, vowing revenge, Austria declared war on Serbia, but only after receiving assurances their chief ally, Germany, would honor their mutual defense pact. If Franz Josef had attacked at once, unilaterally, historians agree their war might have stayed a local quarrel. But securing Germany's support forced Russia's hand, as an ally of Serbia, to mobilize against Austria, and the trip wires began to detonate. Germany declared war on Russia, which drew France in because of its defense pact with the czar. Turkey and Bulgaria threw in with the Germans and Austrians—now known as the Central Powers—while Japan joined the Allies. England, the last domino to fall, came to the defense of France when the Germans moved their forward divisions into Belgium to strike toward Paris.

With nationalist passions aroused, enormous pro-war demonstrations crowded every capital. For the first time movie cameras captured the majesty of assembled military might and those images reached deep into the continent's heartlands. The fever spread. Enlistments soared, conscriptions accelerated, reservists were called to active duty. Hundreds of thousands of young European soldiers eagerly marched down the broad, tree-lined boulevards of the world's most sophisticated cities. Troop trains clattered toward every border. By August 4 bullets were in the air. The dogs were unleashed. The path of twentieth-century history pivoted on this trifling moment.

If not for a wrong turn. If not for a sandwich.

. . .

Newsreel footage and photographs of the archduke's assassination played in movie houses and newspapers across America. Everyone from Bobby Jones to President Woodrow Wilson saw these stark images of the crime. Wilson, the most dedicated golfer who'd ever lived in the White House, had given up the game that summer; his wife, Ellen, was slowly dying. She had suffered a serious fall, and her slow recovery led doctors to suspect that something more serious was responsible. Wilson never gave up hope for her recovery, but by the time they made a proper diagnosis in mid-July—Bright's disease, a degenerative kidney ailment—it was too late.

The Wilsons had been married for twenty-nine years. Ellen was a vibrant, generous, gifted woman—she installed an art studio in the White House for her well-regarded paintings, and sponsored the first serious attempt to rehabilitate Washington's shocking Negro slums—and the brittle Wilson made no secret of his dependence on her. During long nights keeping vigil over her decline, the former Princeton professor read the dispatches describing this string of firecrackers exploding across Europe with the horror of an educated humanist losing his faith in God and man. His ambassadors in France and Great Britain pleaded with him to intervene. When he learned of atrocities committed by the Germans as they marched through Belgium—thousands of civilians slaughtered, priests assassinated, cities burned to the ground—Wilson wept. But intervention did not reflect the national sentiment. Isolationist tendencies dominated every geographic, ethnic, and economic sector of the United States. Hundreds of thousands of recently immigrated Americans had fled Europe to escape this sort of senseless bloodbath; most wanted no part of another. Wilson took the country's pulse and kept quiet, preoccupied with his own private tragedy.

Ellen Wilson died peacefully in her sleep on August 6. She whispered an instruction to her doctor at the end; he must tell her husband that she wanted him to marry again, knowing the loneliness of his job would cripple him.

Ten days after he returned from burying his wife in her native Georgia, two weeks after Germany invaded Belgium, Woodrow Wilson formally articulated America's official response to the European conflict: neutrality in thought and action.

The opening moves of the war played in banner headlines, but the farther one moved from the East Coast the more the conflict felt like distant thunder.

Outside Atlanta, where the Jones family and their friends spent another untroubled summer at East Lake, the news barely registered on Bobby. East Lake's clubhouse had burned down in an electrical fire that spring and its replacement was under construction; the Joneses and new member Pop Keeler, among many others, mourned the loss of their handcrafted golf clubs for months. Stewart Maiden's shop ran overtime to address the crisis; Kiltie personally fashioned a first grown-up set of clubs for Bobby. Donald Ross's newly designed course opened for play that summer and was not an immediate success. Ross had reversed the routing to run counterclockwise, one of his standard innovations. As old East Lake was the only course Bobby had ever played, the new layout confounded him—it was over three hundred yards longer—and his game went temporarily sideways. During their years together the little pro gave him less than ten hours of formal instruction; Bobby learned primarily by watching and repeating. He responded to setbacks by concentrating harder on the details; he noticed that a smaller, heavier ball called the Zome Zodiac flew a little farther and a lot straighter into the wind. A larger, lighter ball called a Black Domino went longer with the wind behind him. He began to study ways to attack a hole strategically rather than just step up to the ball and swing—small but significant advancements to his game, and remarkable in a twelve-year-old.

Pop Keeler was typing up a story at the *Atlanta Georgian* one Friday morning when he overheard a fellow sports reporter named Milt Saul speaking with their chief editor. Like Pop, both men were avid golfers; Saul was a member at East Lake, and he was complaining about a tournament he'd entered there.

"They really ought not to allow kids in these things," said Saul. "We've got three or four youngsters entered, and I've got to play one of 'em tomorrow—Little Bob Jones. He's a squirt, twelve years old. Of course I'll beat the wadding out of him, but what's the point of taking up time beating infants?"

The following week Keeler overheard another conversation between the two men. The chatty Saul had been strangely quiet, and the boss stopped by to ask how the match had gone with Little Bob.

"He licked me eight and seven," said Saul, flustered. "I was right: they ought not let kids play in these things!"

Little Bob Jones: Keeler filed the name away.

. . .

On the day President Wilson declared America's neutrality, American golfers gathered at the Midlothian Country Club outside Chicago to begin play in the 1914 U.S. Open. Francis Ouimet had traveled west to defend his title, heartened by a successful defense of his championship the week before at the Massachusetts State Amateur. He sustained that excellence in the first round at Midlothian with a stunning 69, the finest complete round he could ever remember playing. Fully expecting to find himself in the lead when he made his way to the scoreboard, he was shocked to see someone had posted a 68. Francis was less surprised when he saw the name next to it: Walter Hagen.

The twenty-one-year-old club pro from Rochester, New York, had finished second at Brookline the year before in his first Open, a noteworthy accomplishment overshadowed by Ouimet's big win. Walter still lived a hand-to-mouth existence, and over the winter had nearly given up on golf to pursue his big-league baseball dreams. While he was trying to decide between a tryout with the Philadelphia Phillies and a return to the Open, a last-minute offer from a club member to pick up expenses for the trip to Chicago tipped the scale in the smaller ball's favor. Walter pulled his fancy white silk golf outfit out of mothballs and hopped on the day coach to Chicago from Buffalo, heading that far west for the first time in his life. Determined to travel in style as long as someone was picking up the tab, Hagen arrived the night before the tournament and checked into the first-class Great Northern Hotel. He set out in search of the swankiest restaurant he could find and ordered two dozen oysters and a boiled lobster, like the huge red one on the poster outside. Walter had never tasted lobster before and decided it had been worth the wait. He ate the whole thing, with mayo, then took in a movie.

By the time he got back to the hotel Walter was in agony. Food poisoning. The house doctor couldn't do a thing for him. Nothing did. Hagen felt as if he were retching up meals he'd eaten as a child. By dawn he could hardly stand, let alone play golf. Maybe in a week or so. A friend convinced him to ride out to the course and see how he felt once he got there; if he quit the tournament now, Walter's wealthy patron back home might not buy that story about a bad lobster, and ask for a refund. Walter made it to the train in fifteen minutes. It was a typical late summer Midwestern day; sweltering heat and the soot and cinders blowing off the rails through the train's open windows nearly finished him off before they arrived. Walter staggered into the Midlothian locker room, changed into his fancy silks, staggered out to the range, and tried to hit some balls. It hurt to take a full swing. His body ached, his head and stomach throbbed. He gobbled a handful of aspirins and headed for the first tee, barely able to see.

And broke the course record with a 68.

Hagen made headlines in all the Chicago papers the next day, his first blast of publicity since his strong showing at Brookline. Walter Hagen meeting fame was an open-and-shut case of love at first sight; he ran toward the spotlight. Ouimet played his heart out over the next two days, in some ways a more impressive performance than the year before when he'd snuck in under everyone's perceptions. His every shot was played under intense scrutiny and he stood up to it, finishing in a three-way tie for fourth. Hagen went back to meat and potatoes and led the tournament from wire to wire. The only man who made a run at him was local favorite Chick Evans; with a chance to tie Walter at the last if he could chip in from off the green, Chick missed by less than two feet and finished second, another blow to his fragile self-esteem. Afterward, employing the kind of camouflaged excuse that he had learned to master, Chick admitted, "I had been putting badly, but I could hardly attribute that to my sprained ankle."

Hagen never fully recovered from food poisoning during the Open and decided afterward it was the best thing that could have happened to him. He had a tendency to obsess about things he had no control over, like the weather or competitors' scores. He was in so much physical distress at Midlothian he couldn't focus on anything other than the shot in front of him; if it turned out well, so be it. If it stunk up the joint, that just gave him a chance to make up for it with the next one. Wild recovery shots from impossible locations soon become Walter's bread and butter, and better suited his risk-seeking personality than the missionary-position monotony of a fairways-and-greens style.

"Nobody remembers who finished second," he said.

After his win at Midlothian, thinking too much on the course never troubled Hagen again. The swagger and suave diffidence Walter patented as his trademark style—making him a worldwide icon the likes of which his sport has seldom seen again—can trace its lineage to that Chicago chophouse lobster.

One last stop remained on the game's championship calendar. The U.S.

Amateur Championship was held at Ekwanok Country Club in Manchester, Vermont, during the first week of September. The Amateur drew even less attention than the Open had six weeks before. Coverage of the war's escalating atrocities dominated the newspapers: during the last days of August, the advancing German army destroyed the Belgian town of Louvain, home to an ancient university known as the "Oxford of Belgium." Hundreds of civilians were butchered and forty thousand others driven from their homes. Every book in the school's library, over 230,000 volumes dating back to the Middle Ages, was put to the torch. A city and community that had thrived for over a thousand years vanished from the map. Broad sections of Belgium received the same brutal hammering. By the end of the month, the German army crossed into France.

The amateurs gathered under Vermont's picturesque Green Mountains, but the war cast longer shadows; Francis Ouimet, who three months before had won the French Amateur, spent evenings between matches reading accounts of fierce fighting drawing closer to the course he'd competed on outside Paris. Francis headed for a showdown in the final with defending Amateur champion Jerry Travers. A silver-spooner, Travers had learned the game on a private course his father built on their Oyster Bay estate. He was a notorious playboy—known for squiring showgirls around Broadway—but for the last ten years he had nevertheless dominated the amateur game. The two men had first met in the quarterfinals of the 1913 Amateur; Francis, an unknown making his debut in national competition, took Travers deep into their match before fading down the stretch. Travers went on to win his record fourth Amateur. At Ekwanok Francis again found himself cast as the underdog to the seasoned Travers.

The finals of the National Amateur may be the most nerve-wracking event in American golf: thirty-six holes, the only match on the course with every eye present locked onto every shot. Francis succumbed to pressure early on, while the stoic Travers—who played in a self-absorbed fog of concentration—built a two-hole lead. On the twelfth green Francis realized he was taking his eye off the ball just before he putted. With that correction he steadied his game and closed the gap. The two men stood dead even at the halfway point, and then Francis went on a spectacular run, won six of the next twelve holes, and had

Travers dormie six at the thirteenth. They tied the hole, which won Francis the championship, 6 and 5. The crowd cheered and surged forward, but instead of doffing his cap and offering congratulations, Travers pulled his driver and headed up a hill to the next tee. Francis remained behind, chagrined. The crowd backed away, confused. The man refereeing their match, USGA president Robert Watson, had to hustle after Jerry and quietly point out that the match was over. Travers had completely lost track of the score. He came down the hill and apologized for his lapse in etiquette, and Francis accepted with equal grace.

More than winning last year's Open, this victory in the Amateur fulfilled Francis Ouimet's most enduring ambition and solidified his reputation. He was only twenty-one years old, in obvious command of every aspect of the game. As the first golfer to capture both American championships, Francis now stood alone as the most admired figure in his sport the United States had ever produced. His future was pure blue sky. Distinguished players and the sporting press agreed that Ouimet possessed the skill and determination to dominate golf, both here and abroad, for many years to come.

Less than two years later, in a controversial ruling that split the national golfing community down the middle, Ouimet would be banned from all amateur competition by the game's governing organization. That same summer a cocky young teenager from the South was getting ready to make his debut in national competition.

Francis would not win his third major title for another seventeen years.

Bobby in a Red Cross Match.

Bobby, fourteen, at Merion, 1916.

CHAPTER THREE

Into the Fray

THE ORIGIN OF YOUNG Bobby Jones's hunger to succeed remains slightly mysterious; it appears, from the beginning, to spring from the core of who he was. He owned an only child's conception of himself as the center of the universe, which was certainly a factor. His grandfather's Old Testament willpower at first glance seems to have bypassed the congenial Colonel, but Big Bob drove himself hard in business or any other competitive situation; he just did it in supremely affable style. Bobby inherited aspects of both men. Pleasing his father was important to him, but Bobby had ferocious expectations of his own, etched deep into his neurological and emotional codes. That's a quality which can drive a man to madness, and Bobby would come perilously close to the edge of that road.

In May 1915, Bobby set a new scoring record at East Lake, and club president George Adair decided he was ready for the next level of competition. George and his son Perry had planned a trip to Montgomery, Alabama, where both were entered in one of the South's biggest invitational tournaments, and they wanted Bobby to come along. First they had to convince his father; George offered to pick up all the expenses, but the Colonel hesitated over what would be Little Bob's first tournament away from home. Not until Bobby made an impassioned plea for his dad to let him make the trip did he give his okay.

Bobby distinguished himself in the tournament at Montgomery, but not by his own high standards. Although he missed qualifying for the first flight, he made it all the way into the finals of the second before losing to a thirty-year-old left-hander; a man hitting from the "wrong side of the ball" made his defeat even more humiliating. Bobby pitched a fit afterward and tossed some clubs around, feeling like an absolute failure. He was only thirteen, three months shy of high school, and already expected to beat experienced players more than twice his age.

Provided his game continued to advance, the Colonel had promised Bobby he could enter the prestigious Southern Amateur once he turned fifteen. Bobby returned from Montgomery convinced his career was ruined, only to discover his father had entered him in *that* year's Southern, two years ahead of schedule. What was more, since East Lake was hosting the event Bobby had been tapped for its four-man team in the interclub competition. Kiltie Maiden had now taken the emerging prodigy firmly under his wing and Bobby had thoroughly assimilated his swing. When a friend of Kiltie's from Carnoustie arrived for a visit, he spied Bobby on the course from a distance, mistook him for the wee Scotsman, and could not be persuaded otherwise until Kiltie appeared in person. Kiltie had a word with Big Bob about putting Bobby on the East Lake team—a word sounds about right; a full sentence was an oration for him—and that convinced the Colonel his son was ready.

Little Bob wasn't so sure. The night before the tournament he laid out his first pair of long pants to wear; self-conscious about his appearance, Bobby was afraid he still looked like a stumpy schoolboy in his usual knickers.

Tuesday morning, June 15, a dangerous hailstorm held up play for over an hour. After waiting out the delay in the locker room, Bobby felt so nervous in front of the big crowd gathered at the first tee he had to "keep looking at the ground to keep from falling over." His little round face screwed in a mask of determination, he went out and shot the best round on his team—which won that part of the competition. He finished second for the qualifying medal, one stroke behind the leaders, in a field of 215 of the best players from every corner of the South. Out of that group the top sixty-four advanced to the match-play brackets that would determine the championship. East Lake members crowded around to shower praise on their young hero, while the Colonel proudly held court in the bar; he'd qualified for match play as well. It should have been a red-letter day in the Jones household, but all Bobby could think about as he lay in bed that night was how much better he could have played, reliving his mistakes over and over, establishing a pattern of perpetual dissatisfaction that would torment him for years.

Jones never failed to qualify in any tournament he entered for the rest of his life.

The next day Pop Keeler traveled out to East Lake to cover the Southern Amateur and watched this young Jones kid he'd heard so much about tee it up for the first time. Keeler was recovering from a late spring bout of double-lobe pneumonia—he described it as being "snatched from death feet first"—and found himself short of breath hiking up and down East Lake's hilly fairways. Bobby handled his first-round opponent easily and advanced to the round of thirty-two. He drew a perpetual favorite in his second match, a stocky veteran in his fifties from Houston named Bryan Heard. In his crisp khakis and battered sun helmet he looked like a grizzled African explorer. Friends called Heard the "Commodore." The unlikely duo fought a memorable duel, but the Commodore edged Bobby out with a snaking thirty-footer at the seventeenth, 2 and 1. Keeler observed Bobby closely at the end:

His face flushed brick red and was curiously set for so young a boy, as he watched the Commodore—grim and impassive as a Chinese idol— sink the finishing putt. Then, his expression relaxing into a wide, boyish smile, Bobby went up to his conqueror and held out his hand.

"You're a tough customer," said the Commodore, almost the first words he'd spoken to his young opponent all afternoon.

Once Bobby was out of earshot, Pop asked the Commodore if the young lad had given him a fight. Heard removed his pith helmet and mopped his brow. "I would've shot seventy-six with a par at eighteen. That would have broken the best score ever by an amateur on this course. I only beat him by one." The Commodore watched Bobby mope toward the clubhouse. "That boy's going to be a great golfer. Maybe *the* greatest."

Young Perry Adair avenged his friend's loss that morning, eliminating the

Commodore from the field of sixteen, which pleased Bobby no end. "Too many of these damned kids," muttered the Commodore as he walked off. Bobby, standing near the green, happened to overhear him, which put a smile a mile wide on his face.

The defeat dropped Bobby into the loser's bracket, where he ran off three wins against the best players in the region, the shortest of whom was six feet two and nicknamed Moose. Bobby stood a hair over five feet—and advanced to the finals. Playing over thirty-six holes, Bobby was three down at the end of the morning, because this time his opponent—Frank Clarke of Nashville—did shoot 76 and set a new amateur record for East Lake. Clarke increased his lead to four up by the time they made the turn that afternoon; observers thought the match was over, but Bobby rallied to win the next four holes, squaring the match, and figured he had his man in the bag. He lost the next two holes but still wasn't ready to quit, chipping in for birdie at the fifteenth, only to watch Clarke sink a thirty-foot putt for a half. When Bobby put his second shot in a bunker on seventeen, Clarke closed him out, 2 and 1. His parents, Kiltie, and the crew at East Lake gushed over his resilient comeback. Atlanta papers, with Keeler leading the chorus, raved about the youngster's performance: Bobby was the sensation of the Southern Amateur. In its write-up, *American Golfer* called his battle with Clarke the match of the tournament, and ran Bobby's photo with the story. An article in the sports section of the *New York Times* appeared shortly thereafter: "Georgia's Golf Marvel." It was only the first of many headlines he would make that summer.

Bobby told no one his private feelings: "I felt I was a disgrace to my family, and to Stewart Maiden, and to the Atlanta Athletic Club, and to anybody or anything else convenient to be disgraced."

The lesson Bobby took away from that match was clear: never shake hands with yourself for your fine play before you shake hands for the last time with the man you beat. Bobby showed he'd taken that lesson to heart a few weeks later in Birmingham, at the Roebuck Country Club's invitational, another mainstay on the Southern circuit. Bobby squeaked by Perry Adair in the second round—the first time they'd faced each other outside of East Lake—and reached the finals against Bill Badham, a former collegiate star at Yale. Bobby played out of his skull against Badham, but got madder and madder that he couldn't shake this fancy-pants Ivy Leaguer, a man ten years his senior with a hundred tournaments under his belt.

"I remember thinking how blamed stubborn he was," said Jones later. "It seemed unreasonable to me."

The two were all square after eighteen, but this time Bobby didn't pat himself on the back. He played Badham even to the twenty-first hole, looked him straight in the eye, and stuck a pitch dead at the flag to win his first big tournament. Any golfer who's ever won anything tells you the first win is the hardest. Bobby won twice more in Atlanta before the summer was over, breaking a course record at the Druid Hills Invitational. Then he beat his own father, for the first time ever, in the finals of East Lake's club championship. Big Bob couldn't have been happier; he lifted Bobby off the ground in triumph and they marched home arm in arm, carrying the trophy and singing songs until Clara came out on the porch and yelled at them. Two weeks later, in the Atlanta City Championship, the climax of the local season, Bobby lost in the semifinals to George Adair, who went on to defend his title. The next week Bobby set his soaring aspirations aside and began classes—as a freshman at Georgia Technological High School.

As Bobby's school year progressed, the specter of war drew closer to American shores. President Wilson publicly reinforced the country's neutrality while privately encouraging increased shipments of food and munitions to the Allies. British reinforcements blunted the German offensive in France, which bogged down into trench warfare; the Allied line held firm north of Paris, leading to a stalemate through a long, cold winter. The skirmishing yielded no decisive gains, as 3 million men slugged away at each other over a fifty-mile front.

Americans were supposed to stay neutral, but Bobby later remembered that when the truth of what was happening in the trenches emerged, that got a lot harder. At the Second Battle of Ypres, in April, the Germans fired artillery shells loaded with chlorine gas at British positions, killing hundreds of soldiers. The genie was out of the bottle; an even deadlier gas, phosgene—called "mustard gas" after its vivid yellow coloring—was being weaponized and would kill thousands of Allied soldiers during the next three years.

The Germans unveiled another devastating weapon: the *Unterseeboot*—or U-boat—allowing the Central Powers to enforce a blockade around England in the spring of 1915. Three hundred seventy-five of them saw action, hunting in "wolfpacks," torpedoing Allied warships and destroying cargo ship convoys at will. The rules of engagement allowed a blockading navy to stop and search any neutral ship for contraband that might give aid to the enemy. If it carried munitions or contraband, the ship and its cargo could be seized. Once passengers were escorted to safety, U-boats opened fire and sank the vessel, but such attacks were forbidden against manned ships unless the captain of the target ship resisted search and seizure.

Both sides walked a tightrope on this issue: the Allies needed America to enter the war on their side and hoped to provoke a crisis that would bring them in; Germany wanted to avoid waking the "sleeping giant." As more American merchants risked running the wolfpacks, Kaiser Wilhelm signed off on a cold-blooded directive: any ship entering the waters around Great Britain—enemy or neutral—could be fired on without warning. During the next three months U-boats sank three hundred ships. President Wilson warned that if American lives were lost he would hold Germany accountable.

On May 1 the British ocean liner *Lusitania* sailed out of New York bound for Liverpool, flying under a neutral U.S. flag. A product of the latest engineering, the *Lusitania* was the first ship of its size since the *Titanic* to be labeled "unsinkable." By mid-morning six days later, her passengers could make out the emerald hills of southern Ireland off the port deck; seven hundred yards off the starboard side they couldn't see U-boat 20 lurking below the surface. A single torpedo raced through the water and struck the luxury liner amidships. The hull exploded and the ship sank in less than twenty minutes, sending two thousand people to their deaths—hundreds more than had lost their lives on the *Titanic*—among them one hundred twenty-eight United States citizens.

The unprovoked attack mobilized American outrage against Germany; news of the sinking had been greeted with celebrations in the streets of Berlin. The kaiser's spokesperson expressed sympathy for the loss of American lives but refused to condemn the attack, claiming *Lusitania*'s hold had been laden with illegal ammunition: What other explanation could there be for the explosion that sank the ship? The British damned that claim as a lie, a stance maintained by English historians ever since. The controversy would not be settled until 1980; divers exploring her wreckage confirmed that *Lusitania* had been carrying massive amounts of pyroxylin—an explosive component of nitroglycerin and highly reactive to seawater—disguised as forty-pound packets of cheese.

When he heard about the *Lusitania*, Wilson evaded his Secret Service detail, left the White House, and walked the streets of Washington alone in the rain. Following his late wife's wishes, he had quietly been pursuing a wealthy widow he'd met recently—a jewelry store owner, Edith Bolling, seventeen years his junior—and poured out his tortured feelings about the war to her in a series of passionate letters. (They would marry before the year was out; both keen golfers, they honeymooned at a Virginia golf resort and played thirty-six holes a day.) Wilson decided to answer the Germans with threats of retaliation, but no action. The kaiser promised future restraint and offered compensation to families of American victims. Former president Teddy Roosevelt considered the attack "murder on the high seas" and damned Wilson as a coward for failing to respond with force. French soldiers took to calling shells that failed to explode "Wilsons." Despite condemnations at home and abroad, the president refused to lead the country into war; public opinion narrowly supported his position.

The sport of golf went into hibernation in Britain. Most courses were taken over by the military, their clubhouses turned into convalescent hospitals; fairways sprouted tents, training camps for new recruits. Many were used as gunnery ranges. Seaside links were converted to airfields for the army air corps. Others were plowed over into farmland to support the war effort, sparing only the greens. Dozens of pros past the age of military service left for America to find work, never to return. The upper classes, many of them golfers, filled the officers' ranks, which suffered 70 percent casualties. One private club in Surrey lost thirty-one members in 1915 alone.

Harry Vardon had just turned forty-four, his condition fragile at best; being accepted into any active branch of service was out of the question. Realizing that to be seen practicing his profession might bring offense during a time when death lists filled the newspapers, Harry approached the Red Cross with the idea of playing exhibition matches to raise money, and enlisted J. H. Taylor and James Braid to join him. Their "Great Triumvirate" events proved a solid success, the birth of a tradition in golf that has contributed millions to charities ever since. (Despite their popularity, when traveling to these matches Braid wrapped his clubs in plain brown paper to avoid disapproving looks.) A few months later, a German bomb landed in the garden of Harry's North London home, destroying a wall and killing their next-door neighbor. Asleep at the time, Vardon and his wife escaped injury.

Play went on in America. Four-time Amateur champion Jerry Travers won the 1915 U.S. Open at Baltusrol Golf Club, joining Ouimet as the only man to have won both national titles. A few weeks later, a few days before the Amateur was held at Detroit Country Club, an informal East vs. West team event hinged on a singles match between Ouimet and Chick Evans, which generated more interest than the championship. It was the first time the two "regional champions" had ever met in match play. Chick felt this would provide him the chance to prove once and for all that he was the superior player, and through most of the day he mounted a convincing argument.

Chick reached the sixteenth three up on Francis with three to play. Francis rallied to win the next two holes, but needed to win the par three eighteenth as well to force a play-off. Francis buried his tee shot in a back bunker; when Chick landed his safely on the green, the crowd figured the match was over. Francis played a superb sand shot and sank a ten-footer for par. Evans three-putted from twenty feet, losing the hole and tying the match. Ouimet knew that when his putter went south Chick "couldn't putt for sour apples." Francis beat him on the first extra hole; Chick's longed-for validation would have to wait another day. The next day Francis and two other long hitters were invited to visit the local ballpark and put on an exhibition before a Tigers-Yankees game. As Francis teed it up at home plate a heckler shouted, "Get those tennis boys off the field!" Francis parked his golf ball on the roof of a house across the street, a hundred yards beyond dead center field. The heckler was not heard from again. Ouimet, Travers, and Evans were the overwhelming favorites as the 1915 Amateur got under way, but given the unpredictable vagaries of match play, all three were eliminated by the second round. The trophy was claimed for a second time by 1909's Amateur champion, Robert Gardner—a Yale man, holder of the Ivy League pole-vaulting record—defeating Francis's oldest friend in golf, John Anderson of Boston.

Francis returned home from Detroit and put golf aside for a while. After learning the trade as a sales clerk at Wright & Ditson, in the spring of 1916 Francis opened the doors of his own sporting goods store in Boston. Raising capital from investors that included his father—who had come full circle on Francis's involvement with golf—he took as his partner a fellow member at Woodland, John Sullivan, his future brother-in-law. They offered a full range of equipment, including golf clubs and balls; what hacker wouldn't want to buy his gear from America's first champion? Given Francis's high profile as a Boston celebrity, the firm of Ouimet & Sullivan benefited from a flood of publicity: sales began strong, and the store's future looked bright, but their optimism would be short-lived.

On January 14 the USGA announced it had decided to redefine the rules of amateur status. Any player could, for example, still write articles about the sport for money, or accept a car as a "gift" for winning a big event, and retain his amateur standing. This new interpretation declared that if you had anything to do with selling golf equipment—as an endorser, manufacturer, or retailer—the USGA now considered you a professional. Plans to open Ouimet & Sullivan had been in the works for months when Francis heard about the ruling. USGA president Frank Woodward planned to make Francis a test case for his pet theory of amateurism. He was convinced that the line between pro and amateur had grown dangerously blurred, with nothing less than the integrity of the game at stake.

Francis had invested his life's savings in the store and called upon the goodwill of friends and family to back him. He had been working full-time as a sporting goods salesman at Wright & Ditson when he won the 1914 Amateur and no one had said boo about his status then. He had turned down dozens of offers to take advantage of his championships commercially—everything from performing on the vaudeville stage to appearing in the growing movie industry—because of concerns over apparent exploitation. Wealthy admirers would have been more than willing to set him up in some feather-bed job that paid the bills while allowing him to play unlimited golf as a so-called amateur. He said no to every one of them. From the moment Francis entered the public eye his behavior as a role model and spokesman for the game had been impeccable. He was almost solely responsible for the huge rise in popularity golf had enjoyed since 1913; the number of American golfers had tripled to over a million in three years. Now this decision threatened not only the modest dreams Ouimet had been nurturing but his ability to make a living. Although it wasn't in his agreeable nature to defy authority, make a public protest, or consider mounting a legal challenge—a restraint unimaginable today—Francis felt the ruling was simply unfair. He decided to contest the USGA's policy in the simplest possible way. He opened his store.

In late March, as applications were being accepted for that year's Amateur, Francis received a letter from Woodward, informing him the executive committee had revoked his status as an amateur in good standing. He would be ineligible to play in any USGA-sponsored amateur events until he severed connections with his sporting goods business. His partner, John Sullivan, received an identical letter. Knowing how much golf meant to his friend, Sullivan suggested Francis withdraw temporarily and try to strike a compromise with the USGA. Francis refused. He had given his word to Sullivan that he was in to stay; loyalty came first. Woodward might have won the battle, but he lost the war of public opinion; a storm of controversy erupted, with a majority of people involved in the game leaping to Francis's defense. Kids like Bobby Jones refused to believe their hero would never play again. The greatest amateur of all, Old Man Walter Travis—publisher of *American Golfer* magazine—used his column to blast Woodward's decision.

"Golf is a nice game," wrote Travis, "but one's bread and meat are still just a trifle more important." Recently retired from his great playing career, Travis had also been smacked in the wallet by the new ruling; Woodward decided to lump golf course architects under his new definition of "professional," a calling that had until this moment been exempt. Travis now received the bulk of his income as an architect, and the last thing the four-time champion wanted to be thought of as was a professional.

As they had been in England for nearly a century, professionals in America were still looked down on as second-class citizens. In golf's privileged quarters, particularly the East Coast clubs where the American game took root, referring to someone as a "pro" was tantamount to calling him a hustler, a drunk, or a bum. The Scottish immigrants who made up the first wave of golf men to reach America had all been working-class blokes; more than a few exhibited a fatal weakness for the grain or the grape. Although their skills were valued by the bluebloods who had the time and money to take up the game, they regarded their professionals as the hired help. Scratching out a living in the pro shop or caddie shack remained a last resort for poor men with no other marketable skills or education. Turning their line of work into a respectable profession remained an uphill climb, but in 1916 the activist vanguard of golf workers took their most important step in that direction.

Professional golfers in England organized their first representative body in 1901, the British Professional Golfers Association. American pros followed suit in early 1916; the Professional Golfers of America came into existence when thirty-five members signed its charter in New York City. An East Coast department store mogul named Rodman Wanamaker made a generous donation that allowed them to hire an administrator. The PGA held its first formal meetings in Minneapolis in late June, the same week the U.S. Open was played at Minikahda Country Club. Actively recruiting members from the Open field, they nearly doubled in size. The PGA's first act was to set up a widows-and-orphans fund for indigent pros and their families, but they soon turned their attention to establishing basic employment rights and coordinating the hiring process at clubs around the country for dues-paying members. Fearing retaliation from their wealthy employers, many pros were reluctant to throw in with what might be perceived by the conservative golf community as a labor union. Walter Hagen and "Long Jim" Barnes signed on as the organization's earliest high-profile members.

The PGA held its first pros-only tournament in October that year, a sparsely attended match-play affair that over the course of the next decade would evolve into America's second major professional championship. Rodman Wanamaker was in the gallery throughout the tournament and donated an ornate silver trophy of his own design, personally awarding it to winner Jim Barnes afterward; the Wanamaker Trophy is still given to the winner of the PGA Championship today. Over the previous two decades the USGA had established itself as the guardian of the integrity of the game itself—in Woodward's persecution of Ouimet almost too zealously. With the emergence of the PGA, the often forgotten men who made their living inside the game, the caddies, pros, and greenkeepers who made the game possible at the ground level, at last had a protector of their own.

·   ·   ·

Minneapolis was the farthest point west to ever host a U.S. Open. With the spreading war overseas occupying public attention, only eighty-one entrants made the trek to the championship. Unwilling to incite a confrontation with the USGA, Francis Ouimet declined even to apply. His home club, Woodland Golf Club, petitioned the USGA on his behalf for Francis's reinstatement as an amateur. During a closed-door session during the Open, the executive committee declined the appeal. In the same session the committee addressed an application from Woodland to have its USGA status upgraded from "associate member" to "active," which would have given it a voice in organizational issues like the Ouimet affair. The minutes of the meeting tersely describe the committee's response: "There were no votes in the affirmative." Defending champion Jerry Travers also bowed out of the Open, announcing his retirement to concentrate on his work as a cotton broker on Wall Street; the war had made cotton a volatile commodity, and Jerry was nearing the end of a ten-year spending spree that had depleted his family's trust fund. The absence of these key contenders opened up the field for perpetual bridesmaid, fellow amateur Chick Evans.

Chick brought his caddie with him from Chicago, along with half a dozen putters and his annually reconstructed putting stroke. He had done a lot of soul searching about past failings in major tournaments over the winter, and placed the blame squarely between his own ears. In front of a sympathetic Midwestern gallery, Chick repeatedly whispered the word *"relax"* to himself before every shot—the first recorded use of a mantra by a golfer—and it worked wonders. Chick shot a blistering 32 on his first front nine, ending the day with a three-stroke lead over British expatriate Wilfred Reid, the man Ted Ray made infamous during the 1913 Open by punching in the nose on the eve of the final round during an argument about the British tax system. In searing heat and humidity the next day, Reid faded as he had at Brookline—this time without a sock in the kisser—and Chick entered the final round holding a three-shot lead over seasoned pro Jim Barnes.

His mantra notwithstanding, Open pressure wrapped its fingers around Chick's throat; after a triple bogey at the fourth Barnes caught him. Chick stood on the par five twelfth tee when he learned he was in front again; Barnes had taken a bogey at the ninth and fallen back a stroke. Knowing Long Jim would easily reach the twelfth green in two and be almost assured of a birdie, Chick killed his drive and faced a 225-yard carry over a creek to the green. He rifled a fairway wood that landed twelve feet from the flagstick and two-putted for birdie. Pulling off the shot liberated Evans; he dropped every putt he faced the rest of the way in and won the tournament with a new Open scoring total of 286, smashing the old record by four strokes. That record would stand for the next twenty years, surviving the transition to steel shafts, hotter golf balls, and an upcoming rival named Bobby Jones. Small wonder Chick cried openly when they handed him the cup. After seven years of intense, public, and often self-inflicted suffering in the fields of the golf gods, Chick Evans had broken through.

Pop Keeler had been through a season in hell. During the fall of 1915 he lugged his typewriter all over the South to cover Georgia Tech's football season, often in a cold, driving rain. On one raw, bone-numbing afternoon he watched Tech slaughter Cumberland State by a score of 222–0; that is not a misprint. After that game Pop ended up in the hospital, his tonsils crawling with streptococci. He had barely survived his last bout with pneumonia and feared it was making a comeback, but this turned out to be much more serious. The Friday following his release, Pop was driving home, looked up at the evening sky, and saw two full moons. The following day his feet wouldn't work. A week later he was back in the hospital, paralyzed from his toes to his throat. A neurologist recommended opening up his skull. He was outvoted. Keeler wrote: "I suspect any effort to find something in my skull would have been futile anyway."

Instead they opened up his spinal sheath and discovered he had suffered a cerebral hemorrhage, the blood filtering down from his brain and creating nearly fatal pressure on his spinal cord. They drained the fluid, twice, and saved his life, but could offer little else to ease his suffering. Nerve damage pinched his left hand into a claw with a dropped wrist; he was forced to wear a leather-and-steel brace to prevent further deformity. His tendon reflexes were virtually destroyed, and what muscle tone he'd had to begin with soon wasted away; he couldn't raise either arm above his shoulders. Months into his recovery Keeler volunteered to appear before the Atlanta Neurological Society "as an illustration of what the human body would stand without a complete extinction of the life principle." Pop's struggle lasted six months, including two sanatorium stays where a variety of baths and electrical treatments did nothing but add variation to his misery. When one of his surgeons suggested Pop aid his recuperation by taking up golf again, Keeler responded: "Haven't I been tortured enough?"

When he finally got home and tried to hold a club in his hands, Pop didn't even have the strength to pick it up. For the time being he would enjoy the game only as a spectator. On his first day back at East Lake that summer, Pop witnessed an epic encounter in the finals of the club championship between two best friends, seventeen-year-old Perry Adair and fourteen-year-old Bobby Jones.

Keeler was amazed by the rapid maturation of Jones's game. Bobby had recently broken his own scoring record at East Lake with a 74 and won two local tournaments. He'd put on weight over the winter and looked a little chunky now. Only five feet four, he weighed close to a hundred sixty pounds and could hold his own against any big hitters he went up against. It rained through most of his finals match with Perry, but Jones's golf was so compelling, the fragile Keeler risked his health to hobble around and watch Bobby win his second East Lake title. The kid had come into his own as a player, and Keeler raved about what he'd seen: Pop could barely contain his excitement, which helped him forget his own troubles. Here was greatness, and he was the first reporter to grasp what that might mean to Bobby, Atlanta, and the game itself.

Bobby's win earned him a berth in the first Georgia State Amateur Championship, played in July 1916 at Capital City Country Club in Atlanta. In a match-play field of thirty-two players, the draw pitted Bobby and Perry against each other in the finals. The boys had been going at it in friendly competition for the last six years, and both agreed friendship took a temporary backseat whenever they teed it up, but the pressure of a state championship delineated deeper aspects of their character. Playing as the favorite, Perry took a three-stroke lead into lunch; most agreed he would win out. This sentiment was so widespread that Keeler overheard the chairman of the tournament, Ralph Reed, approach Bobby on the practice green between rounds to make an extraordinary request. So many spectators had traveled from all around the state to watch the afternoon's competition, he wanted Bobby to agree to "play out the bye holes"—that is, the holes remaining in the round after he lost the match to Perry.

Keeler wrote that Bobby replied angrily: "Don't worry, Mr. Reed—there aren't going to be any bye holes!" Jones later denied the conversation ever took place, but Pop stood by his story.

After losing the first hole that afternoon to go four down, Bobby's whole attitude about competitive golf changed completely and forever. He hit every shot harder than he'd ever swung in his life. His concentration took on a ferocity no one watching had ever seen before. He played the final seventeen holes in even par and beat Perry, two up, on the last green. Perry picked up Bob's ball, conceding defeat, and as he handed it to him stammered: "Bob, you are just the best."

Bobby had won Georgia's first Amateur championship and crushed his best friend in the process. Perry was a splendid athlete, accomplished enough to have dominated the sport in his region for the next decade. He had been the Golden Boy of East Lake for over half his life, the fair-haired son of the club's president and former champion. He had basked in Atlanta's uncritical acclaim as the best player the city ever produced. Then, in the course of one summer, his perennial little sidekick had rocketed past him as if Perry had been planted in cement. The difference between their talents remained nearly indistinguishable, but it turned out that the willpower Jones possessed was made of stronger stuff, and coming face-to-face with that obdurate fury under competitive fire wilted some critical part of Perry's spirit. The two remained friends their whole lives, but Perry never quite got over his disappointment at being so thoroughly surpassed. Although he would go on to win a handful of important titles in the South, Adair retired from competition while in his mid-twenties to enter his father's real estate business. He never made an impact in the game on the national stage and, after this loss in the inaugural Georgia State Amateur, he never beat Bobby Jones again.

George Adair took the Colonel aside after the tournament and told him that Bobby's victory earned him an automatic berth into the 1916 National Amateur Championship, to be held a few weeks later at the Merion Cricket Club in suburban Philadelphia. Bobby already satisfied the Amateur's other prerequisites: a verifiable handicap less than six and five dollars for the entry fee. Once again the Colonel hesitated—was his son really ready for the national stage?—and once again George Adair made a persuasive argument: winning the Massachusetts Amateur had been Francis Ouimet's only title before the Open in 1913, why shouldn't it be for Bobby? George was planning to make the trip to Philadelphia—Perry had qualified as well—and insisted that Bobby come along, offering to pick up the tab.

The Colonel wrote a letter to Tech High School, requesting an excused absence for his son; the Amateur was being played right after Labor Day, and Bobby was going to miss the first week of his sophomore year.

Pop Keeler would not be making the trip north to Pennsylvania—budget constraints at the paper—but he made an important personal decision regarding his own future after watching Bobby win the State Amateur: writing about golf in general, and Bobby Jones in particular, was how he planned to spend the rest of his professional life.

During the second half of the nineteenth century Philadelphia's wealthy classes began a long, slow urban flight to the west into Delaware and Chester Counties, where the Pennsylvania Railroad's Main Line served as the spine that connected their new communities to the city center. As trains gave way to the automobile, Route 30 became known as the Main Line, which entered the lexicon as the name for the entire area. It also came to connote a particular kind of upper-crust, old-money, Eastern WASP way of life. Patterned on the English social model, the part of this new American lifestyle devoted to a white-collar city workweek and suburban weekend leisure gave rise to the organization of country clubs, just as it did in the suburbs of Boston and New York. The lush, gently rolling hills of the Main Line provided ideal ground for their creation. Merion Cricket Club, founded in 1865 by sixteen young enthusiasts, reflected that British influence by the sport it featured in its name; taking root at nearby Haverford College beginning in 1835, it became *the* home for cricket in the United States. The Cricket Club's first president, Archibald Montgomery, played the game at a distinct disadvantage; while he was serving in the honor guard at the funeral of President Lincoln earlier that year, a cannon fired prematurely and severed his right arm. Within a few years the club purchased five acres of land to build a private pitch along a road they named

Cricket Avenue, in the town of Ardmore. Another English import, tennis, soon joined the club's roster, and along with the ascendance of American baseball eventually nudged the sport that inspired this small outpost into obsolescence.

Philadelphia's first nine-hole golf course opened in 1893, and the game caught on so quickly that within three years Merion Cricket Club rented a farm near the railway line to construct a golf course on it. The cost of the original outlay was six hundred dollars, with an estimated annual operating budget of twenty-five hundred dollars. The first nine holes opened for play in 1896, for 152 dues-paying members. By 1900 their second nine was completed and the number of golfers topped three hundred, but within a few years the introduction of the hot, solid rubber Haskell golf ball had rendered their short, original course as obsolete as the club's old cricket pitch. By 1910 golf-playing members had decided to invest in a nearby tract of farmland on which to build an entirely new course. They also acquired the old stone farmhouse and barn, to convert those buildings into their new clubhouse.

The members elected Hugh Wilson, a former captain of Princeton's golf team who'd learned the game on the old Merion layout, to spearhead the creation of their new course. Determined to become a serious student of course architecture, Wilson spent weeks studying with American golf's godfather, Charles Blair Macdonald, at the site of his National Golf Links on the north shore of Long Island, just then under construction. Macdonald convinced Wilson that to do his job justice he needed to make a pilgrimage to the shrines of the game in Scotland. Wilson ended up spending half a year overseas and returned with reams of sketches and surveyors' maps he'd commissioned of the holes he most admired. Macdonald had designed National Golf Links as an outright homage to a collection of classic British links holes and moved tons of earth to re-create them as precisely as possible. As he pondered the ground he had to work with back home, Hugh Wilson began to picture something altogether more subtle, original, and demanding.

Upon his return Wilson hired a former groundskeeper from Merion's original course, William Flynn, to supervise construction. A big round Italian immigrant named Joe Valentine worked as Flynn's foreman; he would serve as head groundskeeper for fifty-two years and his son would eventually succeed him. An original thinker and problem solver, Valentine spread white bedsheets on the turf as the men walked the grounds to spot bunkers they planned to install. Turned off by British pot bunkers that lurked out of sight—which had evolved naturally, due to erosion caused by livestock taking shelter from the wind—Wilson insisted his bunkers needed to be seen to affect the greatest psychological impact on a player confronting his next shot. He carved his last three holes in and around an old granite quarry that had supplied the stone for many of the area's big houses, creating a symphonic crescendo to the most dramatic inland course American players had ever seen. Wilson's course opened for play in September of 1912, at a cost of over $180,000, but received such enthusiastic reception from players that plans for a second course began immediately; called the West Course and also designed by Wilson, it opened two years later. Merion thereby became the first private American club to feature two eighteen-hole courses, but from the beginning the original East Course has been considered Hugh Wilson's masterpiece. He would go on to design only two more courses, and the final four holes at nearby Pine Valley—when that storied club's inspired amateur architect, George Crump, died unexpectedly—before passing away himself in 1925 of pneumonia, at only forty-five years of age.

Merion's membership was justifiably proud of their creation, but realized national recognition would come their way only by hosting a USGA championship that would bring the world to their door. With a roster of influential members on its board, Merion secured the 1916 Men's National Amateur. Francis Ouimet missed his first Amateur since coming to prominence; his absence revived the controversy about his status and overshadowed the arrival of U.S. Open champ Chick Evans, who was quick to take offense at what he perceived as a lack of proper deference. When Eastern pundits commented Ouimet would've been the man to beat if he'd been eligible to play, Chick issued this inflammatory gem: "In the West it is generally understood that when a leading player fails to enter an event, he has little chance to win it. There is a certain provincialism about the East, a sort of ostrichlike spirit that believes that when its own eyes are hidden no other eyes can see." With that broadside pasted across the front page of Philadelphia sports sections the day before the tournament, Chick didn't garner much sympathy from Eastern reporters and galleries.

Arriving under the radar during this high-profile wrangling, the Adairs and Bobby Jones checked into the Bellevue-Stratford Hotel in downtown Philadelphia. This was Bobby's first trip out of the Deep South, and his first stay in a grand hotel, where gourmet dining translated to three helpings of pie a la mode. The big city awed and fascinated the wide-eyed fourteen-year-old. Among the unusual sights they experienced was a new means of urban transportation called a "taxi-cab," private cars driven by their owners, who charged riders a nickel to be ferried around town. Originally called "jitneys"—current slang for a nickel— the name eventually became associated with buses. The next day, after a jitney ride to the station, the Atlanta trio boarded a commuter express train out to Merion to get in a practice round. Bobby was not only the youngest player in the field of 157, he was the youngest ever to compete in an Amateur. Bobby loved the pomp and hustle, the tents and colorful banners, the palpable electric atmosphere of a major championship; he had found a home. When they played a practice round it was Bobby's first exposure to lightning-fast bent grass greens; the severe heat of the South prohibited the use of anything but coarser grained Bermuda. He had a steep learning curve; on the fifth hole, facing a thirty-foot putt, he knocked the ball all the way off the green and into a stream.

They arrived early the next day for the first of two qualifying rounds. The top thirty-two players in the field would advance to the match-play tournament. Bobby stepped to the first tee of the West Course that morning wearing a crisp white shirt with a starched collar and a natty bow tie; long light brown wool pants, the only pair he'd brought with him on the trip; a jaunty cap; and a pair of high-topped army boots to which he'd nailed some spikes. He was as tanned and freckled as a farmer's kid, his sun-bleached hair still worn in a schoolboy bowl cut. At five feet four, one hundred sixty-five pounds, he was described as chubby by some accounts, but he carried the weight well, most of it in his legs and rear end, the engine room of his deceptively powerful swing. He seemed a figure of curiosity, even outright amusement for some; Bobby and the Adairs were authentic Southerners, an exotic breed here in the gentrified suburbs of the East. Their sunny openness and lack of guile marked them as country folk out of their element, hayseeds crashing a Manhattan cocktail party. These jaded sophisticates were about to get a first-class lesson in talent.

Bobby shot 74, the lowest first-round score in the entire field. Word got out fast between rounds about what the Dixie Whiz Kid had done, and when he made his way to the East Course for his afternoon round a thousand people waited at the first tee, the largest crowd Bobby had ever played in front of; what would become later in life an almost phobic aversion to big crowds had its start here. He played as poorly that afternoon as he had superbly that morning—although the much more difficult East Course had something to do with that—shooting 89 and landing in a tie for eighteenth place, four shots inside the cut line. Perry Adair came in after him, right on the cut line, and had to endure a play-off to secure the final slot in the match-play field, but he survived. When Bob and Perry met up afterward in front of the big scoreboard, the two hugged each other and jumped up and down in excitement; they were still kids first, golfers second.

They hurried to the bulletin board outside the clubhouse, where the USGA posted the next day's first-round matchups. Bobby drew Eben Byers, a name that meant nothing to him, but one that drew groans from everyone around him. A thirty-six-year-old native of Pittsburgh, Byers had been a National Amateur champion in 1906; he had reached the finals two other times. Sick of receiving condolences from people he hardly knew before they'd even played the match, Bobby cockily fired back a line he'd heard from George Adair: "The bigger they are, the harder they fall."

Grantland Rice smelled a story brewing. A nationally syndicated columnist for the *New York Tribune*, the thirty-five-year-old native Tennessean was considered the country's most influential sportswriter. Sports journalism had just begun to upgrade its image into a respectable profession. Professional teams turned into rallying points of pride for their cities, as all the age-old rivalries taken for granted today were then being born. Historians have dubbed the late teens and twenties the Golden Age of Sports, and much of its popularity and influence can be attributed to the work of a small circle of hardworking New York City reporters, who delivered vivid daily accounts of sporting contests that millions of fans had no other way of experiencing.

The era's best sportswriters—Rice, Ring Lardner, Heywood Hale Broun, Westbrook Pegler, Damon Runyon, and Paul Gallico—were the first to take readers beyond the faceless reportage of facts and numbers and put them inside the worlds and minds of athletes: a first-person, you-are-there style, familiar today but a true novelty then. Each of these men had an inimitable voice and developed a loyal following; most went on to distinguished careers in fiction, poetry, radio, the theater, and screenwriting. Gallico pioneered the participatory brand of sportswriting—sparring with Jack Dempsey for a round in 1922, for instance—that was later elaborated upon and made famous by George Plimpton. Lardner and Runyon pedaled a breezy cynicism about sports and life in general, looking past the rah-rah cant and easy sentimentality of sports to create muckraking portraits of callowness and greed that still seem fresh today. They embodied what became known as the "Aw Nuts" school of sportswriting. The opposite number of these wise guys were the breathless mythmakers, men who looked at these feats of physical achievement and saw a beauty and bravery they wrote about with earnest, wide-eyed wonder—the "Aw Nuts" curmudgeons dismissed them as the "Gee Whiz!" school.

Grantland Rice was the unashamed master of the Gee Whiz school and by 1916 had established himself as a one-man industry. Churning out a staggering volume of articles, columns, screenplays, and installments of weekly epic verse, he published more than 67 *million* words over a fifty-three-year career, the equivalent of 670 average-length novels. Among many other innovations, Rice was responsible for instituting the annual college football "All-American" team. A baseball player, track star, and captain of the football team at Vanderbilt in his youth—and a scratch golfer later in life—he was the only real athlete among his brethren, which explains his empathy with his subjects. Tall, good-looking, a snappy dresser always in superb physical condition, Rice won friends in every sport he covered with his charm, courtesy, and goodwill and struck a chord with readers across the country; he didn't have a cynical bone in his body, which might not play in the salons of the Upper East Side but went over like gangbusters in the heartland. If it turned out athletes had feet of clay, you weren't going to hear about it from him. If people wanted to read about men's failings, the front pages served up a never-ending supply; he believed people turned to the sports page to hear about their triumphs.

Revisionists have not been kind to Rice, pigeonholing him as a cornball shill for the lords of sport, but his approach was grounded in his philosophy for living; he believed that ordinary people—young working-class men in particular—needed heroes, and creating them was his stock in trade. His work made him not only a household name but America's most famous journalist of any stripe during the first half of the century. When Rice decided to write about you—as he would of Jack Dempsey, Babe Ruth, Walter Hagen, and Notre Dame football, all of whom enjoy their cultural immortality in large part because of his interest—it was a benediction from the Pope. You had arrived.

Rice had served a four-year apprenticeship, from 1902 to 1906, at Pop Keeler's future home, the *Atlanta Journal*. During his time there he also struck up a casual acquaintance with a young lawyer named Robert Purmedus Jones; Rice and the Colonel had similar family backgrounds, and both had seen their pro baseball dreams crushed by patrician fathers demanding a more genteel career path for their sons. Because of his interest in golf as a player, he was also the first respected American sportswriter to treat the game as a major sport. When Rice realized that the Jones boy who'd created a sensation during qualifying at Merion was Big Bob's kid, he called Bobby at the Bellevue-Stratford and arranged to take him out to breakfast early the next morning.

Rice took Bobby seriously; he had an instinct for detecting the gifted, and this kid fit the profile. Bobby hardly touched his breakfast; he was about to go thirty-six holes with a former Amateur champion in his debut in a national tournament and couldn't wait to get started. Rice was struck by the fire and confidence in Bobby's manner, but also his gentlemanly manners—a firm handshake while taking off his cap, the courteous and steady cast in the eye. As a fellow Son of the South Rice appreciated the importance of good breeding. He wished Bobby well and said he'd be out to watch him that morning. He didn't voice his concerns about Bobby's displays of temper on the course, nor did he write about them, but he suspected that if Bobby failed to control himself he'd never play the magnificent golf he was capable of shooting.

Most of the gallery attending Merion that day lined up to watch Bobby's match with Eben Byers, who kept his young opponent waiting on the tee in a classic bit of gamesmanship. As they walked off, Bobby stuffed three sticks of gum in his mouth and offered one to Byers, who gruffly shook his head. Bobby shrugged; whatever. The crowd chuckled: with that casual act of innocence Bobby had already won them over. Byers started the match angry—he was a proud man, humiliated that he had to play a boy—and got steadily more steamed all day. Bobby already had a reputation for his temper, but it was never directed at an opponent, only at himself. Anger was the dark side of his bulletproof confidence; he expected perfection on every shot and couldn't forgive himself for anything less. As someone to learn comportment from in his first national match he couldn't have picked a worse opponent than Eben Byers. Early in their match, watching Byers violently reposition his tools after every lousy shot—and he uncorked a lot of them that day—Bobby decided it was perfectly acceptable for him to get in on the act. He'd been tossing clubs around in anger since he was six years old, when that sort of acting out tended to be viewed as "cute." Bobby also had a longshoreman's command of cursing from years of trailing around East Lake after the Colonel and his salty pals, and he unveiled some shockers to the more delicate ears in the gallery.

At one point, already trailing the youngster, Byers hit an approach shot out of bounds, then wound up and hammer-tossed the offending iron over a hedge and refused to let his caddie go after it. The group playing behind them saw so many clubs flying in the air they thought they were following a juggling act. But Bobby was able to discharge his anger and get back to business. Byers stayed in a permanent funk. At the lunch break, Bobby had a three-hole lead, and moved around the grounds happy and carefree. Byers ate his lunch alone in the locker room, out of sight. Bobby's lead grew to five on the afternoon's front nine, but Byers crept back to within three as they made the final turn. The crowd sensed the kid might be ready to crack, that Byers would impose a stronger will, but they'd misread the situation: Bobby's pristine fourteen-year-old nerves were more than up to this task. Byers broke first. Bobby closed him out on the thirty-fifth hole, 3 and 1. The crowd cheered him all the way back to the clubhouse, and he blushed red, waving shyly to his new fans.

Bobby wrote years later, half joking, that he won the match only because Byers ran out of clubs first, but afterward he was his own harshest critic.

"I should have been soundly drubbed," he told George Adair, "I played rotten."

"You won, didn't you?" said George.

Bobby thought about it for a second. "Yes sir, I did."

The next day Bobby went up against Pennsylvania's reigning Amateur champion, Frank Dyer. Untroubled by the attention Bobby brought along with him, Dyer jumped all over his young opponent, winning five of the first six holes. The "Whiz Kid's" club throwing and cursing started immediately. The Byers match had played out as slapstick comedy, and its goofiness had helped defray Bobby's first-round jitters. Frank Dyer presented the kid with his first real test and journalists thought Bobby was close to losing control completely. George Adair recognized it, stepped in, and played surrogate father; he took Bobby aside between holes and told him he'd pull him right off the course and send him home if he didn't behave himself. Chastened, Bobby steadied his emotions and played even par golf the rest of the way. At the seventeenth hole he took the lead from Frank Dyer for the first time.

The eighteenth at Merion is a majestic par four requiring a long drive over an open chasm, the last section of the scenic rock quarry. Dyer and Jones both carried their drives to the fairway but caught bad bounces. The balls were lying by a tall mound; one at the base, one on top, both nestled in high rough. Their referee discovered his contestants were playing an identical brand of ball and neither had differentiated theirs with an identifying mark, as is now the universal custom. Both insisted theirs was the ball in the better lie—an examination once they got to the green revealed that Bobby was correct; his ball had a tar stain on it from an earlier bounce off a road—but to break the stalemate, Bobby volunteered to play the ball at the base of the hill. After hacking it back to the fairway he ended up taking six and losing the hole, which brought them to the lunch break all square, but the advantage was all Jones's. When Bobby latched on to something external to draw anger away from his own performance, he played his best golf, and this incident got him going. He won the opening hole of their afternoon round—after making a point of showing his opponent that he'd covered his ball with "J's"—and never gave back the lead, beating Frank Dyer 4 and 2. Bobby had passed the test.

Bobby's win over Dyer advanced him to the quarterfinals and confirmed his Cinderella status as the darling of the tournament. The evening papers covered his bed at the Bellevue-Stratford that night; Bobby read up about himself and found it a disorienting experience. Many of the stories focused on his temper; he had quickly been stamped as a "hot-blooded Southerner," reinforcing the cultural stereotype of a Dixie hayseed out of his element in sophisticated Yankee environs. Along that same patronizing line, reporters had the nerve to criticize his wardrobe, which hurt Bobby's feelings more than critiques of his temperament. He owned only the one pair of long pants he'd brought with him, and if his boots looked old and dusty compared to what the local swells were wearing, he'd never thought of golf as a "dress-up" game back home and for crying out loud he was only fourteen. But he took the criticism to heart; he swore that nobody would ever make fun of the way he dressed again. Within a few years Bobby would be considered a fashion plate and trendsetter well outside the confines of his sport.

There's a marvelous photograph from one of those sports pages, a posed shot of Bobby setting up for a swing, his gaze slanted down a fairway with Merion's clubhouse in the background. His poised determination, tempered by a wicked Huck Finn smile, suggests a dangerous competitor at least a decade older than his actual age. The club looks as secure in his tanned hands and sturdy, muscled forearms as a scythe in the hands of a harvester. With that hard gleam of confidence in his eyes, no wonder the older players he'd faced found him unsettling. This was only one of many photographs Bobby scrutinized that night, sizing up his image for the first time from the outside, as others saw him. As he put it later: "It seemed sort of indelicate to expose my face in print." He didn't have words to articulate the process at the time, but he had just taken the first step of his transformation from an ordinary kid into an object of fame. One with a face and persona and aura that the public would come to feel they owned more than he did.

Nineteen sixteen was the year Charlie Chaplin burst onto movie screens, separating himself from the pack of antic vaudevillians who made slapstick one-reelers an early staple of the picture business. As Hollywood was discovering, film had revolutionized the creation of public icons; fortunes were about to change hands as a result. Chaplin's skyrocketing popularity pointed toward the mass marketing of stars as the major selling point of entertainment, and not just in the movies. Sports, populated by the strong, fit, and photogenic, would be the next field to feel film's impact so profoundly. Nothing would help Grantland Rice more in his creation of heroes than the mass reproduction of moving pictures confirming the romantic ideals of what star athletes were supposed to look like. The problems all that attention would create for their subjects hadn't even been considered yet; to suddenly see oneself as others do can rip the cover off a young psyche's protective innocence and create chaos for the unprepared mind.

This was the night young Bobby left the Garden of Eden. He seldom made another swing with a golf club in his hand for pleasure or away from the scrutiny of unknown eyes for the next fourteen years. The loss of privacy he was well on his way to realizing would become a crushing burden, but he finally put the newspapers aside and slept soundly that night. Bobby needed every bit of his adolescent confidence the following day; as his next opponent he had drawn defending and two-time U.S. Amateur champion Robert Gardner.

Robert Gardner looked every inch the All-American Ivy League star athlete, from his styled, curly blond locks to the razor-sharp crease in his fashionable slacks. At six one, Gardner had to lean down to shake the schoolboy's hand. Bobby winked at him, which made Gardner laugh. Despite the largest gallery he'd seen in his life, Bobby was over his stage fright; he played crisply all morning. Gardner appeared to be more nervous; he couldn't find a fairway and lost the first two holes. Although Bobby didn't know it at the time, Gardner had a badly infected index finger, which limited his ability to hold on to his grip; the longer the shot the more it flew off line. Despite his wildness off the tee, Gardner executed an impressive variety of recoveries to keep the match close. Convinced the man couldn't keep getting up and down forever, Bobby began to believe he had a chance to beat the defending champ, shot 76, and carried a one-up lead into intermission. The growing legend of the Whiz Kid dominated the grounds; almost every soul who'd made the trip out to Merion crowded around to watch their afternoon round.

They were all square coming to the sixth hole; Bobby stuck his approach close to the pin and Gardner missed the green, leaving himself a delicate downhill chip over a ridge onto a lightning-fast green. He whispered his shot up to within four inches of the cup and got down for a half, when Bobby missed his try at birdie. At the par four seventh, Bobby left his tee shot in ideal position below the flag, while Gardner pulled his well left of the green, staring down at another downhill tight pin; again he chipped to within a foot and knocked it in for the tie. On the eighth, Bobby's approach landed only ten feet from the pin, while Gardner pulled his long and left onto the ninth tee box. This time his pitch onto the green checked up short, outside of Bobby's ball.

"I felt the break had come," said Bobby. "He couldn't keep missing shots and getting away with it."

But Gardner sank his fifteen-footer for par. Although he'd just been shown the line, Bobby missed his third birdie in a row. Another push. Grantland Rice focused on this in his column the next day: "That would have broken the heart of any golfer alive."

"I felt I had been badly treated by luck," Bobby recalled a few years later. "I had been denied something that was rightly mine. I wanted to go off and pout and have someone sympathize with me, and I acted just like the kid I was. I didn't half try to hit the next tee shot, and I didn't half try on any shot thereafter. In short, I quit."

A harsh self-assessment for a teenager playing in his first national event, but typical of Bobby's candor. Gardner handily won five of the next seven holes, and closed him out on the fifteenth when he pulled off another miraculous par after hitting his drive out of bounds. (He was allowed to drop a ball where his ball had gone off the course, lying two; in match play the rule penalizing an out-of-bounds shot with both stroke *and* distance would not go into effect until 1920.)

Looking back on it, Bobby was always grateful that he'd lost when he did. If Gardner had missed any of those chip shots during the heat of their match, Bobby knew he would have beaten him. And if he'd gotten past Gardner, he also knew there was a better than good chance he might have won the 1916 Amateur.

"I had already become a bit cocky because of my success against grown men. I shudder to think what those years might have done to me," he wrote later. "Not so much to my golf, but in a vastly more important respect, to me as a human being."

Grantland Rice wrote this about Bobby's first Amateur: "At his age the game in this country has never developed anyone with such a combination of physical strength, bulldog determination, mechanical skill and coolness against the test. He is the most remarkable kid prodigy we have ever seen."

Although papers reported that "the Georgia schoolboy" took the loss in stride—whistling on his way back to the clubhouse, talking about the big bowl of ice cream he planned to dive into—something much darker and richer was going on inside Bobby. Underneath his smiling sportsmanship this loss hurt him to his core; he had outplayed Gardner almost throughout, but it hadn't seemed to matter. He felt Gardner had only been a stand-in for something else, something implacable and strange, as if the match had been decided by an unseen hand. Herman Melville had written about destiny in a book Bobby had been required to read in school that year. A failure in its day, *Moby-Dick* was being rediscovered fifty years after its initial publication. Bobby developed a lifelong love of literature, but he hadn't appreciated what Melville was after thematically at the time. Now he'd caught an unsettling glimpse of something as slow and powerful as Melville's whale circling in the deep water: the idea that our fate awaits us, foretold like Ahab's, and there was no way of escaping it. What if the result of this match had been written somewhere outside of time or human experience, unconcerned with the playing out of actual events? Bobby ate his ice cream and accepted a hundred consolations as he sat in Merion's clubhouse, but the entire time he couldn't stop wondering why fate, on this day, had chosen the other man. And if that was all that mattered, would it ever turn his way?

The next day Robert Gardner won his semifinal match and advanced to the championship against Chick Evans. Chick had played through without ever being tested, and their final match was watched by eight thousand spectators, including a mesmerized Bobby Jones. The USGA experimented with ropes to control the largest crowd that had ever shown up for an Amateur. Chick started the round with a birdie and built a three-hole advantage by intermission. Gardner came back in the afternoon to close within one on the tenth green, lying two and about to tie the match, when Chick sank a serpentine forty-footer to save par.

As soon as that ball dropped, Bobby knew the match was over; he'd been right there in Gardner's shoes two days before. At this high competitive level, Bobby now knew that winning had everything to do with state of mind; after a blow like that he sensed Gardner was psychologically finished. He was right. Chick won three of the next five holes and closed out the match. Chick's doting mother, who had been in his gallery all week, was the first to throw her arms around him.

Chick Evans had accomplished something no one else could boast about: not only had he captured the U.S. Open and Amateur—as only Ouimet and Jerry Travers had before him—he'd done it in the same year. Boast about it he would, that was Chick's nature, just as it was for him to try to explain to reporters how his was the more impressive achievement. Chick's demons gnawed on him even at the greatest moment in his career. Bobby learned a lot from watching him, some of it negative, about how a champion behaves. He also identified Chick as the man he would someday have to beat, because he now owned something Bobby had during this last week realized he wanted more than anything.

The title of best golfer in the world.

Fate played another hand that day, in a way that delayed Bobby getting his own hands on that title. The game's Grand Old Man, fifty-four-year-old Walter Travis, had been in the galleries at Merion all week. He'd witnessed both of

Bobby's matches and had been impressed by the prodigy. Grantland Rice asked Travis how he thought Bobby could improve.

"He can never improve his shots, if that's what you mean," replied Travis. "But he will learn a great deal more about playing them. And his putting method is faulty."

Rice told George Adair about Travis's comment. Since Travis had a reputation as the greatest putter who ever lived, George sought him out and arranged a putting lesson for Bobby on the practice green the morning before the finals. The early trains coming out to Merion from Philadelphia were packed solid; Bobby and the Adairs were delayed by the crowd and arrived too late to board the express. They caught the next one but arrived twenty minutes late for his lesson with Travis, who had waited only five minutes for Bobby—the thorny Travis insisted on punctuality—then stormed off to watch Evans and Gardner. The lesson didn't take place.

Travis had been right; Bobby's putting method was faulty—the alignment of his stance was off, he swayed his lower body as he made the stroke, and too much hand action knocked the ball off line—but that lesson would now be delayed for almost eight years.

Back in Atlanta, Bobby's schoolmates seemed less impressed by what he'd done than did the steady parade of admiring grown-ups. First among them was Pop Keeler. The two would meet out at East Lake on Saturdays after Bobby's game and hoist a few Coca-Colas, which that summer introduced its iconic hourglass-shaped bottle. Bobby learned that Pop knew a lot more about golf than most people, and he liked talking strategy with him. Bobby also appreciated Pop's interest in him, and his lively sense of humor; he was the silliest grown-up Bobby had ever known, outgoing, socially fearless, and a shameless flirt with the ladies, an enlightening contrast to the shy young Jones. Slowly, steadily, the unlikeliest of friendships was born.

A few weeks later, Bobby's childhood buddy, nineteen-year-old Alexa Stirling, captured the United States Women's Championship, in Belmont Springs, Maryland. After working with Alexa for close to a decade, Kiltie had his first national champion. After Bobby's showing at Merion, the Eastern golf establishment now had two reasons to turn its eye south of the Mason-Dixon Line.

. . .

Bobby and his father read the daily papers about other, less familiar places on maps that in 1916 became forever known as killing grounds: Verdun, the Somme, Kut-al-Amara, Gallipoli. Unable to break through the stagnant Western Front, Germany settled for a strategy of attrition; they would bleed France white. Major cities suffered little damage; for the most part only industrial property was destroyed, and relatively few civilians died; this war, conducted in the fields and forests of the French countryside, had become a perfect threshing machine for killing soldiers. Military casualties, measured in the thousands, reached the hundreds of thousands, and soon thereafter the millions. At the Battle of the Somme, thirty thousand men died in the first *half hour*.

President Wilson had resigned himself to the idea that American participation was inevitable. Despite his efforts to mediate peace in Europe, the Germans refused to engage in meaningful negotiation, and meanwhile twenty-nine more Americans died on ships sunk by U-boats. Facing reelection, Wilson emphasized "preparedness and peace," asking Congress to double the armed forces. Teddy Roosevelt, intent on driving Wilson out of office, dissolved his "Bullmoose" Party to unite behind an obscure Republican, Charles Evans Hughes, who resigned his seat on the Supreme Court to accept the nomination. "Anyone but Wilson" became their call to arms. Less than a year into his new marriage, politically motivated rumors surfaced that Wilson had been unfaithful to his late wife. Wilson was reduced to wrapping himself defensively in the flag; he led the singing of "The Star-Spangled Banner" at the Democratic convention, and, it was noted with pride, held the challenging high note in the final phrase. The Republican attack forced Wilson to campaign not on his positive achievements but only on what he'd avoided; "He Kept Us Out of War" became his slogan, and the 1916 election served as a referendum on that issue.

A confident Charles Evans Hughes went to bed on election night after early headlines declared him the winner. The vote narrowed through the night and remained too close to call into a second day, when it was finally determined that Wilson had carried the pivotal state of California by less than four thousand votes and won a second term by twenty-three electoral votes, one of the slimmest margins in history. Early in 1917 Wilson made one last stab at diplomacy in Europe, asking both sides to lay down their arms and create what he called "Peace Without Victory." His plea fell on deaf ears. On January 31 Germany announced the resumption of unrestricted submarine warfare.

Three days later, after another American ship went down, Wilson finally severed diplomatic relations with Germany, on the brink of war; the final push would come from a most unlikely direction.

On January 16 the British secret service had intercepted a coded telegram from German foreign minister Arthur Zimmermann to his ambassador in Mexico City. In it, Zimmermann outlined a scenario whereby in the event America entered the war, Mexico would launch an invasion from across the Rio Grande. After America was defeated—an outcome about which Zimmermann expressed no doubt—Mexico would be handed back her lost nineteenth-century territories: Arizona, New Mexico, and Texas. Why the Germans thought Mexico, in the middle of a bloody revolution, would be capable of presenting a credible threat to the United States has never been answered. The British sat on this bombshell until after Wilson broke off relations with Germany, then wired it to Washington. Wilson's greatest fear was leading a divided nation into war, but after the Zimmermann telegram became public, the country voiced universal outrage about Germany's treachery. On April 6 President Wilson appeared before Congress and in the most impassioned oration of his life asked for a declaration of war against Germany.

> Neutrality is no longer feasible or desirable where the peace of the world is involved and the freedom of its peoples, and the menace to that peace and freedom lies in the existence of autocratic governments, backed by organized force which is controlled wholly by *their* will, not by the will of their people. The world must be made safe for democracy. To such a task we can dedicate our lives and our fortunes, everything that we are and everything that we have, with the pride of those who know that the day has come when America is privileged to spend her blood and her might for the principles that gave her birth and happiness and the peace which she has treasured. God helping her, she can do no other.

The resolution passed by large but not unanimous margins: 82–6 in the Senate, and 373–50 in the House.

When he was alone afterward with his secretary, Wilson shed inconsolable tears. While Congress cheered him, he knew he had just sentenced thousands of American boys to death.

Red Cross Match, 1918: Perry Adair, Elaine Rosenthal,
Bobby, Alexa Stirling.

CHAPTER FOUR

Finding a Voice

MAJOR LEAGUE BASEBALL CONTINUED play through the summer of 1917 while Wilson instituted the country's first military draft since the Civil War. Boxing and horse racing, the nation's two most popular sports, carried on without missing a beat; a horse called Omar Khayyam won the Kentucky Derby. In the fall of 1917, as the first wave of over a million American soldiers prepared to ship out for France, the college football season proceeded as planned, but Grantland Rice canceled his All-American selections after enlisting himself and leaving for Europe. The Chicago White Sox won the World Series over the New York Giants in October, the same month the first American soldier in Europe fired a shot in anger. The U.S. Tennis Open was held as scheduled but billed itself as the "Patriotic Open." Late that fall, as news of the first American casualties drifted home, the National Hockey League opened its doors for business; Lord Stanley's Cup was won for the first time by the Seattle Metropolitans.

Only the United States Golf Association canceled its scheduled championships in the year America joined the war. Perhaps the lingering public perception of golf as a wealthy man's game prompted the decision. The fledgling PGA soon followed suit and canceled its championship as well. The Western Golf Association in Chicago, four years the USGA's junior and often at odds with its Eastern cousins, announced plans to conduct their tournaments as scheduled. Until the emergence of the PGA, the Western Open was considered America's second major. The WGA went a step further in tweaking establishment noses by inviting Francis Ouimet, whose banishment by the USGA they had refused to recognize, to participate in their annual Western Amateur. Ouimet did not decide to accept until after he made one last appeal to the USGA's executive committee.

Frank Woodward, the man who instigated Ouimet's banishment, had been replaced by the more moderate Howard Perrin, an influential member at Merion. Francis received word through diplomatic channels that Perrin might lend a friendlier ear to his appeal for reinstatement. On June 18, after their regular meeting in New York, the USGA executive committee adjourned to a private dining room at Delmonico's, the downtown power restaurant of its day. Waiting inside were Francis Ouimet and John Sullivan, who had traveled by train from Boston that afternoon. This extraordinary closed-door meeting, the minutes noted, was being held at their request. After what was described as "a friendly and lengthy discussion," the council decided that since no new facts were presented and no change in their status had been made—the two men were still engaged in the sale of "golf supplies"—their application for reinstatement could not be granted. The vote was unanimous.

Bitterly disappointed, the following week Francis accepted the WGA invitation to play in the Western Amateur at Midlothian. In front of a supportive Chicago crowd he won the only formal tournament in which he had competed for the last two years. Although he didn't make it past the first round at Midlothian, fifteen-year-old Bobby Jones told friends his trip to Chicago had been worth it because he got a chance to shake the hand of his idol, Francis Ouimet. They didn't have time for an extended conversation—Bobby was struck speechless when they met, making that difficult—but that would come later.

In the absence of the USGA's championships, the only high-profile golf played in America that summer was at charity tournaments modeled after Harry Vardon's benefits for the war effort. Top players from around the country lined up to participate. One name in particular now dominated golf in the South: Bobby Jones picked up right where he left off at Merion and opened his season in June with a victory at the Southern Amateur, the youngest player ever to win that title. As a result Bobby had been invited to play a series of Red Cross matches, a schedule that would dominate the next two years of his life.

An officer at Wright & Ditson Sporting Goods—Ouimet's old employers—had the idea that a junior version of these charity matches might prove popular. He recruited his key participants straight from East Lake: Bobby, Perry Adair, and reigning U.S. Women's champion Alexa Stirling. Elaine Rosenthal, a talented Chicago teen, completed the foursome. With Miss Rosenthal's mother serving as their chaperone, the kids set off on a whirlwind exhibition tour of resorts throughout New England. While on the road Bobby and Perry experimented with their first grown-up vice, sneaking cigarettes, a habit Bobby was subsequently never able to shake; he claimed they helped settle his nerves on the course. They were treated as celebrities wherever they traveled—and acclaimed as fine young patriots for helping the war effort. These were heady days for Bobby, filled with golf, fawning interviews, and congratulatory dinners, an endless stream of unconditional admiration. Another swing followed through the Midwest and South, where Bobby broke scoring records by the handful. These tours proved such a success—the kids helped raise over $150,000—that invitations followed for them to participate in grown-up events.

Befitting his status as dual U.S. champion, Chick Evans had taken the lead in the Red Cross effort and worked tirelessly on its behalf, traveling every weekend to participate in a match. Chick asked Bobby and Perry to travel to Chicago for a charity match against himself and Bob Gardner, the man who'd beaten Bobby at Merion. Another match followed a few weeks later in Kansas City. Before Bobby established himself as a serious rival, Chick couldn't have been nicer to the younger man, who was flattered by the champion's interest in him. When two players dropped out of a PGA tournament in New York to benefit the War Relief Fund, Chick called Bobby and Perry as last-minute replacements. This time the boys took the train alone, and they received a warm welcome as houseguests of Grantland Rice and his wife, Kit.

The Whiz Kids were shown the time of their lives by the cosmopolitan couple, highlighted, as far as fifteen-year-old Bobby was concerned, by a trip to Coney Island. In addition to his loving, supportive father, Bobby had the good fortune, or uncanny sense, to attract a number of mentors during his early years. Kiltie revealed the secrets of the golf swing. George Adair opened the doors to the regional and national golf scene. Pop Keeler would soon begin serving as the confidant he needed to cope with the grueling demands of fame. Champion Chick Evans had taken him under his wing. Grantland Rice introduced him to the chic, urbane world of big business and high society he would eventually inhabit. Both Rice and Jones later acknowledged that this week in New York formed the foundation for their close, lifelong friendship.

With the cancellation of the Open, the War Relief Fund tournament was the biggest event of the golf season, and its unique format has never been duplicated. On opening day, four teams were chosen from the year's best field: Amateurs, Homebred Pros, Scottish Pros, and English Pros. For the first time Bobby found himself in the company of the game's rough-and-tumble professionals, the rakish Walter Hagen among them. By the start of the war, Hagen had bumped up his price for exhibitions to an unheard-of $150 an appearance. Realizing that collecting paychecks for golf while Americans were readying for war hurt his public image, Hagen threw himself into the charity circuit with gusto. With his unerring nose for a buck, Hagen suspected exposure at charity events would allow him to jack up his appearance fee when the war ended. He was right.

This was the first time anyone charged admission for an American golf tournament, the only obvious way to raise money for charity, but no one had believed people would pay to watch the sport under any circumstances. The War Relief matches proved them wrong. Bobby's amateur team was led by four-time champion Jerry Travers, who came out of retirement to take part. Bobby's host, Granny Rice, was also added to the team, more for press connections than golfing prowess.

The War Relief matches added a master class to Bobby's education: thirty-six holes a day at Baltusrol, Siwanoy, and Garden City against the best golfers in the world. The PGA had settled on an oddly weighted scoring system that substantially rewarded large margins of victory, a huge disadvantage for the amateurs, who were fielding the weakest team. Much of the blame fell on Granny Rice, a nice weekend golfer but miles out of his depth in this company; he got slaughtered in every match and failed to win a single point. Walter Hagen and the Homebred Pros won bragging rights for the week by a wide margin; the Scots finished second, the English third, with the amateurs in distant last place. Those standings fairly represented the state of American golf; homebred golfers had won every U.S. Open since 1911, three of the last four by amateurs. But with Travers retired and Ouimet in limbo, the amateurs' run appeared to be ending, with native-born pros coming on strong. The best performance on the amateur team that week came from Little Bobby Jones, who won all three of his singles matches against older, seasoned pros, and finished 5-1 overall. New York's press corps concluded that Bobby's spectacular debut at Merion had not been a fluke after all. His fluid, natural swing was now hailed as the most elegant move at the ball anyone had ever seen.

There was simply no precedent for this in an American athlete's development. World events had conspired to provide an apprenticeship greater than any golfer in history could come close to matching. A fifteen-year-old launching drives of over two hundred fifty yards, showing unearthly composure under pressure, pulling off high-risk shots no one else dared to attempt, beating pros and amateurs twice his age in national tournaments: no one had ever seen a kid like this. Prodigies had appeared in chess, music, and mathematics but never as an athlete. No other mainstream sport could have produced a Bobby Jones, golf being a non-contact contest where a kid could play straight up against physically and emotionally mature men a generation older. To top it off, as a bona fide Southerner, Bobby had bloomed out of a golfing wasteland in a sport dominated by the Northeast since its inception. His precocity could only be explained as a freak of nature, which was how the press began to slant portrayals of him. Stories and profiles appeared outside the sporting press in mainstream news magazines. Only a handful of articles mentioned, in passing, Bobby's increasingly out-of-control fits of temper directed at his failings on the course. He remained the perfect young gentleman in every other circumstance, but these outbursts were becoming more volatile, and according to one observer were not confined to the golf course.

This was the secret cost of Bobby's skyrocketing reputation; perfection became the only way he could hold up his end of the bargain. He expected nothing less of himself, which set him on a collision course with reality. In their eagerness to spread the word about the phenomenon of early success, reporters almost never bother to note that prodigies seldom enjoy successful second acts. That unhappy task is often left, sometimes sooner rather than later, to the obituary department.

The pressure was growing. The legend of Bobby Jones had begun to take on a life of its own.

In May of 1917, Pop Keeler was still recovering from the previous winter's cerebral hemorrhage. No longer required to wear a brace on his damaged left arm, he had found a way to work around the disability in his golf swing. His scores at East Lake were getting down around 100 again when fortune frowned on him for a third straight year. The diagnosis this time was monarticular arthritis, a devastating infection that took root in his left knee, then rampaged through his system unchecked. Keeler spent ten weeks in the hospital and, as he put it, "sixty hours on the rim of the Big Dark. The doctors assured me solemnly, and I believed them implicitly, that this particular malady caused the most atrocious suffering known to science. This seemed rather piling it on."

They saved his life again, but the infection destroyed his knee, leaving his leg frozen at a forty-five-degree angle. The doctors subjected Pop to months of torturous treatment, breaking his knee on the operating table seven times in an attempt to restore mobility. For six weeks he was forced to lie in bed attached to an experimental device called "Buck's Extension," an elaborate weight and pulley system operated by electric motor that continually raised and dropped the lower part of his leg. He accepted all this punishment with stoic good cheer, and in the end they succeeded in straightening the leg so he could walk, but it remained as stiff as a plank for the rest of his life. The knee joint burned viciously for years. When he went back to golf again in 1918, Keeler played the game on crutches for six months.

With American involvement in the war growing more serious by the day and casualties mounting, Pop felt a deep sense of failing as a sort of "bogus cripple" who didn't deserve the sympathy he often received from strangers who assumed he was a wounded vet. After training himself to walk a short distance without crutches, he tried to volunteer for service overseas but was turned away as physically unfit. He protested that if he could play golf he could carry a gun, but the appeal fell on deaf ears. When, years later, Pop encountered as his opponent in a golf tournament the same doctor who'd judged him unworthy, he took great satisfaction in beating the man soundly.

While Bobby was earning academic honors during his senior year of high school, American boys only two and three years older began dying overseas. Ten million males between eighteen and thirty years had registered for the draft, but six months after declaring war less than a hundred thousand combat-ready soldiers had touched ground in France. President Wilson had put General Jack Pershing in charge of the American Expeditionary Force. A former West Point instructor and strict disciplinarian, Pershing had been nicknamed "Black Jack" by his cadets as a term of derision; he'd commanded a regiment of African-American soldiers during the Spanish-American War. The name stuck, and he embraced its implications with pride. A widower, whose wife and three children died tragically in a fire in 1915, Pershing had spent the previous year chasing Pancho Villa around the hills of northern Mexico. Wilson jumped over a long list of more senior officers to tap him for the job, one of the best appointments he ever made.

Pershing arrived in Paris in June 1917 and applied his implacable will to create the first modern American army. His soldiers adopted as their marching song a snappy tune called "Over There"; its composer, popular Broadway playwright and star George M. Cohan, was awarded a Congressional Medal. The men of the infantry, the army's backbone, became known in Europe as "doughboys," after the fried wads of dough that had been a staple of the foot soldier's diet since the Civil War. Members of the aristocratic cavalry popularized the term, but not as a compliment; it was equivalent to calling their underdog infantry cousins "doughnut heads." The world's most illustrious former cavalry officer, fifty-nine-year-old Teddy Roosevelt, petitioned President Wilson for permission to command his own division. The army's chief of staff refused the request, which never reached the president, but Roosevelt blamed Wilson for the denial and found another reason to despise him.

Francis Ouimet didn't wait for the draft. He became the country's first noted athlete to enlist after America entered the war, and by the fall of 1917 had been assigned to train at Camp Devens north of Boston. Before he could ship overseas, a suggestion came down from command that Ouimet might do the army more good on a golf course than on the battlefield. Francis spent the rest of the war playing fund-raisers for the armed forces, often in uniform, and rose to the rank of first lieutenant. As civic minded as his rival, Chick Evans volunteered for the army air corps, which began life in 1917 with a total of fifty-five rickety training planes and a single combat squadron. Walter Hagen avoided military service; he had a wife and a baby boy, which exempted him from the draft. Although he never lost interest in making a living—some small pro tournaments were still being held—Walter spent half his time during the war playing charity matches. Like many German Americans proud of his heritage Hagen faced closer scrutiny about his loyalties. Courses in the German language had been outlawed nationwide; even the works of long-dead German composers were banned in some cities. The immensely popular newspaper cartoon strip *Katzenjammer Kids* was retitled *The Captain and the Kids* to dodge the growing anti-German sentiment. Henry Ford, the largest employer of immigrants in the country, made sure all his thousands of non–English speaking workers learned this sentence first: "I am a good American."

While the Allies waited for the Americans to arrive, the war entered its darkest days. A five-mile gain at the Battle of Passchendaele cost the British 400,000 men. French dead and wounded passed the 2 million mark with no end in sight; their army was in disarray. Rather than commit suicide in pointless battles, entire units deserted in open rebellion; a few marched on the capital before laying down their arms. Turning its eye away from the slaughter, Paris was transfixed that summer by the trial of a plump forty-one-year-old Dutch divorcée named Margaretha Geertruida Zelle. Her story had all the ingredients of a scandalous potboiler—sex, scandal, espionage—and her case created a sensation around the world. A has-been exotic dancer and courtesan who had been appearing in states of undress on European stages since 1905, Zelle was accused of passing Allied military secrets—picked up during her sexual escapades—to the German secret service. Defending herself at a military court-martial, Zelle admitted passing information to a German spy, but claimed she was a double agent who had been ordered to do so by her superiors in French intelligence. That may have been the case, but no French officials stepped forward to corroborate her story. Although she appears to have been guilty of little more than lousy judgment in lovers—too many of them in German uniforms—the tribunal convicted her as a warning to enemy collaborators. A military firing squad greeted the woman—who had been known for years by her stage name, Mata Hari—at sunrise on October 15, 1917. Zelle faced her firing squad with a performer's bravado, refusing a blindfold and blowing a kiss to her executioners just before they opened fire as the sun peeked over the walls of Saint-Lazare prison. *"Matahari"* is a Malaysian word meaning "the eye of dawn."

Revolutionary forces in Russia overthrew the czar in March of 1917, ending three centuries of the Romanovs' rule. A Western-style democratic republic took control led by moderate Alexander Kerensky and was immediately recognized by President Wilson, but it would not survive the year when an obscure group of radical socialists seized power in Moscow. The rest of the world, and most of Russia, had never heard of the Communist Party or their Marxist ideology. By November, Vladimir Lenin's government cut itself off from its former allies, refusing to recognize Russia's commitment to the war. The Bolsheviks slaughtered the czar and his family, who had been kept in protective custody by Kerensky, dumped their bodies down a well, and began negotiating a separate peace with the Germans. That treachery freed over a million German soldiers for reassignment to the Western Front. By spring of 1918, a revitalized German army climbed out of the trenches and pushed the Allies back forty miles, threatening the outskirts of Paris. A new long-range artillery gun, nicknamed "Big Bertha" by the Allies, could now lob shells into the city from over thirty miles away. Out of fresh recruits, its army in shock, a million Parisians fled the capital; the exhausted French people had reached a breaking point, but for the first time American soldiers were ready to join the fight.

On May 31, on a bridge over a vital crossroads at Chateau Thierry north of Paris, machine gunners from the Third American Division stopped a crucial German advance in its tracks. Days later, at the Battle of Belleau Wood, U.S. Marines of the Second Division rushed into a square mile of hell on earth and rooted out the toughest veteran division in the German army. As they arrived, French officers running back the other way yelled at the Americans to retreat. "Retreat? Hell, we just got here," replied the marines' commander, and entered history. How the untested Yanks would perform under fire had remained the greatest unknown of the war; when the moment finally came they fought like enraged hornets. Nearly eight thousand Americans died in Belleau Wood, over half the men who marched into the engagement, but the Germans lost even more. Over a quarter of a million American soldiers were now landing in France every month. Although they still constituted only a small percentage of the Allied forces, their high morale and bravery in combat reinvigorated the defense of Paris. In September General Pershing launched the first all-American offensive near Verdun; in one day the Germans gave up more ground than they'd yielded in four years.

A meeting of the USGA executive committee, in January of 1918, finally gave Francis Ouimet the news he'd been hoping for. With a divided heart, Francis had decided to give up his sporting goods business when he joined the army. The store probably wouldn't have survived anyway; sales for all "leisure activities" plummeted as soon as America entered the war. His appearances in uniform raising money for the war effort had scrubbed Ouimet's slightly tarnished image. The USGA voted unanimously to restore Francis's amateur status without his requesting it. Ouimet received the news with gratitude; always the good soldier, he never brought the matter up in the press and soon afterward volunteered to work as an officer of the USGA. At that same meeting, the USGA also took one look at what was happening in Europe and canceled its championships for a second consecutive year.

After graduating with honors from Tech High School at sixteen, Bobby spent a second summer on the charity golf circuit, resuming his exhibition schedule with Perry, Elaine Rosenthal, and Alexa. Early that summer he set another scoring record at East Lake with 70, but played his worst round of the season a few weeks later at a charity match near Boston. After a poor shot he scissored his club right over the heads of the crowd, then picked up his ball and chucked it deep into the woods. When the crowd recoiled and Alexa reprimanded him, Bobby shot back: "I don't give a damn what anybody thinks about me." He later apologized to Alexa, but seemed increasingly unable to control his emotions. A *Boston Globe* reporter agreed: "These pranks by Jones will have to be corrected if this player expects to rank with the best in the country. Although Jones is only a boy, his display of temper when things went wrong did not appeal to the gallery."

That same summer, at the urging of his socially ambitious wife, Walter Hagen left the confines of the sleepy old Country Club of Rochester, where he'd spent his entire life, to accept the head pro job at a swank new club outside Detroit, Oakland Hills. The city was the social center of the booming auto industry, fueled by lucrative defense contracts, and Walter felt instantly at home among the club's nouveau riche members, whose company he aspired to join. Walter talked himself into a free set of wheels from a new Motor City chum, beginning a lifelong affair with flashy cars. Although he admitted he was a dreadful teacher—he spent most lessons showing his students how *he* would execute a shot, barely giving them a chance to make a swing—Hagen soon joined Ty Cobb, the Tigers' established star outfielder, as the toast of Detroit.

In September Bobby began his freshman year at the Georgia Institute of Technology, better known as Georgia Tech. Bobby's choice of school, and mechanical engineering as his major, surprised his family, a sign of his growing independence and attraction to precision of mind. An orderly approach to understanding the physical world was something Bobby wanted under his belt, and it would lead to a more profound understanding of the physics of the golf swing than any player had ever possessed. As he left boyhood behind, Bobby's intellectual gifts caught up with the physical. From this point forward his deliberate approach to education followed the classical ideal, shoring up his weaknesses while expanding his sphere of knowledge toward fullness. During his first winter at Tech, consumed with a heavy class load and raising an appropriate amount of hell as a popular young fraternity pledge, he played less golf than at any other time in his life.

The same week Bobby began classes, nearly a million U.S. troops saw action when the Allies mounted their largest offensive of the war. The assault broke the back of the weakening German army. With forces poised to thrust deep into their heartland, the Central Powers unraveled; Austria quit the field and opened negotiations with the Allies for an armistice. Turkey and Bulgaria quickly followed. Germany now stood alone against the Allied advance, and the end came quickly. On November 9 Kaiser Wilhelm abdicated his throne in the middle of the night and fled to Belgium in his pajamas. The next day German officers met their Allied counterparts in the dining car of a passenger train in the forest of Compiegnes and signed the terms of surrender.

The dehumanizing calculus of war reduced the tragedy to cold, hard numbers. Six hundred imperial cemeteries across the fields of France and Belgium housed a million British casualties. In France and England, 36 percent of men between nineteen and twenty-two when the war began had lost their lives. The additional percentage of wounded, disabled, or psychologically damaged can safely be doubled. Add to this a devastating influenza epidemic that swept through Europe in 1918, killing over 20 million worldwide, and it's not hard to see why this soon became known as "the Lost Generation." Germany lost 3 million dead and faced oblivion as a nation and a culture. Its disastrous aggression and subsequent humiliation during the peace process created a seedbed for the rise of a psychotic Austrian named Adolf Hitler.

America got off lightly, losing "only" 120,000 young men during its single year of action, more than half of those to disease. U.S. soldiers had not won the war, but their timely arrival and robust presence in battle had turned the tide and carried the Allies to victory. The domestic economy benefited enormously from the muscle it added to meet the crisis; the United States had grown into a global power. When he traveled to Paris early the following year for the peace conference, President Wilson was greeted as the savior of Western civilization, traveling in triumph through the capitals of Europe; crowds threw flowers in his path on the Champs-Elysées. Only a decade before, Wilson had been laboring in obscurity as president of a small New Jersey college, a man with no political experience or ambitions. After a single term as New Jersey's governor he vaulted straight into the White House. Never had any American political figure come so far so fast. Standing at the high-water mark of his life as he set sail for Paris in early 1919, the speed of Wilson's fall from that peak would exceed his rise; in less than a year his career, reputation, and physical well-being would lie in ashes.

One hundred and fifty tons of paper and ticker tape greeted America's returning soldiers as they marched through New York. Stories spread about men like Tennessee native Private Alvin York, a former conscientious objector who single-handedly captured 132 German soldiers. From coast to coast Wilson's imposed mood of self-restraint and sacrifice ended with the armistice, but in the aftermath of war the economy stumbled and unemployment rose alarmingly. Labor unrest reached violent heights not seen in twenty years; strikes crippled the steel and mining industries. Race riots broke out in twenty cities, and the ghostly Ku Klux Klan resurfaced, boasting 100,000 members; seventy lynchings took place in 1919 in the South and lower Midwest. More than a few victims were soldiers in uniform. Only months before, members of African-American divisions who had served with distinction in France marched in the parade down Fifth Avenue. For many Americans the most alarming news of all came when the Eighteenth Amendment was ratified by enough states to go into effect on January 16, 1920, prohibiting the sale of alcoholic beverages.

In early 1919 the Paris Peace Conference convened, bearing the highest hopes of mankind, fueled by Wilson's naïve faith in his ability to lead Europe into a new tomorrow. Wilson was the first American president to travel overseas while still in office, and he remained in Paris for six months. His hopes for redrawing the map of the world along noble if ill-defined lines of "self-determination" evaporated in a spiteful scrum of score settling and betrayals. The map had already been crudely reconfigured by the war: the Austro-Hungarian Empire was gone, Imperial Russia destroyed from within, the Ottoman Turks on their way to extinction. With the exception of the English royals—a ceremonial shell of their former glory—the last of the ancient regimes had been purged. New countries were being birthed, lost ones resurrected: Poland, Hungary, the Baltic states, Finland now free from Russia, a hybrid Czechoslovakia, the entire Middle East up for grabs, the quarrelsome Balkan republics now lumped into a ticking time bomb called Yugoslavia. In time this new world map looked more like a chain of land mines.

If the end of the war had been a victory of will and purpose, the peace that followed represented a spectacular failure of human nature. Wilson was frustrated and isolated in a hostile environment; his energy flagged and his health followed. He was forced to sign a compromised treaty that brutalized Germany and all but guaranteed the same arguments would be fought over the same ground in another twenty years. The diplomats who sold him out in Paris also managed to pin the perceived failure of the conference on the man who had staked his reputation on its success. His image sullied, Wilson sailed home that summer feeling ill and defeated. During a whistle-stop tour through the States, trying to rally support for America's entry into his League of Nations, Wilson ominously predicted another world war would be inevitable if the free nations of the world failed to unite. He had fatally misjudged the prevailing mood. America, tired of solving Europe's problems, turned him down. Three days after returning to Washington, on October 2, Wilson suffered a massive paralytic stroke.

America turned away from the Old World, eager to immerse itself in forgetting and recreation. The booming war economy meant people had more means to indulge their appetites and more options than ever to feed them. Vaudeville had hit its peak in over four thousand theaters nationwide. Jazz broke out of its cult status into the mainstream, transforming the performing and recording industries with the first mass assimilation of an African-American idiom. Automobiles revolutionized urban lifestyles, encouraging mobility, giving rise to the suburbs and the beginning of a commuter culture. Movies experienced the greatest surge in popularity in history and had developed the talent pool to produce a flood of full-length silent dramas and comedies. Married stars and business partners, Douglas Fairbanks and Mary Pickford were sold as Hollywood's first royal couple; the mass marketing of movie-star glamour was about to become a self-sustaining industry. (Both were avid golfers and, in the style of Tinseltown monarchs, commissioned Donald Ross to build a nine-hole course on their private estate in Beverly Hills. Ross would build another nine on film comedian Harold Lloyd's adjoining estate, thus enabling the A-list crowd to play a full eighteen without rubbing shoulders with mortals.) Women's fashions loosened up, and hemlines began to rise, shaking off the last vestiges of Victorian prudery. Up until now a relatively minor diversion, professional athletics were on the verge of becoming a national obsession.

The stage was set for an explosion in the popularity of organized sports. A small group of superstars who would carry their sports to dizzying new heights had all methodically worked their way toward the spotlight. The Boston Red Sox defeated the Chicago Cubs four games to two to win the 1918 World Series. This was only the fifteenth World Series, and the Red Sox had won five in five tries, this one behind the pitching of twenty-three-year-old George Herman Ruth. A thirteen-game winner, Ruth won twice more in the Series and extended his record scoreless-inning streak, begun in the 1916 Series, to twenty-nine, but the "Babe" was starting to attract more attention for his bat. He earned his nickname while with the Baltimore Orioles farm system, the latest in a series of players discovered by owner-manager Jack Dunn who were known as his "babes." Drafted as a pitcher, Ruth agreed to play outfield because of a manpower shortage caused by the war. In only three hundred trips to the plate Ruth hit .300 and tied for the league lead in home runs with eleven. That fall a former Notre Dame football captain named Knute Rockne took over as head coach and transformed the small Catholic university's program into the most enduring legend in collegiate athletics. Late in the year Jack Dempsey, a charismatic young heavyweight from Manassa, Colorado, fought his way into the ranking of number-one contender for Jess Willard's heavyweight crown, setting up a title fight the following spring. Each of these men, with the assistance of Grantland Rice's typewriter, was about to ascend to America's modern version of Mount Olympus.

The war had done wonders for democratizing the sport of golf. The USGA's restraint in canceling its championships during combat had bought tremendous goodwill and elevated its reputation with the general public. Millions raised by the Red Cross and War Relief matches legitimized the game in the eyes of the common man as a sport for the masses. The box-office success of those events made it clear spectators no longer dismissed golf as an indulgent form of leisure but saw it as a thrilling competitive event. An explosion in golf course construction took place across the country as the newly wealthy hungered for more and better places to play. Club makers and ball manufacturers went back to their drawing boards to produce equipment that made the game progressively more accessible to the average duffer.

The game's American championships resumed in 1919, and when the U.S. Open began play at Brae Burn near Boston in June, the biggest cheers were reserved for local hero Francis Ouimet's official return to the game. Francis shot four under through his first ten holes and electrified the event, but weakened by an attack of pneumonia that winter he faded quickly after his fast start. Bobby Jones declined to travel from Atlanta; the seventeen-year-old freshman wasn't ready to test the rougher waters an Open. Walter Hagen stepped into the breach and the legend of "the Haig"—the fearless, devil-may-care cocktail-swilling roué who created headlines and captivated the public's imagination—officially came to life at Brae Burn.

Hagen arrived in Boston fresh off a solid performance on the Florida winter circuit, and discovered his show-business pal Al Jolson was in town touring in a production of a hit Broadway musical, *Sinbad*. An almost forgotten figure today, Jolson was the entertainment industry's first crossover superstar. Hugely successful in vaudeville, he had become the recording industry's first artist to sell records in the millions. Jolson later made history in the movies when he starred in the first live sound musical, *The Jazz Singer*, in 1927. Born Asa Yoelson, son of a Lithuanian cantor, his trademark style incorporated a high-octane blend of High Holy Day operatics and co-opted black jazz riffs; Jolson frequently performed in minstrel-show blackface, which accounts for his diminished modern reputation. Hagen and Jolson recognized a kindred alpha-dog spirit in each other that led to a series of nightly parties throughout the week of the Open. These revels included a young Bostonian Jolson had befriended by the name of Eddie Lowery, Francis Ouimet's famous ten-year-old caddie at the 1913 Open. Now sixteen and a solid player in his own right, Eddie had just won his first Massachusetts Junior Championship. Another pre-cocious charmer with a love of the spotlight, Eddie had caught Jolson's eye and the star welcomed the kid into his neon-lit world. The fun-loving side of Hagen that had recently started to emerge fit into this scene hand in glove, and he didn't miss any of the heavy backstage action all week. He also took Eddie under his wing, inviting him out to follow the action at Brae Burn where, despite all these recreational distractions, Walter managed to end up tied for the lead of the Open after four rounds with local blue-collar pro Mike "King" Brady.

A likeable, hardworking thirty-two-year-old Bostonian whose best playing days were behind him, Mike Brady carried a five-stroke lead over Hagen into the final round. Although he'd lost play-offs in two previous U.S. Opens, smart money figured the stars had aligned for Mike to finally close the deal in his hometown, but he blew up late in his last round. Hagen had already written off winning halfway through a disinterested front nine when Brady's score drifted back to him; Walter realized he could catch him by playing even par the rest of the way. The ability to turn his game on when he needed it most was a unique component of Hagen's genius, and he played the first eight holes of the back nine at one under. A par at eighteen would win the Open, while bogey would force a play-off. Hagen hit a solid drive, but his second shot flew the green, landing near a wall. As he walked to the green, Walter sent a flunky to the club-house to bring Mike Brady out. Brady arrived in time to watch Hagen coax a delicate chip shot to within eight feet of the pin, leaving a makeable birdie putt for the win. After locking eyes with Brady, Walter stroked the ball firmly at the cup, but it lipped out and hung on the edge, leaving the two men tied. They would play a full eighteen the next day to decide the Open. As he caught a glimpse of the bloodless look on Brady's face, Hagen knew his gamesmanship had taken a big bite out of Brady's brittle confidence.

Al Jolson's musical was closing that night, and, to celebrate, the biggest party of the week had been scheduled. Hagen showed up backstage after the final curtain, planning to make an early evening of it. Here's how he later remembered it: "The party lasted all night . . . champagne, pretty girls, jokes and laughter . . . no sleep, topped off by a trip to an after-hours roadhouse. In the small hours of the morning I recalled that I had an important date in a few hours. I dashed back to my hotel for a quick shower and fresh clothes. Then I wheeled my big Pierce-Arrow out to Brae Burn for the play-off."

Walter spotted Mike Brady standing near the first tee grimly taking practice swings, and ducked into the bar for a quick hair of the dog. Their warm-up techniques proved equally successful; both parred the first hole. Everything about their situation and Brady's hard-nosed determination struck Hagen as amusing. As they stood on the second tee and Brady nervously prepared to hit his drive, Hagen sidled up to him and said:

"Mike, if I were you I'd roll down my sleeves."

"Why?" asked Brady.

"The whole gallery will see your muscles quivering."

Brady snorted like a bull, stood back up to his ball, hooked his tee shot deep into the woods and handed Hagen a two-stroke lead, which grew to a four by the time they finished the tenth. But while he stood on the tenth fairway, looking over a short approach from the rough, Hagen had absentmindedly picked up and discarded an empty matchbox near his ball. An arcane rule at the time prohibited players from moving any loose debris within two club lengths of the ball if it lay within twenty yards of the hole. As they played down the eleventh fairway a zealous local rules official by the name of Frank Hoyt informed Hagen he was assessing him a two-stroke penalty.

As Walter digested the news, a friend in the gallery walked up to tell Hagen he had seen Brady break the same rule on the ninth when he removed a small stone near his ball. Hagen waved Frank Hoyt back over and told him about Brady's infraction. Hoyt marched back across the fairway to Brady to ask him about it and Mike admitted moving a stone but couldn't recall how close it had been to his ball. Hoyt now brought both men together, insisted they stop the match and go back to the scene of *both* alleged violations with a tape measure. Hagen suggested they first finish the hole they were in the middle of playing, which, common sense prevailing, they did. Then, while Brady and Hoyt backtracked to the ninth, Hagen plopped down on a bench to smoke a cigarette and grab a breather: "I needed every minute of rest I could get—this being the morning after the night before."

When they returned after Hoyt's forensic investigation, Brady admitted he had broken the rule. Hoyt was eager to march back to the tenth and apply his same rigorous methods to Hagen's alleged transgression.

"So, Mike, you were penalized two strokes?"

Brady said yes.

"Okay," said Walter to Frank Hoyt. "I'll take two, also." Then he flicked his cigarette away and walked nonchalantly to the tee, his four-stroke lead intact. As he told Brady later, Hagen wasn't about to win the Open because of some damn penalty.

Walter had now been gunning his engines for twenty-four hours and had skipped breakfast after the boozy all-nighter. A delayed-onset hangover hit him like a haymaker; he was struggling to keep his eyes open and lost half his lead on the back nine. Ahead by two, Walter pushed his drive on seventeen and watched the ball sail out of sight on a gust of wind, near a stand of trees. Frank Hoyt allowed only the players and caddies to search for the ball, shouting at the gallery to stand back, then made a show of pulling out his pocket watch to track the five minutes before Hagen's ball would be declared lost. It had vanished in a patch of soft, muddy ground, obviously embedded. Just before the five minutes were up, Mike Brady located a ball buried in the loam about four inches down.

Hagen claimed the ball could only have burrowed so deep if someone had stepped on it, which entitled him to a free lift. Frank Hoyt conferred with USGA officials, but none had seen anyone step on the ball so the claim was denied. Hagen tried another tack; if he played more than two shots with a ball that turned out not to be his he'd be disqualified, so he demanded a chance to identify it before committing himself. Hoyt protested Walter was just trying to finagle a better lie, but Hagen had memorized the rule book. He didn't otherwise have any right to pull the ball out of that muck without first accepting a penalty stroke for an unplayable ball, but they did have to allow him a chance to determine if it was his. After a ten-minute conference, officials used megaphones to explain the holdup to the puzzled crowd; the explanation took almost as long as their deliberations. Hagen dug out the ball, brushed off the mud, and discovered that it was in fact his. Walter gently—*very* gently—set the ball back down, so that it failed to fall back *into* the hole: perfectly legal.

Walter punched the ball into a greenside bunker and got up and down for bogey. He staggered to the final hole with a one-shot lead, where he sank a clutch four-foot putt to win his second U.S. Open. He accepted the five-hundred-dollar winner's check after downing a couple of cocktails and entertaining reporters with his colorful account of the battle with Brady. Then he jumped into his deluxe Pierce-Arrow, drove back into Boston, and partied the night away. The news that Walter had spent the wee hours of the night before whooping it up with Jolson and a bevy of showgirls tore through the press tent. The stories that poured out after this performance did more to create the aura of bulletproof showmanship that now surrounded Walter Hagen than a dozen championship trophies. Bobby Jones was already on his way to becoming a clean-cut, sentimental favorite for sports fans, but Hagen offered an intriguing, R-rated alternative: the loveable rogue.

Not long after Walter returned to Oakland Hills, flush with success, a pushy new member hurrying to make his tee time parked by the clubhouse and whistled for Hagen to fetch his clubs from the trunk. Hagen shot one look at this moron, walked in to see the club's president, and quit. He refused every offer that poured in from other top clubs. Walter had decided to become the first professional golfer in history to earn his keep without a job at a country club, a freelancer living off the fat of the land, which at this point looked plumper to him than a cattle car full of Angus beef. Almost to a man his fellow pros thought Walter was headed for disaster. Nobody could make a living just . . . playing golf. But the plain fact was that, until Walter took the leap, no one had ever tried. It required a man who could stare down ruin with a riverboat gambler's eye and nerves as thick as transatlantic cable. Walter Hagen was the right man, and probably the only man, for the job.

Bobby put down his books at the end of his freshman year in spring of 1919 and picked up his sticks. He had grown to five feet eight, an inch shy of his full height, and had lost fifteen pounds of baby fat—not a kid anymore, but a handsome, winning young gent. His cultivated fashion sense landed him in magazines; in classic Southern gentleman's style he wore cardigans, ties, and two-toned shoes, accessorized with flair and impeccable taste. Only seventeen, Bobby was already the Big Man on Campus at Tech. He struck some people as cocky, but expectations had been rising around Bobby for years and so far he'd backed them up. Fans expected him to win every tournament he entered. Bobby did, too. He dominated his college matches as captain of the Golden Tornadoes, Georgia Tech's varsity golf team—its first, organized because of his presence—but something went awry when the summer circuit began. He chipped away at his East Lake scoring record, lowering it to 69 and then 68, but that wasn't tournament play. This time Bobby stumbled and took a backward step.

He lost the Southern Open at East Lake by a single stroke, furious at losing on his own turf. A few weeks later, as defending champ of the Southern Amateur in New Orleans, Bobby's tee shot at the first hole bounced into an old shoe on a workman's wheelbarrow. Uncertain of the rule governing this odd situation, which allowed him a free drop, Bobby walloped the shoe with a niblick and knocked it out of the wheelbarrow onto the green, where the ball rolled free. But he missed the saving putt, took a bogey, and when told afterward that he'd failed to use the rules to his advantage, blew up in a rage. Bobby lost in the semifinals, disappointing an Atlanta contingent, including his parents, that had traveled south to see him play.

Big Bob's law practice had flourished during the war. While Bobby roomed at his Georgia Tech frat house, the Joneses moved into a rambling clapboard house on Peachtree Road, elevating their lifestyle into the upper middle class. For the first time the Colonel and Clara had the means to travel to Bobby's tournaments and lead his cheering section. Pop Keeler was also on hand his first full season tracking Jones for the *Georgian*. Pop would also be writing pieces for *American Golfer*. Editor Walter Travis had realized there was value in having a correspondent dog Bobby's every step.

A trip to Ontario in July for the Canadian Open yielded another second-place finish, a distant sixteen strokes back. For the first time the luck that had attended Bobby's every move deserted him. He didn't understand, and began leaning on Pop Keeler to help him sort it out.

They made an odd couple: the stiff-legged, lurching, extroverted Keeler, half a head taller and twenty years older than the modest, self-possessed young Jones. Bobby radiated a glow of robust good health; Keeler described himself at this point as "pretty comprehensively dilapidated." Bobby would soon be devoted to the one woman he loved during his lifetime, while Keeler was a compulsive ladies' man. Both had a love of learning, but Bobby remained a quiet intellectual; Keeler broadcast his self-acquired mastery of the classics with a bullhorn, spouting verse or rhetoric suitable to different occasions as if he were a jukebox. What bonded them was a shared passion for the game of golf. As inept a player as he was, made worse by his escalating infirmities, Pop understood better than most who'd ever written about it the inner turmoil of the sport and the incredible strain winning at the highest levels demanded. They also shared a taste for hard liquor, and Keeler helped initiate Bobby's early drinking habits.

Most important, they shared an unstated belief in the future greatness of Bobby Jones. A compelling conviction that he was supposed to conquer this game for some unknown reason possessed the young man. He didn't talk about it much—and only with Pop—but this feeling seemed to derive from that mysterious influence he had begun to sense behind the curtain of human events. Keeler called it destiny.

Their late-night bull sessions might have taken a religious bent, if either man had been inclined in that direction. Although Bobby respected organized religions—and had been raised in and would preside over a traditionally religious home—he was too intellectually curious to swallow unexamined dogma whole. His grandfather's fundamentalism felt like the relic of another age, and Pop was a secularizing influence; his own brushes with death had carried him beyond the reach of conventional piety. He was too much a drinker and skirt chaser to thump Bibles. But as a genetic Scots American who'd been raised as a Scottish Presbyterian, he'd absorbed that church's strict doctrine of predestination. It seemed logical to Keeler that golf, the quintessentially Scottish game, sprang from the same philosophical fountainhead; destiny had been woven into the fabric of golf since conception. Bobby wasn't convinced; his studies in the physical sciences argued toward random chance as nature's governing idea.

The ongoing dialogue of their life together had found its principal theme, and from this point forward the two became inseparable: bonnie Prince Hal and his bawdy Falstaff. Both were convinced Bobby was headed for high achievement, and like a loyal squire Pop pledged he would be there every step of the way to chronicle, aid, and abet the quest. For a man who'd spent an alarming amount of time confronting his own mortality, Keeler presented to the world the blithest spirit imaginable; given all he'd been through it's difficult to know exactly how he'd managed such a burden. But it helps explain Pop's passionate attachment to his young friend; Bobby gave Pop someone to believe in, and consequently something to live for.

Bobby's summer schedule had been designed for him to peak at the U.S. Amateur in late August at Oakmont Country Club, outside Pittsburgh. Oakmont was the brainchild of a Pennsylvania millionaire named Henry Clay Fownes, one of the rocks on which the American game had been built. A steel industry tycoon who didn't fall in love with the game until his early forties—Scotsman Andrew Carnegie arranged the introduction—Fownes became the driving force for its development in his native Pittsburgh. The course he designed and built beginning in 1903 was another of America's early jewels: long, muscular, and layered with the deepest and most hazardous bunkers—over three hundred fifty of them—on any course in the country. He called his most famous creation the Church Pews, which describes perfectly the seven horizontal rows of grass that span its forty-yard length. Few places of such ecclesiastical origins have inspired more taking of the Lord's name in vain. Fownes also designed a peculiar furrowed rake for his bunkers, which left them combed with ridges, making even lies impossible.

When visiting players complained about Oakmont's lack of fairness after their first round, it was the reaction Fownes wanted; he believed poor shots should be punished as if they were criminal acts. Fownes also was one of the first to double-cut his severely sloping greens—which he seldom watered—producing the fastest putting surfaces golfers had ever seen. Henry Fownes was a good player, but his son William became a great one, winning the 1910 U.S. Amateur and assuming Oakmont's reins when his father retired. The younger Fownes made his father's course even more penal over time; if he saw members hitting consistently to some new spot on a fairway to avoid trouble, bam, in went another bunker. The 1919 Amateur would be the first of more than twenty national championships played at Oakmont and it attracted a great field from all over the country. They were about to experience the most terrifying golf course America had ever produced, one that separated the men from the boys.

Bobby Jones made a detour before his trip to Oakmont. That spring Kiltie Maiden had left East Lake—there is a whiff of scandal about the circumstances, a run-in with a member in which alcohol seems to have played a part—to take a job at a country club in St. Louis. After watching Bobby struggle with his swing all summer, the Colonel felt a visit to St. Louis for a consultation with Kiltie was vital, but for the only time in their relationship not even he could fix the problem. Bobby's drives flew so persistently off line that Kiltie joined the entourage to Oakmont, the first recorded instance of a "swing coach" on call during a national championship.

As the tournament began, the biggest story at Oakmont was the return to the Amateur of Francis Ouimet. The happy warrior had driven down from Boston with some friends in a convertible and caught a cold along the way, which quickly worsened. Not wanting to trouble anyone, or bow out when so many had come out to see him play, Francis sought no help and played the first two days with a raging fever. Chick Evans, technically the defending champ, made the trip from Chicago at the last minute. One writer observed his behavior and decided that since both the Open and Amateur had been canceled for two years after he captured them in 1916, Chick seemed to think he'd won six championships in a row. The USGA had tweaked the tournament's format: after a qualifying medal round they would trim the field of a hundred thirty-six starters down to sixty-four and ties. After a second medal round—this time over thirty-six holes—they would cut it further to thirty-two men, who would all advance to the match-play action.

On its first day hosting a national competition, Oakmont attacked this distinguished field of players like a cornered wolverine. Francis shot 77 and considered it one of the finest rounds he'd ever played. Chick Evans carded an 80. Bobby came in at 82, and felt lucky at that considering what had happened early that afternoon. After a clear, beautiful morning, a storm front rumbled in without warning and climaxed with a spectacular twenty-minute hailstorm that dropped golf-ball-sized chunks and sent the gallery running for shelter. Chick dove into a bunker and tried to shield his face from the onslaught. Then, during the second round on Monday, the weather really turned nasty; three separate rainstorms brought howling winds that knocked down mighty oaks and blew the benches on the tee boxes around like matchsticks.

There were calls from stranded golfers for flat-bottomed boats to cross casual water, blimps to journey over occasional lakes, and submarines to locate balls that went into the drink. After shooting 79 in the morning, shaking with fever, Francis was so weak he topped three of his last six tee shots. Facing a ten-inch putt to finish his second round with an 87, a huge hailstone dropped in front of his ball just before it reached the cup and stopped it dead. He staggered off the course into the locker room, where a kind Oakmont member gave up his in-house lodgings so Francis could go to bed. The doctors called in to examine him couldn't decide if he had tonsillitis or pleurisy, but both agreed Francis was a very sick man. Certain he'd missed the cut, he was amazed to discover he was tied for sixteenth. Chick Evans came in tied for sixth. Bobby scratched out an 81-78 in those wretched conditions and finished one stroke behind the leaders; one of them was an Oakmont member, twenty-two-year-old S. Davidson Herron. Herron had been a star golfer at Princeton, the finest collegiate program in the country, due in part to the college's former president Woodrow Wilson's early enthusiasm for the game.

The weather improved and Tuesday's opening matches produced no upsets, but Francis—still weak and playing against his doctors' advice—had to win three of the last five holes to advance. Second-round brackets produced two irresistible matchups. Bobby Jones faced Robert Gardner, the two-time Amateur champ who had ousted him at Merion three years before. Even more anticipated, for the first time Chick Evans and Francis Ouimet would finally go head-to-head in a championship; if Chick was considered the front-runner, Francis was the overwhelming sentimental favorite. For the first half of their match Jones and Gardner replayed the script from Merion, with Gardner more nervous and Bobby carrying a three-hole lead into intermission. Kiltie's final advice to him on Oakmont's range that morning was to stop trying to steer the ball and hit it as hard as he could.

"So what if you end up on the next fairway?" said Kiltie. "On this damn course you're probably better off."

If Gardner thought the kid would collapse again, Bobby quickly put it to rest; he finished Gardner off 5 and 4. Bobby, Pop, and Kiltie rushed over to watch Ouimet and Evans go at each other; their gallery grew to five thousand people. Still fragile and feverish, Francis steeled himself for the most important match of his comeback. Although he felt Chick's resentful behavior fell short of the game's standards of etiquette, Francis was content to let his golf do the talking. Chick remained unfailingly friendly, but there was a disingenuous sincerity to it that rubbed people the wrong way. On this day Chick was all smiles, although he said the heavy weather had intensified his rheumatism and he appeared to have trouble walking. As Francis later wrote: "It was a battle of cripples, and what a battle it turned out to be!"

Evans set the tone by dropping a forty-five-foot eagle putt on the opening hole. Francis won the second and third to surge ahead. They traded superb shots all morning, passing the lead back and forth, never separated by more than a single hole, ending the morning round all square. Evans was so keyed up, and Francis so ill, neither man ate lunch; Francis could only down a glass of orange juice. Both collapsed in separate corners of the locker room and tried to regroup. Francis birdied three of the first eight that afternoon for a three-hole lead, but Chick shaved it to two as they made the final turn. Now the strain on Francis's health came into play; he gave back his lead, and they came to the thirty-fifth hole of the day all square. It was a short, uphill par four, and they both hit perfect drives. Francis stuck his approach six feet from the pin. Chick answered, landing his within three feet. Francis made his birdie, then waited while Chick decided which of his four putters he wanted to use. He picked the right tool and made the putt. The match would be decided at the final hole.

Par four, 456 yards. Elevated tee, uphill second shot. A solemn gallery lined the course all the way to the green. Adrenaline surged; both drives landed in the fairway, Francis slightly ahead. Chick pulled a fairway wood into the rough, short and left of the pin. Francis pushed his long iron into a deep, dangerous bunker on the right. Advantage Evans. When they reached the green, Francis realized his ball had somehow found a decent lie in the furrowed Oakmont sand, sixty feet from the pin. He climbed down into the pit, literally out of sight. He took an explosive swing through the sand and lofted his ball gently onto the green, where it rolled to a stop within the shadow of the flagstick. The crowd roared, then went stone quiet. Chick chopped his ball out of the tall grass and watched it skid fifteen feet past the cup on the glassy green. Advantage Ouimet. Chick stroked his uphill putt for par and came up a foot short. Francis had his left for the win; differences of opinion about the length of the putt reveal the way character affects memory. Francis remembered it as a four-footer. Most reporters placed it in the six-to-eight-foot range. Chick

Evans thought it was ten. In any event, this was how Francis described it: "With no thought on anything but the hole, I stroked the ball accurately and it floated as nicely as you please into the cup for the win I wanted so badly." Which remains the strongest language Francis ever used in print to describe a competitive emotion. Walter Travis called it the most remarkable match in the history of American golf. The crowd rushed to embrace Francis with the same affection it had shown him at Brookline. Evans remembered the ending this way: "I found myself standing entirely alone and went back unnoticed to the clubhouse."

Bobby said he was "pop-eyed and gasping with excitement" after watching this "battle of giants," but the grueling grudge match had left Francis terribly drained. After falling behind early the next day in his third-round match against Philadelphian Woody Platt, Francis once again rallied to even the match on the final hole. The cheers after he sank his tying putt at eighteen could be heard all over Oakmont. As they teed off for their first hole of sudden death the rains came again and they played in a steady torrent. Francis reached the green in two, while Platt was fifty yards short with his second, but he played an exquisite pitch that nearly rolled in to stay alive. Platt's gritty up and down sapped Francis of his last reserves; he lost the match with a bogey on his thirty-eighth hole of the day.

The tournament was judged a huge success. Francis's gutsy comeback thrilled the crowds, and he'd beaten his nemesis, Chick Evans. The weather drew harsher reviews, one critic suggesting that Pittsburgh be referred to in any future golf guides as "a small, blunt town lying between two thunderstorms." Considering that the flu Ouimet battled all week had nearly developed into pneumonia—although he never used it as an excuse—the press decided there was every reason to believe he would be a factor in championships for years to come. But golf's favorite son had other plans; he had married longtime sweetheart Stella Sullivan the previous fall, and after the failure of his sporting goods store he was starting a new career as a banker in Boston.

Bobby won a sloppy, rain-soaked third-round match and advanced to the semifinals against Oakmont's president, Bill Fownes. Despite the former Amateur champ's supreme local knowledge, he was no match for Bobby's all-around game. He had finally found his swing after losing his temper, played the second half of their match in a simmering fury, and dispatched the host club's president 5 and 3. Jones had reached the finals of only his second national championship, the youngest man ever to make it this deep in an Amateur. He was matched against another Oakmont member, qualifying winner Davey Herron. Herron knew every warp and weave of Oakmont's treacherous greens; Pop described him as "a large, plump, curly-haired Pittsburgh golfer with an exquisite putting touch, and built like the proverbial brick barn."

Bobby spent the evening with Pop, trying to relax, but he was as keyed up as a racehorse kicking at his stall before Derby Day. Pop tried talking about it, which did nothing to calm him, then tried not talking about it, which made it worse. Finally he prescribed a single shot of whiskey—and three for himself—then turned out the lights. Both men stared at the ceiling until two in the morning.

"Hey, Pop."

"Yeah, Bobby?"

"This is what we're here for, right?"

"That's right, Bobby."

The next day a boisterous hometown crowd of over six thousand showed up to cheer on Davey Herron, and they weren't all country-club types; Herron spent summers earning college money in a local steel mill and was currently working in a foundry, bending rails into horseshoe curves. Herron's cheering section had a raucous blue-collar makeup, and they failed to grant Bobby some of the game's basic courtesies, cheering when he found a bunker or the rough. The only people wishing Bobby well in that crowd were the Colonel, Kiltie, and, journalistic objectivity be damned, Pop Keeler. Even the marshals seemed partial. The *New York Times* reported one roaring through his megaphone at the crowd to "Get back, get back there; Davey's in the rough and we want to give him every chance!" The Colonel couldn't resist answering back: "And while you're at it, give Jones a chance, too!"

Bobby was the better player tee to green—Herron's swing was not a thing of beauty—which kept them even into the afternoon, but Herron's skill with a putter began to make the difference. Despite the fact that Bobby shot even par on the front nine, after dropping three long-range bombs Herron opened up a three-hole lead by the time they reached the six-hundred-yard par five twelfth.

Both hit decent drives, but Herron pulled his second into a bunker, the first opening to climb back into the match that Bobby had all afternoon. He took out a two wood, intending to crank his second close to the green.

As he reached the peak of his backswing, a marshal standing nearby saw someone moving in the gallery and shouted "Fore!" at the top of his lungs through his megaphone. Bobby flinched, fatally, and topped the ball, which hopped twenty yards into a bunker. Trembling with anger, Bobby failed to get out of the bunker in two tries, then picked up, conceding the hole to Herron. He told Keeler he was usually able to recover from visual distractions during a swing, but there was no defense against a loud, unexpected sound. The damage was done; from a turning point that should have left him two holes in back of Herron, he was down four with only six to play. Pop said Bobby looked so mad that "he could've bitten his ball in half."

"Nothing ever announced to me as distinctly as that megaphone that I was beaten," he said.

Bobby dropped another shot on the next hole and lost the 1919 Amateur Championship to Davey Herron, 5 and 4, who was picked up and carried away on the shoulders of his hometown crowd.

The press worked up a sweat trying to build the megaphone incident into a brouhaha. Even Walter Hagen chimed in; he was covering the Amateur for a newspaper syndicate to pick up a few bucks. The Colonel fed a couple of bitter quotes to reporters about the marshal's breech of etiquette and the ill-behaved partisan crowd, but when others tried to draw Bobby in that direction he declined. Davey Herron had beaten him fair and square, shooting four under par through the fourteen holes of their second round.

"The better man won and he gave me a good drubbing," said Bobby.

Bobby insisted the megaphone had no bearing on the outcome, but even Herron began to react defensively to charges of partisanship. This was the first time in history any member of a country club had won the National Amateur on his home course. It would also be the only major title in Davey Herron's career. His win established a strange pattern that dominated Jones's career: his opponents in championship play often turned in the single best performance of their lives.

As they traveled home to Atlanta, questions about the role of fortune versus fate took on added dimension in Bobby's debates with Keeler. Pop's Presbyterian fatalism slowly appeared to gain the upper hand.

"If someone I can't see is pulling the strings," Bobby asked, "I wonder who was holding the strings attached to that man with the megaphone?"

The USGA soon pulled strings of their own; within a few years they banished megaphones from all future championships.

Bobby was shocked to realize he'd lost eighteen pounds during the week of the Amateur at Oakmont. This wasn't physical exertion; he could play two rounds a day for weeks and never lose an ounce. Nothing like this had ever happened before. He was a well-conditioned athlete just entering his physical prime. Bobby began to realize that golf and championship golf were two different games, and the latter demanded a much more exacting price. There have been many supremely gifted players who simply couldn't stand up to the competitive strain—what Bobby called "that stretching and stretching and stretching inside your head"—and turned away from the full expression of their talent. Grown men had cracked under that kind of pressure; during Bobby's early days the stark example of two-time U.S. Open champion John McDermott's nervous breakdown remained a vivid reminder. Today it's possible to make a living fit for a king from this sport without ever winning at the highest levels; early pros were playing for pocket change compared to modern purses. What would motivate a player today to push himself halfway to derangement when he's already set for life?

Now consider that Bobby Jones never played the game for money, not one penny, during his entire career, at considerable financial hardship. At Oakmont he'd barely stuck his toe in the water, reaching his first final in his second major tournament, and the internal fire it ignited was already burning the flesh off him like wax from a candle. He was under no obligation to take this any further; he manifestly possessed the mind, character, and charm to follow any professional path he favored as far as he wished to go. Bobby already knew he was essentially a private person who didn't enjoy the anonymous adulation or scrutiny visited by fame. He could have walked away from the game, here or at any point in the next eleven years, and lived life on terms entirely of his own choosing. This is where his drive to succeed takes on a mythic dimension; nothing was at stake other than his need to express the gift he felt was in him. Ouimet played the game for love and the joy of competition. Bobby played because he had to, and the price he would pay in physical and psychic pain, belying his external grace, matched the epic scale of his achievements. As 1919 came to an end, that ordeal had already begun.

After returning from Oakmont, Pop Keeler lost an argument about his salary with the editor of the *Georgian* and ended up out on the street. In search of greener pastures he latched on to a job as a publicist for a Hollywood studio and hit the road organizing press tours for stars promoting their new motion pictures. The gig lasted only four months, when he realized that serving at the beck and call of divas like Gloria Swanson would quickly deprive him of his remaining sanity. During Pop's absence Bobby made the acquaintance of another, younger journalist who would bear witness to a crucial phase in his development.

Al Laney was a Pensacola native who'd just been discharged from the army in the summer of 1919 and found himself at loose ends. Riding a train south from Washington he spotted a story in a discarded newspaper about the first Southern Open, then under way at East Lake, and on a whim decided to catch the last day of action. He'd worked for various newspapers before the war, mostly at the copy boy level, and like so many others of his generation he'd been drawn to the sport of golf after Ouimet's victory in 1913. Having witnessed Chick Evans's exciting win in the 1916 Open—although he'd found himself curiously unmoved by Evans himself—he decided to pursue sportswriting in general, and golf in particular, but the war had intervened.

Laney switched trains and made it to East Lake in time to see Long Jim Barnes win the inaugural Southern Open, but he was more impressed by a postgame encounter with its seventeen-year-old runner-up. Bobby and the slightly older Laney, still in uniform, struck up a discussion about the war and golf and Georgia Tech that impressed Laney beyond words. He had sensed something special about Jones, saw it on him as plain as a scarlet letter, but didn't know what it meant. He rode the train home to Pensacola that night and felt something tugging on him. He had vague plans of heading for New York to look for work as a reporter, but this story in a newspaper someone had left on the floor of that southbound train changed everything. He acted on the impulse and secured a job with the Associated Press in Atlanta.

Laney tracked Bobby down at his Georgia Tech frat house, found him in the middle of a cocktail party on the porch, and stood on the street staring at him. Bobby noticed him, remembered their conversation at the tournament, and invited Laney in for a drink. Laney saw that Bobby was the big man on campus and wise beyond his years in the company of those college kids; he lived among them but stood apart without meaning or trying to. Laney had never met anyone so magnetically charismatic. They struck up a conversation about Al's military career; Bobby took more interest in Al than in talking about himself. Over the course of the following fall and winter Laney got to know Bobby as well as anyone in Atlanta. He wrote a piece about Bobby's life at Georgia Tech, enjoyed frequent contact with him, and saw him in many different social situations. Temperamentally drawn to writers like Pop and Granny Rice, Bobby was attracted to Laney for many of the same reasons: his outsider's perspective and a shared respect for the English language. But Laney was fifteen years younger than Rice or Keeler and more of a contemporary, so Bobby let down his behavioral guard more in his presence. Laney, in turn, was a psychologically astute observer, whose insights into Jones provide the clearest window into his state of mind during this period in his life. To most everyone who knew him, Bobby seemed happy and well adjusted, a carefree, immensely popular college kid enjoying the time of his life. According to Laney, who out of respect for their friendship did not write about this until many years afterward, this was an illusion.

"I was fascinated with his personality," wrote Laney. "So gentle, so intelligent and so pleasantly charming in an amazingly mature way on a surface that concealed a strong, almost uncontrolled temper. In young Bobby, passionate emotions were a chaotic mixture with first one and then another in control. They were submerged most of the time, but at certain moments they threatened to dominate his personality, his view of himself and the outside world."

The prevailing belief, later shaped by Keeler, was that Bobby's anger was simply the product of a protracted adolescence. Laney maintains that the truth was much more alarming. Even though he'd broken only one club in anger at Oakmont—journalists kept track of these things—his loss in the finals wounded him much more deeply than his outward forbearance indicated. A few weeks later his pride took another blow when Alexa Stirling won her second consecutive U.S. Women's Championship. Although he never expressed any competitive jealousy about her, Bobby was falling behind his childhood friend. The arrival of his long-awaited greatness had gone off the rails. It was

Laney's conclusion that this gifted young man, perhaps because he was so gifted, had to wrestle with demons. His single-mindedness, this laserlike focus on perfection, was also his Achilles' heel. In the spring of 1920, while he was traveling with Bobby and friends to a tournament in Tennessee, their car got stuck on a rain-slicked, red clay hill somewhere in north Georgia. Laney describes the incident this way:

> I twice had the frightening experience of seeing him come to the very edge of malice in fierce outbursts that neither he nor I understood. I was afraid for him, for I had seen him flushed and shaking in a rage of sudden anger, then drained white a moment later in sudden fear at the nearness of evil. In a sense I shared his deep inner struggle to overcome what, with his intellect, he knew to be ignoble. He knew well that he was poisoning himself with anger, that he must find the inner strength to rise above it. To reconcile this side of his nature with the wonderful young person I knew him to be was a difficult thing for me.

It is telling that these confrontations occurred in the company of Laney and some college kids, and one infers from his account that they weren't isolated incidents. When he hurled a club in anger, those outbursts were easy to dismiss as part of the game; he was hardly the first person to lose his temper playing the world's hardest sport. What Laney describes is a young man fighting for his humanity, struggling with an impulse toward violence that threatened to overwhelm all that was so obviously good about him. Alcohol may have inflamed this loss of control; even Bobby admitted he drank a lot during these years. Whatever the reason, this was a face Bobby never showed Keeler or Rice, his parents, or the other adults in his life. Everyone had expected so much of "Bobby Jones" for so long that he felt he wasn't allowed to fail at any level; he had no outlet for his doubts or fears. Bottled up, they exploded out of him in fits of rage. During a moment of sober reflection Bobby described this battle to Laney as "the critical match I thought I was losing." In the early days of 1920, the outcome of his lonely struggle appeared seriously in doubt.

Championship golf in Britain would have resumed in 1919, as it did in America, but a railroad strike crippled travel throughout the country and caused the last-minute cancellation of both the British Amateur and the Open. The country's courses required months of rehabilitation to render them fit for play. British ranks had suffered heavy losses in the war; Jack Graham, a renowned amateur from Hoylake, died in battle, as did the British PGA's secretary, F. H. Brown. J. L. C. Jenkins, the last British Amateur champion before the war, was severely wounded and never played to the same level. A young tank commander from Edinburgh named Tommy Armour, yet to make a name in golf, lost an eye when he was exposed to mustard gas at the Battle of Ypres and was later sprayed with shrapnel, wounds that left him with a plate in his head and eight chunks of metal in his left shoulder. A tough little Scottish law student named Bobby Cruickshank, and Cyril Tolley, a burly Oxford graduate— both destined to later collide with Jones in historic championships—spent long hellish months in German prison camps.

Harry Vardon turned fifty in May of 1920. The Great War had abruptly ended the Indian summer of his career, capped by his sixth Open victory in 1914. Harry knew that he had reached the end of his run, that a new generation stood in the wings ready to replace him, but, as all great athletes do at sunset, he longed for one last chance at glory. The first Open in six years would be played at Cinque Ports, in Deal, Kent, a seaside links that had hosted the championship once before in 1909. The best of both the old and new generations of British golfers joined the field. There was also one wild card in the deck, from across the pond.

Walter Hagen, reigning U.S. Open champ, had cleaned up during Florida's winter circuit and used the cash to sail over and take on the British Open. As he was an unattached professional, championships were the big game he hunted now, but not for the paychecks, which remained pedestrian; most pros made more from side bets than they did from purses. Public recognition, enhancing name value: that's how Walter planned to drive up his price for exhibitions and make a killing. And he knew that to maximize his reputation he needed to bag the Claret Jug, the game's oldest trophy. He persuaded Dickie Martin of the *New York Globe* to go with him and ensure that American newspapers received a balanced account of his assault on the British citadel; it was another first, a golfer with his own press agent. Walter's luck held on the trip over; he and his wife had separated, and he discovered soon after boarding the *Mauretania* that movie star Constance Talmadge, one of the great beauties of the day, was a fellow passenger. Whether he romanced her successfully during the crossing is unknown—Walter was just enough of a gentleman to decline comment—but he took his best shot.

A mealymouthed reporter from the *Daily Mail* invited Hagen out for a low-key dinner on his first night in London, then penned a hatchet job about Walter's incorrigible boasting, under the front-page headline COCKY DOODLE DOO! When he read the story the next morning, Walter decided not to take this outrage lying down. He picked up the phone and called the *Daily Mail*'s publisher, Alfred Harmsworth, Lord Northcliffe, whom Walter had befriended during the 1913 Open at Brookline. Northcliffe invited Walter for a round of golf on his private estate that afternoon, and greeted him warmly. Over cocktails Hagen shared his distress about the offending story. Northcliffe tried to explain away the lies and exaggerations as a spirited defense of the country's most treasured championship. When Hagen stood his ground, Northcliffe arranged for Walter and the reporter to sit down that evening to discuss the matter. Of their meeting Hagen wrote: "I never came so close to socking a man in my life." Whatever he said or did to the reporter proved effective: the *Daily Mail* printed a front-page apology for the story about Walter the next day.

During the month Hagen spent traveling around leading up to the Open, he became a lightning rod for British disdain of American golf. The refrain was clear: if this loudmouthed dandy was the best the United States had to offer then England had nothing to fear. When they got around to playing the Open at Deal, things really turned ugly. As poorly as professionals were treated in America, the British class system guaranteed theirs got it much worse. Upon arrival at Deal Walter strolled into the clubhouse and asked to be shown his locker. The mortified club secretary whisked him out of the building to a row of rusty nails in the back of the pro shop, above a forlorn pile of shoes, their toes sticking up like skis. The man warned Walter not to set foot anywhere near the members' private area again and told him that he'd be taking his meals in a shabby little caterer's tent out back.

Hagen struck back hard. Every morning he parked his rented limousine—complete with chauffeur and footman—in front of the clubhouse and made a show of changing his shoes on the running board in plain view of the dumbfounded members. He trained his footman to serve as his forecaddie, and instructed his chauffeur to meet him after his rounds on the eighteenth green holding a chilled martini and a tailored Savile Row polo coat. Most British pros still wore the frayed tweeds, knickers, and old boots common to the working class. Hagen had hauled over two steamer trunks filled with twelve color-coordinated outfits, complete with matching bow ties, custom monogrammed silk shirts, and complementary pairs of two-tone spiked saddle shoes.

Walter's wardrobe got better reviews than his golf. As every American in Britain had to learn, when the wind blew hard off the sea on a treeless links their high-flying iron shots lost their spin and couldn't find the greens. Hagen played the worst golf of his life, never broke 80, and finished fifty-third in a field of fifty-four. George Duncan, a rising English player, won the Open Championship. Walter still used his initials W.C. in formal competitions, and columnists suggested they stood for "water closet." The scorn heaped on Walter by press, public, and British players might have broken a lesser man's will, but Hagen never let them see him suffer. A few greats like Vardon could make the game look easy; even when he played his best, with his risky gambles, strange lapses, and daring recoveries, Hagen made the game look frankly impossible. Love him or hate him, you couldn't take your eyes off him. He treated every mistake with equal indifference, held his chin up proudly to the end, and smiled as if he were twelve strokes in front of the field. He offered no alibis; "I tried too hard" was his summary about the ordeal at Deal. As Walter's staff was loading his gear into the limo for the last time, the oily little secretary who'd snubbed him on arrival turned up to gloat at Hagen's departure.

"Sorry you didn't do better, 'Eye-gen, but golf over here is very difficult. I do hope you'll come back in some future year and try again."

"Don't worry about me, pal," said Walter. "I'll be back and you'll see my name on that cup."

Of all the journalists, players, and spectators who'd weighed in on Hagen's failings during his British invasion, only one agreed with that prediction. As Hagen walked off the course after his last round, Dickie Martin overheard Harry Vardon tell a friend in the crowd that "he'll win our championship, not once, but several times." On the heels of this disappointment, Walter traveled to Paris to play in the French Open at La Boulie and beat a Frenchman in a play-off to win it. He wasn't about to sail back to America empty-handed; Hagen never lost a play-off for a championship in his entire career. Walter's gutsy, pioneering one-man invasion of the Old Country not only set up his own triumphant return, it paved the way for a team of American amateurs the following year that would introduce Bobby Jones to a British audience.

He finished a respectable thirteenth place, but Vardon was as disappointed with his own performance at Cinque Ports as Hagen had been with his. His old rival Sandy Herd finished second, and his closest friend in golf, Ted Ray, had come in third; there was still some fight in their generation, Harry was sure of it. When the tournament ended he spoke with Ted about a moneymaking idea; the trip they'd made to America in 1913 remained the most successful of their careers. They had discussed a return trip but the war made overseas travel impossible. They weren't getting any younger—Ted had just turned forty-three—so why not give it a go? They might even take another shot at winning a U.S. Open.

"Crazier things have happened," said Harry.

"And we've both seen 'em," said Ted. "Count me in."

Although Americans didn't realize it, since October 2, 1919, the president of the United States had been an uneducated forty-seven-year-old woman named Edith Bolling Wilson. His protean mind disjointed, Woodrow Wilson had been confined to bed since his stroke. Edith ordered their doctor to tell his cabinet the president had suffered a nervous breakdown; fit enough to rule, but not up to the stress of human contact. Edith controlled all information in and out of the Oval Office. When a bill required the president's signature, she stuck a pen in his immobile hand and swam it around to simulate his writing. She interviewed candidates for cabinet appointments, appointed them, and ignored any element of statecraft she didn't understand; when his presidential corre- spondence reached the national archives years later, entire boxes of vital letters were found unopened. Cabinet members and key senators suspected the truth, but Wilson's vice president, Thomas Riley Marshall—best remembered for the phrase "what this country needs is a good five-cent cigar"—was such a dolt they decided they were better off with an invalid in the job. Although his con- dition would improve over the next year, permitting him eventually to receive visitors and attend a few cabinet meetings, the dynamic intellectual who had led America into the twentieth century had vanished forever.

As the third decade of that century began, America experienced what modern observers would call a generation gap. Men of Wilson and Roosevelt's age had directed the country's affairs for twenty years, their roots planted deep in the Victorian era, their morals and ideals formulated during a time of hoop skirts and robber barons. The young men they'd dispatched to do their fighting in the Great War had returned from Europe no longer content to live in their parents' world. They'd been through their own defining experience, leaving them much more cynical about the way that world worked. They wanted their own music and dances, their own transportation, their own fashions; clothing would no longer function as a rigid marker of class lines. Nothing defined this divide more than the Eighteenth Amendment to the Constitution of the United States, commonly known as the Volstead Act after the Minnesota congressman who introduced the law Congress passed to enforce it. Most referred to it more simply as Prohibition.

Alcohol abuse had been identified by late-nineteenth-century social engineers as the greatest threat to the survival of the family and, by extension, civilization itself. The unregulated production of liquor meant much of the hard stuff being served was truly lethal, and reformers' energies centered on the public saloon as the infected source of all moral devolution: alcoholism, poverty, divorce and family desertion, gambling, criminality, prostitution. A temperance movement arose to shut down the saloons and stamp out this creeping evil, and it grew into a global effort. During the Great War British prime minister Lloyd George identified the three great enemies England was fighting as "Germany, Austria, and drink." Some American states had experimented with forms of prohibition since before the Civil War, but this righteous Victorian impulse reached its apex with 1919's nationwide ratification of the Eighteenth Amendment. What's often misunderstood is that the ban did not prohibit anyone from drinking per se, but simply outlawed the manufacture and sale of alcohol.

Bobby Jones had grown up in a family and around a country-club culture that encouraged social drinking. He tasted his first cocktails as a student at Georgia Tech, and drank in moderation, and occasionally excess, for the rest of his life. When it was finally put into practice in 1920, Prohibition's opposition arose from the younger generation's belief that the cure was worse than the disease. Laws regulating saloons were already in place, and standards in the production of liquor had improved enormously. The young men who had risked their lives in the fields of France and Flanders had come back looking for a good time, and that included the simple pleasure of going out in the evening for a couple of pops. Others who hadn't served in the military, like Bobby, insisted that social drinking was not the problem but part of a new, urbane lifestyle that in American cities was becoming more the rule than the exception.

The Eighteenth Amendment became the most flagrantly violated law in American history. As bootleggers found increasingly ingenious ways to elude authorities, Prohibition led to the rise of the first organized-crime syndicates and corruption among bureaucrats and lawmen charged to enforce it, contributing far more to lawlessness and hypocrisy than it prevented. Hardware stores sold portable stills for home use for as little as six dollars. A large still was found on the farm of a Texas senator who had been one of Prohibition's leading proponents. A new breed of underground watering holes—called speakeasies, for the loose tongues they inspired—replaced the saloon. One of the most popular new cocktails was called Between the Sheets, and it's no coincidence that the first mass-produced contraceptives—Trojans—appeared the same year. But in 1920 the Lost Generation still lacked the cohesiveness and political muscle to lay their hands on the levers of power and turn the world in their direction. Before that could happen they needed to find their voice, and it wasn't long in arriving.

In July of 1918 a twenty-two-year-old former Princeton dropout, fresh out of officer school at Fort Leavenworth, Kansas, reported to Camp Sheridan in Montgomery, Alabama, to complete his training before shipping overseas. Attending a dance at the Montgomery Country Club, he was introduced to the eighteen-year-old daughter of an Alabama Associate Supreme Court justice. The girl had just graduated from high school and was considered the catch of her class; she was beautiful, vivacious, and bold. The young lieutenant fell in love on sight, and in the next few weeks worked his way through a wall of admirers to attract her eye. The young beauty was equally smitten but withheld her affections, uncertain her aggressive young suitor would be able to support her in the luxury to which she had always been accustomed. Lieutenant Francis Scott Key Fitzgerald, the son of shabby genteel Midwestern parents, had only one hope of fulfilling that fairy-tale prerequisite; he was an aspiring author, halfway through his first novel, and its future success carried the burden of his dreams about marrying Zelda Sayre.

After the Armistice and out of uniform, Fitzgerald returned to his native St. Paul to rewrite his now finished book along the lines of encouraging suggestions he'd been given by an influential editor at Scribners, Maxwell Perkins. While writing a nakedly autobiographical story about the harsh social education of a young Midwestern man encountering the upper classes at Princeton and an unhappy romance with an unreliable debutante, Fitzgerald failed to take the lessons of his own book to heart. He kept his stormy passion for Zelda alive with telegrams, passionate correspondence, and occasional visits, but poured most of his energies into the novel. After playing hard to get, Zelda changed strategies and now pressed him to marry; Fitzgerald resisted, unwilling to commit until he knew the fate of his book. In the fall of 1919 he learned that his reworking of *This Side of Paradise* had earned the publication he craved, but his lack of attention to Zelda came back to haunt him. Not long after receiving the news from Perkins, a glamorous photograph of the famous young golfer Bobby Jones arrived in Fitzgerald's mailbox, signed "To Zelda, With love, Bobby." Zelda wrote in an accompanying letter that she'd met Bobby at a dance in Augusta, and he had been avidly pursuing her ever since. This precipitated a crisis and resulted in Fitzgerald proposing and setting a firm date for the wedding.

This Side of Paradise was published on March 26, 1920. Scribners, a venerable and conservative publishing house, had taken a gamble at the insistence of Fitzgerald's editor and champion. The book provoked a torrent of critical response that broke along generational lines. Older critics found it mortifying, incendiary, obscene, an assault on their cherished Victorian values. Younger critics and readers welcomed it as the first articulation of their spiritual dissatisfaction with the world their parents had left them. Scott Fitzgerald had distilled the essence of a troubled time with the voice of a poet and the merciless confidence of youth. He was only twenty-four, and the sensation *This Side of Paradise* created brought him the fame he'd always craved and the title as the leading voice of his generation.

"A new generation dedicated more than the last to the fear of poverty and the worship of success," he wrote in the book's summation. "Grown up to find all Gods dead, all wars fought, all faiths in man shaken."

That message shook the parents of the Lost Generation down to their high-button shoes, but it gave their children a sense of identity. All the cultural fuss aside, Fitzgerald had written his book to impress a girl and it won him his prize: Scott and Zelda were married a week after publication, April 2, 1920, in the rectory of St. Patrick's Cathedral. They honeymooned around the corner at the Biltmore, lighting cigars with five-dollar bills, scandalizing the staff and drinking around the clock until they were tossed out for drunken rowdiness. The tone of their marriage, pickled in gin, had been set. Fitzgerald's prediction that America, led by his young contemporaries, was poised to go "on the greatest, gaudiest spree in history" proved prophetic, and he and Zelda took seats in the front row of the roller coaster. When the Fitzgeralds' personal "spree" degenerated into excess, dissipation and joyless, bloated materialism made them the poster children for "the Jazz Age," the indelible phrase Scott later coined for the twenties. His original title for *This Side of Paradise* had been *The Romantic Egotist*, a revealing glimpse into Scott's mix of literary precocity and emotional immaturity; fame and fortune only poured fuel on his self-destructive fires. The conservative authors of Prohibition wrote their law with juvenile madcaps like the Fitzgeralds precisely in mind. The couple's descent reads as a cautionary tale about the hazards of unchecked hedonism and its toxic consequences: drunkenness, adultery, rootless wanderings, wasted talent, crushing debt, madness, mental institutions, and early death. Until the day he died of a heart attack, only forty-four, his last novel unfinished, a broken man eking out a living as a struggling Hollywood screenwriter, Scott never knew that the signed photograph of Bobby that Zelda used to stampede him to the altar had been a forgery, signed by Zelda herself. Intermittently sane through her last two decades, Zelda outlived Scott by just eight years. She died in a fire at a North Carolina mental hospital where her own mother had warehoused her.

The forgery started with a grain of truth; Bobby had met Zelda exactly once, at a country-club dance in Augusta during the summer of 1919, and her reputation as a party girl had preceded her. Alluring, without question, and dangerous, no doubt, a siren of the highest order; and in the end not the sort of girl who interested Bobby one iota. The younger man, who would by mid-

decade surpass Scott Fitzgerald as the most celebrated member of their generation, possessed reserves of restraint and discipline the doomed author couldn't
hope to approach. And, as it happened, fortunately for Bobby, by the time he
ran into Zelda his heart was already spoken for.

During his freshman year Bobby had met on a streetcar a slim brunette
beauty named Mary Rice Malone, the younger sister of two friends from Georgia Tech, Matt and John. The Malones were Atlanta natives, from the upper-
class Druid Hills neighborhood, Irish Catholic, country-club people like the
Joneses. Mary's father, John, was a tax assessor for the city of Atlanta; her
mother, Mamie, came from an old established Georgia family. Catholics were
relatively rare creatures in the high rungs of Southern society, and the Malones were wary of Bobby. He came from new money, ran a little wild, and his
fame made them suspicious of his intentions. They were members of the Pied-
mont Driving Club, the city's oldest social organization, where Mary came out
as a debutante and joined the junior league, still a sheltered girl.

Bobby was smitten but their courtship proceeded quietly, traditionally.
Bobby visited the Malones at home under the guise of seeing the brothers, taking meals with the family, exchanging shy smiles with Mary at the dinner
table. Gradually he began to spend more time with Mary; he took her fishing,
escorted her to dances at East Lake or Druid Hills in his sleek roadster. Mary
loved to dance, but not the new crazes made popular by the fashion-conscious
"flappers"—another word invented by Fitzgerald—that were sweeping the
country. Mary preferred the traditional waltzes and fox-trots she'd learned at
cotillions. Bobby could dance, too; all those orchestrated evenings growing up
at East Lake came in handy. They were both shy, and not terribly demonstra-
tive, the kind for whom a bond would grow slowly over time until it became
unbreakable. This pace suited their temperaments; they appreciated the
romance inherent in the exercise of self-control. Neither felt any rush to marry
because from early on it was clear they were absolutely right for each other.
They would wait until Bobby was out of school and launched in his career,
whatever it might be; most likely mechanical engineering, at the moment.
Their union was the antithesis of the Fitzgeralds' marriage, more the product
of their parents' values than of the impatient young men who'd marched off to
war. Bobby also wanted to wait because there was a small matter of his future
in the sport of golf to sort out.

. . .

Bobby turned eighteen, finished his sophomore year at Tech in May 1920, and set out to assert himself in the national game. He broke his scoring record at East Lake again that spring with 66. Convinced no one could touch him when he was going right, he decided he would play fewer regional tournaments in order to focus on the big ones; Bobby entered only forty tournaments for the rest of his career, and twenty-nine were majors. Pop Keeler encouraged him down that road; he had just returned to Atlanta after his Hollywood sojourn and had landed a job with the town's most respected paper, the *Journal*. But Pop had come home for a more important reason: Bobby was ready for the Big Show, and for the next ten years he never went into battle without Keeler at his side.

Bobby set the U.S. Open in his sights for the first time in 1920, but he needed a warm-up. In three successive weeks he played the Georgia State Amateur—semifinalist; the Southern Amateur—champion, in a walk; and the Western Amateur, at Memphis. He broke the qualifying record in the Western, and in the match-play semifinals for the first time ran into Chick Evans. Chick was about to turn thirty, in his absolute prime, but Bobby was judged the favorite, which didn't sit well with the proud Evans. As the South's biggest star, Bobby brought in spectators from all over Dixie, and their match attracted the largest gallery of the tournament. Bobby had played dozens of charity rounds with Chick during the war preparing for this moment, studying his every move, but it turned out Chick had been holding something back.

After treating Bobby like his long-lost cousin, Chick came out of his corner trying to knock the kid's brains out. He watched Bobby and his caddie on every shot, guessing from their body language what sort of shot he was facing. When Bobby tried to do the same he realized with a shock that Chick used deliberate misdirection, giving the impression he enjoyed a good lie when his ball was deep in the woods. Bobby picked up the trick and returned the favor later in the match, dekeing Chick into playing a risky shot over a tree. Engaged in more of a street fight than a golf match, the two played dead even through their first eighteen, but in the second round Chick's experience showed; he exploited every mistake Bobby made, played flawless golf, and was up three with seven holes to play. Furious at himself for letting Chick sucker him,

Bobby canned three birdies in a row to square the match. He looked poised to take the lead when Chick's approach at the next hole found a grass bunker and Bobby landed on the green, but Chick got up and down, sinking a twelve-footer. Bobby's putt ran off line, leaving him a six-footer to halve the hole. His next hit the cup, spun all the way around, and spit back out toward him.

"It looked me in the eyes and said you're licked," wrote Bobby. "I was licked, sure enough. Chick out-finished me, and I thought I had him."

Chick won the match, one up. Bobby claimed he learned whatever he knew about the game from losing, not winning, but this was one of his hardest lessons ever. Chick Evans, one of the men he had most admired in the sport, was no friend to him, despite all the past courtesies and the sociable act he put on in front of a crowd. Bobby went back to Atlanta. Chick went on to win the Western Amateur for the fifth time, his crown as the game's top amateur secure for another day.

When Bobby and Pop returned home, Big Bob met them at the station, took Keeler aside, and grilled him about the match with Evans. Pop told him about Chick's gamesmanship, Bobby's comeback, and how Chick had beaten him at the last. The Colonel's face turned red; he almost snorted in anger.

"Well, he'll sure as hell never beat him again," he said, and stormed off.

Pop realized he had just found the source of Bobby's willpower in the iron spirit of his father. The Colonel wasn't just blowing smoke. Bobby never lost to Chick Evans again. Even more startling, during sixteen years on the national stage, Bobby never lost another match to the same man twice.

Bobby and Harry Vardon at Inverness, 1920.

CHAPTER FIVE

Fate and Nothing Else

HARRY VARDON AND TED RAY arrived in New York on the liner *Olympia* during the first week of July 1920. The American press welcomed the old-timers with affection, warming their hands over fond memories of a more innocent age. Their prewar American tour in 1913 had earned the two men legions of friends and they rekindled many of those relationships as they criss-crossed the country. Their American tour manager, an aspiring golf course architect named Arthur Peterson, had scheduled wall-to-wall exhibitions throughout the East and Midwest for six straight weeks, with the men sleeping on overnight trains as they hurtled on to the next stop. This was first and fore-most a moneymaking enterprise—each man would pocket nearly ten thou-sand dollars—but their pace was exhausting. When Harry pointed this out one day, Peterson reminded him that they had wanted to make as much money as possible. Harry never complained again.

Both men were impressed with the improved courses they saw in America and felt that the level of play had risen dramatically: Ouimet's victory had transformed the state of the American game. "Unless Great Britain is able to produce some fresh blood to take our places," Harry told a reporter, "our

supremacy in the Royal and Ancient game is about to be seriously challenged."
Reporters also noticed, not critically, that Harry didn't seem to be the same
player he had been the last time around when they'd dominated their American challengers. Harry was fifty now, and the man responsible for the first great
awakening of golf in America had acquired the nostalgic aura of a treasured
icon. Like Arnold Palmer or Jack Nicklaus at the end of their careers, there was
sufficient reward for fans to simply say they'd laid their eyes on good old Harry
again.

As it had in 1913, their tour was designed to climax at the U.S. Open in
the second week of August, being held in Toledo, Ohio, at Inverness Club.
One of the last stops they made beforehand was in St. Paul, Minnesota, where
Harry's brother Tom had long since settled in as resident professional at the
White Bear Lake Yacht Club. The brothers hadn't seen each other since the
war began and they resumed their family rivalry in a singles match. Harry
nipped Tom by a stroke and broke the club's scoring record, held by Tom, in
the process. Tom groused, not too strenuously, to a reporter: "My damn
brother always goes me one better." Harry reported that after sinking a long
putt on the fifteenth hole his ball had popped back out again like a "jack in the
box." A bullfrog had been hiding in the hole and flinched when the ball
dropped on top of him. After liberating the frog, Tom insisted Harry retry the
putt, which he sank for the winning margin in their match. It wasn't just playing against his brother that rounded Harry into form; as they'd soldiered
through the weeks of their tour he'd felt a sharpness and certainty come back
into his putting and iron play that he hadn't experienced in years. When they
trained on toward Ohio and the Open, Harry confided in Ted that he'd begun
to believe he might just win the damn thing.

"Well, old thing," said Ted. "You'll have to get past me first."

Harry and Ted played their last exhibition at Inverness the day before qualifying began, and beat two local pros, 2 and 1. That evening the two visitors
enjoyed a joyful dinner with Francis Ouimet, but there would be no reenact-
ment of their 1913 showdown; Francis was there covering the action for a
Boston newspaper, a moonlighting angle allowed under the USGA's definition
of amateurism.

The Western Open had been played in nearby Chicago only a week before, so the 286-man field at Inverness included every top dog in the game. Defending champ Walter Hagen slipped into town the day before qualifying. Playing as many exhibitions as he now did, Walter didn't need practice to stay sharp and he liked the challenge of walking onto a course cold. Hagen's controversial defiance of the English at Deal had generated great press in America. When players gathered at Inverness they were greeted with the welcome news that the members had voted to open their clubhouse for use by the visiting professionals. The USGA, mindful of putting on a good show, created a marquee pairing for the qualifying rounds: Harry Vardon and Bobby Jones, playing in their last and first Opens, respectively. Bobby was as much in awe of Vardon as Ouimet had been, and when they were introduced Bobby gushed about the exhibition at East Lake he'd seen Harry play seven years before.

After Harry and Bobby posed for photographers, Pop took Bobby aside and urged him to control his temper while playing with the legend. Bobby had a harder time controlling his excitement; he chatted and bubbled away at Harry throughout their first round. Harry rarely offered more than a distant smile in response, until Bobby got the idea they were there to play golf. Bobby seemed inspired by Harry's presence, desperate to make a good impression, and matched him shot for shot, both finishing with 75. Harry saved his compliments for reporters until after the round, when he pronounced Bobby's methods as sound and predicted a bright future for him. He also wrote, months later, that despite Pop's admonition to him, Bobby "apparently needed a little more time to get his temper under control."

During their second round on Wednesday, Bobby made an effort to adopt Harry's more serious demeanor, and they played the first six holes in silence. At the seventh, after watching Harry nestle a classic bump-and-run shot next to the pin, Bobby skulled a wedge over the green into deep rough, costing him a stroke. As they walked to the next tee, Bobby tried to break the ice with some bashful self-deprecation.

"Mr. Vardon, did you ever see a worse shot than that?"

"No," said Harry, ending the conversation.

When their round was over—both qualified without difficulty—Harry spent an hour in the locker room with Bobby, discussing and answering questions about his iron play. Bobby's trained engineer's mind had been astonished by the faultless mechanics of Vardon's swing and was eager to absorb as much as he could from the master. Although he lacked formal education, Harry had applied more thought and theory to the golf swing than any man alive and he could discuss or write about his conclusions in dizzying detail. (And in spite of Ted Ray's lumberjack persona, he ran a close second, one of the keys to their friendship.) Bobby was equally impressed by Harry's dignity, and vowed to renew his efforts to behave himself on the course. Harry's message to the youngster was as simple as his professional code: learn the trade, not the tricks of the trade. Bobby told Keeler that after this encounter with Vardon, his Open was a success no matter what happened. Pop reminded him that the tournament hadn't actually started yet; beginning tomorrow, sixty-four men would play for the American championship in earnest.

Bobby felt it the moment he walked out to the first tee. This was the same course he'd played the day before, the pleasant weather almost identical, but the air felt electric, knotted with tension, harder to breathe. Bobby's first taste of Open pressure rocked him. His knees shook as he took his stance in front of the massive gallery. He couldn't find his swing, and there was no one to help him. By the time Bobby steadied late in the round he had shot 78, nine strokes behind the leader. Bobby skipped lunch between rounds and loaded up on pie à la mode, a boyish habit Keeler had been trying to break him of that often led to second-round letdowns. In this instance the comfort food helped settle his nerves; he shot a 74 in the afternoon and came off the course seven strokes in back of the leader at the halfway mark. Veteran professional Jock "Hutch" Hutchison, a thirty-six-year-old expatriate Scotsman from St. Andrews, was in front. An eccentric, high-strung twenty-one-year-old American pro from Detroit named Leo Diegel, also making his Open debut, stood alone in second, one stroke back. Tied for third a shot behind Diegel was a trio for the ages: Walter Hagen, Harry Vardon, and Ted Ray.

Seeing all those worthy names in front of him freed Bobby from his pressure to succeed. Sure he was already out of the running, the next day he went out and played what he called "typical kid golf," unconcerned with winning or what anyone else was doing, and shot a third-round 70. When he saw the scoreboard Bobby realized he had turned in the morning's best round: he was only four shots in back of Vardon, who had leapfrogged the other challengers to grab the lead. Hutchison and Diegel were in joint second, a stroke back, with Ted Ray a shot behind them. Of the players clustered at the top only Hagen had fallen out of contention. Chick Evans had crept up from the pack to trail Bobby as low amateur by a stroke. Bobby decided all he needed was another 70 and the Open was his, then helped himself to some more apple pie and ice cream. Harry Vardon marched out to play his final round in a U.S. Open that afternoon convinced he had the title in his grasp. A rowdy crowd of over ten thousand flocked around him, hoping to see history in the making.

Harry played a flawless front nine, and increased his lead to four by the time he reached the twelfth hole. Bad weather hadn't been a factor all week, but at the precise moment Vardon teed up his ball a storm of biblical proportion bolted down across Lake Erie out of a clear blue sky. Hitting dead into the teeth of a sudden gale, he needed four full shots to reach the par five green, and two-putted for bogey. Then the rain came, sideways, lashing, a torrent running off the rim of Harry's hat. Just walking into the wind became an effort. Stretched to the limit of endurance, Harry weakened, and when that happened his vulnerable right hand—nerves ravaged years earlier by tuberculosis—lost its grip on his putter. He missed a two-foot putt for par at the thirteenth when his right hand jumped, banging the ball off the back of the hole; it jumped up and stayed out. Another shot lost. The storm raged around Harry like King Lear on the heath; it almost appeared, one writer observed, to be directing its wrath at him alone.

Harry three-putted each of the next three holes. Not knowing how the storm had affected those playing behind him, Harry knew he needed to par the last two holes to keep his fading hopes alive. The seventeenth faced straight into the storm: 430 yards, the green protected by a brook that now threatened to break its banks. His drive traveled less than halfway, but he had to gamble now and go for that green; he hammered a brassie right on the screws but it ballooned up into the wind. The ball just cleared the brook, then caromed off the far bank and rolled back into the water. Harry's shoulders slumped as he walked forward; he dropped a ball behind the stream, got up and down for six, and collected a par at the last, but the damage had been done. One stroke under par through eleven, then seven strokes lost in eight holes. As he stumbled to the clubhouse, the mysterious storm that had destroyed Harry's chances vanished as quickly as it had come.

Bobby was already off the course by the time the storm hit. The pressure had gone to work on the young man from the start of his final round; he finished with a slack 78, tied for eighth. The 70 he'd thought he needed that afternoon wasn't necessary; even par 72 would've won Bobby his first U.S. Open championship. He finished only four strokes in back of the winner, but with this added indignity: Chick Evans posted a 75 and slipped in to best Bobby as low amateur. Chick had then gone back out on the course and thrust himself into the action, taking Leo Diegel's bag away from his caddie and slinging it himself in an attempt to steady the jumpy Diegel to victory. (The man he replaced, Luke Ross, had been introduced to Bobby during the tournament and, feeling slighted, would end up working as Jones's principal caddie for the next six years.) But Chick's presence on the bag wasn't enough and, although Diegel was too polite to say so, may have been a distraction. With the crowd, Bobby among them, cheering on the only American-born player left with a chance to win, Diegel lost four strokes over the final four holes, ending in a tie with Vardon.

Playing just ahead of him, Ted Ray had survived the punishing squall, the only man in the field sturdy enough to stand up to it. In fact, Ted turned in the round of his life. He drove the 320-yard par four seventh green and cashed in a birdie. During the height of the storm he collected three crucial pars on the same holes Harry had bogied. He caught Harry at the sixteenth, and then moved a stroke ahead of his old friend at seventeen. Facing a five-footer for par on eighteen, Ted learned at this exact moment that sinking the putt would give him the lead. He screwed on his hat, handed his putter to his caddie, refilled his pipe, lit it, took the club back, and calmly dropped the putt to finish a stroke ahead of Harry and Diegel. A pro from Philadelphia named Jack Burke reached eighteen with a chance to tie Ray, but missed his putt. That left only Jock Hutchison on the course with a chance to catch him, but he missed a birdie chip at seventeen and was down to his last chance at eighteen. Hutch was paired with Hagen, already well out of the running. Playing first, taking a casual swipe at his ball, Walter drained a sixty-footer for birdie, then threw back his head and laughed, as the gallery of ten thousand roared.

"I wish that had been yours, Jock," said Hagen.

Facing a putt half as long as Hagen's, his face twisted with strain, Hutchison came up short and missed his chance. Great Britain had carried the day; when Harry faltered, Ted Ray stepped up in his place to win the 1920 U.S.

Open. An immensely popular champion with press and public alike, Ray took the sting out of Vardon's collapse with his gallant charge to victory. When Ted accepted the trophy he spoke at length about the debt he owed his fellow Jerseyman, who had inspired him as a boy and befriended him as a man. The trip had been delayed for seven years by Francis Ouimet, but the U.S. Open's silver cup was going back to Britain for the first time since Vardon had won it in 1900. Absent that astonishing change in the weather, there were many what-ifs; at fifty, Harry would to this day still be the oldest man ever to win a U.S. Open. As it was, at forty-three, Ted Ray would hold that record for an astounding sixty-six years. Vardon's pretournament prediction that American golf was on the verge of dominance over Great Britain in the Royal and Ancient game also proved prescient. A British golfer would not win another U.S. Open for the next fifty years. Harry also predicted that it wouldn't be long before an American player achieved the unthinkable and won Great Britain's Open.

Ted and Harry left the next day to complete their tour, climaxed by a sentimental stop in Boston. They played an exhibition at The Country Club with Francis and Jesse Guilford, commemorating the drama at the Open seven years before. Ted and Harry were determined to put up a game effort in the friendliest way possible, like war veterans from opposing sides reuniting years after the battle. Harry and Ted won the match, 3 and 2, before a crowd that may have been the largest to ever see them. It was the last match Vardon ever played in America. Harry wrote this about his final visit:

> It is with a feeling of pride and satisfaction that I witnessed the enormous popularity which golf has gained in that great country. In 1900, the game had been in its infancy. Now, in 1920, it is the national craze. The skills of the players have increased commensurate with the game's popularity and we have been given further proof of the justly celebrated American hospitality. I hope, in some small way during my three visits, that I helped sow the seeds of all this.

The members of Inverness invited professionals into their clubhouse at the Open and changed the social order in America; Ted Ray's win provoked a watershed event in the British game as well: members of the club that employed him as its professional—Oxhey, in Hertfordshire, north of London—

voted to celebrate his victory by awarding him an honorary membership. Their gesture rocked the foundation of the English sporting establishment; hysterical class-system hard-liners interpreted it as a sign the apocalypse was near. A grateful Ray displayed his U.S. Open cup in the club's trophy case, where a replica still rests today. Harry's employer, South Herts, soon followed suit, as did the home clubs of J. H. Taylor and James Braid. After five decades, their struggle for acceptance had finally broken down the door to the private English clubhouse.

Later in the year, in response to Inverness's generosity, Walter Hagen and a group of pros presented the club with a towering grandfather clock, inscribed with these words:

> God measures men by what they are, not what in wealth possess
> This vibrant message chimes afar, the voice of Inverness.

The author remains unknown, but one suspects Walter had a hand in it. The clock remains in the club's entryway to this day.

When Pop Keeler sat down to write about everything he and Bobby had witnessed on that last remarkable day at Inverness—how that tempest had howled down out of the sky to write a heartbreaking end to the final chapter of Harry Vardon's competitive career—the committed fatalist phrased it this way:

"Fate and nothing else beat Harry Vardon that day."

Bobby didn't feel the same sting of disappointment he had after losing at Oakmont. The compelling finish at Inverness had mesmerized him: five players with a chance to win on the final green. "I concluded right there that the Open championship was the thing; it is my idea of a tournament." He also had no regrets about his finish. "Of all the luck I've had, and I've had a lot, the best luck is that I didn't win at Merion as a kid of 14 at my first Amateur, or at Inverness, in my first Open. I might have got the idea that it was an easy thing to do."

Pop tried to gently steer Bobby away from his unreasonable expectations for perfection. Bobby had watched Leo Diegel closely as he fumbled away his chance to win at Inverness down the stretch, "wondering why his face was so gray and sort of fallen in." The lesson, as Keeler summarized it, was that when you find yourself blowing up in a championship—and you will—just remember "the other fellows are blowing up, too, so keep your own lid on as tight as you can." But Bobby was stubborn and prideful, and still felt he had the game figured out. Keeler saw how much Bobby didn't know and didn't have the heart to tell him. He'd have to learn it the hard way.

The 1920 National Amateur was held in September at Engineers Club, on Long Island. With Bobby having reached the finals the year before—and tasted success in his first Open—everyone from his legion of fans to his own father thought it was time for him to collect a title. The Colonel traveled with Bobby and Pop, so convinced that the breakthrough they'd been waiting for was at hand. They were reunited with Grantland Rice, whose career had gone on hiatus when he enlisted in the Tennessee National Guard at the age of thirty-seven. His superiors tried to keep him behind the lines, and for a while he covered the war for *Stars and Stripes*, but Rice thrust himself into the action. He saw the worst of it, narrowly escaping death on three occasions. Now back on top of the sportswriting world, syndicated to every paper of note in the country, Rice had just taken over the reins of *American Golfer*. One of his first actions was to extend Keeler's contract; Rice knew golf was coming on strong and that Bobby was the game's heir apparent. Rice had long been Keeler's hero in his profession, now he had a chance to befriend and work for him. Pop stuck by Bobby, a hand firmly attached to his coattails as his stock kept rising.

Bobby won the qualifying medal at Engineers, then played his way into the semifinals without breaking a sweat. He appeared confident, boyish and grinning, then found out his next opponent was Francis Ouimet. The two had never met in competition, but a friendship had formed during the previous year. Bobby looked up to Francis more than any man alive, and he served as a role model for Bobby not just on the course, but in life. According to Al Laney, Bobby's struggles with his temper were at their darkest moment, but Francis's approval meant the world to Bobby and he was always on his best behavior in the older man's presence.

A resolutely private and modest man, Francis respected those qualities in others; what Al Laney had called "a deep feeling for unspoken thoughts." It wasn't until spending time together during this tournament at Engineers that the two began to realize how much they had in common: a love of classic literature and thought, a deep respect for the history and conventions of the game, and an ingrained aversion to what Francis called "people making a fuss over me." Although ten years older, Francis granted Bobby the deference of a contemporary, recognizing the brains and sensitivity that made him more than a youthful marvel. Both had been hailed as boy wonders in their sport; although Bobby hadn't won a championship yet, Francis recognized that the longer path he was taking made his journey much more difficult. Bobby never asked for sympathy, only advice, but with Francis fellow feeling came as a matter of course. It wasn't so much what Francis said to him, but who was saying it. Which does not mean that Francis took it easy on him once they stepped onto the course; that was a crucial part of his character as well. Trying your best to win a match against a friend was the ultimate expression of your respect for him as a person. But unlike Chick Evans, for whom winning meant everything, Ouimet believed a hard fight should cause no hard feelings.

Bobby later called this match with Ouimet the end of his boyhood, an assessment that proved optimistic. As mature as he seemed for his age, Bobby was only eighteen, and the easy path he'd had in the draw left him unprepared, while Francis knew exactly what to expect and had readied himself "for the stiffest sort of a contest." To Francis's discerning eye, Bobby had two weaknesses: an uncertain grip on his emotions under pressure, and a shaky putter under any circumstances. Both would come into play.

Francis came out strong and won the first two holes. Bobby appeared flustered and unsteady on the greens, canceling out solid drives and approaches with a cluster of three-putts throughout the morning, which, as he later wrote, "didn't help my youthful conceit of myself." Francis capitalized on every one of those mistakes to either win or halve a hole, and increased his lead to three during the back nine. At seventeen, Bobby's temper flashed for the first time after a poor bunker shot. On the eighteenth green, after Francis made bogey, Bobby missed a two-foot gimme for the win, picked up his ball, and kicked it into the weeds; Francis's lead was three at the halfway mark. Bobby loaded up on pie and ice cream again at lunch and won the first hole that afternoon. Both men played steadily and halved the next five holes. The match turned on the seventh green.

They were both putting for birdie from the front of the green, Bobby slightly away. As he took his stance a flying insect, a bee or yellow jacket, landed on his ball. He shooed it away and prepared to putt again. The bee circled and set down on his ball a second time. When he waved it away this time, the bee flew back and settled on the grass right on his line to the hole. A marshal, trying to be helpful, stepped forward and set his megaphone down over the bee. By now the gallery was beginning to giggle, and when, with impeccable timing, the bee emerged from the open mouthpiece of the megaphone, they roared with laughter. When the bee zeroed in on Bobby's ball yet again, the laughter doubled. Laughing himself now, Bobby pulled off his cap and, wildly waving both it and his putter, theatrically chased the bee off the green and out of sight. Bobby got a round of applause for his antics—even Francis smiled slightly, perhaps for a different reason—but his concentration was fatally blown. Getting back to his ball, he left his putt six feet short and missed the next one. Francis won the hole. As they walked off together, Francis turned to him and said, not unkindly: "Let's just play golf, Bobby."

Bobby burned with shame at the stark realization of what he'd done to himself. "That bee flew away with a good bit of my juvenile fancy for the game of golf," he said later. He couldn't shake the anger out of his system and lost the next two holes as well. Francis's lead was five holes with nine to play, not because of that bee, Bobby knew, but because of how he'd reacted to it: like a child, playful and scatterbrained. Their match ended on the thirteenth green, 5 and 4. As Pop put it, "Francis, in the most solemn and kindly manner imaginable, had given Bobby a thoroughly workmanlike spanking." When the gallery greeted Bobby with gracious applause as he walked off, it brought tears to his eyes; for the first time in his life he felt as if he'd let them down.

Ouimet absorbed a similar beating the next day from Chick Evans before the finals began. Chick had gone on a tear to reach the championship round, and in typically oblique fashion described his easy semifinal win this way: "It was not because he was playing badly that I beat him by so large a margin." Eager to avenge his loss to Ouimet at Oakmont, Chick said, "I am pleased, for I have waited a whole year for the chance of meeting him again. It seemed to me that Ouimet's half of the bracket, excepting Bobby Jones, was the easier, but I am still learning the course." Chick wasn't through. Suffering from sudden amnesia, he added: "Although we have never played together under circumstances that afford a fair chance to judge our games, it seems the unanimous belief of all the golf writers that Francis will win." On this issue Chick was mistaken; the two men's talents being more or less equal, it's safe to say most of them simply would have preferred Ouimet to win.

The USGA let Bobby work as a marshal so he could watch their showdown. He saw Chick win the 1920 National Amateur from Francis, 7 and 6, his third major win, putting him ahead of Ouimet and Hagen. After reaching the finals of the championship for the first time in six years, Francis said this afterward: "His play was magnificent and his putting left nothing to be desired. I had no regrets because I was simply outclassed by a great player." Chick wrote about it this way: "Francis did not putt so well as usual but his real weakness was through the green. I missed many short putts, so I was glad to win, not only because I had waited a year for an opportunity to play against so fine a man as Francis, but because it showed me there was a championship course where careful shot-making was rewarded." Given the choice Bobby had at this point, there was no doubt about which man he preferred as a mentor.

Bobby won a small invitational tournament and played a couple of exhibitions in New York, even beating Vardon and Ray in one of them—although Bobby noted "the old boys were pretty tired"—before returning home to Georgia. But those lesser victories felt hollow to him; the Open and the Amateur were the only titles that mattered now. Soon afterward, Alexa Stirling had won her third straight Women's Championship. Having failed to win any of the four majors he'd entered, and realizing his mental and emotional approach needed an overhaul to succeed at that level, Bobby felt lower about his game than he could ever remember. But when he got together again with Al Laney in Atlanta, his friend noticed a crucial difference in Bobby's temperament.

I could see at once that he had changed. I tried to question him about this and about the Ouimet match. For a while Bobby would say little more than "Francis helped me. You know what I mean." I began to have a certain faint understanding. I began to see that the young Bobby had for Francis what amounted, if not to actual reverence, then to the greatest possible admiration for him as a human being. I was a long time in getting it out of him, and I had to wait much longer to understand that this relationship with an older person of Ouimet's character was the most important thing in the young life of Bobby Jones. Understanding began with his remark, "Francis helped me," and with the feeling of vast relief with which it was said.

Bobby's outbursts would continue, although in the opinion of Laney the time Jones spent with Francis was the turning point in what Bobby had described as the "critical match I thought I was losing." But there were still dark days ahead, and Bobby was about to endure the worst of them.

When Grantland Rice joined the army in 1917 he entrusted his finances to his New York attorney. Returning to civilian life in the spring of 1919, Rice discovered the man had botched every one of his investments and then killed himself. At thirty-nine, with a wife and daughter to support, Rice was left penniless, but never complained. He bought flowers for his lawyer's funeral with the cash in his pocket, and went back to work for the *New York Tribune*. He also took over *American Golfer* because he sensed the sport was making a leap into the mainstream. Upscale urban Americans were picking up the game; golf had become fashionable to the fashion conscious, setting trends in lifestyle and men's and women's clothing. Rice saw another reason to promote the game, because America's favorite pastime was undergoing its worst season in history.

After damning rumors had circulated for months, in September 1920 the Grand Jury of Cook County, Illinois, convened to investigate evidence that the previous fall's World Series—won by the Cincinnati Reds over Charles Comiskey's Chicago White Sox—had been fixed by professional gamblers. The story as it unraveled turned out to be much more devastating: a group of eight White Sox players, fed up with Comiskey's cheap salaries, had initiated the fix and brought gamblers in on the plot. Eight players and two gamblers were indicted on multiple counts of conspiracy to defraud the public and Charles Comiskey. Through shoddy police work and a sharply mounted defense, which portrayed the players as dupes who'd been suckered by professional crooks—the gamblers stiffed them most of their shares—when the case went to trial the following summer the players were found innocent as charged.

The verdict covered no one with glory. Tawdry details exposed at trial left little doubt about the players' complicity or lack of moral fiber. All eight—including two with Hall of Fame credentials, pitcher Eddie Cicotte and outfielder "Shoeless" Joe Jackson—were banned from the game for life. Comiskey, whose profits had gone up during the year of the scandal—one of the main reasons the case failed in court—had been exposed as a tightfisted tyrant. The two gamblers who directed the fix fled the country, and the man everyone knew had bankrolled the conspiracy—New York gambling kingpin Arnold "the Brain" Rothstein—was never even indicted. Rothstein, who once bragged he could fix anything but the weather, decided he'd suffered enough bad publicity from bookmaking and moved his investments into the more sedate profit sectors of drug dealing, bootlegging, and racketeering. During his life he was never successfully charged with any crime, but in the end Rothstein fell victim to his own violation of the code of thieves. After being taken for a sizeable tab in a rigged poker game in 1928, Rothstein welshed on his losses. A week later, after refusing multiple opportunities to make good, an unidentified assailant shot him at a meeting in a New York City hotel room. Rothstein died the next day, at the age of forty-six.

If any sports team deserved a curse on its head, the Chicago Black Sox—as they came to be known after the scandal—rated second to none. But a more benign baseball transaction in 1919 gave rise to an urban legend of ill fate that retains a bigger role in popular folklore. The cash-strapped owner of the Boston Red Sox, Harry H. Frazee, still owed a chunk of money to Joe Lannin, from whom he'd bought the team three years earlier. A New York theatrical producer, the flamboyant Frazee had suffered his worst season on Broadway, and the war had put a sizeable dent in Red Sox ticket sales. Frazee needed cash and had also alienated his most bankable player during failed negotiations for a multiyear contract. That December he sold Babe Ruth to the struggling New York Yankees for $105,000. As part of the deal, Yankees owner Colonel Jacob Ruppert also loaned Frazee an additional $300,000, with the Red Sox home stadium, eight-year-old Fenway Park, serving as collateral.

Frazee had dumped the biggest gate attraction in the game, arguing it was the only way he could afford his other players. He then turned around and invested the cash in more Broadway shows. A few years later, Frazee struck gold with the musical smash No, No, Nanette, which enabled him to pay off the mortgage and sell the Red Sox, pocketing a substantial profit. A happy ending for Frazee, but consider the costs to Boston: Ruth gave up pitching, moved to the outfield full-time, and hit an astonishing fifty-four home runs during his first year in New York. The hapless Yankees, who in twenty years had never won a pennant, went on to take two out of every three league titles—and twenty World Series—during the next forty-four years. And for a while the Yankees actually *owned the mortgage* on Fenway Park. The Red Sox haven't won a Series since, and the Curse of the Bambino was born.

When Babe Ruth joined the Yankees, Grantland Rice realized he was a sportswriter's dream. Larger than life, uninhibited and childlike, Ruth came into his own as a character at the moment his talent exploded. The game desperately needed an antidote to the poison spewing from Chicago; Rice decided Babe was the answer, and he wrote column after column about him during the 1920 season. The mythmaker built the Ruth legend one colorful story at a time. Baseball began climbing back from the Black Sox debacle.

Rice discovered another cornerstone for the dawning Golden Age in the summer of 1919, when Jack Dempsey went into the ring to face Jess Willard for the heavyweight championship. The tall, handsome Willard had defeated controversial African-American champion Jack Johnson in Havana to win the crown in 1915—a fight promoted at a substantial loss, coincidentally, by Harry H. Frazee—but had subsequently done nothing to keep those hopes alive. After decades as an outlaw indulgence of brutal voyeuristic instincts, prize-fighting teetered on the cusp of respectability but needed a popular champion to cement an audience. Willard had spent the years since his win dodging top contenders, grossly over his fighting weight; starring in a movie; and even touring with Buffalo Bill's Wild West Show. The few times he defended his title he was primarily a defensive fighter; the public sensed he was more interested in fattening his wallet than satisfying their bloodlust.

Twenty-four-year-old William Harrison "Jack" Dempsey was six inches shorter, fifty pounds lighter, and fourteen years younger than Willard. As a distant cousin of the Appalachian Hatfields—as in Hatfields versus McCoys—fighting was in Dempsey's blood. A tough kid from a dirt-poor family who'd grown up working the Colorado coal mines, he'd stumbled into boxing as a bare-knuckle saloon fighter under the name "Kid Blackie," taking on all comers and passing the hat for a few bucks. Working his way up to "legit" fights, he won eighty in a row to earn his shot at the title. Dempsey brought a brazen new style to the squared circle; relentless, bloodthirsty, and straight ahead, overpowering opponents with his will. At just under six feet and less than two hundred pounds, he was ruggedly good-looking and charming enough to upset your brutish expectations after watching him tear opponents apart in the ring. Jess Willard accepted the title bout after signing for a record guarantee of $100,000. Dempsey was paid $27,500, and made a point of saying that he'd fight for nothing. Dempsey loved money, but as a public-relations angle there is no more reliable way to get fight fans on your side than to claim you'd climb into the ring for the sheer thrill of compressing somebody's brains.

Willard's showdown with Dempsey provided the template for all the carnivals surrounding heavyweight fights that followed. The promoters sold it as a must-see theatrical event and built an outdoor wooden stadium seating ninety thousand. A ringside seat cost sixty dollars, an unheard-of bounty for a sporting event. Even the cheap seats ran ten dollars. Four hundred reporters traveled to Ohio two weeks early to cover the buildup. Thousands paid a quarter a head just to sit in the boiling summer heat for an hour to watch the two men train. The country had never been so primed for a prizefight.

The temperature hit 110 degrees at ringside when the two men got down to business on July 4, 1919. The heat was so extreme that the uncured lumber they'd used to build the seats bled pools of resin, ruining hundreds of pairs of pants. Grantland Rice had rated the two men even and expected a knockout, but even he was not prepared for the violence of what he was about to witness. In the nine minutes after the opening bell the legend of Jack Dempsey was born. He gave Willard the most savage one-sided beating since the *Titanic* hit an iceberg: seven knockdowns in the first round, with only the bell saving Willard from a knockout. His corner men pulled Willard to his stool, in Rice's words, "as one might drag a sack of oats." They propped him up and sent him out to absorb two more rounds of punishment before throwing in a blood-soaked towel.

The crowd reacted with disbelief. Heavyweight championships tended to be long, strategic affairs with violence doled out in measured doses. There were no round limits; combatants simply flailed away at each other until one man couldn't continue. It had taken Willard twenty-six rounds to dispatch Jack Johnson. To wade in and destroy a man in nine minutes left people feeling cheated, but if the fight had gone on any longer it might have cost the ex-champion a lot more than just his title.

Willard's jaw was fractured on the first punch. Two ribs were broken, one eye completely shut from swelling. He suffered permanent loss of hearing in one ear and he was light-headed from the amount of blood he lost. Dempsey didn't have a mark on him; Willard hadn't landed a single effective blow. Rice realized that Dempsey hit harder, more often, and with greater ill intent than any man who'd ever stepped into a ring. In nine minutes the face of the sport had been more radically altered than that of Willard. Dempsey's unrelenting fury electrified sportswriters, and it was their frenzied accounts of the fight more than the fans' reaction that created a sensation around the new champion. Boxing was about to ride the broad shoulders of Jack Dempsey to legitimacy, and as he had done for Ruth, Hagen, and Bobby Jones, Grantland Rice would serve as his herald.

America's turn away from the Old World completed its arc with the end of Wilson's second term in November 1920. He had recovered enough of his health to fulfill his final ceremonial duties, but the slack-faced, white-haired old man, leaning on a cane, bore faint resemblance to the energetic world leader of recent memory. He slipped quietly out of the White House on the day its new occupant arrived. The country had been clamoring for a new direction in leadership, and with the election of Ohio's Republican senator Warren Gamaliel Harding as the twenty-ninth president, the pendulum could not have swung more violently in the opposite direction.

He was the first sitting senator to be elected to the Oval Office. At fifty-five, he was also the first president born after the Civil War. He had grown up on a farm, come of age in a small Ohio town, played trumpet in the town band, managed the local baseball team, and made his living as a newspaperman. He played golf twice a week, carried a twenty-five handicap, smoked and drank with the boys, and made friends easily with his warm, accommodating nature. Everyone enjoyed his company, but no one predicted greatness for Harding; he was an amiable nonentity. Through his gift for gab he drifted into local politics, serving two terms in the state senate. His staunch editorial support of fellow Ohioan William Taft in 1908's presidential race introduced him to the national stage, and he gave Taft's nominating speech at the 1912 Republican Convention. Two years later he rode his growing popularity to the U.S. Senate. His one term was distinguished by a tendency to duck controversial votes and an uncompromised eagerness to toe the party line. He seemed to have found a home.

There was a darker side to Harding; he had suffered five nervous breakdowns and confined himself to a sanatorium, a secret that would have instantly destroyed him in politics. Harding had married a harsh, shrewish woman five years his senior whom he referred to, not fondly, as "the Duchess." He openly conducted a long extramarital affair with his best friend's wife, which produced a stunningly inconvenient illegitimate daughter. Buying the woman's silence cost the party twenty thousand dollars and a ticket on the proverbial slow boat to China. With those bones rattling around his closet it's no wonder that when his name came up for the 1920 presidential race Harding did little to encourage it. He won almost no primaries and campaigned reluctantly. His primary qualification for the office, as far as his fellow Republicans were concerned, was that Harding looked presidential. His platform consisted of little more than the slogan "A return to normalcy," but he plainly wanted nothing to do with the mess in Europe, which caught the prevailing wind of isolationist sentiment.

The myth of American politics being decided behind closed doors in a smoke-filled room got its start at 1920's Republican Convention. After four inconclusive votes on the floor, party leaders retreated to suite 404 of the Blackstone Hotel in Chicago and by morning had settled on Harding as the man least likely to damage their agenda. Al Jolson wrote and recorded his campaign song, which became a hit record. A few months later Harding soundly defeated an even more obscure Democratic candidate, fellow Ohioan James Cox, a result that was seen as a repudiation of Wilson's policies more than enthusiasm for Harding. Election results were "broadcast" for the first time by a radio station, KDKA in Pittsburgh, a new medium about to explode in popularity. Through no particular ambition of his own, fate had delivered one of the unlikeliest men imaginable to the presidency. He would survive for less than three years.

In 1920 the USGA and R&A (Royal and Ancient) tried to reconcile their differing rule books during a summit at St. Andrews. One of the few issues agreed on during the meeting involved the golf ball. With no established standards, manufacturers had been winding the ball smaller and denser to increase distance. Big hitters like Ted Ray could now pound it so far they threatened to render older, shorter courses defenseless, an argument eerily prescient of today's debate about the game's evolving technology. For the first time since golf began, limits for the ball's weight and measurement were established with pleasing symmetry: 1.62 inches in diameter and 1.62 ounces in weight. The only other idea approved during the summit: an annual international competition.

In the spring of 1921, Oakmont's Bill Fownes assembled a team of American amateurs and set off for England to play their British counterparts. USGA president George Walker, maternal grandfather of future president George Bush, announced he would donate a trophy for the event, which appeared the following year and has since borne his name: the Walker Cup. Bobby made arrangements to finish his junior year at Georgia Tech a month early so he could sail from New York on the last day of April with a team that included Fownes, Francis Ouimet, and Chick Evans. This was the last major golf trip on which Pop Keeler did not accompany him; the cost of the trip came to nearly ten thousand dollars, well beyond the budgets of the *Journal*, *American Golfer*, and Keeler himself. As he watched Bobby's train pull away, Pop had a premonition he should have gone anyway. Bobby arrived in Liverpool on May 9, two weeks before the event, and the English press got their first glimpse of the man Harry Vardon had praised as the rising star of American golf. They liked the look of him and called him "Bonnie Bobby"; his natural reticence played a lot closer to the British house style than Walter Hagen's brassy horn-tooting.

Hoylake provided the perfect setting for the first American-British competition. Built in 1869, Hoylake was the second oldest English links but the first to host some of the game's most historic traditions. The British Amateur had begun here in 1885, defining the line between amateur and professional. In John Ball and Harold Hilton, both of whom grew up there, Hoylake gave the game its first great amateur champions. In 1911 the Royal Liverpool Club bought the Hoylake course for its members, so it has also been known since as

Royal Liverpool. With its tight fairways, tiny greens, and the wind blowing stiff off the Irish Sea, Hoylake provides as harrowing a test as any course in the world.

The Americans needed those two weeks to acclimate to the links style of play. Liverpool had suffered through an eight-month drought and the fairways were as hard as a parking lot. Bobby made the adjustments to bump-and-run shots quickly. Team events were a new phenomenon in golf, but the American squad embraced this locker-room camaraderie and spent their evenings strategizing about how best to attack Hoylake. Two days prior to the start of the Amateur championship, the eight-man teams faced off for their friendly competition. They played alternate-shot foursomes in the morning—a format unfamiliar in America—followed by singles in the afternoon. To everyone's shock the Americans swept the foursomes, took five of the eight singles matches, and won the event decisively, 9 points to 3. The sound of stiff upper lips falling slack with amazement could be heard all over Britain. Predictions that the invaders would march through the Amateur with equal ease filled the newspapers.

The British Amateur's format departed from the American in two significant ways: with an invitation-only field no qualifying rounds were required, and every match in its eight match-play rounds—with the exception of a thirty-six-hole final—was played over eighteen holes. Although this ensured a strong field, it often led to early departures by better golfers when lesser talents got hot, a flaw longer matches tended to equalize. Bobby's gallant, go-for-broke style struck a deep chord with knowledgeable fans. Ladbrokes established him as an early favorite at 5 to 1, with Francis and Chick close behind him. Legal gambling at the touts' open stalls approached the frenzied action at horse races. All eight Americans won their first-round matches, but in the second Francis lost decisively, and Bill Fownes ousted Chick Evans. A battle of two giants, Boston's Jesse "Siege Gun" Guilford and Oxford's Cyril Tolley, turned on a bizarre twist when Guilford's prodigious drive at the twelfth scampered three hundred yards down the fairway and dove into a rabbit hole. Forced to accept a penalty for an unplayable lie, Guilford lost the hole, his composure, and the match.

Bobby went up against an unknown florist from Wrexham named E. A. Hamlet. Employing a quaint, old-fashioned swing, Hamlet displayed the quivering indecisiveness of his namesake and shot a dismal 87. Bobby should have slaughtered him, but after losing his temper at an early mistake he couldn't find a green, couldn't buy a putt, and found himself down two with three to play. Bobby rallied to even the match going into eighteen. Hamlet left his par putt hanging on the lip of the cup. Bobby's putt for par, off line, hit Hamlet's and dropped in. Hamlet's ball stayed out. Match over.

Bobby coasted to an easy third-round win and reached the final sixteen against another obscure Englishman named Allan Graham. Francis watched the match and had to close his eyes on the greens: Bobby couldn't sink a putt over two feet. It ended at thirteen, 6 and 5, one of the worst trouncings Bobby ever absorbed. His anger at his performance carried over into postmatch comments, when he said he wouldn't enter the British Amateur again unless they changed the matches to thirty-six holes. This outburst earned Bobby his first negative reviews from the English papers. He was about to give them a much stronger reason to reconsider their enthusiasm for him.

The last American in the field, Freddie Wright, lost in the fifth round to celebrated British golf journalist Bernard Darwin. A failed career in law had propelled Darwin sideways into journalism, where he fell by chance into writing a golf column in 1907. Darwin had since single-handedly elevated golf writing in England into a respected profession, but few realized what a fine player he was in his own right. His career reached its apex with this win, sending him into the semifinals of the Amateur for the second time. The kindliest man imaginable off the course, Darwin often fell victim to fierce, self-critical temper on it, one of the reasons he responded so instantly and fully to Bobby Jones. With the entire field rooting for him, Darwin lost his last chance to win an Amateur. It was a rousing all-English finals, in any case, won by twenty-eight-year-old Willie Hunter, son of the head professional at Deal.

Despite his disappointment at Hoylake, Bobby's British adventure was far from over. He and four other team members decided to stay on and play in the Open at St. Andrews ten days later. Bobby and Francis made the trip north by touring car, getting lost on remote Scottish roads. A group of American professionals, led by Walter Hagen, had also journeyed to Scotland ahead of the Open to participate in an international team competition against British pros. They met at Gleneagles, an inland American-style parkland course that suited their style of play more than the traditional links. Six years and a few gatherings later this low-key affair would evolve into the Ryder Cup, the most consistently dramatic team competition in the game. At Gleneagles, the British pros defended home turf stoutly, winning 9 to 3, avenging the British Amateur defeat.

This brought together the largest contingent of Americans ever to enter a British Open: fourteen professionals and five amateurs. In 1920 Bill Tilden had become the first American to win the tennis crown at Wimbledon, and golf remained the last unsullied bastion of British sporting might. No foreigner had won the Open since Frenchman Arnaud Massy in 1907, and no other had done it before or since. There was much more English concern about an immigrant Scotsman from the States capturing their title than some homegrown American.

For Bobby and most of the Yanks this was their first visit to the sacred ground of St. Andrews. They found the old gray college town charming, but Bobby couldn't make heads or tails of the golf course. The flat terrain, lack of guiding visual features, blind pot bunkers, and double greens confused him; the layout seemed haphazard to his eye and he decided a good score owed far too much to chance. He kept these reservations to himself, not wanting to offend his hosts, but more practice rounds did nothing to change his opinion. Hagen took a more positive approach; in the year since his dismal showing at Deal he'd played all the best seaside American courses, trying to master the links style. He'd squeezed in as many practice rounds and exhibitions in England as he could with Vardon, Ray, and other British greats, developing what he called a "quail-high stinger": a ball hit hard and low below the wind. But Hagen quickly learned that St. Andrews rewarded precise placement of every shot over raw distance, and that could only be mastered by diligent study of the course and frequent play.

Fourteen Americans survived the Open qualifier, with Bobby low amateur. Expatriate pro Jock Hutchison captured the qualifying medal on the strength of a unique advantage: he had grown up in St. Andrews. His father still caddied on the Old Course, and so had he as a boy before emigrating to the States. Herbert Warren Wind described him as "wearing the map of Scotland on his face." One of the game's most meticulous professionals—winner of the previous year's PGA Championship, his most important victory to date—Hutch had traveled to St. Andrews four months earlier and played every day, sometimes twice, to prepare for this Open.

Bobby paired up with Jock on the first day of the Open and saw an astonishing performance. Jock aced the par three eighth, then teed up his ball on the 306-yard par four ninth and clobbered a drive that ran all the way to the hole, lipped out, and stopped three inches away. The men on the green when his drive arrived told Hutch that only bad luck kept his ball from dropping for a double-eagle one. Those miraculous back-to-back shots have never been equaled in championship golf, and Jock rode them to a two-shot halfway lead. Bobby described Hutch as "set like a piece of flint to win." Playing better than he'd expected after his practice rounds, Bobby came in six strokes behind him, tied for ninth. Hagen was a stroke in back of Bobby, completing a solid American showing. Tied with Hagen was a tall, elegant young English amateur named Roger Wethered.

Bobby woke the next morning with every expectation of having something to say about the Open. Instead, in ways and for reasons he couldn't decipher, the bottom fell out of his game. He topped his first drive and couldn't keep his others on line. The precision of his irons vanished, a death sentence at St. Andrews. His putting woes worsened, and for the first time in his life neither Kiltie nor Pop was around to set him straight. By the time he'd reached the turn — the term originated at St. Andrews; an outward nine holes, then a literal turn back toward the clubhouse for the inward nine — he'd carded a 46 and shot himself far out of contention. The crowd that had gathered to follow the glamorous young challenger slowly drifted away. He took another double bogey at the tenth. Bobby's temper, which had been running hot all day, finally boiled over, and led him into disaster.

The eleventh at St. Andrews is a long par three called High, for it stands on the course's tallest ground, although it is virtually at sea level and barely qualifies as a hillock. The hole features a large figure-eight green set on its side as it faces the tee. The left front is protected by a difficult trap called the Hill Bunker. That's where Bobby planted his tee shot. After digging in to play a recovery, Bobby failed on his first attempt, and then on his second, at which point he said to himself: "What's the use?" What followed next was a matter of controversy only recently resolved; he took either one or two more swings at the ball, which remained in the sand. Some contemporary newspaper accounts claimed he then picked up the ball and tore up his scorecard. Others reported he had done one or the other, but not both. In his column for the *Times*, although he'd been elsewhere when it happened, Bernard Darwin wrote that Bobby teed up his ball and whacked it into the River Eden. Blind with rage, Bobby admitted he picked up his ball, but insisted he only tore up his card in a figurative sense, and denied ever hitting his ball anywhere but onto the twelfth fairway from the next tee. Jones expert and scholar Sidney Matthew recently found an eyewitness whose account appears to settle the dispute: the man claimed to have seen Bobby pick his ball out of the bunker after a third failed attempt, then tear up his card and scatter its pieces in the Eden. Bobby played out the round, completing every hole, and never turned in a card, an automatic disqualification. But no account of the incident, including Bobby's, disputes the fact that he had committed the one unpardonable sin in the game of honor: he quit in the middle of a round.

During his first visit to St. Andrews. In the heat of battle. On the last day of an Open.

Bobby was nowhere near the player or public figure he would become, and with most attention that day focused on prodigal son Jock Hutchison's pursuit of the Claret Jug, his actions didn't generate a fraction of the scandal they would have a few years later, or anything approaching the media firestorm that would have resulted today. A few British reporters took Bobby to the woodshed for it, but most treated the incident as a minor failing, allowing readers to draw their own conclusions about his character. If any other players on the course or in the locker room afterward spoke to him about it, none of those comments have survived. None were needed to reinforce the shame Bobby felt as soon as he walked off the eleventh green. Although players retire from medal competition for a variety of reasons during every tournament, this was the only time in his life Bobby quit in the middle of a round and it scarred him deeply. "I have some sterling regrets in golf," he wrote later. "This is the principal regret—that ever I quit in competition. I've often wished I could offer a general apology for picking up my ball. It means nothing to the world of golf. But it means something to me."

How he reacted in the immediate aftermath said even more about him. Having committed the crime he could have compounded it by leaving town; it would have spared him the whisperings and scrutiny when word spread of his misdeed. Instead he got right with himself and marched out that afternoon to play his final round. Bobby shot a 72 in the fourth round, one under par, but the simple act of showing up did more to address the damage he'd done than a hundred excuses. And had that 72 been an official score, Bobby would've claimed a share of a new low amateur record at St. Andrews, which Englishman Roger Wethered had established that morning. In a calculation of the net effect of Bobby's crisis, that final round signaled a turning point in his life.

Roger Wethered's third-round 72 vaulted him into the lead and the hearts of his countrymen, one stroke ahead of Hutchison, who recorded a third-round 77. Wethered then went out early in the afternoon with the entire gallery behind him and broke his own record with a 71. Bobby played directly behind Wethered and watched him put together that remarkable score as he took his humbling medicine. On the sixteenth fairway he also saw Roger come to grief. Wethered landed his tee shot at the base of a small mound, and to get a clear line to the flag he climbed the mound, then backed down toward his ball to keep the line in sight. He stepped backward onto his ball and was compelled to call a one-stroke penalty on himself for violating Rule 18: thou shalt not move a ball at rest. Without complaint Wethered finished the hole and his round, and the score that should have been his winning 70 turned into a 71. He refused to voice any complaint afterward about the rules or his misfortune, saying only, with a smile: "My feet are just too big."

Bobby hooked up with Ouimet and Hagen after his round and went back out to root Jock on, taking turns as they nipped from Walter's silver monogrammed flask. Hagen finished a respectable sixth, a huge improvement over his embarrassing debut at Deal. Bobby was amazed to hear him dismiss it as just another disappointment; first place was all that counted, anything less made you an also-ran. Hagen's steel-eyed focus on winning made a big impression on Bobby, but so did his casual attitude. Despite the fact that as the world's only unattached pro he was living from one tournament paycheck to the next, Walter appeared to be the most supremely at-ease man in the world.

"What's the point of losing your temper, kid? It's only a game," said Walter. "Isn't that right, Francis?"

"That's right, Walter."

Bobby stared at the two men in disbelief. No one in his deadly earnest pursuit of perfection had ever even posed the question to him in that way before. Crowds love a winner, they were saying, but they'll damn well worship somebody who can show them grace under pressure.

Jock Hutchison helped reinforce both lessons that afternoon. Starting his final round as Wethered had finished his, he found out he needed a mistake-free 70 to force a play-off for the Open championship. In front of three generations of his own family—his father was caddying in the tournament, his own son was in the gallery—and a rowdy hometown crowd, while carrying the standard of the United States as the first American with a chance to win an Open, knowing he needed a nearly impossible three-under-par 70, Jock Hutchison went out and shot his number. His final round remains one of the great performances ever turned in during any major championship. Jock carried that same determination into the next day's thirty-six-hole play-off, where he easily bettered a visibly weary Wethered by nine strokes. Although it was a stretch to say he'd won the title for America—he was a St. Andrews man, born and bred in the grand traditions of the game, and the town took great joy in his victory— Jock had broken the British stranglehold on the game's oldest trophy. The press consoled itself by focusing on Jock's divided heritage; it wasn't as if a *real* American had captured the Jug.

The members of the Royal and Ancient Golf Club, as the Open's administrator and the British game's governing body, took more drastic action, voting to outlaw the square-grooved irons Hutchison had used at St. Andrews, which allowed him to put backspin on the ball and grip the hardened, windswept greens. But even this questionable defense could not stave off the inevitable. Hutch's win turned out to be lightning on the horizon signaling the approach of a deluge; only one British player would win their Open during the following thirteen years. The very next year, an American-born player would win the Open for the first time.

Bobby had tasted the air now at all four of golf's biggest tests. He had experienced the best and worst of international competition, but the poise and maturity he'd seen in Ouimet, Hutchison, and Hagen renewed his determination to wrestle the darker angles of his nature. After his dishonor at the Open, Bobby had not succumbed to self-pity or despair; he faced the music. The last strains of youthful prodigy, driven by unreasonable expectations and emotional intensity, had nearly been wrung out of him, his stubbornness and swollen ego sanded down by experience. The ordeal left him sadder, wiser, more knowing of himself. Pop Keeler recognized the change as soon as he laid eyes on him; Bobby's headstrong, attacking style had failed both on and off the course. For the first time he admitted to Pop his sense of infallibility might be based on a false assumption; the shot that required perfection to succeed was not always the one to play. The road to the top of this game ran longer and a lot rougher than early success had led him to believe. Still only nineteen, Bobby had glimpsed what separated the men from the boys, but his journey across that great divide was not over. Keeler had long ago been humbled by life; his physical weaknesses had nearly broken his spirit. Bobby's belief in himself had nearly been leveled. Pop knew the game could give him the lessons he needed and humble him as it did all others, but Bobby had to submit to it before he could move on. If he didn't yield, acknowledge that this thing might just be bigger than he was, Bobby's confidence might crack open and never recover.

Bobby arrived home in early July with little over a week to prepare for the 1921 U.S. Open. Pop Keeler took the train up to meet him at Columbia Country Club just outside Washington, D.C. America's president took in the championship for the first time in its history. Harding had taken up golf only four years earlier, while still a senator, and had gone golf mad. He played three rounds a week, usually at Chevy Chase Country Club, and resented any responsibilities of office that got in the way of his game. He enjoyed imbibing adult refreshments during and after; less than a year into Prohibition this presented something of a public-relations challenge for the chief upholder of the Constitution. Harding maneuvered around it by playing his liberally lubricated rounds at the private course of Edward McLean, owner of the *Washington Post*, where prying eyes weren't privy to the steady stream of Scotch and sodas flowing in the president's direction. Harding was also the first president to welcome star athletes in for photo opportunities at the White House. He used these occasions as an excuse to meet his favorite golfers—chiefly Walter Hagen and Chick Evans—whom he often tapped to play as his partners in Washington area pro-ams. Hagen became a frequent guest at the White House, and after dinner helped Harding with his swing in the backyard, where the president had installed a practice hole. Walter issued diplomatic assessments of the president's game—he was a first-rate putter, code for "he can't swing"—as if they were State of the Union addresses.

The players put on a rousing show for their president at Columbia. They announced the field of 274—another record number—would be trimmed for the first and only time in Open history by a single qualifying round. This provoked a bitter reaction from players accustomed to the long-standing thirty-six-hole format, which allowed a man the chance to get the bad shots out of his system and give luck time to rebalance his books.

Approaching the first tee in his second U.S. Open, Bobby told Pop he felt as nervous as he could remember. Expectations had reared up in the press again; each time he played a major now he carried more weight. Bobby hooked his opening drive into the woods, which Pop described as "the type written in the story books as impenetrable." Bobby found his ball, and a narrow opening toward the green. His slashing recovery attempt smacked dead into a tree and bounced deeper into the forest. Keeler heard a man next to him mutter: "There goes Bobby." Pop felt a sinking sensation in back of his belt buckle. Disaster. Bobby smashed his third shot as hard as he could toward a thin section of foliage; the ball blasted through the branches and barely trickled onto the fairway. He got down in three from there for double-bogey six. Other flirtations with doom followed—but he squeaked by and barely qualified with a 77, one under the cut line. Pop wrote with sigh of relief afterward: "This was the only time Bobby Jones was ever so close to failure in the qualifying round of any important competition."

Bobby was partnered with Gene Sarazen, a brash young former caddie from Apawamis Club, New York, who was making his Open debut. A stocky five feet five, Sarazen made up for his lack of stature with confidence, powerful hands, and a king-sized personality. Both players knew the other had a reputation for losing his cool on the course, and they made a friendly wager that the first man who threw a club owed the other ten dollars. In the first round Bobby played wildly and posted a 78, but the bet helped both men maintain their cool; neither tossed a club all round. In the afternoon their fortunes reversed; Bobby channeled his anger into a superlative front nine 32 and finished with 71, picking up four strokes on leader Jim Barnes. Bobby appeared poised for a serious run at the lead but in the third round his putter turned skittish; he needed only thirty-seven strokes getting onto the greens, with a birdie putt on all but two of them. He took forty putts getting the ball into the hole. Bobby was right back where he'd ended the first round: nine strokes behind Jim Barnes.

Bobby decided to "shoot the works" in his final round and birdied three of the first four holes. After a towering 280-yard drive at the fifth, a long par five, he pulled his two wood to go for the green and yanked the shot out of bounds. Instead of cooling off he dropped another ball and hooked that one out of bounds. He scored a nine on the hole, and his Open was over. But Keeler watched him closely and never saw Bobby betray a flicker of emotion when those shots sailed left and killed his chances. He didn't quit; no ball was picked up in anger, no scorecard got shredded. Bobby appeared so unconcerned by his demise he might have been mistaken for Hagen. He finished his round without further incident, in fifth place, three slots better than his Open debut the year before.

Sometimes progress, decided Pop, can mean more than victory.

Jim Barnes won the 1921 Open by nine strokes ahead of Hagen—who treated second place with his customary disdain—and 1908 Open champion Freddie McLeod. Chick Evans snuck in ahead of Bobby by a stroke as the low amateur in sole fourth place, the only thing Bobby was mad about afterward. In his second Open, Bobby had been bested by only four men: all former Open champions. More important, he had embraced Pop's advice about the two things a man had to overcome to win a championship, and neither had anything to do with his opponents. They were Old Man Par, and his own damn human limitations.

The newsreel crews asked Jim Barnes to hold off sinking his last putt until they could reposition the president into the frame. Barnes obliged, sank the putt, then marched over to Harding and accepted the trophy from him while cameras cranked away. Harding gave a stirring speech—his long suit—and Pop talked his way out of a minor altercation with a Secret Service man to secure a photo of himself with the chief executive. Writing about the president's golf shortly afterward, Grantland Rice—another Harding favorite and frequent playing partner—observed that he never seemed to mind making a mistake, a fortunate trait because he made so many of them. Which remain the kindest and most revealing words ever written about Warren G. Harding.

Pop ended up in a car with Hagen, driving back to Washington for dinner after the awards ceremony. Knowing that he'd spent a lot of time with Bobby during their trip to Britain, Pop asked Walter for a candid assessment of his friend's progress.

"Bobby's playing some great golf, in spots," said Walter. "He's got every-thing he needs to win any championship, except experience; and maybe, phi-losophy. He's still a bit impetuous."

"I'll drink to that," said Pop, and they did.

"But I'll tip you to something, Pop: Bobby's got more game than anybody out there. He's going to win an Open before he wins an Amateur."

Preparing to board an overnight train for Detroit out of Grand Central Ter-minal, fresh from the finalization of his expensive divorce, Hagen opened a New York sports page and came across a sportswriter's opinion piece stating that Hagen was finished as a force in the game. Rumors had begun to swirl, he claimed, that Walter was on the verge of retirement.

"Where in hell is the next tournament?" he shouted, to no one in particular.

The sports page told him: the Western Open, in Cleveland, later that week. Hagen changed trains in Buffalo the next morning and reached Cleveland in time to enter the Western. Bobby was already in the field, his first appearance in the game's second most important Open, as was Jock Hutchison, everyone's early favorite. Hagen beat Jock by five strokes and Bobby by eight to win the Western, then mailed a banner headline about his victory special delivery to that reporter in New York. Bobby led the field at the end of the first two rounds, a milestone for him in a major tournament, but Hagen's cool professionalism prevailed. Walter marched on from Cleveland to win the Michigan Open, and from there to Long Island for the match-play PGA Championship at Inwood Country Club. Hagen breezed into the finals against Jim Barnes, and beat him 3 and 2, to win his third straight tournament. Even that nitwit New York colum-nist now had to agree that Walter's name still belonged at the top of any discus-sion about who owned the game's greatest talent.

"That reporter did me a big favor," said Walter.

The last chance for Bobby to redeem himself in 1921 came in late Sep-tember at the National Amateur, at St. Louis Country Club in Missouri. The club had opened in 1892, introducing golf to the area, but its new course was only six years old, the work of America's golfing Zeus, Charles Blair Macdon-ald. St. Louis's first pro had been four-time U.S. Open champ Willie Ander-son, who died suddenly in 1910 from alcoholism. Another hard drinker, Kiltie

Maiden, was still the current professional. Bobby's reunion with Kiltie was a warm one that made them both long for simpler times. Wherever he traveled now Bobby carried the trappings of a star: the worshipful press clippings, a growing entourage, an adoring fan base, the dashing good looks and signature style of a fashionable trendsetter. The only thing missing was a trophy to justify all of the above. The title of "best player to have never won a major" began with Bobby Jones; it hung on his neck like a millstone, and the more everyone whispered that a breakthrough must be at hand the heavier it got. The truth was he hadn't come close to winning any of the majors he'd played. The one Amateur final he'd reached ended early; he had never led an Open after three rounds and had yet to seriously challenge down the stretch in the fourth.

Thanks to Granny Rice and the omnipresent newsreel cameras, the idol worship of athletes in the early 1920s was well under way. Bobby did so little to seek it out that all the attention he attracted remained a mystery to him. His magnetism didn't derive from the narcissism of a needy movie star, although he was every bit as handsome, or the boastful crowing of a childish athletic demigod. People were drawn to him by a radiant quality he barely seemed aware he possessed, one that invited the fantasy projections of strangers. He evoked a complex excitement in his fans; the way he held himself hinted at secrets only he seemed to know; a coiled power, withheld, and an emanating decency. He seemed deeply and knowingly amused, without arrogance, rich in human understanding and sympathy. It raises a question of enduring human mystery: What exactly is charisma? In Bobby's case, beyond obvious talents and physical attractiveness, it had something to do with his taut still-ness. Beneath that placid exterior simmered a volcano just barely held in check. People knew that Bobby could erupt, which lent him an element of danger. Bobby was still a troubled young man, and a darker strain of pessimism had seeped into his emotional makeup. As he and Keeler rode the train to St. Louis, they sat on Bobby's berth and quietly talked it over.

"I wonder if I'm ever going to win one of these things," said Bobby.

Pop had never heard him question his chances before. He recognized that Bobby's confidence was dangling over a ledge. Pop took a chance and got tough with him.

"If you ever get it through your head that when you step out on the first tee of any competition you are the best golfer in it, then you'll win this championship and a lot of others. Because it is my honest conviction that you are the best golfer in the world."

Bobby laughed, ruefully. "Please, don't be an idiot. I've seen these fellas play. They're good. They're awful good. And I know it."

"I've seen 'em play, too. And I've seen you play, which you have never done. And I tell you you're better."

Bobby shook his head in disbelief. His mind still ran along the empirical lines he'd learned at Georgia Tech: Where was the evidence? This first admission of doubt was significant and healthy. Perfection was a quality of statues, of marble, not men.

"Men succeed in spite of their flaws," said Pop. "The sooner you realize what they are the faster you'll learn to overcome them. That's when you'll win and not before."

Bobby went off to mull it over; Pop had gotten through. Without ever calling it by name, Pop had added another shingle to his crazy-quilt resume: sports psychologist.

This was Bobby's fourth Amateur. A strong field had gathered in St. Louis: Ouimet and Chick Evans and the others who'd traveled to England on the international team. A rising young player from Los Angeles named George Von Elm made his first appearance, and Tommy Armour sailed over from Scotland. But there was a new name in the field that caught Bobby's eye and riled his competitive fire. The man who had won that year's British Amateur at Hoylake, Willie Hunter, had also made the trip across the briny to compete, amid statements to the press that winning both countries' titles in the same season would make up for Jock Hutchison's win at the Open.

Just let me at him, thought Bobby.

Ouimet shot 69-75 to take the qualifying medal, and with typical modesty said, "It was my good fortune to win." Willie Hunter had no trouble on an American course and finished a stroke behind him; Tommy Armour trailed by another. Defending champ Chick Evans appeared poised to rush past them all, until the twelfth hole of his second round. He stuck his tee shot fifteen feet from the cup. His birdie try drifted four feet past. He missed the comebacker by inches. Then, annoyed, he tried to swipe the ball in one-handed, missed again, and while the ball was still moving struck it a second time, a penalty. Lying one on the green, Chick had to put a seven on his card. Six putts from fifteen feet. From there he was lucky to qualify, and the damage to Chick's brittle confidence would linger. Bobby played cautiously in the qualifier, finishing seven strokes in back of Francis. They posted brackets that evening and Bobby saw that if both men survived into the third round, it set him up for a shot at Willie Hunter.

Bobby couldn't wait; he slaughtered his first man, 12 and 11. He abused his second, 9 and 8. Keeler's pretournament pep talk had gotten through. Based on those beatings everyone, including Bobby, expected him to stomp wee Willie Hunter. Partisan feelings in the crowd ran high and Bobby absorbed the benefit. He shot an even par morning round and stood two up at the lunch break, but found himself saying "Only two up." That worried him; it worried him even more that it worried him. He changed his pants for luck, donning a pair of pin-striped flannels he'd worn in his previous matches. Despite Pop's rants about nutrition Bobby still indulged his sweet tooth between rounds, and this time he went back out after twin helpings of pie à la mode to resume the fight.

In the afternoon Hunter picked up a hole at the third, then gave it back at the seventh. Bobby was still only two holes up with eleven holes left to play.

"He's sticking to me like a bulldog," Bobby told Keeler as they walked the fairway. He couldn't decipher it, but Pop figured it out.

Bobby was playing American-style, high spinning irons to the greens, where they were landing hard and picking up mud from wet pitch marks. The rule allowing players to remove mud from their ball on the green was years away and the mud on Bobby's ball was sending every birdie putt off line, forcing him to settle for pars. Hunter was playing British bump-and-run shots to the green, not to avoid the wind—there wasn't any—but to keep his ball clean by the time it got there. He was sinking clutch putts to save par and stay close. This bulldog had lockjaw.

When they reached the eighth Bobby decided to try something drastic to shake Hunter loose. A short, sharp dogleg right carved through the woods; Bobby had driven straight over the dogleg to the green in practice rounds— about 280 yards as the crow flies—and pulled it off every time, resulting in easy birdies. The risks were obvious: fail to clear the trees and you brought double bogey into play. A rocky ditch below a steep bank protected the green on that side if the shot came up short. He knew Hunter didn't have enough gluteus maximus to duplicate this shot, and picking up a birdie here might just break his obstinate will. When Pop saw his friend teeing up toward the shortcut he had to bite his lip to keep from shouting a warning; Bobby had been lured into playing his opponent, not the scorecard.

Bobby launched a rocket over the tallest tree in the woods, dead on line to the green. At the top of its arc the ball caught the uppermost branch — Keeler called it "a twig no bigger than a pencil" — and fell like a bird shot from the sky into the rocky ditch. Hunter played a safe tee shot down the fairway to the corner of the dogleg then landed his approach on the green. Bobby found his ball in a patch of dense weeds and tried to blast it out; out came a shower of stones, followed by a startled rabbit bounding out of its hiding place, but the ball stayed put. The crowd laughed at the rabbit, and Bobby joined them; Hunter focused on his putt. Bobby's next shot reached the green, but he missed his putt; Hunter collected an easy par and won the hole. Instead of driving a stake into Hunter, Bobby had his lead cut in half, and the failed gamble cut out the heart of his confidence. Hunter won the next hole to square the match, while Bobby was still "reflecting on the mutability of fortune." Nine holes left to play.

The flow leaked out of Bobby's game and with it all his advantages; he was grinding for pars now. They were still all square with four to play. At fifteen, a long par five, Hunter outdrove Bobby for the first time all day. Bobby pulled his two wood to go for the green but pushed the shot to the right, pin high, where it stayed in bounds only by bouncing off a man in the gallery. Hunter's second shot came up well short of the green, but safely in the fairway. Bobby played a superb pitch to the green that rolled to within eighteen inches of the cup, lying three. Hunter pitched up to ten feet, also lying three, and then sank the putt.

Bobby missed his eighteen-inch tap-in for birdie.

Hunter had his first lead of the day, one up with three to play. At the par three sixteenth, both men landed tee shots ten feet away on opposite sides of the cup. Bobby missed his putt; Hunter dropped his and he went up dormie two. At the seventeenth, Bobby ran out of chances when he missed a fifteen-foot birdie. Willie Hunter had beaten him, and Bobby graciously conceded. To demonstrate that good manners ran in the family, the Colonel was the second man to step up and shake Hunter's hand.

But just prior to that, dissatisfied with his approach shot, Bobby had thrown his club back toward his bag, lying on the ground near the gallery. The club glanced off the bag, bounced up, and hit a female spectator in the lower leg. Bobby apologized profusely and appeared more shaken by it than she was; he then missed the short putt that ended the match. Most hardly noticed the incident; some newspapers failed to even report it, but others leaped on it to run out another round of stories about Jones's lack of self-control. Whatever anger Bobby showed was gone the second the club left his hand, but the damage had been done. As he walked off the course Bobby overheard a man in the gallery say to another: "Sure, he's the greatest shot maker we have. But he can't win."

When Pop heard reporters bitching about Bobby's lack of character in the press tent afterward he stood up and delivered a spirited defense. "You'll all be writing headlines about him someday. You'll all be saying it, mark my words; he's the greatest golfer in the world."

Pop went out to drown his sorrows with a few cocktails that night. When he got back to the hotel room he found Bobby waiting up for him, agonizing over the loss.

"Why did I lose?" Bobby asked. "How's it possible for a guy like him to beat me? It was that putt, wasn't it? That God damn little putt on fifteen—"

"Don't you get it? It was the drive, at eight over those trees. You had the lead, you should have sat on it, forced him to catch you. Instead you tried to gamble and let him right back into the match: you handed it to him, Bobby."

"Maybe so, but I don't know how to play any other way. I have to play every shot for all there is in it—"

"That's a laudable frame of mind. And it'll provide you with plenty of chances to get used to losing championships. The best shot's not always the one to play."

Bobby heard him but wasn't ready to absorb the lesson. It would have to come in its own time, the same way he was learning to control his emotions. But for the first time those battles merged into one; if he couldn't master himself he'd never master golf. Something had to give.

"I went away from St. Louis," he wrote, "with a curious ache in my chest."

The pressure was mounting, eating at him, and started to affect him physically. Although he never mentioned it in St. Louis so as not to appear to be making excuses, he suffered from an almost crippling case of varicose veins in his left leg, brought on, Pop felt sure, by internalized stress. Bobby had realized

Hagen was right: nobody gave a damn who finished second. If he didn't like the meat grinder of major championships, nobody was holding a gun to his head and forcing him to jump in. Maybe it made sense if you needed the game to put food on your table, but Bobby still had a year of college to go before he even started worrying about making a living.

"I was still just a boy playing golf," Bobby wrote. "And now in a gradual but apparently universal sort of way, I was expected to win a national championship, not just shoot a fancy round here and there, or beat some classic opponent. Not drubbing the boys back home in a state or sectional tournament. Championship. Championship. So that's it. No matter how prettily you play your shots. No matter how well you swing or how sweetly the ball behaves."

Pop insisted that another element was needed to win one of the Big Shows, in addition to talent and persistence and willpower. Fortune had to smile. Call it luck, call it fate or chance or whatever you like, but you couldn't win without it, that fateful bounce of the ball or turn in the wind that delivered you to victory. The Scots had grasped this mysterious part of their native game long ago, knew how central it was to every outcome. They called it "the rub of the green."

"Chance is bred in the bone," said Pop. "You've no control over it, in life or in golf, and in the end what's the difference between 'em anyway?"

"So what do I do?"

"You wait and prepare, and when you're meant to win it'll happen, not because of your willing or wanting to, but because when it's your turn the outcome's inevitable."

Boston's big-hitting Jesse Guilford went on to win the 1921 Amateur, defeating two-time former champ Robert Gardner 7 and 6. Pop Keeler reported that lightning snaked down out of a moody sky and struck a policeman watching the finals that morning. He was badly shaken, but otherwise uninjured.

Bobby knew exactly how he felt.

Another season was over with nothing to show for it. Bobby returned home to begin his senior year at Georgia Tech. A few weeks later he received a letter from USGA president George Walker. The club-tossing incident in St. Louis may not have generated much local press, but Walker had certainly heard about it. After taking the young star to task for his behavior, Walker warned: "You will never play in a USGA event again unless you can learn to control your temper." As a result of his childish display, the incident at St. Louis, coming on the heels of his surrender at St. Andrews, had brought Bobby to the verge of exile from the game.

Contrite and humiliated, Bobby focused on completing his degree. In need of emotional security as never before, his relationship with Mary Malone quietly deepened; they spent long hours discussing their future together: marriage seemed almost a certainty, but Bobby was determined to finish his education and be able to support a family before they took that step. He had realized a career in mechanical engineering was not going to provide the satisfaction he'd imagined as a freshman. Bobby had traveled a long way up in the world since then, and his ambitions had wider horizons. His father's law practice had continued to thrive—he counted the Woodruff brothers, Atlanta royalty and proprietors of Coca-Cola, as friends and clients now—and the Colonel lobbied hard for his son to join his practice. He had always preached the exalted English ideal of a man embracing a profession; engineering or, worse, professional sports were little better than blue-collar trades. On a personal level, the Colonel was also Bobby's closest friend and liked the idea of him staying close to home.

It's uncertain whether Bobby had made up his mind about his future when he applied that month to Harvard. His stated intention was to round out his college career with a bachelor's degree from their English department. Perhaps he was already looking for a foundation in reading law, while acquiring an institutional pedigree that would improve his prospects. The literary influence of Keeler can also be detected; if technical science hadn't given him the answers Bobby was looking for, maybe he could find them through immersion in two thousand years of literature. Bobby was only twenty, and despite his athletic achievements still struggling with fundamental questions of personal identity. He didn't define himself through his sport, as professionals like Hagen or Sarazen could do. His ambitions demanded more of him than that enviously simple life. Two years at Harvard might provide the perfect harbor, just far enough away from Atlanta, and buy him time to chart his course.

Bobby wrote a sincere response to USGA president Walker, apologizing for his outbursts and resolving to eliminate them, but in private conversations with Pop he seriously contemplated giving up competitive golf. Walker's letter had forced Bobby to confront the question: Was the ongoing strain to his health and mental well-being worth these elusive rewards? The alarming weight losses he experienced during majors had continued. If he didn't break into the winner's circle soon, what possible reason could he have for stepping back into that fire? Scholarship has gone back and forth on the subject of how close Bobby came to abandoning his quest. Bobby later denied it and Pop appears to be the only person he discussed it with directly; years later he had too much stake in maintaining Bobby's legend to confirm it. The approach of the 1922 golf season forced the issue. That spring Bobby underwent four medical procedures to repair the varicose veins in his left leg. It was a more serious problem than had first been diagnosed, and he ended up spending two weeks in the hospital. During his stay, Perry Adair came to see him, with a request.

Perry's father, George Adair, Bobby's first patron in the game, had died suddenly in November of 1921, at the age of forty-eight. His friends in golf had decided to dedicate a new trophy for the Southern Amateur in his name; that year's tournament, where the Adair Trophy would debut, was scheduled to take place at East Lake. Knowing he had sworn off regional tournaments, Perry had come to ask whether Bobby would agree to play in this one as a tribute to his father. The Southern was scheduled less than two weeks after his release from the hospital and his doctors warned against putting any strain on his leg. But Bobby couldn't say no to Perry; he got in four hours of practice—his only golf in three months—and snuck out to play nine holes the day before the tournament began. With his leg heavily bandaged, Bobby finished in a tie with Perry for the qualifying medal, then breezed through five match-play rounds to win the championship easily.

Bobby's name became the first to grace the George W. Adair Memorial Trophy, and in a satisfying coda, Perry would follow him in victory the next year. This was the proudest accomplishment of his career; Perry soon retired from competition to run the family's thriving real estate empire. Bobby's effortless victory had convinced him he shouldn't turn his back on golf, but from this point on he would concentrate exclusively on the Big Shows. He had just turned twenty-one and graduated from Georgia Tech near the top of his class. The chase was on. He had one week to get ready for the 1922 U.S. Open.

During the week that Bobby won the Southern Amateur and decided to continue in the game, Walter Hagen was making history overseas. He had traveled to England to play in their Open for the third straight year. After laying siege to Britain's upper-class clubhouses during his last visits, this time Walter was determined to march in and seize the crown.

The 1922 Open was played on the links of Royal St. George's in Sandwich, Kent. So high was Hagen's confidence in his game—featuring a now mastered punch shot, the key to surviving the hard coastal winds—that at two in the morning on the eve of the championship he was spotted conducting a putting clinic on the carpet in the bar of the Ramsgate Hotel. When reminded that everyone else in the field would already be sound asleep, Walter said: "They may be in bed, but they aren't sleeping."

The weather behaved and Hagen coasted through the first three rounds just off the lead. Three of the top four on the leader board were Americans; Long Jim Barnes was tied with Walter, two strokes in back of Jock Hutchison. In between them stood fifty-three-year-old J. H. Taylor, mounting a last courageous run at a major. Five strokes behind and seemingly out of contention was Britain's only other hope, Scotsman George Duncan, the last son of the realm to win the Open, in 1920.

An early tee time put Walter out ahead of his pack in the final round. He hired half a dozen caddies to track his competitors and report back to him; this flood of information might have driven any other player crazy, but Hagen needed to know exactly where he stood, and that defines part of his greatness: pressure actually *helped* his game. On this day it produced one of the great rounds of his career, an even round 72 played in heavy weather that gave him what looked like an insurmountable lead. A dozen reporters rushed to the press tent to fire off dispatches that Hagen had won the Open. Knowing better, Walter lit up a cigar and planted himself near the eighteenth green to keep an eye on the finish.

By seven o'clock that evening, only George Duncan had a chance to catch him; he had thrown an inspired round at St. George's and reached the final tee needing a three to win and a four to tie Walter and force a play-off. Duncan cracked a drive down the heart of the fairway and appeared to hit a perfect approach; his ball hopped up dead on line, rolled onto the green, but broke sharply left and drifted into a grassy depression forty feet from the pin. Now Duncan needed a chip and a putt to catch Hagen. Walter had just played the same shot and knew the slope to the hole was steeper than it looked from there. But did Duncan or his caddie know that?

He didn't. Duncan's ball stopped eight feet short of the hole. Eight feet to keep the Claret Jug out of Hagen's hands. As he watched from the gallery, those hands were trembling as Walter placed them on the shoulders of an English reporter standing in front of him. The crowd fell silent.

The putt rolled by the hole. In spite of a heroic 69, Duncan's comeback had fallen one stroke short.

Hagen said he felt "too weak and too shaky to move." He managed to stagger out onto the green and offer sympathy and congratulations to Duncan for his valiant effort. Walter had just become the first native-born American to win the British Open. When they handed him the Claret Jug, in a short, modest acceptance speech he promised to return and defend his title the following year. His surprising humility scored points with the British and helped ease the pain caused by his victory.

Only a few minutes later Hagen made a second gesture that erased the goodwill his first one had created: he signed over his winner's check to his caddie. Hagen estimated he had spent $10,000 on a round-trip visit to England. When they handed him his check Walter realized that winning the game's oldest championship had netted him $375. Pocket change, tip money, and Hagen treated it accordingly. His action suggested that the point of winning their Open had nothing to do with the purse so proudly offered by the R&A. Guilty as charged. What mattered to Walter was the effect this would have on his name and reputation, and he knew for a fact it would do a whole lot more for his bank account than this paltry sum.

Three years had passed since Hagen cut his ties to Oakland Hills and ventured out on his own as an unattached professional. At twenty-nine he had joined Vardon and Ray as the only men ever to capture the national championships of both their countries. In the nine years since he'd first left Rochester to play in the Open at Brookline, Walter had transformed himself from a callow kid into a swashbuckling celebrity of universal fame. For the moment, alone among all the emerging, accomplished sportsmen in the American landscape, Walter Hagen had entered the rarified realm of legend. And that, as it turned out, would be worth its weight in gold.

The 1922 U.S. Open was being played at a new venue, Skokie Country Club just north of Chicago. Bobby and Pop boarded another train north, in the usual cramped sleeping berths, not a roomy Pullman compartment, a hard and wearying way to travel. First class was well out of reach of Bobby's budget and would remain so for the next five years. Now reinstalled at East Lake as resident professional, and back on the team as Bobby's swing coach, Kiltie made the trip with them. After talking it over with Keeler, the Colonel had decided to remove himself from his son's entourage, feeling his presence added too much pressure. Pop took on the added responsibility of sheltering Bobby from increasingly aggressive reporters who chased him for quotes; he let it be known among his brethren in no uncertain terms that if they wanted any words from Bobby to spice up their stories, from now on they were going to have to go through him. If Pop hadn't been so likable they might have hated him for it.

The voluble Pop and the taciturn Kiltie added comic contrast to Bobby's inner circle. Pop's nonstop chatter and perpetual good cheer rubbed Kiltie the wrong way, particularly in the mornings before the first drink had wiped away the cobwebs. Forever trying to improve his own desperately impoverished game, Pop constantly badgered Kiltie about his theory of the golf swing. Although few men alive knew more on the subject, Kiltie just plain hated to talk; the more questions Pop fired at him the more reticent the little Scotsman became, and the more he clammed up the harder Pop pressed him for answers. This aggravated dialogue would continue, the mutually frustrated outcome unchanged, for years.

On the train Keeler noticed Bobby poring over Cicero's *Orations Against Cataline*. One of history's great advocates of culture and conservatism, an accomplished trial lawyer in the ancient Roman courts, and the man credited with defining the modern principles of rhetoric, Cicero represented a new role model for Bobby. He recognized something of himself, or a vision of who he'd like to be, in these words written over two thousand years before: "An eloquent man should be able to speak of small things in a lowly manner, of moderate things in a temperate manner, and of great things with dignity." Bobby admired Cicero's modest but unshakeable self-respect and told Pop, "I wish I could think as much of my golf as he did of his statesmanship. I might do better in these blamed tournaments."

Skokie Country Club, developed from a homemade nine-hole course recently transformed by Donald Ross into a modern track, was making its debut as a national championship venue. Scorched bone-dry after a spring drought, the course was torched by players in practice rounds with record low scores. Bobby found the layout surprisingly easy, giving rise to optimism in the Jones camp that this might be his week. With over 320 entries, qualifying rounds took three days, with thirty-six holes restored as the standard. Bobby cruised in with a 72-76, and on the first day of the Open proper found himself paired with Walter Hagen.

Walter had returned in triumph from England with the Claret Jug. Hundreds of fans and a military marching band greeted his boat as it docked in New York. In the first parade ever given by the city to a sports personality, Hagen claimed he rode in a fleet of limos down Broadway escorted by a squad of motorcycle policemen as crowds lined the streets. With most of Hagen's accounts, dividing his estimates by half is a safe way to arrive at reliable numbers; it was more likely one limo, escorted by two motorcycle cops. A raucous dinner followed that night in the ballroom of the Biltmore. After a few days of round-the-clock celebration, a bleary-eyed Hagen caught a train to Chicago and showed up at Skokie on the eve of the tournament. He wasn't about to miss a chance to become the first man to win both Opens in the same year.

Based in large part on the box-office success of Hagen's exhibitions, the USGA had decided for the first time to charge admission. After a heated debate over whether selling tickets would drive people away, ten thousand showed up willing to plunk down $1.10 at the gate. With paying customers walking the grounds, the USGA decided to pair the two biggest names in the field; the marquee matchup of Bobby and Walter drew thousands to the first tee. Hagen threw down a flawless 68 in the first round to take the lead, besting Bobby by six strokes, but his frenetic travel schedule caught up with him that afternoon; he fell back to a 77, tied with Gene Sarazen in third place. Bobby shot a steady 72 to settle in one stroke behind them in fifth.

The next morning found Bobby paired for the final rounds with the dashing Scotsman George Duncan. Now the harsh lessons of his last few years began to pay dividends. With every club in the bag working, Bobby shot his best round in an Open, 70, landing him in a first-place tie with a young Chicago pro named "Wild" Bill Mehlhorn, nicknamed for his fondness for high-stakes poker and cowboy hats. Bobby had climbed another step up the mountain: he held a share of the lead at a major going into the final round. Hagen was three strokes back. One shot behind him, almost unnoticed, stood Gene Sarazen.

The path to Bobby's first big win looked wide open. His game felt sure and steady and, keeping the promise he'd made to George Walker and the USGA, Bobby held his emotions in check throughout the week. He'd improved by two shots during every round and told Keeler he thought he could shoot 68 in the final and win going away. Bobby played well but 68 proved optimistic; two missed putts gave him 36 for his outbound nine. As he reached the tenth, word drifted back to him that Sarazen, playing ninety minutes ahead, had just finished with the 68 Bobby had hoped for. The math was simple, and brutal: Bobby needed a 71 to beat Sarazen and win the championship. That meant he'd have to play the long back nine in 35, one under par.

Bobby crushed his drive at ten, but his approach ran through and over the green. He pitched back to the pin and rolled ten feet past it. Pop and Kiltie stood next to each other in the gallery watching Bobby line up the putt. He struck it firmly, on line, but it caught the lip and spun out. A stroke lost to par. "Kiltie and I looked at each other under the long, moaning sigh the gallery exudes on such an occasion," wrote Keeler. "The little Scot was ghastly under his tan. He shook his head slightly. Bad business."

Bobby described the pressure bearing down on him now as "the iron certitude of medal competition. You *know* what you have to do in that last round. It is not one man whom you can see, and who may make a mistake at any moment, with whom you are battling. It is an iron score. Something already in the book."

He needed to par in now just to tie Sarazen, but lost another stroke at the twelfth, flying the green, pitching back long, and missing a thirty-footer for par. After missing the green again on thirteen he chipped up and sank what Pop called "an ugly little four-footer" to save par. That seemed to revive him. Bobby pounded his drive at fourteen straight down the middle, nearly reaching the green. As a grim Keeler trudged down the fairway he felt someone come up from behind and clap him on the back.

"Don't let your chin drag," said Bobby. "It's not as bad as all that."

His tone sounded chipper, but despite the attempt at bravado Keeler said Bobby's "face was gray and sunken and his eyes looked an inch deep in his head." The iron certitude was eating at him. Bobby thought that Pop looked even worse than he did: it was working on both of them. Just after this exchange, Bobby's caddie had pointed to a man he didn't know hopping along after them in the gallery.

"Here comes our jinx again," he said.

He was nodding at Pop, which gave Bobby a much-needed laugh.

Bobby misplayed his easy pitch at fourteen, leaving himself a tough thirty-five-foot putt for the birdie he desperately needed. As he made the stroke Bobby put so much unconscious body English to it that by the time the ball dropped in the hole he was lying flat on the green. The crowd roared in approval. One of those lost strokes had come back, but he still needed a second birdie to catch Sarazen. The eighteenth was his best chance, a reachable par five, but he had three tough holes ahead to get there. At fifteen he just missed a long putt for birdie. Kiltie and Pop could barely breathe when that one stayed out, but Bobby calmly marched on. He collected another workmanlike par at sixteen. Make par at seventeen, then that birdie at the last would get him into a play-off.

Bobby cut off the dogleg with a booming drive on seventeen, carrying a strategic bunker at the elbow. That should have left him with an easy second shot, but when Bobby reached the fairway he discovered the ball had taken a dreadful kick, dead left, out of the fairway and onto a dirt service road, where it came to rest under a low-hanging tree. That such a bold, well-executed drive could end up in such a rotten lie seemed cruel, inexplicable.

Bobby betrayed no emotion. He worked himself into position over the ball, visualizing a low runner under the tree to the green over one hundred and fifty yards away. The shot came off perfectly but ran out of gas just before it crested a small slope to the green and rolled all the way back down to the fairway. But Bobby left his crucial chip to the hole short, and his putt for par came up short as well. Bogey five.

Standing on the tee at eighteen, Bobby needed a miracle eagle three for the tie. He walloped another drive, then pulled his three wood to try for the green and set up an eagle putt. The ball was struck so purely it ran through the green into the gallery standing off the left side. The chip he needed to drop into the hole rolled right over the cup. Bobby made the six-foot putt for the birdie he'd been banking on, but the bogey at seventeen had killed his chances.

Gene Sarazen had won the 1922 Open, with Bobby in second by a stroke.

In three Opens he'd gone from eighth to fifth place and now second by a single shot. He'd never been low amateur in the championship before; at Skokie he finished thirteen ahead of Chick Evans, who was playing in his own hometown. The previous year's Amateur champion, Jesse Guilford, was sixteen strokes behind him and Bobby beat the reigning British champ, Willie Hunter, his nemesis at St. Louis, by seventeen.

No amateur ever finished ahead of Bobby in an American or British Open again.

Most important of all, Bobby never once lost control of his emotions. In years past, that horrendous bounce at seventeen, which cost him the tournament, might have sent him into a blind rage.

The next morning, Bobby and Pop ran into Sarazen on the train headed east. Sarazen was holding court in an upgraded first-class compartment around the large silver trophy, as the two men walked past to their second-class berths. In later years Sarazen told the story of the encounter two different ways: in one he claimed Bobby, half kidding, offered to play Gene straight up for the trophy the following day. Gene gave the impression that if he'd said yes Bobby would've jumped at the chance. The other version had Gene teasing Bobby as he passed: "Hey, Jones, bet you'd like to play me for this again tomorrow." Bobby responded with another simple and gracious congratulations.

This second account sounds a stronger ring of truth. At twenty years and four months, Sarazen and Bobby were almost exactly the same age, but their lives could not have followed more divergent paths. The son of Sicilian immigrants in New York named Saraceni, Gene changed the name in his midteens, worried the original made him sound too much like a concert violinist. He'd worked as a caddie since the age of eight, and dropped out of school in his early teens. Cockiness was an essential part of the young Italian's Dead End Kid makeup. Coming up the hard way had given him a helping of Hagen's bluster and braggadocio—his best friend during childhood, an Irish kid named Ed Sullivan, didn't do too badly in life either—and as the shortest pro in the game Gene felt the constant need to make a big impression. A few weeks after his breakthrough at Skokie he would follow with a victory over Hagen in the PGA Championship. After these early back-to-back major victories in his career Sarazen cashed in aggressively on all the deals that came his way; his future seemed assured. At that moment Bobby, the modest, educated young man from a loving and supportive family, could not say the same.

Bobby didn't let anyone see how low his spirits had sunk until he was on the train with Pop and Kiltie. All three felt tired and discouraged. As Bobby put it, "this championship quest was getting a bit thick." For all the great golf he was capable of playing, Bobby had clocked forty rounds in ten national championships and never once broken 70. Other players, lesser talents by any measure, managed to do so repeatedly, often winning because of it. The game seemed to select its winners by nothing more sensible than the random conferring of lucky breaks. Neither Kiltie nor Pop could argue with that point; they'd seen it happen too often, and that was a bitter pill to swallow. Trying to offer consolation, Pop asked Bobby what he'd do if he played the game as poorly as Pop did.

"I'd probably get a lot more fun out of it," said Bobby.

Bobby was brushing up his Latin and studying Einstein—whose startling theories of relativity were in the popular news—a month later when the three men took another train north, this time to Long Island and the National Golf Links. Bobby was scheduled to play in the first official Walker Cup competition with Great Britain. The event would serve as a final tune-up for the National Amateur, played a week later at The Country Club in Brookline. Bobby won both his matches and the American team prevailed, 8 to 4. The evidence was mounting that American players had caught, if not surpassed, their British counterparts on both the amateur and professional levels, but one unlikely old soldier put up quite a fight.

When British team captain Robert Harris came down with tonsillitis on the eve of the tournament, forty-six-year-old Bernard Darwin stepped in as his emergency replacement. Making his first trip to America since 1913, Darwin had come to cover the event for *The Times* of London but instead found himself losing a first day match against his old friend Francis Ouimet. The next day Darwin rallied to beat American captain Bill Fownes in singles. Both days were played in the heart of a stultifying heat wave, and Darwin attributed his team's ill fortune during the first Walker Cup to their playing in shirtsleeves: "It is at first a bewildering experience, and I shall not forget my first coatless drive. It was one of the grandest hooks it has ever been my fortune to see."

A raucous dinner marked the end of the festivities—fueled by their host C. B. Macdonald's extensive wine cellar—and the next morning both teams ferried across Long Island Sound to Connecticut, where they jumped a train bound for Boston. The Colonel traveled up from Atlanta and rejoined Team Jones, ready to put his fear of being a jinx to the test. The American favorites qualified easily, with defending champion Jesse Guilford capturing the coveted gold medal. Playing on the hallowed ground of The Country Club meant a lot to Bobby; he got in a practice round with Francis before the start of competition and heard firsthand the story of his friend's great victory in 1913.

Bobby won his first three matches in the Amateur. In the semifinals, he came up against Jess Sweetser. Bobby joked afterward that on the first tee he shouldn't have reminded Sweetser, 1920's collegiate champion from Yale, that he was about to enter Harvard. They halved the first hole, and then Sweetser played a blind shot from ninety yards to the second's elevated green. The roar of the crowd told them what had happened; Sweetser had holed out for an eagle. Bobby then played his second shot to the green, and heard another roar, followed by a groan; his ball landed six inches from the cup but stayed out. Bernard Darwin called them "the greatest little shots" he'd ever seen. Bobby was already one down. It was like a punch in the face, and five years later Bobby wrote, "it still makes me groggy when I recall it."

His eagle propelled Sweetser into a rampage while Bobby was still reeling. Seven holes later Bobby found himself six down. A tall, handsome, and, some said, excessively cocky player, Sweetser went on to break Ted Ray's nine-year-old course record with 69. Bobby steadied to shoot two under par on the back but could only pick up a single hole on his streaking opponent. Five down at intermission, Bobby tried to continue the fight but this was Sweetser's day; after lunch Sweetser parred the first eleven holes and the match was over, 8 and 7, the most lopsided, decisive defeat of Bobby's entire life.

"Jess Sweetser chopped my head off," said Bobby. "I remember thinking it was adding insult to injury, beating me at the most distant point from the club-house, so I would have to haul my bedraggled self nearly a mile before I could sit down and rest."

The next day Sweetser won the 1922 Amateur by beating Chick Evans, 3 and 2. When Bobby congratulated him, Sweetser said: "Thank you, Bobby. I beat the best man in the field yesterday." Not much consolation; Bobby had failed to reach the finals and, after Skokie, felt he'd taken a step backward. He felt even worse that his father had come all that way to Boston only to see him get trounced; the Colonel left Brookline convinced he was jinxing Bobby. Pop tried to defuse their frustration by suggesting Bobby always brought out the best in his opponents, that an inspired performance like Sweetser's only confirmed his greatness.

Bobby took no comfort from it. Sweetser was a month younger than he was; for the first time he had lost to a player catching up with him from behind. As they summed up the Amateur at Brookline, golf writers echoed that sentiment; there hovered around Bobby now an air of disappointment, as if people had begun to tire of his perpetual promise, seeing no payoff for the long-term investment of their affections.

Bobby began to believe he lacked what it took to win championships. He could hit great shots with the best who ever played, and the mechanical perfection of his form took your breath away, but he seemed to be missing a key ingredient to put him over the top. What was it? Luck? Mental toughness under pressure? The will to win? More than one observer of the sport had concluded that a big brain wasn't an asset in golf. Could intelligence and emotional sensitivity, among his most valuable human qualities, actually be holding him back? The questions haunted them all on the trip back to Atlanta; if he had greatness in him, would it ever show itself when it mattered most? Only Pop Keeler's faith was unshaken; he was convinced that the toughness Bobby needed could be acquired only through defeat in the heat of championship competition. Metals were strengthened in the crucible through the stress of forging. Pop noted that Brookline erased all talk of Bobby quitting the game; it only increased his resolve.

On Saturday, September 16, a week after returning from Brookline, Bobby went out with his dad and regular weekend foursome to play a round at East

Lake. He had broken the scoring record six times since he was thirteen; it stood at 66, a number he'd subsequently matched three times. That day Bobby shot his seventh record score at East Lake, a 63. This was 1922, the era of hickory shafts and irons with sweet spots the size of a pea, on one of the toughest courses in America. Bobby never shot a better round in his life and that record would stand at East Lake for seventy years. It became the talk of the town when Keeler wrote it up in the papers. Pop raved to Bobby about what he'd done when he saw him the next day, but he was in no mood to hear it.

"The place for that round was at Brookline—or Skokie," said Bobby.

He took no pleasure from his achievement. Although he empathized with his young charge's anguish, secretly Pop couldn't have been more pleased. He could see the striations forming in Bobby's steel-blue eyes. Still only twenty, he'd been cured by the fire and shaped by the lathe, iron, and hardwood, battle-tested. Strong enough, at last, to carry his burdens. It won't be much longer now, thought Pop.

Four days later Bobby left for Boston, and Harvard.

PART TWO

THE CHAMPIONSHIP YEARS

No virtue in this world is so oft rewarded as perseverance.

—BOBBY JONES

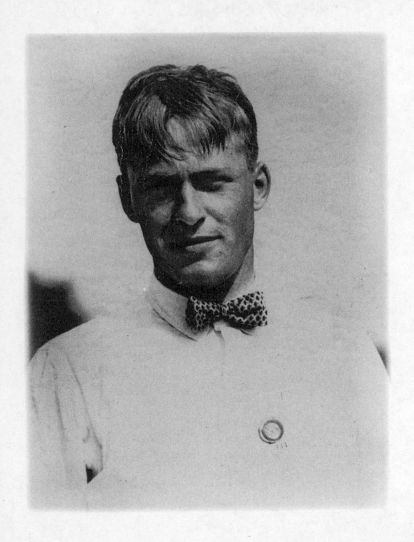

Bobby, twenty-one, at Inwood, 1923.

CHAPTER SIX

Breakthrough

PRESIDENT WARREN G. HARDING played his final round of golf during the last week of July 1923. On his way back from a campaign trip to Alaska— the first chief executive to set foot in that vast American territory—he stopped in Vancouver and snuck in a round between meetings. The demands of the presidency had worn the genial man down; he looked two decades older than his fifty-seven years. By any standard, Harding's tenure in the White House had been the most calamitous in half a century. As promised he had slashed taxes and raised protective tariffs, which fostered a favorable business environment in the aftermath of the war, but his problems began much closer to home. Lacking the intelligence or strength of character to champion a vision of leadership, he'd appointed a squadron of suspect friends and supporters to key positions, more than a few of whom had proceeded to freely, almost pathologically, steal everything in sight. He named Albert Fall, a disreputable former colleague from the Senate, as secretary of the interior. Fall hounded Harding to hand control of the navy's strategic oil reserves to his department, then secretly auctioned off their commercial exploitation to the highest bidder. One of those oil fields sat under a distinctive, bulging geologic formation in Wyoming called the Teapot Dome—Fall accepted a bribe of $300,000 for it from oil magnate Harry Sinclair—which gained lasting fame as a catchall phrase for the ensuing scandals. Later that year Fall bought a pricey ranch in his home state of New Mexico with a briefcase full of hundred-dollar bills. Fall eventually took the fall for his crimes and in 1929 began serving a one-year sentence in federal prison, the first cabinet member in American history ever to go directly from the White House to the Big House.

The chief of the Veterans Bureau, a Harding crony named Charles Forbes, was convicted of embezzling $200 million from the agency's coffers. Harry Daugherty, Harding's attorney general and chief officer of the law, narrowly escaped joining them in prison for a variety of shenanigans—including the selling of government-produced alcohol for profit during Prohibition—but walked away when he successfully bribed his jury. Two lesser appointees accused of graft avoided trial by committing suicide. Not one of these lengthy investigations produced any evidence linking the president to his friends' crimes, but to say he was only guilty of poor judgment hardly does justice to the scale of his ineptitude.

Death spared Harding the spectacle of seeing his friends stand trial. He was so weak from congestive heart failure, he only had the energy to play six holes of that last round in Vancouver. To avoid speculation about his physical condition, he ordered his foursome and their Secret Service detail to cut over to the seventeenth tee and play in from there. A typical Harding decision; claiming to finish his "full" round in less than two hours raised more questions than if he had walked off the course.

Harding did a lot to popularize golf during his term. Unlike his predecessor, William Taft, who concealed his obsession with the game for fear of appearing elitist, Harding never missed an opportunity to have his picture taken on the course. But golf had in the years after the war entered the mainstream of American life; thanks to Ouimet and Hagen and attractive young players like Bobby Jones it was now viewed as a wholesome, healthy pastime to be enjoyed by the middle class. Harding helped establish that legitimacy when he lent his name to the USGA's Public Links Championship and became an honorary member of its executive committee. This small legacy from his association with the sport remains a more striking contribution to the public good than just about anything else he achieved in office.

After taking ill in Vancouver, Harding and his entourage traveled south, stopping in San Francisco to let the president rest. At the Palace Hotel, on the evening of July 29, Harding collapsed after dinner and died four days later. Reports of the cause of death vary because, curiously, no autopsy was performed, which has given rise to some intriguing conspiracy theories. They started when it was disclosed that while in Alaska Harding had received a mysterious coded message from Washington—likely involving word of the impending Teapot Dome scandal. Although the first official accounts blamed food poisoning, the death certificate identified an embolism and cerebral hemorrhage. Others believed it was a heart attack. One paranoid school of thought suggested Harding had been poisoned—with cyanide or arsenic—by his domineering wife, Florence. Believers point to the fact that Florence demanded no autopsy be performed, not uncommon at the time but suspicious in the case of a president dying in office. His frequent philandering and the illegitimate child his longest affair produced make some sense as a spousal motivation for murder, and that scandal was just about to become public. The country would soon be exposed to such indelicate details as Harding's predilection for making love to his mistress in the White House cloakroom. Frequent calls to exhume Harding's body in order to conduct a definitive autopsy have to date been resisted.

Whatever went on between them, Florence never hesitated to give Warren an earful, and that continued unto death; a week later, as his body lay in state in the White House, the Duchess spent over an hour alone with him, witnesses said, talking a blue streak to his corpse. Warren Harding had spent only 882 days in office, but it would take seven years to sort out the malfeasance and misdeeds left by his administration. Among the harsh assessments of Harding that appeared after his death, even Grantland Rice had to hedge his bets: "Harding was a poor president, but he was quite a fellow and, I think, an honest man."

The Roaring Twenties in America are often depicted as a nonstop cocktail party, a far cry from the truth. The early part of the decade brought tumultuous upheaval, when the furious rate of societal and technological change we take for granted today thrust the country into a future it was not prepared to embrace. The rapid transition from nineteenth-century stability to churning postwar turmoil threw two generations into disarray and created a combustible mix of anxiety amid a world of newfound freedoms. Small wonder that sports and sporting heroes offered a comforting refuge.

The Golden Age of American sports reached its first full flowering in 1923. Babe Ruth's Yankees had captured the last two American League pennants but lost both World Series to their crosstown National League rivals, the Giants. (Both Fall Classics were played entirely in the teams' shared stadium, the Polo Grounds.) The 1922 series was for the first time broadcast live on WJZ Radio in Newark; Granny Rice provided the play-by-play, the perfect master of ceremonies. Through a jerry-rigged configuration of amplifiers and signal boosters—and a gentlemen's agreement with other New York–area stations to suspend operations in order to avoid potential interference—Rice's account of the game reached out from the Polo Grounds in a three-hundred-mile radius to over a million people. Hundreds on street corners and post offices in Manhattan huddled around radio sets to hear for the first time Rice's spare, deliberate narrative and the startling immediacy of a stadium crowd reacting to the crack of the bat. The broadcast electrified the public; in that one afternoon, the future of radio as a commercially viable medium—which until this moment had by no means been decided—became assured. Major corporate sponsors jumped in to finance programs in exchange for advertising time, and the modern media industry was launched.

In April of 1923, the Yankees began their season in a new state-of-the-art stadium in the Bronx: Yankee Stadium, the House That Ruth Built. Seventy thousand filled the stands on Opening Day. John Philip Sousa and his band wowed the crowd with a rousing rendition of "The Star-Spangled Banner" and New York's popular young governor Al Smith threw out the first ball. Then, in what would become a tradition as reliable as Christmas, the Yankees beat the Red Sox, 4–1, on the strength of a two-run homer from Ruth. The Babe would go on to hit forty more dingers that year, drive in an additional 129 runs—both league-leading numbers—and hit for an average of .393, the highest of his career. Among those marching in pregame festivities on Opening Day was Harry H. Frazee, the man who sold Ruth to the Yanks. The Red Sox owner had continued selling off his best players for ready cash. When they took the field that afternoon, half the Yankees' everyday lineup were ex–Red Sox. Only three months away from selling the Boston franchise, Frazee had turned the former dynasty into the laughingstock of baseball. The night after completing that final transaction, Frazee slipped out of Boston on a midnight train to his home in New York. Three months later, on the strength of three Ruth home runs—a new record—the Yankees beat the Giants, four games to two, to win their first World Series. It is small comfort to Red Sox fans that Harry Frazee died young, only six years later, of Bright's disease, at the age of forty-nine.

Jack Dempsey had defended his heavyweight title four times since destroying Jess Willard in 1919 but no one had come close to challenging him; in order to ascend to the mythic realm Dempsey needed an opponent who could test his limits. That man arrived in September 1923, in the unlikely form of Luis Angel Firpo, the South American heavyweight champion from Argentina. A crude, bestial fighter—billed as "the Wild Bull of the Pampas"— Firpo stood four inches taller than Dempsey and outweighed him by thirty pounds. The fight took place in the infield of the Polo Grounds, two weeks before the start of the World Series, and was also broadcast on radio.

Firpo had fought exhibitions during a tour of the States, but no one knew how he'd match up with the American champ. The answer came quickly: Dempsey knocked Firpo down seven times in the first two minutes. Aside from an avid willingness to inflict pain, Firpo, it turned out, had no boxing skills whatsoever. Each time the big man hit the canvas Dempsey stood over him, pummeling him again the moment he stood up. (New York's boxing commission afterward added the rule ordering boxers to a neutral corner after a knockdown.) But Firpo had a few components useful in the sport: a granite chin, a fair measure of courage, and a right hand like an anvil. When he got up for the seventh time, Firpo reared back, and as the champ rushed in to resume his attack he caught Dempsey with a right to the jaw. The punch sent Dempsey flying through the ropes onto the press table a few seats down from Rice, a look of stupefied astonishment on his face. Nearly unconscious, Dempsey staggered back into the ring just before the referee's count would have ended the fight. Firpo mauled him for the final minute of the round as Dempsey hung on desperately to survive, then both men returned unsteadily to their corners. The packed Polo Grounds crowd stood screaming between rounds at the naked savagery their unbelieving eyes had just witnessed.

Dempsey's head cleared as the second round began: Firpo went down twice more, and then a third time at the one-minute mark. This time the Wild

Bull couldn't find his legs and the fight ended with Dempsey on the shoulders of his corner men. Writing the next day, Grantland Rice summed up the general reaction: "Four minutes of the most sensational fighting ever seen in any ring back through all the ages of the ancient game."

Dempsey had conquered his Minotaur, in a fight so dangerous and thrilling it changed the way people perceived the sport and made him an icon of his age. Along with Dempsey, Hagen, and Ruth, the public also embraced running back Red Grange and Knute Rockne's championship Notre Dame teams in football, Big Bill Tilden in tennis, and racehorse Man o' War, who won twenty of his twenty-one career starts at the track. These figures bore no resemblance to the spoiled, airbrushed celebrity pitchmen manufactured by today's sports-entertainment complex. They were all colorful, quixotic individuals who'd risen to the top through hard times. The public responded as strongly to their personalities as to their achievements in the arena, which made the sportswriters' jobs that much easier; who needed to pump up the details when Ruth or Hagen were so much larger than life? Not to suggest these sly pros weren't interested in money, but compared to today's casually tossed around millions there was still a heady air of innocence and fun to the proceedings. This was the twentieth-century sports industry inventing itself from scratch, and everyone involved was making it up as they went along. Olympus was quickly becoming a crowded pantheon, but Granny Rice knew there was always room for one more.

In the spring of 1923 the recent unearthing of King Tutankhamun's tomb had set off a craze for all things ancient and Egyptian. John Barrymore's Hamlet electrified Broadway, where the annual edition of the Ziegfeld Follies dominated the box office, while a young playwright named Eugene O'Neill shocked audiences with the social realism of *The Hairy Ape*. Immortal actor-director Buster Keaton joined Chaplin and preppy gagman Harold Lloyd as the movies' reigning Kings of Comedy, while a former screen lothario named Rudolph Valentino (né Rodolfo Alfonzo Raffaelo Pierre Filibert Guglielmi di Valentina d'Antonguolla) reinvented the archetype of the Latin lover and rescued Metro Pictures from bankruptcy. Kids saved their pennies to buy a new frozen treat called Popsicles, when they weren't gorging themselves with Milky

Way and Butterfinger candy bars. A two-thousand-year-old Asian table game called mah-jongg swept the country; exports of the game's colorful white tiles from Shanghai to the United States exceeded $1.5 million. (Ironically, most were manufactured from cow bone shipped to China from American slaughterhouses in Kansas City and Chicago.)

The kooky side of the Jazz Age was in full swing; marathon dances, raccoon coats, and the inexplicable fad of flagpole sitting were all the rage. Bandleaders Paul Whiteman, Jelly Roll Morton, Bix Beiderbecke, and a young trumpet virtuoso from New Orleans named Louis Armstrong topped the booming record charts. The annoying novelty song "Yes, We Have No Bananas" ended up stuck in everyone's head, spreading around the world faster than an influenza virus; serving as a policeman in the English colony of Burma, an aspiring young writer named Eric Blair—later known by his pseudonym, George Orwell—heard natives in remote upland villages singing it obsessively. The world was shrinking; Pan American Airlines opened for business and commercial air flights moved toward the mainstream, while a four-month around-the-world luxury cruise would set you back a thousand dollars. In Mexico, the old retired revolutionary Pancho Villa was assassinated by political rivals. A wild-eyed thirty-four-year-old Austrian radical named Adolf Hitler attempted and failed to overthrow the shaky German government from a Munich beer garden. Halfway around the world, on the West Coast in California, the landmark HOLLYWOODLAND sign appeared in the hills above Los Angeles, advertising a new housing development.

A widespread backlash to the excesses of the Lost Generation coalesced across America. One of the most popular figures in a growing religious revival, glamorous evangelist radio broadcaster Aimee Semple McPherson established her gospel-thumping empire in Southern California. As would happen often in decades to come, the movie industry became a favorite conservative target for its explicit films and off-screen scandals, personified by the rape trial of comedy giant Roscoe "Fatty" Arbuckle. In order to dodge the threat of government censorship, the movie industry created a self-regulating review board that came to be known as the Hays Office, for its sour chief executive, former postmaster general Will Hays. Hays took his new job more seriously than moguls expected; he cracked down on the sex and violence flooding American screens and instituted a draconian code of moral accountability that counted every bullet and legislated every inch of exposed flesh. Small wonder that a German shepherd named Rin Tin Tin, rescued overseas by an American soldier during the Great War, rocketed to stardom in a popular serial that same year. The previously unknown breed quickly became one of the country's most popular dogs.

Boston banned Isadora Duncan for dancing in a see-through Greek dress, and likewise Richard Strauss's operatic rendition of *Salome* for its heroine's salacious romp over the severed head of John the Baptist. A number of emerging American writers and artists rebelled against this rising wave of conformity by abandoning their country for an expatriate's bohemian life in Paris; the avant garde California poet Gertrude Stein established herself as their center of gravity. After two gin-soaked years living beyond their means among the landed gentry of Long Island—where he absorbed source material for his masterpiece, *The Great Gatsby*—F. Scott Fitzgerald and Zelda, with infant daughter Scottie in tow, moved their dysfunctional sideshow to the City of Light and accelerated their long, slow downward spiral. While in Paris Fitzgerald befriended an imposingly self-possessed he-man journalist from the Midwest named Ernest Hemingway—Pop Keeler's former colleague at the *Kansas City Star*—who had just published his first collection of stories and verse.

Bobby Jones turned twenty-one on March 17, 1923. He'd spent the fall and winter immersed in Harvard's rigorous academics. Having exhausted his collegiate eligibility at Georgia Tech he'd been turned down by the Harvard golf team, but he worked and traveled informally as their assistant manager. They needed him: Bobby once played a best-ball match against the entire six-man squad, and beat them soundly. (The school awarded him an honorary letter, and later voted him into their Varsity Hall of Fame.) He resisted joining the Harvard chapter of his old Tech fraternity, evidence of his focus on education, but still had time to daydream; Bobby drew up designs for an ideal driver he hoped to build someday that he called the Dreadnaught. The girl he'd left behind was also much on his mind; after almost four years together, Mary Malone and Bobby had decided they would marry the following spring, but held off making a formal announcement until he returned home. He played a few rounds of casual golf with Francis Ouimet around Boston, on one occasion setting a course record at the Charles River Country Club, but when he asked the school for permission to leave early in order to participate in the British Amateur and the second Walker Cup, they said no—this was Harvard, where final exams trumped championships.

This brought Bobby to the eve of the year's U.S. Open without a single warm-up, and scarcely any practice. His game had never been in worse shape, to such an extent that Kiltie met him on Long Island, where the Open was being played at Inwood Country Club. A long, harrowing, penal course carved out of an old potato farm on the marshy shores of Jamaica Bay—across from the future site of Idlewild Airport, later JFK International—Inwood offered one of the toughest layouts in championship history. The course anticipated the USGA's future template for Open setups: narrow fairways, impenetrable rough, and glassy greens. The trip also allowed a sentimental reunion for Kiltie with his older brother, Jimmy, the resident pro at nearby Nassau Country Club since leaving East Lake in 1907. As Bobby's game continued to languish during his practice rounds—he couldn't even break 80—the Maidens consulted with each other about where to turn him around. On the greens, they decided. Build up his confidence there and the full swing must follow.

Jimmy pulled a battered old putter out of a barrel in the back of his pro shop and handed it to Bobby. It was an unlovely instrument, with a long history. Built by a storied Scottish club maker named Robert Condie, the club had come over from Carnoustie with Jimmy nearly twenty years before. Its goosenecked blade bore a number of nicks and rust in spots. The hickory shaft had partially splintered at some point in its life; three bands of black whipping just above the neck held it together. With a face bearing two degrees of loft more than standard, Jimmy thought it might help Bobby get the ball rolling better on Inwood's undulating greens. (When he held it in his hands years later, Jack Nicklaus said it felt more like a three or four iron than a putter.) Before the mass manufacture of clubs, these handcrafted tools often acquired affectionate nicknames. Jimmy Maiden called this one "Calamity Jane."

Bobby liked her the moment he took Jane in his hands. One account claims he went out to the practice green and sank twenty-four of his first twenty-five putts. That may not be true, but there's no question she boosted his confidence over the ball at a crucial moment. Pop thought Bobby was sagging under the weight of expectation at Inwood more than ever before, so worried about disappointing expectations that he'd forgotten he'd come to play golf. Although he'd mastered his temper, Bobby still lacked Hagen's ability to laugh off a loss or forget a bad shot; he felt every ounce of pressure acutely and knew he'd reached a turning point in his ability to stomach it. Although he never came out and said so, Bobby dropped enough hints for Pop to conclude that if this Open ended badly for him—in second place or anywhere south—they might have reached the end of the road. Winning a major, as the two now agreed, wasn't up to the players anyway. Fortune cast the final vote.

"I was fearfully depressed," wrote Bobby the following year. "The full heft of responsibility hit me at Inwood—the idea of being a great golfer (as people kept saying) who couldn't win. And more and more it was getting on my nerves. Instead of regarding my game as a pleasant diversion and a fine sport, I was thinking of it as a possible means to championship; not so much because I wanted to be a champion as because everybody seemed to have concluded I ought to be one."

Three hundred and sixty golfers from around the world showed up when qualifying began on Monday, July 9. Rounds were split over the next four days, and only seventy-seven would advance to the Open proper. When they published the draw on Sunday night, Bobby found out he would have to wait until Thursday to play his way in. The smartest decision Bobby made before the tournament was to break his customary routine of bunking in a hotel with Pop; several weeks before, Bobby and Francis Ouimet had agreed to share a room in the attic of the Inwood clubhouse. Francis had played well that spring, leading the U.S. team to victory in the Walker Cup at St. Andrews, then reaching the semifinals of the British Amateur. They spent their spare time watching early qualifying, getting in practice rounds, and discussing the tough Inwood layout. Both agreed there were no breather holes; every shot demanded discipline and a sound game plan. Patience would be rewarded, but not panache. More than any other Open in memory, this tournament would be won by the man most willing to measure himself against Old Man Par.

Bobby broke 80 for the first time at Inwood twice on the day he qualified,

77 and 79, six strokes in back of the lead in the middle of the pack. The perfect pace and positioning, Keeler decided, no point in shooting your best rounds now. Qualifying medal winners almost never won an Open or any other tournament, so the prevailing superstition said. Bobby had a chance to confront another superstition the next day, Friday the thirteenth, when he was paired with Walter Hagen for the Open's first two rounds.

Hagen had just returned from defending his British Open crown, interrupting the most lucrative exhibition tour of his life, a yearlong run with a unique performer named Joe Kirkwood, an Australian-born pro and the game's first trick-shot artist. He'd developed this unusual talent while entertaining his country's wounded war veterans back home and soon realized he'd found a way to supplement his spotty income as a touring player. Kirkwood's repertoire astonished galleries; he could launch booming drives with the ball balanced on the crystal of a volunteer's watch—without leaving a scratch—or a woman's open-toed shoe, without removing a digit. He could close his eyes and stroke twelve perfect five irons in a row, or chip ten stymies consecutively into the cup. He could take full swings with an iron, pop balls straight into the air and land them in his caddie's pocket. Left-handed, right-handed, wearing a hood, standing on his knees, Joe wove a brand of magic that no golf ball could resist. He attributed his unique ability to steady nerves, regular exercise, and strict clean living. How he managed that during years on the road with Hagen is an even bigger mystery. Walter and Joe charged five hundred dollars an appearance—which could easily double if they had a piece of the gate—appearing six days a week and sometimes twice on Saturday.

After a two-year courtship, Walter had also remarried three months earlier, which, given his perpetually wandering eye, can only be categorized as a triumph of hope over experience. The second Mrs. Hagen was a sophisticated, well-heeled Philadelphia widow named Edna Crosby Strauss. Their honeymoon, such as it was, took place during Hagen's return to Great Britain, where he finished second by a single shot in the 1923 Open to an obscure English pro named Arthur Havers. Despite the gains made by Hagen and other pros for social acceptance, the members at Troon were one of the last pockets of diehard resistance. Once again Walter had the last word; after denying him entrance all week, when the club secretary asked Hagen to come into the clubhouse to hand Arthur Havers the Claret Jug, Walter led a tremendous gallery right to the doorway, then stopped, turned, and addressed the crowd:

> I've been asked to come into the club house with Arthur Havers for the presentation. At no time have we Americans been admitted to the club house, not even to pick up our mail. At this particular time, I'd like to thank you for all the many courtesies you've extended to us. And I'd like to invite all of you to come over to the pub where we've been so welcome, so that all the boys can meet you and thank you personally. If the committee likes, they can present the trophy to the new champion over there.

Walter then led a crowd of hundreds to the neighborhood pub, leaving only a handful of people to join the old guard inside for the trophy ceremony.

During their tour Hagen and Kirkwood made a significant technological advance to the game. There years before, a New Jersey dentist and frustrated hacker named Dr. William Lowell had whittled a small wooden peg on which to place his ball on the tee box, forgoing the traditional molded pile of wet sand. Lowell patented the gadget and took it to market, painted fire-engine red and sold in paper packets as the Reddy Tee. Despite advertising in every golf publication the doctor's novelty hadn't caught on until the desperate Lowell offered Hagen and Kirkwood fifteen hundred dollars to use it on tour. They stuck hundreds of the eye-catching pegs in their bags, handing them out as they walked the fairways, where kids scrambled after them as souvenirs. Before long so many people were clamoring after them, according to Hagen, that the USGA had to start roping off tee boxes and fairways. Within months the Reddy Tee started showing up in pro shops around the country; even cynical old pros grudgingly admitted they were useful. A wealth of imitations flooded the market and the little wooden tee became a universal accessory; Hagen took the Reddy Tee to England and it caught on there as well. The reason tees aren't all still red today is that their paint ran off in high heat and humidity. The first time Hagen went out with a pocket full in those conditions he saw a stream of crimson running down his tailored plus fours and thought he'd been shot. Not about to turn his back on Dr. Lowell's endorsement money, Walter took to carrying a spare Reddy behind his ear.

During the first round of the Open on Friday the thirteenth, 1923, Inwood stood up to the most accomplished field ever assembled, yielding only two scores under par. Jock Hutchison fashioned a flawless 70. Clicking with Calamity Jane on the greens, and chipping brilliantly, Bobby needed only fourteen putts on the back nine to finish with 71. No other player managed even par; Hagen came in with a loose 77, in twentieth place. Francis Ouimet, who had barely qualified, shot himself out of contention with an 82. The afternoon rounds saw Hutchison follow his fast start with a solid 72. Bobby stayed on his tail with 73, two strokes back at the halfway mark. Hagen improved to ninth with a 75, nine strokes back but teetering on the cusp of irrelevancy. Alone in third place, one stroke behind Bobby, stood Robert Allan Cruickshank.

Standing five feet four, an inch short of Sarazen and fifty pounds lighter, Cruickshank had built a solid reputation as an amateur in his native Scotland before the war. Enlisting early as an infantryman, he'd been thrust into the thick of the fighting. In the trenches at the Somme, from only a few feet away, he saw his younger brother torn apart by an artillery shell. Eventually taken prisoner, he spent months in a German prison camp, giving half his rations to fellow prisoners suffering from dysentery. Cruickshank organized an escape, led three other men to freedom, rejoined his unit, and refused reassignment back to Britain, finishing out the war on the front lines. When the war ended he returned to university, finished his degree, and emigrated to the States in 1921, intent on starting a law career. When he realized it was possible to not only make a living at golf in America but be considered a first-class citizen, he detoured back into his sport and turned professional. He reached the semifinals of the PGA Championship during his first two tries, losing to eventual champion Gene Sarazen. Cruickshank could play, and after all he'd been through, if any man in the game could stand up to the pressures of a U.S. Open, Bobby Cruickshank ended the search.

"Inwood was separating the tigers from the rabbits," wrote Pop that night. The Open was already down to a three-man race: Jock Hutchison and the two Bobbys. At the end of the first day a press tent straw poll gave Jock the edge. This surprised and alarmed Pop; faith among the press corps that Bobby could close the deal had begun to fade.

Bobby's old friend Al Laney, recently hired as a golf writer by a New York newspaper, was at Inwood covering his first U.S. Open. He hadn't seen Bobby since leaving Atlanta two years earlier, and had been unable to find a chance to approach him. On his way to the course Laney spotted Bobby chatting on the clubhouse steps with Granny Rice and Francis Ouimet. Laney couldn't summon up the nerve to say anything and was about to walk away when Bobby saw him and called him over: "Come meet Francis Ouimet."

"So at last I shook the hand of the hero of Brookline," wrote Laney later, "and it was revealed to me immediately why this man I had never seen had so caught my affection and that of thousands of others. And why he could help Bobby. It was his goodness. This was a 'good' man in the real meaning of full of goodness."

Bobby went out ahead of his closest competitors that morning paired for the final rounds with Sarazen. Cruickshank followed ninety minutes later, playing with Hagen. Jock Hutchison went out last in a pairing with Joe Kirkwood. Bobby had momentum and a hot putter in his bag. He then shot a five-over 41 on the front, including two penalty strokes, but never lost his composure and didn't relinquish hope as he had in the past; everyone blows up during at least one rough patch during an Open, he'd banked that knowledge now and relied on it. This was his bad round, and that was all, not fate turning its back on him. "Stick to your business and save all the strokes you can," he kept saying to himself.

For the first time in such critical circumstances Bobby held firm: Bobby carded a superlative 35 on the back nine to finish with 76. With the third round complete, Bobby was shocked to discover that both Hutchison and Cruickshank had blown up worse than he had, with 78 and 82, respectively. Hutchison stood four strokes back and was running on fumes, his rabbity energy spent. Bobby led Cruickshank by three. Expecting to find himself mired in third place, Bobby held the lead going into the Open's final round for the second year in a row, this time all by his lonesome.

He took his lunch break with Ouimet and Pop—tea and toast, no more indulgences at the dessert tray—all three keeping a healthy silence about his situation. Privately Bobby calculated 73 would be enough to hold off Cruickshank and Hutchison; that was the number in his head as he set out for his final round. Somewhere between the lunchroom and the first tee he fudged that number upward, figuring 75 marked the edge of his margin for error. His eternal battle with Old Man Par had been momentarily forgotten; sometimes the last lesson you learn is the first one to slip your mind.

Was his name already written in the Book? Did the gods want him to win a championship? How much control did he have over what was about to happen? A skittish Pop put it this way: "He was playing against something besides famous professionals and amateurs, and narrow fairways and terrible traps. He was playing against a grim fate that in every start had ridden him and crushed him to the turf in tournament after tournament when it seemed his time had come."

Bobby bogeyed the first hole, chalked it up to nerves, and moved on. He reclaimed that lost stroke with a bold birdie on the par five fifth, when two tremendous woods put him on the green and Calamity Jane did the rest. So far so good. Then trouble at the seventh, a challenging 223-yard par three: he smacked a three wood down the right side of the fairway; it took a wicked bad hop off a spectator's foot and jumped out of bounds. Two strokes lost to par, which might once have been a crushing blow to his confidence; but again he stood firm and didn't let it rattle him. Three strokes to finish the hole, then two straight pars to reach the turn with 39. The course's toughest stretch was behind him; he'd never shot higher than an even par 35 on the back all week, which would put him at 74, smack in the middle of his safety zone.

A short par four began the inward nine. Reaching the green easily in two, he dropped a twenty-foot putt for birdie and the crowd roared. Word spread over the course that Jones was about to close the deal; his gallery swelled and snaked around the fairways. They saw him knock off three more pars in a row, confident and strong. Playing with the house's money now, he gambled at the long par five fourteenth and came up aces: a birdie four and he was back to even par for his round with only four holes to play. Pop limped along after the exultant gallery, gasping for air, not allowing himself to believe the moment could be at hand.

Bobby dropped his tee shot in a bunker at fifteen, a par three, then lofted a soft recovery to within four feet and dropped the putt dead center for his save. Luck appeared to have thrown in with him at last. Three holes to go; three par fours. Twelve strokes to a 72; Cruickshank would have to card a tournament best 69 just to tie him, and news had already filtered back that the Scotsman was stumbling on his first couple of holes. The worst Bobby had played these finishing holes during the Open was even par; twice he'd birdied the eighteenth. Numbers and calculations cascaded through Bobby's head, colliding with the clear cold intentions he needed to finish the job.

Pressure is a hazard in the game as plain as sand or wind or water and all the more insidious for being out of sight. Bobby landed his drive at sixteen in the middle of the fairway. A simple mid-iron would put him on the green with a chance at birdie and almost certain victory. Bobby rushed his swing, came over the top, pulled the shot left, and watched it sail out of bounds. The crowd froze in their tracks. Dead silence. He never changed expression, dropped another ball, went through his routine, and rifled it right of the green toward a bunker. The ball kicked left off a mound on its first bounce, rolled onto the green, and stopped six feet away from the cup. Calamity Jane came through for him again; he made the putt for bogey, a sensational up and down from one hundred and fifty yards out. The crowd reacted as if he'd bagged another birdie. Only one stroke lost after a potential disaster; Pop listened to the buzz as the gallery tallied up the cost of Bobby's stumble, deciding it was an extravagance he could afford. Pop wasn't so sure; he saw a shade of gray come over Bobby's face and felt his stomach flop over like a trout out of water.

Again Bobby's drive at seventeen found the short grass, long and on line, leaving an even simpler iron shot to the green. The crowd gasped when he overcooked the easy approach, watching his ball bounce over the green into a patch of deep rough. After a ticklish pitch back toward the flag he was left with a ten-foot putt for par.

He missed it.

The buzz turned to solemn stillness, broken by whispers of concern: *He couldn't. Not again. He mustn't, he can't.*

His gallery didn't want to see this; not another soul on that course did. If Jones shot himself out of this lead with so much riding on it he might never recover; no one knew or felt that more acutely than Keeler. He found his mind involuntarily wandering back to a tournament Cruickshank had played in two years earlier: Cruickshank had trailed Jock Hutchison and Jim Barnes by nine strokes with eight holes to play, and he'd caught them both and forced a play-off, and then beaten them decisively the next day.

But he hadn't been playing for the national championship, Pop reminded himself. Bobby could still make par at eighteen for 74, the edge of his safety zone. Cruickshank would then still need to break par in the last round of an Open to tie.

The eighteenth at Inwood stretched 425 yards, the fairway a narrow chute closely lined with trees. A shallow lagoon protected the front of the green, forcing a key decision on the second shot: go for it or lay up. Bobby steered his drive onto the fairway. He was nearly two hundred yards out with a strong breeze in his face, but he had no choice; he had to shoot the works. He pulled his three wood out of the bag. Pop went pale; the shot screamed for an iron, a hard crisp iron over the pond, straight at the flag. Bobby tried to finesse the wood, and pulled it left, over the green and just beyond a nasty pot bunker. They found the ball nestled down in short rough beneath a decorative chain that marked the boundaries of the twelfth tee box.

Now fate truly did seem to conspire against him; the position of the ball prompted a paralyzing five-minute discussion among a covey of rules officials about what to do with the chain. Bobby sat on a mound behind them and brooded while they deliberated; his eyes smoldered, his mental gears seized up. Pop watched from a distance, helpless, sensing Bobby's collapse would become complete. Ouimet joined him, speechless and equally stricken. When officials finally decided the rules allowed them to remove the chain—a clear-cut option Jones had pointed out at the start of their filibuster—Bobby had already talked himself into the cellar. He halfheartedly chopped the ball out of the rough and dumped it in the pot bunker. Another swipe at the ball in the bunker put him on the green, and he used two putts to get down for a double-bogey six.

Disaster. Four shots squandered in three holes. He'd finished with 76, one stroke outside the margin he'd set himself at the start of the day.

The crowd looked away, reluctant witnesses to a one-car accident. Pop hauled himself forward to meet Bobby coming off the green.

"His face gave me such a shock that for a moment I forgot what I meant to say. His age seemed to have doubled in the last half hour."

"I think you're champion, Bobby," he said, after swallowing hard. "Cruickshank will never catch you."

Pop later catalogued two different quotes as his response. The more sanitized version in the "authorized biography" has Bobby saying, "I'm afraid I finished too badly. I had a great chance to shut the door, and I left it open."

Bobby remembered seeing Pop standing before him as he left the green, blinking repeatedly, unable to speak. Bobby's unvarnished version of how he responded, sharp and bitter, shows up only in Pop's earlier drafts.

"Then I said what was in my heart and had been there longer than I like to admit: 'Well, I didn't finish like a champion. I finished like a God damn yellow dog.'"

Bobby walked inside to his room in the clubhouse to wait for the jury to come in. Francis decided to follow him, after a respectful interval. He found a scene that would recur frequently during the next seven years: a haunted young man, pacing the floor of some small, spare clubhouse room, spent and shaken after running the gauntlet, a strong drink in hand to blunt his jangled nerves, waiting for word about some other poor bastard's battle with fate.

Pop found Grantland Rice and the two struck out across the course with the rest of the gallery to find Bobby Cruickshank. They caught up with the little Scotsman on the sixth green, just in time to watch him sink a birdie putt, the same moment news about Bobby's dreadful finish reached Cruickshank. It energized him; he made the turn in 36, a stroke under par, began the back stretch with two no-nonsense pars and then picked up another birdie at the twelfth.

Cruickshank was three shots ahead of Bobby with six holes to play.

"I was good and sick and utterly empty," wrote Pop. "I had passed up breakfast and lunch and was rattling like a gourd. Also my feet hurt. If there was any less happy person in the world than I, he inevitably was looking for a red barn with a rope over his arm."

But Cruickshank still had to finish those last six holes. He bogeyed the thirteenth and then dropped another stroke at the fifteenth; his lead had been reduced to a single shot. He reached the sixteenth tee confronting the same test Jones had encountered two hours earlier: par the last three holes and the championship was his.

Cruickshank double-bogeyed the sixteenth.

"I felt as if the burden of the world had rolled off my shoulders," said Pop. He slipped away from the gallery, frantically wheeling his bad leg back to the clubhouse and up the stairs to Bobby's room. News of Cruickshank's breakdown had preceded him. Ouimet and several others were already congratulating Bobby. Keeler took Francis aside to ask him in confidence if he thought Bobby's win had been salted away.

"Absolutely," said Francis. "No man on earth could play those two holes in seven shots under these circumstances." But Bobby knew at least one man who had, Francis had done exactly that himself ten years earlier to win his Open.

A USGA official entered the room and asked Bobby to come downstairs and prepare himself for the trophy ceremony. Bobby said he'd rather wait until Cruickshank had finished and the last putt was in the hole.

Pop decided to go out and watch the finish. As he walked back onto the course word filtered in that Cruickshank had secured his par at seventeen, at 405 yards the easier of the last two holes. He still needed to birdie the treacherous lagoon hole to tie Bobby and force a play-off. Pop reached the gallery in time to see Cruickshank land the long, accurate drive he needed. From 175 yards out the Scotsman pulled the iron Pop had been praying Bobby would use earlier. The ball left the club straight, low and perfect, touched down on a dead line to the flag twenty feet away and rolled to a stop within six.

"The cheer of the gallery crashed out like artillery," wrote Keeler.

Bobby and Francis could hear it in the clubhouse: Cruickshank had given himself a chance. Pop knew the ball would drop before he hit it. So did Bobby, watching from his high window.

Cruickshank's stroke was sure and solid and the putt fell for a birdie three. Brave Bobby Cruickshank had caught him, and deserved to. Bobby called it "one of the greatest holes ever played in golf." Their eighteen-hole play-off was scheduled for 2:00 p.m. the following day, Sunday afternoon.

Now Francis stepped in. With the help of two friends he cleared some space around Bobby, cordoning off their section of the clubhouse, leaving Pop the job of feeding quotes to the clamorous press. At first Bobby seemed inconsolable and couldn't shake his finish at eighteen out of his mind; unless that pattern was broken, this was a fatal psychology. Francis suggested a change of scene, away from the bustle at Inwood; they went downstairs, avoided the crowds, and climbed into a friend's borrowed car. Francis drove them a good twenty miles through the open countryside, all the way to the northern side of the island and Roslyn, New York, where they shared a quiet dinner at the Engineers Club, the course where Francis had beaten Bobby after his encounter with the bee in the semifinals of the 1919 National Amateur. His selection of Engineers was deliberate and thoughtful; this was the scene of one of Bobby's last self-destructive juvenile meltdowns. He was a man now, with an opportunity to demonstrate a wholly different reaction to the current adversity. Over the course of their dinner, in thoughtful and spare discussion about the game and his situation, Bobby worked his way around to a crucial mental adjustment that allowed him, as he put it, "to get square with myself."

"If Cruickshank had bogged down at the finish, and I'd been left in front, I'd never have felt I won the championship," he told Francis.

"How so, Bobby?"

"I'd have felt that Cruickshank lost it. This wasn't between Cruickshank and me, though I made the mistake of thinking so. It's between me and Old Man Par. Like it will be tomorrow."

By the time they drove back to Inwood through the gathering dusk, Bobby seemed at peace. Francis sang a couple of popular tunes to relax, in his pleasing light tenor. The crowds were long gone by the time they got back to the club; they went up to their room without interruption. There wasn't a better man on the planet for Bobby to share these hours with, or one who better understood what he was going through. This was the tenth anniversary of Francis's win at Brookline, the last time an amateur had faced a professional in a play-off for the U.S. Open title.

Although when they met, Bobby was still a teenager, Francis didn't consider himself a mentor to him, and out of modesty would have refuted the claim earlier. He was only thirty-one, hardly a graybeard, and Bobby was a remarkably mature twenty-one. Neither man was given to effusive or emotional statement of the obvious; both appreciated a silent, deeply felt sympathy that only established friends could share. On this occasion that understated, slightly distant ease did Bobby a world of good, more so than the turbulent emotions Pop was going through. Francis was a fellow competitor, another shared experience that needed no underlining; he'd walked this lonely path and come out the other side a champion.

It's tempting to imagine Francis dispensing detailed advice to Bobby about how to handle himself in an Open play-off, but that doesn't fit either man's character. There was nothing he might tell him that Bobby wouldn't have already considered; few men as gifted as the young Georgian had ever applied more effort to understanding the game they both loved. Bobby was facing a trial by fire that would decide his entire future, and precisely because Francis was the only other man alive who had lived through that same ordeal he didn't presume to know he had the answers. When the stakes were this high a man's response could emerge only out of the deepest part of who he was. Francis's presence was more effective than anything he could have said; sometimes the greatest advice is best expressed in silence.

According to Francis, the evening ended this way: "Bobby picked up a book, read a few chapters, and turned in for a fine night of rest."

An afternoon start presented its own set of challenges. The next morning Francis appointed himself a policeman "to keep well-wishing friends away from Bobby; one of the most tiring things in the world is to talk golf just before a big match." He ordered breakfast brought up to the room, and then barred the door to anyone but Bobby's closest friends. When Pop came in, Francis reported that Bobby had slept well, and Bobby insisted he felt fine and ready, but the sight of his young friend gave Pop a jolt. "The boy's face was drawn and pinched and his eyes were far back in his head, and introspective, with the look of a chess player exerting all the powers of his mind."

Bobby's appearance under stress seemed to be forever setting Pop on his heels. Pop was feeling pretty unsteady himself—he'd hardly eaten the day before and had medicated his jangled nerves with late-night cocktails—so his view that morning was colored by the queasy lens he was looking through. "I was not feeling all right nor anywhere near it. I was sick with a nervousness that had my stomach gripped in a vise. I could not sit still and my legs shook when I tried to walk."

Cruickshank had been established as the betting favorite, with odds running 10 to 7; the arbiters of chance had ruled that catching Bobby from behind gave Cruickshank some moral advantage. This was the kind of chuff Francis and Pop were determined to keep from Bobby's ears. Shortly after noon caddie Luke Ross came to collect Bobby and take him down for his warm-up. He seemed calm and centered, but reported later that he felt "kind of numb." Pop appeared to be in much worse shape; he felt like hell hit with a ripe tomato. Francis grabbed Pop and a couple of his newspaper friends and took a walk out onto the course. Keeler suggested they try to alleviate their anxiety by singing, so the four men sat alone on a bank behind the third green and self-consciously sang a couple of little songs.

"It was silly, of course," wrote Pop, "but there was an utterly indescribable tension in the close air. The sky was overcast. I could not get it out of my mind that fate was closing in."

Pop's mind kept wandering and then got stuck like a phonograph needle on a line from Kipling's poem "Danny Deever": " 'I'm dreading what I've got to watch,' the Color-Sergeant said." (The poem was one of hundreds rattling around in his magpie mind, about a royal regiment forced to execute one of their own for shooting an officer in his sleep.) Until the match began, Pop could not keep that phrase from repeating obsessively in his head. Seven years since Bobby had made his debut at Merion, seven years to reach this cross-roads.

For a few moments the day before, the USGA had considered delaying their play-off until Monday; there was still a lingering puritanical bias against playing golf on Sundays, particularly the closer one got to New England. A forecast of foul weather tracking toward Long Island decided the issue; it might arrive as early as that afternoon, and Monday looked to be a washout. The play-off's late starting time was a compromise to allow people to first attend church. Neither the threat of a storm nor religious feeling seemed to stop anyone from attending: as noon approached there were close to ten thousand people around the clubhouse. Distant lightning flashed occasionally through a forbidding thick blanket of clouds; rumbles of thunder and high humidity added to the oppressive, brooding atmosphere. This was before the USGA provided organized security, so as the players moved toward the first tee Francis recruited a couple of large acquaintances to help him surround Bobby and prevent spectators from accosting him during the match. Jones and Cruickshank walked out to the tee right on schedule, at 2:00 p.m. Both men wore plus fours, white shirts, and bow ties. They posed for pictures together, on either side of USGA president Wynant Vanderpool.

Then a brisk handshake with words of mutual good luck were exchanged, both men contained and determined, and off they went with two perfectly played tee shots. Unless someone blew up under pressure this would be match play disguised as medal. Both somehow had a handle on their nerves. The front nine featured more back-and-forth action than singles at Wimbledon; they wouldn't halve a hole until the eighth. The start went like this: advantage Jones, even, Cruickshank one up, even, Cruickshank up one—his third birdie in the first five holes—then Cruickshank went two up at the sixth despite Jones playing even par. Cruickshank's lead fell back to one when Bobby attacked the seventh with a tremendous three wood to the long par three green; protecting his lead, Cruickshank played safe and short off the tee, chipped up, and missed his putt for par. Bobby later felt that unerring tee shot at seven, down a tight tree-lined chute to the tiny green, was his most important shot on the front nine. Their first half came at the eighth, and then Bobby won the ninth with a solid par when Cruickshank missed a five-foot putt. That squared the match at the halfway mark. Both had shot 37, Bobby matching par for the first time on the front nine all week. Dead even.

Pop saw a contained ferocity in their focus; the strain felt palpable, crushing, but neither man gave in to it. They played swiftly, with purpose, in silence, the gallery staying as quiet when they were over the ball as if they'd never left church. Thunder rolled closer. The wind picked up, announcing a genuine threat of rain. Ouimet had to take his role as bodyguard seriously; in the middle of play as Bobby walked down a fairway, a man approached and invited him to spend a week at the fellow's summer home. Bobby had never seen the man before and politely told him to come around after the match was over. The man wasn't satisfied and insisted on an answer; Francis and his friends stepped in to distract him and Bobby slipped away. Another stranger greeted him like a long-lost brother as they walked between holes. This time Francis and company intervened; the man lost his temper and was hustled out of sight.

Now the tension began to creep into their heads and hands and arms; Jones seized the lead again with a bogey at ten when Cruickshank doubled badly. Both bogeyed the eleventh with sloppy approach shots, the worst hole of the day for both. Bobby recovered quickly; at the par three twelfth he landed his towering approach two feet from the flag and watched it roll right by the cup; he made his birdie, Cruickshank settled for par, and the younger Bobby's lead was stretched to two. For the first time Cruickshank looked as if he might be on the verge of breaking.

They halved the thirteenth with pars, only the third and last time that happened all day. Then, coming off the ropes, at the par five fourteenth Cruickshank nearly holed a brilliant approach shot for an eagle, settled for birdie, and halved Jones's lead. Almost like a boxing match now, thought Pop; that shot seemed to stun Bobby momentarily. He double-bogeyed the par three fif-teenth with two loose shots—Cruickshank took a bogey—and just like that they were back to square with three holes left to play.

The sixteenth had given Cruickshank trouble the day before and it did again on Sunday; he recorded a bogey to Bobby's par. Advantage Jones. Both missed the fairway at seventeen and pitched up short of the green; Bobby appeared to gain a formidable edge when Cruickshank's recovery crawled into a greenside bunker. Bobby chipped up toward the flag but left it ten feet short; Cruickshank came out of the bunker, landing just outside Bobby's ball, and then sank his par-saving putt; Bobby missed his, losing the hole and his lead. Three hours and seventeen holes into the match and they were back in a flat-footed tie. Both men appeared completely out of bullets; the gallery looked nearly as spent as they did. Friends like Pop, Francis, Kiltie, and Rice didn't know what to do with themselves. No one had ever seen a play-off like this.

They staggered to the eighteenth. Either the fearful lagoon hole would decide the match or they'd have to play another eighteen, on another day by the look of the dark clouds rolling overhead as Cruickshank stepped to the tee. The wind picked up severely, dead into them; the storm appeared to be no more than half an hour off. Cruickshank intended to hit a low draw to stay below the breeze and catch as much roll as he could toward the green. Instead he misplayed a tee shot for the first time since the tournament began, a half-topped hook that sizzled through the rough, traveled less than 150 yards, and skidded to a halt behind a tree near a service road. The green was completely out of reach from there; he'd have to lay up shy of the lagoon and hope his short game could salvage another par. A perhaps fatal unforced error. But could Bobby capitalize?

Bobby stepped to the tee and cracked a long high fade down the right side, setting up the preferred approach to the green. Losing its energy, the ball just dribbled off the fairway to the right and looked as if it would settle in the rough, but an extra roll carried it onto a patch of dry, hard ground, surrounded by loose dirt. When his gallery reached the spot, Ouimet felt a chill run up his back at the choice he saw Bobby faced. Two hundred yards from the green, over water, a clean lie but one that demanded perfect contact to pull off. He could lay up short and try to outpitch or outputt Cruickshank to the flag, but Jones wasn't playing Bobby Cruickshank now, in fact hadn't given him a moment's thought all afternoon; he was in the ring with Old Man Par, and that meant he needed to be on that green in two.

The work of seven long years all narrowed down to this one swing, one that Francis and Pop already knew Bobby was about to try, and dreaded having to watch.

The crowd, stacked ten deep behind them and stretching in a long curve across the fairway, paused long enough for Cruickshank to punch his second shot out of trouble and short of the lagoon.

Jones later claimed he remembered nothing about the decision or the shot itself. By everyone's account he didn't waste a second, as if not wanting to give himself time to consider how many ways this could go wrong. He glanced over and made eye contact with Kiltie for the briefest moment, then pulled a driving iron—the equivalent of today's two iron—stood up to the ball, and swung the club back. Francis shuddered when he saw the club selection and closed his eyes; Pop couldn't take his eyes off it. All three men later said they'd never seen Bobby hit a ball with less deliberation or more decisively. Francis heard the crisp click of the club as it made contact, opened his eyes, looked up, and found the ball soaring like an arrow straight for the flag. Pop said it "went away on a ruled line." While it was still in the air, Kiltie took off his new straw hat, raised it up, and smacked it down on caddie Luke Ross's head. Ross claimed he never felt a thing.

The ball cleared the water, bounced twice on the green, checked up, nearly hit the flag, and stopped just six feet past the hole. Now the thunder came from the assembled congregation, and they wouldn't let up.

Bobby saw the ball lying near the hole and for the briefest moment wondered how it got there. The next thing he remembered was Francis grabbing him by the arm and propping him up as the gallery stampeded around and past them to surround the green. Grantland Rice shook his hand as they moved forward; Bobby didn't even see him.

"Finest shot I've ever seen, Bobby," said Francis. "Finest shot I've ever seen."

Luke Ross took the club back from his boss before someone tried to steal it. Bobby and Francis shuffled ahead, jostled by the crowd, in a daze. Pop, tears in his eyes, took his other arm; Kiltie was grinning from ear to ear—there's a first time for everything—holding his ruined hat.

I don't care what happens now, Bobby thought.

Cruickshank had to hole his pitch or land stone dead and hope that Bobby missed the putt, but the bell had already tolled; he hit the ball thin, ran it into a bunker, rolled twenty feet past the hole coming out, and missed the putt. Double-bogey six.

Bobby putted twice to collect his par. Cruickshank walked straight over and held out his hand, and the world followed hard on his heels.

Bobby Jones. U.S. Open Champion.

"And now that he had won I could say things that had been locked up in my heart for four long years," wrote Pop Keeler. "I could not say them before. They would have been misunderstood as alibis by those who did not know Bobby as I knew the boy. And one of the things I had wanted to say was this: All those years he had been the victim of too keen a mind and too fine an imagination. It was never his heart that was at fault. In his breast beat the heart of a lion. And the world knew it now. But to me, Bobby Jones was no greater on that day than he was the day before, or than he was last year. He had showed the world—that was all."

Cruickshank had been turned away at the last. He would finish four more times in the top five of a U.S. or British Open, but never came this close to winning one again. He later became the oldest player, at sixty-eight, ever to qualify for a U.S. Open, and shot his age in PGA events twelve times between 1971 and 1973, two years before his death. Beloved throughout his life, a sentimental figure in the game, he slowly slipped from memory. But it was not his turn that day at Inwood, and he accepted it with grace. The other Bobby's name had been written down first.

"Man, it was a bonnie shot," Cruickshank said to Pop as they waited for the trophy presentation. "There never was such a golfer, and I'm proud to have stepped so close to him. He is now what Harry Vardon was at his best: the greatest golfer in the world. To be defeated by him is glory enough."

"Taking into consideration the lie of the ball, the club selected and the distance," said Francis, who could speak to the subject with some authority, "it was the finest shot I've ever seen."

In 1986, the members at Inwood planted a plaque in the ground to commemorate the spot where Bobby hit his fateful approach to eighteen.

Pop asked Kiltie what he was thinking while Bobby was standing over the ball at eighteen. Kiltie said he wasn't thinking at all. "Well," said Keeler, keeping after him as usual, "then why did you bust your new straw hat over Luke's head when the ball hit the green?"

"How the hell should I know!"

Bobby and Pop sat on the clubhouse steps a short time after the play-off, waiting for the ceremony to award the trophy, a day later than he'd hoped for, but infinitely better now, on his own terms. "How do you feel?" Keeler asked him.

Bobby looked at him for a moment, as if puzzled by the question, and took his time answering. "Why, I don't care what happens now."

When they handed him the cup, when he saw Ouimet's name engraved there, and Hagen's and Chick Evans's and Vardon's and Ted Ray's, when he felt the great shining weight of the silver in his hands, he couldn't speak. He managed to croak out a couple of modest thank-yous before his voice broke. A bagpipe was playing somewhere as the crowd swept forward to lift him on their shoulders.

Pop Keeler.

Bobby and Mary Jones at the Atlanta Athletic Club.

CHAPTER SEVEN

Halfway There

Pop and Kiltie decided to splurge on the way home and reserved a first-class drawing room on the train south. Pop bought all the New York morning papers—there were seven of them then—splashed with stories about Bobby's win, and spread them out around the compartment so they could look at the photographs as they rolled out of town. Pop kept catching Kiltie staring at the cup in the corner, wearing "an expression similar to that of a cat who has recently come across a pan of cream uncovered." None of them remembered talking a great deal—a novelty for Pop, a welcome relief for Kiltie—but for once few words were necessary. Every once in a while Bobby took out the gold medal he'd won in addition to the silver cup and said in his dry, understated way: "You know, it's remarkably hard to get one of these things."

When they stepped off the train in Atlanta the town had turned out to greet him with flags and a brass band, and when they cheered and Bobby saw them all filling the station he had to turn away to compose himself. His mother, Clara, rushed to him, the Colonel crushed him in a hug, and then Bobby shyly kissed Mary in front of all those people, and they all piled into an open car and his city paraded him home. Pop Keeler couldn't remember the last time Atlanta had given anyone such a welcome. The state of Georgia was damn proud of Bobby too, and passed a resolution that week saying as much.

Bobby decided he couldn't feel too badly treated by fate. His first big win had come when he deserved it, and not a moment sooner, and he basked in the warmth of an extended welcome home. A grand dinner at East Lake a week after his return honored his accomplishment, followed by a program of speeches and salutations: the mayor of Atlanta expressed the city's gratitude and pride in Bobby, and the Colonel contributed an emotional salute to his son's tenacity. Bobby had always dreaded public speaking, but he capped the evening with a brief, eloquent speech summing up his deep feelings for the place that had nurtured his dreams:

> You gentlemen have said some beautiful things about me and what I've been fortunate enough to do. But one thing they all have absolutely wrong. They spoke of my honoring the Atlanta Athletic Club. No man can honor a club like this. The honor lies in belonging to it. I am prouder of being a member of this club than I could be of winning all the championships there are.

Bobby spent two months catching his breath, enjoying unhurried days out at East Lake. He played only ceremonial golf the rest of that summer with family and friends and various dignitaries—nothing close to the pressurized ordeal of a championship, and a welcome respite from it. There was a full life to be lived outside of the game, time to spend with the Colonel and his cronies at the club, plans to make with Mary. Bobby wouldn't put himself back into the heat of competition until it was nearly time to return to Harvard that fall and finish his degree.

They played the 1923 U.S. Amateur in September at Flossmoor Country Club, a tough seven-thousand-yard layout just south of Chicago. Bobby arrived as the prohibitive favorite, and he tied Chick Evans for the qualifying medal. Pop couldn't remember seeing him more relaxed before a championship. Bobby spent his evenings reading the English translation of Giovanni Papini's controversial best-seller *Life of Christ*; not exactly light bedtime fare, although at that moment he had a specific, personal interest in this particular title.

The American Amateur title would continue to elude him. In the second round Bobby ran into a red-hot golfer named Max Marston, a thirty-one-year-old veteran from Pine Valley—amateur champion of both New Jersey and Pennsylvania—who went on to beat Ouimet and then win the title against defending champion Jess Sweetser. Bobby lost the match, 2 and 1, his earliest exit from the Amateur in six appearances.

Bobby sank into melancholy as he reviewed his performance, convinced that match play would always bring him up against a golfer who played out of his mind and knocked him out of the Amateur. Now the only round in which he'd never been eliminated was the first.

Pop countered by pointing out that Bobby had also *won* a match in every round of the Amateur, except the last. The tournament was headed back to Merion in 1924, where he'd made his debut in 1916. Maybe his luck would change there. Bobby remained convinced that his game just wasn't suited to match play.

Chick Evans had suffered an even more shocking defeat, losing to Willie Hunter in the first round. When they ran into each other on the night Bobby lost to Marston, neither man with any official golf left to play, they agreed to square off informally the next day, with the gold qualifying medal for which they'd finished in a tie at stake. There was sportsmanship in the gesture, but also a trace of spite. Bobby's loss meant Chick's 1916 record of winning the Open and Amateur in the same year still stood. Bobby couldn't help but be aware of the envy Chick radiated toward any amateur who threatened to surpass him. Chick seemed completely unaware of what he conveyed to his competitive peers; envy appeared to be an unconscious part of his makeup. What rankled Bobby was Chick's inability (or unwillingness) to acknowledge those natural, aggressive feelings face-to-face—every player in the game felt them—or make a joke of them as Hagen or Sarazen would have done. Instead he offered his Eagle Scout grin and the usual bland, cheerful homilies, while his eyes said something different, and the resentful words he expressed out of their presence always drifted back to them.

"Why, of course I'll play you for the medal, Chick," said Bobby. "Looking forward to it."

The next day, with the USGA squeezing their match into the Amateur schedule at Flossmoor, Bobby broke the medal-play course record with a 72

and spanked Chick by four strokes. Pop watched the contest closely and realized that Bobby paid no attention to what Chick was doing all day long; he was
playing the course, not the man. "That's the way to win at match play," he told
Bobby afterward. "You're out there against Old Man Par and no one else."

For Bobby the insight was a revelation. He had always followed the conventional wisdom of treating each hole in a match-play event as a separate
entity, like the rounds of a prizefight. It didn't matter what score you had by the
end of the match as long as you won more holes than your opponent. As a
result his concentration wavered whenever holes got away from him, which in
the long run negated his greatest strength: the power of his mind. Bobby
worked through every stroke of a medal-play tournament as the trained
engineer-artist he had become; with a structure, a design, a plan of attack.
That discipline focused and freed him to work wonders when called upon to
improvise. In match play a savant like Walter Hagen, who excelled at it like no
one else in history, could switch his game off and on at will as fortune dictated
with no emotional erosion, but Bobby needed his engine room stoked from
start to finish. Playing against Old Man Par, the one opponent who never faltered, kept him on that edge.

During his round with Evans, Bobby found his mind circling back to the
first time he'd ever seen Harry Vardon play at East Lake in 1913. Ted Ray's
showy drives were the shots people tended to take away, but the memory of
Vardon quietly collecting par after par was what won the match for the Englishman that day, conclusive evidence that his was the ideal approach for the
format. What if he could sustain the mental effort demanded by championship medal golf throughout an entire match? He left Chicago determined
to give it a try, next year at Merion. He had his recollections of Vardon, and his
growing friction with Chick Evans, to thank for that idea. And his first gold
medal from a National Amateur to remember them by.

Eager to get back to Atlanta and Mary and launch the career he'd decided
on, Bobby increased his class load and finished his degree in English literature
at Harvard by the start of the New Year, a semester ahead of schedule. He limited his golf that fall to a few charity exhibitions, including a match against
Francis to benefit the Caddie Welfare Fund. A few weeks later Bobby and

Sweetser bettered Hagen and Sarazen in a best-ball match at Winged Foot in suburban New York, raising seven thousand dollars for the Rotary Club's crippled children fund. After disappointing finishes at the British and U.S. Opens, Hagen had lost the 1923 PGA Championship to Sarazen and slipped from the top of the professional rankings for the first time in five years. In addition to a dizzying tournament schedule, Hagen's ongoing tour with Joe Kirkwood had kept him on the road for the last two years; Walter decided that for the first time in his life he was golfed out. He climbed into his chauffeured Cadillac with his socialite wife and drove down the Atlantic coastline to winter in Florida.

The Florida land boom rewrote the book on get-rich-quick schemes in the early 1920s. Until the end of the nineteenth century the Sunshine State had remained the most backward corner of the former Confederacy, an underdeveloped tangle of old plantations, small farmsteads, and sleepy seaside towns, until a dynamic Yankee real estate mogul named Henry Flagler began carving out a railroad down the length of the peninsula. While extending the line all the way to Key West—home to ten thousand, it was the most populous city in the state—Flagler decided to build a town near Biscayne Bay that he christened with the Native American name for a nearby river, Miami. He built a private estate for himself in neighboring Palm Beach, inspiring Gilded Age millionaire friends to build more winter palaces in the area, and articulated a vision of prosperity for the state that he never lived to see. After Flagler died in 1913 a Midwestern millionaire named Carl Fisher—creator of the Indianapolis Motor Speedway and its famous championship race—dredged an idea called Miami Beach out of a coastal mangrove swamp. Florida began marketing itself as the antidote for anyone looking to escape the harsh Northern winters. Two other factors made what followed possible: since the end of the Great War, the middle class had experienced an unprecedented rise in investment income. Combined with the new mobility made possible by the automobile, Florida emerged as the perfect destination for the new phenomenon of resort living and second homes.

Land was abundant, credit was cheap; waves of speculators moved in to corner the middle of those transactions and walked away with millions. The Florida legislature did its part, voting to outlaw state income and inheritance taxes, and legalized horse and dog racing to attract high rollers. All of it worked: the state's population doubled in less than five years. Resorts lined the pristine beaches on both coasts and golf courses figured prominently in the lifestyle; they sprang up on every corner of the state, so it's no wonder Walter Hagen swooped in to grab a piece of the action. He accepted an offer to serve as professional at a private golf club near Pasadena, on the Gulf Coast. For four months of work each winter, during which he played golf with prospective buyers on a course he helped design, Hagen signed the richest deal a pro golfer had ever negotiated: thirty thousand dollars a year and a prime corner lot to build his own home. For every well-publicized exhibition he played—drawing thousands of potential customers to the complex—he received another lot in the development, collecting ten over the next three years.

Walter set himself up in an office across the street from the development and hired a knockout blonde secretary; whenever they spotted potential customers wandering their way, he and the girl would go out on the veranda and break into song—she played the ukulele—to lure them in for the sales pitch, selling memberships at five hundred dollars a pop. Walter closed deals with the instinct of a cat playing with a mouse; Pasadena-on-the-Gulf would prove to be the most successful business venture of his life, a checkered record at best. Finding an equally successful follow-up proved elusive; he plunked a lot of his profits from Pasadena into a nearby golf club manufacturing company. They soon discovered that the heat and high humidity warped and swelled an alarming percentage of their hickory shafts, which caused the heads to come flying off when customers took the clubs north into cooler weather.

Bobby Jones had also chosen real estate as his game off the course. When he returned from Harvard in the spring of 1924 he accepted an offer from Perry Adair to join his thriving family business. Perry had given up competitive golf, and along with his older brother, Forrest, assumed the reins of Adair Realty and Trust. They quickly became major players in the Florida frenzy, buying up huge tracts of coastal property near Sarasota. Bobby set golf aside, rolled up his sleeves, and went to work on the company's lowest rung, looking after a portfolio of minor rental properties. Beating the pavement collecting rent checks while living at home with his parents was a far cry from the glamorous professional beginning he'd envisioned.

Although he had collected a postgraduate degree, Bobby's education in golf was far from over. Over the winter, while visiting the nearby resort area of Augusta, Georgia, Bobby ran into the game's Grand Old Man, Walter Travis. In failing health, Travis wintered in the South to keep his fragile lungs away from the cold. One afternoon, in the basement of Augusta Country Club, Bobby cashed in an eight-year-old rain check and collected the putting lesson Travis had planned to give him on the practice green at Merion back in 1916.

In his brisk, no-nonsense manner, Travis diagnosed that Bobby's stroke had been tooled for the South's grainy Bermuda grasses; it functioned as a hit at the ball, rather than a smooth stroke through it. Travis told him that style would never hold up on bent grass greens. He changed Bobby's setup drastically, placing his feet closer together, heels nearly touching, with the weight shifted toward the left, which stabilized him and prevented any swaying that could throw the club off line. He adjusted his grip to the standard reverse overlapping, creating more of a hinged stroke, and encouraged him to feel the sensation of tapping a tack into the back of the ball. He also suggested Bobby practice a form of breath control to neutralize the nervousness that sometimes afflicted him while standing over a putt. Knowing Travis's reputation as the greatest putter in history, Bobby took these alterations seriously. Although he needed most of the year to assimilate the Old Man's instruction, from this moment forward putting would never again be the weak link in Bobby's game. By the end of his career some mentioned him in the same breath as the game's greatest clutch putter, Travis himself.

Bobby took away something else from his day with Walter Travis. The Old Man was often described as possessing the perfect temperament for golf: he was such a congenital pessimist that whenever anything went wrong during a round it only met his underlying expectations. Bobby never drank from the full, saturnine richness of Travis's perpetually half-empty glass, but the encounter helped his ongoing effort to accept the vagaries of the game without heaping all the blame on himself.

When Warren Harding died unexpectedly in 1923, Vice President Calvin Coolidge was sworn in by his own father, a notary public, at 2:47 a.m. in the sitting room of the old family homestead in Plymouth Notch, Vermont. The fifty-one-year-old former governor of Massachusetts became the first and only president who shared his country's birthday, July 4. Raised on a farm, educated in a one-room schoolhouse, Coolidge embodied every cliché of the tight-lipped and tightfisted New Englander. Challenged by a female companion at a White House dinner that, on a bet with a friend, she could extract more than two words from the president during the evening, Calvin gave her a ghost of a smile and said only: "You lose."

Coolidge attacked the waste and extravagance that he believed had ruined the Harding administration. If Harding's reckless personality personified the excesses of the Roaring Twenties, for the rest of his time in office Coolidge stood in stark opposition to them. His values, born around the cracker barrel of his father's general store, recalled the stern, uncompromising rigor of his Pilgrim ancestors. Coolidge's still waters ran deeper than they appeared. He had a dry, self-deprecating sense of humor and a glamorous, vivacious wife named Grace, the source of whose attraction to Calvin became an enduring mystery to the Beltway's intelligentsia. Silent Cal didn't fit in with the capital city's smart set. Teddy Roosevelt's socialite daughter Alice remarked of the country's new leader: "He looks like he was weaned on a pickle."

Although the game had become an established ritual among politicians and captains of industry, Coolidge, left-handed, played golf poorly and reluctantly. To dedicate the number of daylight hours required for a full round ran contrary to his Yankee nature. No other sport ever caught his fancy either, and the only exercise he regularly enjoyed was riding an electric mechanical horse he had installed in the White House's basement gym. The stone-faced image of Silent Cal is never contradicted by anything he did more than this, riding that horse three times a day, and whooping like a cowboy. His antipathy to exercise and sports in general was hastened by the tragic 1924 death of his sixteen-year-old son, Calvin Junior, who developed a septic infection from a blister on his foot, contracted while playing tennis without a pair of socks on the White House court. Although he would easily win reelection later that year, most who knew him said that whatever appeal the land's highest office held for Coolidge died with his son.

The 1924 United States Open was played at Walter Hagen's last stop as a resident pro, Oakland Hills outside Detroit. Only two months before, the USGA announced their decision to allow clubs with steel shafts into competition. They had first appeared in 1920; advances in metallurgy created by the wartime steel industry made them possible, fueled by manufacturers' concern that the supply of hickory needed to meet the demand of the golf boom might run dry. No pro or amateur of any note played with steel shafts yet; Bobby wouldn't until after his retirement. He arrived a week ahead of the tournament to sharpen his game and defend his championship. Hagen showed up at the same time, and the two played some competitive practice rounds together. Although always professing great respect for Bobby as a person and a player, Hagen felt being beaten by any amateur to be a blow to his professional pride. At Oakland Hills, as he came off the course after losing a practice round to Jones, that pride prompted Hagen to make a side bet with a local big shot that he would come to regret.

The tournament began on June 5, and for the first time in USGA history qualifying rounds had taken place at various regional locations prior to the Open. The eighty men who began play at Oakland Hills had already earned their way into the field. Bobby sent a clear signal he was ready to become the first man since Johnny McDermott in 1911 to repeat as Open champion; shooting 74-73 on the first day, he held a share of the lead with Wild Bill Mehlhorn. Hagen played well on his old turf and landed three strokes back in fourth. Between them, alone in third and only a stroke out of the lead, stood this year's designated unknown, a prototype for the obscure, intriguing figures that the Open's format annually thrust into the spotlight.

His name was Cyril Walker, a thirty-year-old native of Manchester, England, working as a professional out of a country club in Englewood, New Jersey. Only five feet six and unhealthily wizened at 118 pounds, Walker had done nothing during a decade in the States and dozens of tournaments to suggest he belonged on the leader board with Jones, Mehlhorn, and Hagen. He didn't look like championship timber; he had a crooked smile, squinty eyes, snaggled teeth, and big ears that stuck straight out from the sides of his head. He suffered from severe nerves during competition, which deprived him of sleep, disrupted his digestion, and decelerated his pace of play to an aggravating crawl; Walker was the slowest pro in the game. But the wind was blowing hard off Lake Michigan that week at Oakland Hills, and Walker had served his apprenticeship on the links of Royal Liverpool near the Irish Sea. In spite of his size he had large hands and powerful wrists and had mastered the British art of punching the ball below the wind. He had also undertaken a rigorous exercise program prior to the Open and felt his game had reached rare form. Cyril had brought along his little wife, Elizabeth—he called her by a pet name, Tet—who kept Walker away from late-night drinking sessions with the "boys." After full nights of sleep he woke every morning "feeling fit as a fiddle, clear-eyed and with my nerves absolutely under control." Although he'd told a friend when he arrived he didn't have much of a chance in the Open—"It's too much for me. The course is too big. I haven't the endurance"—Walker returned from his last practice round at Oakland Hills and confided in Tet he felt eerily certain he was going to win the championship. She replied: "I know you are."

Cyril Walker caught Bobby by the end of the third round with his third 74 in a row. Hagen, Mehlhorn, Macdonald Smith, and Bobby Cruickshank all lurked within three strokes. The wind kicked up fiercely that afternoon and picked off the contenders one by one. Hagen stayed in contention until the sixteenth, when he dumped his drive in a water hazard. Mehlhorn finished with the early lead. Bobby came to the final hole needing a birdie to get past him. Unlike his "yellow dog" finish during the last round at Inwood, Bobby bagged his birdie and grabbed the lead. But this time the tenacious little Brit playing an hour behind him didn't falter down the stretch.

Pop watched from Walker's gallery and was "hypnotized by his methodical determination. I have never seen anything like it, in sport or out. His work in that last round displayed the peculiar inevitableness of a natural phenomenon, and it impressed less by mechanics than by the invincible spirit, the grim determination, which sent that seemingly frail human machine along hole after hole." Throwing down the round of his life, Walker had two strokes in hand over Bobby by the time he reached the last three holes, and confronted the dire challenge of knowing exactly the score he had to beat. Pop became obsessed with the idea that as Walker stood on each successive tee he seemed to be saying to himself: "This one golf hole is the single problem of my career. It is the problem of my existence. There never has been any other problem. There never will be any other problem. I was created, developed, trained, drilled, to play this one hole in par. It shall be done."

Cyril Walker played those last three holes in one under par and won the Open like a man whose hour had come.

"Any man who can shoot that last nine in par today deserves to be champion," Bobby told Pop. "My hat's off to Cyril Walker."

Offering Walker nothing but compliments, Bobby demonstrated that a sportsman treats defeat and victory with the same good grace. After ending up in fourth place, Walter Hagen was nowhere near as sanguine; he forked over a much larger amount than Walker had won, in cash, to that unidentified high roller from Oakland Hills. Their bet: that Hagen would finish ahead of Bobby Jones.

Cyril Walker capped the unlikeliest week of his life by collecting the cup and one thousand dollars, the biggest payday of his career. For the sweet-natured little pro it would unfortunately be all downhill from here. No record of why or how it happened appears to have survived, but by 1941 Tet was out of his life and Walker was scratching out a living at a driving range in Miami, Florida. After long periods of homelessness and a protracted illness, he died in 1948, at fifty-six. Walker's was the saddest end of any Open champion since Johnny McDermott.

Bobby rushed home from Detroit, and on June 17 he married Mary Rice Malone. His earlier interest in Papini's *Life of Christ* takes on retroactive significance; Papini had been a lifelong agnostic who embraced Catholicism later in life and wrote his book as a deeply felt embrace of his new religion. Bobby had been raised as a Sunday-school Southern Baptist; the Malones were strict Irish Catholics. Bobby had been considering a conversion to Catholicism and reading Papini served as part of his decision-making process. The Jones family patriarch from Canton, Bobby's formidable old grandfather, R.T., caught wind of this and put his foot down. Under no circumstances would a Jones from Canton hold truck with the Church of Rome. There's no record of exactly how this went down inside the family, but in the end Bobby declined to convert to Mary's faith. So the wedding took place in the evening under a full moon on the lawn of the Malones' family home, and not at Atlanta's Catholic Church of the Sacred Heart, although one of their senior priests conducted the ceremony. Bobby's celebrity attracted the interest of all the local and regional society pages, every one of whom remarked on the warm, romantic mood and the couple's obvious devotion to each other. Hundreds attended, spread out across the broad moonlit lawn, the trees aglow from a thousand glittering lights, some in the shape of shamrocks symbolizing the Malones' heritage and Bobby's St. Patrick's Day birthday. A full orchestra played throughout the preamble to the ceremony, then began the traditional wedding march as Mary walked down the flower-strewn aisle.

A nervous Pop Keeler stood in the audience, his attention wandering fearfully: "Queer what vagrant thoughts get in your mind at times. I catch myself thinking it is a well-behaved gallery, but packed awfully close. Will the players have room to swing!" He spots his little mock antagonist Kiltie Maiden standing on tiptoe near the back of the audience, struggling to see the couple as Mary reaches Bobby at the altar; he swears the stoic little Scot looks closer to tears than most of the dowagers around them. Then Pop finds his own glasses fogging up. Solemn silence as the young couple exchange their vows, voices barely above a whisper. "Orchestra again—it's all over! Crash of music and congratulations and the gallery is all over the green—no, confound it all."

After five years of courtship, Bobby and Mary were at last husband and wife. As Pop makes his way toward them in an endless reception line he never sounds more like Shakespeare's Falstaff, ill at ease with his princely companion's new worldly status, agonizing over what he's going to say. "Old friends always say something supremely foolish at important junctures."

When Pop finally got to them all that came out was "Hello, Bobby."

"Say, O.B.," said Bobby, "I found your belt in my trunk when I was unpacking."

Pop beamed at them both: "And looking from Bobby to Mary standing there together—really together, under the flowers—I wished I knew words delicate and happy and graceful enough to say something fitting of the culmination of this charming romance. There is something beautifully old-fashioned and tender about it. It is not a matter for words, perhaps, but rather for the thoughts and hopes and emotions that are never spoken but lie deep in the heart. God bless them both!

"There have been many champions; there will be many more. There has been only one; there will be only one Bobby Jones."

There stood Bobby alongside his new bride. The once sickly infant born into a middle-class Atlanta home, deep inside the borders of a dispirited, reconstructing culture, had grown up to become the South's first twentieth-century hero: a modest young champion whose feats were about to transcend any claims of regionalism and astonish and inspire the world, and who by virtue of his gifts would become a friend to princes, presidents, and kings. And, every bit as remarkable, his destiny had been foretold by one lonely, limping prophet; Oscar Bane Keeler had prophesied all this years before when Bobby was just a boy. There's a minor note of melancholy to Pop's spirits that night as he hovered on the edge of the Malones' broad green lawn. Now Pop would have to share his friend with Mary and the multitudes.

Bobby was invited to meet his first president, Calvin Coolidge, at the star-studded opening of the Congressional Country Club in Bethesda, Maryland, one of his few golf excursions that summer. As the season wound down, the third annual Walker Cup matches were played on Long Island, at Walter Travis's masterpiece, the Garden City Golf Club. The United States won the Cup for the third time in a row, 9–3, which served as a final tune-up for the National Amateur Championship. With travel costs proving too onerous for amateurs on both sides of the Atlantic, it was agreed that from this point forward they would play for the Walker Cup every other year.

From Garden City Bobby, Pop, and caddie Luke Ross traveled to Philadelphia and suburban Merion. Instead of the downtown Bellevue-Stratford they checked into the Greenhill Farms Hotel in Overbrook, closer and more convenient to the course. When it rained heavily during practice rounds, Bobby told Ross to stop polishing his irons, a tactic he would employ in rough weather for years to come; his engineer's training told him that letting a light coat of rust form on the forged steel encouraged friction, increased spin, and prevented the ball from slipping off the clubs' wet faces.

Dozens of articles and magazine profiles couldn't resist contrasting the brash boy from Dixie who'd charmed them all so thoroughly in 1916 with the sleek, confident young conqueror he'd become. The course at Merion had matured over those years as well, a fitting test for the game's improving amateur field: longer, tougher, and featuring over a hundred new bunkers. Chick Evans, the returning champion from 1916, would lose in this year's first round and in a classic sound bite afterward said: "The course isn't so tough, unless those *white faces* get you." They *had* gotten Chick, and the name he applied has stuck to those bunkers ever since. This was Bobby's seventh Amateur, and armed with his recently completed education in classic literature, he recognized a perfect opportunity to dramatically complete his journey. Keeler agreed; winning the Amateur at Merion, where Bobby's career had begun, would bring a satisfying wholeness to the story.

Bobby had also taken to heart the lessons he'd absorbed about Old Man Par; he vowed to stay focused on playing the scorecard, not his human opponent. Analyzing his own record, Bobby had determined that if he'd followed this disciplined strategy he would have already won at least one Amateur and a second Open. If anybody he went up against could match or beat par with more success than Bobby did, they deserved to win. But theory wasn't practice and this new philosophy would be quickly put to the test.

Bobby finished second in qualifying, two strokes behind Clarke "Ducky" Corkran, a veteran who broke the course record his first time around Merion with a 67. Bobby looked up after an easy first-round victory to find Ducky Corkran waiting for him. This made him more determined to stick to his new strategy, and no one could argue it wasn't working when Bobby went four up through twelve. At the thirteenth, a short par three, Bobby airmailed a dart at the flag and stopped four feet shy; the match poised to end right there, Corkran answered with a pitch only six feet away. Both made their birdies and the match moved to the fourteenth, with Bobby up dormie five.

Pop felt so confident of the outcome at that point he wandered off to watch some other matches—and half an hour later was shocked to hear that Jones and Corkran were still playing. Ducky had won both the fourteenth and fifteenth; they now stood dormie three. The sixteenth is an extraordinary hole, a long, serpentine par four, its fairway navigating a sinuous curve around the course's old marble quarry. Beating Old Man Par on sixteen demands a long, accurate drive just short of the quarry, and then asks for a nerve-wracking iron that must carry the yawning rock pit to an elevated green or find disaster. Pop scuttled back to the quarry just in time to see the two men hit their approaches; Corkran went first and found the front of the green. The pressure shifted to Bobby. He rifled a four iron that bracketed the other side of the flagstick; both men lagged close, made their pars, and Bobby finally bid Ducky adieu.

The next day it looked like Bobby might fall victim to another golfer gone wild. After playing each other dead even through the morning, Bobby's third-round opponent, Rudy Knepper, began the afternoon with three straight birdies. Bobby never faltered, and fired away at the scorecard. Under pressure Knepper collapsed and Bobby won handily, 6 and 4. So Pop Keeler was shocked when he returned home to their hotel room that night to find Bobby sitting on his bed, distraught and near tears. The draw had conspired to send Bobby into the next day's semifinals against his greatest friend in the game, Francis Ouimet.

"I don't want to play Francis," said Bobby. "I'm going well and his game's all shot to pieces—"

"Then you should be able to beat him—"

"Damn it, I don't want to beat him."

Pop realized he was serious and chose his words carefully. "Well, do you want to win an Amateur championship?"

He did. He just couldn't think of climbing over Francis to get there.

"And how's your plan coming along, shooting at par and letting the other fellas take care of themselves—"

"It's working just fine," said Bobby, impatiently. "Keep shooting pars at them and they'll all crack, sooner or later."

"All right," said Pop. "When you go out there on the first tee tomorrow, you're not playing Francis Ouimet. You're playing the card of the Merion Cricket Club's East Course. And so is Francis. And whoever plays it closest goes into the finals on Saturday."

Less than twenty hours later, the two men walked off the eighth green— their twenty-sixth hole of a thirty-six-hole match—with their arms around each other's shoulders. Francis was smiling happily and Pop thought Bobby "looked like a man who had just been notified his bank balance was overdrawn." Bobby had played the scorecard and showed it no mercy. Francis had been systematically destroyed, 11 and 10. So completely did Bobby dominate the match that when he looked upset after losing the eighteenth with a double bogey, the last of only two holes Ouimet won all day, Francis smiled gently at his young friend and said: "Bobby, you could afford to lose that one."

"What Bobby did to me was criminal," said Francis to Keeler afterward, good-natured as ever. He predicted there would be no stopping him in medal or match play from then on.

One last man had something to say about the 1924 National Amateur. Making his second appearance, George Von Elm meant as much to the game of golf on the West Coast as Bobby did in the South. Born and raised in Salt Lake, he'd been a star high school athlete in three different sports and won Utah's amateur championship at fifteen. After wearing out local competition, George had recently relocated to the sun-drenched playgrounds of Hollywood. The twenty-three-year-old Von Elm had dispatched defending champ Max Marston in the semifinals, becoming the first golfer representing California, or anywhere west of the Rockies, to make it this deep into the Big Show.

It was as if central casting had supplied the perfect man for the role of the Formidable Opponent; sun-bleached blond, tanned, Teutonically fit, impeccably dressed, formal to the point of hauteur in manner and bearing. Keeler later said of Von Elm that as he swaggered down a fairway you could practically hear his saber rattling. Von Elm and Bobby, diametric opposites in style and temperament, would over the next few years become bitter rivals, equaling Bobby's simmering differences with Chick Evans. But when they met in the finals of the 1924 Amateur it was the first time they'd ever played each other. Von Elm had a bone-crushing handshake and a habit of staring down opponents on the first tee, like a boxer's prefight psych-out. Neither cut any mustard with Jones. Pop had never seen Bobby look more cool, confident, or businesslike at the start of a match; the Californian's bristling arrogance brought that out in him. Once they teed off he paid no attention to Von Elm, which seemed to bother him more than anything else Bobby did that day.

Von Elm won the first hole, the only time Bobby had trailed in a match since the first round. It would also be the last. By the turn Bobby was two up, and he stretched it to four by intermission. After a light lunch Bobby hammered Old Man Par, and Von Elm absorbed a beating by proxy; Jones won five of the next nine holes. On the tenth green Bobby was about to putt out after George had finished, when Von Elm stopped him.

"Don't putt that one, Bobby. I've had enough."

They shook hands. The final score was 9 and 8, and wasn't that close. Bobby had collected the second half of the American double championship that only Ouimet, Evans, and Jerry Travers had won before him. The circle had been rounded, back at Merion, where he'd rocketed into public consciousness as an unknown boy wonder. This fairy-tale quality of Bobby's career was something Pop didn't even have to underline, and it contributed to Pop's conviction that his future was all in the hands of destiny. Hard to argue with, given what would follow, but from a practical standpoint Bobby had won at Merion by sticking to his strategy of playing against par and ignoring his opponent. Not only had it reduced his stress, but it didn't even require him to play his best golf; focusing on the scorecard kept him from feeling obliged to produce something heroic on every shot.

As they handed him the Havemeyer Trophy he'd sought so fervently for the last eight years, Bobby experienced a curious pang of guilt. "I don't really feel like I did anything," he told Keeler.

"No fireworks, no blood and guts, no abject suffering," said Pop.

"That's right."

"Bobby, you might want to keep that to yourself."

People would still play over their heads against him on a regular basis no matter the format. He tended to bring out the best in opponents and always would. But it had come to him at last that all he had to do to win the damned thing, any tournament against any man in the world, was go out there and play like Bobby Jones.

Bobby and Walter Hagen, 1926.

CHAPTER EIGHT

The Battle of the Century

Atlanta turned out at the Brookwood train station, and the crowd that welcomed Bobby home from Philadelphia was even larger than after his Open victory. Pop reported that he was "blushing, speechless and inexpressibly happy." They threw another big party at East Lake, giving speeches and reading telegrams that poured in from all over the world. When dinner was done they dimmed the lights, lowered a screen, and showed a movie someone had found: rare footage of Bobby and Alexa playing at East Lake as youngsters, followed by footage of Bobby winning at Merion. All wide shots and silent, not tight enough to convey the action or excitement, but a thrilling novelty. Pop spotted himself limping through the foreground and felt a lump in his throat, as if Bobby was going to have to win the title all over again. Just as the Open cup had the previous year, the Havemeyer Trophy went on display in East Lake's lobby, with Bobby's name newly engraved at the top, the last of twenty-eight carved on the cup itself before they added a ring around the base to accommodate the future. Both of American golf's greatest prizes had now traveled south of the Mason-Dixon Line.

. . .

Bobby spent the first few months of 1925 in Sarasota, Florida, where Adair Realty and Trust had opened an office to handle its real estate holdings, over two thousand acres of land. The Adair development was called Whitfield Estates, one of the first in the state to anchor around a golf course: Whitfield Estates Country Club. Perry hired Donald Ross to design the course, construction began in 1925, and he named Bobby as sales manager for the adjoining lots. Bobby went to work selling lots and homes to customers, but Perry soon realized that his friend's greatest value was out on the golf course, so that's where he spent his afternoons, wooing potential buyers.

The Florida land boom had reached its peak; the state had experienced a frigid winter, which kept vacationers away. So many new houses had gone up so fast that demand for building materials overwhelmed the railways, which slammed the brakes on construction at new developments. When prices stopped ramping up, speculators who'd piled onto the pyramid late in the game found themselves strapped for cash. The result was rampaging inflation, which sent the cost of living through the roof; many of the middle class who had migrated to Florida in pursuit of affordable housing discovered they couldn't afford to stay. Newspapers picked up the theme and ran with it, warning buyers to keep their distance. Hustlers rushed for the exits. That bad winter of 1925 was followed by a blistering hot summer and then disaster: an early fall hurricane that killed four hundred, left twenty thousand families homeless, and caused $80 million in damage. This kicked the state into severe depression. Although the rest of the country remained buoyant while the stock markets thrummed, Florida's collapse served up a chilling foreshadow of what was in store for the rest of America only four years down the road.

Bobby spent two winters as sales manager of Whitfield Estates. Although his writing about the experience remains circumspect, it was clear to him from the beginning that he was desperately ill suited to the life of a salesman. While Hagen was bamboozling buyers at nearby Pasadena and chuckling all the way to the bank, Bobby couldn't summon up the forced cheerfulness that comprises so large a part of every real estate transaction. He didn't find fault with the industry or pass judgment on it; Bobby wasn't a prig, he just didn't have the sales gene in him.

"I had to sell a little piece of myself with every sale," he wrote later.

There were other privations. He was newly married and away from his bride, who provided the emotional bedrock on which his increasingly demanding life would center. Mary was in the late stages of expecting their first child in April and stayed home in Atlanta while Bobby went south. He returned briefly when she gave birth to Clara Malone Jones. Beginning a family raised new anxieties about making a living; the fact that he felt miscast in real estate did nothing to allay them.

The best thing that happened to Bobby during his seasons in Sarasota was his decision to room with Tommy Armour. The suave young Scotsman and war hero had immigrated to the States in 1921, hoping to start a career in business. Walter Hagen introduced Armour into the upscale golfing universe of Westchester County. Short on cash but with faultless British manners more useful than a resume, Armour landed a job as social secretary at the Westchester-Biltmore Country Club in suburban Rye. The Westchester-Biltmore was America's first gargantuan golf complex, built in 1922 with two golf courses, a polo field, a racetrack, and twenty tennis courts at a cost of $5 million. Many resorts built to this epic scale would follow. While working at Westchester, Tommy was introduced by Bobby Jones to Perry Adair; Adair soon afterward offered Armour the job as resident professional at Whitfield Estates. Tommy jumped at the chance and announced he was turning pro. The loss of his eye during the war had little effect on his golf game; he often wore a black patch instead of his glass replacement, which contributed to his piratical look. He'd gone into the army a private and come out a major, with a reputation as the fastest gunner in the entire tank corps. A larger-than-life figure in the carousing Hagen mold, he had a capacity for liquor that was even more legendary. Whereas the Haig often watered down drinks to polish his reputation as a boozer, Armour's glass was never half empty. Armour's strength was legendary, leaving alone the fact that he'd killed a German officer with his bare hands after their tanks had been reduced to scrap metal. Those hands were so powerful he could grip a billiard cue by the tip with only his thumb and forefinger with his arm extended and hold it straight up in the air. Try that after a half dozen cocktails.

Armour's move to Florida gave him a chance to play its informal pro winter circuit, where he fell in with Hagen and the other free-spirited scoundrels who gravitated around him off the course. Armour not only matched or beat Hagen drink for drink, he could also hold his own with him in a lying contest; the antithesis of the stoic Scot, Armour loved to gab and was a dazzling raconteur. At first glance Hagen didn't seem the type of alpha male to tolerate the presence of another equally outlandish character, but the two developed a mutual appreciation without either feeling threatened. The fact that they were starting to make a decent living on the golf course had a lot to do with their tolerance. Realizing they needed each other to draw spectators to their exhibitions went a long way toward keeping the peace in the professional ranks; these low-key tournaments in Florida were the seeds of what would eventually become the PGA Tour.

That largesse didn't always extend so generously to Bobby Jones, although the pros all professed to like him personally, and he never had any trouble fitting into their towel-snapping locker-room culture as one of the boys. Even though Bobby never cashed a check from a victory, and his winning never reduced the amount anyone received—first-place money simply went to whichever pro finished second—whenever an amateur won a tournament the pros viewed it as a blow to their pride. Winning the biggest championships had huge economic repercussions; a victory in either Open boosted a pro's exhibition fee by hundreds of percent, and no one profited more from that than Hagen. As the decade progressed, and Bobby's reputation continued to grow, Hagen increasingly became the spokesman for the anti-Jones point of view.

The next chance the pros had to beat their amateur nemesis came in the 1925 Open at the Worcester Country Club outside Boston. Nearly 450 players from around the country attempted to qualify; Bobby traveled to Long Island and worked his rounds in during a business trip with Perry Adair. He played his way into the Open on one of the country's most unusual new courses, the Lido, recently built as part of a real estate development on the island's marshy south shore by the Methuselah of American golf, Charles Blair Macdonald, at an unheard of cost of $800,000. Macdonald called it "the most daring experiment undertaken in the world of golf course construction." A marvel of engineering, water management, and land reclamation, the design for its finishing hole had been chosen from among eighty-one entries submitted to a contest run by an English weekly magazine, *Country Life*. The winner was a thirty-four-year-old former British army surgeon, Dr. Alister MacKenzie, who had dabbled in course design as a hobby for nearly twenty years. As one of the developers of the military use of camouflage, he had original thoughts about putting those devious concepts to work on a golf course. A decade later,

MacKenzie would gain lasting fame as the principal architect, with Bobby Jones, of Augusta National Golf Club. Bernard Darwin called the end result at Lido "the finest course in the world." The legendary Lido, alas, would not survive the coming Depression, its lagoons drained and rolling fairways abandoned when the real estate development failed.

Bobby shot two brilliant rounds at the Lido, the second a 70 in a blinding rainstorm that he considered one of the best rounds of his life, four strokes ahead of Hagen, adding fuel to their pro-am rivalry. Mindful of box-office appeal, the USGA paired the two titans together at Worcester during a practice round—where they charged admission for the first time, and lucky patrons who paid a buck witnessed a new course record 66 by Bobby and the first hole in one of Hagen's career—and again on the first day of the 1925 Open.

The USGA had set up the course for maximum difficulty, par had been lowered two strokes to 70, and at 7,100 yards it was the longest parkland layout most had ever faced. Ouimet knew the course well, but business and family obligations had recently limited his competitive golf; so he astonished everyone by seizing the lead with a first-round 70. Boston papers had a field day. Bobby got his bad round out of the way, a 77 that he attributed to the desertion of his irons. It was his action between shots on the eleventh hole that morning that would come back to haunt him.

Bobby's approach to the elevated green fell short, settling in deep grass on a steep embankment. As he took his stance to play a short pitch up to the flag, his club head grazed the grass and to his eye caused his ball to move a fraction of an inch. No one else saw it happen, but after playing the shot he informed his partner, Hagen, and the USGA official covering their match that he was calling a penalty stroke on himself. Hagen was dumbfounded and tried to talk Bobby out of it before he spoke to the official, but Bobby insisted he had broken Rule 18—moving a ball at rest after address—and had to pay the price. He finished his round, and then argued again with USGA officials afterward, who tried to dissuade him from assessing himself the penalty, which wouldn't be written in stone until he signed and turned in his scorecard. Bobby remained convinced he had caused the ball to move, end of story. His 76 turned into a 77. Hagen walked away shaking his head; although he played by the rules and was never accused of bending them, given an identical dilemma it's safe to say he wouldn't have felt the same ethical compulsion to confess to an unwitnessed crime.

Many writers later trumpeted this act of contrition as a wonder of sportsmanship, praise that made Bobby furious. Rules were rules and he was astonished anyone who knew the first thing about the game would expect him to do anything less. His widely reported quote to Pop afterward was: "You'd as well praise me for not breaking into banks." Keeler felt even more strongly about it, and told him so. "If it turned out that one stroke stood between Bobby and the championship, I would be prouder of him' than if he had won." Given the game's Presbyterian predilection for punishing anyone who flirted with fate, Pop would soon be given a chance to test the limits of his pride.

Bobby's first round left him in thirty-sixth place, dead and buried according to one Boston front page, which led their early edition with this banner: JONES OUT OF NATIONAL OPEN. Whoever slugged that headline underestimated the effects of self-disgust on Bobby's game; he shot his way back into contention during the afternoon with a 70, climbing all the way back into a tie for tenth, six strokes behind this year's surprise leader, a thirty-five-year-old transplanted Scotsman named Willie MacFarlane.

He was an even more unlikely figure than Bobby Cruickshank or Cyril Walker, a thoughtful, slender, bookish professional from Oak Ridge Country Club in Tuckahoe, New York. MacFarlane was a bit like a legendary jazz musician who never played public gigs. He had a reputation for shooting unbelievable rounds among the Westchester County cognoscenti, setting scoring records at many tough courses in the area, including an eye-popping 61 on his home track, but even the most ardent fans of the sport had never heard of him. Content to ply his trade from behind the counter of his pro shop, Willie had never won a tournament in the United States and had played in only one other Open, Inverness in 1920, where he finished in eighth place tied with Bobby Jones. Willie had neither the time nor the ambition to play golf at this level. He preferred teaching, particularly children, consistent with what Keeler described as his "pedagogical" appearance. Reporters turned up the fact that Willie had recorded only thirteen scores in the last nine months. Despite the layoff—or maybe because of it—Willie MacFarlane turned in one of his genius rounds that afternoon at Worcester, a 67, the lowest single round ever recorded in U.S. Open history. (The average score that day was 78.) He ended tied with Leo Diegel for the lead and found himself exposed to the hot glare of the public spotlight.

More sweltering heat and high humidity greeted the sixty-six golfers who made the cut for Saturday's final two rounds; these were the hottest June days on record in Boston. Before the advent of air conditioning, heat waves presented the gravest health hazards; hundreds had already died throughout New England. Growing up in the South's semitropical summers gave Bobby a big advantage; while others wilted, the heat never seemed to bother him. Although Bobby had never broken 70 in an Open, he matched that number in the morning's third round and moved into a tie for fourth. MacFarlane appeared to be on his way back down to earth after carding a 40 on the front, but hit his stride on the way in again with a 32 and maintained his lead by a single stroke over a handsome young club pro from White Plains, New York, named Johnny Farrell.

This set up the most wide-open finish in tournament history. Eight men had a chance to win the Open that afternoon. Seven had a shot going into the final hole. Leo Diegel went out in 34, found himself in the driver's seat, began twitching again, and shot himself out with a dreadful eight at eighteen. He looked so debilitated over the ball that Bernard Darwin began using his name as a verb: nattering nervously over any task became "to diegel." Hagen and Sarazen both made late runs; Sarazen fell short with a par at eighteen when he needed birdie. A par would have secured the lead for Hagen, but his lust for birdie led to a bogey five; Walter finished tied for fifth with Sarazen. Johnny Farrell's par at eighteen gave him the clubhouse lead. Ouimet reached sixteen a short while later, needing only three pars to jump ahead of Farrell; his bid for a second Open win in his home state fell one stroke short, but he tied Farrell for the lead.

Bobby played solidly down the stretch against Old Man Par; his pairing with Tommy Armour seemed to steady him. He matched the best final-round score turned in by any of the contenders, 74, and he slipped in a stroke ahead of Ouimet and Farrell. Only one man who could catch him was still on the course. Playing half an hour behind Bobby, MacFarlane was barely hanging on to his lead when he made the turn. After playing his worst back nine of the week he needed a par at eighteen to catch Bobby.

MacFarlane reached in two, forty feet from the cup. His long lag stopped five feet short and settled in a divot mark; this was before players could lift and replace balls on the green. He was forced to putt with a mid-iron to get the ball rolling, but it dropped. The next day Bobby and MacFarlane would "play off" for the U.S. Open title. One can always look back on a dozen misbegotten shots over the course of four rounds that could have determined a championship, but that playing field levels over time. An act of character, not fate, had made the difference here. As Pop had predicted, the penalty stroke Bobby had called on himself during his first round had cost him first place in the 1925 Open.

Sunday's play-off appeared a complete mismatch on paper; Bobby was not only over a decade younger but infinitely more seasoned in high-stakes tournaments. He looked strong and solid next to the bespectacled, Ichabod Crane–like Scotsman. Bobby had drawn his usual adoring galleries and had his team at his side: Keeler, Maiden, caddie Luke Ross. MacFarlane's caddie, a friend of a friend, was a man he'd only just met, Bill Savage. Turning down Willie's first offer of ten dollars a round, Savage had taken pity on the unimposing MacFarlane, suggesting lightheartedly that he'd get paid only if Willie won the Open, in which case they would split the purse down the middle. Willie accepted. At least he had a highly motivated caddie.

By now experts should have realized that MacFarlane had an undetected gift for upsetting expectations. Sunday morning's eighteen-hole play-off ended in another tie. Both men shot 75, and Bobby felt fortunate to still be in it. The heat intensified through the day, 90 degrees when they teed off at 11:00 that morning. Already down a stroke, after duffing his approach on fourteen Bobby slam-dunked a miraculous thirty-yard pitch from the rough for a birdie to even the score. Willie took another lead at sixteen; Bobby birdied seventeen to get back to even. Then a gift: Willie missed an easy five-footer for birdie at eighteen that would have won it outright. Bobby had to sink a side-winding five-footer for par to send them into a second overtime.

For the first time an Open play-off had been extended to thirty-six holes. As they broke for lunch the mercury crawled to over 100 degrees in the shade. When Bobby mentioned this to Willie on the first tee that afternoon, he said cheerfully: "Thank goodness we don't have to play in the shade." The odds all favored Bobby now. The saunalike heat and accumulated strain would wear the older MacFarlane out. That missed putt for the win at eighteen was bound to rattle around in his head and knock something loose. On the front nine that afternoon those predications looked accurate; Bobby matched Old Man Par with a 35. MacFarlane slowly faded to 39; Jones had a four-stroke lead with nine to play. Watching from the gallery, Francis told Pop as they made the turn that he "would not give MacFarlane a nickel for his chances."

They should have checked the scorecards and remembered how MacFarlane had been torching the back nine at Worcester all week. He birdied the par three tenth. After two halved pars, at thirteen Willie sank a twenty-footer for another birdie, while Bobby, pressing now, three-putted for bogey. His lead had shrunk to a single stroke. At the par five fifteenth, Bobby tried to push his advantage in length off the tee and break Willie's back with a birdie; he went for the green in two and got buried in a greenside bunker. Playing conservatively, Willie reached the green in regulation and collected an easy par. Bobby's bid for par came up short and they were dead even with three to play. Now Bobby appeared drained, while MacFarlane looked fresh as a daisy. As they walked off the fifteenth green, the amiable Scotsman told Bobby that given the great response to their battle they should try selling this act in vaudeville.

"I'd rather we get jobs as a couple of ice men," said Bobby.

Both men parred sixteen. After their drives, as Bobby waited for MacFarlane to play his approach from the other side of the fairway on seventeen, he walked over to Keeler.

"This thing's getting funny," he said, lighting up a smoke. "Still tied after a hundred and six holes."

"Looks like a third play-off," said Pop.

Bobby's face turned grim. "There won't be another play-off. I'll settle it now one way or another."

They halved seventeen and came to the home hole tied—335 yards, uphill, to a small green cut into the ascending slope like a shelf. The hole was set four steps from the front edge, fiercely protected by a long, deep bunker that ran across the front. Bobby outdrove Willie by twenty yards. MacFarlane played his approach long and safe to avoid the bunker, leaving himself a forty-foot downhill putt to the flag. Good as his word, Bobby tried to end the ordeal by sticking his short pitch a foot beyond the front edge and letting it trickle close to the hole.

The ball landed four inches short of his target, but instead of rolling forward, sucked slowly, painfully back off the green, down the slope, and into the bunker. His blast out of the sand left him a ten-foot putt for par. Completing his role as tortoise to Bobby's hare, Willie coaxed a perfect lag to within inches and collected his four. Bobby needed to sink his putt to force a third play-off. To nearly everyone's relief, he missed.

MacFarlane had defended his profession's honor and beaten Jones to win history's longest Open. Bobby had finished second in America's championship for the third time in the last four years, but 1925 was Willie MacFarlane's turn, the first Scotsman to win a U.S. Open since Alex Smith in 1910. Willie cashed his winner's check, and as promised paid half to his caddie, Bill Savage, in crisp fifty-dollar bills. Over the next decade MacFarlane periodically emerged from his sanctuary to win five more tournaments, but only one more of Willie's countrymen would win a U.S. Open in the next eighty years. American domination of the old Scottish game was now nearly complete.

Walter Hagen declined to defend his British Open title in 1925, but fellow American pro Jim Barnes went over alone and won his fourth major. That Open was played at Prestwick on Scotland's Ayrshire coast, Old Tom Morris's professional home, where the first ten Opens had been played. A huge, unruly crowd showed up on the last day, swarmed the fairways, and severely disrupted the final round. The resulting chaos cost third-round leader, expatriate Scotsman Macdonald Smith, his best chance to win a major; he bobbed like a cork in those jostling galleries and shot 82, when 78 was all he would have needed to win. The R&A afterward dropped the storied course from its rotation, the end of an era. Aside from two brief stretches during the next forty years, before and just after World War II, when American pros gave up traveling overseas, from this point forward they would dominate the British Open.

Bobby hadn't captured either of the game's oldest championships, but they were coming back into his thoughts. The day after his disappointment at Worcester, he and Pop stopped for a day in New York. Bobby had lost twelve pounds during the play-off, and for once he could blame that on the weather. Sixty-seven New Yorkers had died from the heat, and Pop feared he might be the sixty-eighth. To avoid the sweltering heat they accepted an invitation to dine at the Player's Club. Over dinner in the cool refuge of Edwin Booth's old brownstone, inspired by the actor's library of English literature, Bobby and Keeler discussed a return to Britain. Bobby's withdrawal from the Open at St. Andrews in 1921 remained the sole blemish on his sporting escutcheon. He was determined to erase that first impression from the British public's mind. The Walker Cup would be played at St. Andrews in the summer of 1926, and the USGA paid travel expenses, a vital consideration for Bobby. The British Open and Amateur were both scheduled within weeks of the Walker, so being named to the team would allow him to play in all three. Although there was little doubt Bobby would be invited onto the Walker Cup team, a good showing at the 1925 U.S. Amateur would guarantee it.

The Amateur returned that September to Oakmont. A change in format had been announced: only sixteen men would make it through qualifying, and all ensuing matches would be played over thirty-six holes. Before Bobby made the trip to Pittsburgh, he made a decision closer to home that affected that year's championship even more directly.

Since Bobby's arrival at the top of the game, the golf hothouse of East Lake Country Club had produced another young wonder. Twenty-year-old Watts Gunn—one of the greatest *names* in sports history—was a student at Georgia Tech, a Georgia amateur champion in 1923, and an unabashed admirer of Bobby Jones, the local legend who had first inspired him to play. Although only three years his junior, when in Bobby's company Watts looked and acted like a high school kid. Bobby referred to him as his protégé, and Watts felt flattered by it. He was a wiry, sheltered son of a noted judge from nearby Macon, who had refused Watts's request to qualify for the National Amateur. Bobby pleaded with Judge Gunn to let Watts come along to Oakmont; Pop attended the same meeting to lend his support. Bobby's account of his own debut at the Amateur—when he was six years younger than Watts was now—proved persuasive. A few weeks later, Watts was on the train with them to Pittsburgh.

When he found out they'd been awarded the Amateur, Oakmont's patriarch, Bill Fownes, decided that his pet project, already the hardest course in the country, needed toughening up. He sprinkled in bunkers like birdseed, shipping in train cars full of sand. The obstacle-course layout combined with the new format eliminated a boatload of strong players from the field who contended for the final sixteen; five former Amateur champs, including Ouimet, failed to qualify. Bobby made the cut, and to everyone's surprise, none greater than his own, so did Watts Gunn, with the fifth best score in the field. From that point forward the Amateur title required only four wins, each played over the thirty-six-hole length that Bobby favored. The penal ordeal of Oakmont increased his advantage; nobody else seemed up to it. Bobby walked through his first three matches without being tested; in the semifinals he beat George Von Elm for the second year in a row. Imagine his surprise when he looked up and realized that in the finals he'd be going up against none other than Watts Gunn.

Something wild had gotten into Watts. He was either too smart or too simple to be bothered by the depth of these new waters. Pop thought he was play-ing as if the kid had a spell cast on him. He was too unworldly to comprehend what he was up against; there was something kind of mechanical and uncom-plicated about Watts's game that just clicked at Oakmont. Watching him at work Pop said, "There didn't appear to be anything on his mind but his hair," and meant it as a compliment.

When he was three down after eleven holes in his first-round match against Pennsylvania's champion, Vincent Bradford, something wild got into Watts; he won the next *fifteen holes in a row* and beat Bradford, 12 and 10. A streak like that had never been produced in an Amateur before. Watts faced former champ Jess Sweetser in the second round during a savage rainstorm and gave him the worst beating of his life; Sweetser was gone before he knew what hit him, 11 and 10. Afterward Bobby asked Watts about the match and he couldn't remem-ber any of it in the proper order, the holes all jumbled together. When Pop asked him how he felt, Watts stared at him with a dreamy look in his eye and said: "Gee, I'm awful hungry. I'm so hungry my pants are about to fall off."

In his semifinal match against a player named Dick Jones from New York, Watts found himself up by only a hole at the lunch break. Based on his experi-ence to date this wasn't how big-time matches were supposed to go. He ran into Bobby in the clubhouse, who asked how he was coming along.

"Gee, I got a tough one today," said Watts. "I'm only one up."

Watts pulled himself together that afternoon and dispatched Jones of New York, 5 and 4. First to greet him coming off the green was Jones of Atlanta, whom he now had to face in the finals of the 1925 Amateur. This is what Watts told the assembled reporters afterward: "I'm scared stiff. I'm awful hungry. I'm tickled stiff to be playing Bobby. He gives me four strokes in our matches at home, but I reckon he won't do that here."

Bobby made it clear that his protégé would get no special favors. Much as it upset him to beat a friend, he had found a way to do it against Francis at Merion; his game was played against numbers on the scorecard, not his endearingly goofy sidekick. An hour after their match was set, Watts ran up to Bobby and Pop, remembering that he should cable Judge Gunn in Macon that he'd made the finals.

"Don't worry," said Bobby. "He knew it long before you did."

After dinner that night, Bobby ran into Watts in the hotel trying to sneak out for a date he'd made with a girl who'd flirted with him that day in his gallery. "I'm just going out for a bite," said Watts. "I'll be right back."

"Oh no, you won't," said Bobby. "I'm going to lick hell out of you tomorrow and I don't want any excuses when I do."

Bobby walked Watts back to his room and changed the course of his friend's life in an even more profound way: Watts eventually married *another* girl who'd been in his gallery that day.

Watts had made possible a record in the Amateur that has never been equaled: two members from the same club facing each other for the Havemeyer Trophy. To this point, no two contestants from the same *city* had ever reached the finals. Atlanta newspapers fell into a lather at the prospect, the story splashed across their front pages, sports pages, and human interest pages. Church bells rang. Civic pride hit a high-water mark; if any athlete could resuscitate the self-respect of an entire city, Bobby was the man. He especially looked the part standing next to his youthful opponent. Watts's childlike nature made it easy to forget that Bobby was only twenty-three; in comparison he seemed like the Ancient Mariner. The entire experience still felt like a lark to Watts, but Bobby was all business. Watching him prepare, Pop was reminded of an older brother preparing to beat up on a sibling. As they warmed up the next morning before their match, Watts joked again with Bobby about being given his customary two strokes a side. Bobby smiled, looked him straight in the eye, and said: "I'm going to lick you today." That was the sanitized Keeler version. According to Watts, Bobby grinned and told him: "I'm going to give you hell, you little SOB."

It would be dramatically pleasing to report that Watts continued his inspirational run and gave his mentor the match of his life, and for the first eleven holes he did exactly that; Bobby was one under par, and one down. Watts didn't seem to know what he was doing, but there's no space on the scorecard for state of mind; Pop described Watts's play as "strangely able" and worried that he might never wake up. The match turned on the same hole at Oakmont where the megaphone incident had derailed Bobby's first trip to the finals in 1919, the long par five "Ghost Hole." Watts had reached the green in regulation and looked certain to collect a par. Bobby was lying three in a calamitous Oakmont bunker to the right of the green; he had an intuitive suspicion that if he couldn't match Watts for par here the kid might sprint away on a hot streak and disappear in a cloud of dust. He splashed his shot to within ten feet and drained the par-saving putt. Watts's putt for birdie hung on the lip and they halved the hole. Watts looked perplexed. Momentum swung hard in Bobby's direction; he evened the match on the next hole and played the next six in two under par to carry a four-hole lead into the lunch break. From there the outcome was not in doubt; Watts never gave up, but the meter on his beginner's luck had run out. He lasted until the eleventh hole that afternoon, where Bobby collected his second consecutive Amateur championship, 8 and 7, then put his arm around his young friend and consoled him all the way back to the clubhouse. But Watts didn't need much consoling; he was happy as a clam in mud just to be there.

Watts gave an impromptu speech after collecting his second-place silver medal. "When I came up here, I didn't expect to qualify, but everybody was so nice to me I wanted to stick around as long as I could. That is, until I got to Bobby. You know nobody can beat our Bobby."

"I don't think I'll be urging Judge Gunn to send you to any more championships," said Bobby.

Watts grinned: "Jones, you are one tough kid."

An Atlanta crowd lifted both favorite sons onto their shoulders when they returned home the next day, and East Lake threw another celebratory dinner. Bobby included Watts in every speech and interview he gave, allowing the younger man to feel as if he'd won a share of the championship. Watts Gunn thus became a permanent part of the lore of East Lake Country Club—there's a room named after him to this day—and he would go on to win both the Southern Open and Southern Amateur in 1928. If he never followed Bobby to become a consistent presence in national championships, Watts cherished the memories of that one marvelous week at Oakmont throughout his life, and he had Bobby to thank for it.

Bobby had successfully defended an Amateur title for the first time since Jerry Travers did in 1913 and had now won an Open or Amateur for three straight years. After they got back to Atlanta, Bobby shared a confidence with Pop: if he could win either cup for six years running—only three more—he'd be satisfied enough to walk away from the game. They didn't speak of it again for a while, and Keeler never pressed him on the point, but for the first time the subject of the end was in the air.

Although his sport had given him a huge head start in life, like most young men his age Bobby was wrestling with fundamental issues of adult responsibility. At this point he and Mary were still living with his parents in their big white house. With the birth of their first child he felt the daily pull and obligation of providing for his family; Bobby knew that unless he turned pro a day would come when golf would be only an obstacle to that end. Although he already knew selling real estate made him miserable, he still had to put bread on the table; Bobby agreed to spend another winter in Florida working for Adair Realty at Whitfield Estates. This year he went down in late October and took Mary and baby Clara with him.

Grantland Rice continued to feed the culture's ravenous appetite for sports heroes. Knute Rockne coached Notre Dame to two more college football championships, his 1924 team riding on the legs of a backfield that Rice dubbed "the Four Horsemen of the Apocalypse," a grim allegory for a country nearing the peak of the decade's manic high. After breaking every collegiate rushing record, a running back from the University of Illinois named Red Grange quit school to play pro ball in 1925, picked up eighty thousand dollars in an exhibition tour, and joined the Chicago Bears of the nascent National Football League. Rice dubbed Grange "the Galloping Ghost" and his box-office appeal solidified the shaky status of professional football; its rise as the country's most popular sport can be traced from this point forward. Al Capone, a sociopathic strongman who had just ascended to control of the Chicago underworld, bought season seats, lived openly like a Medici prince, and achieved perverse celebrity as a publicity-seeking villain. A couple of years later, after Grange and owner-coach George Halas won their first championship, the team was invited to meet President Coolidge, who didn't spend much time reading the sports page. When informed he was about to see George Halas and the Chicago Bears, Coolidge replied: "Great. I love animal acts."

During the sweltering summer of 1925 the world turned its eye to rural Dayton, Tennessee, where two giants in the twilight of their careers debated the sensational case of a high school substitute science teacher who had dared to include the evolutionary theories of Charles Darwin in his curriculum. (Darwin was the grandfather of English golf journalist Bernard Darwin.) Chicago's legendary lawyer Clarence Darrow agreed to defend twenty-four-year-old John Scopes against a charge of violating the Butler Act, a new state law that forbade teaching evolution as scientific fact because it contradicted the biblical version of creation. Former secretary of state and three-time Democratic presidential candidate—now turned evangelical Christian—William Jennings Bryan arrived to head the prosecution, after working as a shill for a Florida real estate developer. The recently formed American Civil Liberties Union took strong interest in the Butler Act as a landmark free-speech issue and placed ads in Tennessee papers soliciting teachers willing to break the law, offering to pay for their defense. Scopes had already agreed to be arrested and serve as a test case at the behest of some progressive Dayton businessmen, not because of their politics, but because they sensed the publicity of a trial would revive the town's flagging economy.

They got their wish; the so-called Monkey Trial turned into a media circus we would recognize instantly today, but back then it carried an air of novelty. The judge allowed newsreel cameras into the courtroom and much of the proceedings were broadcast on live radio, both justice system firsts. The European press had a field day satirizing the primitive customs and beliefs of the Old South, a disgrace for a region struggling to change its image as a cultural backwater populated by, as Yankee reporter H. L. Mencken called them, morons, yokels, and rubes. Even Pop Keeler wrote columns about it, and as a Southerner expressed his enlightened big-city scorn for the Butler Act.

The trial created such a powerful furor because it brought into focus an ongoing conflict between two powerful, warring influences in American daily life: urban modernism versus rural fundamentalism. Over half of America now lived in big cities, a seismic shift in population and demographics. The Scopes case was a turning point for a society that had embraced science and free thinking, striving to break free of patriarchal frontier tradition. In the end Scopes was found guilty of violating the Butler Act—a point Darrow never denied—but his minimum sentence of a one-hundred-dollar fine was considered a victory for Darrow's strategy of putting the Butler Act itself on trial. Bryan, exposed on the witness stand during cross-examination as an ignorant, narrow-minded opportunist, died five days later of a heart attack. Scopes declined to continue teaching in Dayton. H. L. Mencken paid his fine. A few months later Scopes accepted a scholarship to the University of Chicago made possible by a collection of newsmen and scientists. His conviction was reversed by the state supreme court a year later on a minor technicality, but the Butler Act remained on Tennessee's books until 1968.

In April of 1925 the man who had lit the fuse of the Jazz Age published a melancholy novella foretelling its demise. F. Scott Fitzgerald had marshaled his wayward talents long enough to write *The Great Gatsby*, a cautionary fable about the wages of greed, materialism, and sexual obsession on a group of Midwesterners climbing the slippery social ladder of Eastern society. Not interested in their former master of the revels turning in this gloomy Cassandra act, the reading public gave it a cold shoulder. Fitzgerald and Zelda trudged back to Europe, the quick cash of magazine writing, and drinking; the book's status as an enduring American masterpiece would not emerge until a decade after his death. On Broadway a wackier take on the excesses of the upwardly mobile found a much more receptive audience; four scrappy veteran vaudevillians in their Great White Way debut made the satiric musical *Cocoanuts* the surprise smash of the season, and the Marx Brothers were on their way to stardom. The play's story line, about rampant corruption and swindling in the Florida real estate market, prefigured the implosion of the state's gold-rush economy by a matter of weeks.

Walter Hagen won his second consecutive PGA Championship in the summer of 1925, reaffirming his status as the supreme professional. When he set up shop in Florida for the winter and bumped into Bobby, an irresistible idea arose out of the frothy last days of the real estate frenzy. Bobby spent a lot of his time on the links with Walter, Tommy Armour, and the other hearty brutes who comprised the emerging pro tour. There's no question Bobby privately considered joining their ranks during that season. Less than a decade removed from underclass status, professional athletes in every sport had garnered unprecedented legitimacy, and their income continued to rise. Bobby's fame had never been higher; he was nuts not to cash in on it, in the opinion of his freebooting friends. He was so damn good in their private matches he still had to give Tommy Armour a stroke a side.

The temptation was almost irresistible: he was chained to a demeaning salesman job he despised, he had mouths at home to feed, and the minions of corporate America were eager to open their checkbooks to the commercial exploitation of the decade's Golden Boy. While Bobby mulled this over, an electrical fire destroyed East Lake's clubhouse; among the losses were all of Bobby's favorite clubs—except Calamity Jane; he'd become so devoted to her that he slept with the club under his bed—and the original Havemeyer Trophy, which Bobby had let the club keep in its lobby. A duplicate trophy was ordered—at a cost of fifteen thousand dollars—and work began on rebuilding the clubhouse, but the unique, ornate, silver-wedding-cake style of the original Havemeyer was never precisely duplicated. The question of whether Bobby's amateur status would disappear with it remained, for the moment, unanswered.

Bobby weighed the idea. He listened to Hagen and Armour check off a pro's bountiful advantages. He even made plans to play in the Florida Winter Golf League. There's no question he discussed the idea with Mary at home, but he never brought it up to Pop Keeler or his own father, a telling indication that his traditional upbringing as a Southern gentleman—in a line of men born to follow careers, not practice common trades—still occupied the high ground of his conscience. The Colonel had made it clear once again there was a place for Bob in his law practice, should he see fit to follow that path. The events of 1926 would finally make up his mind for him.

The Winter League was canceled abruptly in January for lack of interest, a clear sign the number of people wintering in Florida had dropped precipitously. Perry Adair had a hand in the idea that followed, but Hagen came up with it first. He was the sport's reigning professional champ, Bobby was on top of the amateur game; why not arrange a grand exhibition match to settle the issue of who was the game's best player? The press and public had been clamoring for a match like a heavyweight title fight. The idea took shape: thirty-six holes on Bobby's home course at Whitfield Estates followed by thirty-six the following week at Hagen's home at Pasadena, drawing well-heeled crowds to help both struggling developments move some inventory.

His own promoter advised Walter not to go up against Jones. Hagen's stock was sky high on the exhibition circuit; losing to Bobby carried more risk than winning brought benefit. Nonsense, argued Walter: everybody wins here, particularly me. He was assured of a $5,000 guarantee; as an amateur Bobby wasn't playing for anything but his Adair Realty salary. He couldn't share in the gate with Hagen either, and they were planning to charge an unheard-of $3.30 for tickets. Bobby agreed to the match largely out of a sense of obligation to Perry; he saw it as part of his job. Hagen loved reading that the press predicted victory for Jones, the Polly Purebred amateur—while the scallywag pro was inevitably cast as the black-hatted villain. When they tossed a coin and Bobby won the right to play the first thirty-six at Whitfield Estates, Walter realized he'd be playing the first half of the match in front of a hostile gallery cheering against him on every shot. He had Bobby right where he wanted him.

They had never played a head-to-head match, but Walter knew enough about Bobby's emphasis on perfection to believe he carried a huge advantage; he could forget a bad shot the moment he hit one. Bobby couldn't shake off a mistake with anywhere near the same facility. Hagen also felt that in this version of a street fight, away from the niceties and rituals of a USGA event, he could get into Bobby's head. Psychology was the extra club in his bag. Hagen knew that in match play nothing mattered but who won the hole, and it didn't matter how. Bobby had come up against an opponent who didn't give Old Man Par the time of day, a clash of philosophies as much as of style and credentials. Pop Keeler traveled down to watch. So did Grantland Rice and a squadron of important writers from New York. They billed it as the Battle of the Century.

Promoters limited ticket sales to 750, but hundreds more crashed the gate on the last day of February to watch the battle's first round at Whitfield Estates. Hagen hit one fairway out of the first nine and built a two-hole lead. His recovery shots were even more supernatural than usual and his putter was hot as a pistol; twenty-seven putts in the first round. Bobby appeared off-key from the start. Although he drove beautifully, his irons were loose and uncertain. He compensated by pressing around the greens, as Walter predicted he might. Bobby worked the lead back to one with a birdie on twelve, but Walter pushed his lead to three as the morning round concluded. While Bobby sweated and strained to place every shot perfectly, Walter continued to hook, slice, push, and pull everything off the tee, and still Bobby could gain no ground until canning a birdie on the afternoon's fifth hole.

At the sixth Hagen hit another terrible drive to the edge of the rough, dead behind a towering pine. Bobby played a flawless tee shot and a solid iron to the elevated green, leaving himself a good chance for birdie and a possible turning point. Hagen stood up to his stymied ball, half topped a wicked slice that ran a hundred yards at an altitude of three inches, hopped through a greenside bunker, climbed a steep embankment and came to rest on the green twelve feet from the pin. Bobby missed his birdie putt; Walter was getting under his skin. A disheartened Pop believed the match turned on this hole. Hagen held on to his three-hole advantage through the final turn and then decided he might as well try to put his foot on Bobby's neck. Walter shot 32 on the back nine. When the smoke cleared he had shot a two-under-par 70 and built an eight-hole lead. Asked to analyze the reason for his success that day, Hagen pointed to his putter; both men played well but he had taken exactly eight fewer putts than Bobby.

The match resumed the following Sunday, on Walter's course at Pasadena. His big lead put a dent in attendance, but for once Hagen was more interested in pride than in his pocketbook. Bobby played golf only against the problems of the course in front of him, trying to match the blueprint of perfection he carried in his head; he was his own worst critic and the presence or absence or behavior of galleries made no difference to him. Hagen was a born performer who fed off the energy of a crowd like a Broadway ham milking curtain calls on opening night. He confessed later that he used to set up shots like a movie director, trying to extract every last ounce of drama and suspense. After putting so beautifully at Whitfield Estates, Walter went mad on the familiar greens at Pasadena. He sank a fifty-footer to go up nine on the second hole. Twice that day his drive hit a tree and bounced into the fairway, and he got up and down for birdie. Somewhere during that morning round, out of frustration, Bobby abandoned his strategy of playing the scorecard and tried to match Walter shot for shot. His game actually improved. Bobby played the last twenty-five holes at Pasadena in even par but he still lost ground. For this match, Hagen's name had been written in Keeler's Book of Predestination, although it was only natural to suspect Walter had snuck in the night before under cover of darkness and jotted it down himself.

By the time they reached their twenty-fourth hole of the day, Walter was up twelve with twelve to play. Both men were just off the green, lying two. Bobby chipped in from forty-five feet for birdie. Walter stepped up to his ball, pulled a three iron, and chipped it toward the flag.

"My little sweet potato went for that hole as if it had eyes," he said.

His ball hit the stick, dropped for a birdie to halve the hole, and the Battle of the Century was over. Technical knockout.

"Walter chopped my head off," wrote Bobby soon afterward. "He played the most invincible match golf in those two days I had ever seen, let alone confronted. And I may add that I can get along very comfortably if I never confront any more like it."

Hagen had won the match decisively, 12 and 11, and established new scoring records at both Whitfield Estates and Pasadena. He needed only 69 strokes that last day; Bobby joked that he needed 69 cigarettes, but he'd shot a respectable 73. For his troubles Hagen collected the largest single check ever paid to any golfer for an exhibition match, $7,600. As a show of gratitude he went out and bought Bobby a set of diamond and platinum monogrammed cuff links, so his net was reduced to $6,800.

"Sure I grandstanded," Walter wrote later. "But don't get the idea I was merely being amusing and brassy. To me that stuff was all part of my game. It helped fluster my opponent as much as it delighted the gallery, and was equally important in releasing the tension from my game."

The disappointment of his loss to Hagen produced several positive effects on Bobby. The experience humbled him to such an extent that any thoughts of turning professional were shelved. He realized that stepping down off the altar of amateurism would drop him into an arena where no holds were barred in the scramble for a buck, and clashed with his evolving self-image. Bobby had been raised from birth to fit the Victorian ideal of a professional gentleman; that was not only planted in his genes but conditioned into all his social reflexes. Make an honest and honorable living, raise and provide for your family, and in your spare time pursue those things that hold your interest. As an amateur. Our modern perception of "amateur" suggests someone who does something poorly or with a lack of professionalism, but the Latin root of the word "amateur" is *amor*, someone who pursues a pastime out of love. Bobby embraced his amateurism as more than a label; it defined him as thoroughly as "professional" described Hagen. Fate had not tapped Jones only to send him out on the road nine months a year with a bunch of scruffy nomads chasing penny-ante purses in half-assed tournaments. He wanted a life centered in Atlanta as part of a community, a solid wage earner supporting his wife and children and family. Bobby's status as a dominant part-time player among the professional elite is unique in the history of the game, and that identity had become too big a part of who he was to cast aside. Four to six tournaments a year was all he could afford to play; his nerves couldn't have taken much more than that as it was.

Walter's masterful performance also increased Bobby's desire to keep climbing the mountain; there were still many goals ahead of him, chief among them winning a British Open. The match with Hagen had also exposed a weakness in his game that could prove fatal overseas—faulty iron play. After the match Bobby asked his former roommate, Tommy Armour, for help. Armour observed that Bobby was trying to steer the shots with his right hand instead of pulling down and through impact with his left. Bobby made the correction and noticed a startling improvement; his iron shots flew so straight that Bobby found it was almost impossible to hit them *off* line. Armour also talked him through a shot-by-shot tutorial on how to play St. Andrews, the course that had baffled Bobby in 1921, where the coming year's Walker Cup would be played. Bobby began to understand the singular strategic genius of the Old Course and went to work developing a detailed plan of attack.

The friendly sparring with Hagen wasn't quite finished. A couple of weeks after their epic match they met again in the Florida West Coast Open, played at Pasadena, a medal-play tournament that was part of the winter tour. Hagen won, but only by a single stroke, with Bobby second; he was already gaining ground. When Bobby was named to the Walker Cup team and planned his return to Great Britain, he and Walter made one last sociable wager: whoever scored the lowest in both of that year's Opens and qualifiers would buy the other a hat. The joke was that Bobby seldom wore a hat when he played, and Walter never did; he was being paid a fat endorsement fee by Brylcreem hair gel to keep his lustrous, groomed black mane out in the open air whenever he stepped on a course. A serious money rematch between the game's two heavyweights seemed certain to follow, but the USGA put an end to the speculation. They issued a ruling that if Bobby played Hagen for another cash match it would compromise his amateur status. There would be no rematch.

Who was the better golfer? Despite Hagen's convincing win the question still hung in the air. Walter had this to say about it: "The closest I can come to an answer is that any champion golfer—with his nerves steady, his game at its peak, the weather and course conditions equalized by his skill and luck—can beat any other champion golfer on any given day. I happened to play Bobby on my particular days."

Bobby was too modest to compare his game to anyone's; that was someone else's job. Because he always insisted he learned more from the matches he lost than those he won—and it's clear he learned a great deal from losing to Hagen—the memory of this loss remained a far from unpleasant one. Years later, in his final book, Bobby wrote a fond reminiscence about their famous match, with the two combatants depicted as a couple of "old geezers sitting before the fire on a cold winter night" with snifters of brandy in hand. As they recall the details of their combat "way back in '26," their memories diverge hilariously, Walter chortling with glee at the way he beat Bobby, with Bobby chiding Walter that he's embellished his account of the match so often he's come to believe all the improvements. What comes through loud and clear is that despite their radically different personalities and playing styles, the two men had forged a relationship in the heat of competition to stand the test of time.

"When you play a lot of intense and interesting competitive golf with and against a man," wrote Bobby, "you develop a real affection for him. The respect and admiration you have for him as an immediate adversary ripens through the years because of the memory of the tense and thrilling experiences you have shared. I have seen many a lesser champion become snobbish in the moment of opulence and glory. Walter never forgot for one instant what he owed to the public. He was the greatest competitive athlete I have ever encountered."

Bobby and Walter both left Florida in the spring of 1926. The real estate bubble had burst and the remainder of the decade would pass before it turned around. For once in his life Hagen got out of a failing investment with his nest egg intact, while Bobby went back to work as a low-level wage earner in the Atlanta office of Adair Realty. He had privately made up his mind he was going to leave the business soon, and told Mary so. According to sportswriter Paul Gallico, who spoke about the matter with him later, Bobby "became convinced he and his golfing titles and prowess were being employed merely as a front to dispense wastelands." A bigger transformation was in the offing, but first there was the matter of an extended trip overseas to attend to.

What he was about to do that summer changed everything.

*The 1926 Walker Cup team, with Francis Ouimet, third from the left,
and Bobby, second from the right.*

CHAPTER NINE

The Americans Are Coming

THE WALKER CUP TEAM sailed out of New York for England on May 5, 1926, on the *Aquitania*. Francis Ouimet was on board, along with Jess Sweetser and Jesse Guilford, team captain Bob Gardner, Bobby, and the imperious George Von Elm. Thanks to his showing at Oakmont, so was twenty-one-year-old Watts Gunn, a true innocent abroad. And along to record all their adventures on his first trip away from American shores was Oscar Bane Keeler. The USGA threw them a grand dinner in the ballroom of the Waldorf-Astoria the night before they departed and the city arranged a big send-off at the harbor with flags flying and trumpets blaring. Irving Berlin contributed a special version of his hit "Always," with lyrics rewritten to predict the team's success. Bobby's parting from Mary had been more difficult than usual; she was four months pregnant with their second child. When they boarded the ship that night Pop found Watts Gunn on the top deck, and together they looked down on the crowd covering the dock below. At midnight the ship's steam whistle bellowed to announce their departure, lines were cast off, the anchor weighed, and propellers thrashed until the *Aquitania* inched away from shore. As they steamed through the harbor past the Statue of Liberty and into the open sea,

Pop looked back until the light of her lamp disappeared from sight. He wrote his first column that night; Pop would wire back to Atlanta a series of colorful dispatches chronicling their travels throughout their trip, less than half of them about golf, many about the comic challenges of chaperoning the unpredictable Watts Gunn. As he lay down in his bunk that night Pop's mind was filled with musings on man's mastery of the oceans and the march of human progress. His transcendent mood was short-lived; he woke up with a start at 3:00 that morning. The ship had slipped into the rough open Atlantic and he was suddenly, catastrophically seasick.

Small intrigues broke out on board through the crossing. Watts read *The Great Gatsby* and wondered aloud what all the fuss was about. Bobby caught a cold and gave it to Jess Sweetser. Francis battled a bout of seasickness to rival Pop's. Together they haunted the infirmary and experimented with a variety of remedies, but they found no relief until somebody slipped them a white powdered remedy in a blue bottle called Carlsbad #2. Pop felt revived enough afterward to take his first walk around deck in the bracing fresh air, and even downed a cautious lunch. Then the powder wore off and "I went back down to my room to die." But when he woke from his next nap the seasickness had vanished, and didn't return. The boys got a kick out of investigating a rumor that Marion Davies, William Randolph Hearst's notorious movie star mistress, was on board; it remained unconfirmed. On the third night out Francis organized a singing squad and regaled the dinner guests with a barbershop quartet version of "Moonlight Bay." At dinner that night the discussion revolved around the general labor strike that had paralyzed much of Britain, affecting everything from food delivery to basic transportation. There was real uncertainty that the tournaments they were traveling to take part in would even be allowed to take place; shipboard editions of Lord Northcliffe's *Daily Mail* appeared every evening, keeping them apprised of the degenerating situation. It wasn't until the *Aquitania*'s last night out at sea that they received a cable from the Royal and Ancient confirming that the British Amateur, the first of their events, would proceed as scheduled.

On the morning of May 11 Pop went topside at 3:45 a.m. to steal a look at the town of Cherbourg off the starboard bow, his first glimpse of a foreign country; he'd never even seen Canada before, and the romance of those distant lights affected him deeply. (This was also the same season in which American Gertrude Ederle became the first woman to swim the English Channel, although she wasn't in the water at the time.) They docked a few hours later that morning in Portsmouth, and discovered the general strike had canceled their boat train, so they made their way into London by motor coach. As they drove out of the harbor onto the highway, Watts was terrified by his introduction to English street traffic: "Good Lord, Pop, they're driving on the wrong side of the road!" The team checked into the posh Savoy Hotel on the Strand, spent a whirlwind day and a half sightseeing, and then heard the news that the strike had been settled. Britain went back to work and so did the Americans; they climbed into their motor coach and drove southwest to Kent, where the team played a one-day exhibition at Rye and decisively defeated a composite Oxford-Cambridge team.

They bunked in a hotel near the golf club, a converted country manor next to an old monastery, now a dance hall. Bobby, Pop, and Francis became even more intrigued by the place when they learned the old house was allegedly haunted, and over the course of their stay they tracked down a sorrowful legend. Centuries before, the young lady of the house, daughter of the resident lord, had been promised in marriage to a rich, older local squire. During their engagement she fell in love with a young monk from the monastery; the two eloped, and the squire pursued them with a vengeful mob. The monk killed the squire in self-defense. Rough justice followed. The lovers were dragged to the basement of the manor house. The girl was forced to watch as they chained the monk inside a niche and walled him up alive. The squire locked his daughter in a room on the other side of that wall and left her to starve to death. The ghostly voice of the monk calling to his doomed love as they both wasted away could supposedly still be heard echoing through the halls. Pop devoted an entire column to their investigation. When Watts heard the story at dinner he turned pale and didn't sleep all night.

Making their way north the team spent one day back in London, where Pop and Bobby visited Ye Olde Cheshire Cheese, Samuel Johnson's famed eighteenth-century hangout on Fleet Street. The organizational genius behind the first English dictionary, and subject of James Boswell's legendary biography, Johnson had long been a literary hero of the language-loving Keeler.

Within a few years he was himself routinely being referred to as "Bobby Jones's Boswell." Bobby got a big kick out of the pub's atmosphere, but when they got back to the hotel that night Bobby confessed to Pop he was terribly homesick for Mary and their baby. He had decided to drop out of the British Open, the last event on their agenda, and return to Atlanta two weeks earlier than originally planned. Pop was disappointed but understood the decision; he was already yearning for home and hearth himself. The next evening the team boarded the Flying Scotsman and rolled north out of Victoria Station toward Edinburgh. Occupying an entire car and a half, they covered four hundred miles in nine hours and arrived at Muirfield the next morning. After checking into the Marine Hotel in nearby Gullane they got in a single day of practice rounds, attended a dinner in the team's honor that night, rested on the Sabbath — still the custom in Scotland — and on Monday, May 24, play began in the British Amateur.

Lying inland near the Firth of Forth, the venerable Muirfield layout felt more hospitable to the American players than the links courses that run along the shore. Although Walter Travis had won the 1904 event as an American, he was originally from Australia; no American-born player had ever captured the British Amateur, but the British oddsmakers established Bobby, George Von Elm, and Chick Evans as the early favorites. Bobby was less sanguine about his chances; with the eighteen-hole limit on every match in the first six rounds of the event the format posed what he felt was the toughest challenge of all the major titles. He was also shaking off the effects of the persistent cold that had bothered him since the crossing; Jess Sweetser was in even worse shape. The sturdy Ivy Leaguer nearly collapsed during the practice round, but a last-minute withdrawal of his first-round opponent allowed him to spend a day in bed and regain his strength.

Ouimet edged Von Elm in a close second-round match, then came up against Sweetser in the third. Despite his advancing illness, Sweetser rallied to win their match on the eighteenth hole. Bobby drew an easy path through the first few rounds, his game gaining an edge as keen as Pop had ever seen. In the fourth round Bobby drew the reigning British Amateur champion, Robert Harris. It was the first time in the event's history — in either country — that a current American champ met his British counterpart head-to-head. In one of the commanding performances of his life, Bobby dispatched Harris in twelve holes, 8 and 6. Little doubt remained in experts' minds that Bobby would march through the rest of the field to win the title. He and Sweetser were the only Americans left in the semifinals.

Bobby felt unaccountably restless after winning his match with Harris. The weather had been unusually warm, and this far north so close to the summer solstice the sky remained light until eleven at night. Bobby left his window open and slept with only a sheet covering him; a chill wind crept in off the sea overnight, and he woke with muscle spasms and a severely stiff neck. He felt, and thought he heard, the left side of his neck "give a loud, rasping creak like a rusty hinge." He could barely lift his arms to his shoulders and seriously considered withdrawing from the tournament. Pop Keeler consulted with the hotel and they summoned a local physical therapist, who worked on Bobby for over an hour. Accounts about the results differ; Bobby claimed he felt loose enough afterward to at least go over to the course, hit a few shots, and make up his mind about playing, but he first made Pop promise not to say a word about the injury to anyone. Muirfield had no practice range, so Bobby hit a few balls in the eighteenth fairway and was soon called to the first tee; during that hundred-yard walk to the tee he made up his mind to play the match.

"It is the player's business to come to the tournament not only in proper practice insofar as his golf is concerned, but also in proper physical conditions. If I had failed in either respect, it was the fault of no one but myself. I would go out and do the best I could, so long as I could lift the club at all."

Bobby's opponent in the fifth round was a twenty-year-old from Glasgow named Andrew Jamieson, making his debut in the Amateur. He was a nervous, fragile lad, who rode his bicycle to the tournament every day from the nearby village where he was staying. Jamieson had spent three hours the night before working on the putting green with a brother who was caddying for him. Without question he was the lowest regarded golfer still in the tournament, the unlikeliest figure to knock Bobby out of the Amateur. Bobby never mentioned his physical problem as an excuse—he didn't even write a word about this difficulty in his first autobiography—and wouldn't bring it up at all until his final book, written half a lifetime later in 1958. But it was clear from the start that his injury made it impossible to swing freely or avoid flinching at impact. Still, Bobby at 60 percent was good enough to beat 95 percent of the men in any field; his reputation alone by this point was worth two strokes. Jamieson showed up wearing a novice's blinkers and cobbled together a cautious, risk-free round of thirteen pars and one birdie. Bobby didn't win a single hole from him. He felt his neck begin to loosen as the match advanced, and if they'd been playing thirty-six holes he probably would have felt enough improvement to mount a comeback. This was exactly the worst-case scenario he had dreaded going in: Andrew Jamieson, complete unknown, had ousted him, 4 and 3. Jamieson didn't stick around long; after losing in the semifinals that same afternoon the mild-mannered giant-killer climbed back on his bicycle and rode quietly out of town.

Bobby's devoted Scottish caddie, twenty-nine-year-old lantern-jawed Jack McIntyre, cried his eyes out after the match and pledged that his new boss would find him waiting on the tee a few weeks later at Royal Lytham & St. Anne's for the British Open. "I know he's the greatest of them all," said Jack. McIntyre's nickname among the caddying class was "Soldier" for his manner of slinging a club around under his arm like a rifle, but they might as well have been describing his fiercely loyal heart. Gunga Din would not have manned his post more faithfully. Bobby didn't have the heart to tell Jack when they parted that he was going home before the Open. Pop Keeler felt even worse. He walked out onto the links alone that evening among the tall gray dunes by the sea, listening to "the plaintive sound of those strange little birds called Pee-wits, from the cries they made. In all my life I have never heard anything as lonely as the cry of the Peewit in that long English twilight, nor was I ever so lonesome."

Alone in his room, Bobby got to thinking about his last early exit from a British tournament, five years earlier. He felt depressed and disappointed, but not angry. "And I didn't want people to think so. If I went home now it would look somewhat as if I were sulking. I had little hope of winning the British Open. No amateur had won it since 1897, five years before I was born. But I thought maybe I could make a decent showing. I was determined, no matter where I finished, that I'd not pick up this time. The British are a wonderful sporting people, and I wanted them to think kindly of me and to believe I could shoot a little golf."

He told Pop of his change of heart when Keeler returned from his rueful stroll, and Pop's spirits revived instantly. They spent the next twenty-four hours supporting Jess Sweetser, the last American in the Amateur draw; Pop functioned as his nurse. Jess had been carried to twenty-one holes before winning the semifinals, and sprained his wrist during the match. Pop wrapped his wrist and tried to treat his fever, but Jess rejected any suggestion he withdraw so close to the summit. Only able to down a few sips of orange juice, Sweetser marched out the next day to play the thirty-six-hole final match and defeated Scotsman Alfred Simpson, 6 and 5, to win the British Amateur championship. His teammates carried Jess, elated but on the brink of exhaustion, all the way back to the clubhouse. Walter Travis had found a worthy successor.

A remarkable scene followed in the hallowed chambers of Muirfield's clubhouse. This was the sacred home of the Honourable Company of Edinburgh Golfers, the oldest organization in golf—founded in 1744, a decade before the Royal and Ancient Golfing Society of St. Andrews—whose walls were covered with portraits of redcoated captains that predated the American Revolution. The club's members, some of them prominent British golf writers, stood by in wide-eyed amazement that night as the victorious Americans, filled with high spirits of both the emotional and distilled variety, broke into song. Francis led them through the repertoire they'd been working on since the crossing, tight harmonies echoing through halls that had never heard a note sung in its history. (Keeler called Francis and Jess Sweetser "occasional singers: they sing at every occasion.") Their formal hosts warmed to the idea that their distinguished forebears looking down from on high might not be spinning in their graves. By the end of the evening Ouimet and the boys were taking requests from some of the Honourable Golfers.

On the last day of May the team traveled eighty miles north by coach, around the Firth of Forth to St. Andrews, and checked into the Grand Hotel to prepare for the Walker Cup competition, which followed three days later. Pop spent his off day touring, and wrote a column about the dungeon of St. Andrews castle. Sufficiently recovered from his neck injury, Bobby reacquainted himself with the Old Course, looking at it with fresh eyes acquired during his winter's work with Tommy Armour. He began to grasp the genius of the place, and each successive round he played reinforced his conviction that here was the world's greatest test of golf.

One idle afternoon Pop, Bobby, and some of the other Americans paid a visit to the St. Andrews factory of legendary club maker Tom Stewart. In the aftermath of the East Lake fire, Bobby had cobbled together a set of mismatched clubs to replace those he'd lost; a handful turned out to be the products of Tom Stewart's forge. The son of a blacksmith, Stewart had been crafting irons for over thirty years. Entering the anonymous shop on Argyle Street from off an alley, identified by only a single sign, Bobby and Keeler witnessed "twenty hardy Scots toiling like a platoon of Vulcans in the forge room, sixteen more at the finishing wheels next door." Out of these grubby, cramped rooms emerged what those in the know considered to be the game's finest instruments. Old Tom Stewart seemed equally impressed with Bobby's knowledge of club design and mechanics; their meeting signaled the start of a significant relationship. Stewart provided Bobby with a duplicate set of clubheads before he left England—they wouldn't be fitted with shafts until he returned to East Lake—and continued to supply him for the next few years. Ouimet, Gunn, and Von Elm all ordered clubheads as well at a cost of $1.25 apiece, stamped with a small round dot signifying Stewart's personal seal of approval and his now legendary trademark, the silhouette of an old clay pipe.

The Walker Cup began on June 2. The entire town of St. Andrews shut down for the duration and over five thousand turned up to watch; Keeler thought it had the feel of a national holiday, which was close to the truth. In alternate-shot, two-ball foursomes in the morning Watts Gunn paired with Bobby and helped him gain revenge against Andrew Jamieson and his partner, the powerful Oxford man Cyril Tolley. Watts struck the decisive blow, an improbable 120-foot putt for birdie to win the thirteenth. The American team took three of the four foursome matches and a 3–1 lead. That afternoon the English struck back in singles, winning four of the first six matches and halving another. Only Bobby had an easy time of it, clobbering Cyril Tolley 12 and 11, with his finest burst of golf since arriving in Britain. It was left to George Von Elm to eke out a heroic half in the final match against a gigantic military man named Major Hezlet, which allowed America to retain the Walker Cup for the fourth straight time, 6½ to 5½, the narrowest victory in the event's history.

The teams marked the end of the event with a formal dinner that night, but Jess Sweetser excused himself early; after winning two matches in the cold winds at St. Andrews he appeared spent. At midnight Jess knocked on Pop's door, white as a sheet and holding a bloodstained handkerchief to his mouth;

he had suffered a severe lung hemorrhage. Doctors were summoned. They debated at length about whether Jess was fit to travel; he was gravely ill with tuberculosis. He took the news calmly but insisted on being allowed to return home; if he was going to die he didn't want to go on foreign soil. The team helped him onto the train the next day; Keeler shared his compartment. The doctors had prescribed morphine and gave instructions to Pop on how to inject him with it. When the Americans sailed home the following day, Francis took charge of Jess and saw him safely on board. He suffered another hemorrhage during the crossing; the British Amateur champion returned home as an invalid and was carried off the *Aquitania* in New York on a stretcher. He spent nearly a year recuperating in a sanatorium before he could resume work as a New York stockbroker.

Bobby and Pop took a long walk along the Thames marveling at some colorful Dickensian street urchins before they parted company. Bobby and Von Elm left that night for the Lytham & St. Anne's Club to begin their practice rounds for the Open; Pop made a side trip to Paris, taking with him the madcap Watts and another youngster from the Walker Cup team, eighteen-year-old Roland Mackenzie. "I don't envy you," said Bobby.

Keeler whizzed the boys around Paris for three days, the better part of one spent in the Louvre, where Watts was less than impressed with his first look at the Venus de Milo, but suggested that if she took up dancing the Charleston and lost a little weight she might be easier on the eyes. A night at the Moulin Rouge watching the cancan dancers proved more to Watts's liking. Pop enjoyed the show, too; he saved their ticket stubs in his scrapbook. Keeler snuck away from his young charges long enough to take a solitary tour of Notre Dame, snapping pictures of a gray Paris afternoon from up among the gargoyles and "feeling the spirits close at hand." The next morning they flew back to London in a sleek Handley-Page biplane, the only regular air passenger service between Paris and London. With everybody in England driving on the wrong side of the road, Watts felt safer in the air; he whooped and hollered as they bounced across the turbulent channel. Pop fortified himself with a pitcher of gin fizzes and gripped the arms of his wicker chair until he thought the bones would burst from his hands.

A second group of American golfers made the passage over on the *Aquitania*. Walter Hagen was captaining a team of top professionals coming to compete in the biennial international matches, the event's last edition before these matches officially became known as the Ryder Cup in 1927. Whether they were still groggy from the crossing or looking ahead to the Open, the American pros struck out against the British, who were captained by Ted Ray. The U.S. team lost 13½ to 1½—their most lopsided defeat in international competition. The victory helped soften the blow struck by Sweetser at the Amateur; press and public alike now reckoned the issue of which country held supremacy in the sport would be settled at the Open.

Bobby told Pop he had played "moderately well" at Lytham & St. Anne's before traveling to Sunningdale, Surrey, where his thirty-six-hole Open qualifier was scheduled. There were three regional qualifiers that year—in north, south, and central England—an R&A experiment, the first time qualifying rounds had been played away from the site of the Open. Fresh from their Paris sojourn, Pop Keeler and Watts joined Bobby there.

Considered Britain's finest heathland course, Sunningdale was set on gently rolling sandy terrain southwest of London. Sunningdale's beauty belies its demanding combination of precision and menace. Bobby befriended the resident professional, 1904's British Open winner Jack White, who presented him with a superbly crafted driver that he had named Jeanie Deans, after the heroine of a nineteenth-century Sir Walter Scott romance, *The Heart of Midlothian.* (The character is a supremely virtuous and self-sacrificing creature who saves her condemned sister's life by gaining the king's pardon.) Bobby appreciated the literary reference and fell in love with the club; he hadn't yet found a driver he liked to replace the one he'd lost in the East Lake fire. Jeanie Deans took her place in the bag beside Calamity Jane, a dignified Scottish redhead next to an Old West firecracker.

This was actually Calamity Jane II; Bobby had retired the first Jane a few months earlier. He had a good friend by the name of J. Victor East, an Australian pro who had emigrated to England with fellow Aussie Joe Kirkwood after the war. On Bobby's recommendation Victor ended up working as resident pro at the Vanderbilts' retreat in Asheville, North Carolina, the Biltmore Forest Country Club, where Bobby and Mary spent their honeymoon. Victor East had a touch of mad scientist in him and spent years tinkering with original ideas about how to improve golf clubs. Watching Bobby putt during a trip to Biltmore Forest, Victor became convinced that the face of the original

Calamity Jane had been warped by caddies applying an emery cloth to clean the blade after a round. Bobby refused to believe him until Victor set up a pendulum putting device he'd invented on a billiard table in the resort. He attached a regular putter to the machine and set it swinging, and ball after ball rolled right straight where he'd pointed it. After he hitched up Calamity Jane, the golf ball hooked dead left into the corner pocket. Bobby commissioned East to build him six replicas of Calamity Jane before he sailed to England. The original Jane was retired; Jane II was in his bag at Sunningdale when Bobby went out to qualify for the 1926 British Open.

It was June 18, a sunny, breezy, beautiful day. The course record at Sunningdale for competitive play was 70, par was 72. That morning, a powerful Welsh pro named Archie Compston lowered it a notch to 69. Bobby began his round at noon and proceeded to play the one single perfect ball-striking round of his entire life. He hit every fairway and green in regulation, save one—his only mistake of the day—a 175-yard par three where he got up and down from a bunker. He hit all four par five greens in two. This was no driver–wedge course; he was usually hitting a four iron or more to the greens. He shot 33 on the front and 33 on the back, six birdies, no bogies, for a record-shattering 66. He took 33 shots from the field, and 33 putts on the greens; Pop fantasized afterward what he might have done if Calamity Jane had been equal to Jeanie Deans and his irons. He missed two birdie putts of five feet or less, and holed only one over ten feet. The cheers went on long and loud after Bobby holed his last putt beneath the magnificent oak that frames the eighteenth green. Bernard Darwin wrote that the crowd looked awestruck, "realizing they had witnessed something they had never seen before and would never see again."

That night Bobby still felt keyed up after his round so he, Pop, Von Elm, and the gigantic Archie Compston took a long walk after dinner. They went out a rear gate of the Wheatsheaf Hotel, where they were staying in the town of Virginia Water, and walked toward a lake in nearby Windsor Park. After passing a lovely little waterfall, they followed a winding path near the shore, and as they neared the site of an ancient wharf came upon an astonishing sight: four large carved marble faces, beautiful, feminine, and severe, with serpentine hair like the locks of a Medusa. Battered by time, a curious repose in their old stone eyes, they stared eternally out across the shores of the quiet lake. They found faint inscriptions carved at the base of the columns, and between Bobby and

Pop's schoolboy Latin were able to decipher the text. The statues appeared to be an entreaty to the God of Love, from an adoring wife longing to have her husband returned to her. The man, a Roman officer in Caesar's army, had been sent to some distant land—Africa, they thought—and his wife had built this memorial to him over two thousand years before. This was her face, reproduced, eyes eternally trained to the southeast, waiting for sign of his return. The power of that testament to lost love felt timeless and utterly contemporary. Bobby had gone out that evening worrying that his record-breaking performance might be peaking too soon. The realization of what they had found moved the four men deeply and they walked back in silence, reaching the hotel just after midnight. His cares had dissipated: Bobby shot a 68 during his second time around Sunningdale the next day, ahead of every other qualifier for the 1926 British Open by seven shots.

After passing a rigorous inspection process that had begun in 1923, the Lytham & St. Anne's Golf Club was hosting its first Open. (The "Royal" prefix, which Lytham & St. Anne's now carries, is attached to a club that at any point in its existence has counted a principal from Great Britain's royal family among its membership.) Named after two nearby villages, it first opened for play in 1897 and was at inception a true links course from which you caught an occasional glimpse of the Irish Sea. Situated a few miles south of the Victorian seaside resort town of Blackpool and a mile inland, it had seen civilization steadily encroach on it, until by 1926 the course ran along a railway line in the middle of red-brick suburbia. There was beauty in the turf and true menace in the test offered by the course's superb green complexes and canted fairways. Among its eccentricities are an opening par three and back-to-back par fives on the front. Bernard Darwin called it "a beast, but a just beast."

This was also the first time the R&A charged admission for its Open championship—as they had weeks before at the Amateur—a change spurred by the unruly mob that had run amok at Prestwick the previous year. The plan was put into play to limit attendance and keep out the hooligans, but with Bobby in the field they sold over eleven thousand tickets each day. The championship began on Wednesday, June 23. Good as his word, caddie Jack McIntyre had paid his own way to St. Anne's to carry Bobby's bag; Bobby felt Jack's stalwart, Sancho Panza–like presence was as good as a four-leaf clover. Just as

THE AMERICANS ARE COMING | 259

they had at the Amateur, touts established Bobby as the early favorite at 6 to 1. By the time they teed it up and word of Bobby's qualifying performance had sunk in, the line on him had fallen to 3 to 1, the shortest odds on record for an Open. The weather held through all three days of play, just as it had at Sunningdale, one of those glorious streaks of sun during a dreary English summer. The wind stayed up and steady, prevailing off the ocean from the northwest, which rendered the shorter back nine the tougher passage. Thirteen Americans qualified: all four of the amateurs who had remained behind—Gunn, Mackenzie, Von Elm, and Bobby—and the entire professional team who had made the trip over.

Hagen led all qualifiers who played their way in at St. Anne's. Walter was fresh off a stunning victory in an exhibition over top British pro Abe Mitchell. Considered Britain's finest match-play golfer, Mitchell had earlier that year offered an open challenge to any American: one thousand pounds Sterling— about five thousand dollars—winner take all. Naturally Hagen was first to take him up on it; it was, in fact, his main reason for coming to England. After finishing the first day down four to Mitchell, the next morning Walter's chauffeur took him to the wrong golf course; after a navigational correction that included a frantic stretch of off-road driving, Hagen ate a leisurely breakfast, changed his shoes, shook a lot of hands, and showed up on the tee forty minutes late, scandalizing the punctual, well-mannered British fans, and purposefully messing with Mitchell's mind. In front of a huge partisan crowd, Hagen came back to clip Abe down the stretch and pocket one of the biggest checks of his life.

Still on a high from that win, Walter led the Open after the first round with a dazzling course record 68. Bobby wore the same sweater, shoes, and socks he'd had on at Sunningdale. "My sixty-six outfit," he told Pop. On this day he came up six strokes shy of that number and four strokes behind Hagen, alone in fifth place. He wore a different outfit the next day, but for the rest of the tournament carried around a smooth old English penny he'd won from J. H. Taylor, when he bet that Walter would make his last putt to break the record.

The wind swirled unpredictably on the second day. Hagen fell off during his second round with a 77. Bobby snuck past him with a steady 72, landing in a tie for the lead with fellow American Bill Mehlhorn, with Walter only a stroke behind. This looked like America's week as Yanks crowded the top of the leader board; the nearest British player, Archie Compston, sat all the way back in a tie for seventh. With no homegrown heroes to root for, the crowds lined up behind Bobby; Hagen's negative press after his shenanigans in the Mitchell match had earned him a black hat. If an American had to win their Open, the galleries made no secret that they preferred the modest, sportsmanlike amateur over the mercenary Hagen. They had already begun to perceive Bobby as more English than the English—well mannered, reserved, self-contained—while Walter was easy to cast as the soon-to-be-clichéd Ugly American. Oblivious to public opinion, Hagen was eager to make a good showing against Bobby in the only British Open the two men ever played together.

Bobby teed off at 9:00 a.m. Friday with a brawny twenty-six-year-old pro from Yonkers, New York, named Andrew Albert (Al) Watrous. A rising player at home, Watrous stunned the galleries that morning with a 69 to take the lead from his famous partner, who stood alone in second two strokes behind him. Fifty-six-year-old legend John Henry Taylor, the last of the Great Triumvirate still playing competitive golf, had announced this would be his last Open. He stirred the hearts of his countrymen that morning by shooting 71 and putting himself into the hunt. Hagen finished two strokes in back of Bobby and four off the lead, a sound position from which to close if he put together one of his finishing kicks. After a magnificent run in the third round, Von Elm sat a stroke in back of Hagen. These were the only men left with a chance at the 1926 Open.

When they finished their third round, Bobby saw Al staring in shock at the scoreboard, took him by the arm, and led the young pro back to the room he was sharing with Pop at the Majestic Hotel. Pop yanked the shades and ordered tea and cold ham sandwiches from room service while the two men lay on the twin beds and tried to rest; Bobby warned Watrous that whatever he did, "For God's sake, don't take a nap." According to Open tradition, a nap between rounds was fatal. They chatted fitfully. All Watrous could manage to eat was a single slice of ham. As they walked back to begin their final round an hour later, Pop heard Bobby tell Watrous: "Remember, Al, the winner and the runner-up are in this pair." Reaching the players' entrance Bobby realized he had left his identification badge on the dresser in his room, and the guard minding the gate, apparently fresh off the boat from another galaxy, didn't recognize him. Bobby refused to make a fuss, hurried around to the public entrance, and bought his way in with a ticket.

Bobby's old friend Al Laney, who had landed a job on the *New York Herald Tribune* and spent the last two years working from Paris, walked the third round following Bobby and Watrous and picked them up again that afternoon. The wind was whipping. Bobby had every part of his game working at peak efficiency, except Calamity Jane II. Jeanie Deans was finding the fairways, and his irons threatened every flag, but he didn't one-putt a single green all day. This was before sprinkler systems; with the greens dried and hardened by constant wind and sun, Bobby said it was like putting on ice. Watrous put his head down and played sturdy, determined golf, twice yielding half his lead to Bobby, but Jones gave it right back with three-putt greens. Both men played the front in even par. Starting an hour after them, Hagen made a move on the front nine and closed into a tie with Bobby. Watrous took back his two-stroke lead at thirteen with a solid par. The players and gallery walked to the next tee in heavy silence. Pop was so distraught he walked away for a while.

The rest of the round would be played dead into the wind. Although Pop missed most of it, other writers on hand felt that Bobby now put on the finest demonstration of skill from tee to green in his career. He parred the 455-yard fourteenth; showing the strain, Watrous took three putts and bogeyed, cutting his lead back to one. With the wind whipping their pants legs both men reached the 463-yard fifteenth in two, but again Watrous three-putted; the two Americans were tied for the lead with three holes to play.

After matching pars at sixteen, they stepped to the seventeenth: 462 yards, a slight dogleg left, the left side protected by a run of pot bunkers. Watrous hit a perfect drive down the right side, leaving an ideal angle to the green. After outdriving Al all day, Bobby came over the top and hooked it into the waste area down the left side. When they found his ball he'd salvaged a small piece of luck: it had avoided the deadly bunkers and come to rest cleanly on a firm patch of sand. Watrous was away and played a safe long iron to the front of the green. Upset at Bobby's impending defeat, Bernard Darwin remarked gloomily to a friend about what his successful approach might do for Watrous's career: "That shot may be worth $100,000." Meanwhile, Pop was back in the clubhouse bar, "taking in a liberal dose of antifreeze."

Bobby's ball was 175 yards out, all of it hazardous, not a foot of fairway between this spot and the hole. His view of the green was almost completely obscured by sand dunes, gorse, and heather. He had heard the crowd's reaction, knew that Watrous was on the green, and knew what he had to do in response. He walked to the fairway to get a look at the flag, then marched back and didn't hesitate. In moments like this, Bobby consciously slowed his languid backswing even more than usual, taking it back a notch farther to avoid the tendency to rush. Al Laney was standing close enough to see Bobby's face and said, "What I remember more acutely than the shot itself was how drawn and almost ill Bob's face appeared as he stepped into the sand and settled his feet." Bobby asked Jack McIntyre for his four iron; Laney noted that the similarity in lie and distance to the shot that had won him his first Open at Inwood in 1923 was uncanny.

This time he hit an even better shot. He nipped the ball cleanly off the sand; it barely cleared the dunes, then made straight for the flag like a sniper's bullet. Benefiting from the resistance of a stiff headwind, the ball landed on the front edge, bounced twice, and snaked to a stop ten feet inside of Watrous's ball. The crowd went mad.

The blood drained from Watrous's face as they walked to the green. When news spread to the clubhouse, Pop rushed out from the bar to the eighteenth green in time to see Watrous three-putt for the third time in the last four holes. Bobby got down in two for his par and took a one-stroke lead, his first of the tournament. He never glanced at Watrous, so fierce was his concentration on the next tee. He closed his final round with another par; Watrous gave away another stroke.

Bobby left the course in first place with a final score for the championship of 291, matching the Open's all-time low set by James Braid in 1908. But Hagen was still out on the course with six holes left and a chance to catch him. Bobby locked arms with Al Watrous and walked him into the clubhouse. They poured stiff drinks and waited for word. Rumors flew around them. Walter had finished his front nine two under par. He was mounting a charge on the back. Pop grew worried enough to start for the press room; on the way there a reporter informed him that Hagen had bogied twice down the stretch. Pop went right back into the clubhouse to shake Bobby's hand. Still, Hagen came to the final hole needing a par to tie Watrous for second place. Walter, it was widely known, had no interest in second.

While Bobby, Pop, and a hundred others watched from the clubhouse balcony, and thousands waited in the gallery, Hagen paced off his second shot from the middle of the fairway to the edge of the green and back again, over 150 yards; he made it melodramatically clear he was trying to drop his second shot in the hole for an eagle from the fairway, a last-ditch attempt to tie Bobby for the lead and force a play-off. Walter's caddie, also his valet and wearing a uniform color-coordinated with his boss's outfit, asked the official following their match to hold the flagstick. The man didn't understand. Walter marched closer to the green and shouted so that everyone around the green could hear: "I want you to hold the flag!" The man took hold of the flagstick with the gravity of an undertaker.

Hagen let the tension build, then took out his five iron and swung—time stood still while that ball was in the air—and almost pulled off a miracle; the ball landed less than a foot from the hole, jumped over it, and skipped into a flower bed behind the green. Bobby later told Walter he had to turn his back, unable to watch because he knew Hagen was just lucky enough to make a shot like that. With his chance gone, Walter took three more strokes for a diffident bogey, dropping into a tie for third with George Von Elm; it was his worst finish in a British Open in the last four he had played.

There's an urban legend quality to this account. Although it became a treasured anecdote in the lore of the game, Al Laney said he remembered Walter's final shot landing nowhere near that close to the hole. When decades later Laney finally got around to asking the Haig about it, Walter laughed and said: "Don't you remember, son? Never deny any story about yourself. I don't go around breaking down my image this late in life." Whatever the truth, the crowd around the eighteenth green that day cheered mightily when Hagen's shot went astray. This was no salute to Walter's histrionics; the man they loved to hate had fallen from contention. Bobby Jones had won the British Open, and he was the first champion who ever had to buy a ticket in order to play his final round.

Bobby stepped in off the balcony, and the clubhouse around him filled with the living history of the sport. The Great Triumvirate was there to shake his hand: Vardon, Braid, and Taylor, along with former champions Ted Ray and Sandy Herd and George Duncan and fifty-seven-year-old Harold Hilton, the last amateur to win the Open, in 1897. Pop calculated that at least forty national championships had crowded around his young friend, and they weren't acting all that British either, slapping him on the back, even hugging him. This was

Bobby's official welcome into the great fraternity of his sport. The balance of power, still a subject worthy of debate over the previous few years, forever shifted during that English summer. An American had won their Amateur for the first time and their Open for the fifth time in the last six years, but all these glorious champions of a passing age recognized that Bobby was a player who transcended nationality. He knew what a blow this was to their collective pride, yet there they were paying him gracious tribute. In his speech awarding the Claret Jug to Bobby shortly afterward, with tears running freely down his face, J. H. Taylor gave perfect voice to the sentiment that crowd was feeling. "We have just watched the greatest golfer in the game win the game's greatest prize."

Bobby never lost his dread of public speaking, but in these moments he was often at his best, shy, sincere, and emotionally vulnerable. He told the crowd, and all those assembled British champions, his greatest honor was simply adding his name to a trophy that already held so many who had done so much. Turning to Taylor, he paid tribute to the old warrior's third-round 71 and said it was "better than I could do." Hagen added a moment of lightness moments later by handing Bobby a comically oversized niblick, with a face the size of a shovel, saying: "If you ever get into another bunker, try this one." Walter then drove out of St. Anne's in his chauffeured convertible Rolls-Royce, tossing golf balls and tees to a crowd swarming around him; resent him they might, but it was hard not to love a man who could make an exit like that.

A Scottish writer asked Keeler if Bobby would be willing to donate the iron he'd used to strike that winning shot at seventeen to the club. Pop not only promised Bobby would hand it over, he volunteered to go collect it for them; that iron still hangs on the wall of Royal Lytham & St. Anne's clubhouse today. Not long afterward the membership added a plaque to the seventeenth fairway honoring the spot from where he'd struck his historic blow.

When Bobby and Keeler left their hotel in the early evening to begin the trip back to London, they stepped off the elevator and there was Bobby's faithful caddie, Jack McIntyre, come to say good-bye; but as he held out his hand and tried to speak the little speech he'd rehearsed, he couldn't get the words out. Bobby put an arm around his shoulders, and with his own voice faltering, told him: "Jack, old man, I'd never had done it without you."

Jack sat right down on the floor of the hotel lobby and sobbed like a baby.

Bobby and Pop made the fifty-mile drive to Liverpool through the "soft

English twilight" to catch a night train back to London, the two of them alone with the Claret Jug in the back of a cab. Both men later described this drive as the happiest hour of their lives.

"I think Bobby and I were not especially coherent on that ride," wrote Pop. "We sat up and grinned idiotically at each other frequently; and at times pounded one another on the back. And we talked a lot about what the folks at home were doing at that moment. That really was the best of all, thinking of the folks at home."

"When I see that old *Aquitania*," said Bobby, "I'm going to pick it right up in my arms and hug it."

During their final day in London, Bobby gave a series of interviews to the English papers that underscored his humility and sportsmanship. Walter Hagen, on the other hand, shot off parting remarks about the sorry state of British golf—the word "lazy" was mentioned—and spent the better part of a month trying to extract a size-twelve, two-tone saddle shoe from his mouth. British pros didn't have the luxury of abandoning their club positions to pursue freelance careers; no organized system of tournaments that would have allowed them to support themselves yet existed in Britain or Europe, and wouldn't for decades. Hagen's unflattering implication was that they lacked the initiative to create such a system themselves. Their fixed, inferior position in the British class system still made such a step impossible.

If Hagen thought the English lacked enterprise, he trailed them by a greater distance in graciousness. Bobby received a telegram at his hotel that day from Andrew Jamieson, the young amateur who had defeated him in the Amateur at Muirfield. It was in Latin, but Bobby and Pop deciphered it this way: "Congratulations from a small nobody who was impudent enough to beat you."

The next day, Sunday, June 27, Bobby, Pop, Hagen, and the rest of the American invaders boarded the *Aquitania* and set sail for home. A hundred cabled messages of congratulations were waiting in his cabin for the champion. By the time they reached New York, the American players had been gone for nearly two months. A relentless schedule of celebrations on board gave Bobby a chance to regain the pounds he'd dropped at St. Anne's, but precious little time to get the rest he needed.

There would be even less after they arrived. The U.S. Open was scheduled to begin in two weeks.

Francis Ouimet and Bob.

*Bob and Von Elm
at Baltusrol.*

CHAPTER TEN

The Double

As THE *AQUITANIA* PASSED through the Verrazano Narrows into New York Harbor, the city's municipal steamer, a small packet ship called the *Macom*, sailed toward them. Pop called Bobby up on deck for a wonderful surprise. Close to a hundred friends and family had made the trip to New York and sailed out on the *Macom* to welcome him home: Mary, both his parents, even his crusty old grandfather, R.T., who claimed to already be in town on business; God forbid he make a special trip for such frivolity. (The old man had just imported Chinese silkworms to his textile factory in Canton, Georgia, and doubled his fortune by becoming one of the first domestic producers of the exotic fabric.) Also among the welcoming committee was Pop's boss, owner of the *Atlanta Journal*, a senator or two, over forty reporters and photographers, and a band playing "Dixie" as they pulled alongside. The *Aquitania* came to a stop while Bobby and company went on board the *Macom* and were taken to Pier A on the Battery. Everyone in the city knew he was coming: ships saluted him with their whistles and horns, a fireboat trailed them spraying water like the Tivoli fountain.

A wall of newsreel cameras greeted Bobby as he stepped off the gangway. The party was waived through customs, a privilege reserved for visiting royalty, and thousands cheered as they climbed into open cars and began a three-mile trip toward the heart of the city. With their sea legs still wobbly beneath them, they got out to walk behind a succession of marching bands when they reached Broadway as a phalanx of motorcycle cops cleared the way, sirens blaring. "Ticker tape flying in white spirals from the skyscrapers, and a continuous road echoing like thunder through the canyon of downtown New York," wrote Pop. He estimated a million people lined the parade route to city hall, and that as they walked along Bobby looked like "an embarrassed, happy little boy." Although the city had thrown something similar for Hagen after his first British Open win, it didn't begin to approach the scale of this reception. No single individual had ever received anything like this procession through what would become known as the Canyon of Heroes.

New York's flamboyant playboy mayor Jimmy Walker gave a speech on the steps of city hall that was broadcast live on radio. Visibly overwhelmed, Bobby added a few simple words before cheers began anew. In newsreel footage, Hagen stands among the dignitaries beside him and looks infinitely more at home basking in all the attention, which wasn't even directed toward him. Bobby and Mary couldn't steal a moment alone together until they checked into the Vanderbilt in mid-afternoon, where a gala dinner was held in his honor that night. Attendees remarked that their guest of honor had a solemn look on his face throughout the evening. Keeler chalked it up to exhaustion, but Bobby felt dazed and disoriented.

He couldn't put a name to it yet, but Bobby was experiencing the strange alchemy of transformation from a local hero into an utterly famous household name. He didn't belong to just Atlanta or Georgia or even the game of golf anymore; now the whole country laid claim to him. He wasn't an actor; the public wasn't responding to a role he was playing, or to a politician peddling some brand of charismatic flimflam. Bobby was exactly who and what he appeared to be. The elegant way in which this young man played an incredibly difficult sport without expectation or reward of a single red cent in return appealed to people in a way no athlete had ever done before. Ouimet had put golf on the map and Hagen had created the game's first larger-than-life personality; Bobby was the first American to transcend his sport in a way we would recognize today as a superstar. Bobby was hot; he was cool. He was like us, only better. The air around him felt charged with the dreams of millions of strangers, but his modesty made him still seem as approachable as the kid next door; after being humbled by his struggles with the game, none of his success seemed to have affected his hat size. This was a dynamite combination, and the hysteria in New York was only a taste of what life had in store. Pop described the entire experience of that day as "stepping off the *Aquitania* and into one of the Arabian Nights."

The glare of the spotlight spilled over onto everyone close to Bobby, particularly Mary. Romance magazines wrote about their marriage; fashion magazines wanted to photograph her clothes and their home. Mary knew she had married a man on a mission, but until their tumultuous welcome had never realized that from this moment forward she would have to share her husband with the multitudes in ways no bride in her right mind would have imagined. Huge life decisions hung in the balance. The next day Bobby and Mary boarded a westbound train together, along with his parents and Pop, bound for Columbus, Ohio, and Scioto Country Club. During the trip Bobby sat down with the Colonel and discussed his leaving the Adairs' real estate business and entering the law.

Six hundred ninety-four players attempted to qualify for the 1926 U.S. Open, requiring seventeen sectional events, both record numbers. One hundred forty-five survived the cut and would tee it up at Scioto; the more than one hundred credentialed reporters who flocked to the Midwest to cover the event were interested in exactly one of them. Bobby's landmark win in England had touched off an avalanche of interest. No golfer, of any nationality, amateur or professional, had ever won both the British and United States Opens in the same year. He was about to try to turn the trick within three weeks.

Scioto was a Donald Ross design, just over a decade old and already considered one of his better efforts. The club's head pro was forty-six-year-old George Sargent, a founding father of the PGA who had been Ouimet's playing partner during his final rounds in the 1913 Open. As players arrived in town so did a heat wave and a rigid band of high humidity. When practice began on Monday, Sargent told the press to expect high scores; a monthlong drought had left both fairways and greens hard and unforgiving, but the rough he'd cultivated had somehow flourished. Jock Hutchison told Keeler he had lost a ball in the stuff, dropped another and lost that one, and when he went to look for that one he lost his caddie. The city of Columbus sent over emergency water wagons to spray down scorched areas of the fairways. During the middle of

Bobby's practice round on Tuesday a thunderstorm blew in off the Great Lakes and chased everyone off the course, canceling the scheduled pro-am event. Bobby didn't mind; he needed rest more than practice.

He might have appeared sharp to the undiscerning eye, but to Pop he looked "stale, jaded and dull." Bobby told Pop that after two months of steady pressure and constant travel he was used up and longed to be home. Just before his tee time on Thursday morning he said something Pop had never heard from him before: "I wish this was over."

Then Bobby went out to play his first round, breathed in the electricity and adrenaline crackling in the championship atmosphere, and shot 70. The assembled reporters, many of them newcomers to golf who had been sent to cover Bobby as a general news story, fell all over themselves. "The perfect golfing machine at work" summed up the sentiment in dozens of stories. Bobby and Pop knew differently; this had been a sweating, grinding piece of work that further exhausted him. Pop watched him slump to the showers, his shoulders broken out in heat rash; Bobby leaned his wet head on Pop's shoulder and asked with only half a laugh: "Why can't I play this damn game?"

But that 70 left him in second place, two strokes off the lead behind Wild Bill Mehlhorn. The son of an immigrant German bricklayer who once plied that trade himself, Mehlhorn had established himself as one of the decade's toughest pros. Bobby spent a restless night; Grantland Rice encountered him before the second round and was shocked at how exhausted he looked. That morning Bobby couldn't sustain his high-wire act. Where he had caught good breaks and bounces the day before, this time they went against him. He was forced to take a penalty stroke at ten to gain relief from a stone wall next to a water hazard. He rallied, briefly, until he reached fifteen. He was playing in a steady wind, and after grounding his putter in front of his ball to square his line, he moved it behind the ball to begin his takeaway and the exposed ball wobbled and turned over. Once again, no one else saw it move. Once again Bobby called a penalty stroke on himself; once again he expressed dismay that people should compliment him for following the rules.

He was barely hanging on by the time he reached eighteen, a reachable par five birdie opportunity; he needed one to finish with 76. After pushing his drive into the right-hand rough Bobby tried to make up the day's sins with an overly aggressive swing that came in too steeply; the hosel of his two iron snagged in the grass and the ball advanced twenty feet. Annoyed at himself, he swung again without changing clubs and hooked the ball into light rough on the opposite side of the fairway. His pitch to the green came up short. A chip from there left him a five-foot putt. He rushed it, and missed it, and took double-bogey seven for 79, his highest single-round score ever in a U.S. Open. At the halfway point Bobby trailed Mehlhorn by six strokes, four shots behind a twenty-five-year-old pro from Elmsford, New York, named Joe Turnesa. His father, a Neapolitan immigrant named Vitale Turnesa, had sailed to America at the age of fourteen in 1875. After knocking around New York for twenty years as a manual laborer, Vitale heard about possible work at a golf course being built in Westchester County and walked twenty-six miles from Manhattan to get there. The course turned out to be Fairview Country Club, where Vitale caught on and later became head greenkeeper. He and his wife raised seven sons at Fairview, all of whom grew up caddying and, to their father's dismay, fell in love with the game Vitale considered a frivolous waste of time. All but one of the seven Turnesa boys turned pro, and he might have been the best player in the bunch. But Joe was the first brother to make an impact on the national scene, and Scioto was his coming-out party. When his father, who still didn't approve of his profession, was told the next day that Joe was in the lead in the final round of the Open, Vitale responded: "He damn well should be. All he ever does is play golf!"

The USGA had changed the format that year, extending play to three days, with the final two rounds played on the last day of competition. The field was trimmed after the second round to the top fifty players and ties. The added box office helped increase the prize money; the purse had grown to $2,145, with the top twenty players finishing in the money. First place earned you a check for $500, unless you were Bobby Jones.

Bobby felt disgusted by Friday's performance, particularly the final hole, where he had lapsed into the kind of juvenile mistakes he thought he'd put behind him. Mary and his parents worried that Bobby was driving himself close to collapse. When he woke Saturday morning, Bobby was violently ill, vomiting repeatedly. Pop rushed him to a local doctor's house at 7:00 a.m. Dr. Earl Ryan couldn't diagnose the problem precisely—it was symptomatic of exhaustion, but he wasn't about to tell Bobby Jones not to play the last rounds of the Open—and gave him something to settle his stomach. Refusing payment or free tickets, Dr. Ryan said he was coming out to watch the last rounds and asked Bobby only for a ball he used that day. Returning to Scioto, Bobby summoned his best golf of the week, an error-free third round of 71. He picked up a stroke on Joe Turnesa, trailing him by three in third place, behind Wild Bill Mehlhorn by one shot. Bobby rested in the clubhouse between rounds and tried to eat a light lunch of tea and toast but couldn't keep anything down despite the medication. He would have to play the Open's final round on borrowed energy, a bad stomach, and wobbly legs.

The wind picked up, heralding the approach of another Great Lakes blow. Rain fell in spurts. Mehlhorn fell out of contention quickly, creating a two-man race. Turnesa teed off two groups ahead of Bobby, but two-thirds of the crowd was in Jones's gallery. Following him all week at Scioto was a teenage drugstore clerk named Charlie Nicklaus who idolized Bobby. Two decades later, raising his son Jack on the fairways of Scioto, where he was now a member, Charlie held up Bobby as the game's ideal both on and off the course. Jack never found a bigger hero in the sport.

Joe Turnesa was an unflappable character and didn't seem to mind playing with the lead. They played the first eight holes dead even with each other and the scorecard. On the short par three ninth, protected by a large tree overhanging the right side of the green, Bobby made his first mistake for bogey while Turnesa got his par. Joe's lead increased to four, with nine holes left to play.

Bobby could keep track of Turnesa just by listening to the reactions of his gallery. Joe parred the tenth and the eleventh. Bobby matched him. But as Bobby teed off on twelve, Turnesa tried to gamble at the par five thirteenth; he went for the green in two, but playing into the wind came up a bounce short and got caught in the high grass. An aggressive gamble at this stage of the tournament, it ended up costing him a six. By the time Bobby reached twelve he knew Joe had given back a stroke; now he went all out to grab another one from him. His drive was long and low, shearing like a clipper into the wind. His second cleared the patch of rough that had trapped Turnesa and kicked onto the front fringe of the green. A simple chip and putt and he had his birdie.

Turnesa's lead had been trimmed to two. A sudden absence of wind cost him another stroke at the 445-yard thirteenth, when it failed to move his approach off line as he'd intended and found a greenside bunker. Another bogey.

Bobby's second shot ran into a bunker on the other side, pin high. But the bunker had a low lip, and Bobby elected to putt the ball out. That got him to within four feet and Calamity Jane saved his par. The roar that went up reached Turnesa on the fifteenth tee. He realized his lead over Bobby was down to a single stroke.

They matched pars on the next two holes. At sixteen, Turnesa bounced his approach through the green and left his chip short coming back. He missed a nine-foot putt for par. Bobby capitalized, recording a routine four: they were tied. On the par three seventeenth Turnesa betrayed his only sign of tension all day; short with his tee shot, short with his chip, and just like that another bogey. When Bobby came through and collected his three he had his first lead of the tournament.

It lasted all of thirty seconds. Just ahead, playing the par five eighteenth, aware he needed a birdie to stay even with Jones, Turnesa went for the green in two and pushed into the rough. But his pitch from there was nearly perfect, leaving him an eight-footer for birdie. He sank the putt for four. The roar reached all the way back to the eighteenth tee.

Tied for the lead.

He looked focused and strong to the seasoned observers crowding around him, but only Bobby knew how deeply the exhaustion had wormed into his bones. He felt nauseated and weak and hadn't eaten a bite of food all day. He'd burned off the twelve pounds he'd regained on the *Aquitania* and then some. Another eighteen-hole play-off the next day might just finish him; he knew he didn't have the strength to win one in his weakened state. He'd lost two Open play-offs in the last three years when he was on top of his game. Today, sick as he was at this moment, offered his best and only chance.

Winning the Double Open, history, was in his grasp. All he had to do was match Turnesa's birdie at eighteen and he could close his hand around it.

Into that whistling crosswind, Bobby smashed a 310-yard drive that split the seam of the narrow winding fairway. Some estimates claim it was even longer; Pop paced it off to be certain. Pop said the only sound you could hear among the crowd of ten thousand as Bobby reached his ball was the racket of typewriters from the clubhouse roof; reporters had been stationed up there all week to watch the action. Even the typewriters stopped as Bobby ripped another fateful mid-iron on the Open's final hole. His knees were shaking as he swung; they nearly buckled as he walked after it.

The crowd began cheering before the ball reached the green, then exploded as it touched down on the front edge and rolled twenty feet right past the flag. Bobby lagged his eagle putt to within four inches. Four inches left to win the Open. His mind played tricks on him over the ball, the imp of the perverse taunting him to stub his putter on the ground and whiff. Ha-ha! Bobby clamped down those thoughts, held the putter a half inch off the grass, and tapped the ball home for the win.

Double Open champion. Pandemonium broke out around him, and it stayed that way for a while.

But the celebration was slightly premature; there were still two players on the course with theoretical chances to catch him. Bobby dragged himself out of range of all the well-wishers and backslappers—remembering to slip the last ball he'd used to Dr. Earl Ryan along the way—and staggered back to his hotel room. His father found him outside, clamped both hands on his shoulders, and told him: "It doesn't matter if you win now; what matters is that you finished at all, and finished the way you did."

"Thank you, Dad," he said.

When Bobby reached his hotel room his mother, Clara, was already there, packing his suitcases. He filled her in on the round as he poured himself a highball with his hands shaking so hard he could barely hold the glass. Then he slumped into a chair, and burst into shuddering, convulsive sobs.

All the strain and tension of the last three months lived in the glare of that spotlight. All the uncertainty of his real life in such stark contrast to the "conquering hero" of the newsreels. Empty, bewildered, lost. He was twenty-four, soon to be a father of two, between careers, and short of cash. An idol to the nation in a sport from which, as a matter of principle, he had firmly decided he would derive no financial reward. Adored by uncomprehending thousands still celebrating less than a hundred yards away, and millions around the world. As far as Bobby could remember it was the only time in his life he'd ever broken down like this, at the exact moment of his greatest triumph and the most remarkable achievement in the history of golf. In front of his own mother, no less. If he could only stop bawling his eyes out for a second he'd burst out laughing.

Clara took a long, puzzled look at him. Not the warm, cuddly type, she had always been the backbone and disciplinarian in the family, keeping Bobby on the straight and narrow while the Colonel stayed his pal. The sight of her only son falling apart didn't make any sense, and she pressed him on it. This was supposed to be his idea of fun, wasn't it? That's why he did this, isn't that right, Bobby? He couldn't even answer her.

"Well," said Clara finally, "I think that's about enough championship golf for you."

The larger question he was confronting, when Bobby could get his mind around it, was simple, and every person comes to it at some time or another in life. He nearly killed himself to win these damn things, and now that he'd finally done it, all he could ask himself was: *Is that all there is?*

The phone rang. It was Pop calling from the clubhouse with confirmation: By the way, you've won the Open. Come and get it.

An equally dramatic scene was unfolding in Scioto's locker room. Walter Hagen had played poorly in the Open; he finished a distant sixth and had never been a factor. That didn't stop him from marching in after it was over and lashing out at his fellow pros as they were packing up to leave.

"Whenever I fail to stop Jones the rest of you curl up and die, too. All that goddamn amateur has to do is show on the first tee and the best pros in the world throw in the towel. If we don't stop him he's going to walk all over us." Dead silence. "Well, I'm going to ask you all this: What are we going to do about it? It's about time we stand our ground!" Then he stomped back outside to pose for pictures and sign autographs.

Bobby pulled himself together and walked back down to the eighteenth green. He put on a weary smile but told USGA officials he preferred to just collect the trophy and not give a speech; he was afraid he might break down all over again. When officials saw his ashen face no one put up any objection. Fresh from his private rant against him in the locker room, Hagen stepped in and offered Bobby a gracious public congratulation.

The champ held the cup for photographers while the cheers began again. He'd never been part of a more incongruous moment; torn to shreds inside, a champion, standing alone on a mountaintop no one had ever reached before. Not one of those ten thousand people looking on ever questioned for one second how lucky they were, how happy it made them feel, to be if only for a fleeting moment in the presence of a god.

BOBBY'S BRINGING HOME THE BACON.

That was the banner headline waiting for him in Atlanta. His two Open trophies, Claret Jug and silver cup, rode on the back of a flatbed truck, together for the first time, as the parade wound through downtown and ended at the Atlanta Athletic Club's posh new headquarters. Pop's eyes filled with tears at the sight of that crowd; he described in his column how hard it was to get tired of these affairs. But Bobby was tired, period. Tired of golf, tired of traveling, tired of being on constant display, knowing the demands on his time and attention would only get worse.

For the first time in his career, Bobby felt compelled to give Pop an "official interview" for national syndication, to satisfy the public's hunger for insights into "Bobby Jones." Just as he and Pop had always been able to discuss his swing and golf game as if it belonged to some neutral third party, they now began to think of his public image as a creation distinct and separate from himself. The interview reads as exactly what it was, a friendly chat between two old pals over a couple of cocktails.

Bobby attributes his success to luck—principally, the luck of growing up next to East Lake and the presence of Kiltie. (The word "fate" is never mentioned; Keeler felt it might come across as too deep dish for broad consumption.) When prompted, Bobby talks about technique, reluctantly, but it's clear how deep and precise his thinking about the golf swing had become. The self-deprecation he displays in describing his game never reads as false modesty; his faults still pained him and he despaired of ridding himself of them. He uses the words "wretched" or "terrible" more often than any superlatives. When Pop brings up the great shots that had won championships and were starting to crowd his resume, Bobby can recall thinking about what he wanted to do as he assessed a situation, but "that was before I swung. I didn't think of anything consciously while I was swinging." All he could remember about the winning shot at Inwood was looking up and seeing the ball outlined in the sky against a black cloud.

His most revealing comments come on the subject of nerves. "I do not think nervousness hurts my game. The more nervous I am, the better I play, usually. I suppose it means being keyed up. Some of the sloppiest rounds I have played, I wasn't nervous at all. As to the strain, I don't seem to be conscious of it during a round. Afterward—well, I know something has been done to me." He insists you have to be nervous to play golf well, the one quality that made certain you wouldn't play a mediocre round. The man who could keep himself on edge was a hard man to beat.

"Nerves are what differentiate a thoroughbred from a plough horse," he says.

Despite which, Bobby also mentions that he's trying lately to learn how to relax between shots, chatting with his partner or some friend in the gallery—usually Pop—to relieve the tension. "Then when I get to the ball I can snap on the concentration as hard as I need to."

When Keeler tries to bring up the subject of the penalty shots, Bobby feels an invitation to moral flattery approaching and holds up a warning hand. "There is absolutely nothing to talk about," he says, "and you are not to write about it. There is only one way to play this game."

Pop decided to risk violating Bobby's confidence, and used that line to close the interview.

His ethical rigor on the course would continue, but there would be no more uphill fighting on the private side. The decision had been made between Scioto and home that in the fall Bobby would attend Emory University's law school in Atlanta, the finest program of its kind in the South. The choice of Emory seems dictated by an overwhelming desire to spend time close to home, but the Colonel grilled him about the bigger decision: Was Bobby sure about the law? He said he was. The mental challenge, the precise rigor of the language, the clean crease between right and wrong, all felt like a tonic to the life he'd been living. And after Emory's three-year program, once Bobby passed the bar he knew a desk would be waiting for him at the firm known as Jones, Evins, Moore & Powers. The Colonel's fondest lifelong wish had come to pass.

In August Bobby traveled to Sarasota for a vacation with Keeler and his father. They went fishing, socialized, and relaxed, and had almost nothing to do with golf. Sarasota organized a small parade in Bobby's honor, then presented him with a brand-new Pierce-Arrow touring car in gratitude for his contribution to the growth of the city. After checking carefully with the USGA and being assured that accepting the gift wouldn't violate his amateur status, Bobby decided to keep the car, and drove home in it.

Bobby picked up his sticks again in August and began preparing for the season's final test. The 1926 Amateur Championship was held at Baltusrol Golf Club, in Springfield, New Jersey. Founded in 1895 by the publisher of New York's Social Register on a large spread of farmland at the base of Baltusrol Mountain—it had once belonged to a farmer named Baltus Roll, until he was murdered in 1825—the club had played host to two Opens and an Amateur. After the 1915 Open, adjoining land was purchased and members brought in architect A. W. Tillinghast to construct two entirely new courses, but no other amenities: this was a *golf* club, not a country club. Completed in 1920, the Upper and Lower courses enjoyed equally strong reputations; both would host future championships, including four more Opens, but the 1926 Amateur was the first major to be played on either.

For the first time the USGA introduced the concept of seeding the top amateurs, and Bobby claimed the first spot. Behind him came Jess Sweetser, still recuperating from tuberculosis and unable to play, then George Von Elm, Francis Ouimet, and Chick Evans. Bobby arrived with a chance to become the first man ever to win three Amateur championships in a row, and to match Chick Evans's 1916 Open-Amateur double in the bargain. Qualifying began on September 13, and Bobby won the medal at one over par, a shot off the Amateur record. Seeding determined brackets for the top thirty-two survivors, who would play two eighteen-hole matches on Wednesday. The final three matches leading to the championship, all thirty-six-hole affairs, would follow on Thursday, Friday, and Saturday.

Bobby breezed through both of Wednesday's matches without incident. On Thursday, in his first thirty-six-hole match, he met Chick Evans. The two hadn't played each other in a tournament for six years, since Chick had psyched him out at the Western Amateur in Memphis. Chick did an unseemly amount of crowing at the time; then only eighteen, Bobby had vowed to even the score. Chick had now gone six years without a national title, while Bobby had become the king of the game. Although as friendly as ever to Bobby's face, the envy rose off Chick like a vapor and Bobby saw no reason to let his advancing dislike of the man stand in the way of beating his brains out. Bobby opened a two-hole lead after the first eighteen, but Chick stuck close and Bobby was tempted to fight him head-to-head. But he kept to his disciplined approach, Chick cracked on the final nine, and Bobby finished him off at their thirty-fourth hole, 3 and 2.

Friday morning's semifinal brought Bobby together again with Francis Ouimet. Francis had barely qualified, squeaking in through a play-off, but his game had come back to life since his poor showing against Bobby at Merion two years before. Both played a superb first round, Ouimet at even par, no easy achievement at Baltusrol. Bobby shot three under, which on this course seemed superhuman. After lunch together the two friends went back to battle in the afternoon; Francis opened with an eagle to get within two, and closed out the front nine with a phenomenal 34. Bobby shot 33 and stretched his lead to four. Francis parred the next four holes, and lost the match, 5 and 4. Because they so enjoyed playing with each other, they finished the round together and hardly a soul in the gallery deserted them. Francis shot 69, a stroke off the new club record 68, which had just been turned in by his opponent, Mr. Jones. Francis could only shake his head and laugh.

Saturday's final brought Bobby up against that bristling Californian fashion plate George Von Elm. After spending the summer in Great Britain together the two men were getting on each other's nerves. Von Elm felt he had established himself as the country's second best amateur—he was right; even Hagen said he was the only other nonpro who ever worried him—but the gulf between Bobby Jones and second place was so vast Von Elm felt permanently slighted. As a regional champion George ruled California, but without any major titles that hadn't translated to national respect, the same provincialism that colored Midwesterner Chick Evans's attitude toward the Eastern establishment. Both men always forgot that, as an outsider coming from the South, Bobby had faced far more innate prejudice at the start of his career than either one of them. He was simply a better player, something neither Evans nor Von Elm was ever willing to concede. He was more socially adept, less egotistical, and a more pleasant person to be around. Chick's high-energy boosterism and hunger for approval could prove wearying, and Von Elm bristled with Prussian disdain; all that was missing was a monocle and a dueling scar. His rivals often seemed perplexed by Bobby's regard for their feelings, none more so than Von Elm. Although Bobby made repeated efforts to be friendly with him as a fellow competitor, Von Elm's resentment of his greater stature continued to grow. This would be their third match in the last three Amateurs. Given that both of Bobby's previous wins had been lopsided, everyone expected him to trounce George again; everyone except Bobby. He'd seen too much of this tough-minded son of a bitch's game. On their way to the course that morning, Bobby told Pop: "Nobody's going to keep beating a golfer as good as George Von Elm."

Von Elm sat glowering on a bench at the first tee waiting for Jones to arrive. He brushed off reporters with a snarl and refused to pose with Bobby for photographs. Both men were at the peak of their games. Both had a personal stake in beating the other. Von Elm stood between Bobby and a trophy case of previously unapproachable records: three Amateurs in a row, the Open-Amateur Double, and three major victories in the same calendar year, which sportswriters had started to call "the Triple Crown." Bobby stood between Von Elm and the legitimacy he craved. Pop called it one of the best and hardest matches ever played in the history of the Amateur.

They were dead even through sixteen, both playing even par golf. On the seventeenth green, after Bobby missed a long birdie attempt and sank a tough comebacker for par, the huge gallery rushed ahead to the next tee. But Von Elm still faced a tough six-footer for par to halve the hole, and he stepped away from his ball when the gallery made its move, visibly upset. As Bobby described later, "I don't know exactly what prompted me to do it, but I felt that there was no way to stop the crowd and that it was definitely unfair for Von Elm to have to putt with all the commotion going on." Bobby walked over and knocked Von Elm's ball toward him, saying: "I'll give you that one, George." George thanked him as they walked on to the next hole. On the next green, Von Elm returned the favor; while Bobby was studying a four-footer, Von Elm picked the ball up and stuffed it in Jones's pocket, halving that hole as well. Their referee, Bill Fownes, called them together as they left the green and said: "Now listen, boys, this Alphonse and Gaston stuff has gone on long enough. Let's play golf." In the best amateur tradition, their private feelings about each other were not going to get in the way of sportsmanship.

Von Elm played relentless golf over the second eighteen that afternoon; he never faltered. Bobby appeared to have slipped past his peak, but never gave up. George opened up a two-hole lead—the only one either had been able to build all day—as they reached their thirty-fifth hole. A par five, over six hundred yards in length, it was the longest hole in the history of USGA competition. Bobby hit his drive in the rough. After advancing it back to the fairway he tried to land a knockout punch while practically lying on his back, and nearly holed his third shot from 170 yards, but the ball rolled twenty feet past the flag. When he missed his birdie putt and both men settled for par, the match was over, 2 and 1. Bobby had shot one over par for thirty-five holes but his reach for history had been turned away by Von Elm's steady brilliance, and for the first time an American golf title belonged to a man from west of the Mississippi.

Pop later wrote: "Of all his championships, I loved him best in that long and losing battle."

Bobby offered no excuses, and gave Von Elm credit for the win he deserved. "It was George's turn," he said. Visibly relieved, Von Elm collected the new, restored Havemeyer Trophy and appeared to have gained the respect he needed, but the feeling was short-lived; most of the next day's newspapers blamed the result on subpar golf by Bobby, rather than George's masterful one-under-par performance. He realized it would take more than one win over Jones to earn him a place beside him up on the pedestal.

Two weeks later Bobby traded his clubs for law books and began his first term at Emory University. That same week he learned that the Royal and Ancient of St. Andrews had named him an honorary member for his win in their Open. Bobby accepted proudly, but announced with regret that because of his studies he would be unable to travel overseas the following summer to defend his British Open title. There would soon be more distractions: Bobby and Mary's second child, Robert Tyre Jones III, was born less than two months later.

The greatest year anyone had ever played in golf was over. It was impossible to imagine a player could ever match it, let alone surpass it. And for the first time in history, all four of the game's major titles belonged to American-born players: Sweetser, Jones, and Von Elm.

As Bobby turned his hand to the building blocks of a future career that winter, in the back of his mind an impossible thought began to take shape. Something had been missing in his matches at Baltusrol, particularly in the finals against Von Elm; for the first time in any national championship he hadn't felt nervous. He told Pop about this alarming loss of competitive edge, but privately interpreted it as a sign that the time was coming, sooner rather than later, for him to move on in life. He began to look for a way out of golf, one that would both satisfy his ambition and allow him an exit with his dignity intact that no one would argue with.

And then it came to him: What if all four major titles could be won in the same year . . . by the *same* American-born player?

Bob at Minikahda, 1927.

CHAPTER ELEVEN

Consolidation

BOBBY SET THE GAME aside that fall and well into the winter of 1927; his course load was simply too demanding for the other kind of course work he was more accustomed to. He played only two and a half rounds of golf between November and late February. The layoff didn't seem to hurt his game; during one of his earliest spring rounds, with Kiltie at East Lake, Bobby scored the first hole in one of his life. Pure luck, he called it. A month later he won the Southern Open, played at East Lake against a field of the game's best professionals and amateurs, by eight strokes. The longer he played, the luckier he got.

There's no record of the two men ever settling the bet they'd made after their Battle of the Century in Florida, but Walter Hagen owed Bobby Jones a hat. Bobby had outplayed him in the two Opens and their qualifiers by a total of eighteen strokes. Hagen finished the professional season by winning his third PGA Championship in a row, then embarked on another lucrative exhibition tour. But while Bobby was establishing a new domestic routine in Atlanta with Mary and their two kids, Walter's second marriage ended up on the skids. Edna Strauss Hagen filed for divorce in April of 1927, accusing her husband of abandonment. Given the amount of time Hagen spent on the road it was a difficult charge to dispute, but Walter turned around and charged Edna with abandoning him. There's no question that Hagen was by nature about as faithful as a free-range rabbit, but that issue never came up during the proceedings. Although it would take years to finalize the divorce, Hagen had come to grips with his essential wandering nature and remained a solo act for the rest of his life.

During a decade of exclusivity, Bobby had used Pop as a shield from the inquiring national press; Pop in return received unfettered access to the private thoughts of his friend and became a respected national sportswriter. Along the way a lot of journalistic feathers got ruffled. A false perception had started to form that Bobby considered himself to be bigger than the game. The resentment directed toward him from professionals like Hagen was well documented, although underpublicized by reporters maintaining the day's looser journalistic standards. In 1927 some of Bobby's fellow amateurs—principally Chick Evans and George Von Elm—started to get into the act.

Evans and Von Elm believed that the USGA danced to Bobby's tune, organizing tournaments to suit his schedule and handing him preferential starting times. They also complained that they let him handpick his playing partners. Some of those grievances had a foundation in fact, but not because Bobby was asking for them. The USGA needed to sell tickets to its championships to survive and Bobby had become the sporting world's biggest attraction. They needed him on the golf course when the most people had a chance to see him. If that meant pairing him with someone he knew or had developed a rivalry with, so much the better. One of the eternal axioms of show business is the star gets his name in lights and the biggest dressing room. That never stops the grumbling from the second rank, but if anyone felt slighted all they had to do to change it was beat him a few times. Most never beat him once. It's interesting to note that these same complaints would surface later regarding Ben Hogan, Arnold Palmer, Jack Nicklaus, and Tiger Woods during their primes.

Bobby heard the gripes and decided that there was no percentage in addressing them publicly, but he did tell Pop he felt ready to accept the responsibilities of stardom, which included dealing with other reporters on a one-on-one basis. He also let everyone around him know that from now on he preferred to be called Bob, a name more suited to the grown-up he had become. His friends and family accommodated him, even some journalists complied, but his identity as "Bobby" was too firmly established for that to ever change public perception. (Pop took to calling him "Rubber Tyre," but he was the only one who could get away with that.) Seizing additional control of his image while struggling to subsidize his education, Bob accepted an offer from Jack Wheeler's Bell Newspaper Syndicate to write a series of first-person columns about golf. Bob discovered he enjoyed the work, and the columns would continue until 1935. He also began contributing to Grantland Rice's *American Golfer* on a semiregular basis. Something of a loophole in the USGA's definition of amateurism, a person sportswriting for a paycheck without turning pro had well-established precedents; both Francis and Chick Evans had taken similar jobs after winning their national championships. No one complained when their articles first appeared, but some sticklers did so about Bob's; for the rest of his playing days he would remain under greater scrutiny, and be held to a higher standard, than any other amateur in history.

The general interest in Bob had grown so great that he signed a contract with a New York publishing firm to cowrite his autobiography with Pop Keeler. In his introduction to *Down the Fairway*, published later that year, Grantland Rice pointed out that "one person in ten million might have an interesting autobiography to put out at the age of twenty-five." The book is still a wonderful read, and although Pop had a major hand in shaping it, Bob's voice comes through clearly. This was the first of four books Bob would publish during his lifetime, and he already possessed a distinctive literary style, in some ways typical of the better writers from the South: lyrical, ironic, understated, with a keen eye for the unexpected detail. His writing on the sport in this way resembled his golf swing: powerful and precise, with a touch of poetry. It's no exaggeration to say that by the end of his life he had become the most insightful writer on the subject of golf who had first been an outstanding player. Most sportswriters remained heavily invested in the business of mythmaking about him, but in his version Bob wanted no part of that process. The point of view he offers of himself in *Down the Fairway* remains grounded, self-deprecating, and refreshingly clear-eyed. One detail on which he agreed with his less modest profilers: Bob expressed shock at realizing he'd already been competing at the national level for thirteen years, more than half his lifetime. He'd won five major championships and astonished the world. They hadn't seen anything yet.

Pop Keeler's personal life took an unexpected turn that summer. At forty-five, a decade removed from his failed first marriage, he was the definition of a dedicated bachelor. While still a beat reporter at the *Journal*, in 1918 Pop had covered a tragic story about two Atlanta boys, Mack and Jack McAuliffe, both under ten, who died when a tunnel they were digging in a vacant lot collapsed on them. When he learned that the boys had been playing a war game, imagining that they were fighting Germans, he gently cast their story as a eulogy for fallen heroes. The boys' mother, Eleanor McIntosh McAuliffe, was deeply affected by the story and called Pop to thank him for it. A friendship evolved, and then, slowly, an autumnal romance. In a pleasing bit of serendipity, Eleanor was a professional sportswriter herself, and golf was her favorite subject; she was later instrumental in helping organize the Georgia Women's Golf Association. Both were lively, lonely people who discovered they had a lot to talk about, and both loved to talk. She called him Pop, he called her Mommer. In the summer of 1927, Pop confided his feelings for Mommer to Bob, and his young friend gave them his blessing. With Bob having already announced he was skipping the British events, Pop and Mommer planned to marry in New York, right after the U.S. Open, and then honeymoon in Paris.

After the beatings it handed the Amateurs in 1919 and 1925, Oakmont Country Club learned the USGA wanted it to host the 1927 Open. Bill Fownes once again went to work, adding more hazards and obstacles to his ongoing experiment in testing the limits of the human spirit; in many spots he let the rough grow up over a man's knees. Of the heavy rakes he'd invented to carve two-inch furrows into the sand—perpendicular to the line of the hole—and turn his 220 bunkers into death traps, Jimmy Demaret would later say: "You could have combed North Africa with 'em and Rommel wouldn't have got past Casablanca."

Among the men in the field that year were members of Great Britain's first Ryder Cup team. After the 1926 matches at Wentworth, the international competition between American and British pros found a sponsor in a former nursery owner from Hertfordshire named Samuel Ryder, who had made his fortune peddling seeds for a penny a packet. A golf nut in his mid-sixties, Ryder could afford to hire England's top pro, Abe Mitchell, as his private instructor. After watching Mitchell and the British team trounce the Americans at Wentworth, Ryder invited members from both sides to tea. Ryder offered to provide a trophy if the teams would agree to formalize the event as a biennial affair, played in alternate years with the Walker Cup. Shortly thereafter Ryder commissioned the delicate gold chalice that bears his name and has since become one of the world's most fiercely contested trophies. In June of 1927 the first official Ryder Cup competition was played at Worcester Country Club outside Boston. Ted Ray captained the British side, with Hagen his American counterpart; the Americans prevailed 9½ to 2½, gaining revenge for the bloodbath at Wentworth.

As play began at Oakmont the talk filling the air was less about golf than a twenty-five-year-old aviator named Charles Augustus Lindbergh. Just weeks after his heroic solo transatlantic flight to Paris, Lindbergh had returned to New York and followed Bobby's route down the canyons of Broadway to the grandest reception ever given a citizen who wasn't in uniform. Both Jones and Lindbergh were private, shy, attractive young men whose conquering exploits fulfilled the heartland's yearning for public figures whose deeds spoke of values more simple, pure, and selfless. The material excesses of the Jazz Age had spawned a spiritual exhaustion in the American upper classes; fed up with a string of drug and sex scandals flowing out of Hollywood and New York's café society, people wanted to believe the country's best young men rejected hedonism and were fundamentally good and morally sound. Lindbergh and Jones both rejected substantial offers of material gain to exploit their personal achievements, but years later, after Lindbergh's ill-considered flirtation with fascist Germany in the 1930s, Bob would retain people's affection decades after the Lone Eagle lost his luster.

A lot was expected of Bob at Oakmont. Although he was speaking to reporters, he refused to offer any forecasts, despite having won the Amateur on this course two years earlier. He knew going in that his game was a long way from what this monster layout demanded. Bob had recently won the Southern Amateur in a walk against nearly the same field, it was true, but that was at East Lake, the track he knew so well he could kick a ball around it in par. Oakmont punished anything less than perfection without mercy.

He must have sensed something. Bob's tournament ended, in effect, on the fourth hole of the first round when he hooked his drive into one of those furrowed bunkers. Not just any hazard, but Oakmont's most feared one: the sixty-yard-long Church Pews. Bob needed four shots to get out of church. He shot 76 that day, and 77 the next. That should have been the end of the Open for him, except that Oakmont was kicking every other behind in the field. Only six shots out of first he told anyone who would listen he had no chance to win, then supported his prediction with 79 in the third round, eight strokes out of the lead. When he finally put together a decent stretch during the final round, the field drifted back toward him, and as he reached the thirteenth tee he learned he was only a single stroke behind the leader, "Lighthorse" Harry Cooper. Bob looked to be on track to shoot 70 or 71, and word spread that he was making a run at his third Open. The nerves of every other player in the hunt rattled and pinged, while Bob's gallery inflated back to its normal size.

The thirteenth at Oakmont is a par three, the shortest on the course. Bob yanked a five iron into a narrow ditch way left of the green. From a lousy lie in the ditch he hacked it into a massive bunker. He needed two to get out of the sand and onto the green, leaving himself an eight-footer for five. "Then," said Bobby, "I carefully missed the putt."

Triple-bogey six. Pop saw the air go right out of him. Two holes later he double-bogeyed the fifteenth. Bob finished with 79, tying his personal worst for an Open round. He ended tied for eleventh, his lowest finish ever in a U.S. Open. His exit cleared the stage for one of the most exciting back nines in the history of the championship.

Harry Cooper was a twenty-three-year-old transplanted Englishman, the son of a golf professional who'd taken a club job in Texas when Harry was a boy. A sleek and stylish character who earned his nickname from Damon Runyon for his quick stride and lightning-fast speed of play, Cooper was considered a real comer in the professional ranks. He appeared to have this Open all wrapped up, until he faltered down Oakmont's brutal home stretch. Gene Sarazen nearly caught him, but he failed to sink a fifty-foot birdie at eighteen and fell a stroke short. Wild Bill Mehlhorn and Emmett French both had shorter putts to tie at eighteen but failed to capitalize. Only Tommy Armour — the Black Scot, as they'd taken to calling him — was left with any hope of catching Cooper. With six holes left to play he trailed Lighthorse Harry by three. By the time Armour reached eighteen Cooper's lead was down to one.

Pop and Bob stationed themselves on the edge of the green and watched Tommy drill a four iron to within ten feet; he needed that putt to force a play-off. The tension was so thick they could feel it in their ears. Two men argued behind them that under these circumstances no one could make that putt. Bob reminded them that a man who had snapped the neck of a German tank officer with his bare hands knew a little something about pressure. Armour made the putt.

Keeler couldn't stick around to watch the play-off. He had a train to catch to New York, where he was scheduled to be married the next day. Bob left the same day for Atlanta, upset but philosophical about his poor performance; law school had demanded too much of his time, but his four-year streak of consecutive championships was in jeopardy. He vowed to return home and prepare for the Amateur later that summer.

Both missed a great play-off the following day, won by Tommy Armour for his first major victory: the professional ranks had held serve against Jones. The Black Scot proved an enormously popular champion with press, public, and fellow players. Instead of cashing in on his victory with an exhibition tour, Armour took a longer view. He would spend the remainder of his life working as the resident pro at a succession of upscale private clubs in and around Palm Beach, whose members lined up to be charged outrageous sums of money for lessons. After the win at Oakmont Tommy's fee went up to one hundred dollars an hour. Twenty years later, he would be able to ask, and eagerly receive, one thousand dollars a lesson from his rich, eager clients.

After their civil service marriage at city hall in New York, Pop and Mommer had two days to kill before boarding the *Aquitania* to begin their honeymoon. Pop wandered into the midtown headquarters of the USGA to give his regards to the organization's secretary, Tommy McMahon. McMahon said: "You might be interested in this," and handed him a telegram.

The telegram was from Mr. Robert Tyre Jones, of Atlanta, asking Mr. McMahon if to his knowledge the entries to this year's British Open at St. Andrews—scheduled to begin in just over two weeks on July 11—were officially closed. And if they weren't, would Mr. McMahon mind cabling Mr. Jones's entry to the R&A. "It's cabled," said McMahon.

Pop broke into an ear-to-ear grin, and walked back to their hotel where, with the same poetic finesse with which he'd wooed her, he explained to Mommer that there was going to be a slight change in their honeymoon. It was a good thing she loved golf; an Open at St. Andrews sounded like more fun than Paris to her anyway.

Bob hadn't told Pop or anyone else his plans because he needed to talk it over with Mary. After three years of marriage, the former sheltered schoolgirl had begun to assert herself in Bob's life, particularly with regard to any decisions about golf that affected her family. Bob knew that if he wanted to take off for a month overseas on a moment's notice it wasn't going to happen without Mary's blessing. With two young kids at home she couldn't go with him, but it would be the last trip of this kind on which she didn't. The Colonel, Kiltie, and two other Atlanta friends jumped at the chance to see Bob defend his championship at St. Andrews. They caught a night train to New York, sailed over on the *Transylvania*, and landed in Glasgow only five days before the Open.

Local qualifying had been restored after the previous year's regional experiment; a round each on the Old and New courses would advance a hundred players to the championship. Entry fees for professionals were 1 pound; twice as much for amateurs, as they were historically men of more means. The pros would contend for a purse worth 275 pounds, with 100 of that going to the winner, the largest payday in Open history. With a healthy surplus in hand from last year, the R&A decided not to sell tickets. The Old Course was so open and easy to access from every direction they couldn't keep anyone out who wanted to watch anyway. But there would be no repeat of the mob scene at Prestwick; the fans at St. Andrews were the most knowledgeable in the world and cared too much about their game to breach its etiquette.

With no Walker Cup competition that year, Bob was almost the only American in the Open. After a poor practice round on Saturday, team Jones moved to an American-style course at nearby Gleneagles to get in more work before the tournament. (St. Andrews still prohibited playing golf on the Sabbath; there was no such law in effect at Gleneagles, a resort dependent on the American tourists.) Bob regained his touch, setting a new course record of 67, but it left him again the following day during his first qualifying round on the Old Course. For one nervous night there was concern he might not make the cut. That worry vanished the next day when he tied the New Course record with a 71 and qualified easily.

Pop Keeler had arrived with his bride from their interrupted honeymoon, so the entire group that had been with him from the beginning — his father, Kiltie, and Pop — was on hand, along with Jack McIntyre, his faithful Scottish caddie, back on his hero's bag. The night before the tournament began, Kiltie told Keeler in an abnormal burst of enthusiasm that if Bobby kept hitting the ball this way there wasn't a man alive who would beat him. As long as Pop had known him, Kiltie had never predicted anything about golf before in his life.

Since his first visit to St. Andrews six years before, Bob had schooled himself in the traditions of the Auld Grey Toon and embraced them as a student of the game. He had also grown to love and appreciate the nearby course that started it all.

The Scots had been playing the game on this long, narrow fishhook of seaside ground at St. Andrews a hundred years before Columbus discovered America, two centuries before Shakespeare, before Queen Elizabeth I or Henry VIII. Golf is the oldest sport in the Western world, and St. Andrews is not just the physical and historical center of the game, it is its spiritual home. The city takes its name from the ancient cathedral at its center, which accepted relics of the apostle Saint Andrew in the eighth century. Golf appeared not long afterward. Open to the public from the beginning, St. Andrews lays undisputed claim to the oldest continuous site of play anywhere in the world. The village of St. Andrews developed as a medieval university town, the second oldest in Scotland after Edinburgh, and over the centuries its students absorbed the culture of the local game during their school years, disseminating the sport of golf around every corner of Great Britain and Europe when they departed. Nature, not man, was the Old Course's principal architect, and these greens and fairways evolved as slowly and deliberately as the sport itself.

The genius of the Old Course lies not in its inherent difficulty but in the overwhelming number of options it presents a golfer. Standing on the tee you are seldom if ever directed to follow any specific path to the green; what more often confronts you is a flat, featureless landscape — alive with hidden dangers — through which you must carefully plot your way. With its seven huge double greens — some of them over an acre in size — varied pin positions, and the infinitely changeable wind you are almost never asked to play the same course twice. The Old Course requires great skill, but more than that it demands precise thinking and strategy; you first beat this golf course with your mind by creating a disciplined plan of attack, one shot setting up the next as if in a chess game, and then you had to go out and execute it. Bernard Darwin meant it as a compliment when he said he thought that Bob was "amused by its problems." Talent, nerve, a relentless mentality: not many players had all these weapons in their arsenal. It was no wonder that by his third trip to St. Andrews, Bob had decided that this primal testing ground where the game had taken root represented the greatest challenge golf had to offer.

By his own admission, Bob had disgraced himself here in 1921. His second trip in 1926 had brought forgiveness and redemption, and deeper understanding on his part of what riches the place represented. During his third tournament at St. Andrews, Bob earned the undying love and admiration of the British sporting world. Following the exacting approach he'd been formulating since his discussions with Tommy Armour, in the first round of the 1927 Open Bob tied the Old Course scoring record with a 68. Par at this time was 73; it was the first time Bob had ever broken 70 in any Open competition. Along with his 66 at Sunningdale, it stands as one of the great single rounds of golf ever played. Calamity Jane II came into her own: at the fifth he canned a putt of 120 feet for an eagle. At the eighth he dropped a 30-footer for birdie. He saved par from 20 feet at thirteen. He did not miss a single putt of under 12 feet, needing only twenty-nine in the round. Six came from more than 100 feet out on those oversized greens and he didn't three-putt once. In his room at the Grand Hotel afterward, overlooking the eighteenth green, Bobby refused to give in to the rest of his brain trust's cautious optimism. Somebody would go crazy. Somebody would catch him.

Nobody did. Bob had grabbed a commanding lead he would never relinquish; the rest of the field seemed to part in stunned silence and let him pass. The next day in the second round he shot 72 while playing what felt to him like even better golf. Everyone fifteen or more strokes behind him at the halfway mark failed to make the cut; he had gone so low the smallest number of players advanced since the Open introduced mid-tournament elimination. On the morning round of the final day Bob shot 73—even par—and although his score had gone up, he felt he played his best golf of the week. He began his fourth round that afternoon at six under par and held a four-stroke lead. That may not sound like much to fans of the modern game, so accustomed to the routine abuse of par, but at the time, and particularly in an Open at St. Andrews, this number was shocking. The weather had stayed fair, as it will sometimes do in July, and there hadn't been much wind all week, but Bob still had to make the shots.

He stumbled at the start of the final round. Pop and the Colonel feared the strain was catching up with him. By the time he'd played eight holes he was four over par for the day and for the first time since the Open began his lead looked vulnerable. The Colonel couldn't take the tension and headed back to the hotel; Pop stayed in the gallery. Bob was entering the part of the course known as the Loop, a stretch of four holes at the tip of the fishhook that criss-cross each other at the farthest outward point before beginning the return journey to the clubhouse. During his searing first round Bob had played this difficult passage at even par, 4-4-3-4, and distanced himself from the field. Summoning up a ferocious burst of shot making he went 3-3-3-3. He followed a twenty-foot birdie at nine by driving the green at the 312-yard tenth. After narrowly missing a third straight birdie at eleven, he ran his approach at twelve within two feet. He collected two more birdies on his way in to finish with a 72. The year before, while winning at Lytham, Bob had tied the lowest winning score in the history of the Open with 291. He had just shattered his own record by six strokes, which turned out to be his winning margin over the nearest pursuer.

When Bob sank his final putt on the great open stage at eighteen, Bernard Darwin was there in the crowd as twelve thousand people swarmed the green, covering its broad green expanse in an instant.

"Not even when Francis Ouimet beat Vardon and Ray was there such a riot of joy," wrote Darwin. "Personally I thought Bobby was going to be killed in the very hour of victory. It was a real relief when, after what seemed whole minutes, Bobby reappeared, his putter held high over his head, borne aloft on admiring shoulders." As the mob closed in on him Pop shouted in alarm to anyone who would listen: "They're going to kill him!" The film and photos confirm they weren't exaggerating; it was a dangerous moment, resolved only when Bobby appeared hoisted above the crowd, still holding Calamity Jane. Six local policemen fought their way into the scrum, pulled him down, and saw him safely to the doorway of the Grand Hotel, where the Colonel was waiting for him. At the sight of Bob hugging his father at the door, Pop discovered an urgent need to clean his glasses; all of a sudden, he wasn't seeing clearly.

For a second straight year Bob had decided to play in the British Open at the last minute because of a disappointing performance in another event. In winning the way he did at St. Andrews he captured the undying affection of the true guardians of the game. The Scots had discovered in Bobby Jones the manifestation of their ideal golfer rendered in flesh, blood, and bone. It no longer mattered where he came from or what flag he played under. He was "their Bobby" now.

Neither did he do himself harm with his acceptance speech a short time afterward. When they handed him the Claret Jug for the second year in a row he said: "Nothing would make me happier than to take home your trophy. It was played for here thirty years before I was born. I had rather win a championship at St. Andrews than anything else that could happen to me. You have done so many things for me that I am embarrassed to ask for one more, but I will. I want this wonderful old club to accept the custody of the cup for the coming year."

If there were any die-hard nationalists left in that crowd who resented seeing the Claret Jug go to another American, those objections vanished on the soft westerly breeze.

"I have achieved the ambition of my life," he told them. "Because I have won at a place where golf was played nearly five centuries ago. This wonderful experience will live in my memory until my dying day. If I never win anything again, I am satisfied."

This was as fine a feeling as a competitor in his sport or any other could ever hope to have, and given the perfection of the moment, he could be forgiven the slight overstatement. He felt he had atoned for his poor performance at Oakmont.

But he was a long way from satisfied.

Bob, the Colonel, Keeler, and Kiltie made a sentimental journey the next day to nearby Carnoustie, the little pro's old hometown. They boarded a ferry boat and crossed the Tay River to Dundee, where a thousand people had gathered to welcome the Open champion. After a short drive to Carnoustie they were greeted by the mayor, who presented Bob with the key to the city. While

Bob went out to play an exhibition round on the course that is the town's namesake and its enduring pride and joy, Pop observed: "About 6,000 of the population—which is estimated at 6,000—went along with him." Pop then accompanied Kiltie to the home of his parents, taking pictures of the Scot with his mother and sister, who happily doted on him. While they lingered there, a half dozen old acquaintances from the neighborhood happened by, almost all of whom hadn't seen Kiltie since he'd left for America twenty years before. All knew of his success, and the legendary exploits of his famous pupil, but it never colored their reactions: it was as if he'd just returned from buying a carton of milk. As he watched and listened to their monosyllabic greetings and conversations—marked by a "curious lack of demonstration"—for the first time the voluble Pop grasped the cultural and genetic depths of Kiltie's reticence. Pop never hounded him again for an answer he wasn't willing to give.

Although Bob had won his second straight Open overseas, his unprecedented streak of holding a USGA championship for four straight years was in jeopardy. He had confided in Pop two years earlier that he might walk away from the game if he could extend that streak to six. That ambition had already begun to evolve into something even more audacious, but achieving the original objective meant a lot to him nonetheless. After returning home to another grand reception, Bob and company spent less than two weeks in Atlanta before leaving for Minneapolis and his last chance to keep the streak alive at the 1927 U.S. Amateur.

The tournament boasted the strongest field the Amateur had attracted since the Great War. After studying local weather patterns over a fifteen-year period, the USGA had decided the week of August 22 offered their best chance for perfect weather in Minneapolis, where the tournament was scheduled. The Minikahda Club played host to the event, site of the 1916 U.S. Open, where Chick Evans won the first half of his historic double championship. Chick was back again; at thirty-eight he was no longer ranked among the game's elite and longed to restake his claim to the national limelight. Francis Ouimet was on hand, as was the reigning champion, George Von Elm, whose sleek feathers were ruffled once more when the USGA announced its seedings. Despite beating Bob in last year's Amateur, Von Elm still came in ranked behind him at number two. Although he told reporters he wasn't bothered by the slight, aggrieved complaints about the USGA's favoritism for Bob filled the air immediately. Von Elm was further irritated when it was announced Minneapolis-area golfers would be honoring Bob at a testimonial dinner two days before the Amateur began. No one planned even so much as a lunch for George.

Bob's arrival on August 18 generated front-page headlines in the Twin Cities. Evidence of her increasing role in Bob's life, Mary traveled with him to a championship for the first time. His presence created waves that reached beyond the tournament itself. When it was announced that Bob and Watts Gunn would play an exhibition against two local stars at Minikahda the Saturday before qualifying, another local course canceled a scheduled exhibition that day between Walter Hagen and Tommy Armour. Hagen was in town to cover the Amateur for the North American Newspaper Alliance, a moonlighting gig that had become an annual tradition for him, although he spent more time signing autographs and chatting up potential dates than he did at the typewriter. The contest to become Bob's caddie during the tournament also made the front page because every one of Minikahda's 175 caddies had requested Bob's bag. A lottery finally settled the issue and veteran Pat Doherty won the honor. "I'm mighty proud, and I guess I ought to be," Doherty told a local sportswriter. This was his first national event and he vowed to do everything he could "to help Bobby win the title."

Bob had climbed to the pinnacle of America's sports pantheon, and for the moment he stood there alone. After five years as champion Jack Dempsey had lost his heavyweight title in a 1926 upset to Gene Tunney; he was training hard for a September rematch; but it would also end in defeat and lead to his retirement. He would eventually open a popular restaurant in New York and live high off his reputation. Knute Rockne's Notre Dame football team had fallen off after their "Four Horsemen" years; he would win two more national titles before dying in a plane crash in 1931, at the age of forty-three. Red Grange was slowed by a knee injury after turning pro and his reputation was tarnished by greed and blatant commercialism; he sold his name to dolls, sweaters, soft drinks, candy bars, and a host of less savory products. In case any confusion remained about his motivation, Grange publicly stated: "I'm out to get the money and I don't care who knows it." Only Babe Ruth and the Yankees, who were nearing the end of their greatest season—that summer the Babe hit sixty home runs and Lou

Gehrig joined the lineup known as "Murderer's Row"—could compare to the national acclaim now directed toward the Golden Boy from Atlanta.

The Twin Cities got their first look at Bob when he faced a press conference before playing his first practice rounds in a driving rainstorm. More than 150 journalists and correspondents from around the country and as far away as Great Britain were on hand to cover the event, and a thirty-five-hundred-square-foot wooden shed had been put up to serve as their press center. When asked if anything was wrong with his game, Bob laughed and said: "Everything." Despite his win at the British Open, he claimed he'd been off form for months and had hardly played at all, but his radiant tan belied that statement; he'd put in many hours at East Lake to prepare for the Amateur. He also said that because he enjoyed the competition he planned to keep playing in major tournaments indefinitely. "I don't know of any particular reason why I should quit," he said.

As many as fifty thousand people were expected to attend during the week; tickets sold for $1.10 a day, until the semifinals, when the price went up to $2.20. A pass for the entire week set you back $5.50. (As per the usual arrangement, Minikahda would split the proceeds fifty-fifty with the USGA.) As it did now wherever he played, Bob's presence attracted thousands who'd never seen a golf tournament before. Believing that their well-bred Midwestern crowds would be better behaved than most, the club eliminated megaphones and whistles for the marshals, equipping them instead with a system of white, yellow, and red flags to handle the galleries; local papers published guides detailing what behavior the various flags were supposed to inspire. Pioneering local radio station KSTP announced plans to issue regular updates from the course throughout the week, with Saturday's thirty-six-hole final match being broadcast live for the first time in its entirety.

It was a busy news week in Minnesota: President Calvin Coolidge was visiting nearby North Dakota, and state resident Charles Lindbergh was returning home for the first time since his historic flight; he was to be honored with a parade through the Twin Cities on Tuesday morning. Lindbergh's presence in town didn't diminish Bob's drawing power. His practice rounds were played in front of galleries estimated in the thousands. As eager as they were to see him, his game was still sour—he was hooking his drives badly—so he arranged to practice the next day in private at nearby Golden Valley Golf and Country

Club. When he returned to Minikahda the following day, rain washed out his round after nine holes, but after an hour on the range with Kiltie, Bob announced himself ready to start the tournament. Local handicappers positioned Jones as the front-runner, laying odds of 3 to 1 that he would reach the final.

Carrying the standard for Minnesota golfers was thirty-one-year-old Harrison "Jimmy" Johnston, winner of seven straight state amateur titles and a two-time Walker Cup teammate of Bob's who had turned in an impressive performance in the Open at Oakmont. A World War I veteran who'd been gassed in battle and suffered from intermittent health problems, Johnston played out of White Bear Lake Yacht Club in suburban St. Paul, coached by resident pro Tom Vardon, Harry's younger brother. In a last-minute interview before the Amateur Bob rated Johnston and Von Elm as the two men he was most worried about. George again took offense that Bob had expressed concern about anyone but him.

One hundred fifty-nine other men attempted to qualify for thirty-two match-play positions, beginning on Monday, August 22. Included in the field was the current amateur champion of Massachusetts, twenty-seven-year-old Eddie Lowery, Ouimet's friend and caddie from the 1913 Open. Bob shot 75 in his qualifying round on Monday, tied for ninth, four strokes off the lead established by an unknown from New Jersey named Eugene Homans. The only man more upset than Bob at the end of the day was George Von Elm, who despite weeks of studying the course shot 79, which put him right on the cut line. Bob told Pop that night he wasn't going to risk flirting with the cut by playing a cautious round the next day. Although he believed the old superstition that the man who won the qualifying medal never went on to win the championship, Bob went out on Tuesday afternoon determined to shoot the works.

Bob asked Keeler to walk the first few holes with him the next day to settle his nerves, and Pop's steadying presence got him going. Two holes later Bob signaled Keeler he was back on track and Pop could move on. Bob's four-under 31 on the front nine shattered the record at Minikahda. He birdied the eighteenth and broke Minikahda's course record with a 67; he had won the qualifying medal and tied the Amateur record for lowest qualifying score, which earned him a headline on the *Tribune*'s front page, just below Charles Lindbergh's homecoming parade.

Von Elm scratched and clawed his way to a 75 and narrowly advanced to match play. So did George Voigt, local favorite Jimmy Johnston, Chick Evans, the leader from the day before, Eugene Homans, and Francis Ouimet. (His erstwhile caddie, Eddie Lowery, failed to advance.) In his syndicated column the next day, Walter Hagen wrote: "Personally, I felt a little bigger thrill watching Von Elm as he struggled over the last nine in a frantic effort to land himself among the qualifiers than I did in watching Bobby Jones, who was just having a little fun giving the course record a battle." Walter worried that George was "putting too much body into his swing." But Von Elm could hear the roars from the big gallery behind him as Bob made birdie after birdie. In other words: he was pressing.

For his Wednesday morning first-round match Bob drew a youngster from New York, Maurice McCarthy, who gave him a scare. McCarthy was one up through nine and held that lead through fifteen, when the pressure hit him; he lost the last three holes, and the match, down two. Von Elm survived his first-round match, and in the afternoon played a veteran from Minikahda by the name of Harry Legg. Their battle went down to the wire, when Legg booted out the defending champ on the final green to the biggest cheers of the day. That afternoon Bob edged the other surviving youngster, Eugene Homans, 3 and 2, to advance to the final eight. Joining him were Chick Evans, Francis Ouimet, and Bob's next opponent, Jimmy Johnston. The presence of Legg and Johnston in the quarterfinals generated excited speculation about an all-Minnesota/all-Minikahda final, but Jones would have something to say about that. The eighteen-hole matches were behind him and Bob hadn't come close to playing his best golf. Hagen, the journalist, thought Bob had been "fortunate" to advance.

Jimmy Johnston's dreams of glory died fast on Thursday morning, as the Jones they'd all come out to see showed up. As he was able to do now whenever the stakes were highest, Bob came onto his game and played untouchable golf. He was eight up by the end of the morning after winning seven holes in a row and nearly equaled his two-day-old course record with a 68. When they resumed play after lunch, Bob made quick work of it and won the match, 10 and 9. Johnston won two holes all day. Bob explained to a local reporter his merciless philosophy about match play as they set out that morning: "If you get an opponent one down, try to get him two down. If you have him two down, try to get him three down. And don't stop trying until he shakes your hand." Harry Legg also lost his quarterfinal match, eliminating the last local favorite.

Four men were left standing, and three were former Amateur champions. On Friday Chick Evans faced current intercollegiate champion Roland Mackenzie. Two old friends made up the other side of the bracket: Jones and Ouimet, meeting in an important match at the Amateur for the fourth time in the last seven years. Ten thousand people followed them that day but of all the accounts written about their match, Ouimet left the most expressive:

> Those of you who think Bobby is a bargain in a semifinal match should take him on sometime. Bobby was positively ruthless. If you play well, he will go you one better. He gives you no openings whatsoever, and you have to make your own bed. I made mine and was put to sleep by a margin of eleven down and ten to play.
>
> I can only describe a match against Bobby in this manner: It is as though you got your hand caught in a buzz saw. If the young man were human he would make a mistake once in a while, but he never makes mistakes. He can drive straighter than any man living. He is perfectly machinelike in his iron play, and on the greens he is a demon. If you can beat that type of man, I should like the recipe. But he is more than a great golfer. He is a grand competitor.

Only Chick Evans now stood between Bob and his third Amateur title. The pairing offered an irresistible story line: the veteran campaigner mounting a late-career comeback against the sport's reigning king. The men had split their two previous encounters in USGA competition and had never met in the finals of an Amateur; but the behind-the-scenes drama was just as compelling.

Although the rivals appeared friendly and sportsmanlike when they were face-to-face, Bob had heard about the backstage grumbling from Evans, Hagen, and Von Elm for years. As Von Elm confessed to journalist Lester Rice a few years later, by this point he "hated Bob's guts" and Bob sensed it. The reasons may have been more complex than simple envy: Von Elm was a teetotaler who took Prohibition seriously, and he disapproved of Bob's casual drinking, smoking, and occasional locker-room cussing. Discussing their relationship with Lester Rice years later, Bob wrote that he had "no illusions about Von Elm's real feelings toward me. He always impressed me as having a chip on his shoulder, and I am sure you know that neither of us was the type to attract the other. We just did not speak the same language."

Chick Evans was a different story. A prim thirty-eight-year-old businessman still living with his mother, he never fit in to the locker-room culture that was such a big part of the off-course atmosphere. When they went out to play their finals match on Saturday morning, Chick was all smiles to Bob's face in front of reporters and photographers. Bob had a hard time reconciling that behavior with the deeply bitter feelings Chick expressed about him to so many others. He always respected what Chick meant to the game as a player, but as two people they simply repelled each other. As they stood on the first tee being photographed that morning, Chick put on what Bob called a "typical Evans performance . . . he draped his arm around my shoulder, flashed that big grin and rattled on in a loud voice about how much fun it was going to be to have a game with me, that neither of us cared who won. We would just go out and have a real good time, and all that sort of bosh." Bob knew exactly how much Chick wanted this win. More than any other opponent he ever faced, on this day Bob took satisfaction not just in beating Chick, but in crushing him.

The match began at 10:30 Saturday morning. The Colonel, Clara, Mary, Pop, and Kiltie were all in the gallery. After they finished the morning round, the *Tribune* opened its front-page account the next day with the story of a determined Minneapolis matron who had stationed herself at the eighteenth green in order to secure a spot to watch the end of the championship. She was seven holes too late. Chick shot 75 in the morning, which would have kept him close to any other competitor, but Bob was already up three, and two under par, when they reached the ninth hole.

The ninth at Minikahda is 560 yards long, a par five that plays steeply uphill to a small fast green. Before the tournament began a Minikahda member offered a substantial bet that no one would make an eagle three at the hole during the championship. To do so required a long, perfectly placed drive and a phenomenal second to reach and hold the green. A few birdies had been recorded to date, but nothing close to an eagle. In fact, to that point in the club's history, no one had ever made three at number nine.

Bob hit a booming 300-yard drive that flirted with the out of bounds on the right but cut 50 yards off the path to the green. From 230 yards out he powered a fairway wood that soared straight up that hill, bounced twice, and came to rest a foot from the hole. Chick conceded the putt, but Bob sank the ball for eagle anyway; he putted out on every hole to stay sharp. The member lost his bet, and Chick was down four. Pop quickly canvassed his fellow reporters, who agreed they had just seen the finest fairway wood shot a man ever played in a championship.

The stark difference in the two men's personalities was on display all afternoon. The extroverted Chick laughed and joked with the sympathetic Midwestern crowd, on a few occasions "dancing a little jig" when he sank a putt or pulled off a tough shot. Bob remained a study in composed concentration, going about his business while appearing substantially more relaxed than he actually felt inside. They spoke hardly a word to each other and some reported the tension between them as "thick." Chick looked annoyed at one point when Bob didn't concede him a breaking three-foot putt for a half, and when Bob's back was turned Chick sarcastically tipped his hat. Whenever Chick conceded him a putt, Bob putted out anyway, prompting Chick at least once to look away and roll his eyes. Chick won his first hole of the day at the eleventh with a twenty-foot birdie, then turned to the crowd and shouted: "Taking a hole from him today is some record, but he can't beat that one!" Oakmont's Bill Fownes, who was refereeing their match, considered talking to Chick about toning down his antics. Bob picked up one more hole during the back nine to stretch his lead to five; for the second time in less than a week he had shot a five-under-par 67.

Dark clouds rolled in and threatened as they began their afternoon round. Content to coast on his lead, Bob bogeyed two of the first six holes and Chick trimmed the deficit to four while playing his steadiest golf of the day. At the seventh, as the first rain started to fall, Bob turned it on and captured the next three holes in a row, capped by a birdie at nine, to stretch his lead to seven. After halving the tenth, both reached the par three eleventh green with their tee shots when the day's most controversial incident occurred.

The rain that had been threatening all afternoon came down in buckets as they walked onto the green. Bob lagged his first putt close and tapped in for his par. Chick left his first putt a foot short. As he took his stance to tap in for par he seemed annoyed that Jones hadn't conceded it to him; it would have halved the hole and left Bob seven up with seven holes to play. But if he missed it the match was over, and the rule of thumb in match play is you always make your opponent sink any putt he needs to extend a match. Chick knew that, and Bob knew that, and when Chick looked up at him he claimed Bob was glaring at him.

What happened next became the crux of the dispute: Chick's putter nudged the ball and rolled it slightly ahead as he addressed it, a clear one-stroke penalty if he had caused it to move. But according to Chick, his ball hadn't moved at all; Bob corrected him, politely but firmly. Bob's account was slightly different: he thought Chick had moved the ball *intentionally*—perhaps to get the match over with—then looked up and said: "I guess it moved." Bob answered that he agreed, and Chick stuck out his hand to congratulate Bob on winning the Amateur.

Both men smiled, seemed to put the awkward moment behind them, and walked back to the clubhouse as the skies opened and the crowd ran for cover. Neither mentioned it to reporters, and they paid proper, sportsmanlike respect to each other. No one covering the event made anything more out of it than an unintentional accident. But thirty years later this moment and his whole history with Chick still rankled Bob. When a television network was putting together the first comprehensive retrospective of his career, Bob asked that only one man be excluded from the list of people they planned to interview: Chick Evans.

In his column Walter Hagen summed up Bob's performance by saying the gallery had been treated to "an exhibition of the greatest golf that had ever been played anywhere." In the next paragraph, a world-class non sequitur, Hagen explained why he had so thoroughly enjoyed his journalistic assignment by pointing out that "there are more pretty girls in Minneapolis than any other city per thousand of population." Walter spent a good portion of the final round walking the course with the Colonel, who kept to the back of the gallery to stay out of his son's sight. As they parted once the match was over, Walter admitted wistfully to the Colonel: "I'd rather beat him than all the golfers in the United States and Britain put together."

Bob slipped on a thin black slicker and stood in the rain during the ceremony outside the clubhouse. Chick Evans, who had changed into a dapper
business suit, stood under an umbrella. USGA president Bill Fownes brought
out the Havemeyer Trophy and said, "Here, Bob, you better hold the cup."
Chick stepped forward and said, "Gee, I'd like to hold it for you." He got a big
laugh from the crowd, then Chick unintentionally summed up the last six
years of his career: "But Bobby has me stymied." Bob later said that a photo
taken of him a few minutes later, standing in the rain, his hair all messed up,
holding the Havemeyer Trophy for the third time, was his favorite shot taken of
him during his playing years. There's a sly, mischievous twinkle in his eyes—
you can still see the boy in him—due in no small part to the fact that he had
just decisively surpassed Chick Evans once and for all.

The autobiography he'd written with Pop, *Down the Fairway*, was published that fall to positive reviews and five printings, more proof of his growing
popularity. It was time to begin his second year at Emory. Applying himself
with characteristic single-mindedness, by the end of the fall semester—
halfway through the three-year program—Bob decided to try to pass the Georgia state bar exam. Living hand to mouth had worn him down, and living with
his parents had created inevitable tensions at home between his wife and
mother. Mary wanted her own home, and she wanted Bob in it with her, not
roaming around the golf courses of the world. Just after Christmas he learned
that he had passed—no one could recall anyone passing the bar after only
three semesters of law school—so when 1928 began he left Emory and
manned the desk that had been waiting for him all these years at his father's
law firm.

Atlanta loved Bob Jones because he had done more to put their city on the
international map than any other citizen in the twentieth century. In years to
come he would often be referred to as Atlanta's ambassador to the world, but
their gratitude was about to get him in hot water with the USGA. In November, at another dinner in his honor, his friends presented him with a check for
fifty thousand dollars to help Bob and Mary build their own house. The money
had been raised as a charitable fund at the Atlanta Athletic Club, and thousands had contributed, their thanks for all Bob had done in promoting their
city. News of the gift prompted a vigorous debate in the national press about

the nature of amateurism in general, and Bob's unique status in particular. Two months later, after meeting with the USGA in New York during their annual convention, Bob returned the check to his friends. The USGA did not order him to turn down the money—nothing in their bylaws covered this situation; there was no precedent for it—but they hadn't hesitated to point out the negative perceptions that could result. The example of his friend Francis Ouimet losing his amateur status over his ill-fated sporting goods store in 1917 was in the forefront of Bob's mind. With a new career and a growing family to care for, he couldn't risk tarnishing the reputation he'd worked so hard to establish as an amateur sportsman. He was never a rebel by nature; as he matured Bob received too many benefits from conformity and working within the system, and he kept to this path until his playing days were over. Bob's decision was greeted with universal approval and cited as further proof of his exceptional character.

Soon afterward he turned down another offer for help with their housing situation, from his own grandfather. When R.T. heard about Bob returning the Atlanta money, the old man quietly offered to lend him whatever he needed. Most assumed Bob accepted, but this part of the story wouldn't surface for decades: Bob and Mary talked it over, wrote to thank R.T. profusely, but declined, explaining they were determined to make it on their own. The young couple did buy their first home in Atlanta, at a substantially more modest price, in the spring of 1928. Bob also invested in a real estate project with his father and some others from the Atlanta Athletic Club. They had their eyes on a property in the mountains of North Carolina that they hoped to develop into a golf resort called Highlands Country Club. Upon completion the following year, Highlands became one of the Jones family's favorite retreats.

Bob had begun to feel the weight of another burden. During his rise to the top of the game he became aware that many close friends from Atlanta and around the country had begun gambling substantial sums of money on him in major tournaments. The betting was legal in England, under the table at home; he never encouraged anyone to put down a bet, but while many of these friends were wealthy enough to treat whatever they wagered as recreational fun, more than a few were not. Whenever he lost now Bob was keenly aware others around him were paying for it out of pocket.

After trying, and winning, his first trial that spring, Bob turned his attention back to preparations for the summer golf season. He had already announced he wouldn't travel back to Great Britain to defend his Open title. This would prove to be the shortest competitive season of his career: only two events, with a month to practice in between, the U.S. Open and the Amateur.

The 1928 U.S. Open was played during the third week of June at Olympia Fields Country Club, twenty-five miles south of Chicago. Ten years before, the club's founders had bought over 670 acres of undeveloped farmland and created the largest golfing complex in the world. Four golf courses—old Tom Bendelow designed the first and consulted on the second, and before he died Willie Park Jr. designed the third—spread out in all directions around a mammoth English Tudor clubhouse that covered two square acres of land—including the country's largest locker room—anchored around an eighty-foot-high, four-sided clock tower, each side visible from the first tees on the four courses to regulate starting times. Its fourth and most recent course was the site of the Open. Olympia Fields had already played host to a Western Open in 1920 and the 1925 PGA Championship, but this was its introduction to the Big Show. For the first time the USGA eliminated qualifying for the top thirty finishers from the previous year's Open. Bob arrived a few days early for practice rounds on a course he'd never played before.

Walter Hagen didn't show up until the day before the Open began. The Haig had just returned from England, where he'd won his third British Open at Royal St. George's. The current captain of St. George's, Edward, the Prince of Wales, presented Walter with the Claret Jug. The two hedonistic playboys had met that week and realized they were cut from the same cloth. After handing Walter his prize, the prince invited him into the clubhouse for cocktails. One of the last citadels of the class system, Royal St. George's members sent their secretary in to remind their country's crown prince that professionals weren't welcome on the premises. The future King Edward VII gave the secretary a blistering earful and sent him on his way; Walter and Edward formed a friendship that lasted for decades, and another social barrier had fallen to Hagen's fearless personality.

Hagen arrived in Chicago a slight favorite over Jones: he had won the only two championships previously played at Olympia Fields, the reason he felt he could forgo any practice rounds. But Walter was now thirty-five years old, and given the mileage he'd put on himself, he was an old thirty-five. Hagen started slowly on the first morning of the Open, with a 75, while Bob shot 75 that afternoon. The USGA reversed starting times on the second day and Bob returned an even par 71 to grab the halfway point lead. Hagen played a lousy front nine, and then, as a torrential storm blew through, he shot 32 on the back nine to land in fifth place, a stroke behind George Von Elm. Behind Bob in second place was twenty-seven-year-old Johnny Farrell, a stylish short-hitting pro from Quaker Ridge Club in New York who'd had three top-ten finishes in the last five Opens.

The narrow Olympia Fields #4 course was slaughtering the rest of the 150-man field, and Bob's presence had gotten into the heads of more than a few professionals. As Pop made his way around he could hear the cry of "How's Jones going?" flying back and forth between pros as they passed each other. Because of the swarming crowds that followed Bob everywhere, playing with him almost always translated into a two-shot deficit, but not one of these men ever registered a complaint in public or private about Bob as a partner. Gene Sarazen made the point that even if you didn't know him, you felt you were playing with a friend. When Bob recorded what was, by his standards, a mediocre 73 in the third round, he still held a two-stroke lead. Hagen was three shots behind Bob, Farrell and Von Elm were five back. An unheralded twenty-one-year-old pro named Roland Hancock from Wilmington, North Carolina, stood six strokes back. Everyone else had already punched their ticket home.

Bob began his final round with a birdie and picked up another at the fifth. He was cruising, and with the toughest stretch of the course behind him he had at least a five- or six-stroke lead to play with. Pop felt more certain this thing was in the bag than at any other event in his career, but Bob had been scrambling for pars all week, and the effort had worn him down. He admitted to Pop that at this point he made "the fatal mistake of telling himself that he would just coast in." Bob wasn't built for coasting—he had to feel he was grinding to sustain his concentration—and the moment he took his foot off the gas disaster struck.

Bob hooked his drive on the sixth into the weeds. He punched out and salvaged a bogey. Leaking confidence, he began steering his shots, double-bogeyed the seventh, and followed with three more straight bogeys. Seven shots lost in five holes, he dropped from two under to five over par. Word of Bob's collapse whipped around the course, but only Johnny Farrell took advantage. Playing ahead, Farrell finished with 72; his total of 294 was now the number to chase. Hagen fell away, then Von Elm. Sarazen made a late rush but came up shy. After struggling through those awful five holes, Bob played eleven through seventeen in one over. He reached the eighteenth knowing he could still beat Farrell with a birdie, hooked his drive into deep rough, then punched out into a narrow, muddy ditch that ran across the fairway a hundred yards short of the green. Forced to take an awkward stance with his right foot planted in the mud and the other hitched up onto the bank, he slammed a wedge as hard as he could down at the ball. It barely cleared the lip of the ditch. Ten thousand heads craned toward the green, where the ball sailed in, dropped, and stopped twenty feet from the hole. A miraculous recovery. Making the putt would win him his third Open, a miss would drop him into his third play-off in the last six years. His ball had a clump of mud on it from the ditch, and the rules still didn't allow a player to lift, clean, and replace it on the green; that wouldn't change until 1960.

Bob missed the putt.

Everyone was about to call it a day and prepare for the play-off when word came in that all young Roland Hancock needed to do was par the last two holes for a course record 69, and the Open would be his by two strokes. A crazed gallery rushed back toward the seventeenth fairway. As Hancock walked over a small bridge leading to the tee, unaware of where he stood, he heard people shout "Make way for the new champion!" The cat was out of the bag. He was forced to wait twenty minutes while marshals tried to clear the fairway, and all the while the knowledge of what was at stake punched holes in his confidence. Hancock pushed his drive onto a patch of bare ground he thought might be part of a hazard. Instead of waiting for a ruling—it wasn't a hazard— he tried to advance the ball without grounding his club and topped it fifteen feet into heavy rough. Two more shots to reach the green and then two putts and just like that he had double-bogeyed. Par at eighteen would still land him in the play-off with Jones and Farrell, but the patient died on the operating table; Hancock made back-to-back sixes and finished in third place, never to be heard from again.

After 1927's play-off win by Tommy Armour, the USGA had decided that in the event of a tie, eighteen holes didn't provide a definitive test for identifying the game's best player. This year's play off would go thirty-six holes, played on the same day.

A light mist was falling as the two men stepped to the tee on Sunday, June 24. Johnny Farrell pulled an electric-green sweater out of his bag. He had a reputation as the most fashionable player in the game, but it wasn't all for show. In order to encourage a higher standard of professionalism, during the 1920s the PGA handed out an annual award to the best-dressed player and Farrell had won more than a few of them. The last check he collected for it was fifteen hundred dollars, 50 percent more than first place in the Open. You'd have thought Walter Hagen would win this award in a walk, but he was considered too flashy; the refined elegance the judges preferred just wasn't his forte.

Johnny Farrell also had a deserved reputation as a cool customer, but a play-off for the Open raised the ante on anxiety. He looked flustered on the first hole, where Bob collected an easy birdie. After halving the second, Bob double-bogeyed the third, a hole that had been giving him fits all week; Farrell collected his four for a one-stroke lead. By the time they made the turn it was clear Farrell had better command of his game; Bob made a series of unforced errors and was forced to scramble to stay even. Farrell finished the morning round with a brilliant kick, four birdies in a row for a one-under-par 70. He led Bob by three.

Farrell appeared energized and Bob looked beyond exhaustion; Pop wondered if he'd even be able to finish. He should have known by now that Bob's pale, haunted look was the signal his friend was about to catch fire. He opened the second round with a birdie; Farrell slipped to double bogey. They were all square. Then it was Bob's turn to falter, with another double at the third, his jinx hole. Again, he climbed back into a tie that lasted until the ninth, where he lost two strokes to Farrell once again. A steady rain was falling by now but the gallery hardly seemed to notice. This was like watching a duel fought with rapiers.

With nine holes left, Farrell's nerves frayed; picking up a stroke on three straight holes, Bob took the lead for the first time since the first hole that morning. Farrell birdied the thirteenth to square them again with five to play. That held until the sixteenth, another par three, when a rub of the green intervened:

Bob's picture-perfect tee shot to the green ricocheted off the flagstick and bounced into deep rough. Two holes to play and Farrell had a one-stroke lead.

The par four seventeenth. Bob outdrove Farrell, who pulled his into the rough. Playing his second over a low bush directly between him and the green, Johnny hit a beauty that rolled to within three feet; a certain birdie. Bob reached the green in two as well, but left himself a twenty-foot putt. He looked at the line from every angle and calmly sank the putt. The weight shifted to Farrell; he dropped his matching birdie and carried a one-stroke lead to eighteen.

The sky had turned black, the belly of the storm about to unleash a downpour. The eighteenth was 490 yards, a reachable par five with a dogleg left to an elevated green. Farrell pushed his tee shot right, in light rough just short of a bunker. Bob split the fairway. Farrell played a wood, trying to reach in two, but the ball crossed the fairway and landed sixty yards short in the left-hand rough, halfway up the hill. Bob hit a rocket off the deck toward the left side of the green, but it nicked someone in the crowd near the green and kicked left. As the crowd scrambled out of the way, a policeman shepherding the gallery stepped on the ball, squirting it into the rough; an alert USGA official spotted the incident and allowed Bob to replace the ball in its original lie on the closely mown collection area.

Farrell played a dead-hands pitch out of the rough that arced right on line to the flag and stopped eight feet short, lying three. The pressure shifted to Bob: he clipped his ball neatly off the turf and sent it running straight for the flag. For a fleeting moment an eagle three seemed in the offing, the gallery gasped . . . but the ball stopped two feet short. Bob holed out for his birdie and stepped away.

Farrell walked to his ball, studied the green, crouched down low to look at the line. As he took his stance a row of photographers opened fire, shutters shattering the graveyard silence. Farrell stepped away and quietly asked their referee to hold off the picture taking until he completed his work. Then he walked right back to the ball, and without a moment's hesitation rolled it slowly into the heart of the cup.

Johnny Farrell had won the 1928 Open. Bob shot 73-71 in the play-off and came up a stroke short. Given the high level of play, with both men canning birdies on the last two holes, most considered it the finest play-off in USGA history. There was more rejoicing in the locker room afterward; for the second year in a row a professional had prevailed in the Open against the relentless amateur from Atlanta. Pop thought Bob seemed more relieved than disappointed; he hadn't lost this title; Farrell had won it.

Slipping on a stylish beret, Johnny Farrell collected the Open trophy and his winner's check for one thousand dollars. Although a few dollars shy of his "best-dressed" check, his performance that day changed Farrell's life for the better forever. He'd not only won the U.S. Open—he had joined the most exclusive outfit in the sport of golf:

The "I Beat Bobby Jones" club.

After six weeks back and in his law office, Bob returned to Chicago to captain the United States Walker Cup team. During the ten practice rounds leading to the event, Bob worked out any lingering frustration about his loss to Farrell. He broke the scoring record at four different courses, shot eight of ten rounds under 70, averaging 68.5 for the stretch. In 1928 numbers, this was a level of play no one had ever approached. In the last tune-up, Bob won a one-day medal event at Flossmoor Country Club with a course record 67. At one point in that round—Pop kept the card—Bob recorded seven straight threes. A scary thought circulated through the press and among his amateur teammates: twenty-six-year-old Bob Jones, the world's greatest golfer and not yet at his physical peak, was actually *getting better*. Looking at his career from a distance, from the Open through the upcoming Amateur, this was his greatest sustained period of play. If further proof of Bob's mastery was needed, the U.S. team won the most lopsided victory in the five Walker Cups to date, 11–1. Bob won his singles match against Philip Perkins, the current British Amateur champion, by a score of 13 and 12.

Both teams hopped on to the Twentieth Century Limited afterward and trained to Boston, where the 1928 National Amateur was held at Brae Burn. This was the last bachelor outing for Bob with his Atlanta contingent and Walker Cup buddies; Mary would accompany him on every subsequent expedition but the last. Rated the top seed, Bob qualified easily, in fifth place. Then came what for Bob now almost constituted a phobia: Wednesday's dual eighteen-hole matches. He survived the first, 4 and 3, then faced an old foe of

Ouimet's from Boston, Ray Gorton. Gorton was a multiple Massachusetts Amateur champion and longtime member at Brae Burn who knew the course intimately and held its scoring record: the definition of a dangerous match-play opponent. Both men played dreadful front nines. Then, wrote Pop, "came the fireworks." Bob birdied the tenth, a short par five; Gorton topped him with an eagle to grab a one-hole lead. At the eleventh, Bob sliced his drive behind a stand of towering trees, two hundred yards from the green in deep rough. The odds dictated punching back into the fairway and trying to get up and down for par, but Gorton had hit a perfect drive after his eagle and was heating up; Bob couldn't afford to hand him another hole.

Pop: "Bobby took a 4 iron, swung as hard as he could, tearing up a great strip of turf and long grass, and the fascinated gallery saw the ball soar over the trees and descend on the green, five yards from the hole."

A shot eerily reminiscent of the one they'd both seen Ted Ray pull off at East Lake fifteen years earlier, Bob called it the best iron he ever played in competition. It didn't faze Gorton; he played his second to twenty feet and sank the putt for birdie. Bob dropped his putt as well to halve the hole, and for the moment blunted Gorton's momentum.

After trading holes, Bob squared the match at fifteen. They halved the sixteenth. At the 255-yard par three seventeenth, Gorton missed the green short; Bob went long into a bunker. Gorton chipped close and assured himself of par. Bob blasted out to the edge of the green, leaving himself a ticklish downhill eight-footer. He barely tapped the ball; it seemed to take a minute as it tracked toward the hole and then fell. When it did, Pop, watching from the hilltop behind the green, realized he was suddenly sitting on the grass. "I had dropped, too," he said.

At the eighteenth, Bob made a routine par. Gorton carded a stupendous four after popping up his drive to force sudden-death extra holes. The pressure finally hit Gorton. He sliced his drive behind a woodpile, while Bob played two safe shots to the green. Gorton reached the green in three, but his attempt to extend the match lipped out. Bob advanced to the field of sixteen, and the welcome refuge of thirty-six-hole matches.

Bob was never threatened again. He won Thursday's match with England's John Beck, 14 and 13. In the semifinals he pounded Phil Finlay, 13 and 12. The finals brought him together with Philip Perkins, the British Amateur champion he had recently demolished at the Walker Cup. Perkins had made a lot of noise in the press after Chicago about how he wasn't going to let that sort of thing happen again. The beating he took at Brae Burn only differed by a matter of degrees; Bob won his fourth U.S. Amateur title, 10 and 9.

Bob had tied Jerry Travers's record of four wins in the Amateur, and he'd done it in only five years. Add two wins each at the U.S. and British Opens and he now owned eight major titles. No man had ever won so many; the few who came close took decades to accumulate them. Bob had done it in only six years. He had also reached the goal he'd once set for himself of winning either a U.S. Open or Amateur for six years in a row. Pop didn't dare remind him; they were having too much fun, he didn't want it to end. But if fans and journalists felt there was a creeping sameness to Bob's domination of the game—the press had grown fond of calling him a "golfing machine"—no one experienced it more acutely than he did.

As he returned to Atlanta and settled into work, content to spend time with Mary and the children, and weekends with Dad and the boys at East Lake, the public persona he'd created felt increasingly like an intrusion. The spotlight didn't keep him warm, and he was forced to spend more time trying to avoid ways in which he might be perceived as exploiting his status than he did enjoying it. He turned down big cash offers for movies, exhibition tours—including an invitation to visit from the Japanese Foreign Ministry, where golf was just catching on—personal appearances, even a Broadway musical set at a country club; saying no, politely, became a full-time job. The conflict arose out of the good news that he had started to define and discover who he truly was: family man, Atlanta lawyer, dignified member of his community, gentleman athlete. In that order. A low-key life of quiet satisfaction suited him best; he soon realized he didn't feel suited to trial work. Confrontation wasn't his style, and he could never walk into a courtroom and be certain his celebrity wasn't exerting an undue influence on a judge or jury. That tilted the playing field and upset his sense of sportsmanship; shortly afterward he settled on civil and contract work as his métier. The irony of his predicament was inescapable; by virtue of playing a sport he loved in pursuit of realizing a private, personal excellence, he had become one of the century's most utterly famous human beings, which in turn made a private life that much more difficult to manage. There had always been a degree of detachment in Bob, a sense of a man observing life from a slight remove, one of the qualities that made him such a superlative golfer; he could maintain that detachment without ever losing his passion to succeed. His life resonated with contradictions.

Mary had begun to question his pursuit of this chimerical quest. She had a touch of the mystical about her, an offshoot of her Catholic faith. She read tarot cards, and showed an interest in the current trend of spiritualism, which gave her an appetite for the answers her parochial high school education hadn't provided. Mary was proud of Bob but knew the price he paid during these ordeals more than anyone: the extreme weight loss, the physical pain and private anguish. She wanted what any loving spouse wants for their partner: happiness, contentment, well-being. If all he got from soldiering out there was suffering and a fame he didn't seem to enjoy, what exactly was the point of all this? What more could he hope to learn or gain? Most important: What would it take for him to feel satisfied enough that he could set this madness aside and get on with the rest of his life? The life he now shared with her and the children and their family and friends at home?

Bob had owed her an answer for a long time, and now he finally had one to give. It had been percolating in the back of his mind for nearly two years. Casting his eye ahead he had settled on 1930: the next time the Walker Cup team traveled to England. The British Amateur was scheduled to be played at St. Andrews, his favorite course in the world; the British Open followed at Hoylake, where he'd made his overseas debut in 1921. The U.S. Open would be held a few weeks later, on a course called Interlachen in the Midwest near Minneapolis. And at the end of that summer the U.S. Amateur was returning to Merion, where Bob had arrived at fourteen and where he'd come back to win his first Amateur title eight years later. What better stage to set the climax of the boldest assault on the record books anyone had ever imagined? He could close the circle with perfect symmetry, but if he thought he'd climbed mountains before, this was a trek to Everest.

Four majors. Four wins. That was his ticket out of the game and into private life.

If he lived to tell about it.

Bob and Mary return to New York.

The Colonel, Clara, Mary, and Bob, 1929.

CHAPTER TWELVE

Preparation

By 1928 THE NATIONAL mood had turned frantic. The music grew louder, faster, more insistent; Benny Goodman, Gene Krupa, and Fats Waller epitomized the hot jazz style; a dreamy Swede named Greta Garbo ascended to her place as the last great siren of the silent screen. As the Jazz Age passed its peak and teetered toward disaster, the pursuit of pleasure and novelty for their own sake began to curdle. With the growing defiance of Prohibition came trouble; speakeasies multiplied, teenage drinking became a major social issue, and bootlegging had given birth to organized-crime outfits whose bottom lines rivaled major corporations'. The top twenty companies in America now controlled over half the country's wealth. Unions had taken a terrible beating, metaphorically and literally; the labor movement of the early century had all but disappeared. Everybody seemed to be chasing a buck, on the make, looking for a killing. Cynical columnist H. L. Mencken began referring to the upwardly mobile middle classes as the "booboisie."

When Al Jolson opened his mouth in *The Jazz Singer* and his singing voice emerged, the novelty of the talking picture took the moviegoing public by storm and flipped Hollywood on its ear. The careers of stars once assumed to be secure for decades vanished at the speed of sound. A conservative back-lash gained momentum nationwide, demanding more rigid enforcement of Prohibition; a bill to permanently ban the publication of "dirty books"—like James Joyce's *Ulysses*—nearly passed in the Senate. Provocative actress and playwright Mae West—the Madonna of her day—was arrested and briefly jailed on obscenity charges for her titillating play that she titled, not by acci-dent, *Sex*. The elevation of celebrity backstage gossip into front-page news had begun with the nationally syndicated Broadway column of Walter Winchell; the mindless idolatry of pop-culture figures took center stage of the public's attention, and the line dividing the public from the private began to disappear.

Calvin Coolidge had seen enough of Washington. Silent Cal stuck to his promise that he would not run for reelection in 1928 and retired to a quiet life in Massachusetts. He bought a big house—the only extravagance of his life—lived off his presidential pension, wrote a few magazine articles, served on a couple of corporate boards, and died as quietly as he lived, in 1933, at the age of sixty-one. The two remarkable men vying to replace him offered a study in American originals.

The Democrats nominated the governor of New York, Al Smith, the first Irish Catholic in American history to run for the presidency. An unabashed big-city liberal, populist, and opponent of Prohibition—they called themselves "wets"—Smith offered a best-case scenario of the American immigrant jour-ney. A child of the tenements, Al grew into prominence as part of the Tam-many Hall political machine in Manhattan. Once in office, his record as governor was spectacular. His progressive legislation improved the quality of life for millions of New Yorkers and he lowered taxes by eliminating waste. A hit play about his life ran on Broadway, named after the famous tune he used as his campaign song: *The Sidewalks of New York*. The coalition he formed—for the first time uniting Northern urban and Southern rural voters—revived the flagging fortunes of the Democratic party, garnering them the most votes they'd earned since Wilson's heyday, and set the stage for the ascendancy of his close friend Franklin Roosevelt.

His Republican opponent was Herbert Hoover, a fifty-four-year-old self-made millionaire from a small town in Iowa, son of a Quaker blacksmith. Orphaned at seven, raised by an uncle in Oregon, he hustled into the inaugu-ral freshman class of Stanford University and worked his way through college by running half a dozen entrepreneurial businesses. He met and married a fellow geology student—also from Iowa—named Lou Henry. Graduating with a degree in engineering, Hoover took a job managing a British mining operation in the wild Australian outback. When he recommended his bosses buy a prospective site he scouted on camelback and it turned out to be a literal gold mine, Hoover banked his first serious money. The company sent Hoover to China, where he worked as chief engineer for the Imperial Bureau of Mines. When the Boxer Rebellion broke out, Hoover and his wife, Lou, strapped on sidearms and manned the barricades, smuggling supplies to six hundred trapped Christian refugees and saving their lives. After hostilities ended, Hoover found an ancient map showing the location of a legendary silver mine in Burma. He tracked it down and claimed it for his company. When the Hoovers left China for London, his British employers rewarded him with a 20 percent stake in their operation. Although comparisons to Teddy Roosevelt's larger-than-life persona would become inevitable, Hoover always resented them: TR had entered life as the pampered son of a wealthy Eastern establishment family; Hoover had pulled himself up from nothing, and was damn proud of it.

By twenty-seven, Hoover was earning more money than any other man his age in the country. He had the Midas touch; when the Great War broke out, his net worth was well into the millions. Eager to move beyond accumulating capital for its own sake, Hoover entered public service. He headed the Commission for Relief in Belgium, saved the country from starvation in the wake of the German invasion, and was the only man involved in the Paris Peace Conference who emerged with an improved reputation. After he served successfully as secretary of commerce under Harding and Coolidge, there was no man in America more respected or prepared for the rigors of the nation's highest office. Hoover was a firm believer in individual initiative and believed there was no problem on earth that people of good will couldn't solve if they committed themselves. He trusted technology's ability to transform the future, was an enthusiastic booster of radio, and appeared on-screen in the first public demonstration of a newfangled invention called "television" in 1927.

The American people liked that Hoover had never held elective office; they called him the Great Engineer, and faith that he could fine-tune their unwieldy government like a well-oiled machine carried him to the White

House in November 1928 in a landslide. With his financial wizardry and business expertise at the country's helm, experts saw this current Golden Age of prosperity extending indefinitely into the future. At his inaugural speech the following spring Hoover offered visionary optimism about the prospects for his country: "We in America today are nearer to the final triumph over poverty than ever before in the history of any land. The poor-house is vanishing from among us."

Seven months later, the roof would fall in on the American dream.

After twenty-two consecutive match-play victories in the PGA Championship—and four straight years' custody of the Wannamaker Trophy—Walter Hagen finally lost in the third round of the 1928 event to Leo Diegel. The frantic Diegel, who some felt had the most talent in the pro game and the nervous system least equipped to service it, had consulted a psychiatrist to help him handle his anxiety issues. His victory in the PGA testified to its effectiveness, but he would have to wait to get his hands on the Wannamaker. Hagen had misplaced the huge trophy—he'd left it in a cab—and it would be two years before it turned up in a Detroit sporting goods factory.

Walter had been chosen to captain the second official United States Ryder Cup team, and he led them across the Atlantic at the end of April 1929. For the first time the team arrived in England sporting identical uniforms—a Hagen innovation—and the 1929 Ryder Cup, played at Moortown near Leeds in Yorkshire, proved to be the closest and most exciting in history. It came down to Hagen's final match against British captain George Duncan. A victory by Hagen would allow the defending American champs to retain the trophy, but Duncan hammered Walter decisively, 10 and 8, and the Ryder Cup for the first time stayed home in England. That was only one of the British trophies that Hagen had packed for this trip.

An early start date ensured the 1929 British Open at Muirfield would be played in the worst weather the sport's oldest championship had ever seen. On opening day, intermittent squalls brought down sheets of rain, and wind cold enough to freeze water buckets on the tees. Hagen shot 75, six shots off the pace set by Leo Diegel. The next day, in slightly warmer weather, Walter not only broke the course record with 67 but scored the lowest round ever recorded in a British Open. The field was cut to sixty-four men, and Hagen stood second among them, two strokes behind Diegel.

Journalist Al Laney covered the Open for the *Herald Tribune*, and before the tournament sat down to interview Hagen, who told him to forget what had happened at the Ryder Cup; he was going to win this Open. There was no ambiguity about the prediction, as there was later when Babe Ruth allegedly called a home run shot in the 1932 World Series. Walter stated it flat-out, but because Laney was writing what was called a "mailer," a feature sent to New York by mail to avoid cable costs, the story wasn't published until the tournament was over.

The next day, an epic gale blew in off the North Sea. Laney wrote that "it howled and screamed and sent huge combers rolling onto the beaches. It seemed to come from all directions, and if you did not brace your feet you could be blown off them." Laney couldn't believe his eyes when he went out after breakfast and ran into Hagen coming in off the course. With no long johns to wear, Walter had put two pairs of pajamas under his regular clothes and stuffed them with newspapers for insulation. The Haig had been out in the storm for over an hour to watch the early starters; he winked at Laney and told him he figured a score of 150 for the day should do the trick.

With golf balls flying every which way, Hagen kept his lofted irons in the bag and played the entire third round without lifting his "quail high stingers" more than twenty feet off the ground. Supremely confident in his short game, he left his low approaches short of the greens, then chipped up and putted down for pars. Fifty-nine-year-old Harry Vardon, playing in his last Open and in obviously declining health, barely survived the ordeal. Golfers passed Hagen going backward and others withdrew just to get out of the storm. Hagen finished with 75 and took a four-stroke lead into lunch before his final round. When he ran into a thoroughly frosted Al Laney in the clubhouse, Hagen asked: "Where were you? It was a lot of fun out there."

That afternoon the weather degenerated, the wind rose, and a freezing rain added to the misery. Hagen kept smiling; if it hadn't been so cold he probably would have whistled. Thousands of hardy Scots in attendance that day paid him the ultimate compliment and walked the entire round in his gallery as he laughed and chatted with them. He always played his best in front of an audience, but he also had a practical reason: standing on the perimeter of the fairways, they created a windbreak for his punch shots. Walter matched his morning 75, hitting the number he'd predicted to Al Laney, and won his fourth British Open by six shots. In his speech after they gave him back the Jug, Walter graciously told the crowd that he hoped he had never done anything to offend them. After that heroic performance, as far as Hagen and the British were concerned, all had finally been forgiven. At thirty-six, although he didn't know it yet, Walter Hagen had just won his eleventh and last major championship.

Pop Keeler estimated that Bob played ten rounds of golf between the 1928 Amateur and the 1929 U.S. Open. He was admitted to the Federal Bar in May, and studying for that exam in addition to his regular workload kept him off the course more than ever before. During a brief business trip to New York City in late May, after a practice round at Winged Foot with Forrest Adair, Bill Nye — a recently retired Secret Service agent—and businessman Fred Trabold, they retired to Trabold's Park Avenue apartment for a game of bridge. Sometime during the evening thieves broke into the car and stole both Bob's and Adair's golf clubs. Calamity Jane, Jeanie Deans, and his thirteen other sticks had been kidnapped.

It appeared to be an inside job; Bill Nye called Grover Whalen, the New York police commissioner. Whalen suspected members of the Mob had followed them home from dinner and knew exactly whose clubs they were stealing. Instead of waiting for a ransom demand, Nye and Whalen sent word through the New York underground that the perpetrators of this crime would be dealt with severely. The story made front-page news in New York and around the country: for curiosity value the theft of Bob Jones's golf clubs nearly rivaled the recent St. Valentine's Day Massacre in Chicago. Scheduled to leave town the next day and with the U.S. Open only a few weeks away, Bob urgently wired Old Tom Stewart in St. Andrews, asking him to build a duplicate set at once and ship them overseas. (Stewart forged a number of extra sets, and later got into trouble for stamping them with the initials "RTJ" and selling them as "Bobby Jones' clubs.") By the end of the following day Bob's clubs and bag appeared, intact and untouched, in the office of a local garage owner; the thieves turned out to be two young kids who had robbed the car at random, with no idea what they'd taken. When they realized the trouble they were in they tried to sell them on the cheap to the garage owner; he recognized the clubs and called the police. The man collected a handsome reward, the kids were never named or arrested, and the clubs were put on the next train to Atlanta and followed Bob home.

In the middle of June Bob returned to New York to spend ten days preparing for the Open at Winged Foot Golf Club, in suburban Westchester County. Home to two courses built in 1923, Winged Foot was the handiwork of another inspired amateur and one of the game's great eccentrics, Albert W. Tillinghast, or Terrible Tilly, as people who often played his courses called him. Tillinghast came from money, and happened upon golf course architecture purely by chance when he discovered he possessed a gift for transforming raw real estate into big, brawny fairways and greens.

Winged Foot's name derived from the ankles of the Greek messenger god Mercury, symbol for the New York Athletic Club, whose members had decided to add a pastoral outpost to their Manhattan stronghold. These socially prominent physical fitness fanatics were alleged to have told Tillinghast: "Give us a man-sized course." He delivered. Tilly moved 7,200 tons of rocks and cut down 7,800 trees to create the West Course, where the thirty-third Open would be played. The end result was a tight, torturous, 6,900-yard test of manhood; of its twelve par fours, ten measured more than 400 yards, protected by deep frightening bunkers. Tillinghast himself said about these holes: "They were of a sturdy breed." Translation: Bring your best game.

Bob appeared to have done just that, turning in two 69s during practice rounds. Mortal men simply did not break par at Winged Foot and Jones did it twice. Bob figured if he could master the greased-lightning greens he had a good shot at the trophy; he spent the entire last day of practice on the putting green. The next day, Bob pinned another 69 on the West Course and led the first round of the Open by a stroke over Al Espinosa, a slow-footed thirty-four-year-old pro from the Monterey Peninsula in California. Hard as it is to believe, this was the first time Bob had ever broken 70 in a round at the U.S. Open. The next day a thunderstorm dampened Bob's assault on Winged Foot; he fell back with a 75. Playing in the morning before the rain, Espinosa and Gene Sarazen ended up tied for the lead at 142, two strokes ahead of Bob.

Saturday, the final day, dawned bright and sunny. The USGA's raising ticket prices to three dollars a head discouraged no one from showing up to watch when Bobby Jones was in the running. The rain of the day before had slowed the greens but done little to dampen the fast-draining fairways. Advantage Jones. Pop watched the morning round, noting that Bob "played with great confidence and boldness." Nothing troubled him, no one seemed to be in his way. He returned with 71, good for a three-stroke lead over Sarazen and four over Espinosa. Five strokes was then, and still is, considered the outside limit for comebacks in the final round of an Open. Although two men were inside that mark, there wasn't a soul at Winged Foot who would have bet against Bob. As he ate his traditional lunch of tea and toast, both Sarazen and Espinosa went out ahead of him; Gene shot six over on the front and waved good-bye to his chances. Espinosa played the front in a respectable 36, but a disastrous eight on the twelfth hole appeared to sound the death knell for him as well.

Bob sailed through his first seven holes, showing magisterial command of his game, and stepped to the eighth tee needing only to par the next two holes to match Espinosa's front side. Knowing Espinosa had tanked at twelve, Bob blasted his drive around the dogleg, leaving a four iron to the green. With the wind blowing hard from the right he sent his approach toward that side of the green, but the wind didn't move the ball. It stayed dead on line, caught the edge of the green, and bounced into a deep bunker.

The recovery didn't look difficult; he had a good lie and room to work with on the green. He even liked the shot as he hit it, but the green sloped away from him and a full day of sunlight had dried out the surface. The ball ran and ran, past the flagstick, off the green, and didn't stop until it trickled into another bunker on the other side, settling just under the lip. Now he needed to get up and down for bogey.

Bob decided to blast the ball out to get past that lip. He did. All the way back across the green and back into the original bunker. The crowd reacted as if they'd been punched in the gut. After trudging across the green for the third time like a weekend duffer, he lofted the ball softly out of the sand and it stayed on the short grass, but he needed two putts to get down for a triple-bogey seven.

He appeared to shake it off with a birdie at the ninth. Bob had gone out in 38 and still held an insurmountable lead over Espinosa. But playing ahead, after his catastrophic twelfth, Espinosa figured he was out of it and had nothing left to lose. Nothing better illustrates Bob's oft-repeated maxim that golf is a game played entirely on the six inches of real estate between the ears. Thinking the pressure was off, Espinosa marched through the last six holes of his final round in one under par and finished with a 75.

Bob's escapades in the bunkers at eight had the opposite affect on his psyche. He called his back nine "an agony of anxiety." He finished the twelfth hole with a six-stroke lead over Espinosa, but instead of sprinting for the finish he started playing not to lose. Doubt crept into his mind, and spread to his arms and hands. He started steering the ball. He lost a stroke at thirteen, scrambled for par at fourteen, then sliced his drive on fifteen behind a stand of trees. After knocking a recovery back to the fairway he flew his next over the green into knee-deep rough, flubbed his pitch onto a little knoll between himself and the green, and ended up recording another triple-bogey seven on the hole.

Most of his lead over Espinosa had been squandered. To hold on to the single stroke that remained he needed to finish with three fours, and his next hole, the sixteenth, was a par five. With the wind behind him Bob killed his drive, then played a splendid long iron onto the green only twenty feet from the flag. It was Calamity Jane's turn to go south. He left his first putt five feet short, missed his second, and made five. Now Bob had to finish with two fours just to tie Espinosa, already in the clubhouse and more shocked than anyone at Winged Foot when he learned that he still had a chance at the title.

Bob collected his par at seventeen without incident. He hit a serviceable drive at the 440-yard eighteenth, leaving himself a long iron into a devilish, undulating green. He pulled the approach slightly and the shot came up less than a yard short of where it needed to land to hold the putting surface, then slowly rolled back down, stopping just short of a bunker in deep rough. The crowd surrounding the green stood five deep as Bob reached his ball. Pop Keeler managed to see Bob play his delicate pitch up to the green; it rolled and stopped a dozen feet from the flag. Downhill, sidehill, on a surface that had turned to glass; if he missed it, Al Espinosa would win the Open.

Pop got swallowed up in the crowd, lost sight of the green, and found himself standing next to a photographer perched on a stepladder. Keeler quickly ran through all the calculations: Bobby needed the putt not only to force a play-off but to keep his score under 80. He'd never scored below 70 or above 79 in an Open, and he'd already broken the record on the low side. If he failed on the high side Bob would be the first to say he didn't deserve to win. But what would it do to his confidence? Six strokes lost on the last six holes? What would such a collapse do to his ambitious plans for 1930? "I knew in a sort of bewildering flash that if that putt stayed out," wrote Keeler, "it would remain a spreading and fatal blot, never to be wiped from his record."

Pop couldn't even watch, afraid somehow that the ball wouldn't find the hole if he did. A heavy silence descended. Somewhere, very far off, Keeler thought he heard a church bell slowly ringing. Then a gentle click from the green, Calamity Jane meeting the ball. He heard another click, the shutter of the camera in the hands of the photographer above him, as the ball started its journey. A faint stirring from the crowd, no louder than the intake of ten thousand breaths . . . which grew steadily in volume, then started to change to a fatal gasp—the ball had tracked ever so slowly straight for the hole and then stopped on the rim—

It was over, it stayed out—

No, the gasp changed to a roar loud enough to wake the dead—the ball made one last turn and dropped.

Bob had salvaged a 79 and his tournament. Because of everything that followed, Pop later called that putt the most important shot of his friend's career. Al Watrous, who had dueled so memorably with Bob at the 1926 British Open, later told Keeler that Bob's last putt was so perfectly calibrated that if the hole had been a circle drawn on the green, the ball would have rolled to a dead stop right in the middle of it.

"Bobby was not accessible," wrote Keeler. "The crowd had him."

It would be his fourth Open play-off in seven years; for Espinosa, his first. Thirty-six holes, scheduled for nine o'clock Sunday morning. But Bob knew that Al Espinosa was a devoted Catholic, from one of the founding Spanish families of California. Would the USGA mind delaying the start until ten so that Al could attend Mass? He meant it as a courtesy, but somewhere in the back of his mind another subliminal message must have gotten through to Espinosa: if any man hoped to beat Bob over thirty-six holes, he needed divine intervention. Both men attended the same service, as it turned out, and both took their wives.

Al Espinosa was a combat veteran of the Great War, but he admitted he'd never faced anything like the pressures of an Open play-off before. When Bob stumbled coming out of the gate that morning—playing the first three holes in four over par—Espinosa's hopes rose to meet the wind for one brief shining hour. Then Bob remembered who he was playing—Old Man Par, not Al Espinosa—and restored the balance of nature.

Bob won the play-off by twenty-three strokes.

He shot 72-69. Al Espinosa failed to break 80, twice. It remains to this day the greatest margin of victory in a play-off of any important championship. Bob stamped his name on the big silver cup for the third time, and his national championship winning streak reached seven years. If Pop's estimate is accurate, he had done it after playing ten rounds of golf in the previous six months.

Once they were home in Atlanta, Bob told Keeler that his quest for all four major titles in 1930 was officially on, but Pop was not to say a word to anyone. For the first time the city decided to hold off throwing a parade; maybe they sensed something bigger was on the horizon. Bob practically owned the deed and title to the Amateur, and that tournament was only six weeks away. It was being played for the first time on the West Coast, at a nine-year-old course on the Monterey Peninsula in northern California that was part of the area's first big tourist destination, the Del Monte Hotel and Resort. They called the course that had been drawing such ecstatic reviews Pebble Beach. Bob's work schedule didn't allow the luxury of practicing full-time, so he started going into the office early and squeezed in as many afternoon rounds as he could.

During one of those rounds at the end of July, Bob experienced his close encounter with the thunderbolt that took down the chimney at East Lake. Feeling lucky that he and his foursome escaped serious injury, if not death, he reported no ill effects from the blow he absorbed to the back of his neck; in the books he wrote later he never mentioned suffering any injury. But Bob was also never one to complain, and there were hints of persistent neck and shoulder problems that had lingered since the Amateur at Muirfield in 1926. If he felt any the worse for wear from the chunk of masonry that nearly took his head off after the lightning strike, he told no one about it. On the other hand, lightning of one kind or another had been striking Bob since he was a boy, in the form of uncommon talent, experience, or fame. The odds of real lightning hitting you were only 300,000 to 1; he'd been paying off longer shots than that all his life. The question of what this bolt had done to him wouldn't be answered for twenty years.

A little over two weeks later, on August 17, Bob, his parents, Mary, Pop, and the rest of his Atlanta entourage—along with the Havemeyer Trophy—boarded a private rail car and headed west to Los Angeles.

Traveling by private rail car sounds glamorous, but this was a decade before air conditioning. By the time their train hit the Southwestern desert in the late summer heat, Bob and the rest of his party felt like they were traveling in a portable oven. They stopped for a day to take in the spectacle of the Grand Canyon—where they witnessed a Hopi Indian rain dance ceremony, followed immediately by a teeth-rattling thunderstorm—then rolled into Los Angeles in the early afternoon and checked into the downtown Biltmore Hotel. Bob drove out to Lakeside Golf Club in the San Fernando Valley to get in a private round of golf. When word spread through the Toluca Lake neighborhood that Jones was on their local course, hundreds lined the fairways by the time he reached the back nine. Bob's celebrity could now get him through any door in the Western world, but there were few places he enjoyed more than laid-back, luxurious Southern California. The Joneses spent a couple of days hobnobbing with Hollywood royalty—Bob also played in an exhibition at Los Angeles Country Club, a conservative outpost on the western side of town where flashy show-business types weren't welcome—and renewed the acquaintance of action movie kingpin Douglas Fairbanks, whose private Donald Ross–designed course in his Beverly Hills backyard met with Bob's approval.

After another day spent in the company of celebrated cowboy humorist Will Rogers at his ranch near Santa Monica, the Jones party took the train north to San Francisco. This visit to Hollywood laid the groundwork for a big part of Bob's future; he would return less than two years later to begin a career in movies.

The golf course at Pebble Beach opened in 1919, and like so many other classic American courses it was primarily the handiwork of a passionate amateur. Jack Neville was a real estate salesman and former California State Amateur champion, and Pebble Beach was the only golf course he ever produced. As he modestly described the effort years later: "Years before it was built, I could see this place as a golf links. Nature had intended it to be nothing else. All we did was cut away a few trees, install a few sprinklers and sow a little seed." Although he'd found an extraordinary canvas to work on, there was obviously a good deal more artistry to Neville's creation than he was willing to take credit for, and the stunning result has been stealing the breath away from visitors ever since. A professional long-drive specialist named Douglas Grant had consulted with Neville during construction, and former National Amateur champion Chandler Egan also supervised a renovation in preparation for the 1929 Amateur.

Jones added his voice to the chorus of admirers. His first time around Pebble Beach, Bob tied the course record and spoke enthusiastically to reporters about it afterward. Hundreds watched him that day and thousands more flocked from all over the Bay Area to see the Emperor Jones practice his craft. By this time he had become much more than a sports hero; Bob had acquired the status of a cherished national landmark, and even if you had no interest whatsoever in his sport, just saying you'd seen him swing a club had become the kind of thing you wanted to be able to tell your grandchildren. A few days later some of them were treated to the sight of Bob breaking the record at Pebble with a 67—at one point collecting seven straight birdies—and shooting four under par on its picture-postcard back nine. Already established as the number-one seed, when Bob tied for the qualifying medal with Eugene Homans—one of his victims the previous year at Minikahda—predictions for a fifth Amateur title filled the columns of every golf writer in America. Pop thought Bob had never played better leading up to any championship, but he found the air of invincibility that had been conferred on his friend by the world at large more than a little annoying. As great as Bob had become, not even he could ever master the world's hardest sport.

"No man ever has had golf under his thumb," wrote Keeler. "No man ever will have golf under his thumb. The game is greater than the man. Golf is like the game of life. No man ever will be its master."

Something was nagging at Bob, and had been ever since they first arrived at Pebble. Those early-round eighteen-hole matches were staring his man in the face; Bob might have four Amateur titles to his name, but he had also lost in every round of the tournament now but the first. This would be his nineteenth eighteen-hole amateur match of the last five years and he had lost only one of them—to Andrew Jamieson at Muirfield in 1926, when he played despite his injured neck.

Enter Johnny Goodman: a blond, handsome twenty-year-old from Omaha, an orphan who had grown up poor and more or less stayed put. Part of the mythology that quickly sprang up around him was that, unable to afford regular train travel, Goodman had borrowed a friend's cattleman pass and ridden the rails to the tournament in a cattle car. The record shows that did happen at least once, earlier in the year on his way to the Open at Winged Foot, but after a good showing there he was riding in coach on his way to the Amateur with the rest of the human beings, although some reports still insisted that he reached Pebble Beach by hitching a ride on a cattle truck. After working as a caddie through childhood, Goodman had developed into the best player ever produced by the state of Nebraska. He was cocky, but he could also back it up. The qualifying score that earned him his invite to the Amateur was the lowest of a thousand entrants from around the country, and he had recently finished as low amateur—after Jones—in the Open at Winged Foot. Goodman was no fluke, no Andrew Jamieson; he was a tough, seasoned competitor who was desperately hungry to put his name on the map. He was also a devoted admirer of Mr. Bobby Jones, and Goodman had maintained his amateur status in order to emulate him, at considerable hardship.

After a brilliant week of play, Bob started their match by missing every shot of the first three holes. When Goodman sank a ten-foot putt for birdie on the third, Bob was down three to his unheralded opponent. Bob rallied, birdying two of the next three to whittle Goodman's lead to one. Both men reached the green on the par three seventh; when Bob tried to press for advantage and jam his putt home for a birdie, it ran six feet past and missed the comebacker for par. Goodman went two up and showed no sign of nerves. Bob fought back again and finally squared the match at twelve. On the thirteenth green, when Bob lofted a stymied putt over Goodman's ball and dropped it straight into the cup to halve the hole, the crowd went mad, certain Bob would capitalize on the momentum and sweep this persistent challenger from his path.

The match turned at the par five fourteenth. When Goodman's drive landed in the rough, Bob decided to shoot for the green in two and instead found a deep greenside bunker. Goodman recovered brilliantly; short of the green in three, he chipped up and saved par. Bob missed his putt to stay even and went one down again. They matched pars for the next three holes, Goodman standing tall against the mounting pressure of the Jones mystique. Needing a birdie at the long seaside eighteenth to get back to square and force extra holes, Bob's last putt died two inches short. Goodman calmly two-putted for his par and eliminated Bob Jones from the 1929 Amateur.

Shock waves reverberated from the stunned gallery at Pebble Beach to sports pages and radio reports across the country and around the world. Bob's devoted fans went into mourning. Initially irritated at himself for throwing the match away on those careless opening holes, by early that afternoon Bob had adjusted his reaction to one of relief. With the Open already in his pocket for the year and his string of championship years intact at seven, he'd lost nothing he couldn't afford. Most importantly, he'd purged that phobia about losing an early eighteen-hole match from his mind; the aftereffects were nowhere near as dire as he'd imagined. In fact, his loss at Pebble had one last positive effect: Bob was more determined than ever to capture the four championships up for grabs in 1930.

Bob gave Johnny Goodman all the credit he deserved for beating him and told Pop he was looking forward to relaxing and watching the rest of the action at the Amateur; he'd been so good for so long he hadn't had a chance to watch much of the event in person. That same afternoon he saw Goodman lose his second-round match to a talented newcomer from Rhode Island named William Lawson Little. Most observers concluded that the game's reliable old guard was giving ground to an emerging group of younger players. George Von Elm lost his first-round match as well, and Francis Ouimet went out in the third round against Lawson Little; Bob ended up refereeing that match for his old friend. When he walked out on a green late in the match to determine who was away from the hole he was greeted with the biggest ovation of the day.

The next day Bob and Francis decided to forgo the Amateur and accept an invitation to play at a new course nearby they'd heard everyone at Pebble raving about. A few years earlier a former American Amateur champion—she'd ended Alexa Stirling's reign in 1921—and wealthy Eastern socialite named Marion Hollins had fallen in love with a heavenly slice of seaside land just north of Pebble Beach and hired the gifted Scots architect Dr. Alister MacKenzie to transform it into a golf course. Hollins named the result Cypress Point for the striking windswept trees that adorned the rocky coastline. Bob decided at first glance it was the most dramatic layout he'd seen anywhere in the world. So impressed was he with MacKenzie's routing and masterful eye for detail that when the moment came a few years later to select an architect for a dream course he planned to build, Alister MacKenzie was the man Bob tapped for the job.

The 1929 Amateur ended in disappointment for everyone but the eventual champion, Minneapolis's Harrison "Jimmy" Johnston, who defeated a dentist from Oregon named O.F. Willing to win the title. With Jones, Von Elm, Ouimet, and many other leading contenders eliminated so soon, attendance suffered drastically. More than any other sport, as it would years later with Arnold Palmer and Tiger Woods, by the end of the 1920s golf in America had become a one-man phenomenon.

Johnny Goodman had a bright future, and he joined George Von Elm, Cyril Walker, Willie MacFarlane, Johnny Farrell, and Andrew Jamieson in the game's most exclusive company: the "I Beat Bobby Jones" club.

Only one more name would ever join the list.

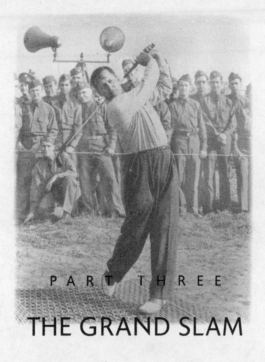

PART THREE

THE GRAND SLAM

The price he pays for his success is too high.

— BERNARD DARWIN

*No one knows what will happen in golf until
it happens. All you can do is work and
suffer and wait for fate.*

— BOB JONES

Bob with the British Amateur Trophy.

CHAPTER THIRTEEN

The Amateur, St. Andrews

BOB AND HIS ENTOURAGE took the scenic route home from San Francisco, traveling through Yellowstone National Park and arriving in Atlanta near the end of September. Bob had noticed during their California stay that the state's housing market appeared to be in serious trouble; similar to what had happened in Florida four years before, speculators had driven prices out of the reach of buyers. The Golden State's land rush had turned sour, supply exceeded demand, and entire developments languished. The same phenomenon had hit Wall Street. The stock market had until recently been the exclusive province of the country's wealthy elite; the middle class simply couldn't afford to gamble with its money. In a country of 120 million people, fewer than 2 million invested in stocks and bonds. But just as they had in real estate, in the last few years speculators had moved into the market, over half a million of them, driving up stock prices artificially and buying on margin; the volume of trading since 1927 had doubled. A creeping amorality had infiltrated the practices of many brokerage houses and businesses; making money through stock manipulation turned into a casino game, and more and more people were willing to put their chips in play. The idea of carrying debt, even mortgaging a house, was a brand-new phenomenon for middle-class people, and many had become dangerously overextended; personal debt doubled in the second half of the decade. While the national economy showed signs of weakening, the market's gyrations grew increasingly volatile through 1929, experiencing sharper downturns and steeper recoveries. By September, the wildly overvalued Dow Jones Industrial Average had hit an all-time high of 381. Seasoned investors knew the market had reached its top and began quietly pulling out their money.

Toward the end of the month the market took another severe dip and for the first time prices didn't bounce back. Within three weeks what began as a trickle of investors leaving the market turned into a flood. On the morning of Thursday, October 24, stockbrokers were overwhelmed with sell orders, and no one wanted to buy; over $9 billion in losses was recorded in less than a day's trading. They closed the doors to the Stock Exchange to avoid a panic, and the six leading Wall Street bankers poured $20 million back into bellwether stocks to staunch the bleeding. President Hoover spoke on national radio the next day to reassure the nation that the market's valuations remained sound; trading stabilized on Friday and through the half day Wall Street then stayed open on Saturday. On Sunday very few investors rested; the soul searching that took place led to a collective panic when the opening bell rang on Monday morning.

Prices plummeted from the opening bell. Investors lost $14 billion—1929 dollars—by the end of the session. Solid blue-chip companies sold off like penny stocks. Experts threw up their hands. Prices kept dropping and no one could find the floor; it was bucking and rolling beneath them like a barrel in a Coney Island fun house. The six Wall Street titans who had stemmed the tide on Thursday jumped out in front of everyone else, making a mad dash for the door; they pulled their money out just in time, but half of them would later wind up in federal prison for previous financial shenanigans.

October 29. Black Tuesday. Sixteen million shares sold. Another $15 billion lost. The single worst day that any publicly traded stock market had experienced in human history. Stock tickers broke down trying to keep up with the frantic selling. As the smoke cleared, the cold hard ground rose up to meet them fast; the market had crashed, but despite persistent legends to the contrary, no investors or brokers threw themselves out of Wall Street's windows. There would be a legion of suicides in the months and years to come, not only in the financial capitals but around the country and the world, but on that day the hundreds of thousands who'd been burned by the Crash were too numb with shock to drag themselves over the windowsill.

The Roaring Twenties ended two months ahead of the calendar. The Jazz Age was over.

Bob Jones hadn't put together enough of a nest egg to risk losing any of it in the stock market. The Crash didn't affect his personal fortunes, nor did it catastrophically affect his father's law practice. Coca-Cola, the Colonel's biggest client, was and would remain for the next ten years the definition of a Depression-proof company; no matter how low their spirits sank, most people still wanted and could afford a cheap, refreshing beverage. But grandfather R. T. Jones's textile business in Canton, Georgia, was hit hard; his homegrown silk operation went bust, so he went back to harvesting cotton and manufacturing generic blue denim. R.T. refused to let his workers suffer the consequences, kept them all on his payroll, swallowed his losses, warehoused his surpluses, and hunkered down to wait for a better day.

Bob's sole focus now became the 1930 championship season. Throughout the 1920s he had averaged no more than three months in tournament competition, but this plan required a once-in-a-lifetime effort. He took the Colonel into his confidence and received his blessing to take time away from their practice to devote most of the coming seasons to the campaign.

The strain of winning nine championships during the last seven years had left Bob progressively more fragile physically and emotionally. In addition to the increasing mental stress and severe weight loss, digestive problems were a regular part of any tournament now. He suffered from severe muscle spasms in his neck and right shoulder, the legacy of his injury at Muirfield, or perhaps the first symptoms of the injury caused by the lightning strike. He hid these traumas from everyone else in his life, but Mary could plainly see the toll they were taking on him. When Bob shared with her his goals for the coming year she insisted on going with him to Britain. She was staking her claim; she wanted Bobby back, for herself, for his own good, and for the good of their children. He welcomed the idea. His closest confidante would be there either to console him in defeat or share his greatest triumph. Bob had come to believe in the role of fate in human affairs, but Mary never needed convincing. Her religious convictions rested on the bedrock of destiny, and not long before they sailed for Europe she actually dreamed that Bob won all four tournaments. Clear about the magnitude of what he was going after, she wanted to support him whatever the outcome, as long as Bob kept his promise to walk away from the game. Although she never showed it in public, Mary had inherited a fiery temper from her father and now had the confidence to fight for what she wanted. The world had already taken much more from her husband than she had ever been comfortable watching him give.

For the first time in his life Bob began a rigorous training regime to condition himself for the coming ordeal. He made at least two trips to Highlands Country Club in North Carolina to get in some uncharacteristic early winter rounds, where he also played tennis to stay in shape. Back in Atlanta he also spent an hour each day playing an aerobically intense indoor variation on tennis invented by his movie-star pal Douglas Fairbanks. In his honor they called the game "Doug": it was played with tennis rackets and a heavy badminton shuttlecock on an enlarged court, over a net hoisted somewhere between tennis and badminton standards. Bob set up a "Doug" court on the stage of an empty theater owned by a friend in downtown Atlanta near his law office and stopped there on his way home every afternoon. Between Christmas and March, when his playing season officially began, Bob lost over twenty pounds and was in the best shape of his life. When the weather improved and he could comfortably play golf on a daily basis, he matched his own course record of 63 during one of his first warmup rounds at East Lake. Sufficiently encouraged, he entered his name in the Savannah Open, a mid-March tournament and an important event on the professionals' developing winter circuit.

Bob decided to room in Savannah with a twenty-one-year-old player from Missouri named Horton Smith, who had just taken the pro ranks by storm. Smith was a member of the game's new breed who'd grown up playing steel-shafted clubs, one of the first to follow in Hagen's pioneering footsteps. Unattached as a resident pro at a country club, Smith was convinced he could earn a living playing in tournaments from the start of his career and he was right. The leading money winner on the pro circuit in the 1928–1929 winter season, Smith won eight of the nine tournaments he entered and took home over eleven thousand dollars. His smooth, syrupy-tempo swing owed a lot to Bob, and the two hit it off at once, talking theory and exchanging pointers, the beginning of a lifelong friendship. Bob picked up a pointer from Smith about cocking his wrists at the beginning of the downswing, which he felt allowed him to strike the ball more crisply with his short irons. Although they were never paired together once play began, the tournament at the Savannah Golf Club turned into a personal battle between them. Bob broke the course record during the first round with 67; it stood until Smith's second round the next day, when he lowered it to 66. Smith carried a five-stroke lead into the final day. In the third round, Bob dropped the record another notch with a 65. When Smith finished with 70 the two men were deadlocked going into the fourth and final round.

Playing half an hour ahead of Smith, Bob set the pace at par and Horton stayed with him, maintaining the tie through sixteen holes. The break came at seventeen. Trying to reach the long par five in two, Bob hooked his approach out of bounds and carded a bogey. Despite recovering with a birdie at the last hole, he'd left an opening that Smith exploited; he finished birdie-par to beat Bob by a single stroke, at ten under par, and miles ahead of the rest of the field. Horton Smith collected the winner's check for one thousand dollars; the tournament awarded Bob a customized twelve-gauge double-barrel shotgun that over the years became his favorite hunting gun. The press decided that at long last a young pro had arrived who could give the Emperor Jones a fight for his crown.

Two weeks later, just after Bob celebrated his twenty-eighth birthday, he and Horton Smith renewed their rivalry at the Southeastern Open, played on two courses in Augusta, Georgia, a longtime winter retreat for residents of Atlanta and the South. The tournament sponsors had persuaded Smith to enter at the last minute, hoping to create another duel with Bob like the one they'd put on in Savannah. They paired the men for the first two rounds in anticipation of fireworks, but Bob had played these two courses since he was a teenager; Smith had never seen them before, and arrived by private plane too late to get in a practice round. They were tough, tight tracks, with frighteningly fast greens, cut so quick the sun glared off them as if they were stainless steel. Benefiting from the hard work he'd put in over the winter, Bob came into full possession of his game at Augusta, months earlier than he'd ever done before. While he arrived fresh and rested, the pros were at the end of their winter schedule and showed signs of fatigue.

Bob led after the first two rounds, three shots ahead of Horton Smith. On the second day he lapped the field and finished thirteen shots ahead with Smith in distant second place. Bob had stretched his lead to eighteen with only three holes left, when a half-hour delay on the sixteenth tee blunted his concentration. While killing time with Keeler, Granny Rice, and a privileged, interested spectator by the name of Ty Cobb, Bob ignored the fiery Cobb's suggestions that he stay on his feet and swing a club to keep loose. Instead Bob lay down on the grass and lounged while he chatted with his old friends. When play resumed he hooked two of his final three drives into the weeds and tossed away three strokes on the finishing holes. Later that evening over cocktails at Cobb's house in Augusta, the recently retired baseball immortal took him aside and, as Bob later described, "I got the dressing-down of my life. It was not Ty's idea just to win, but to win by the most you could. That's what made him such a great player." But Cobb assumed Bob had let down because he'd refused to follow his advice and let his muscles get cold. Bob wrote years later his lapse had been due to an even worse offense that in the face of Cobb's wrath he couldn't bring himself to confess: mental complacency.

Bob had avenged his loss to Horton Smith faster and more decisively than usual; this was the greatest margin of victory in his career. Superlatives rained down in the wake of his performance, with Keeler and Rice leading the chorus; sportswriters were running out of adjectives to describe him. The most extravagant compliment came from one of Bob's favorite former adversaries. After watching Jones dominate both courses at Augusta, destroy one of the best pro-am fields of the year—and wallop him personally by twenty-nine strokes— the man Bob had beaten to win his first U.S. Open in 1923, Bobby Cruickshank, took Pop aside and predicted that Bob would not only win the British Open and Amateur, he would return to the United States and win the Open and Amateur back home as well. Pop was so astonished anyone had hit on Bob's secret intentions, even inadvertently, that he didn't even mention the audacious wager to Bob. This proved to be much more than idle locker-room chatter on Cruickshank's part; he cabled fifty dollars to his father-in-law in England, instructing him to place a bet with a London bookmaker that Jones would win all four of the year's major championships. The gamble was so outrageous it wasn't even on the touts' boards; when they finally calculated probabilities, Cruickshank received odds of 210 to 1. Inspired by the gesture, a group of Bob's friends in Atlanta cobbled together a much larger wager—

twenty-five hundred dollars—that they placed on the same unlikely bet. The British touts who booked it asked Lloyd's of London to insure their long-shot gamble; Lloyd's weighed the odds, and agreed.

Before he left Augusta, Bob made a crucial discovery that would substantially affect the sport's future development. Right next door to Augusta Country Club stood an overgrown, decaying 365-acre property called Fruitlands Nurseries. An indigo plantation before the Civil War, the property was sold soon after the war ended to a visiting Belgian nobleman, Baron Louis Mathieu Edouard Berckmans. Under the direction of Berckmans and his son Prosper, it had served for close to fifty years as one of the principal suppliers of exotic fruit trees and flowers in the country, but Fruitlands Nurseries' fortunes died with the younger Berckmans in 1910. After a decade of struggle the business shuttered its gates in 1918. Five years later a Miami developer bought the property out of bankruptcy with the hopes of turning it into a grand hotel and golf resort, but in the aftermath of the Florida real estate crash his plans never came to fruition. Bob saw that the grounds had obviously gone to seed, but the lushly flowered landscape, its azaleas, magnolias, and dogwoods, just then in the early bloom of spring, lingered in his mind long afterward as the possible site for a project he had begun to envision for after his retirement: building the perfect golf course.

Horton Smith also benefited from Bob's survey of that old, abandoned nursery, which more than made up for the drubbing he absorbed on the course next door. A few years later when Augusta National opened and Bob decided to host a friendly gathering to introduce his creation to the best players in the country, Smith would go on to win two of the first three tournaments that soon became known as the Masters.

The journey began with a grand send-off thrown by his friends at East Lake on April 21. The city presented him with a gilded four-leaf clover for luck, and Augusta National Golf Club contributed a grandfather clock in honor of his recent win there, which sits in the lobby at East Lake to this day. The Colonel and Clara wouldn't be on this trip; they had been recruited to stay home and babysit the children. Bob, Mary, Pop, and Eleanor Keeler and the rest of a small Atlanta entourage left a few days later and arrived in New York on April 28, where members of Bob's Walker Cup team had gathered.

After a celebratory lunch hosted by the USGA at Engineers Club on Long Island, two days later the Americans boarded the *Mauretania* (the *Aquitania*'s sister ship, fastest in the Cunard fleet) and set sail for England. Bob's teammates included Francis Ouimet, George Von Elm, current Amateur champion Jimmy Johnston, runner-up Dr. O. F. Willing, and two promising newcomers, nineteen-year-old Donald Moe from Oregon and George Voigt from New York. The stock market crash had sufficiently disrupted the life of Wall Street broker Jess Sweetser that he'd been forced to drop off the team; he was replaced by first reserve Roland Mackenzie.

In addition to the golfers a number of other luminaries were making the crossing, including Bob's friend Douglas Fairbanks, celebrated French entertainer Maurice Chevalier, and a beloved sixty-year-old Scottish music hall comedian named Harry Lauder. Mayor Jimmy Walker came down to see them off and newsreel cameras covered their departure at the gangway; most of the event consisted of these bigwigs praising the Great Jones to the sky while Bob stood by smiling uncomfortably. The dashing Fairbanks, who had recently lowered his own handicap to four, announced he was looking forward to watching his friend compete overseas, not just once at the Walker Cup but a second time at the British Open. And with business bringing him back to New York in between events, he was prepared to make the crossing twice. Maurice Chevalier contributed a charming little song. Harry Lauder, decked out in a full kilt and tasseled Scottish cap, announced that he adored watching Bobby Jones play golf but that he himself had given up the game years ago because he'd "lost his ball."

After a convivial voyage, during which Bob kept himself in trim playing improvised games of "Doug" with the original Doug on the ship's topside tennis court, the *Mauretania* docked in Southampton on May 6 at 5:00 a.m. With ten days to prepare for the Walker Cup at Royal St. George's, the team took a motor coach into London and checked into the Savoy. Bob spent the rest of the day showing Mary the sights. He led the team out for practice the next morning at a local London course, which also served as their initial meet-and-greet with reporters. The English press welcomed Bob back like visiting royalty, while the bartender at the Savoy reported with pride that Bob and Francis had enjoyed a new cocktail he'd created called "a Bosom Blush": no record of its original inspiration survives. The following day Bob enjoyed the company of genuine royalty; he and defending U.S. Amateur champ Jimmy Johnston were whisked out to Sunningdale to play a match with Edward, the Prince of Wales, and Sir Philip Sassoon, a prominent ruling-class social fixture. The prince picked Bob for his playing partner; they won the last three holes on the strength of Bob's play to end the match in a diplomatic draw. One London columnist praised Bob's matchless command of etiquette by pointing out that, unlike Hagen, at no point in their match did Bob refer to his partner, the heir to the British throne, as "Eddie."

The next day the entire team traveled to Sandwich, Kent, to begin practice rounds on the velvety turf at Royal St. George's. The weather held calm and clear—"American weather," sniffed Bernard Darwin—and even Bob, speaking in his capacity as team captain, felt compelled to express a desire that the weather turn foul, if only to prove that Americans could play under "English" conditions. Bob was privately more concerned about his own swing, which he told Pop he'd lost somewhere crossing the Atlantic.

The R&A charged admission for the first time and drew huge crowds for the two-day event, but for the sixth straight outing the Americans made the Walker Cup no contest. After agonizing over his pairings for the first day of foursomes, Bob's selections won three of the four matches. Bob and his own partner, short-hitting Oregon dentist "Doc" Willing, took their match, 8 and 7. In his capacity as captain he also unselfishly named Jimmy Johnston as the team's number-one player for singles. The next day, with Doug Fairbanks and the Prince of Wales walking side by side in his gallery—prime specimens of New and Old World royalty—Bob won his singles match against British team captain Roger Wethered, 9 and 8. Six of his teammates followed suit and the United States retained the Walker Cup by a score of 10 to 2. Don Moe, America's youngest player and presumably weakest link, came back from four down to shoot 67, break the course record at St. George's, and equal the lowest score in Walker Cup history. In the locker room afterward, as they were changing their shoes, Moe's British opponent, Bill Stout, ambled over to him and said sincerely, "Donald, that was not golf; that was a visitation from God."

Some of the British sporting press began to grumble that there wasn't much point in continuing this event if the only result was biennial humiliation. Bob had never lost a singles match in five competitions. As the end of play approached, Keeler overheard two Englishmen in Don Moe's gallery musing on "the futility of murdering Jones when they always have another prodigy coming on." The strangest moment of the tournament occurred at the final hole of Roland Mackenzie's match with William Campbell. Mackenzie pushed a well-hit approach shot sharply to the right, straight toward the gallery 180 yards away. Afraid he might have killed someone, Mackenzie ran down the fairway when word got back to him that the shot had in fact struck a man in the crowd; the fellow was uninjured, but no one could find the ball. After a five-minute search the victim suddenly cried out: "Here it is!" and lifted the ball out of a coat pocket.

Three days later on Saturday, May 19, the Walker Cup team participated in a popular, relaxed annual amateur outing at Sunningdale sponsored by *Golf Illustrated* called the Gold Vase Tournament. Bob had agreed to appear for social reasons more than competitive ones—he partnered with Dale Bourne, an old friend and a former British Amateur champion—but after shooting 75 in the morning round, six strokes off the lead, his competitive fires kicked in.

"Although enjoying a little relief from the competitive strain," Bob wrote later, "I realized I was going to have a hard time shaking myself out of the lethargy of indifference I had permitted to take possession of me."

He made a friendly lunchtime wager with Dale Bourne; Bob bet a single pound that he would break seventy that afternoon. Although reluctant to tax himself so close to the start of the British Amateur, only a week away, this was his last tune-up before the championship run began; just playing for that small a stake focused Bob's aggression like sun through a magnifying glass. He birdied three of the last four holes to shoot 68, break the tournament scoring record, and win the Gold Vase by a single stroke.

"Even though the competition was more for good fellowship than for the record," wrote Bob, "it was never unpleasant to have another trophy."

He would get in one last day of golf before the Amateur at Sir Philip Sassoon's private estate, paired again with Prince Edward, against their host and another future king, Edward's younger brother Albert, later George VI. Pop looked on from a small, invited gallery of lords and ladies, and could only marvel about the experience afterward. The little Dixie Whiz Kid had come a long way from short pants and playing golf holes fashioned out of wagon ruts on the dirt roads of suburban Atlanta.

The foundation of the Grand Slam was all riding on the British Amateur, the only major title in the sport Bob had never taken. He later called it the most important tournament of his life. His loss to Johnny Goodman at Pebble Beach had softened his distaste for eighteen-hole elimination matches, but the British Amateur threw seven of them in his path over five days before the thirty-six-hole final, the toughest and most physically demanding test in the sport. The bookmakers had established him as a 5-to-1 favorite to win the Amateur, but he knew he would need more than incomparable shot making and mental toughness, more even than good luck to climb that mountain. Fate would have to smile.

Play in the British Amateur began at St. Andrews on Monday, May 26. Bob arrived a few days earlier in time for a practice round on Saturday and die-hard Jack McIntyre showed up to carry his bag every step of the way. The next day, just as he had three years earlier to get a round in on Sunday—when golf was prohibited on the Old Course—Bob and company motored the 120-mile round trip to Gleneagles.

Monday morning dawned gray and benign; the sun would break through later, and the wind never stirred off the Eden all day. A dry, cold spring had left the Old Course in poor shape for the championship. What little grass there was had been mown to the nub; the fairways ran like parking lots and bare patches appeared on almost every green. The draw sheet listing every contestant's name was big enough to cover the side of a house. The enormous size of the field required some to play two matches on the first day, while others waited until the following afternoon to hit their initial drives. Bob began play as the top seed in the second bracket, which earned him a bye in the first round. He walked out onto the first tee of the Old Course at 3:00 that afternoon to meet his opponent, Henry Sydney Roper, a former coal miner, described by Bernard Darwin, the venerable correspondent for *The Times* of London, as "a player hitherto unknown to fame."

Sid Roper was the prototype of the player Bob dreaded facing in short matches. Most of his British friends had assured him Roper wasn't capable of anything better than bogey golf. Bob always believed he could accurately size up an opponent when meeting him on the first tee, not the quality of his game so much as the man's ability to withstand the scrutiny and pressure that a match with Bob guaranteed.

"What I observed of Mr. Roper in this respect," Bob said, "was not at all reassuring."

About the same size as Bob, Roper had an efficient, athletic swing and a calm look in his eyes. This young man was not just a golfer, Bob decided at once, but a competitor. When Roper pummeled his first drive, Bob signaled his own engine room to crank up the power to full speed ahead.

He rattled in a long downhill putt to birdie the first hole. Bernard Darwin, watching from the gallery, thought he detected signs of tension in Bob's putting stroke. That diagnosis appeared sound when he missed a much easier putt for birdie at the second. He gently dropped a short pitch shot at the third right next to the flag for another birdie that he could have putted with his eyes closed. After his 300-yard drive at the fourth dribbled into the infamous Cottage Bunker, Bob played one of the ten best shots of his life and holed a six iron off the sand from 150 yards out for a double-eagle two—the rarest of all golf's avian deeds: an albatross. Pop heard a man in the gallery near him mutter, "He's a witch. They ought to burn him at the stake." Bob followed that thunderbolt by reaching the green of the par five fifth in two, and two putts later had another birdie.

At the end of five holes Bob was five under par.

Any other man might have fled for his life after witnessing such an assault, but Roper, who played the first five holes in even fours, was one under par and only down three to Jones. What was worse, he looked utterly untroubled by the way Bob had just vaulted the first furlong at St. Andrews. In fact, he hardly seemed to notice.

Roper won the sixth hole when Bob three-putted. Bob restored his lead to three with another birdie at seven. After pushing his drive wide right at the eighth, Bob found himself stymied on the green; Roper had won his second hole of the last three and showed no signs of cracking.

They halved the ninth. Bob had played the outward nine in 33 strokes in a burst of supernatural golf. His lead over Roper was only two.

Another half at the tenth. On the short eleventh, the scene of his unbecoming retreat nine years earlier, Bob nearly holed his tee shot for an ace; another birdie and the lead was back to three. At the twelfth Bob recorded his seventh under-par score of the round and his lead for the first time grew to four.

Again Roper came back. They halved the thirteenth and Roper won the next with a superbly played approach. After halving the fifteenth, the match finally ended at sixteen, 3 and 2, when both men took fives. If they had continued, and Bob had finished with two fours, he would have equaled his own amateur record for the Old Course.

After predictions that Roper would play bogey golf, the man had made exactly one of them in the entire match, on their last hole. Bob told Keeler later that Roper would probably have beaten him on any other day of the tournament, but once again Bob had played his best when he needed it most. Thanks to the size of the field and the luck of the draw, on Tuesday he rested. He would have to play thirty-six holes, two matches a day, from this point forward through the finals, if he made it that far.

On Tuesday night the weather turned bitterly cold, wind whipping from the west, the direction that made the Old Course play the hardest. Spectators went overnight from shirtsleeves to coats and mittens. Bob arrived at the first tee at twelve minutes after eight, blowing on his fingers to restore feeling, looking cold and miserable. His third-round opponent was Cowan Shankland, not the most promising name for a golfer, and for the better part of the morning he lived up to it. Playing slightly down to the level of his competition, after handily winning the first three holes Bob appeared to let his concentration drift. A bogey at the ninth meant he had played the front nine in 40 and held only a one-hole lead. Bob won the tenth with a par, then watched his opponent putt off the green and nearly into the Eden on eleven. Three more routine pars were all he needed to dispatch Cowan Shankland, 5 and 3.

If Bob had been conserving his energy during his morning match, he had good reason. After lunch that day the fourth-round draw brought him up against current British Amateur champion Cyril Tolley.

Cyril James Hasting Tolley was thirty-five years old, a tall, burly, powerfully built natural athlete who had lettered in three sports at Oxford, after surviving thirteen months in a German prison camp. Since winning the British Amateur in 1920 he had become a mainstay of their international teams. An aristocratic version of Ted Ray or John Daly, he possessed both intimidating power and exquisite touch around the greens; he was an all-or-nothing man, which led to wild fluctuations in the quality of his golf. After having played with Bob numerous times in and out of formal competition in both countries, Tolley had become his closest friend in the game on this side of the Atlantic and there was no one Bob feared or respected more in the entire field. Since the brackets had been published, revealing the two men were in the same quarter of the draw, the possibility of this meeting had made it the most anticipated match of the tournament. A local holiday in the nearby town of Dundee created an unwieldy crowd of over twelve thousand people, who crammed around them on the first tee—the rest of the matches on the course that afternoon went almost entirely unwatched—and it would play a crucial, some would later say regrettable, part in the outcome.

The two friends were masters of studied indifference under fire, but tension showed on both men's faces as they shook hands at 1:35 and teed it up. Tolley topped his first drive forward less than a hundred yards, and it cost him the hole when Bob collected a routine par. The gallery stampeded ahead to the next tee and down the second fairway, a pattern that would be repeated all afternoon, which led to aggravating delays, some as long as twenty minutes, before every shot they played. The wind had picked up, blowing ever harder, a three-club gale that swirled sand out of the bunkers and sent people scampering for cover between shots. For the first time in the tournament, the Old Course confronted them armed with all its defenses intact.

When Tolley won the second to square the match after Bob sliced his approach, it was clear neither man intended to yield an inch. Bob had beaten Tolley decisively in their only other head-to-head match, during the 1926 Walker Cup, but the Englishman showed no signs of remembering that encounter. This quickly settled into a primal battle that evoked allusions to every kind of combat from assembled sportswriters; a duel to the finish, fought with the brutality of bare-knuckle boxers summed up the prevailing point of view.

Tolley took his first lead at the fourth, when Bob again sliced an iron approach, this time into the crowd, and failed to get close with his recovery. Bob pushed his second shot into the gallery on the next hole as well, but after a lucky bounce back into the fairway saved his par and the hole was halved.

After the sixth was halved Bob squared the match at seven when Tolley three-putted. Bob seized his second lead with par at the eighth. The 306-yard par four ninth was playing dead downwind and Bob tried to carry it with his drive but pulled it into the gorse; Tolley stepped up and slaughtered a ball that ran all the way onto the green. After his birdie the match was squared again.

The tension twisted tighter with every stroke. The immense crowd grew so still that as each man stood over his ball ready to strike, all you could hear was the eerie whistling of the wind. After halving the tenth, both stumbled at eleven, but Bob stuck his third shot next to the hole and Tolley could only manage bogey. Bob had a one-hole lead for the third time, and for the third time gave it right back; both men hit magnificent drives on the 314-yard twelfth that bounced over and through the green, but Bob flubbed his second coming back, while Tolley chipped dead to the hole for another birdie.

All square with six to play. The crowd churned around them like an immense school of fish: quiescent for long periods then startled into whirling, scrambling motion whenever a shot was played. The stewards toiled and strained to shepherd them but they were overmatched. The constant delays were hard enough for Bob and Tolley and downright impossible for anyone else. Every other match they encountered on the narrow links was forced to stand aside until the whole great throng had passed by. Some greens stood empty for half an hour with players and caddies forced to stand guard over their ball against any mischief from the advancing masses.

As the end approached, the two men started banging at each other like two heavyweights going toe to toe. Bob sank a putt of nearly forty feet for birdie at the thirteenth; he had his fourth lead of the match. Tolley answered at the 512-yard par five fourteenth with his best shot of the day; after another booming drive he launched a soaring three wood that landed on the fringe and rolled to within three feet of the flag: eagle. All square. At the long par four fifteenth Bob stuck his approach inside of five feet; from twenty feet Tolley took a dead run at birdie, missed coming back for par, and conceded Bob his putt. Bob had his fifth one-hole lead of the match.

Bob knew every bunker on the Old Course, open or concealed. One of the most dangerous of them all, a series of three actually, guards the right side of the sixteenth fairway and is known collectively as the Principal's Nose.

Attempting to blast over the bunkers with the wind at his back and take a run at the green, Bob landed his ball in the Nose. Tolley scrambled for a par while Bob paid the price for his gamble with bogey.

All square through sixteen.

Now every living soul on the course converged along the 467-yard par four Road Hole; estimates run as high as fifteen thousand, a nightmarish collision of flesh and shouting stewards. The wait to restore order before the match could resume took more than twenty minutes. A photo of the two men waiting on the tee is a portrait of strain and battle fatigue, two boxers collapsed on the stools in their corners waiting for the final round to begin. Long celebrated in Britain as one of the game's greatest holes, what was about to happen would elevate the seventeenth at St. Andrews into enduring legend.

Both drives flew long with the wind behind them, Bob's to the left, Tolley's right center and slightly longer. The hole was cut close to the front, and right behind the deep and deadly Road Bunker. Bob had no direct line to the flag from his position, while Tolley's angle in appeared to be ideal.

Bob stared at the green and studied his options for nearly a minute, an eternity given his usual brisk pace. He then motioned the stewards to move the gallery away from the left side of the Road Bunker and all the way to the back of the green. A buzz ran through the crowd. No one ever played in at this flag from that side of the fairway; the traditional path from Bob's position was to shoot for the front of the green and hope to roll the ball in from the right, pin high.

Pop was standing in the gallery with Alister MacKenzie, the golf architect whose work at Cypress Point he and Bob had so admired the year before, and who knew the Old Course as well as any man alive. Keeler wasn't reassured to see MacKenzie shaking his head, a mixture of disbelief and admiration.

"It's a very bold conception," he said.

Bob waited until the stewards had edged the crowd back as far as they showed any willingness to move. He stood to his work and drilled a four iron exactly on the line he'd visualized, toward the swale just left of the Road Bunker, where he hoped it would roll up onto the green and down the slope, but it took a huge hop off the rock-hard ground and looked as if it might bounce toward disaster, either onto the road behind the green or to the left toward the next tee. But the stewards had not moved the crowd as far as Bob had requested; the ball hit someone in the gallery on that first bounce and dropped straight down onto the fringe a few feet off the green, about hole high. Some complained afterward that Bob had aimed for the crowd intentionally, but he had clearly just asked the stewards to move them out of the way; they were just so eager to watch Bob they weren't willing to move far enough. And as he wrote years later, "I should never have been so heedless of the possibility of inflicting injury upon a spectator."

"Men call it fate," added Pop.

The pressure shifted to Tolley and weighed on him; his short iron approach landed short, ran forward, curled a few inches just short of the top of the swale leading up to the green, and rolled back down to the front edge. The cavernous Road Bunker now sat directly between his ball and the flag. Bob was away. He chipped up to within eight feet, leaving himself an uphill par putt from the left. Tolley had only one spot he could land his ball with any hope of ending near the hole: just over the edge of the bunker, dangerously close to the lip, at the top of the slope that ran from there down to the hole. Keeler felt sure no man alive would be able to negotiate that shot under these conditions. "I could see nothing but a win for Jones."

Tolley hit his target as surely as if he'd floated over and dropped it by hand, and the ball gently trickled down the slopes to within two feet of the flag. He told Bob and Pop afterward it was the finest shot he had ever played. Neither man argued with him. Bob years later wrote that it was the best finesse shot he'd ever seen.

The pressure shifted again. Bob took one look at his "eminently missable" putt and dropped it for par. Tolley matched him. All square through seventeen. "Although it had been as tense a hole as I had ever played in my life," wrote Bob, "the result only served to increase the pressure."

With the wind behind them and no trouble in front of them, both men ripped their drives 340 yards to within thirty feet of the enormous eighteenth green. Another long wait ensued as the crowd poured in to surround the green, in some places standing ten or twelve deep. Bob was away and played a strong pitch that ran twenty-five feet past the hole. Tolley failed to press the slight advantage; his chip came up short through the Valley of Sin to about fifteen feet. Bob putted first and left it on the edge of the cup, then went through "the most agonizing moments of that entire year" as he waited for Tolley to try his putt for the win. Bob fully expected him to make it.

Tolley's ball came close but stopped just short of the hole. Both men tapped in for pars. The match headed for extra holes and sudden death. The crowd turned and made a mad dash toward the first green while the players and caddies headed for the tee. By the time they reached it, the crowd stretched all the way along either side of the fairway.

Both hit strong drives. Bob played his approach first to the left front of the green, a splendid piece of iron work, landing gently about ten feet from the hole. Tolley pulled his second to the left of the green, then pitched up short, leaving himself seven feet to the hole, inside and on the same line as Bob's ball.

Bob rolled his ball right on that line. It came to a stop a few inches short of the hole. With a gasp the crowd realized that Bob's ball had left Tolley's line to the hole almost completely stymied. He attempted to cut his ball around Bob's with an iron but it wasn't meant to be. Bob tapped in for his par. The match was over on the nineteenth hole. Policemen stepped in to escort both players back to the clubhouse as the crowd surged in on them. In one photo they appear to be holding Bob up on his feet.

"The release from the tension was almost unbearable," wrote Bob. "It was the kind of match in which each player plays himself so completely out that at the end the only feeling to which he is sensitive is one of utter exhaustion."

Bob and Tolley remained great friends, and the two men corresponded about the match three decades later, when Bob was writing his autobiography and asked Cyril for his recollections. "I have graven on my soul," Bob said, "the completely brutal ferocity of that man-to-man contest."

That night he told Pop he'd had a funny feeling out on the course against Tolley, not just once but a few times. There had seemed to be something inevitable about the outcome, as if whatever he did had almost nothing to do with the final score. That uncanny certainty did nothing to reduce the strain that had melted twelve pounds off him already; his belt tightened a notch, Bob looked gaunt, his eyes recessed in his head. His appetite had vanished alto-gether, but he seemed haunted by that strange sensation he'd had and couldn't stop talking about it.

"Please, don't talk about golf or anything to do with it just now," Pop asked him politely. "Just go get some rest. You have to play thirty-six more tomorrow."

Thursday morning, the fourth day of play. The western wind had vanished overnight, the skies cleared, the air warmed again; St. Andrews had drawn in its teeth. Bob's fifth-round opponent was an Englishman named G. O. Watt. After letting him hang around for a few holes, Bob threw down a string of four birdies in six holes and dispatched Watt, 7 and 6. He was grateful for a breather match, one that exerted no more than "ordinary pressure," requiring only twelve holes and forty-five shots, because another battle loomed after lunch that afternoon.

By the sixth round only three Americans were left in the field. Both Ouimet and Von Elm had fallen in the fifth; in addition to Bob, Jimmy Johnston and George Voigt had won through to the sixth round, both with comparative ease. For the first time the draw brought two Americans together when Bob faced Johnston, the reigning U.S. Amateur champion.

Johnston had begun his tournament by ousting fifty-three-year old Bernard Darwin, who was covering the event for *The Times* of London, referring to himself in his account of their match only as "B. Darwin." B. Darwin took Johnston to eighteen before bowing out. From there Johnston's path had grown progressively easier, until now. Darwin set out to follow their match with a bit of wishful thinking, stating he was eager to watch the two Americans "cut one another's throats before a big crowd." Johnston started well, but Bob played slightly better; Jimmy made only two slight mistakes through the first eight holes, and Bob made him pay for both, playing, as Darwin observed, "without fault and without mercy." Bob took a two-hole lead into the ninth, drove into a bunker and lost half his lead, then drove the tenth green and took it right back. When Johnston missed birdie by an inch at the eleventh, the match turned; after leaving his man stymied on twelve and Johnston's bunkered approach at the next, Bob's lead had grown to four with five holes to play. The gallery began to drift away to follow other players. Pop went off with them. This match was clearly over.

That's when the fun started.

Johnston played two superb wood shots to birdie the par five fourteenth for a win, and then Bob made a gift of fifteen with a missed four-footer for double bogey. After Bob collected par at sixteen, Johnston displayed his nerve by sinking a brilliant twelve-foot putt to halve the hole and extend the match; Bob's lead was two, with two holes to play, but with Johnston suddenly on his game the result looked far from secure.

The Road Hole again. After a solid drive, Johnston found the green in two, while Bob's approach came up short of the Road Bunker, just as Tolley had done the day before. Bob couldn't match Tolley's miracle pitch and had to settle for bogey; Johnston two-putted for his par and the lead was down to one.

Both men hit solid drives at the Home Hole. Playing first, Johnston showed the strain on his second shot, pulling his pitch to the upper left corner of the green, a leave of nearly ninety feet from the cup. But the strain was working on them both; Bob followed with an only slightly less egregious pitch toward the same corner, thirty feet inside and to the right of Johnston's ball. Bob had the advantage; Jimmy's putt would inevitably show him something of the line.

The colossal crowd that had earlier abandoned them came roaring in when they heard about Johnston's comeback. Ouimet, Von Elm, and the other members of the American Walker Cup team looked down on the eighteenth green from the balcony of the Grand Hotel. They watched Johnston putt first; the ball rolled and rolled and rolled, then curled right for the hole and stopped only a few inches short of a miraculous birdie.

Bob's touch failed him; Francis could see he was grinding even from this distance. His putt stopped nine feet short. Downhill, sidehill, with a foot of break from left to right. Nine feet to halve the hole, stave off Johnston, and win the match. The moment of crisis.

"He'll make it," said Von Elm to Ouimet. "He's made hundreds like it. He'll pop it right in."

Bob looked nowhere near as certain. He later told Pop it was the longest nine-foot putt he'd ever seen.

He hit it. The ball rolled right on line and dropped dead center. Match over. That was Thursday.

Friday, May 30. Again no wind, but the day broke damp and cool. Bob's seventh-round opponent was a tall young Englishman from Stourbridge, Eric

Fiddian. Darwin described Fiddian as a good driver and putter who "lacks a solid middle to his game. When I see him with an iron in hand, I do not expect to see the ball finish very near the hole." For the first time all week Bob lost the opening hole when he dunked his second shot in the Swilken Burn. Fiddian's only lead of the match would last until the fourth, at which point Bob passed him as if Fiddian was carved in marble. Bob went four up by the eighth. Bernard Darwin concluded "the rest of the game was of purely academic interest. Fiddian postponed the evil day with a birdie at twelve, but there could be only one end and it came at fifteen." Bob eliminated Fiddian, 4 and 3, and "it was all done without the faintest apparent effort." The gods had arranged another breather.

A curious episode followed. Bob had played his way into the semifinals, and a longer than usual break followed as he awaited the results of the match that would produce his opponent. After a light lunch, Bob and Mary walked upstairs to the living room of their suite at the Grand Hotel. Word arrived that Bob would be playing George Voigt, the only other American left standing, in the semifinal round. Bob felt tired unto collapse, unaccountably agitated, his stomach roiling. A fugitive suggestion entered his mind that a short nip of something bracing might settle his nerves and revive his dulled senses. A decanter sat on the living room sideboard, only it didn't contain Scotch, the bracer he'd been craving, but sherry, for which he'd never shown any previous appetite. If Pop had been in the room he certainly would have talked him out of it. Bob poured a glass for Mary and one for himself; he couldn't explain afterward why it seemed like a good idea at the time.

He had never touched a drop of alcohol before playing a tournament round.

"I could not have made a greater mistake," he wrote. "The wine flushed my face and caused me to be very keenly aware that my eyes were the slightest bit out of focus."

He couldn't shake the deleterious effects, even as he went down to prepare for the afternoon match with Voigt. He told no one at the time, reluctant as ever to use anything as an excuse, and kept the whole experience to himself for years afterward, but as his starting time approached he came close to panic. The slight blurring of vision would persist until more than half the match had been played.

Bob had been feeling the influence of something like providence playing a hand at St. Andrews all week. The improbable eagle against Roper. The fortunate bounce off the crowd at the Road Hole with Tolley. The final putt on the Home Hole to beat Johnston. Bob had edged continually closer to the date he'd made for himself with destiny, and then, out of nowhere, came this casual, almost willful act of self-destruction. He'd had a few cocktails before playing casual rounds at East Lake with the boys, but there was no precedent for this kind of behavior in any tournament he'd ever played. Even decades later he never arrived at an adequate answer. But the thought occurs that his intention might have been both crystal clear and entirely unconscious: Was he testing fate?

George Voigt was thirty-five, a mature, steady competitor who didn't shrink from the spotlight. Working as a bank executive and then as private secretary to the publisher of the *Washington Post*, he had dominated amateur golf in the Mid-Atlantic region for most of the 1920s as thoroughly as Bob had in the South. Many felt he had passed Von Elm to become the second best amateur in the game, and Grantland Rice thought he might be the best clutch putter in the world. A few compared not only his confidence and breezy manner to a slimmed-down Walter Hagen but also the quality of his golf. His swing was compact, machinelike, repeatable, and he never faltered on the greens. He gave the impression of a man who had nothing to fear from his enemies, and he and Bob were friends. In fact it was no exaggeration to say that Bob was his hero.

The wind had picked up by the time they teed off, the temperature stuck in the low forties. Voigt arrived wearing a heavy sweater and fingerless gloves to keep his hands warm. After both men reached the opening green in two, Voigt dropped his fifteen-foot putt for birdie. From about ten feet out, Bob matched him, rattling the ball against the back of the cup.

Bob walked away from the first green aware that he'd been lucky again; his putt had been badly judged, only the wrong speed had kept it on line into the hole. The alcohol hadn't affected either his drive or approach, and wouldn't all day, but as he stood looking down at the green, he'd realized he couldn't focus his eyes on the ball. He wouldn't make another putt of any consequence for over two hours.

Voigt gave away the second hole with a bunkered drive. Jones up one. They halved the third, and then the fourth when Bob missed his first short putt of the afternoon but Voigt failed to capitalize. Voigt squared the match with a birdie at the fifth, when Bob missed his own birdie putt of less than four feet. He missed another near gimme of the same length two holes later, failing to take a hole that Voigt had all but handed to him. His play from tee to green remained flawless, but at the short eighth, Bob missed his third makeable birdie putt of the front nine. Another half. No one watching understood what had gone wrong with his putting stroke. When yet another birdie putt at the tenth hung on the lip, Darwin decided that his "aggregate of misses was decidedly criminal."

At the par three eleventh, just as his vision started to clear, Bob began paying the price for his mistakes. Voigt was on the green with his drive, while Bob overshot his into the Eden. Voigt had his first lead of the match.

After halving the twelfth, Voigt extended his lead to two at thirteen with a delicate pitch and run and a single putt. Bob flubbed his chip and missed his par putt. For the first time all week Bob trailed in a match by more than a single hole.

Voigt was two up with five holes to play. Even he started to believe he might win. Bob looked beaten and downcast; the way he had played, most of the gallery now expected him to lose. But there's a peculiar, age-old superstition at St. Andrews that says the golfer who is two up with five to play never wins his match. Francis Ouimet, who had been following the match all afternoon, heard at least a dozen local spectators spread the word with religious certainty that Voigt would now falter because he was two up with five to play. Bob heard the whispers too and found no comfort in them. George Voigt was not the kind of man who tossed away a lead.

As they stepped to the fourteenth tee the wind kicked up, blowing in off the water from the left across the long fairway. The gallery crowded in around them on the tee. Maybe that was the reason Voigt couldn't feel the freshening wind. He elected to play his ball down the right side of the fairway and cut the corner, but the moment it climbed above the crowd the wind took hold and it drifted like a balloon just over the nearby stone wall, out of bounds into the gorse. Voigt couldn't believe his eyes; he'd been hitting the ball dead straight all day. Bob watched this unlooked-for gift arrive, then deliberately aimed way left, all the way onto the adjoining fifth fairway, where he safely landed his drive. Stroke and distance penalties applied to Voigt's mistake; he lost the hole and his lead was cut in half.

They halved fifteen when Bob missed another short putt that would have won it and evened the match. At sixteen, Bob played safely left again into the adjoining third fairway. Voigt aimed his drive down the left side as well, but again the wind grabbed his ball, blowing it all the way across into the dreaded Principal's Nose. He couldn't recover. The hole went to Jones, and the match was all square with two to play, just as it had been against Cyril Tolley when they reached seventeen.

An enormous gallery again surrounded the Road Hole, but as Darwin noted, a bit sniffily, "this was a St. Andrews crowd, not a Dundee rabble, and all was well." Bob at last appeared to have full possession of his faculties; he followed a fine drive favoring the left through the rising wind with a solid approach that landed just short, kicked forward, but then rolled back down into the swale when it failed to crest the small slope to the green. Desperate to seize the advantage and break Bob's momentum, Voigt went for broke, pulling a one iron and hitting a stalwart second that ran up the swale and onto the front of the green, only ten feet past Jones, but with a clear line to putt. Bob played a bump-and-run chip toward the flag; it lacked conviction and stopped twelve feet short. Voigt ran his birdie attempt straight at the hole: it stopped less than a foot from the cup. He was assured of par; Bob was assuredly not. Voigt was certain Bob couldn't make that putt under these circumstances.

Francis watched Bob's behavior closely as he walked to his ball. "Ordinarily he takes a quick squint at the line, steps up and hits his ball. On this occasion he consumed quite a bit of time and looked his line over carefully from every angle."

An English lord with whom Keeler had been walking as he watched the match chose this moment to announce to Pop: "The stars are with Bobby in this tournament. His luck is as fixed as the orbit of a planet."

Bob had an eerie feeling as he stepped up to the ball. "I could see the line as plainly as if it had been marked on the green. I knew before I swung the putter that I would surely hole the putt."

It dropped dead center. Darwin decided that with this putt Bob had just demonstrated "true greatness of soul."

The crowd broke ahead to line the eighteenth fairway. With the wind against them, Voigt left his drive twenty yards short of Bob's. Smelling blood, an energized Bob ran up and leaped across the Swilken Burn on the way to his ball. Visibly shaken, Voigt had a tough decision to make. He carried no iron between an eight and a five and the distance put him dead between them. He elected to use the eight and punch the shot in low, but the coolness he'd shown all day had gone out of his touch after losing his lead. The ball missed reaching the plateau green by six inches, hit the bank, and rolled back into the deadly hollow guarding the front edge that since time immemorial has been known as the Valley of Sin. Bob clipped a gorgeous high pitch that banked off the wind and gently fell within eight feet of the hole. Voigt's chip up from the Valley was sound, but he was six feet shy of the flag and lying three.

Bob's eight-foot putt to win the match outright ran so straight and true he stepped forward with his hand out to pluck the ball from the hole, when it hesitated on the last blade of grass and hung outside the lip. Voigt still had his six-footer for par to extend the match into extra holes. He took his time, but his moment was gone. The putt lipped out. Bob had reached the finals of the British Amateur.

Ouimet rushed out to congratulate both teammates before the crowd closed in. He overheard Al Laney commiserate with George Voigt as he walked off the green, saying he felt sure that most everyone in that crowd felt, as he did, that George should have won the match. Voigt smiled wearily and said: "Just remember, Al, it's only a game, after all." Voigt later wrote that he'd replayed the match a thousand times in his mind and could never quite figure out where he'd gone wrong. But he had no regrets; it was enough for him, he said forty years later, to know Bob as a friend and teammate, and to have played a small role in his larger story.

Two up with five to play; you would have heard that as the dominant theme running through conversations in all the pubs afterward and long into the evening, where all were comforted by the warm reassurance of a fable confirmed. Why, the outcome was foretold!

Bob's diligent study of the Old Course had paid dividends on the one day his opponent had by all accounts outplayed him, but the strain had caught up with him; he told Pop as he walked off the course he felt more dead than alive. A drink, a hot bath, dinner with Mary and to bed, ordered Pop; tomorrow is another day.

This much was clear: whatever mysterious influence had been looking after Bob Jones all that week at St. Andrews watched over him still. If he had deliberately set out to test fate that afternoon, where temptation appeared in the unlikely guise of a glass of sherry, he'd just received as emphatic an answer as a man could ever hope to have.

Bob's opponent in Saturday's final would be thirty-one-year-old Englishman Roger Wethered. He had grown up and learned the game on the storied links at Dornoch in the north of Scotland, where his family summered. Universally admired as the model of a sporting gentleman, he had appeared on the scene in 1921 while still an undergraduate at Oxford, losing the British Open in the play-off to Jock Hutchison. He had gone on to win the British Amateur in 1923, reach the semifinals twice, and lose in the finals in 1928. He had also become a fixture on Britain's international teams, and his record in those matches showed he was equal to anyone. The knock on Roger Wethered, if it can be called a criticism, was that he was so nice a person he lacked a killer instinct. He wasn't even considered the best player in his family; his younger sister Joyce, four-time British Women's Champion, claimed that title without argument. To this point in the game's history, she was the greatest female golfer who ever lived. After playing in an exhibition against Joyce at East Lake the previous year, no less than Bob Jones had this to say about her: "I have not played golf with anyone, man or woman, amateur or professional, who made me feel so utterly outclassed."

Joyce Wethered might well have given Bob a harder time in this final; she could drive the ball as far as any man, equaled Bob's own formidable powers of concentration, and never backed down from a challenge. On the other hand, according to Bob, Roger was "a completely charming person without any semblance of aggressiveness on the golf course." Bob had been among a group of Roger's friends standing near the eighteenth green on the final day of the Open at St. Andrews in 1921, who'd had to persuade Roger that it was more important for him to stick around for the play-off with Hutchison than to return home for an amateur cricket match in which he'd agreed to play. They nearly failed to convince him.

Estimates of the crowd that gathered in St. Andrews from all over Scotland on the morning of Saturday, May 31, run as high as twenty thousand. With their favorite "Bonnie Bobby" facing an upper-class Englishman, the native Scots handed Bob something he'd never experienced before in an overseas match: home field advantage. Over thirty-six holes, a distance where Bob had lost only once in the last six years, not many thought Wethered could stand up to him. Bob considered his opponent a close friend but took one look on the first tee and concluded "Roger himself held very little hope of winning."

The sun was shining, a modest wind blowing from the east to keep things interesting. After introductions, as they waited for the gallery to settle, an official of the Royal and Ancient addressed the crowd at the tee with the following: "During the hundreds of years in which golf has been played at St. Andrews, every one of the greatest golfers in the world has at some time or other played the Old Course. Wonderful scores have been made, but no one had ever been able to play a round without having at least one five on his card." Francis Ouimet was standing close to Bobby and saw his mouth tighten at the comment, although he said nothing. But the challenge, whether that was the official's intention, waved in the air like a red flag before a bull.

Just what Bobby needed to hear, thought Francis.

After splendid first drives, Bob foozled his second shot short of the Burn, then played a flawless pitch to within a foot and halved the hole for par. Darwin refused to waste words on describing Bob's play for the outward nine since it never varied from "a vast straight drive down the course, a good second with some iron club and then a putt which was generally stone dead and seldom more than four feet away." Bob recorded seven more fours on the front, and a three. Hitting erratic drives, Wethered had to work considerably harder to achieve the same result on the card, and after nine the match stood even, each man going out in 35. But this was where the longer length of the match served as a balm to Bob's nerves; time was on his side, he could hammer away at Old Man Par and let Wethered worry about his own problems. After they made the first turn, Roger began to crack.

On the tenth green, Bob holed a six-foot putt for par. Roger missed for par from five. Bob had the first lead of the match. As Roger turned after picking up his ball, Bob read on the Englishman's face "his belief that he could not keep this up much longer."

They halved eleven, when Bob holed a side-winding eight-footer, and twelve, where Bob missed an easier putt for birdie. As they turned into the home stretch Bob went to the whip: with three pars sandwiching a birdie at fourteen, he won the next four holes in a row. Wethered's driver had already faltered; now through this crucial sequence his putter started to balk. Bob seized on each mistake ruthlessly. They reached the seventeenth, the eventful Road Hole, with Bob up five.

A quick glance at the scorecard at this point in their match reveals that Bob had made two threes and fourteen fours. He had yet to make a five.

Both men's drives at seventeen were perfect. Forced to gamble, Wethered played a three wood toward the Road Hole green. The ball pitched into the ascending bank to the right of the Road Bunker, took one hop, and settled on the green twelve feet from the hole. Bob pulled his three wood and played his shot along the exact same line, but it had a touch of draw on it, and instead of hitting the bank it dove straight into the gaping, sheer-faced Road Bunker.

Bob's ball was no more than fifteen or twenty feet from the hole, but the front edge of the bunker looked over his head as he took his stance. This was still a year before Gene Sarazen, tinkering with a wedge, some scrap metal, and a soldering iron, invented the modern sand wedge, with a flange below the leading edge designed to slice down through the sand. Players as accomplished as Walter Hagen still tried to pick the ball clean out of bunkers, like a chip shot. Bob took one look and knew if he tried that here the ball might very well scamper across the green and end up on the road. But as he dug his feet in he also realized the ball was lying on only a thin layer of sand. He split the difference.

With perfect pitch he cut the legs out from under the ball, and it rose up on a whisper of sand, barely cleared the top of the bank, hit the downslope carrying so much backspin it nearly came to a stop, then trickled down to pass the cup by two feet. An old St. Andrews caddie standing next to Ouimet uttered an unprintable oath, followed by "the finest shot I've ever seen." Wethered left his putt for birdie hanging on the edge. All Bob had to do to keep his streak of fours alive was can the two-foot putt.

"Bob hurriedly took his stance and just as hurriedly hit his ball and—horroro!" wrote Francis. "He missed. Missed the two-foot putt. He whaled his drive a mile up the eighteenth fairway. He was mad!"

Bob finished the round with his four at the Home Hole and maintained his five-hole lead at the halfway point of the match. He had shot a flawless, textbook 71, besting Wethered by five strokes.

Bob crossed the street to the Grand Hotel. Francis went after him and followed him up to his room. The minute the door was closed Bob paced, cursed, and kicked a chair. "He was wild," wrote Francis. "He looked at me with disgust and I could not understand his attitude."

"What in the world's got into you, Bob?" asked Francis. "You're five up."

"Did you hear what that official said on the first tee?"

Francis thought for a moment, and then it came back to him.

"And I had to make a two-foot putt at seventeen to be the first man to play St. Andrews without taking a five."

Bob had forgotten all about Roger Wethered or winning the British Amateur. Throughout that whole morning round—about which Bernard Darwin the next day wrote "I do not think I ever saw golf so well played in all my life"—Bob had set his sights against a scoring record that had never been reached in five hundred years. One careless slip had cost him the achievement. That he used this spur to push himself forward in the finals of a championship he had to win says more about his essential nature than anything else he ever did on a golf course.

Outside, spectators kept pouring off the trains. When they returned to the tee for the second round, the crowd had increased to twenty-five thousand, the largest ever gathered at the Old Course. The town was so thoroughly emptied that a popular English mystery writer later set one of his best-selling stories in St. Andrews on this very day; the deserted village presented the perfect setting for a quaint British murder. Ouimet and some of Bob's friends from Atlanta stepped in as his personal escorts to keep him from being stampeded to death between holes. With anger still staining his mood, Bob took three putts for bogey at the first when Wethered stymied him and won the hole. That was Bob's second five of the day; there would be no assault on the "all-fours" record that afternoon, but then Bob had no intention of playing a full second round.

At the second Wethered hit a perfect drive. Bob hooked his into the crowd and the ball ended up on the road, just short of the out-of-bounds wall. After Roger played up to the green, Bob hit a phenomenal recovery shot that cleared all the trouble and stopped on a bank behind the green. From there he chipped down and nearly holed his third shot, laying a perfect stymie between Wethered's ball and the hole. Roger three-putted. Bob's lead was back to five.

They matched scores until the sixth, where Roger's birdie trimmed the lead to four again. At seven Bob grabbed it right back with the help of another stymie. Two more halves and the lead remained five, with nine holes left to play. Wethered was running out of real estate.

Bob drove the front edge of the green at ten, took two putts for a birdie, and his lead was six. After they both parred eleven the lead was six with only six to play. Par at twelve was all Bob needed to close out the match. He drove three hundred yards to the green and after an easy par put an exclamation point at the end of his day—thirty holes played in two under par and the job was done.

Hats filled the air. The crowd swallowed him, a full mile from the clubhouse. A friend of Bob's was nearly trampled in a bunker. For a brief moment they lifted their hero up on their shoulders. Francis saw Bob's face turn white as the throng rushed at him, so he, Von Elm, and the two Atlanta friends dug him out of a great pile of well-wishers—Pop said they "apparently wanted to take the new champion apart to see what made him tick"—and formed a cordon around their friend until six burly Scots constables joined them in the eye of the hurricane. The cheering wouldn't stop. Bob turned to Francis when the police arrived and asked him to make sure that Wethered was all right. A brass band that had dutifully assembled to serenade the victor arrived too late; they broke apart on the human wave sweeping back toward the town and never played a note.

Pop knifed his way into the crowd to reach him about halfway back to the clubhouse, and they hugged and pounded each other on the back and shouted words that both men could hardly hear.

"I'm satisfied!" Bob shouted. "I'm satisfied! I don't care what happens now!"

When they reached the clubhouse doors Bob fell into Mary's waiting arms, and Pop saw to it that they were left alone for a while.

Only the third American to ever win the British Amateur after Travis and

Sweetser, Bob had added the last and most elusive championship to his collection. All the jewels of golf now sparkled from his crown. They soon called him out of the clubhouse for the trophy ceremony. He threw on a jacket and slicked back his hair and took the old silver cup, topped by the small stout figure of Old Tom Morris, into his hands for the first time. (Within hours a photo of him holding the trophy reached New York from London, via radio waves and a new technology we now call facsimile transmission.) As exhausted and spent as he was, Bob couldn't stop smiling. He spoke of his love for St. Andrews, and how honored he was to be a member of the Royal and Ancient.

"I was lucky to win," he told the crowd. "I never have been happier to get any cup, and I never worked so hard, nor suffered so much either."

Over three hundred matches had been played in five days. In every round Bob played he turned in the best score in the field. Victory had required him to play a total of 143 holes; he did so in six under par.

"He has now caught up to Alexander the Great and has no more championships to win," wrote Bernard Darwin.

He had no idea how wrong he was.

Bob with the Claret Jug.

CHAPTER FOURTEEN

The Open, Hoylake

A SPECIAL NIGHT TRAIN carried them away that evening from St. Andrews, the Americans all sharing a car and celebrating halfway to London, where they arrived at dawn. Bob and Mary left later the same day for a week in Paris, a change of scene to rest and restore his weary mind and body. He slept long hours and built his weight back up with five-star meals while they took in the sights of the city. France was a sound choice for seeking refuge; golf was a minor sport here — too quintessentially British for the Gallic soul — so the only people who recognized him on the street were visiting Americans and Brits. He made room in his leisurely schedule for an exhibition match, pairing with Jimmy Johnston against a pro-am team of the current French champions — playing in a light rain, Bob and Jimmy beat them one up — and a few days later spent an afternoon taking in the French Amateur Championship, which was won the next day by George Von Elm.

When they returned to England and made their way to Liverpool for the start of Open qualifying, Bob found to his dismay that the respite in Paris had recharged his spirits but his swing had been left in the lurch. He hadn't anticipated it, but a letdown was inevitable; with the win in the British Amateur the pressure had slipped from his shoulders. All four major championships were now or had been his in the last six years, a claim no other man living or dead could make. Since his plan to capture all four championships in a calendar year had never been made public, no one would know if he fell short. Bob said as much in a published interview with Keeler: "My little expedition is a success, no matter what happens at Hoylake."

Bob and Mary arrived in Liverpool and checked into the Adelphi Hotel on Wednesday, June 11. Bob jumped in a taxi and went right out for a practice round at Hoylake. He shot 71 but claimed he couldn't find a fairway or green; Calamity Jane did most of the work, saving half a dozen pars. Bob had played in his first international competition here in 1921 but hadn't laid eyes on it since. Hoylake is a long, flat, and testing course that demands and rewards honest, straightforward drives and long irons. Bob spent over an hour on the driving range after his practice round—an eternity for him—trying to put things right with Jeanie Deans. His swing with the big clubs still felt awkward; Keeler took one look at his game and saw it had gone "stale."

On Saturday the press announced that Pop had agreed to present daily radio summaries of the action at the Open back to America, the first live transatlantic sports broadcast. The BBC provided its local facilities in Liverpool; once they reached across the sea Pop's reports were to be beamed across the United States by David Sarnoff's National Broadcasting Company. Sixteen years earlier, Sarnoff had been a struggling twenty-one-year-old Russian immigrant working as a radio technician. On the night of April 14, 1912, he happened to be manning the control booth of New York City's most powerful radio station, atop the roof of Rodman Wanamaker's Department Store. Sarnoff picked up a faint distress signal from the *Titanic* and remained glued to his chair for the next seventy-two hours, relaying up-to-the-minute dispatches from the scene, the world's primary link to the unfolding tragedy. Rewarded for his resourcefulness with rapid promotion, three years later Sarnoff came up with an idea for a "radio music box," the first commercial radio receiver for the home consumer. Sales remained sluggish until 1923, when Sarnoff, now general manager of the struggling Radio Corporation of America (RCA), pulled off the first national broadcast: the Dempsey-Firpo heavyweight title fight. The coverage created a sensation. Over the next three years RCA sold $80 million worth of what came to be called "radios." Five years later, Sarnoff founded the

National Broadcasting Company radio network. This live broadcast from the Open at Hoylake—primarily to keep the country informed of Bob's progress—was the latest of Sarnoff's innovations.

After a brief spring rally, the American economy resumed its steady downward spiral. Unemployment had hit 3 million in America, small-town banks were starting to fail, farms went bust, and the first soup kitchens appeared in the inner cities. It seemed only Babe Ruth was making more money; his 1930 salary jumped to an unprecedented eighty thousand dollars. When fans complained he was now cashing a bigger paycheck than President Hoover, the Babe replied: "I had a better year." Against this darkening backdrop, the attempt by a handsome, self-possessed amateur golfer to capture both of the world's oldest sporting trophies on the links of Great Britain offered welcome distraction from such relentless bad news. Times might be tough, but they didn't seem to affect "our Bobby"; his undiminished brilliance remained a comforting constant in a firmament that had been turned on its ear.

Fifteen other Americans attempted to qualify for the Open at Hoylake, a fraction of a record 296 entries. Some had traveled from as far away as Mexico, Greece, and South Africa; the Open was becoming an international event. Walter Hagen, on a lucrative exhibition tour of Australia, New Zealand, and the Far East with Joe Kirkwood, declined to defend the title he'd held for the last two years. He did, however, make certain that the Claret Jug arrived at Royal Liverpool in time for the tournament.

Two days of qualifying began on Monday, June 16, at Hoylake and a nearby course called Wallasey. The field was split between them, each side scheduled to change courses for their second round. When their names were called to the first tee at Hoylake, Gene Sarazen and Tommy Armour didn't report; no explanation was given. On the amateur side, Jimmy Johnston and George Voigt were last minute scratches, serious losses to the American cause.

Bob played his Monday round at Hoylake, paired with a golfer from Havana, Cuba. A warm sun and only the slightest breeze greeted him—this uncanny weather had followed him throughout Great Britain for weeks—and Bob responded with an effortless 73. Pacing himself, thought Bernard Darwin, holding back his reserves. At 6,750 yards, the course was in spectacular shape, but like many of the classic British tracks offering narrow fairways and small greens, it depended on wind to enhance its defenses. Bob said that the only fault he could find was that the greens were running so true it gave a man no excuse for a missed putt. The galleries were large and some local fishermen had been recruited to help with crowd control, carrying ropes and clad in bright blue jerseys. Headlines were made that day by two others who tied the Hoylake course record of 70: Leo Diegel, the wiry, high-strung American terrier, and Archie Compston, the towering thirty-six-year-old Welsh giant, England's best hope in the Open.

Compston's strapping personality was scaled to his six-feet-five-inch frame. Admired as a dashing if not great golfer, he was also something of a national hero for standing up to the Inland Revenue, England's uncompromising tax bureaucracy. Rumored to have won considerable sums by betting on himself in matches played against some aristocratic amateurs, the taxman had taken him to court for a share of those alleged winnings in 1929. When Compston emerged victorious, his popularity was considerably enhanced. Archie was wild and unpredictable, yet capable of mad streaks of red-hot play; two years before, he had annihilated Hagen in a match-play exhibition at Moorpark, handing Walter the worst defeat of his career: 18 and 17 in a thirty-six-hole match. He was equally capable of losing his temper over nothing and blowing up like a hand grenade. He had never been able to rein in his disposition long enough to close out a four-round major, but his fans lived in hope this would be the week. Leo Diegel, on the other hand, had to be considered a legitimate contender in any event he entered. After long struggles to contain his jangly nerves, Leo had won the last two PGA Championships and finished second to Hagen at the British Open the previous year. The eccentric, elbows-akimbo putting style he'd developed to control his anxiety on the greens—Darwin described it as "a washerwoman at work over her tub"—endeared him to knowledgeable fans, who always reserve a special place in their hearts for any poor soul who suffers the yips.

The second day of qualifying reduced the field to 112, eighteen of them amateurs. At Wallasey, a short, hilly course featuring a number of blind shots, Bob shot a limp 77. Most of his gallery from Hoylake had followed him over to Wallasey and began to wonder if Bob had left too much of himself out on the Old Course during the Amateur. Darwin decided he was saving himself for the Open, "playing golf, rather than slaving at it," but some began to question the pretournament installation of Bob as the 2-to-1 favorite, an unprecedented vote of confidence. British fans took comfort in seeing that only eight Americans qualified to play on, with only two among the top twenty, the weakest qualifying performance for the invaders in five years. Diegel finished third behind Archie Compston and a stylish twenty-three-year-old named Henry Cotton, whose swing and relentless work ethic on the practice range put many in mind of a young Harry Vardon.

Henry Cotton was a groundbreaking figure in British golf: the first man from the upper classes to turn professional. He had spent the last two years playing in America, where Tommy Armour took him under his wing and taught him the secrets of the right-to-left-draw. Although weak from a recent bout of influenza, Cotton had been dubbed someone to watch by no less than Bernard Darwin. The second American in the ranks, George Von Elm, finished fifth, tied with Cyril Tolley for low amateur. Macdonald Smith, the old warhorse, shot the best round at Hoylake on the second day with 71, and came in eighth. Nine strokes behind the leaders and all the way back in twenty-ninth place was Bob Jones, and behind him by a stroke was the other American favorite, Horton Smith.

Bob headed out onto the first tee to begin his first round in the 1930 Open at Royal Liverpool early on Wednesday, June 18. The tradition of amateur champions in the British Open had started and ended at Hoylake; aside from Jones, the only two who had ever won it were both born and bred there: John Ball and Harold Hilton. Now seventy and sixty years old respectively, both Ball and Hilton were on hand to watch Bob hit his opening drive. So were Harry Vardon, J. H. Taylor, James Braid, Ted Ray, George Duncan, Sandy Herd, and seventy-six-year-old Allan Macfie—another Hoylake native and winner of the first British Amateur in 1885—virtually every citizen of the British Empire who'd won a major championship in the last fifty years. Watching them assemble near the clubhouse, Darwin remarked that it was as if all the gods of Olympus had descended to earth. With their presence, and in light of the Americans' poor showing during qualifying, expectations for a British revival in the Open ran high.

Bob could not have felt less prepared to face their scrutiny. He wasn't much of a nationalist by nature; he'd grown too fond of all the British greats and had no interest in showing up the English because they played under a different flag. On this day he was worried only about embarrassing himself.

Before moving to the tee Bob told Pop that on the practice range he had no idea where the ball was going with the driver. He looked as close to being undone mentally at the start of a tournament as Pop had ever seen him. Thunderclouds rolled in from the west, reinforcing Bob's gloom.

The first hole at Hoylake is called Course, a 458-yard par four that demands one of the most delicate and difficult opening drives in golf. All along the left side of the narrow fairway sits the clubhouse, out of bounds. Two hundred fifty yards from the tee the fairway dogs to the right, along a low mud wall called a "cop" that borders the practice ground, also out of bounds. The cop runs all the way in to hug the right side of the green. A hook off the tee, a slice on the first or second shot is deadly. Hit it straight, or else.

As Bob took his club back to swing "some imbecile clicked a camera at him, and he had to begin again," reported Bernard Darwin. He then pushed his drive to the right, flirting with the out of bounds, and rolled into the shallow ditch in front of the cop. Digging it out from there to the fairway, Bob steered his third onto the front edge of the green. As he was about to chip up "a lady spectator made explosive noises behind him and he had to break off, walk around like a caged lion and begin again." Bob chipped close and sank his putt for bogey. After another bogey at the third—the hole called Long that would plague him all week—Bob found his stroke for the first time since the Amateur.

"One hole in par followed another in monotonous perfection," wrote Darwin. "Not a single exciting thing happened for a long time."

He finished by tying the course record with 70. "Not too good to be terrifying to others, and yet good enough to inspire confidence in himself," pronounced Bernard Darwin.

When he returned to the hotel late that afternoon Bob saw a headline that read EIGHT INCHES OFF A WORLD'S RECORD; his final putt had failed by that distance to break the Hoylake scoring record. He couldn't for the life of him imagine that they were describing his round; as a subjective experience his golf had felt miserable. Nervously preparing for his radio broadcast debut, Pop had seen less of Bob's play that day than usual and was surprised when all Bob wanted to talk about afterward was how rotten he'd played. His game felt hopeless; even when shots ended up where he wanted them to go it felt like an accident.

Two other men matched Bob's opening 70: steady old Macdonald Smith, still chasing his first major title at forty, and the young Englishman Henry Cotton, shaking off his influenza and the thunderstorm that passed through in the middle of his round. (The same storm system moved on to drown out Derby Day at nearby Ascot Racecourse, the climactic event of the English racing season, reducing the lords and ladies in their smart frocks to bundles of dripping rags.) A few local favorites played decently but there was no avoiding the fact that of the eight Americans who'd qualified, six had placed in the top ten; Horton Smith stood two off Bob's pace.

The weather cleared and warmed on Thursday; the British hoped for a wind that never blew. On the scorecard Bob's second round looked like a portrait of consistency: even par 72. But this was misleading; fine recoveries out of deep rough near the greens concealed the fact that Jeanie Deans had again lost her way. Time and again he scrambled to the green, where Calamity Jane saved par. Without her he might not have broken 80. In conversation with Keeler that night—which Pop declined to share with his radio audience—Bob said he hadn't been "sure for six collected minutes what my game would do. I simply don't know where the damn ball is going to go when I hit it. The fairways are so tight I keep trying to steer the ball off the tee, and it's the most hopeless job I've ever tackled." His win at the British Amateur had played like a forced march with intermittent pitched battles; the Open at Hoylake was going to be a war of attrition.

A veteran English pro named Fred Robson slipped into second place, a stroke behind Bob and two ahead of Horton Smith. By midday the air had grown unseasonably warm, and without a cooling breeze it sapped the strength of Macdonald Smith and a visibly ailing Henry Cotton; with 77 and 79 they tumbled down the leader board. Archie Compston improved his position with 73, five strokes off Bob's pace, tied with Macdonald Smith and Leo Diegel. Late that afternoon the heat claimed the life of an elderly English spectator— one Clem Todd from Sheffield—who pitched forward while seated on his shooting stick by the eighteenth green and never regained consciousness. Pop predicted for his radio audience that evening that this Open would come down to the two Southerners who'd dueled earlier that season in Savannah, Bob Jones and Horton Smith.

The halfway cut reduced the field to sixty-one men who would contend on the final day: fifty-two professionals and nine amateurs. The focus of every surviving player remained firmly fixed on just one man, the polestar everyone was chasing. Not only national pride was at stake for the British, but also professional; like Hagen, British pros were tired of Jones having his way with them. Americans had won the last six Opens in a row, eight of the last nine, and Jones two of the last four. Someone had to stand up for the Union Jack and stop this man in his tracks. Whoever found it in himself had two rounds on Friday to try.

One man resolved to do something about it publicly. In the breakfast room of his hotel on Friday morning, Archie Compston told anyone who would listen he was going to march out and beat Bobby Jones. He was quoted as saying he felt "good enough to go around Hoylake in nothing." Compston was prone to issue this kind of brawny pronouncement from time to time—and nothing had come of them—but a man of Archie's dimensions was hard to ignore.

The final day began, and according to Pop would produce "battle, murder, sudden death and devastation." Horton Smith teed off at eight, the first contender out on the course in the third round. Bernard Darwin, also working a double shift as a radio commentator for the BBC, had overslept; he watched Smith three-putt the first green from the window of his hotel bathroom. Smith's fortunes unraveled and after a 78 the young American was out of the running in his first major. Englishman Fred Robson soon followed Smith onto the course, and into the also-ran category: another 78.

Gray scudding clouds threatened rain as Bob reached the tee a little before nine. After another wayward drive that just missed the ditch, he recovered for his first par of the tournament at one. At two he pushed his drive into the hay, hit his second in a bunker, and was lucky to make bogey. At the par five third he hooked his drive out of bounds, then pushed his third shot into the cabbage; he ended up, by drilling a long putt, with six. Then the evil spell that had affected his starts all week lifted again and he played out the front nine like an avenging angel at 37, distancing himself from Smith and Robson.

The cheers started behind Bob at five and quickly rippled forward to him: Archie Compston was going crazy. After par at the first, the Welshman ran off three straight birdies; playing the first four holes in thirteen strokes, he had chewed up all of Bob's five-stroke lead. The crowd, waiting for any British-born human being to play like this in an Open for nearly a decade, went nuts right along with him. Compston fed off their energy, striding down the fairways like an enraged highlands chieftain who couldn't wait to clobber his ball another fatal smash. He made the turn in 34.

Bob stepped to the fourteenth tee, the first of five monstrous finishing holes that cover over a third of the course's total yardage. During the first two rounds Bob had saved his best play for last; par was twenty-two for this brutal stretch and he'd taken twenty and twenty-one strokes respectively. During the third round, with cheers for Compston ringing in his ears—after missed drives, timid irons, and a three-putt green—he played them in twenty-four.

Compston wasn't through. He carried his mad streak into the back nine; three more birdies in the first four holes. "And at every fresh exploit a wild yell of defiance or exultation rent the air," wrote Darwin. The Welshman looked invincible; wild rumors of impossible scores reached the old champions in the clubhouse. Some were seen jogging out onto the course to join the thousands watching Compston come in. He faltered only once, a bogey at sixteen after a missed short putt, then finished strong with two fours and was nearly carried off the course.

Compston had played Royal Liverpool in 68 strokes, smashing the course scoring record by two, and in four hours had revived the spirits of a sporting nation that had stood by helplessly for years as America hijacked their native game. After playing one of the greatest rounds in the history of the Open, Compston pulled ahead of Jones by a stroke and led Leo Diegel, the next closest competitor, by three. Seated in the clubhouse eating a sandwich, Bob watched Compston finish: "As he left the eighteenth green after his great sixty-eight and made his beaming way to the clubhouse through a myriad of well-wishers, he was about as happy a figure as I have ever seen." Compston jumped into a waiting car and sped off to a nearby village to rest for an hour. Bob walked to the first tee to begin his final round a few minutes later.

The morning's gray sky shaded toward black and a light mist started to fall. Bob knew he didn't have anything close to his best game. Tension and uneasiness had been gnawing at him without relief since his arrival in Liverpool. As popular as Bob was throughout Great Britain, after Compston's charge no one there was wishing him well. He felt he had less energy and sharpness of mind at such a crucial moment than at any other tournament he'd ever played, but it wasn't in his nature to back off from a fight. After winning the Amateur he had told Pop it didn't matter what happened at Hoylake, but now that the moment was here it mattered like life and death. Darwin had observed that Jones never seemed greedy for victory, but once he was in the arena he could not help fighting to the death; that's what separated him from every other golfer alive, that force of will. If he was going to keep his chances for the Slam alive, he had to win this thing on guts and nerves alone. He put the whip to his resolve by telling himself that no matter what the outcome, he was about to play his final round in a British Open.

Bob parred the first hole for the second time that day. At the second he smashed a high towering drive that drifted right toward the gallery. From the tee it appeared to be tracking toward a steward (identifiable by his red skull-cap), standing with his back to the play. The ball bounced right off the man's head and shot dead left for fifty yards, rolling into a bunker on the adjoining fourteenth fairway. The steward was uninjured; Bob said later, "I have often wondered what that fellow's head had been made of."

His ball was sitting cleanly in the sand, a huge break compared to the knee-deep rough surrounding the bunker. The longer Bob examined his next shot the more he liked it. The distance, lie, and angle to the green were nearly identical to the eagle he'd holed at St. Andrews in his first-round match. Fixing the memory of that shot in mind he played one nearly as good, landing the ball twenty feet below the hole. He knocked in the putt for birdie; the bounce off that steward's head turned out to be the only luck he'd had all week. After a par at the third he had traversed the minefield where he'd blown up in every round at a stroke under par. That steadied him through the seventh; if he could par eight and nine he was on track to match his best nine of the tournament.

Archie Compston returned from his lunch hour still fired up and brimming with confidence. Crowds swarmed around him and he welcomed the attention. Instead of regrouping before setting out on his final round, against the advice of his caddie he decided to warm up again. Compston strode to the practice ground, pulled balls out of his bag and belted them with his driver and long irons for fifteen minutes. Darwin watched with dismay as he hit close to fifty shots. "To us it looked he was doing the hitting as an outlet for sheer joy. It was a tiring business right on the edge of such a critical test."

When Archie reached the first tee, still laughing like a buccaneer, he learned about Jones's strong start; Bob had pulled back in front of him by two strokes. For the first time that afternoon Compston's broad grin disappeared.

Ahead at the eighth, a 480-yard par five hole called Far, Bob followed a strong drive with a three wood that rolled off the left edge of the green and down a small slope. His ball came to rest in a shaved hallow, twenty yards from the cup and fifteen yards from the edge of the green that perched on a small knoll; from there the fast surface ran straight down toward the flag. He badly wanted birdie here, feeling he could ride the momentum all the way in and build a lead that left Compston in the dust.

Bob tried to finesse a chip just over the front edge of the green and trickle it down to the hole. He misjudged it by a fraction and came up inches short of the crest. Worried about the speed of the green he decelerated his second chip and left the ball ten feet short of the hole. His putt for bogey slipped a foot past the hole. Unsettled, he tapped carelessly at the ball and missed the putt coming back. Five strokes to get down from twenty yards. Double-bogey seven. He felt as if someone had just hit him with a mallet.

As I walked to the ninth tee, I was in a daze. I realized that in one brief span of only a moment or two, all the effort of the past three days had been just about washed out. I wasn't looking at any Grand Slam, only one championship.

I was badly shaken and knew it. I was even confused mentally. At this point I was completely incapable of making any calculation either of what score I might ultimately achieve or of what it would be necessary to do to stave off the challenge of others. I simply resolved to keep hitting the ball as best I could, to finish the round in an orderly fashion, if possible, and let the result be what it would.

It was the worst moment Pop had ever seen Bob experience. Darwin remarked to a friend that only one man had ever missed a putt of less than a foot in a final round of an Open and gone on to win the championship. The man walking with him, Harry Vardon, didn't need to be reminded; he'd been the one to do it.

Unaware of Bob's gaffe at eight, Compston hit a good drive off the first tee, came up short with his approach, and left a long putt from the fringe less than two feet shy of the hole. A gimme. He took a quick stroke, reached down to pull his ball from the hole . . . and saw it still hanging on the lip. He stepped back and stared at it in disbelief, and in that moment the magic that Archie had conjured up and carried with him all day vanished. The missed putt stunned him worse than a physical blow. At the second, after another decent drive, he shanked a short iron dead right and ended up taking double-bogey six.

"And so began the rot," wrote Darwin. "One hooked shot followed another and there was a long and gloomy string of fives. The story is too sad to tell at length, even if it were worth it. The thunder clouds overhead were no darker than his expression."

From the high peak he'd reached during his heroic third round, Compston fell like a stone down a well. There would be no suspense, no struggle or last-minute reversal, only a quick and violent tumble from the summit. The crowd that had set out to follow him with such high hopes slumped away from his gallery in droves. Archie Compston shot 82 in his final round, a fourteen-shot swing from his record 68. He would finish in fifth place, but the hangover lingered long after this Open; Compston never seriously contended in another major during his lifetime. Within a few years, on a recommendation from Walter Hagen, he took a job as private instructor to the Prince of Wales. He and Prince Edward would be spotted cruising the Mediterranean on board the Royal Yacht, knocking golf balls off the top deck into the sea.

Unaware of Compston's disintegration, Bob climbed to the ninth tee looking like a beaten man, shoulders sagging, inexpressibly weary. A brisk wind had arrived with the advancing storm clouds, toughening the obstacle course in front of him. There would be no more thoughts of attacking holes or defending a lead, scoring above or below par. All he could focus on now was playing one shot at a time until this ordeal was over. Unable to remember playing the hole afterward, he somehow managed a birdie at the ninth and finished his front nine in 38, the highest he'd scored there all week.

He began the final nine with four straight plodding fours, barely strong enough to put one foot in front of the other. Pop looked so lost and forlorn it helped bring Bob out of his melancholy; feeling badly that he'd caused such discomfort he started joking with him to lighten Pop's mood as he walked between shots.

It wasn't until he reached the fourteenth tee and Hoylake's strenuous finishing stretch that word reached them about Compston's meltdown. Bob inhaled the news like pure oxygen. He played two outstanding shots just short of the green and got up and down for a birdie. He handed that stroke right back over with a bogey at fifteen.

The sixteenth, par five, 532 yards. Dogleg to the right around the corner of a dike, leaving 270 yards to a wide, flat green. Bob's last realistic chance for birdie in the round. A well-placed drive hugged the right side, then he went all out for the green with his brassie. The shot bounced into a bunker guarding the left side of the green. The ball had rolled out of its pitch mark, sitting up, twenty-five yards from the hole, but close enough to the steep far wall of the bunker to seriously limit his swing. He would have to stand with his right foot on the bank outside the bunker, then chop down at the ball with a sharply descending blow. It would come out low and hot; it remained to be seen if he had enough green to work with.

Bob pulled a large, concave-faced wedge from his bag that Horton Smith had given him at Augusta. An early forerunner of the sand wedge, it weighed twice as much as an ordinary club. He'd used it only twice in England, but it was built for exactly this kind of situation. If he dropped it just behind the ball, making contact above the center of the clubface, the loft would be just about right to play a running shot across the green. He placed his right foot on the bank, dug in with his left and practiced the move down at the ball a few times. Then he played it for real.

The ball popped out of the sand, barely cleared the face of the bunker, hopped onto the green. Backspin grabbed the grass, acting as a brake; the ball slowly rolled and rolled, tracking straight for the hole. It just missed falling in the side door and came to a stop two inches past the cup. He had the birdie he needed.

Bob dropped a testing six-foot putt to save par at seventeen. Hitting both fairway and green, he closed out the final round with one last par for a score of 75. Newsreel footage of his finish shows a shockingly small group of people around the eighteenth green. When his last putt fell there was no celebration or rejoicing from either Bob, Jack McIntyre, or his gallery; there was no reaction whatsoever. He shook his partner's hand and walked off, signed his card in the scorer's tent, then ducked into the clubhouse and, as he had done so often over the years, fortified himself behind closed doors in the secretary's room upstairs to wait and see if anyone would catch him.

When Pop joined him, Bob looked as white as a sheet. His hands were ice cold, his eyes darted around like a caged animal. He asked Pop to pour him a stiff whiskey, but his right hand trembled so severely he couldn't hold the glass. He had to steady it with both hands, downed it in a couple of gulps, then asked for another and slumped into a chair looking like a man twice his age. He was utterly spent, past speech. Pop watched with more pity than pride. Bob had survived the round, but at what cost? He sat beside him for a while before saying anything.

"When are you going to quit this foolishness, Bob?" he finally asked.

"Pretty soon, I think," he said. "No game is worth these last three days."

Two Americans still had chances to catch him and were closing fast. Leo Diegel, playing an hour behind him, and then Mac Smith, alone and unwatched near the end of the field. Diegel had been two strokes behind Jones starting his final round; Smith was six back, a lot of ground to make up, but Bob had left the door wide open.

When Pop went on the air for his radio broadcast three hours later, this is what he had to say: "It is possible that I will be forgiven if this brief broadcast of the conclusion of the British Open Championship is a trifle confused, or even incoherent. It is not every day, or every year, in the history of sports that an American homebred amateur can add the British Open title to the British Amateur title on the same campaign. And with Bobby Jones on top of his eleventh major championship, and the first four competitors all from the United States, I feel sure you will be patient with a very tired and bewildered war correspondent, who for two of the longest hours that ever crawled across a clock this afternoon, wondered what was happening."

A cold rain finally fell from those sullen clouds shortly after Bob finished his round. Leo Diegel played stoutly all afternoon, picked up two strokes on Bob by the turn, and stood in a flat-footed tie with him when he reached the sixteenth. Knowing he needed to match Bob's birdie, Leo put every ounce of his 140 pounds into a second shot that found the same bunker Bob had been in earlier, but he failed to get up and down and ended with a bogey six. Now Diegel needed two birdies to catch Bob, and the best he could manage were pars. One down, one to go.

Mac Smith mounted a valiant run, shooting even par on the front, and one under on the back for 71, the lowest round of the day, but he'd started too far back. Smith reached the eighteenth hole needing an eagle to tie Bob for the lead. From the clubhouse window Bob watched Smith's caddie walk ahead to the green to pull the flag. When he saw Smith's approach fail to find the hole he knew this Open was his. He put down his drink. Pop saw no joy, no happiness, only relief. Bob's hands finally stopped shaking and the color slowly returned to his face.

Eleven major championships in eight years. He had equaled John Ball's forty-year-old record—winning the Open and the Amateur in the same year—and the grand old man was the first of the long line of British champions to congratulate him. (Shortly after the tournament, Bob invited Mr. Ball's great-grand-nephew Erie to come to America, as an assistant pro at East Lake.) It was the highest score Bob had shot in any British championship. Keeler wrote afterward: "If experience and patience and philosophy and grim determination were enough to produce that score from his game at Hoylake, I will say he never played a greater tournament, perhaps never one so great."

For the first time reporters began to contemplate the scale of what Bob was halfway to finishing. He was already the only man who had ever won all four of the sport's major titles, and as defending U.S. Open champion he held three of them simultaneously. Speculation about what he might do in next month's U.S. Open filled columns around the world. Some dared to wonder if he had it in him to win all four in the same year. Bernard Darwin, the game's most perceptive and sensitive commentator, wrote this the next day:

> As far as I know, Bobby Jones has no more records to equal or worlds to conquer. He can retire with a quiet mind, and well he may, for I don't know where anyone ever suffered more tortures in winning any championship than he did in winning this. It was a triumph of courage. If he has played better he has never played more bravely. It was all agonizing hard work for him, and he was longing for it to be over. But he kept his teeth gritted and never for one moment allowed himself to give in. For him, I

believe the strain is an ever-increasing one. Experience has taught him not to crack under it, but it surely grows ever more acute.

It was not a banner day for British golf. With only eight men in the field, America had captured the first four spots and five of the top six; only tragic Archie Compston, in fifth place, had cracked the American ranks, and done it going backward. Despite England's disappointment, given Bob's character and modesty, Darwin added that "even the golf ball cannot help but like him." He ended his coverage by predicting that Bob would match these accomplishments back in America, and win all four of the year's major tournaments.

When they called him down to receive the Claret Jug, Bob felt so disoriented at first he hardly knew why he was there. The club secretary saw him crumpled in a chair just before the ceremony, his face pinched and ghastly. Bob rallied long enough to offer a small speech, nearly identical to the one he'd given at St. Andrews, and smiled as he posed for the traditional photographs holding the trophy. A permanent weariness looked etched into his features. He hinted to reporters that given how exhausted he felt, his returning to defend his titles the following year seemed unlikely. Mary hovered protectively; Pop realized she'd never seen Bob look like this before.

A few hours later, slightly revived, Bob leaned out the window of his train as it left for London that night to tell his friend Al Laney he could now write about the idea of his winning all four majors. There was no point in keeping it a secret anymore. As the train pulled away, Bob called back to him: "But don't forget to keep your fingers crossed!"

Eager as he was to start the voyage home, Bob had one last commitment in England he was determined to honor. During qualifying rounds at Royal Liverpool, Ted Ray had asked if he'd be willing to play a charity match at Ray's home club before he left the country. As Bob put it, "The proposition suggested the possibility of a most enjoyable game."

Bob said he would be glad to participate but only if Ted played with him and invited Vardon, Taylor, or Braid to complete the foursome. What better way to complete his final visit to England than a best-ball round with Ted Ray and two-thirds of the Great Triumvirate?

On Saturday, June 22, Bob paired with James Braid against the grand old partnership of Ted and Harry in a best-ball match at Ray's home course of Oxhey. Playing his first carefree round in nearly six weeks, Bob shot 66 and broke the course record. He and Braid edged Harry and Ted at the last hole. Bob nailed his drive on a par three within a foot of the pin, and as old Harry stepped forward to tee up his ball Bob heard him say in his soft quiet voice: "Ah, Master Bobby's 'ot today."

This turned out to be the last round Bob ever played with Harry, Ted, or James Braid. A game played among friends, who just happened to be four of the ten greatest golfers who'd ever lived, away from crowds and competitive pressure, with no trophy or national pride at stake. Ted presented him with a gold cigarette case after the match, inscribed: "To a great golfer and a great sportsman." A fitting conclusion to Bob Jones's British career.

Bob.

CHAPTER FIFTEEN

The U.S. Open, Interlachen

THERE WAS NO MORE telling sign of Bob's mental and physical exhaustion than this: when he and Mary departed London for the cruise ship home he left his golf clubs behind at the hotel. An enterprising bellboy at the Savoy found them in the lobby, jumped in a cab, and tried to catch Jones at Waterloo Station. He arrived just as Bob's train was rolling down the tracks, so the bag followed him to Southampton on the next train, but Bob and the *Europa* sailed for New York ten minutes before it arrived. After an urgent exchange of ship-to-shore cables, officials sent the clubs steaming after him the next day on the *Aquitania*. The British amateur Cyril Tolley, on short notice heading over to compete in the American Open and Amateur, accompanied the Joneses on the trip. On board the train to the harbor, Tolley asked Bob how long he'd been in England. Six weeks, Bob answered. Tolley then asked him, as a friend and fellow competitor, if he had ever before played as poorly for so long a stretch of time. Bob thought it over carefully and answered no.

During the last day at Hoylake, news about Bob's final round reached his friends in Atlanta via radio and hole-by-hole telegraph updates. Newspapers reported that the city came to a standstill as the bulletins arrived, with crowds gathering in the early morning hours around newspaper and Western Union offices. A former Georgia Amateur champion and playing partner of Bob's named Chick Ridley camped out at the *Journal* all night and kept Big Bob up-to-date with constant phone calls. At home, the Colonel paced the floor from well before sunrise until the results were conclusive. When the news finally came across the wire that Diegel and Smith had failed to catch Bob in the final round there were "wild scenes on downtown streets, in office buildings and out at East Lake." Reporters were immediately dispatched to the Colonel's house and noticed that little four-year-old Bob the Third and five-year-old Clara were "romping with glee," resonating with the unbridled delight being expressed by their grandfather. Plans were organized by Atlanta's mayor, John Cohen, to greet Bob and Mary with a hometown reception when the *Europa* docked in New York on July 2. A special train carrying well-wishers north from Atlanta was arranged; the railroad called it the "Bobby Jones Special." Over two hundred fifty Atlantans would be waiting for him by the time he stepped off the boat.

Kiltie Maiden had recently given up his position as resident professional at East Lake for the second time, striking out on his own to open a golf instruction school in suburban New York City. When a reporter rushed out to inform him that his most famous pupil had just completed a sweep of the British majors, Kiltie broke down in tears. When he collected himself he summed up his feelings with his usual economy: "There are no words for me to use to tell how pleased I am. But one who has never been through the terrible strain of a championship cannot realize what it takes out of the players. Bob, it seems to me, suffers more than most. I'll bet he hasn't eaten a real meal all week nor had a full night's sleep."

The greeting New York gave him this time around dwarfed the reception he had received after his British Open win in 1926. During a crossing Bob described as restful and tedious, he made so few appearances that members of his party felt compelled to issue a public statement denying rumors that he had experienced an unspecified physical breakdown. As the *Europa* sailed into harbor, twin fireboats sprayed geysers, and hundreds of Atlantans sailed out on the *Mandalay* as a brass band played "Valencia." After he had bypassed customs and given a mass interview to the assembled press, a police escort hurried Bob and his party to city hall, where Mayor Walker greeted them again on the front steps and then introduced him to a nationwide radio audience as the crowd cheered wildly. Nothing he'd ever experienced, no acclaim or excitement from his fans, prepared Bob for the adoration they showered upon him this day. The crowd would not stop shouting for "our Bobby." Newsreel footage shows him looking stunned by the depth and scale of their tribute. The mayor called New York the "Atlanta of the North" to express how deeply his city had embraced their mutual hero. When Walker turned over the radio microphones to him, Bob's voice sounded husky with emotion, and he could only offer a few gracious sentences in response.

> I have not experienced anything like this before. When I came up Broadway I tried to figure the reason for it. All I can say is that I am overwhelmed by the welcome I have received from the people of New York and the people of Atlanta. I have never been so impressed.

To this day, Bob Jones and John Glenn are the only two individuals ever to receive two ticker-tape parades down the canyons of Broadway. This was a hot and humid midsummer afternoon, and in surviving film of the spectacle it appears as if the entire city had shut down to greet him; on Wall Street, Wednesday, July 2, turned out to be the slowest trading day in two years, and not only because of the deepening Depression. The wild party of the 1920s might be over but Bob's accomplishments and personality had touched a primal chord in the American soul, and their gratitude for the thrills he'd given them would now pour out of every village, town, or gathering he moved through. Although he played his part without complaint and endured the rituals of championship with grace and courtesy, this outpouring of unconditional devotion ran deeply contrary to Bob's modest instincts. One reporter described him as "gasping for breath and looking about almost wildly as if for some avenue of escape." A grand dinner for four hundred followed in his honor that night at the Vanderbilt Hotel, where despite his efforts to look engaged he seemed equally uncomfortable.

Grantland Rice, who acted as the dinner's master of ceremonies, caught up with Bob after the festivities that night. In his column the next day Rice compared the greeting Bob had been thrown by New York to those Ancient Greece gave to victorious Olympians. He added that he thought this day of celebration had been even harder on Bob than his final rounds at St. Andrews or

Hoylake. "In spite of the few days' boat rest, which helped a lot, it was easy enough to see that Bobby Jones was a rather tired young man. There was a look in his eyes that indicated a deep yearning to find the top of some distant mountain where he could forget golf and the plaudits of the crowd."

Bob let his guard down with his old friend Rice and talked about his toughest moments in the Amateur and Open. He said tournament play is often "a matter of who gets the breaks and there are times when the final result seems to be beyond your control. Things can happen before you know they're happening. They break your soul before you know what has taken place."

He sidestepped the question of retirement but did say he would not return to England the following year—"I have to get back to work and make a living"—then added he was looking forward to the Open at Interlachen, against the toughest field in the world, but refused to predict another victory. "No one knows what will happen in golf until it happens. All you can do is work and suffer and wait for fate."

Bob left by train for Minneapolis at two o'clock the following afternoon. His parents, grandfather, Pop, Rice, and a large percentage of the "Bobby Jones Special" crowd traveled on with him, while Mary returned home to Atlanta to take care of the children. His golf clubs, fresh off the *Aquitania*, were rushed through customs and conveyed by police escort to Penn Station, where they showed up minutes before the Broadway Limited was scheduled to depart. Bob carried his own bag onto the train and kept it in his compartment the whole way. Not quite so fortunate in his timing was Cyril Tolley, who had made plans to join Bob on the trip west; officials held up the train at Bob's request for two minutes in the hope that the Englishman would appear, but Cyril had misunderstood Bob's directions, taxied to Grand Central, and bought a ticket on the Twentieth Century Limited.

"I was certain he said Grand Central," Cyril told a reporter. "Oh well." In between inquiries about his train, Cyril made the following prediction: "Bobby did not play well in Britain—that is, for Jones—but I am confident he will be Bobby, himself, again in the west. And if he is, this championship is over before it starts."

In 1909 six members of an informal golf club in Golden Valley, Minnesota, just to the west of Minneapolis, decided civilization had crept too close to their playing ground; they didn't own the fields where they'd laid out their original course, and houses kept popping up on the fairways, which required constant rerouting. The men pooled a thousand dollars together and after an exhaustive search bought an option on 146 acres of gently rolling meadows, woods, and small lakes a half hour's streetcar ride south of downtown. While the founding members went about the bureaucratic monotony of incorporation and soliciting members, one of the farmers found out that his land was about to be purchased and developed into a golf club for the well-heeled. With dollar signs dancing in his head, the farmer announced to his friends that he planned to stall and then severely jack up his price once the option expired. When they got wind of this eleventh-hour tactic, the club founders decided to pay the man their originally negotiated price of twelve thousand dollars in full, in person, and in gold. Two of them boarded a streetcar one dreary February afternoon in the middle of a driving snowstorm, then trudged the last two miles through building drifts to the farmer's house, arriving well after dark. When the farmer saw them dump out a bag of gold bullion on his kitchen table he nearly fainted. Upon sober reflection he agreed to accept the payment and live up to the original contract, but fearing robbery refused to keep the gold in his house overnight. The two founders lugged their bounty all the way back to the streetcar stop through the storm, rode back to town, then sat up all night with a loaded shotgun protecting their investment until the bank opened the next morning.

The clubhouse and eighteen original holes opened in July of 1911, and Minneapolis had its first real country club. The members named their club Interlachen—German for "between the lakes"—a fitting description for the lovely piece of land they now called their own. After playing host to a Western Open in 1914, and a Trans Mississippi championship in 1916—won by the area's first local hero in the sport, Harry Legg—the members decided their golf course needed an upgrade. They did what so many other upscale clubs in the postwar era decided to do: they hired architect Donald Ross to redesign and shape a new layout. The peripatetic Scotsman reversed the nines and reworked half a dozen holes; his resulting parkland masterpiece opened in 1921 to universal acclaim. That same year the members hired their third resident professional, Willie Kidd, from Monefieth, Scotland. A gifted player and teacher, much beloved by the membership, he would remain on the job for the next thirty-seven years.

Bob said he felt right at home the minute he laid eyes on Interlachen; the massive Tudor clubhouse bears more than a passing resemblance to East Lake's, and the two courses share not only a similar landscape but many of Ross's signature designs: sinuous fairways, strategic bunkers, and small canted greens. Bob arrived in Minneapolis early on Saturday, July 5, and when the train pulled in at 8:50 that morning a throng of well-behaved Midwesterners crowded the downtown station; his friend, competitor, and Walker Cup teammate Jimmy Johnston headed the greeting committee, and Bob's arrival was carried live on local radio. Weary but buoyant, Bob smiled and waved to the crowd as they posed for photographers. He claimed to be sufficiently rested for the Open but denied that he had his heart set on winning all of the year's championships; he pointed out that no one had ever won three of the majors in the same year, let alone four.

After checking into his downtown hotel Bob drove out with Tolley and Johnston for a practice round at a local country club called Woodhill, where he matched the course record with an effortless 69. As they would all week, reporters and photographers dogged Bob's movements every step of the way.

Every golfer in the country of any consequence poured into the Twin Cities that weekend; Walter Hagen motored in from Detroit in the latest of his extravagant touring cars with Tommy Armour, Al Watrous, and twelve-year-old Walter Jr. along to watch his father compete in an Open for the first time. Jock Hutchison, Don Moe, Chick Evans, Willie Hunter, Leo Diegel, George Von Elm, Long Jim Barnes, George Voigt, Bobby Cruickshank, Johnny Farrell, Gene Sarazen, Johnny Goodman, Willie MacFarlane, Al Espinosa, Lighthorse Harry Cooper, Joe Turnesa, Ralph Guldahl, Wild Bill Mehlhorn, and Macdonald Smith were all in the 150-man field: a roll call of the game's past and future champions, all of whom had at one time or another memorably locked horns with Jones in a major. With Bob halfway to the Slam, everyone sensed something special was in the air. The question among the players was whether this Open would end up a fierce battle or a Jones coronation. Figuring in the endorsement income of the last few years, an Open championship could mean as much as $100,000 in extra income to a victorious professional. Even fifty-nine-year-old Tom Vardon, resident pro at nearby White Bear Lake Yacht Club, played his way into the tournament, his first Open in fourteen years. One slogan united all the pros: "Beat Jones."

Bob's quest attracted an equally star-studded cast of American sportswriters to join Pop Keeler in the press corps: Rice, Paul Gallico, Bill Richardson of the *New York Times*, Westbrook Pegler of the *New York News*. Two hundred twenty-six reporters covered the event from papers all across the country. One hundred fifty typewriters, dozens of telephones, and scores of telegraph transmitters were installed in a large wooden shack built beside the course that would serve as a temporary press headquarters. An extra twenty-five long-distance operators were added to the local phone system to handle the increased traffic. The Open was the single largest sporting event, and maybe the largest of any kind, ever held in the Twin Cities. In anticipation of enormous crowds, the *Minneapolis Tribune* reprinted a primer written by Granny Rice on gallery etiquette for the uninitiated. ("Don't walk across the course if any player is on the tee. You may be hit.") That same day the paper reported the approach of an ominous heat wave that broke long-standing records in Oklahoma and Kansas and appeared to be headed toward Minnesota.

On Sunday Bob picked up his local caddie, a teenager named Donovan Dale, whose name had been pulled from a hat, and played his first two practice rounds at Interlachen, matching even par 72 each time. Only club members and their families were allowed on the course that day to watch, but Bob still drew a gallery numbering in the hundreds. The only international player in the field, gregarious crowd pleaser Cyril Tolley, drew appreciative reviews from the locals, a proper Oxford Englishman still something of a novelty in the area's Lutheran/Scandinavian culture. On Monday Bob and Leo Diegel played together and both equaled the course record with 70; Johnny Goodman finished right behind them with 71 on his first circuit around the course. Hagen broke the front nine's record that morning with 32, pronounced his swing ready for action, called it a day, and drove off to go fishing with his son. (Walter also announced he planned to challenge Johnny Farrell's title as best-dressed professional; the Haig sported a pair of sharply creased cream colored flannel slacks, after the fashion of tennis stars, and announced afterward that plus fours were now "passé.") Interlachen's members, who had hoped their course would put up a stout defense, worried that the visitors might be preparing to have their way with their pride and joy. Bob had to remind an anxious local reporter that these were practice rounds, with occasional conceded putts, free of the heavy Open pressure that would descend on Thursday morning.

Two long days spent in the rising heat wave gave Bob a painful case of sunburn, and he played Tuesday's practice round with a wet table napkin wrapped around his neck like a bandana. In an exclusive interview, he revealed to Granny Rice that he had still not regained control of the driver and long irons that troubled him at Hoylake. Growing larger every day throughout the week, crowds continued to center and swirl around Bob; when he hit his tee shot on the long downhill par three thirteenth into a greenside bunker, an unidentified souvenir hunter jumped in, grabbed it, and ran off. Bob nonchalantly walked on to the next tee; just another day in the life.

By Wednesday morning the heat wave had parked on top of the upper Mississippi River Valley; temperatures edged over one hundred degrees. Accustomed to spending the final day before a tournament resting and reading quietly in his room, Bob had to seek relief outside due to the hotel's lack of air conditioning. He spent the morning fishing with Jimmy Johnston on nearby Lake Minnetonka—where even the fish were too overheated to bite—then played a late afternoon nine with Johnston, Tolley, and Moe. Over a thousand people followed them around in the stifling heat, which seemed to bother everyone but Bob; he told Pop after he came off the course that for the first time since Augusta in the spring his game felt as if it had all come together. As he had at Hoylake, Pop shared that confidence during a radio broadcast beamed back to New York that night: fifteen-minute radio summaries of each day's action.

"This battle will be the hardest championship that any man ever won," Hagen told Rice that night. "Here are one hundred fifty of the best golfers in the world, the survivors of twelve hundred entries, and yet it is the field against one man—Bobby Jones. Nothing like this has ever happened in golf, from the days of Vardon and Taylor and Braid to the present moment. It is almost unbelievable, but it is true."

Everyone of note on the grounds was asked to pick their favorites by reporters that night. A surprising number failed to name Jones as their first choice; many felt he would buckle under the strain of his battles in Britain. Hagen was mentioned by most; although eleven years had passed since his last U.S. Open win, he had arrived in the best physical condition he'd displayed in years. While most of the field rested or played abbreviated rounds on Wednesday, Hagen played thirty-six in the scorching heat and walked away none the worse for wear. Even Pop Keeler talked up the old pirate as a man to look out for, noting that he had recently converted to steel shafts and revitalized his iron play—Bob was now one of the last in the field still playing hickory. Many pointed to the meteoric rise of Horton Smith; as the last man to beat Jones at Savannah and the heir apparent to Hagen in the professional ranks, he posed the greatest threat to Bob's quest. Others liked the chances of the two men who chased Bob down to the wire at Hoylake, Leo Diegel and Macdonald Smith.

Plans to accommodate ten thousand fans a day were in place; how many would show up beyond that was anyone's guess. The chairman of the gallery committee spent the final evening going over last-minute instructions on how to shift the crowds around with his 150 marshals, studying a map of the course like a field general looking over a battlefield. Workmen spent the long northern twilight stringing rope through the posts hammered into every fairway. In anticipation that ropes alone would not prove sufficient, volunteers assigned to Jones's gallery were equipped with sixteen-foot-long bamboo fishing poles that they would extend like toll gates to hold back the hordes; marshals rehearsed snapping them into position that evening like members of a precision drill team. Two dozen Interlachen caddies who had not caught on with players in the field were armed with red flags and assigned to spot drives that missed the fairways and landed in the ankle-deep rough; on the course's sharp dogleg holes they were told to stand in the fairway and serve as human targets for players teeing off. Last-minute checks verified each station of the radio recording system installed to relay scores from every green to a large central scoreboard near the clubhouse. Small platforms were erected next to the ninth and eighteenth greens, where announcers would be stationed, shouting out the halfway and finishing scores of each player as he came off the course. So many festive tents dotted the landscape it looked as if the circus had come to town. The Big Show was about to begin.

Professional Jack Burke from Houston, Texas, led off the 1930 Open at 8:30 in the morning on July 10, teeing off in front of a few dozen spectators. By the time Bob was called to the starting line with Jock Hutchison at a few minutes after ten, the crowd around the first tee had grown to over five thousand and the temperature had reached 93 degrees. By noon it was 103 in the shade, on its way to a high of 108. Humidity hovered between 80 and 90 percent all day, with no afternoon thunderstorms to alleviate the pressure; the smothering peak of the heat wave had arrived. This was the hottest day on which a round of the U.S. Open had ever been played, setting a record that would stand for thirty-four years. One writer described the galleries as "lying in casual water from start to finish, and it all came from open pores." The heat rendered viewers so placid and pliable as they followed their favorites around that marshals reported it left them almost nothing to do. The Red Cross tent treated at least twenty for heat prostration, and a small number of golfers withdrew, too dizzy to finish their rounds. Twenty-six spectators reported that they had their pockets picked on the course, including two rubes from South Dakota who lost one hundred dollars apiece.

Bob's teenaged caddie, Donovan Dale, had signed on with a national newspaper syndicate to provide a ghostwritten, first-person account of each day's round. In his first column Dale professed amazement at Bob's patience with his gallery. The vast crowd pressed in around them from every angle and shut out any breath of fresh air, adding to the oppressive atmosphere. Bob's playing partner, forty-five-year-old Jock Hutchison, was more adversely affected; he shot 84 and would never be a factor in the tournament, but his good-natured attitude helped keep the round lighthearted. After his introduction at the first tee, Bob hit a perfect drive, then had to gesture for the sustained applause and cheers to stop as Jock walked out to play his first shot. Jock plucked Bob's tee from the ground, dropped it in his pocket, and then made a show of looking around for more, drawing a big laugh. When an official asked again for quiet, Jack said to the crowd: "That's all right, this doesn't bother me a bit." Then he laced his drive down the middle just short of Bob's.

As they set off, two friends from East Lake flanked Bob, acting as his escorts, bodyguards, and water boys: Chick Ridley and Charlie Cox, adjutant general of the State of Georgia, the commanding officer of the Georgia National Guard. A former Georgia Amateur champion, Ridley was huge, built in the Ted Ray mold, and a good man to have at one's side; he was known for improbable feats of strength, like driving a golf ball clear through the Atlanta telephone directory. Each tee at Interlachen was being patrolled by members of the Minnesota State Militia, and General Cox struck up conversations with most of them while they waited for the gallery to settle. Bob later heard one of the local guardsmen say to another: "I don't know what sort of golfer this Jones fellow is, but he's got the goldangest highest-ranking water boy I ever saw."

Bob had it going from the jump. Using fifteen of the seventeen clubs in his bag—he never called on his one iron or oversized concave wedge—Bob carved a 34 out of Interlachen's front nine by collecting seven pars and two birdies at the par fives. Jeanie Deans was back at the top of her form; he missed only three fairways all round, and two of those by only a foot. His only bogey of the day came at the par four tenth, his last missed fairway, when a middling recovery from the rough found a greenside bunker. Young Mr. Dale was amazed by his speedy, no-nonsense pace. He realized that Bob seldom spoke during a round because he was sizing up his next shot as he walked to the ball. By the time he reached it he'd already decided what he was going to do, asked for his club, made the shot, and moved on. Dale could find no fault with his master's game, but thought Bob could have bettered his first-round 71 by at least three strokes; wary of playing the fast greens too aggressively, three short birdie putts had hung on the front lip and failed to drop. The blast-furnace heat, as far as he could tell, failed to trouble Mr. Jones for a moment. In spite of his lifelong exposure to extreme Southern summers, Bob later said this was the hottest day he could ever remember, with the air so humid it must have been "only a very little shy of liquidity."

When Bob and Jock came off the course, their soaked clothes hung off them as if they'd jumped into one of the state's ten thousand lakes. People in the clubhouse thought Bob had wounded himself; his red foulard tie had bled the front of his white shirt crimson, and the paint from the Reddy Tees he carried in the pocket of his light gray plus fours had sent a red streak all the way down his leg. When he met Pop in the locker room, he was so worn out and cramped from dehydration that his fingers couldn't undo the soaked, shrunken knot of his tie; Pop had to clip it off him with a pocket knife. (The severed tie was quickly snapped up by a souvenir seeker.) Bob had lost ten pounds by the time he came in that afternoon, and for once couldn't attribute it all to nerves. Only after twenty minutes under a cold shower, and a few glasses of ice water, did he begin to feel human again. Some wondered out loud after his clockwork performance in that blazing inferno if he was human at all: Bob had established the early first-round lead.

Almost the entire rest of the field yielded to the heat. Englishman Cyril Tolley went out in the noonday sun, was besieged by swarming mosquitoes, lost nine pounds, and shot 80; by the time he dragged in, his crisp white flannels looked limp as dishrags. Long Jim Barnes carried around a huge umbrella to keep the sun off his face. Chick Evans nearly had to quit after nine because of light-headedness and shot an 81. But the game's other old lion announced he wasn't ready to be put out to pasture yet: attracting the day's second largest gallery, Walter Hagen finished with an even par 72. The Haig played without a hat; he was still under contract with Brylcreem, but endorsement be damned, Walter announced he wouldn't be venturing out into that inferno again tomorrow without a big straw boater covering his head. Harry Cooper and Horton Smith joined Hagen at 72 a short time later; Horton said afterward he intended to have words with a local friend who had issued a warning about Minneapolis's unpredictable weather and urged him to "bring an overcoat."

Johnny Farrell began his round with an eight and a six, then played out of his mind to finish the front nine at even par and ended with a 74. A salty old pro from a public course in Brooklyn, with the irresistible golf name of Wiffy Cox, matched Bob's 71; a former sailor with a gravelly Popeye voice, Cox seemed immune to the blistering heat. Minneapolis golfers fared poorly; Tom Vardon withdrew from the tournament, exhausted after an 81, and local favorite Jimmy Johnston struggled to an 80, his worst competitive round in years. Willie Kidd, Interlachen's resident pro, scraped together a 77, then, alone among the men who'd finished their struggles that day, went back out into the flaming heat to watch the rest of the action. The rest of the field remained huddled inside Interlachen's "Sobbing Room," a chamber set aside for members to tell sad stories about their rounds, which on this day had been converted into a cooling oasis with lounge chairs, pitchers of ice water, and electric fans. Tolley summed up the prevailing mood when he shuffled in and asked no one in particular: "So, what did the Great Man do today?" Everyone knew exactly who he was talking about.

Beginning his round after noon under the full hammering zenith of the sun, Tommy Armour sent a messenger scurrying back to the clubhouse after four holes to ask for a big bag of ice. Before every subsequent shot Armour rubbed down his face, neck, and forehead with chunks of ice wrapped in a handkerchief; it seemed to do the trick. The Black Scot blistered the back nine in 33 to match the course record 70, and edged ahead of Bob by a stroke. Later in the day another native Scotsman made news; Macdonald Smith came to the eighteenth tee needing only a par four to shoot 69, break the course record, and take sole possession of the lead. His approach to the elevated final green fell a foot short and rolled back down the hill into a thick clump of clover. Smith's bogey five netted him 70 and tied him with Armour for the first-round lead in the Open.

Sixteen people in the Twin Cities succumbed to the intense heat on Thursday. Scores of others died all across the Midwest and the Deep South, where the high pressure had started to intrude. Some small measure of relief arrived in Minneapolis when a drier wind blew in from the east on Friday morning and moderated the humidity; temperatures ran about seven degrees cooler and attendance at Interlachen increased by 30 percent, with over twelve thousand tickets sold. Many of those ticket holders started out to follow first-round leaders Macdonald Smith and Tommy Armour, but by the end of the morning nearly the entire crowd had circled around two men playing in con-secutive pairings: Horton Smith and Bobby Jones.

Granny Rice bounced back and forth between their twosomes all day long and had this to say about Horton Smith: "It was as fine a round of golf as any-one has ever seen in an Open championship when you consider the way he went about it. Horton adopted a unique idea and put it into effect. This idea consisted in hitting his drive smack down the middle and then rapping an iron shot six or eight feet from the pin. It is a system that seldom fails, even if you are putting with a broom."

After their battles at Savannah and Augusta, no other professional in the field seemed more eager or unafraid to take on the Emperor Jones. The lanky young Missourian sent an early message to the famous amateur playing just behind him with every shout that issued from his gallery. Riding a birdie at the second and a steady string of pars, Smith had picked up a shot and pulled into a tie with Bob by the time he reached the 485-yard par five ninth. After another rifle-shot drive Horton gambled on his second and spanked a two iron that cleared the lake then ran up onto the green, coming to rest only twenty feet from the hole. While Smith advanced to his ball, Bob played an equally strong drive behind him and was waiting to play his second in the fairway when a huge cry went up from thousands packed around the distant green; Smith had dropped his putt for an eagle and jumped ahead of Jones.

Bob stared at the distant green but betrayed no reaction. His caddie watched him closely as he pulled his three wood and stood to the ball; Bob had reached this green in two in every round he'd played, and birdied it the day before, but today the wind was directly in his face; the shot demanded both power and precision, a carry of two hundred yards over the lake then up a thin throat to a green protected by a deep bunker on the left. The gallery narrowed around him, forming a human tunnel down the line of flight. Bob stepped away from the ball, urging the crowd to move back and give him more room, then took his stance again. As Bob reached the top of his backswing, two little girls in the gallery just behind him broke from the crowd to run across the fairway; their motion disrupted his peripheral vision, and he came down to impact a fraction of an inch off plane. He struck the ball thin and it shot off, low and hot, toward the water.

The crowd gasped. They watched the ball hit the surface of the lake at tremendous speed sixty feet short of the far bank, but instead of sinking it skipped forward, hit the water a second time, then bounced out onto the grass on the opposite side and rolled to a stop only thirty yards short of the green. Bob's caddie, Donovan Dale, said it reminded him of "skipping a rock down at the creek." "The crowd's groan," wrote Rice, "before it reached full utterance, took a queer turn into a frenzied shout."

They cheered him all the way as Bob walked around the lake—given what they'd just witnessed, some might have expected him to walk across it—and a legend immediately arose from some eyewitnesses who insisted they'd seen the ball bounce forward off a lily pad. Although it came to be known forever after as the "Lily Pad Shot," Bob always maintained that no vegetation was involved, simply the elementary laws of surface tension and aerodynamics. Whether the beneficiary of luck, fate, a lily pad, or a hardheaded bullfrog, Bob regrouped during his stroll to the ball, pitched up to within two feet of the cup and sank his putt for a four. What could easily have ended up a bogey score or worse had, in a moment's act of grace, turned into a birdie. The ovation that arose from around the ninth green did not go unnoticed by Horton Smith, standing on the tenth tee; when he saw Bob's ball bounce across the water, this exact thought entered his mind: "It is not destined for me to win this championship." After a good drive, Smith jacked his approach over the tenth green and wrote a bogey five on his scorecard. The two men were back in a tie. After a 40 on the front nine, explaining that he didn't want to slow Bob down, his playing partner, Jock Hutchison, called it a tournament and withdrew; Bob would play the back nine alone, which further underscored his head-to-head battle with the man in front of him.

With a sizeable percentage of the gallery shuttling between them on every hole, Smith steadied down and played the last eight holes in perfect par. Bob's game was less solid; he ground out pars, bogeyed the thirteenth, then stumbled badly at fifteen, missing a four-foot putt and taking double bogey. By the end of the round Smith had bested him 70 to 73 and seized a two-stroke lead at the halfway mark of the tournament.

"Bobby had very little to say as he marched along," reported Donovan Dale afterward. "I don't understand how anybody can think easily with that gang watching, but he apparently isn't bothered and appeared ready to play more when he finished the eighteenth. Bobby has been behind before—half of the tournament's yet to be played. I pity old man par for the rest of the way."

The duel between Mr. Smith and Mr. Jones dominated the day's head-lines; GALLERY QUITS FIRST ROUND LEADERS FOR NEW GODS sums up the tone. Their golf had provided such compelling theater everyone else seemed to shrink back and grant them center stage. Tommy Armour and Mac Smith shot 76 and 75 respectively, still in the running but unattended by galleries by the time they finished their rounds. Lighthorse Harry Cooper clung to par for the second straight day and stayed two shots back. An obscure twenty-three-year-old expatriate Englishman named Charles Lacey, resident professional at Pine Valley, stepped into the role of this year's dark horse; he matched Smith's best round of the day and jumped into a second-place tie with Jones and Cooper. Hagen had struggled manfully to a second-round 75 and stood five shots back. The second-round leader board ended like this:

Horton Smith	72-70—142
Bobby Jones	71-73—144
Harry Cooper	72-72—144
Charles Lacey	74-70—144
Macdonald Smith	70-75—145
Johnny Farrell	74-72—146
Wiffy Cox	71-75—146
Tommy Armour	70-76—146
Walter Hagen	72-75—147

Sixty-nine men survived the halfway cut, ten amateurs among them. All the important professional names would play on during Saturday's two final rounds, but Interlachen's host pro, Willie Kidd, was going to have to watch from the sidelines. He would be joined there by amateurs Jimmy Johnston and Cyril Tolley, the tournament's two biggest disappointments. Chick Evans withdrew even before the cut, halfway through his second round; he had a contract to cover the event for a Chicago newspaper and spent the rest of the tournament working as a journalist.

That evening during his radio broadcast, Pop Keeler did his best to dispel the growing legend of the lily pad but did remark that the fortunate bounce boded well for Bob's chances: "That's the way it goes in championships. If your name is up, the ball will walk on water for you." He stopped well short of saying Bob's path to the title was clear, and fretted that the pros were really gunning for him this time; he had a premonition that somebody was about to go crazy and close this thing out before it was over. Horton Smith, who had shown an unprecedented willingness to stand up to Bob's game, worried him the most.

If Bob shared his friend's concern that night he didn't show it; he and his father joined Jimmy Johnston for an excursion on a private yacht around Lake Minnetonka during the warm, lingering twilight. Horton Smith spent the evening at his downtown hotel, where he joined a large group of other golfers at a screening in the ballroom of some newsreel footage from the first day of the Open. He turned in early to rest for Saturday's final two rounds with four former U.S. Open winners, and two others who had lost them in play-offs, within five shots of his lead; he didn't sleep very soundly.

So Bob woke early on Saturday morning, July 12, knowing with absolute certainty he was about to play his last two rounds in a U.S. Open. He already owned every record of consequence in the game's history and had won the admiration of hundreds of millions of people, for his character as much as his championships, yet Bob remained less ruined by success than any other athlete in memory. Remaining true to the best principles of his game, he never once coasted on his reputation or took the easy money. Every step he'd made during his immortal season of 1930 had taken him deeper into uncharted waters. Now, having done more to define the vast gulf between the very good and the truly great, as the end of his journey came into view, tired, buffeted, and bruised, did he have the strength and reserves to reach for greatness one last time?

He was scheduled to tee off early in the third round, at 9:15, and saw it as a chance to make a statement, set the tone before any other contenders were on the course. He had always liked playing just off the lead, preferred it; he could go flat-out without feeling he had something to protect. He would be partnered for both rounds that day with Joe Turnesa, the man he'd battled to the wire in the U.S. Open at Scioto in 1926, another advantage; Turnesa was a friend, a pro's pro, steady, respectful, and solid. For the next few hours, hardly a soul at Interlachen even noticed Joe was playing.

The mercury fell a few more notches that morning, but the humidity returned; the air was thick, a mix of clouds and sun with a constant threat of thunderstorms. Ten thousand people had already assembled, a sea of white shirtsleeves and hats, to watch Bob tee off. Chick Ridley and Charlie Cox were on hand, armed with full canteens to act as his seconds; the Colonel stayed toward the back of the crowd, still leery after all these years of letting Bob see him watching. Pop was there for him, as he had been from the beginning, front and center. Maternally fixated player-turned-reporter Chick Evans encountered Bob's mother, Clara, near the clubhouse and wrote this about her later: "Bob's devoted and darling mother has suffered dreadfully from the heat, but wants to be present at his triumph. Her heroic efforts to keep well must be an inspiration to Bob, greater than the championship itself."

The golf swing is as pure a reflection of personality as any athletic action a person can perform, as unique as a snowflake, more telling than a signature. Bob's swing never said more about him than it did that morning at Interlachen, languid and unhurried, equal parts poetry and power, a portrait of efficiency with no wasted motion or energy. He sank a ten-foot putt for par at the first, collected effortless pars at two and three, not pressing for anything, like an orchestra tuning up, and then came the music; his second shot to the par five fourth found a bunker. He clipped the ball off the sand to within six feet, then holed the putt for birdie.

After a scrambling par at the fifth, he left his drive at the sixth in deep rough a hundred yards short of the green. After a short iron pitch to five feet of the hole he canned his second birdie of the round. On the seventh he improved his odds; his approach landed only three feet from the cup. Another birdie. Two routine pars followed at eight and nine. Bob had played the front nine in 33.

The announcer at his post beside the ninth green shouted out the result for all to hear as Bob moved in. The crowd at the clubhouse erupted in a sustained cheer. Horton Smith was on the practice green near the first tee preparing to begin his round when the mob swept around him at a gallop. As Smith moved upstream to his starting line, Bob walked ahead to the back nine.

By this point in the round Bob was hitting with full power, his tempo on the downswing increasing with nearly every stroke. Gone was any thought of safe or conservative play; he couldn't afford to let up for a second, not when his swing felt like this. His features looked set and determined, unstoppable; he hardly spoke a word. After another easy par at ten, he crossed the street to the par five eleventh, a reachable dogleg right with a pond in the crook of its elbow protecting the shortest route down the right side. Bob placed a mammoth drive in the perfect spot to the left of the water, and then played just short of the green with his second; he chipped up to within three feet and collected another easy birdie. Horton Smith could hear that roar on the second tee half a mile away.

The twelfth hole mirrors the eleventh, another par five, 535 yards long, a narrow, tree-lined dogleg left that ends in a steep climb to an elevated green. Bob blasted his drive 290 yards, then stood over the ball and debated whether to wallop a wood to the green or lay up short with an iron. He chose the latter; a ripple of disappointment ran through the crowd. He played his wedge shot to level ground and a perfect lie at the foot of the hill. Looking up at the green, he could barely see the top of the flag and waited for his caddie to climb up to show him the line; he played another short wedge and watched it arc up and disappear from sight. The gallery packed in around the green up top let out another roar; the ball grazed the flag on the fly and came to rest eight feet from the hole. Bob climbed the hill, and when he saw the result he cracked his first smile of the day. A minute later he rolled in that putt for a birdie four.

Five under par.

After a wayward drive he saved par at thirteen with another brilliant chip.

At fourteen a twenty-foot putt for birdie missed by an inch. Routine par at fifteen. At sixteen, a challenging short par four, he planted his approach within inches of the pin. He could have fanned it in for birdie with a feather.

Six under par. Two more pars coming home would bring Bob in at 66 and shatter the U.S. Open single-round scoring record.

The crowd danced around him, delirious with excitement; as word spread about his round he'd drawn nearly every person on the course to his gallery and was being followed by the largest audience who'd ever followed one man in American golf. They stood ten or twelve deep, shoulder to shoulder; most could barely catch a glimpse of him, but no one wanted to miss the opportunity to say they'd been there on the day that Bobby Jones made history. He still had to fight his way through a human wall to reach every tee and green, and without ropes to restrain them on the tees they thundered after every drive down every fairway. Kids darted around between shots, but after yesterday's lily pad incident the gallery had become more self-policing; whenever Bob stood over his ball, marshals stared at the crowd like bird dogs, no one moved, and the air grew as still as church.

The hole has since been shortened, but in 1930 the seventeenth was a terrifying par three, downhill, at 262 yards the longest of its breed in the USGA directory and perhaps the world. Surrounded by bunkers, the green is further defended by a small lake on the right and a stream to the rear. From the tee the available target area appears about the size of a dinner plate. Bob's tee shot with a two wood came up twenty yards short and landed in heavy rough beside the slope of a bunker. He negotiated another delicate pitch to twelve feet, and then watched the putt slide just by the hole for his first bogey of the day. The way the field played this hole, anything less than four felt like a birdie.

The finishing hole at Interlachen is a big, brawny test of character; the fairway favors a fade, leaving a steep uphill second to a severely contoured green tucked against the side of the clubhouse. Bob applied a touch more fade than he wanted to his drive and watched it bounce off the fairway into a cluster of trees. For the first time all day, Pop saw a hint of fatigue in Bob's face, the toll he would pay for this burst of perfection. His stance was problematic, leaving barely enough room to swing a club, but with an abbreviated action he slugged the ball back out onto the fairway near the base of the hill. His third shot, a short pitch to the green, took a hard bounce and kicked into a bunker dead behind the flag. He settled into the sand, lofted the ball gently onto the edge of the green, then watched it trickle slowly toward the hole and stop one roll short of dropping in for par. Bogey five.

No person in any form of competition had ever broken 70 at Interlachen. The average score on this day was 77.96. Bob had just shot 68 in the pivotal third round of a U.S. Open, his personal best in the event, the one and only time he felt he had reached and sustained his highest level of excellence in a national championship. He had hit three approach shots during the round with seven irons; each landed less than a foot from the hole. He had eleven one-putt greens. Driver, irons, putter; everything clicked. He likened the experience afterward to how a halfback feels when he breaks through the line of scrimmage into the open field and knows he has the speed to reach the end zone. Now his only anxiety was whether anyone would catch him from behind.

Horton Smith stood up to this hurricane for a while. He played the front nine in even par 36, remarkable under the circumstances, but after he made the turn, as more and more of his gallery deserted him and the booming shouts and cheers for Bob's heroics continued to rise in volume and frequency and echo across the course, he began to falter. Not obviously, but with a slow leaking of confidence. A double bogey at seventeen ended Smith's slide. He played the back nine in 40, for a grim 76. He'd gone from a two-stroke lead to a six-stroke deficit in less than four hours.

While Bob went into the clubhouse to rest and repair for the final round, news of his thunderbolt spread through the tournament; players collapsed internally at the news, gave up, couldn't stand the gaff, decided to call it a day and wait till next year. Walter Hagen, for so long the pro game's standard-bearer against the great amateur, could only match Horton Smith's 76; thirteen strokes down, he was out of the running. Halfway through Hagen's third round even his own son deserted him for Bob's gallery. Toward the end of the back nine, playing to an empty house, Hagen was so bored and dejected he started putting left-handed; he would shoot 80 that afternoon and finish tied for thirteenth place. Walter told Chick Evans the awful truth about his game afterward: he had lost command of his putter and could no longer deny that his decline had begun in earnest. The twin curiosities of Charles Lacey and Wiffy Cox vanished into history. Johnny Farrell and Macdonald Smith both faded; they were seven strokes back. Tommy Armour stumbled to 75; nine back, over and done. Chick Evans reported that the locker room was deathly silent; that was the sound of men packing it in.

Only two men remained within striking distance of the lead: Horton Smith was six strokes behind, and given the way Bob had just passed him no one gave a nickel for his chances that afternoon. His closest competitor was Harry Cooper; with a steady third-round 73, the Texan sat five strokes in back of Jones.

That was it. Bob Jones had blown everyone else in the field off the golf course.

The Midwestern heat wave had spread to Atlanta; 103 degrees that Saturday afternoon. The *Journal* reported that every human being over the age of ten spent the entire day glued to a radio set. Mary huddled in Bob's parents' big house with their kids, receiving or passing on regular updates from friends on the phone, the radio turned up full blast so she could listen as she chased the toddler from room to room. With all the windows open for the heat and every radio within a hundred miles turned on, you could have walked down any street in the city and never missed a word of the coverage.

The same scene was repeated in hundreds of other cities and towns around the country. Four thousand miles to the east, Bernard Darwin woke up in the middle of the night and dialed his primitive radio up and down trying in vain to find any report of how Bobby was doing.

Could Jones do it? Could he hang on?

He walked out of the clubhouse to the first tee at 1:15. The crowd had grown as large as sixteen thousand; some estimates put it closer to twenty thousand. No one could read it on his face but Bob was spent, dead tired; the relentless pressure, the incessant attention and lack of privacy, fighting the crowds and himself and this cruel, intractable game. He had spent a restless hour inside, nibbling at some chicken salad and a glass of iced tea, trying to prepare mentally. He knew he couldn't hope to repeat what he'd done in the third round; the bill for his morning's burst of brilliance was about to come due.

His first drive betrayed no unsteadiness; nearly three hundred yards long just right of center. His long iron approach found the back of the green; two putts for a routine par. The crowd roared its approval. Two good shots landed him on the second green, but he three-putted for bogey, the first symptom of trouble. At the short par three third he pulled his drive twenty yards left into a bunker. He recovered onto the green, but three-putted for the second straight hole. Double bogey. Three strokes lost to par after three holes. A shudder rippled through the crowd.

At the par five fourth Bob cracked another soaring drive, three hundred yards dead down the middle. A strong three wood left him just short of the green; he later called this his most important shot of the tournament because it staunched the bleeding. Bob pitched up close and sank the easy putt for a birdie. Steadied, he played the next four holes in even par, but still gave the gallery cause for concern; during that stretch he missed two makeable putts for birdie. As Bob teed up his ball on nine, the immense mob trampled over the right-of-way of Walter Hagen, playing his second hole of the afternoon, alone and unnoticed; the Haig had to wait until Bob played on before he could proceed, which told him all he needed to know about his current status.

Bob collected par at the ninth without aid or comfort from a lily pad. Out in 38, two over for the first half of the ride. Far from disastrous, but five strokes worse than his morning effort. And he was about to hear footsteps coming up behind him.

Macdonald Smith teed off half an hour behind Bob at 9:45. After falling two strokes short of Bob at Hoylake, Smith, now forty-two, knew this might well be his last chance to win the major that had eluded him for over twenty years. Each of his older brothers had a U.S. Open title to his name, but Mac had come up short so often people tended to disregard him. Eight times he had finished within three strokes of the lead in a British or American championship. He'd lost his best chance at Prestwick in 1925, when the out-of-control mob ran wild on the fairways and ruined his final round. Fate had never smiled on him, but Mac Smith was a buoyant, cheerful man by nature and had never given up.

Starting seven strokes in back of Bob, with only a small gallery watching, Mac began his final round with two pars, then birdied the par three third—the hole Bob double-bogeyed—with a drive that nearly went in the hole.

Almost no one on the course knew it, but Bob's lead was already down to three.

Even before he had any inkling about Smith, Bob's face was a mask of worry as he made the turn. His energy and concentration were flagging, and when he called on them, his reserves hadn't answered. The crowd jostled him, claustrophobically; Chick Ridley and Charlie Cox had to muscle through a human wall to forge a path for him. Starting the final nine he found a rhythm with his driver and played the opening third of the side conservatively for three straight pars. He felt better, but the two par fives he'd birdied that morning, the last obvious chances on the back, were behind him. His strategy was obvious: take no chances. Make pars. Force the men behind him to go for broke.

As Bob walked onto the thirteenth tee, word reached his gallery for the first time that Mac Smith had birdied the ninth and finished his front nine in 34. Only three strokes separated them; the crowd thrummed with news of this dawning threat.

A difficult, downhill par three, the 192-yard thirteenth hadn't presented Bob any problems all week, but now he pulled his drive to the left and watched it bounce down a steep bank toward Mirror Lake behind the green. He tried to shave his recovery from the rough too closely; it hit the crest of the hill and rolled back down a few feet shy of the green. His next chip found the green, twelve feet short of the hole, but the putt wouldn't fall. He had to tap in his second to get down for a double-bogey five.

Bob's lead over Mac Smith in the final round of the Open was down to a single stroke. Messengers began sprinting back and forth between the two players, forming a network of nerves.

Rice and Keeler looked at each other in the gallery at fourteen as the crowd bustled around. They both watched Bob closely as he passed, eyes to the ground, deep in concentration. The dangerous moment had arrived. Fate and will were about to collide. If Bob faltered one more time from here on in both of the men who'd watched him play his entire career knew that the game, the Open, the quest for the Slam, would all be over.

The fourteenth hole is an intimidating, uphill, 444-yard par four. Bob's drive soared up the right side of the fairway but got no forward kick off the hill. He had 210 yards left to the green. He roped a three wood that bounced up and rolled to a stop within fifteen feet of the cup. When he sank the putt for birdie the biggest shout of the day went up. Mac Smith heard the eruption from a few hundred yards away, where he was lining up his putt on the twelfth green. Ten seconds later, he responded by sinking the eight-footer for birdie, and the cheer echoed back toward Jones.

Bob's lead was back to one stroke, and he knew it before he teed off again. He smashed a fine drive and iron to the green at fifteen. His bid for birdie, from only eight feet, lipped out. Par four, but given the lost opportunity it was hard to feel good about it. The crowd tried to rally him, shouting encouragement, slapping him on the back as he walked to the next tee. Then word arrived that Smith had bogeyed thirteen; the lead was back up to two. The news lifted his spirits; Bob decided to press the advantage at the short par four sixteenth. He pounded his drive over the trees protecting the dogleg, going for the green as he had that morning, but as so often happened when he swung too hard he pulled it left. The ball settled in the rough, short of a string of bunkers, thirty yards shy of the putting surface.

He walked up to the green to examine the surface around the flag, headed back to his ball and took out his lofted, heavy wedge, the only time he used it in the entire Open. A short, crisp swing; the ball lifted cleanly out of the tangled grass . . . and dropped and stopped dead less than three feet from the hole. His birdie putt would've gone in from there on the desire of the gallery alone, but Calamity Jane did the job for them.

Three-stroke lead, two holes to play.

Hope came out of hiding. At last Bob had closed the door, all his fans assured themselves. Two birdies in three holes would stop Mac Smith in his tracks. Bob was now even par through the back nine; surely that would be enough to see him to the finish.

Bob climbed up to the elevated tee at seventeen, a narrow chute perched on a plateau dug out of the hill, the launch pad to the mammoth 262-yard par three. He studied the green below and the lake to the right. He glanced up at the treetops; a brisk wind blew from the left toward the water. He pulled his two wood and lined up to start the ball at the right edge of the green, then draw it back into the wind toward the flag.

He hit it on the heel of the club; the ball didn't hook. The gallery watched in horror as it arced out, found the wind, and faded toward the lake. It appeared to encounter a tree as it neared the swampy waterline, then disappeared. With fifteen thousand eyewitnesses looking on, not one could say for certain what had happened to the ball. The crowd followed Bob down toward the water. Even the forecaddie who'd been stationed there to watch drives couldn't locate it. They dug and poked around for minutes. Someone finally came across a ball embedded in the mud on the shore of the marshy water, and the rejoicing began; they knew he'd get a free drop from such a lie and suffer no penalty at

all. Bob had a better suggestion: "I think we'd better make sure that's my ball."
After prying it out of the muck with an iron, Bob determined that it wasn't his.

A clutch of local and national officials descended to consult about how to
proceed as Bob and the crowd waited breathlessly. A lost-ball ruling would send
him back to the tee, playing his third shot. A triple-bogey six seemed almost
guaranteed; his entire lead over Smith could vanish with this one mistake.

The senior official, former USGA president Prescott Bush, emerged from the
huddle to announce that the lake had been designated a parallel water hazard by
the committee, and cards had been given to all players stating the rule when the
Open began; therefore Bob was entitled to a drop within two club lengths of the
hazard, at a penalty of one stroke. No loss of distance. No return to the tee.

Knowledgeable observers questioned the ruling. Didn't the ball have to be
found first to receive the lesser penalty? This was clearly a lost ball. Didn't that
call for loss of stroke *and* distance?

Bob didn't question the ruling; that wasn't his job now. He dropped a ball
in the fairway and pitched to the green, lying three. He needed two strokes to
get down for his double-bogey five. His third of the round on a par three.

The lead was back to one. Mac Smith was still alive.

Bob heard grumbles all the way to the eighteenth tee. Doubts that he
could rise from the canvas for a third time in the same round. Questions about
whether he'd been given another favorite's advantage by the ruling at seventeen. If that uncalled penalty turned out to be his margin of victory, he knew
that controversy threatened to taint his win and the entire campaign for the
Slam. It made him mad. It was a good mad.

His drive at eighteen carried three hundred yards, ideally placed down the
right side, leaving the angle he needed to the hole, perched on the green's
upper tier, back and left. Bob asked for an iron; Donovan Dale handed it to
him, a look of reverence on his face. A wild roar rose from the crowd as he
made his swing; after overshooting this green that morning, his approach faltered in the opposite direction; the ball hit the apron of the putting surface and
reached the green but failed to kick up onto the back tier.

The crowd stampeded to the green, forming a dense wall up and around
the hill. The empty green seemed to be a stage waiting for the lead to appear;
a break formed in the crowd like a curtain parting, and as Bob came through
the opening he was greeted with thunderous applause. His ball sat on the front

of the green, forty feet from the hole, breaking hard right to left up the slope. He looked it over. A four for par from this spot was a long way from guaranteed; this was three-putt territory. Three putts for bogey here and Smith could easily close the gap to force a play-off, or even win the Open outright.

Newsreel cameras cranked away from the clubhouse and the back of the green as Bob walked all the way up to the hole and back, examining the contours and the line. Pop, Rice, his parents, his friends, and countless thousands of strangers looked on; people surrounded that green and spread out in every direction almost as far as the eye could see. Bob took his stance, looking cool and collected. "I was quivering in every muscle," he admitted to Pop later.

The last shot Bob Jones ever hit in a U.S. Open rolled up that hill, took the break of the slope as if it were riding a rail, turned right six feet from the hole, gently clicked against the center of the back of the cup, and stayed down for a birdie three.

It took five minutes to clear all the hats that were tossed into the air off the green so his partner, Joe Turnesa, could putt out. Bob and Joe shook hands. A reporter named Ted Husing had been broadcasting live for the last two hours on a portable thirty-pound backpack radio transmitter that he carted around—the first live coverage of its kind—but the getup was so cumbersome he hadn't quite been able to catch up with the action. Then, just as Bob was about to play eighteen, the station decided to cut away to the live call of a high-stakes horse race in Chicago. Husing hustled to try and get Bob for a live interview afterward but missed him.

Ridley and Cox wrestled a path for Bob through the crowd to the scorer's tent, where he turned in his card: 37 on the back, for a final round 75 and a total score for the Open of 287. He had finished only one shot off the all-time Open record set by Chick Evans at nearby Minikahda in 1916. Alone in that enormous crowd, Chick heaved a small sigh of relief.

Bob had scouted out a small room upstairs in the clubhouse between rounds as the private sanctuary where he would sweat out the results from the rest of the field. Pop arrived moments later with a whiskey and soda, and the news that Mac Smith had parred seventeen. Bob's lead was two. The rest of the news was good: Horton Smith and Harry Cooper had been unable to mount a charge on the final nine. Only Mac Smith was left with a chance to catch him, and he had one hole to do it.

Bob's hands weren't shaking this time as he held his highball. Pop thought he looked completely worn out, but peaceful in a way he hadn't seen for some time. Maybe years.

"So, what do you think, Pop?"

"I think it's almost over, Bob."

Outside the clubhouse, in Bob's absence his caddie, Donovan Dale, was mobbed by reporters. "Besides being the world's best golfer, Bobby is a real gentleman to caddie for," he told them. "And that, if you know the things a caddie runs up against, is saying plenty." In his pocket were the eighty-five dollars Bob had tipped him. The average wage for a caddie was less than a dollar a round. Dale apologized for what he felt were inadequate answers to some of the reporters' questions, but just now he was "too tired to think."

Just as he had at Hoylake only two weeks earlier, Mac Smith came to the final hole needing an eagle two to tie Jones for the lead in an Open championship. His drive found the fairway and left him 150 yards to the green; the same gallery that had followed Jones now surrounded Smith. He waited for his partner to play up to the green, took his time, stared down the flag, then made his swing.

The shot looked good all the way. It bounced on the front of the green and started rolling up the slope on line to the hole . . . and hit his partner's ball, knocking them both sideways. That was the end. Two putts later, just as it had at Royal Liverpool, Mac Smith's four at eighteen secured him first-place money, second place on the scoreboard, and a footnote in history. Horton Smith, just as he had at Hoylake, finished third.

Pop came back to the room—known today as the "Bobby Jones Room"—with the news. They grinned at each other and Pop asked him how he felt.

"Well," said Bob. "I'm pretty happy."

Back-to-back U.S. Opens. His fourth American Open, tying Willie Anderson's record, established back in the days when a hundred caddies and rough club pros played a few rounds for a hundred bucks and the amusement of their upper-class employers. Counting both British and American events, his seventh Open win overall, tying Harry Vardon's record. His third major championship in the last seven weeks, and twelfth of his career in eight years; alone and in the clear now, ahead of anyone in history who ever played the game.

"So tell me," asked Pop, "are you going to quit this damned game now?"

"I'm going to play in the Amateur in September at Merion, anyway," he said, and smiled. "Don't print it yet, but that's going to be the end."

Pop held back the news when reporters pressed both men on the subject of retirement in the locker room a short time later, but something about the way Bobby smiled set the rumor mills into motion. He cued Pop to give them an answer. Pop stood up—clad only in a towel—and recited some verse extolling the virtues of the quiet life. Speculation about Jones quitting the game after Merion would dominate columns for weeks to come.

Almost no one left the grounds before the awards ceremony. Bob had time to shower, change his shirt, and put on a coat and tie. Players and officials from Interlachen and the USGA walked out in formal procession onto the broad green lawns below the clubhouse, the happy throng arrayed above them all in white. Horton and Macdonald Smith both paid tribute to Bob but vowed to keep on fighting as they collected their checks. When they handed him the silver cup, Bob gave his thanks on live radio; reporter Ted Husing had abandoned his portable gear, and Bob spoke into a regular microphone. He returned the compliments given him by the company of Smith and Smith, but couldn't quite explain how he managed to better them.

"I was just a little lucky, that's all," he said.

"Make that plucky," Horton Smith interjected, and got a big laugh.

When the ceremony ended, a tired, humbled Walter Hagen told Ted Husing that after Bob's display of greatness at Interlachen and throughout that summer, it would no longer be appropriate to criticize any golfer who got himself into trouble by saying that he "played like an amateur."

Another reporter elicited a rare word from Bob's grandfather. During the last couple of year even old R.T. had come around to appreciate the wonder of what Bob was doing, even if the credit should go elsewhere. "The arms of the Lord are around the neck of my boy this day," he said. "God be praised."

Bob Jones played in eleven straight U.S. Opens. He won four of them, finished second in four others, tied for fifth, eighth, and eleventh. For eight of the last nine years that he competed in the national championship, he finished either first or second.

In spite of the heat, frenzied celebrations broke out that evening in the streets of downtown Atlanta. Plans were set for the greatest homecoming Bob ever received.

Bernard Darwin awoke early in England after a sleepless night, saw the newspaper waiting on his breakfast table, opened it to read the news about Jones, and shouted for joy. A short time later on his morning walk he ran into J. H. Taylor and they grinned and slapped each other's back like a couple of school kids: Bobby had done it!

Lighthorse Harry Cooper returned to his Minneapolis hotel room only to discover that while he'd been out someone had robbed his room. His wife's jewelry was stolen, and over a hundred dollars in cash, a healthy chunk of the money he'd just won for finishing fourth in the Open.

A few hours later that evening, not long after dark, a reporter ran into Bob standing by the tracks of the Great Northern railway station. A private rail car had been requisitioned to convey Jones and his friends to Chicago and from there home to Atlanta, and he was waiting patiently for it to be coupled onto the train. Many other players from the Open, those from the East, had boarded that same train. There was no explanation as to where the other members of Bob's party had gotten to, but for the moment he was alone and almost unnoticed.

The reporter wrote there was little to catch the eye in the young man, a very tanned young man, in modest gray coat, white plus fours, and gray turn-down hat, quietly checking over his traveling bags and a black leather golf bag. From the way he carried himself—bone weary, self-contained, lost in thought—he could have been any of a hundred thousand men traveling by train that night across America, for business or a convention somewhere. A salesman, perhaps. Or a lawyer. Homesick. Tired of travel.

Bob graciously answered this last reporter's questions—he was "sorry to leave" so soon; he had enjoyed Minneapolis and the tournament, but he was "anxious to get home."

A porter arrived to help with the bags; the special car had at last been coupled onto the train and they were ready to depart. Would Bob mind posing for a final photograph? Not at all, said Bob.

There was one last burst of flashlight powder, and a pair of gray-stockinged legs beat a hasty retreat to the sanctuary of a railroad car.

Bob with his Marine escort.

The last putt.

CHAPTER SIXTEEN

The U.S. Amateur, Merion

HE HAD PUSHED HIMSELF to the limit of endurance. He lost seventeen pounds in three days during the Open at Interlachen. His neck and shoulders ached; he was constantly beset by muscle spasms. The stomach problems that had troubled him since his trip to Paris, the weak link in his system since childhood, had now become chronic and continued to plague him throughout the rest of the summer; by the time he reached the Amateur championship he was treating it with doses of paregoric acid. He had not slept in his own bed, sat at his desk, or held his children since the last week in April, having spent nearly three months on the road. He never gave voice to any complaint and refused to let his closest confidant ever write a word about these trials. He had enjoyed far too much good fortune to ever ask for public sympathy, he told Keeler. It wouldn't seem fair: "Other fellows have their troubles, too."

After years of philosophical discussion with Keeler about the role of fate in his game and in life, the incredible events of that summer convinced Bob he had been delivered into the influence of forces larger than himself, a destiny over which he could no longer pretend to exercise any control. What does one do in those circumstances? Pulled by the currents of such powerful forces, how do you make decisions? If he had any last lingering doubts about fate's govern-ing presence in his life, as his train sped from Minneapolis toward Chicago that night, they were about to be removed altogether.

A pioneering aviator named "Mail" Freeburg had been flying the airmail route between the two cities for over three years, a round trip each day, morn-ing and night. He was headed south to Chicago on that same Saturday night—they called it "the milk run"—using the major rail lines to navigate as pilots liked to do. Skies were high and clear, visibility good. As he neared the Wis-consin border a little after midnight, where the rails crossed the Mississippi near a town called Trevino, he noticed an unusual reddish glow on the horizon and banked down toward it to investigate.

The wooden railway trestle spanning the river was on fire and near col-lapse, engulfed in flames. Freeburg remembered that he'd flown over a train about ten minutes before, the regular night train to Chicago, and it was headed directly for that bridge.

Freeburg turned around and sped back along the tracks, flying low. When the headlight came into view he swooped down repeatedly toward the locomo-tive, dipping his wings, trying to attract the attention of the engineers. The train was closing toward the bridge, but it was around a distant bend; they couldn't see the fire. Freeburg flashed his lights, but the train didn't respond. He made one last run, leaned out the window, and dropped a series of lit flares on the tracks ahead of the train. The engineers responded at last and slammed on the brakes. The train came to a halt just as it rounded the curve toward the river, stopping less than a quarter of a mile from the burning bridge.

The members of the party that was in progress aboard the special car stepped out to have a look when the train stopped. Bob and his father and Keeler and Cyril Tolley watched the fire for a while until the engineer received his orders to reroute the train and cross the river farther to the south.

Mail Freeburg landed in Chicago a few hours before the train arrived on Sunday morning. No one made that big a fuss about Freeburg's actions at the bridge: it didn't even appear in the papers for a couple of days, and then only as a small item in the back pages. Freeburg was hard to grab for an interview because he was already back in the air, flying the mail.

Bob never got a chance to thank the man who had saved their lives.

. . .

Reporters at Interlachen filed over 1.3 million words with Western Union telegraph service during the Open. At least half of those concerned Bobby Jones, sent out to every part of the civilized world. If interest in Bob had been at an all-time high before the Open, after his win it became an obsession. Hundreds turned out at Union Station in Chicago in the hope he would briefly step into view while they transferred his car to the train that would take him the rest of the way home. Bob appeared long enough to sign some autographs and grant a quick interview to a local reporter.

As they headed south on Sunday, airplanes kept regular track of the train's progress, reporting back to his hometown. A legal holiday had been declared on Monday in Atlanta and plans created for the biggest parade of all to welcome Bob home. Those plans were telegraphed ahead to his train as they traveled through the night. The train stopped a few miles short of the downtown station early Monday morning so Bob and his party could climb into waiting cars and be escorted to the start of the parade route. Mary and the kids greeted him as he climbed down, and Bob the Third delighted his dad with a demonstration of his newfound ability to whistle.

GREATEST DEMONSTRATION IN CITY'S
HISTORY MARKS GOLF KING'S RETURN
TO NATIVE HEATH

That was the headline on the front page of the *Atlanta Constitution* on Tuesday morning. Half of the population of the city turned out to see him; with businesses closed that morning, over 125,000 people crowded the parade route on Peachtree Street. The heat wave lingered, muggy and oppressive, but there were rain clouds on the horizon. The parade began at the stroke of noon. The guest of honor was preceded by a procession of three hundred caddies from courses all over the city, marching bands, motorcycle police, veterans of the Great War, politicians, friends and family. On every block thunderous ovations greeted Bob, perched on the backseat in the first open car, adorned by the American flag and the Union Jack. Mary, in white and wreathed in smiles, sat below him. The Colonel, Clara, and the children rode in the next car. Just in front of Bob's car rode the three trophies he'd brought home, grouped for the first time, arrayed on the back of a flatbed truck with a sign that read: BOB IS

HOME—HERE'S THE BACON! Confetti and ticker tape billowed from overhead office windows—"pity the poor street cleaners," wrote Pop—as Atlanta tried to outdo the welcome their favorite son had received in New York two weeks before. When the parade ended at city hall Bob and the principals climbed onto a dais draped in bunting. The mayor presented Bob with a key to the city. Pop said a few words—the event was carried on radio—and introduced the phrase he'd come up with to describe the championship sweep that his friend was one win away from completing: he called it the Grand Slam. Pop showed off the trophies and then called the young hero to the podium. Bob's brief, modest speech thrilled the crowd, cheering every sentence. He spoke, as had become his custom, from the heart, no prepared or written words, with the same sincerity and economy he showed with a club in his hand.

"Your welcome makes it impossible for me to say much. It has fairly taken my breath away. I had no idea any such affair was planned. I appreciate all the things you have done for me, and I just want to say you don't think any more of me than I do of you," he told them before taking his leave.

The band played "The Star-Spangled Banner." Bob and his family were whisked off to the Atlanta Athletic Club for an intimate lunch with a few friends. The wind kicked up, and it finally started to rain as the heat wave broke and everyone headed for home.

Bob didn't touch a club until the following Saturday, when he played his regular game with the Colonel and his buddies at East Lake. He went back to work at the office, tried to rest and settle into his normal routine, but there would be nothing close to normal for him now, not this summer. A barrage of requests for interviews from around the world poured in; he accommodated as many as his schedule allowed, answering them all in prose as crisp and efficient as his golf swing. Bags of fan mail collected at his door. He never used a press agent, never hid behind a flack or a mouthpiece, despite having become one of the world's most famous people. He remained startlingly accessible; if you wanted to correspond or talk with "Bobby Jones," and you weren't an obvious crank or crook, he would most certainly write back or speak to you. He had lived with fame for so long that the greater magnitude of scrutiny he encountered now he treated as just a heightened inconvenience; what he craved was peace, diligent work, a quiet life with his family and friends. The unending assault he experienced on his privacy that season may have been possible to bear only because he knew it was so close to being over.

He took Mary and the kids for a quiet vacation at Highlands Country Club in North Carolina, played recreational golf with his dad and some friends, but for the month of July he mostly left the sticks alone. As the weeks passed he began to feel restored, the reservoirs of energy he'd depleted during the quest slowly seeping back to level. Then, out of nowhere, came another stark reminder that fate wasn't through with him yet.

On a warm Friday near the end of July, he had a lunch engagement at the downtown Atlanta Athletic Club and set out to walk the eight blocks from his office. He had just turned from Cone Street onto Carnegie Way and was nearing the entrance to the AAC building. Preoccupied, his mind elsewhere, he registered that the sidewalk was empty ahead of him and was halfway down the block to the door of the club when he heard a voice from somewhere behind shout: "Look out, mister!"

He turned, startled: a speeding car had just jumped the curb and was bearing directly down on him. He stopped and leaped backward—pure athletic reflex, his powerful legs carrying him close to ten feet—as the car rushed right over the spot on the sidewalk where he'd been passing and crashed into the side of the building. No one was behind the wheel of the smoking wreck. When Bob looked around, he was unable to spot the person who'd shouted out the warning to him. The street was empty.

Reacting to the sound of the crash, people came rushing out of the Athletic Club. After the police arrived it was determined that the car had been parked at the top of the hill a block away without the handbrake having been set. At some point, for some unknown reason, the car began to roll and missed maiming or killing Bob by no more than eighteen inches.

The lightning bolt. The train. Now this. His third close call in less than a year. At which point he had to ask: Was fate putting him in harm's way, or delivering him from it?

LAST STOP: MERION.

Granny Rice's headline summed up Bob's private thoughts after Interlachen. Speculation built through the summer about the possibility of Bob leaving the game, while emotional investment in his completion of the Grand Slam built to a fever pitch. As the Depression's chill settled into the bones of everyday life, shaking faith in the American dream, the prospect of this young man from Atlanta completing his impossible mission offered a ray of hope. His success seemed to imply there was still a path that could lead them out of this deepening darkness; if Jones could do this thing, so could they overcome the crippling forces that had assailed their way of life. Thousands hitched their fading dreams to his, in a way all too familiar to us now but unheard of at the time. This wasn't some cynical marketing campaign co-opting a championship athlete's image to sell tennis shoes or soft drinks. It happened as a kind of spontaneous combustion; people possessed the common sense to realize that the reasons driving him toward this goal came from a place both authentic and good-hearted. That he sought no obvious profit from it made his effort all the more meaningful and real; this was a man worth emulating, strong and unhurried in the face of adversity, patient, resilient, and unassuming. There was more to life than money. Throughout a life lived almost entirely in the public eye he'd never tried to exploit his fame. He had quietly gone about his business, and without ever setting out to do so, when his country had never needed it more, Jones now showed the world how to stand up to troubled times. The man had crossed over into myth.

Bob remained mute on the subject of withdrawing from the game, but as he began practicing again in earnest for the Amateur the pressure grew almost unbearable. They had recently learned Mary was pregnant with their third child; she would not be going with him to Philadelphia. He would feel her absence acutely; she had replaced Pop, naturally and appropriately, as the emotional rock in his life. As the date drew near, Bob's stomach pains resumed, and he found it increasingly difficult to concentrate on work and suffered through many sleepless nights. He became fixated on the idea that another accident might strike and end the quest a few steps from the summit: every time he shaved he remembered a friend who'd been forced to withdraw from a tournament because he'd grabbed instinctively for a razor blade he'd dropped and severely cut his hand. Always mildly superstitious—he wore a gold shamrock on his watch chain and liked to wear the same outfit every day when he was playing well—for Bob the simple act of shaving, along with a dozen other mundane daily rituals, became infused with unseen danger. Fixation shares a border with obsession; thoughts of completing the Slam consumed his waking and sleeping hours.

Pop estimated that he and Bob had logged over 120,000 miles together during his playing years, but in terms of life experience they had traveled a much greater distance. With the dramatic wholeness characteristic of his entire career their last trip would take them back to where it all began. By the time they were ready to leave for Merion, Bob's stomach problems had grown so severe that he was under constant medical care. He had agreed to play in a charity exhibition for war veterans at East Lake on Sunday, September 14, the day before departure. The night before, he was stricken with such severe stomach pain he couldn't stand and was rushed to the hospital; the first diagnosis was acute appendicitis—for two tense hours the Slam appeared in jeopardy—but another round of tests revealed that this was the result of a nervous disorder. Bob was given new medication and cleared to travel to Philadelphia, but only if a doctor accompanied him. Refusing to cancel his commitment to the exhibition, Bob left the hospital for East Lake, played the event, and helped raise over five thousand dollars for the charity.

On the way, Bob stopped for a day in Washington to play in another charity event at Columbia Country Club with Horton Smith, to assist a young pro who'd been paralyzed in an automobile accident. Earlier that day Bob visited the White House for the first time, where President Hoover offered his congratulations and best wishes for continued success. (Hoover was not and never had been a golfer: far too time-consuming. For exercise the Great Engineer played a game of his own invention called Hoover Ball—an amalgam of volleyball and basketball—that he ordered younger members of his staff to play with him.) Bob played the round at Columbia in a steady rain, then boarded a night train. By the time he arrived in Philadelphia early the next morning, slightly hungover, the muscle spasms in his neck and shoulder had flared up again. A crowd of journalists and photographers were waiting for him; every paper in town had assigned at least one reporter to follow his every step. The *Philadelphia Evening Bulletin* assigned sixteen writers and photographers to Bob and the Open.

Among them was a young cub reporter named Joseph Dey Jr., who nailed an exclusive when Bob arrived; as they wheeled Bob's bags into the lobby of the downtown Barclay Hotel, a bellman dropped one of the packages and the unmistakable odor of bootleg liquor filled the room. Pop spread a little cash around to keep the incident quiet and recruited the guilt-ridden bellman to find a local source for their hootch. (Joe Dey, who hadn't covered golf before, became so intrigued by Jones and his performance at Merion that he pursued golf writing full-time; a few years later, when the USGA was looking for its first executive director, Dey applied for the job, and stayed at his post for the next thirty-five years, thereafter serving as commissioner of the PGA Tour.) Security was heightened at the Barclay, with extra men stationed at the stairwells leading to their famous guest's room. Bob's two-bedroom suite offered the only privacy he would experience for the next ten days.

He had five days before qualifying. When Bob arrived at Merion on Wednesday for his first practice round he discovered that over four thousand people had paid a dollar apiece for the privilege of watching him that day. Although a few marshals had been assigned to his twosome in anticipation of a crowd, the massive gallery that showed up made the kind of concentrated work Bob needed impractical. Every time they surrounded him he was left with a ten-foot-wide corridor through which to make his next shot and he lived in constant fear of injuring someone if it went off line. Marshals carried ropes and were supposed to stay ahead of the crowds, directing their movement. When they stampeded forward after every shot the marshals failed to stay in front of them; Bob could never try the same shot twice, a primary objective in practice rounds. He shot 73, three over par, and felt completely out of sorts afterward. A new sprinkler system had been installed and the rough had grown to six inches in some spots, more severe than Bob had ever seen at Merion. The greens were cut to three-sixteenths of an inch, a championship standard for putting surfaces that would endure into the 1960s.

The next day the crowd around him grew even larger and more unruly. A nineteen-year-old caddie named Howard Rexford had won the Jones lottery at Merion and would carry his bag throughout the tournament. During his practice round on Thursday, a hot and humid day, the crowd's rowdy behavior and his own loose play prompted Bob to toss a few clubs back to Rexford after some poor shots, the closest he'd come to his old temperamental ways in almost a decade. Bob shot 78 that day and despaired about his game; as well as he knew this course he couldn't get a handle on it, and the greens baffled him. He tried one putt ten times before it dropped. His close friend Jess Sweetser, eighth seed in the amateur field, joined Bob's gallery for the final two holes. He had read in the morning paper about Bob's mediocre outing the previous day and could see for himself that the crowd made it impossible for him to practice. He called Bob that night and invited him to the private sanctuary of nearby Pine Valley. The stock market crash had crippled Sweetser's business as a Wall Street broker but did nothing to harm his manners.

Bob, the Colonel, and Pop traveled to Pine Valley with Sweetser on Friday morning. With no one watching them but the ducks, Bob began to settle down. He shot a two-under-par 33 on the back nine. After they returned to the hotel that night after dinner, Bob grew ill again, vomiting repeatedly. Rumors had begun to spread that he was seriously ailing. Despite feeling weak, he knew the only way to quell those reports was by showing up at Merion. He played a four-ball match on Saturday morning with Sweetser, Jimmy Johnston, and Max Marston, shooting 71. When asked how he was doing by a reporter, Bob replied, "Terrible." He wasn't referring to his golf, but his fine round put a stop to the chatter about his health. Sweetser's hospitality didn't stop there; after the round he took Bob, the Colonel, and Pop out to a local ballpark to watch the Phillies lose to the first-place Cardinals. Both Bob and his dad were lifelong baseball fans—Bob had recently been named the vice president of a minor league team in Atlanta called the Crackers—and the game relaxed him even more. By the time they got back to the hotel, Bob's stomach pains had subsided for the first time since Atlanta, and his neck and shoulders felt pain-free.

For the second consecutive tournament Bob decided to forgo his habit of relaxing in his hotel on the day before play began; he felt on the verge of coming into his game but needed confirmation more than rest, so when the USGA asked him if he would play one more practice round in order to pad their box-office take during troubled times, Bob agreed to appear. That Sunday morning, when he hit the opening shot of his final practice round at Merion, another emergency presented itself on the first tee. The ball made a peculiar sound coming off his driver, and upon examination Bob realized the duckhorn plate on the face of Jeanie Deans had cracked. A small crack had also started to appear at the back of the club's persimmon head. The Colonel took charge and rushed her into the pro shop, where resident pro George Sayers diagnosed the problem; Bob's unerring ability to hit the ball on the center of the club every time had worn a small hole where the edge of the tee met the inset. The fracture had turned into a fissure, but Sayers assured them he could handle the repair. Knowing that Jeanie Deans might be as close to retirement as he was, Bob played with his second-string driver in the bag and shot 69 on Sunday. The swarming crowds, now under more efficient control, didn't seem to bother him. He even made a small bet with his English friend Dale Bourne that he could shoot even par that day.

"With a little luck, I may qualify," he told a reporter afterward, with a twinkle in his eye. On the eve of the tournament Bob had found his game.

Realizing he was going to be facing galleries at Merion larger than any he'd ever seen before, Bob's Interlachen bodyguard, Charlie Cox—commanding officer of the Georgia National Guard—had placed a call to colleagues in Washington and Philadelphia. By the time the qualifying for the Amateur began on Monday morning, a contingent of fifty U.S. Marines in full dress uniform had arrived from the Philadelphia Navy Yard to supplement the USGA's marshals and serve as Bob's last line of defense. Chick Ridley and Cox would once again be at his side, walking stride for stride, carrying his water. Forty policemen would also be roaming the grounds; the USGA wanted no repeat of the pickpocketing spree that had taken place at Interlachen.

That night at the Barclay, Bob received a telegram from Johnny Boutsies, owner of a Greek restaurant that the Jones family frequented in Atlanta. Johnny knew that with Bob's grounding in the classics he would be able to decipher the cryptic message, which read: E TON E EPITAS. Bob shared it with Pop; he had translated it but wasn't sure of the reference. WITH IT, OR ON IT.

Pop told him it was the traditional farewell that wives and mothers in ancient Sparta gave to their warrior husbands and sons when they buckled on their shields and sent them off to battle.

One hundred and sixty-eight contestants would attempt to qualify for thirty-two match-play slots. The second floor above the clubhouse, originally the old farm's barn, was converted into the pressroom for over one hundred fifty reporters who descended on Merion; Rice's nationally syndicated column was carried by far fewer papers than normal because so many had sent their own scribes to witness Bob's final leg of the Slam. Fourteen years earlier, when

Bobby made his debut, twenty-nine sportswriters had covered the entire tournament. Six telegraph operators had been sufficient then; now there were thirty. Three radio networks arranged for live hookups, and three motion picture outfits had sent crews to cover the event, including Grantland Rice Newsreel, a company Rice owned and operated. A telephone system had been installed on the golf course, with a station every three holes, so scores could be constantly related back to the press and the big scoreboard. When Rice showed up to watch the action on Monday he'd forgotten his press credentials at his hotel; he was so famous now he required no identification at any sporting event in America, but the marine manning the gate failed to recognize him. Unwilling to pull rank, Rice plunked down two dollars for a ticket. Early in the week he sat down with Bob for a meal and afterward wrote a column marveling about the breakfast he'd shared with a freckle-faced kid from Atlanta back in 1916. Neither man could quite comprehend how so much time had passed so quickly.

Bob began his first qualifying round at 9:18 on Monday morning. Not one of the seven thousand people who bought tickets and followed Bob around that day had come to see his playing partner, Emory Stratton from Brae Burn. Jeanie Deans had been returned to Bob's bag by Merion pro George Sayers as promised and appeared as good as new, but Bob pushed his first drive down the right-hand side and found a bunker. A long recovery shot landed within ten feet of the flag, and the par he collected appeared to steady him. With a phalanx of marines providing security, Bob settled into the brand of cold-blooded concentration that had always separated him from the pack. He assayed a superlative round: nine pars through the front, two birdies and a bogey on the back for the day's best score of 69. The drone of a passing airplane overhead, dogs barking, the clicks and whirrs of motion picture cameras, nothing seemed to bother him. Only sixty other men in the entire field broke 80 that Monday. Getting out early ahead of the field, Bob's round took him only three hours. Avoiding a crush of reporters, he left for the Barclay and spent a quiet evening with Pop and his father.

The next day Bob wasn't scheduled to tee off until nearly one in the afternoon. With final positions on the line, many of the players ahead of him on Tuesday slowed their pace to a crawl. His second round became an exercise in patience, waiting on nearly every tee for the fairway to clear. His gallery grew so enormous it spilled over into adjoining fairways, disrupting other twosomes; one exasperated player pleaded with the crowd to step aside so he could play his next shot: "After I fail to qualify, you can come out and watch Bobby all week."

Bob stayed within himself and shot even par on the front. At the fifteenth a man in his gallery broke into applause as he stood over his putt; Bob looked up and glared at the man—the only time he ever showed anger at a spectator—then missed the putt for bogey. He came to seventeen needing only to par in for 71. He also knew that score, added to his 69 in the first round, would lower his existing record for an Amateur qualifier. These smaller accomplishments within the context of his larger pursuit helped keep Bob in the moment, and he was determined to break this record. The wait at the seventeenth tee, a long, dangerous par three that played down and over Merion's old quarry, dragged on for half an hour, testing his patience to the breaking point. Bob got his par at seventeen but had to wait again at eighteen. Five groups were bottlenecked between tee and green. The home hole at Merion asks for a knee-knocking drive that must carry two hundred yards to the fairway back across the quarry. When Bob finally stepped to the tee, he took out all his frustrations on the ball.

The tee shot rocketed across the quarry, kicked forward down the descending slope of the fairway on the far side, and carried close to 350 yards, leaving him a blind, uphill shot into the green. This was an unfamiliar distance to a target he couldn't see; no one could ever remember a drive landing here before. Bob misjudged the shot and the ball bounced into the rough behind the flag. He left his chip coming back short and then missed the eight-foot putt for par that would've broken the record. He had tied his own record for lowest qualifying score in the Amateur and won the gold medal for a record sixth time, but as he walked off the green he was furious at himself for failing to capture the record outright.

The final field of thirty-two included ex–Amateur champions Francis Ouimet, George Von Elm, and Jess Sweetser. Also reaching the match-play rounds were Watts Gunn, Johnny Goodman, and George Voigt. Five former Amateur winners failed to make the cut, including defending champ Jimmy Johnston, Jesse Guilford, Chick Evans, and Cyril Tolley. If Bob hadn't been on the verge of making history, which he stuck around to watch, Cyril would have preferred to stay home in England.

Bob couldn't sleep again that night. Wednesday would bring the two eighteen-hole elimination matches of the tournament and reduce the field to eight, the last obstacle he feared on the path to the title. He called Pop after midnight, and Pop came in and sat with him for a while.

"There's something on my mind I can't shake off. I go to sleep all right from fatigue, but then around midnight I wake up and have to get up. I've always been able to sleep. Something's bearing down on me in this tournament that was never there before."

Pop knew it was the specter of the fourth championship and all it implied, bearing down on him like a horseman he could not see. He called it the Fourth Horseman of the Apocalypse of Championship.

Bob wasn't sure. After all he'd been through, it may have been his own mortality. Death had brushed him with its wings three times in less than a year. What price was he ultimately going to pay for this perfection?

The next morning Bob encountered Jess Sweetser in Merion's locker room on his way out to play his first match. Jess asked him who he was going to play.

"Sandy Sommerville," said Bob.

"Phew! What a guy to get in the first round."

"I know."

Charles Ross "Sandy" Somerville was considered the best golfer ever to come out of Canada. A triple-threat athlete — varsity halfback in football at the University of Toronto, first-string center on the hockey team with offers to turn pro — he had already won three Canadian Amateur titles on his way to a total of six, and he would go on to become the first Canadian ever to win the American title. Only twenty-seven, a physically impressive specimen, Somerville had a deserved reputation as a pressure player. The gallery of ten thousand strangers who greeted them on the first tee at ten o'clock that Wednesday morning didn't seem to bother him at all.

The weather was ideal for scoring: no wind, warm, and oppressively calm. Bob and Somerville played the first two holes even; Sandy bogeyed the third to send Bob one up. The next three holes were halved in par; at one under for his round, Bob was still only one up. Bob had an instinct that the match would turn at the seventh, a short par four, after both hit good drives and solid approaches to the right of the hole; Bob was eight feet out, Sandy seven, on a slightly different line.

Bob walked all the way around the green, viewing the line from every angle, grateful he had to putt first; if he could hole this birdie Sandy's putt would get a lot tougher. If he missed Sandy would almost certainly make his and pull even; then all bets were off.

"I never worked any harder on any putt than I did on this one," Bob wrote later.

The green was scary fast, slightly downhill, with an undetectable right and left break that Bob knew was there only from experience. He tapped the ball gently and watched it crawl down to the hole, hesitate, then curl and drop in through the side door. Somerville saw the line from Bob's effort but didn't embrace it with the same conviction; his ball grazed the top of the cup and stayed out by an inch.

Bob was two up. The swing in momentum elevated his game. He birdied the par four eighth, then rammed in a twenty-five-footer right past a partial stymie at nine for his third birdie in a row. Somerville kept making pars but it wasn't enough; as they made the turn Bob was four up. The Canadian never challenged again. The match ended on the fourteenth green, 5 and 4. Playing flawlessly, Bob had taken care of Sandy Somerville in only two hours and ten minutes to advance to the field of sixteen.

Bob drew the tournament's remaining Canadian in the afternoon's second round, Fred Hoblitzel, a far less accomplished player than Somerville. Bob's nervous stomach was acting up; he ate only toast and iced tea during a brief intermission.

From the moment they walked out to play that afternoon the immense gallery terrified Fred Hoblitzel. After a scrambling par at the first, he picked up at the second, conceding the hole. He bogeyed the fourth, then double-bogeyed both the sixth and the eighth. He scratched out only three pars on the entire front nine. The larger surprise at this point was that Bob was only three holes up. As brilliantly as he'd dispatched Somerville that morning, Bob's game went slack that afternoon; playing down to the level of the competition, he shot 41 on the front—including a drive he shanked out of bounds at the sixth—eight strokes more than he'd taken earlier, but Hoblitzel was so hapless that Bob held an identical lead. No one, including both contestants, appeared to have any doubt about the outcome from their opening drives. Bob finished Hoblitzel off by the same score—5 and 4—and at the same hole—the fourteenth—where he'd earlier ended his match with Somerville. Jones had advanced to the quarterfinals, and the last of the eighteen-hole elimination matches was behind him. Despite his aversion to them, in the last four years his record in those short sprints was 17–2.

Sensing that Hoblitzel wasn't capable of putting up a fight, by the time they reached the back nine a large percentage of Bob's gallery had deserted the match in search of bigger thrills. They found them in a second-round battle between George Von Elm and New Yorker Maurice McCarthy. McCarthy needed a miraculous hole in one on Tuesday to qualify. After beating Watts Gunn over nineteen holes in the first round, McCarthy and Von Elm reached the end of their match dead even. They slugged out nine extra holes shot for shot, putt for putt, the longest battle in the history of the Amateur. As darkness fell, on the twenty-eighth hole—his forty-seventh of the day, another record— McCarthy finally knocked out Von Elm with a birdie.

By Wednesday night they were calling the action on the course that day the greatest collection of upsets during any Amateur in memory. Ouimet and Johnny Goodman both bowed out in the first round—Francis to an eighteen-year-old-from Detroit; he owned socks older than that—and now Von Elm was gone. George Voigt lost a second-round match to an unknown kid from California named Charlie Seaver. Of all the former champions and top-ten seeded players who had started the tournament, only Jones and Sweetser were left standing in the field of eight.

Immediately after his dustup with McCarthy, George Von Elm announced his retirement from the amateur ranks. He would elaborate a few days later when the tournament ended—perhaps hoping to upstage a similar announcement some speculated might be coming from Jones—in a printed statement remarkable for its thinly veiled bitterness.

> I have retired from amateur golf because competing in the American and British Amateur and Walker Cup international match isn't worth the $10,000 a year it costs me. For ten years I've had the "Mr." stuck in front of my name, and that insignia of amateurism has required more than $50,000 of hard-earned money.
>
> I propose hereafter to play golf in such open events as I choose, and on such occasion gamble my skill against the prize money. I want it under-

stood at the same time that I have a business of greater value to me than I could ever hope to equal as a golf professional. I am a businessman first, last and all the time. That business has paid for my amateur golf, and now I propose on my ability as a golfer to be placed in a position to earn something for the business.

It isn't nice to treat the subject of my amateur status in cold terms of dollars. The USGA's Amateur Championship is a highly organized commercial project, while the thirty-two performers play their hearts out for honor and glory. Not a penny of the money the USGA makes is contributed to the expenses of the players. Tournament golf today is show business in a big way. The finger of suspicion points to many players of amateur golf today, but the show must go on, and the USGA is busy a good part of the time straining at gnats and swallowing camels.

True to his word, George Von Elm never played in another amateur event, nor did he ever win an Open or professional title of equal consequence.

A heavy rain soaked the greens and fairways late Wednesday night; Bob woke up during the storm and was unable to get back to sleep until after 3:00 a.m. This time he declined to call Pop, sitting out the long hours before dawn alone. The morning papers predicted an open run for Jones to the title, which was exactly why he didn't read them. He might have been particularly upset by a small article that claimed that a Hollywood movie studio was about to sign him to a contract worth $200,000 for some unspecified film work. When he was questioned about it by reporters that day Bob denied any such offer had been made, although if one of that magnitude were to come along he said he wouldn't turn it down. Years later Chick Evans revealed that he had been the source of the rumor, and still believed it to be true. It wasn't. The idea had been floated to Bob, but he cut off the man making the offer and refused to discuss it until after the tournament was over.

On the same day Bob played his quarterfinal match, tennis great Bill Tilden was honored in Philadelphia by the Penn Athletic Club. The members voted Tilden an honorary membership—Bob had received one days earlier—and threw a luncheon in his honor. During his speech Tilden went out of his way to credit Jones, saying that because of his sportsmanship and modest attitude Bob had done more to popularize the United States overseas than any man alive, and if Americans realized it he would be even more of an idol at home than he was already. He said he hoped Bob would go on to win at Merion, and thereby "hang up a record that no man can hope to equal."

First he had to get by a golfer from Culver City named Fay Coleman, the current Southern California champion. For years golf writers had leaned on the idea of describing Bob as a "mechanical man," a "robot of the links"; all you had to do was wind him up and send him out there, click-clacking along like an automaton. Although worlds away from the truth of the turmoil he experienced internally, when playing at his best he did appear to be functioning at machinelike efficiency. With all the stresses tearing at him at Merion, as he progressed deeper into the Amateur that image began to break down. Against Coleman in the quarterfinals, he bogeyed four of the first nine holes and still led the match one up. Anyone walking out to face Bob in this tournament was up against a host of obstacles in addition to the man himself, but Coleman hung tough; when Bob hooked his drive out of bounds and double-bogeyed the fifteenth, Coleman evened the match. The young man played capable golf, but at no point did he persuade the thousands watching that he could seize control of the match. Bob settled down to par the final three holes; Coleman recorded back-to-back bogeys to end the morning round two down.

Bob was pacing himself, thought Pop, like a long-distance runner. Saving his kick for the decisive moment when he could sprint ahead and finish the job: classic match-play strategy. When they went back out after lunch, overcast skies threatened rain all afternoon but Bob bent to his task. They halved the first with pars. Coleman won the second hole with a stymie to draw within one—Bob tried to chip over his ball into the cup and failed—but he had reached his high-water mark. Starting at the long par five fourth hole, Coleman began to crack: three straight bogeys to Bob's perfect line of pars. Smelling blood, Bob called on the kick; with a birdie-par finish to close out his front side, Bob seized a commanding six-hole lead with nine to play. When it grew to seven after the tenth the match was all but over; Bob coasted for two holes, which Coleman won, then closed him out on the thirteenth, right next to the clubhouse, 5 and 4. As they shook hands and walked off the green the heavens opened in a heavy downpour and sent thousands scattering for cover.

When he reached the shelter of the locker room, Bob learned he would be playing his old friend Jess Sweetser in the semifinals; Jess had outworked an exhausted Maurice McCarthy, spent from his battle against Von Elm. The other bracket was a surprise: nineteen-year-old tournament rookie Charlie Seaver against the former Princeton champion Eugene Homans.

Eight years earlier, Sweetser had handed Bobby the worst match-play beating of his career—8 and 7—in the semifinals of the 1922 Amateur at Brookline. Sweetser had gone on to win that title, and added the British Amateur four years later, the gallant effort that nearly cost him his life when he contracted tuberculosis. His health, and his golf, had never been the same. The two men had become great friends during their Walker Cup experiences, but had never met a second time in match-play competition until now.

With two young and relatively inexperienced golfers in the other semifinal, experts agreed that Sweetser remained the last serious threat to the completion of the Grand Slam. They also sought comfort in the startling fact that Bob had never lost a match to the same man twice, and in every rematch he avenged his earlier defeat. Sweetser knew the only way to beat Bob—as he had done at Brookline—was to get him down early and keep the pressure on. He also knew that the ten thousand in attendance—with the exception of his own wife and parents—and millions around the world listening by radio or reading coverage in print were unanimously hoping he would fail. Even the waiters at Merion were pulling for Bob; one famously threatened to remove a reporter's soup because the man was slurping while Bob prepared to putt on a distant green.

Homans and Seaver teed off at 8:30 on Friday morning. Bob and Jess began their match a half hour later. Thousands who set out with the two younger men came rushing back to the first tee after they'd played only a single hole. On every hole during their match, including the long par fives, the gallery would reach all the way from each tee to the green. The full-dress marine escort stood at attention around the first tee as Jones and Sweetser walked out to begin the first round.

Sweetser stumbled out of the gate; he found two bunkers on his way to the green and lost the hole with a double-bogey six. Bob calmly sank a fifteen-footer for birdie. At the par three third, Jess half topped his drive into another bunker and couldn't recover; another par for Bob and he was two up. Sweetser hit his approach short at four for bogey; a second birdie for Bob. Three up. At the fifth, Jess hooked his drive into a brook and had to accept a penalty stroke: double-bogey six. Another par for Bob and he was up four. *Well*, thought Jess, *so much for a fast start*.

But after they halved the sixth, the "mechanical man" sputtered, slicing his drive over a fence out of bounds; when Bob missed his approach to the green he conceded the hole. They halved the eighth with pars, then Bob put his tee shot in a bunker on the par three ninth, chipped out short and two-putted for bogey. Sweetser took advantage and made par; he was two down as they made the turn. After Bob made his second straight bogey at ten, which cut his lead to one, the crowd murmured its disapproval. Heads wagged, eyebrows raised. Most of these people were watching Bob play for the first time—many were watching *golf* for the first time—and didn't understand: Bobby Jones wasn't supposed to make mistakes, was he? It got worse: two more bogeys followed at eleven and twelve. What the heck was going on here? Sweetser double-bogeyed because of a well-laid stymie to lose the eleventh, then scratched back to one down again with a par at twelve.

The least concerned man on the grounds appeared to be Bob; as he'd been able to do all that week, he let the bad shots go and flushed the mediocrity from his system. The next two holes were halved with pars, both men hitting fairways and greens, with Sweetser laying his approach inside of Bob's on both occasions. The crowd warmed up with the Indian summer sun; they were starting to feel they might be about to witness something special.

At the fifteenth, both men found the green in two, but Bob ran in a fifteen-footer for his third birdie of the round to go two up. They halved the sixteenth, but the tone of the action was changing. Bob had mastered himself and withstood Sweetser's run; in the gallery Keeler could physically feel the pressure shifting back onto Jess. Their tee shots at the long par three seventeen would be crucial: Bob, playing first, found the green, while Sweetser came up just short. Facing an uncomplicated chip, Sweetser stumbled again; he came up short and missed a four-foot putt for par. Jones made par. Up three.

Bob kept the pressure on with a spectacular drive across the quarry at eighteen. Sweetser's effort ended up twenty yards behind him, increasing the pressure on his long approach to the green. He watched it flare to the right and land in a bunker: another bogey, while Bob cashed in for his par. At the intermission, Bob had regained all of his early four-hole lead. In the other match ahead of them, young Californian Charlie Seaver had taken a commanding lead over Eugene Homans, up five.

Bob followed his lunchtime rituals: a few bites of chicken salad on toast, iced tea. He looked calm, collected, didn't talk much. Resting for the final kick, thought Pop, and didn't even try to speak to him. Not today.

On their opening drives of the afternoon, both men found bunkers, both reached the green. Bob missed an easy six-footer for birdie and they halved the hole with fours. At the long intimidating par five second, Bob striped another bullet down the center; Jess popped his drive up high to the right and watched it soar onto adjoining Ardmore Avenue, out of bounds. Just like that, Bob was five up, but he handed that gift right back by overshooting the green at the third. Sweetser saved his par; Bob's scrambling putt failed to find the hole. Four up.

They halved their twenty-second hole of the day. When they reached the next tee, the par four fifth, Pop saw something come into Bob's expression: eyes set like stone, his movements a fraction slower and more deliberate.

Here comes the kick, thought Pop.

Sweetser hit a serviceable drive down the middle. Bob's ball passed him on the fly and kept running another fifteen yards. After Jess played to the front, Bob stuck his approach twenty feet from the hole on the challenging, right-to-left sloping green. Sweetser missed his long try for a three and took par. The putt Bob faced was downhill, sidehill, and fast, with a break of at least two feet; he rammed it dead into the center of the cup for birdie. The lead was back to five.

Another half at six. At the seventh, Bob drilled an eight-foot putt for birdie. Jones up six. Jess looked dazed. At the short eighth, Bob stuck his iron second on the green. Sweetser's approach flew over the flag and bounced into a pot bunker; he failed to get out, and conceded the hole. Jones up seven. At the par three ninth, both men reached the green. Bob took a quick look at his line, feeling it now, and his twenty-four-foot birdie putt tracked straight for the hole and dropped.

Jones up eight, with nine to play.

Both men hit good drives at the par four tenth, with Jones the longer again.

Jess hit a high pitch second to the right side of the green, twenty feet from the hole pin high. Bob took his wedge in hand and played an elegant pitch and run that landed on the front edge, rolled and rolled toward the flag, and came to rest four inches from the cup and an eagle two. Over fifteen thousand had jammed into their gallery by this time and most of them went berserk; the marines snapped to their task, holding back the throng. Walking to the green, Bob looked over at Sweetser and grinned sheepishly. When Sweetser missed his last birdie attempt he stuck out his hand, conceding Bob's tap-in. The match was over, 9 and 8.

As they walked to the clubhouse Bob put an arm around his old friend and said, "I feel sort of mean about that last shot. It was like a stab in the back, or a shot in the dark."

"Bob, it wasn't any shot in the dark. It was a great shot." Jess patted him on the back, and mopped his own brow. "I'd about had enough anyway."

In reaching the finals Bob had also avenged the most lopsided defeat of his career; for the two matches they'd played together, over fifty-seven holes, Sweetser now stood one down to Bob Jones, a fact Jess was proud to tell you for the rest of his life.

The gallery rushed ahead of them to catch up with the Seaver-Homans match, which had turned into a barn burner. Five down at the halfway mark, Homans chipped away at Seaver's lead during the afternoon; he stood three down at the turn. Homans won the eleventh with a par. They halved the next two holes, at which point Seaver stood two up with five to play: the dreaded St. Andrews match-play lead. An unforced error by Seaver led to bogey at fifteen and his lead was one. Another half and then Homans won seventeen when he putted around a stymie. They stood all even on the eighteenth tee and had by now inherited most of Jones's gallery. Seaver's collapse became complete after a pulled approach and a long chip left him with a ten-footer for par that wouldn't drop. Homans sank a two-footer for par and advanced to the finals. Only nineteen and playing in his first Amateur, great things were predicted for Charlie Seaver, but alas, they weren't to be; athletic glory skipped a generation and was fulfilled decades later by Charlie's son Tom, the future Hall of Fame pitcher.

Only Eugene Homans now stood between Bob Jones and the Grand Slam.

.   .   .

Bob soaked in a hot tub back at the Barclay and drank his first highball. He had a second afterward, sitting with Pop and his dad. Despite the relative ease with which he appeared to be winning his matches, he told them this was the toughest, most grueling campaign of the four he'd been through that summer; it wasn't the golf—getting to the course was almost a relief. He felt like a creature in a zoo, on constant display wherever he went. His natural inclination to polite, sincere interaction was under constant assault by strangers pushing and pulling at him for favors or autographs. Bob was by nature an observer, a reactor, who felt as if he'd ended up on the wrong end of a microscope. He would have been happy to go on playing, but much more than the satisfaction that playing well and winning gave to him he wanted his life back. He spoke with Mary on the phone before retiring to bed, said good night to his kids. Downstairs at the front desk a snow drift of telegrams wishing him luck accumulated through the evening. Reporters huddled in Merion's pressroom churning out copy late into the night. Families gathered around their radios all over the country, eager for any news about Jones. Atlanta papers prepared hourly editions in order to update Bobby's progress. Extra operators were called on duty to handle the anticipated crush of telephone traffic the following day. Granny Rice said it was no exaggeration that you could almost hear the entire country holding its breath. Herbert Warren Wind described it memorably as "multiply the tension of a no-hitter by fifty." Bob was one step from the summit.

The USGA had added an innovation to the match-play segment of the tournament; standard-bearers carrying signs mounted on six-foot poles bearing each player's name and their score now accompanied each pairing to show their gallery where they stood in their match. Late that night, someone broke into the caddie master's hut and stole the sign with Jones's name on it.

Bob slept better that last night than he had all week, uninterrupted, then woke half an hour before sunrise. Another rainstorm had passed through during the early morning and sweetened the air; you could taste the first hint of fall, cool and bracing. He ate breakfast alone, in his room, then drove out to Merion, arriving at 7:30. The match was scheduled to begin at 9:00. He changed shoes at his locker, then followed all his small, daily rituals, as if this was just another round of golf. Outside, the USGA braced itself for a record crowd. They underestimated.

Eugene Homans and Jones weren't strangers. Eugene had played Bob tough in a second-round match at the 1927 Amateur at Minikahda—losing 3 and 2—and he tied Bob for the qualifying medal the previous year at Pebble Beach. Homans's nickname on the course was "Gabby" because he never opened his mouth during a match unless spoken to. He was only twenty-two, bespectacled, scholarly, and painfully slender; some thought he looked anemic. To the contrary, he was under normal circumstances a capable and tough-minded opponent, as his comeback win against Charlie Seaver demonstrated. But when he walked out to the first tee on Saturday morning, the eighteen thousand people who were already packed around the first fairway felt little else for Homans than pity. He looked frail next to Bob, a commoner beside a beloved and handsome crown prince. In fact, another wave of nausea had fluttered into Bob's system just prior to the match that was so strong he couldn't button his collar. Bob may have been more adept at concealing it, but the nerves of both men were frayed to the seams as they teed up their first shots. No Amateur championship in the game's history had ever attracted a crowd like this.

They were off. Homans hit a driver in the fairway; Bob outdrove him with a three wood. Homans pulled his approach into a bunker; Bob pitched to within twenty feet. Homans's recovery left him thirty-five feet from the hole and he missed the putt for par. Bob lagged his close and took his par. Jones up one.

They halved the second with bogeys, both men showing the strain; Homans found two bunkers along the way. Bob three-putted from the front of the green, and failed to capitalize. At the par three third, Bob steered his drive onto the green. Homans, needing a three wood on the 195-yard hole, found yet another bunker. He failed to get up and down. Bob calmly two-putted for par. Jones up two.

At the par five fourth, Bob drove into a bunker but hit a brilliant three wood far down the fairway. Homans found the fairway but pushed his second into the rough. Both reached the green in three. Homans three-putted; Bob needed only two. Jones was up three.

The overcast weather had brought in a stiff wind; blowing across, it pushed both tee shots at the fifth into bunkers. Jones's recovery was stronger, but he missed a four-footer for par. Both men bogeyed the hole. Five holes into the match Homans had failed to record a par. Pop took a nip from a flask; Bob looked more relaxed than he did. Homans got his first par at the sixth for another half. After both men reached the seventh green in two, Jones left his first putt three feet short. Homans putted to within a foot and stymied Bob's ball; Jones couldn't get around or over him. Homans tapped in for par and won his first hole. Jones up two.

They played the eighth even. At the downhill par three ninth, Homans's drive found the creek short of the green. Bob gently dropped an iron off the tee within twenty feet. After taking a drop, pitching up, and missing his putt, Homans conceded Bob's second putt for par. Jones had played the front nine in three over par and was up three. Homans had 43 on the front and showed no signs that would have encouraged anyone to think he could turn himself around.

Bob kept the heat on with a perfect drive at the par four tenth. Homans hooked his drive into the rough, then pitched over the green into a bunker, where it rolled into a heel print left by the retreating gallery. Bob pitched safely to the middle of the green. Homans misplayed his shot out of the bunker and needed two putts for bogey. Another two-putt for Bob for par. His lead increased to four.

The 378-yard par four eleventh hole asks for a downhill tee shot to a blind landing, bearing slightly to the left. The green sits in the elbow of a stream called the Baffling Brook; trees protect its right side and a bunker the left, asking for one of the most demanding second shots on the course. The premium is on accuracy over distance off the tee and Bob used his three wood to find the fairway; Homans outdrove him slightly using a driver. Bob's approach stopped twenty-five feet past the hole. Homans pitched to within eight feet. Bob looked the line over from both sides, unusual for him, then drained the putt for his first birdie of the day. The crowd erupted. Homans missed his birdie try. Jones up five.

They halved twelve and thirteen. At the 412-yard par four fourteenth, Bob was on in two, fifteen feet from the hole. From the same distance Homans hooked a three wood into the rough. He left his chip seven feet shy of the flag. Bob lagged close. Gene missed his putt. Bob tapped his in. Jones up six. Whatever fight was left in Homans appeared to leak away; Bob brought the hammer down. At fifteen, he stuck his approach six feet from the flag. Homans's found a bunker; he failed to get up and down and conceded Bob's putt. Bob knocked it in one-handed for birdie. Jones up seven. At sixteen, both hit good drives, then spanned the quarry to reach the green with their second. Homans three-putted from sixty feet. Bob two-putted from twenty-five. Jones up eight.

A brief respite: Homans collected his first birdie of the day at seventeen to trim the lead to seven, and it stayed that way when both men parred the eighteenth. Jones had shot 72 and Homans 80, but after Bob's birdie at eleven and his hard, implacable play coming in, the crowd knew the match wasn't even as close as the score. Jones was tough enough to beat anyone who'd ever lived; on this day, on the brink of this triumph, there wasn't another man alive who could have beaten him.

The two men stepped back out to start their second circuit at half past one. The overcast had cleared, large white clouds and blue sky appeared overhead. The sun warmed and the wind diminished. For the rest of the way, it would play out as more spectacle than contest. Once the crowd realized the outcome they craved was not going to be in doubt, a party atmosphere took hold. Celebration replaced anxiety. They cheered wildly after Bob's every shot. Marshals and marines and police and state troopers did everything they could to contain them, but hundreds broke ranks on every hole, rushing ahead to line up on the next one.

They halved the first two holes in par. Bob used his oversized wedge to carve out a sensational bunker shot at the third that stopped within a foot of the hole. Homans putted past the hole and left himself stymied behind Bob's ball; he missed for par, Jones sank his. The lead was eight. At the fourth, their twenty-second hole of the day, Bob played every shot safely to a smooth five, while Homans struggled for bogey. Jones up nine.

Bob took a breath, content to match shots with Homans for a beat. They halved the next four holes without incident. A plane circling overhead snapped pictures of the galleries. The pilot was on a job documenting a nearby real estate development from the air. Heading home, he had some film left over in his wing-mounted camera and fired away when he saw the vast crowds below. The man wasn't even aware of what he was shooting, and the pictures didn't reach the public eye until years afterward. He recorded the crowds arrayed around each of the next three holes, as the match drew to a close.

Homans bagged his second birdie at the twenty-seventh hole, holding off the end for a moment. By now the crowd's excitement was impossible to contain. Slack with emotion and the weight of what was coming, both men played the tenth/twenty-eighth as a comedy of errors. They found bunkers with their second shots; Bob failed to get out on his first try, while Homans skulled his across the green into another bunker. Both took double-bogey sixes; Bob later wrote "ha-ha" next to his score for ten on the card.

He was eight up with eight to play.

They walked to the eleventh tee. Homans still held the honor from his birdie at nine and drove deep down the right side. Bob crushed his final drive long and down the left, leaving the best angle to the green. The gallery packed into the tightest corner of the course surrounding the eleventh green. A solid mass of people who didn't make it there in time backed up the hill halfway back to the tee box.

Silence. Homans played first, a neatly judged wedge shot that rolled to a stop twenty-five feet past the hole. Bob's drive had nearly reached the stream, traveling close to three hundred yards. He asked for a wedge from his caddie, Howard Rexford, took his stance, and fired a precise pitch that landed on the front and bounded forward to within thirteen feet of the flag. An enormous roar crashed around them as he traversed the small bridge to the green. Pop thought Bob looked haggard and drawn, but he was white as a ghost himself, the enormity of the moment crushing.

The crowd settled. Eighteen thousand people. The Colonel was in that crowd, and Pop Keeler, Grantland Rice, Francis Ouimet, Cyril Tolley, and four-time Amateur champion Jerry Travers, the man whose record Bob was about to break. All the people who'd watched him grow into the man he was gathered in solemn silence around this sylvan green, the quiet broken only by the gentle splash of water flowing in the stream.

His caddie handed him Calamity Jane, the world's most famous golf club, then pulled the stick. Bob lined up the putt, cocked his head, that familiar quizzical last glance at the line and the hole, then the slight economic hinge of the wrists, and Bobby Jones's last putt rolled forward to within six inches of the cup.

Gene Homans knew the moment wasn't his, this crowd wasn't there for him; it wasn't his turn. Bob Jones's name had been written in this Book, perhaps as long as fourteen years ago. He took hardly a moment to line up his putt, just this side of careless, and then let it go, and even before it creased the side of the hole and rolled past, Homans started walking toward Bob with a big smile, extending his hand, the first to reach him.

And then shouts and cries and tumult filled the air. They all came at him in a wild rush, hundreds and thousands. Only the quick reaction of Ridley and Cox and the fifty marines who leaped to his side protected him from certain harm. In the middle of the chaos Howard Rexford had the foresight to replace the stick and pick up Bob's ball. The cheering would not dissipate for five full minutes. Runners dashed back toward the clubhouse, a call was placed from the phone at the twelfth tee to the pressroom, but the crowd was so loud the man on the other end of the line couldn't hear a word; he didn't have to. The cheer had traveled the half mile back to the clubhouse; operators were already toggling their telegraph keys, spreading the news around the world.

Jones had won the Grand Slam.

Chick Ridley and Charlie Cox had rehearsed this drill earlier with their fifty marines; they formed a corridor and Bob edged his way back through it inside their protective cordon. The trip to the clubhouse felt as if it took forever, but Bob didn't seem to mind. He smiled and waved to the crowd and their cheers attended him all the way back in.

> All at once I felt the wonderful feeling of release from tension and relaxation that I had wanted so badly for so long a time. I wasn't quite certain what had happened or what I had done. I only knew that I had completed a period of the most strenuous effort and that at this point, nothing more remained to be done.

Before he went inside, Bob slipped $150 into Howard Rexford's hand, a small fortune for a caddie. Rexford hung on to Bob Jones's last ball for thirty years, until for some reason he put it in play during a match and lost it in the woods. Pop Keeler fought his way through to Bob as they entered the clubhouse, and there was some whooping and hollering to do and songs to sing as his friends crowded him one last time. Any thoughts about Prohibition went out the window as they broke out the champagne and the hootch and the forty-dollar Scotch. This was better than winning the World Series on Christmas. No one on those grounds or in that building ever forgot the moment.

The Colonel couldn't locate Bob in the crowd and finally made it into the building, shouting: "Where's my boy? Where's my boy?" They found each other just inside the locker-room door; the Colonel threw his arms around his only son and wept, tears in both their eyes—and Keeler wept when he saw them crying—just as there had been twenty years before when Bobby had shown him the scorecard for his first 80 at East Lake.

Pop hustled everyone away. For a few moments, the only solitude Bob had had since his arrival that morning, everyone left him alone with his dad.

Bobby, Mary, and their children.

Bob, the businessman lawyer.

CHAPTER SEVENTEEN

Retirement

ALL THREE NATIONAL RADIO networks carried the live presentation of
the Havemeyer Trophy at Merion. After he'd said all his thank-yous, Bob was
asked about retirement, but this was neither the time nor place to make an
announcement of that magnitude; the joyous mood of the crowd and the
moment would have been shattered. Bob answered diplomatically: "I expect to
continue to play golf, but just when and where I cannot say now. I have no definite plans, either to retire or as to when and where I may continue in competition. I might play next year and lay off in 1932. I might stay out of the battle
next season and feel like another tournament the following year. That's all I
can say about it now."

He was letting them down easy, and with that he quietly stepped away.

Jubilation broke out in Atlanta, but he let them know that this time he'd
prefer to return home quietly, without a parade. He'd had enough of crowds
and noise and cheering that summer to last a lifetime. The inevitable dinner at
East Lake was all he would allow, when the four trophies of his conquest were
for the first and only time in their colorful histories united, with the Walker
Cup as a chaser.

National interest in Bob crested with his final victory; the win at Merion made the front page of every newspaper in the country. No single sports figure in history had ever received the attention or affection that he attracted now. The USGA reported record receipts for the tournament of over $55,000, a windfall that would help sustain them through the difficult years ahead. Reporters announced that Bobby Cruickshank had cashed his winning long-shot bet on the Grand Slam—Pop's phrase quickly became omnipresent; others later took and were given credit for it, but it started with Pop—and collected $10,500. According to some estimates, the group of Atlantans who had pooled their resources on a similar wager split a small fortune worth $125,000. Bob never knew about the bet, or who had put the money down, until afterward.

As he looked back on the experience, his final season took on an air of unreality. He attributed his success during the Slam to perseverance more than skill. He felt he had played his best golf of the year at Augusta, before the quest officially began. Aside from a few stretches at the British Amateur and his stunning third round at Interlachen, he had never sustained his highest level of excellence. Even when he was being outplayed, which by his reckoning had happened in three of the four tournaments, the decisive element had been his ability to think his way through the patches when his swing deserted him. He never gave up, and that in the end had made all the difference; his mentality and will carried him close to the top. Then, during the toughest part of the climb, when each step was burdened with the weight of the world's expectations, he never trailed during his fives matches at Merion for a single hole.

Bob had won his first British Amateur, his third British Open, his fourth U.S. Open—a new record—and his fifth U.S. Amateur, another record. He had won thirteen matches in a row, and three medal competitions, including the Amateur qualifier at Merion. He had tied both countries' records in winning the Double; he had won the Double twice over no matter which way you counted them. He knew he could never duplicate such a feat and he had no intention of trying. Bob had now captured thirteen major wins, more than any other player in history. Darwin's words after the British Amateur at St. Andrews that he had no worlds left to conquer had come to pass.

He rested. He took stock. He went back to practicing his profession and enjoying quiet time with his family. He played casual weekend golf at East Lake with his dad and their friends and found a natural rhythm to his life again. He fielded questions about his future on a daily basis and politely deflected them. Eventually they slowed.

He still played the game with the old hickory shafts he grew up with at a time when almost every other man had changed to steel. During the 1920s he played an average of only four tournaments a year against full-time professionals, generally practiced for only a few weeks to prepare himself, and was still, without argument, the greatest player who ever wore cleats. Since 1923, Bob had played in twenty-one major championships and won thirteen of them, a winning percentage of 62 percent. At the time of this writing, in early 2004, golf's all-time leading money winner, Tiger Woods, is the same age Bob was in the second half of 1930. Counting his three U.S. Amateur titles as majors, Woods has played in thirty-six championships and won eleven of them, a winning percentage of just under 31 percent. When he was Bob's age, Jack Nicklaus had nine majors under his belt. Arnold Palmer had won one Amateur. Ben Hogan hadn't won a single major. No one in their right mind could imagine Jack or Tiger or Hogan retiring at that point in their lives, and it's important to remember that no great athlete in any sport up to that time had ever quit the field at the top of his game. Bob Jones was about to blaze another trail. He called in Pop Keeler one day to confirm the news with him. They met out on the porch at East Lake, over a drink. Pop had been expecting the moment, dreading it, longing for it himself.

"I'll never give up golf," Bob told him. "I love it too well, and it has meant too much in my life. But I think I'd like to play the sidelines for a while. It'll be an easier and more gracious trail from now on."

Pop found that he couldn't speak for a moment. He just held out his hand.

"It was grand, Bob. Wasn't it grand?"

"Yes it was, Pop."

"I was happy, in a way," Pop wrote afterward. "And I was—well you don't come to the end of 15 years with the grandest sporting competitor, and the greatest boy who ever lived, without something that hurts."

Keeler had been at his side from the first step, through the darkest days and the greatest glory. His devotion to Bob Jones had carried him from an obscure corner desk of a small-town news department to a deserved reputation as one of the most respected sportswriters in the world. He had devoted himself to making this young man realize his extraordinary potential, the net effect of which made him one of the world's most famous men. The way had been long and uncertain for years, but Pop's faith had never wavered and the riches he'd derived from the journey were more precious to him than gold. He was forty-eight now and would work and live on, a much-beloved figure, for another two decades; his friendship with Bob would never falter, and their time together still had one of its brightest chapters to come, but their paths would inevitably start to diverge.

Pop knew all that; Bob's good-bye to golf was, in effect, his own as well. Shortly after Merion, foreshadowing what was to come, Pop announced his retirement from writing about championship golf.

"I could still say what I had said to people all over the world," wrote Pop. "They could see for themselves if he was a golfer, but I could tell them that he was a much finer young man than he was a golfer. Wholly lacking in affectation, modest to the degree of shyness, generous and thoughtful of his opponents, it is not likely that his equal will come again. It would be immeasurably more pleasant to write of Bobby Jones himself than of his exploits, but you cannot pick out the details of a winsome personality, or properly hold up for inspection the graces of modesty and the strong heart. Besides, good-natured as he is, he would be furious if any chronicler who knew him should attempt a thing like that."

Bob found himself as an athlete before he even knew who he was. He had only recently found himself as a man, but what he'd found was solid and sure and grounded. Having lived a fantasy life, reality demanded his attention; he had a family to support and another child on the way. Times were tough and about to get a lot tougher. Fame was fleeting. An Atlanta friend who owned a string of movie houses interested him in exploring the idea of a series of instructional films about the game. He could teach what he knew to the masses in a way that had never been done before; Bob warmed to the idea at once. He was determined that any commercial effort to which he lent his name be of the highest quality, guided by his direct involvement. When he entered into active negotiations with Warner Brothers—and met with Harry

Warner, who ran the family business in New York—Bob knew the time had come to issue a public statement.

Bob signed his Warner Brothers contract on November 13, 1930. The deal called for him to create and star in a series of twelve short films, ten minutes in length, a staple in the motion picture business at the time, the appetizer course to an evening at the movies, which usually included a newsreel and a cartoon as well before the main feature. In success, the contract included an option for six additional films. Bob was scheduled to receive ten thousand dollars a film, and 50 percent of the net receipts from distribution over the next five years, potentially worth a great deal more. With his father's help he made arrangements to put most of the money into a trust for his children.

Teaching golf was a job reserved for the professional golfer. About to tread in a very gray area, Bob decided he couldn't in good conscience announce the movie deal without first renouncing his amateur status. He did both in the statement he released on November 17, read to the press in New York by a USGA official, less than two months after his win at Merion.

Upon the close of the 1930 golfing season I determined immediately that I would withdraw entirely from golfing competition of a serious nature. Fourteen years of intensive tournament play in this country and abroad has given me about all I wanted in the way of hard work in the game. I had reached a point where I felt that my profession required more of my time and effort, leaving golf in its proper place, a means of obtaining recreation and enjoyment.

My intention at the time was to make no announcement of retirement, but merely to drop out quietly by neglecting to send in my entry to the Open Championship next spring. There was at that time no reason to make a definite statement of any kind; but since then, after careful consideration, I have decided upon a step which I think ought to be explained to the golfers of this country, in order that they may have a clear understanding of what the thing is and why it is being done.

He goes on to explain the details of his arrangement with Warner Brothers and his hope that the films improve people's ability to play and increase interest in the game.

The matter of monetary compensation enters into the discussion at this point, and it is for numerous reasons that I wish to be perfectly understood on this score. The amateur status problem is one of the most serious with which the USGA had to deal for the good of the game as a whole.

I am not certain that the step I am taking is in a strict sense a violation of the amateur rule. I think a lot might be said on either side. But I am so far convinced that it is contrary to the spirit of amateurism that I am prepared to accept and even endorse a ruling that it is an infringement.

I have chosen to play as an amateur not because I have regarded an honest professionalism as discreditable, but because I have had other ambitions in life. So long as I played as an amateur, there could be no question of subterfuge or concealment. The rules of the game, whatever they were, I have respected, sometimes even beyond the letter. I certainly shall never become a professional golfer. But, since I am no longer a competitor, I feel able to act entirely outside the amateur rule, as my judgment and conscience may decide.

With that, Bob Jones let the game of competitive golf slip from his hands. His statement inspired stories and editorials from around the country and Britain praising his decision. Most approved of the timing and agreed that leaving the game at the peak of his highest achievement ensured Bob's immortality. There was great sadness that the game's brightest star was passing from view, but the impact of his absence would prove to be far more profound than anyone anticipated. In spite of their disappointment, no one could deny that he left in the same style and spirit with which he had thrilled his fans for so long. A few, like Walter Hagen, refused to believe it—why would anyone voluntarily give up the spotlight?—and predicted Bob would be back once he'd had a good long rest. The Royal and Ancient of St. Andrews went a step further; since they had received no notification of Jones's retirement from him directly, they decided not to rule on the issue until such time as it pertained to Bob playing in one of their championships. In the meantime, they announced that "the decision does not affect Mr. Jones's position as a member of the Royal and Ancient Golf Club."

He had made his entrance on the world stage fourteen years earlier as a

callow, cocky boy. He took his leave from it as golf's greatest player and a gentleman, in the best and truest sense of the word.

Bob and Mary's third child, a daughter named Mary Ellen, was born on
January 29, 1931, and their family was complete. Just after finalizing the deal
with Warner Brothers, Bob agreed to appear on a weekly radio series for David
Sarnoff's NBC Network, and he called on Pop Keeler to cohost the show with
him; it ran for twenty-six weeks, with episodes re-creating his greatest triumphs. A personally satisfying business arrangement came soon afterward
with the Spalding Sports Goods Company, the same firm that had sponsored
Harry Vardon's original tour of America in 1900. Spalding was now the largest
manufacturer of golf clubs in the country. Working with his favorite designer,
J. Victor East, and using his own Tom Stewart set of clubs as a model, Bob
drew up plans to create a mass-produced set of irons. Applying his considerable skills and knowledge as an engineer to the process, the result was the first
high-quality matched set of irons ever produced on American soil. He took
great pride in them, put his name on them, and appeared in advertisements to
endorse them. Bob joined Spalding's board of directors; his relationship with
the company would last for over thirty years.

In late February of 1931, Bob and Pop ventured out to Hollywood to begin
work on his film series for Warner Brothers. (Pop's luggage included eleven
typewriter boxes: ten of them contained jugs of corn liquor.) They began
shooting in early March, turning out the first twelve films at a rate of four a
month. George Marshall, an avid golfer known for his steady hand at the helm
of Mack Sennett's slapstick comedies, was hired to direct. With typical modesty Bob wanted to call the series *How I Play Golf* — not how *to* — starting with
the putter and working his way up through the bag to the driver. In a unique
amalgam of entertainment and instruction, each film folded a fluffy incidental
comic scenario around a more nourishing nugget of Bob's advice on the subject under discussion. Warners recruited their own contract players to round
out the casts that surrounded him, but interest in working with Bob was so
great that for the first time every studio in town signed releases for their own
stars so they could appear in the series. Almost all appeared without benefit of
salary, but the golfers in the group received a much more valuable in-kind

remuneration: hands-on personal instruction from the Great Jones about their games. A group of actors and directors who became friendly with Bob during filming soon began inviting him into their weekly fun-filled scrambles. In mocking tribute to their deficient skills, they called themselves "the Divot Diggers." Bob played with them frequently, and their tradition carried on for years after he left.

Traveling each day from nearby Warner Brothers studio in Burbank, filming took place at Flintridge Country Club in nearby La Canada, an off-the-beaten-path track where they were able to work without attracting an unwelcome crowd. (Later scenes and inserts would be filmed at Lakeside Golf Club, right next door to Warners, and also at Bel-Air Country Club over the hill in Los Angeles.) With his experience in turning out copy under deadline pressure, Pop proved to be a valuable everyday presence on the set, banging out story lines on his Underwood—and working as their announcer—but much of the dialogue was improvised on the spot, including Bob's. James Cagney, Edward G. Robinson, Loretta Young, Walter Huston, Douglas Fairbanks Jr., W. C. Fields, and Joe E. Brown were only a few of the luminaries who pop up in the films; a dozen other big stars of the day who have since faded from view appeared as well. They usually played fictional characters, and on occasion themselves, but in every instance Bob played himself without any introduction, on the reasonable assumption that everyone in the world already knew who he was. Each story contrived to bring its principals, suffering from some urgent and quickly defined golf deficiency, into contact with the famous golfer while out on the course. Watched in succession, the series suggests that Bob is an almost mystical being who materializes from out of the woods to offer soothing words of advice and a laying-on of hands to his anguished supplicants. They bump into him—he's forever strolling by in the middle of his own never-ending round of golf—he applies his gentle ministrations to their troubles, and the stars depart as if magically healed by their friendly neighborhood holy man.

The curious effect of these films today is that all these Hollywood big shots, busily hamming it up or acting their hearts out, come across as utterly synthetic when juxtaposed with Bob's self-possessed authority. He's good-natured, game for whatever the films demand, and never condescends to any of the goofy proceedings around him; but his own relaxed personal magnetism and natural gravity exude more genuine "star quality" than everyone else on-screen combined. After all his years in the public eye, he appears completely at home in front of the camera. When each film gets past the clunky plot and requisite clowning to the meat of Bob's instruction, his advice is first-rate: clean, precise, and practical. Taken as a whole—and visually reinforced by one startling demonstration of his masterful skills after another, often with the experimental use of slow-motion photography—the approach Bob presents to the game remains as fresh and useful today as when it was first filmed over seventy years ago. As silly as most of the stories seem now, there isn't a golfer alive who couldn't profit from seeing what Jones had to say about playing the game. The films are the best surviving record of his understated charisma—despite all the movie stars, there isn't a better-looking or more interesting person on-screen in the series—and his powerful physical vitality. Pop wrote that at the height of his powers Bob could tear an entire deck of playing cards in half with his hands. When you see his swing repeatedly from every angle and in slow motion as often as you do in these films, you begin to comprehend how he was able to accomplish so many of the unbelievable things he did with a golf club in his hand.

The first twelve films in the series rolled out in April of 1931 and continued through the summer at a rate of one a week. Screened in over six thousand theaters, they were an immediate smash, well reviewed and financially successful; it was later estimated that with his back-end profit participation, Bob doubled his up-front salary. Warners picked up his option for the additional six films, which due to scheduling conflicts didn't go into production until early 1933. Warners titled the second series *How to Break 90*, still one of the staples of every golf magazine. One of the Hollywood trade papers reported that by mid-decade the eighteen films Bob shot for Warners had been seen by over 40 million people, and for most audiences this was their first real introduction to the sport. Bob always looked back on his two brief seasons in Hollywood as one of his happiest professional experiences. More films would undoubtedly have followed, but the deepening Depression put an end to the movie-short business. Like so many other perishable products of the early studio system, the films disappeared from circulation and nearly died from neglect; over forty years later a distant cousin of Bob's by the name of Ely Callaway—having already made a fortune in wine, he was just then getting in the golf business—found what were believed to be the last surviving celluloid prints slowly decomposing in a storage room. They were restored and transferred to video just in time, and are still readily available to anyone curious about seeing the real Bob Jones.

They say a great athlete dies twice, the first time when he leaves his sport, but Bob never regretted his decision to retire or indulged in nostalgia for days of glory past, something that plagued a born showman like Hagen, who craved the spotlight. Bob was happy in his own skin and had also learned to live in the moment, one of the master skills in life; playing a game for so long that demanded that ability in order to succeed helped give it to him. He would still have enjoyed the personal satisfactions that came from winning championships but was no longer willing to pay the costs he had to endure to experience it: the travel and time away from his family and home, the profound loss of privacy, and the physical and mental stresses that brought him to the edge of collapse. Twice during the Grand Slam year alone only the timely intervention of friends, police, and the U.S. Marines had saved him from serious injury at the hands of a jubilant mob.

One of his closest friends, Francis Ouimet, wrote this about his retirement: "I think Bob was so fed up on the galleries, excitement and notoriety which comes under the heading of publicity, that he was sick and tired of it all. There is great satisfaction in playing in and winning golf championships but when the appetite has been whetted and satisfied, then a fellow likes to sneak off by himself in friendly fourball match and have some fun. He does not want to feel that his very life depends upon playing a perfect shot. He wants some kind of relaxation. I think he wants to golf with friends in a friendly way, without the blare of trumpets."

After reaching and losing in the semifinals of the National Amateur five times during the 1920s, Francis was the first to benefit from Bob's absence. Even Watts Gunn, a loyal friend to both men, came to Francis before the next Amateur began and said, "Francis, I feel like a new man altogether with Bobby and George Von Elm out of the way." Francis Ouimet won the 1931 National Amateur at Beverly Country Club, near Chicago, at the grand old age of thirty-eight. After beating four golfers nearly half his age to reach the finals, seventeen years to the day and almost to the minute after capturing his first Amateur title, Francis bookended his career by defeating Jack Westland to win his third major championship. Bob walked in his gallery that day, reporting on the action for *American Golfer*, and shared in his old friend's triumph. A short time after his own last great victory, Francis announced his retirement and joined Bob on the sidelines. Like Bob, he hungered for a private life and a business career. For the rest of his life, a beloved member of the Boston community until he died in 1967, whenever he was asked why he hadn't won more championships he always reminded people that they had no idea how good Bob Jones really was.

George Von Elm, the self-declared businessman-golfer, made it into a play-off for the 1931 U.S. Open with New England professional Billy Burke. Overshadowing even Von Elm's own memorable overtime battle at the 1930 Amateur with Maurice McCarthy, their titanic struggle remains the longest contest of its kind in USGA history. Von Elm birdied the seventy-second hole in regulation to force a play-off, then did it *again* during the play-off on the thirty-sixth hole to force another two rounds the following day. After 144 holes of golf, Billy Burke finally edged Von Elm to win the tournament by a single stroke. Although he continued to compete in the event throughout the decade, George never again came so close to another Open title. He remained in the Southern California area, a prosperous businessman, for the rest of his life, and played golf as a member of Lakeside Golf Club, where as the years passed he was feared a good deal more than he was liked.

Despite thrilling finishes and popular victories in both championships that year, with Bob out of the picture attendance at USGA tournaments fell by more than 50 percent. A trend began; without the electrifying presence of stars like Jones or Hagen, general interest in the sport gradually sank to its lowest levels since the Great War. In Great Britain, where thirty-six-year-old Tommy Armour won the 1931 Open at Carnoustie, attendance suffered similar declines without Bobby on hand to defend his title. As the Depression hit bottom during the middle of the decade the golf industry suffered considerable hardship; country-club incomes dropped by 65 percent. Many were forced to scale back the sports and services they offered their members and reduced their annual fees. Dozens of clubs failed to react quickly and went under. The repeal of Prohibition in 1933 helped slow the losses, when liquor sales could once again legally supplement club income, but along with the rest of the country, the sport would not fully find its footing again until after World War II.

Bob took in a few of the major tournaments during the early part of the decade as a spectator. Reluctant to steal any player's thunder by calling attention to himself, he could occasionally be spotted watching from a hill or distant vantage point away from the galleries. As the public's hopes for a comeback slowly faded, people relinquished the idea of Bob as a player and champion. Fans' memories are notoriously short-lived and unreliable, and soon his image became anchored to the past, part of another less complicated time. Deprived of the most compelling player in its history, golf in America would not come close to enjoying the same level of popularity it had experienced during Bob's heyday until the arrivals of Ben Hogan and Arnold Palmer.

If he didn't miss the pressure and strain of championship golf, Bob's love for the game never diminished. After returning home from Hollywood in June of 1931, he found the ideal outlet for his affection in the design and creation of Augusta National Golf Club. He remembered that languishing old exotic nursery next door to Augusta Country Club, and with the partnership and guidance of a New York investment counselor named Clifford Roberts purchased the property for $15,000 cash and a $60,000 mortgage. Bob hired Dr. Alister MacKenzie, whose designs for Cypress Point he had so admired, to help him transfer the course he had in his mind onto paper and then sculpt it from the grounds they now owned. Roberts took control of the club's business and they began soliciting members from around the country; charter memberships cost $350, with annual dues of $60. Grantland Rice was one of the first to be invited and accept; his own fame and enormous popularity proved indispensable as a recruiter of additional members. Those new members were slow in coming; Jones and Roberts could not have picked a less promising moment to open their doors. For the first few years of its existence Augusta National's survival was far from assured; with the Depression at its worst, the club nearly went under more than once, but during each successive crisis Jones and Roberts persevered.

The process of bringing to life all the theories and beliefs Bob had accumulated about golf course design became his consuming passion. Built at a cost of $115,000, Augusta National opened for play in January of 1933; Alister MacKenzie died suddenly at the age of sixty-three before ever seeing it completed. Routings and features from dozens of immortal courses echo throughout Augusta National, but the total exceeds even the sum of its extraordinary parts; the passage of time has confirmed that with MacKenzie's help Bob had created something unique and transcendent, an American original that can be copied but never duplicated. Volumes have been written about the course and its genesis, but a neglected point in understanding its finest quality is this: the many ways in which the course suggests nothing so much as the man who conceived it; graceful, guarded, fair, tough-minded, and touched by a mysterious divinity.

When the USGA declined to move the date of its championship forward into April and hold the 1934 Open at Augusta—where it was conceded that greens and fairways would not hold up under midsummer Southern heat—Jones and Roberts decided to organize a tournament of their own. Bob agreed to serve as the host, and he called on all his friendships within the sport to attract a field of the game's greatest players. From the beginning Roberts wanted to call this event the Masters; Bob's modesty prevented him from approving, but Rice and other sportswriters started using the name and it gradually caught on. Six years later, Bob relented and it became official.

Sixty-nine amateurs and professionals played in the First Annual Invitation Tournament at Augusta National in late March 1934. For the first time at any tournament in memory, the traditional "Mr." prefix in front of amateurs' names did not appear in any of the printed material. Since his own status fell somewhere between the two definitions, Bob felt there was no longer any need to make that distinction. Whatever the reason, the message it sent was clear: golfers capable of playing at this elevated level were seen, at last, as equals; friends, competitors, and social peers. The news that Bob intended to play in the event generated enormous heat and attracted reporters and spectators from all over the country, as did news that he had set an early course record at Augusta with a 65 during a practice round. Bob felt compelled to clarify that this was the only tournament in which he intended to compete and did not signal his formal return to the game.

Although he was only thirty-two years old, after four years away from competitive golf Bob quickly discovered that he possessed neither the keen mental focus nor the overriding desire that would allow him to perform to the standards he'd set during his championship run. His inimitable flowing swing looked as rhythmic and powerful as ever, but just as it had spelled the end for

Hagen—with whom he was paired in the third round and compared sorrows afterward—his extraordinary putting touch under pressure had vanished. "I grew nervous when I played in the Masters," he said, "and it hurt my game. It's perfectly obvious why. I wasn't keyed for the tension anymore." Bob finished in a tie for thirteenth, eight strokes behind eventual winner Horton Smith, and made it clear he would thereafter be playing in his own tournament in a purely ceremonial capacity. After the tournament, refining his vision after testing it in the field, Bob decided to reverse the nines at Augusta, creating the lineup of holes down the stretch that's been creating dramatic finishes ever since.

The following year, trailing late in the final round, Gene Sarazen made up a three-stroke deficit and forced a play-off with leader Craig Wood after one of golf's greatest shots; he holed a miraculous double eagle from two hundred yards away on the par five fifteenth. Both Bob and Hagen, who was paired with Sarazen that day, were among the few witnesses who actually saw the ball roll into the cup, a fact that delighted the fiercely competitive Sarazen. Sarazen went on to win a thirty-six-hole play-off with Wood the following day, and thus completed what's now referred to as the first professional career Grand Slam: both Opens, the PGA, and the Masters. Bob finished in twenty-sixth place that year; there would be no more talk of him seriously contending in the Masters. Although both Bob's spring tournament and Augusta National would continue to struggle for the next few years, Sarazen's shot helped solidify early interest in the Masters and helped set it on its path to eventual inclusion as the sport's fourth major championship.

Through the 1930s Walter Hagen contended in occasional tournaments but never bagged another major; his life trailed slowly away in an endless succession of attempts to recapture past glories. In 1934, while in St. Paul, Minnesota, for a tournament, he accidentally killed a young boy who ran out in front of his car. He was cleared of any wrongdoing in the official inquiry that followed, but some who knew him said the Haig was never quite the same afterward. He did make a concerted effort to get closer to his own neglected son as a result, and a decade later with his only grandson. His last twenty-five years were spent in affluent retirement and slowly deteriorating health, the bill coming due for his hedonistic lifestyle. An almost forgotten figure by the end, Walter Hagen died of cancer on October 6, 1969.

. . .

In 1936 Bob and Mary traveled to Europe with Mr. and Mrs. Robert Woodruff, the president of Coca-Cola, and Granny and Kit Rice to attend the Olympics in Berlin. They made a stop in Scotland on their way at the Gleneagles resort to relax and play some golf. Finding himself less than sixty miles from St. Andrews with a free day on his hands, Bob could not resist the idea of heading over to play the Old Course again; that afternoon the hotel sent a driver over to St. Andrews to put in a request for a tee time under the name "R. T. Jones Jr." When Bob and his partners arrived the following day and ate lunch at the Marine Hotel before their game, Bob noticed a substantial crowd gathered on the Old Course and feared they'd come to play on a day when an important local tournament was scheduled. It wasn't until they reached the clubhouse that Bob realized this crowd had come for him; word had spread about his impending visit, businesses shut their doors, and the entire town had turned out, over six thousand people by the time he teed off. Rice reported seeing grown men cry simply at the sight of Bob. Winner of the 1893 Open and one of the grand old men of the game, St. Andrews's resident pro, Willie Auchterlonie, came out to join Bob, Rice, and Gleneagles's professional, Gordon Lockhart, for their round. Bob was playing with steel-shafted clubs now, his own Spalding design, but after a lifetime with hickory in his hands he felt he hadn't quite mastered them yet. Inspired by the town's affection and the lighthearted holiday mood, Bob turned back the hands of time and shot a 32 on the front nine.

"Whatever the cause, and very much to my astonishment, I played as well that afternoon as I have ever played in my life," Bob wrote afterward. "I shall never forget that round."

After he capped off his afternoon with a birdie at eighteen, for a 71, the gallery cheered and crowded around as if he'd won the Open all over again. Bob retreated to the clubhouse for a drink with his partners, then stood on the portico and signed autographs for an hour as people lined up around the block.

He never played another shot on the Old Course again.

He continued to make his yearly appearance at the Masters, and on a few occasions played in exhibitions to support various charities, but he turned down most invitations for public speaking and showed no interest in pursuing life as a public figure. Now a pillar of the Atlanta business community—he was named president of the Chamber of Commerce in 1938—his role at the family law firm became as ceremonial as his playing career. He spent the majority of time attending to various business ventures, which now included seats on a number of corporate boards, an active role as vice president of Spalding, and controlling interest in three Coca-Cola bottling plants. As they grew older he also spent more time with his three children, with whom he was by all accounts a strict but affectionate father. When his only son, Bob the Third, showed an early interest in competitive golf, Bob tried to gently discourage him, aware that terrible expectations would attend his every effort. He even sent him to Kiltie Maiden for lessons, after secretly instructing Kiltie to try and discourage him. The younger Jones inherited the family gene for persistence, won the Atlanta Junior Championship in 1941, and went on to qualify for three National Amateurs; in his last appearance he was ousted in the first round by a young Jack Nicklaus.

Bob remained accessible to presidents and paupers alike, serving as an advisor to Franklin Roosevelt on the Works Progress Administration, and answering every letter written to him with the help of a full-time secretary. By 1939 Bob's rising income afforded a move into a luxurious Italianate four-bedroom house in one of Atlanta's best neighborhoods, on Tuxedo Road; Mary called their new home "Whitehall." They owned a second home in the resort at Highlands, North Carolina, and spent part of every winter in nearby Augusta. As their city grew with them, Bob and Mary moved in national social circles unimaginable to their fathers' generation; the South truly had risen again, with Atlanta leading the way, in no small measure because of the achievements of its most famous native son. After leaving competitive golf behind less than a decade earlier, Bob Jones had become the man he once and always hoped to be.

In the aftermath of the attack on Pearl Harbor and the outbreak of World War II, at the age of forty-one Bob lobbied for and received a commission as a captain in the United States Air Force. Too young to serve during the last war, he was determined to see action in this one, but found himself stuck for months on an air base in Florida. Resisting entreaties from higher-ups that he stay home and play exhibition golf to raise money while keeping an ocean away from the line of fire, Bob kept pushing for an overseas role and eventually entered training as an intelligence officer, specializing in prisoner interrogation. In 1943 he was promoted to major and received a posting to an air base in northwestern England with the Ninth Air Force, where he served under a man who would become one of his greatest friends, General Dwight D. Eisenhower. Bob landed with his division at

Normandy Beach on June 7, the day after D-day, and he spent the next two months working near the front lines under constant threat of artillery fire. By the time he was discharged and sent home near the end of 1944—the Colonel had fallen ill back in Atlanta, and he wanted to help care for him—after two years of active service, Bob had earned the rank of lieutenant colonel.

Along with the rest of the sport's major championships on both sides of the Atlantic, the Masters was canceled during the war years and once again Augusta National nearly went under; the course was literally put out to pasture, with a herd of cows grazing on its fairways. After six months of intensive work to put the course back in shape, much of it done by German prisoners of war from nearby Camp Gordon, the Masters tournament resumed in 1946. Just coming into his own as a player after a decade of hard knocks, thirty-four-year-old Ben Hogan finished in second place by a stroke to Herman Keiser, just as he had to winner Byron Nelson four years earlier in the last Masters. In the immediate aftermath of the war, Bob became involved in the creation of another golf club even closer to home, Peachtree, in Atlanta. Like everything else he touched in his career, it became a great success. He could still turn in extraordinary stretches of golf; as late as 1946, he played the front nine at East Lake in 29 strokes, six under par.

His businesses were thriving, he was all but set for life financially, happily married for nearly a quarter of a century with three healthy children, and looking forward to grandchildren, who would not be long in coming. He hunted and fished and played tennis and golf as he pleased with a select and favored few whose company he adored. He had friends in the highest places around the world, many more who were nearer and dear to him, and the universal regard of anyone who'd ever seen him play or followed his career as the greatest sportsman of his generation, if not the century. After nearly twenty years of struggle, Augusta National and the Masters were on the cusp of achieving the recognition and reverence that they enjoy today as a cornerstone of American sport.

Bob turned forty-six on St. Patrick's Day in 1948. His lucky streak had held; he had made the turn onto the back nine and should have been looking forward to the best years of his life.

Fate had different plans.

Bob's return to St. Andrews at Freedom Hall.

CHAPTER EIGHTEEN

Decline

In the summer of 1950, the USGA held its fiftieth annual U.S. Women's Amateur Championship at East Lake. As part of the festivities the club announced a plan to host a dinner honoring the anniversary and the amateur tradition. The winner of three of those first fifty titles, Atlanta native Alexa Stirling Fraser, accepted an invitation to attend. She was now fifty-three years old, a happily married mother of three, living in Toronto with her distinguished physician husband. Long retired from the game and the spotlight, Alexa had not returned to Atlanta in over twenty years, and decided to go primarily out of a desire to see her old childhood friend Bobby Jones. Perry Adair, the third member of their Dixie Whiz Kid trio, would be there as well; Alexa felt it was time for a reunion. When Bob learned she was coming he insisted on meeting her at the train station with a sportswriter friend, who found Alexa as she came off the train and escorted her to where her old friend was waiting at the top of a flight of stairs.

She had been expecting the handsome, vibrant champion she'd enjoyed watching in newsreels and newspapers all through his great sporting years. Alexa refused to believe her eyes. This man standing at the top of the stairs was a physical ruin, his face a pale and deathly gray, swollen by the use of cortical steroids. He carried a cane in each hand, and wore a cumbersome metal brace on his right leg. Bob took in the shock on her face without alarm, kissed her warmly, and told her not to worry. When they started for the car Alexa realized with another jolt that Bob could no longer walk. "He dragged his feet along without being able to lift them, his face set against the pain each movement cost him."

Over the next few days, Bob shared with his old friend details of his still undiagnosed illness that he had never confided in anyone. He could no longer drive or climb stairs; he needed to be carried to his fourth-floor office in a wheelchair. He had lost all feeling in his hands and could write his name only by using a pen attached to a tennis ball that he gripped in his palm.

"One morning a few weeks ago, I woke up without remembering my condition," he told her, "and I stepped out of bed to walk to the bathroom. I fell flat on my face, of course. I lay on that floor and beat it with my fists and cursed at the top of my lungs. For ten minutes nobody dared come near me. I would have bitten them."

Over the course of her visit, Alexa's profound sadness at Bob's condition slowly changed to admiration. He had been stripped of his magnificent physicality in the cruelest imaginable way, but somehow his spirit, fine mentality, and sharp sense of humor remained untouched. How had he done it? she wanted to know.

"There were times I didn't want to go on living," he told her. "But I did go on living, so I had to face the problem of how I was going to live. I decided I'd just do the very best I could."

"And he'd be damned if he was going to have any soupy sympathy," wrote Alexa afterward. "About this point he was profanely specific."

Two years earlier, during the first rounds of the Masters in 1948, the pain in Bob's neck and shoulders had flared up again. He had endured similar discomfort on many occasions ever since the "crick in the neck" injury he suffered during the British Amateur at Muirfield in 1926, and paid it little mind. Bob played poorly but finished the tournament without generating undue concern, promising his friends that he'd be seeing them out on the course again the following year.

This time the soreness didn't go away. He experienced a six-week spell of double vision for distant objects, like greens or flags. He became aware of an alarming tendency to stumble, particularly with a right foot that seemed reluctant to follow orders. A creeping numbness in his right hand followed; one day while fishing a friend noticed a fishhook deeply embedded in his thumb. Bob hadn't felt a thing. He began searing his fingers with cigarettes that burned down too close to the nub without his noticing; he began using a cigarette holder to avoid injury, joking that he had to "tee them up." The numbness and tingling spread to his arms and legs.

His doctors sent him to specialists, who were baffled and sent him to surgeons. He was x-rayed, poked, and prodded. A precise diagnosis remained elusive, but there was agreement that what appeared to be clusters of bone spurs were massing in and between his cervical vertebrae. None of the physicians he consulted had a definitive idea of how to treat the condition; it seemed to depend on how much pain Bob felt he could tolerate.

Within months he could no longer take a full swipe at a golf ball without severe burning pain in his back. His long graceful swing shortened and soon lost its music. That August, during one of his regular rounds at East Lake with two young protégés—Charlie Yates, the 1938 British Amateur champion, and Tommy Barnes, winner of multiple Southern Amateurs—both men noticed that Bob couldn't get around on the ball. He was shuffling his feet when he walked. Not long afterward, on the final hole of his regular weekly game, Bob hooked his drive into the trees and neglected even to go in after it. He confided in Tommy Barnes after the round was over that he wouldn't be playing golf again for a while. He had decided to have an operation.

The head of surgery at Emory University hospital performed the work on October 30, 1948, and in a seven-hour procedure removed a number of bony growths from between his fourth, fifth, and sixth cervical vertebrae. Bob's doctors were quoted in the local papers saying that the operation had been a complete success; they believed the growths they'd found had been pressing on his nerves, creating constant pain and inhibiting movement. Bob began an aggressive rehabilitation program soon afterward, but in truth it was two weeks before he could even attempt to walk again. Another cruel blow came while he recuperated in the hospital; Bob was shocked to learn about the sudden death of his old friend and mentor, Stewart Maiden. After decades of heavy drinking, during which Bob repeatedly come to his aid—paying for stays in hospitals, at times his only financial support—Kiltie died of heart failure.

Within a few months it became clear that the operation had not alleviated Bob's symptoms; on the contrary, the numbness and atrophy in his right leg and arm only grew worse. By early the next year, the loss of motor control began spreading to his left side. He continued a rigorous program of physical therapy but soon he could no longer walk without the use of a cane. Before long, he needed two of them; a friend ordered some made of hickory from the same firm that used to make the shafts for his golf clubs. After consulting with the best surgeons and specialists around the country, he underwent a second operation at a clinic in Boston in early 1950; doctors there seemed to feel his troubles derived from a damaged cervical disc and put him under the knife for five hours. For the second time extensive surgery did nothing to alleviate his condition, leaving his upper back and neck a welter of ugly scars. Shortly afterward, his right side became almost completely paralyzed.

Not long after seeing Alexa Stirling, Bob had another encounter with an old friend while visiting New York City for the USGA's annual meeting. Before the meeting convened, Bob was sitting on a low chair at the end of the dais when Al Laney—who had not seen him since before his illness—stopped by to pay his respects.

"He took my hand in both of his and pulled me down toward him in a semblance of an embrace, and as he did I saw steel braces showing below the cuffs of his trousers. As soon as I could I moved away from him for fear he would see the shock of it on my face."

A few months later at the Masters, Laney was walking the course when Bob pulled up alongside in a small motorized cart that he now used in order to get around. They exchanged small talk, then "in his gently understanding way he placed his not yet gnarled hand on my knee and said quietly, 'You ran away from me at the meeting.'"

Laney tried to explain, awkwardly saying that he hadn't wanted to impose.

"Never mind that," said Bob. "I want my old friends to impose on me. I love my old friends and I want to be bothered by them."

Encouraged, Al asked about his condition and Bob quietly explained all that he'd been through, and then spoke of his prognosis.

"I've known you now longer than anyone in golf, Al," he said. "I can tell you there is no help. I know I can only get worse. But you are not to keep thinking of it. You know, in golf we play the ball as it lies. Now, we will not speak of this again, ever."

Bob smiled, and soon after dropped Laney off. As he drove away he said: "Remember now: Bother me!"

A precise diagnosis would not come until 1956. After examining his voluminous case history, Dr. H. Houston Merritt of the Columbia Medical Center Neurological Institute in New York informed Bob that he was suffering from an extremely rare illness called syringomyelia. Striking fewer than one out of a million people each year, for reasons that are not fully understood, the disease causes the spinal cord to expand: the result is a slow strangulation of the nervous system, as nerves are compressed into dysfunction, with atrophy and complete paralysis the inevitable result. The pain this causes is widespread, severe, escalating, and unrelenting; it is, in short, a living hell. Although there is still no cure, subsequent medical advances now make earlier diagnosis and treatment considerably more effective, but at the time the average life span for a person diagnosed with syringomyelia was five to seven years after onset. By the time they figured out what he was suffering from, Bob had already been living with the disease for eight.

The most common form of syringomyelia is congenital, a defect inherent from birth that reveals itself in childhood. Far less common, but more often the case in instances involving adult onset, it can be induced by severe trauma to the neck or spine. Because of the late diagnosis in Bob's case, the precise cause of his disease could never be pinpointed, but Bob's mind went back to the injury he had suffered in the British Amateur at Muirfield. And three years after that, to the cluster of bricks and mortar that had struck him on the back of the neck when a lightning bolt blew up the chimney at East Lake.

The disease was a one-in-a-million shot; he had been struck by lightning again.

Pop Keeler finally retired from the *Atlanta Journal* in April 1949 at the age of sixty-seven and received a magnificent send-off from his friends in Georgia and around the country: a sit-down dinner for three hundred, with speeches, medals, and a gift of a brand-new Buick. Bob spoke last and presented Pop with the keys, remarking on "all the suffering I caused poor old Keeler and how he held my hand through the critical moments of my career. I thought he might need someone to hold his hand tonight, and I am glad to be here to do it."

Pop had lost weight; he looked tired, his face drawn. He announced he'd given up drinking recently—"because of the wife and the kidneys"—but there were suspicions that he wasn't well. After fighting back tears, when he finally got up to speak, for one of the only times in his life O. B. Keeler found himself at a loss for words: "Life has been good to me, but this is the finest moment of all. I can't thank you folks for this night. I can only say God bless you."

A little over a year into his retirement, Pop was diagnosed with liver cancer. He spent most of his last summer at home with Mommer at the big house they called "Distillery Hill," once the sight of a nineteenth-century gin mill. After all his close brushes in the past with what he referred to as "the Old Man with Hour Glass," Pop didn't have much left to fear from death. He faced it with the same humor and grace he'd shown to every setback or triumph that came his way.

Bob visited him in the hospital on a Saturday afternoon near the end. Pop came out of a coma, lucid and calm.

"I'm glad you're here," said Pop. "I'm well down the eighteenth fairway." He closed his eyes. "Hold my hand a minute. I'm sick, I'm so sick I'm almost crazy."

Bob told him that Georgia Tech had just beaten LSU in football that afternoon.

"That's really remarkable," said Pop.

A short time later Bob let go of his friend's hand, and the next day the man with the hourglass arrived. Oscar Bane Keeler died at 2:40 Sunday morning, October 15, 1950.

Bob received word late the next day at the Greenbrier Hotel in White Sulphur Springs, West Virginia, where he'd just arrived with a group of friends.

"He was my dearest friend," said Bob, then excused himself from the reporter who'd told him about it, too emotional to say another word. Bob returned to Atlanta at once and, along with Grantland Rice, served as an honorary pallbearer at Pop's funeral.

His colleague at the *Journal*, Ed Danforth, wrote this about Pop the following day: "He has done his best to be old, yet he never could suppress the eternal youth in his heart. He tried to be cynical without success. He loved people. He never attended a gathering that he did not instantly become the center of attraction with no effort at all on his part.

"Everyone was his friend."

Determined to continue living his life, Bob remained as active as his deteriorating condition would allow. He suffered a mild heart attack in 1952 that further defined his limits. He hunted until he couldn't feel the trigger with his finger and accidentally discharged a round that could have killed somebody. He fished until his crippled hands could no longer hold a rod and reel. Denied those former pleasures, he poured his competitive instincts into bridge. Stripped of all vanity, he held his head up and never hesitated to appear in public. His annual role as the host of the Masters became increasingly important to him. He held court in his cabin near the tenth tee, a warm, august presence to old friends and a patient mentor to new players. His regular appearances during the green jacket ceremony on television introduced him to a whole new generation of Americans who had never known him as a golfer.

A registered Democrat his whole life, for the first and only time in his life Bob became active in politics, supporting his friend Dwight Eisenhower's successful 1952 campaign for president. The two men had discovered an affinity for each other's common sense and selfless, old-fashioned decency that went far beyond political values or party affiliation. Four years earlier Bob had been instrumental in bringing General Eisenhower into the fold at Augusta National and their deep friendship now became one of the enduring joys of his life. Knowing better than most others alive the trying demands of public life on a private man, Bob arranged for a special cabin to be built at Augusta for the president, which became his favorite retreat.

After the death of Pop Keeler, Grantland Rice assembled *The Bobby Jones Story* from the vast stockpile of columns and stories he'd written through the years, a project Pop had left unfinished at the time of his passing. The book was published in 1953, the same year that Perry Adair died, only fifty-three. Granny Rice himself passed in the summer of 1954 at the age of seventy-three, after suffering a stroke. Bob attended the funeral in New York, which took place not long after the USGA announced that they were creating an annual award for sportsmanship that would bear Bob's name. The first recipient, fittingly, was his old friend Francis Ouimet, who agreed to accept the honor only because it came to him in Bob's name.

Two years later, in July of 1956, Bob's father died at the age of seventy-six. With the Colonel gone, he had lost his dearest friend.

In 1958 Bob accepted an invitation to serve as the nonplaying captain of the American team in the first World Team Championship, a bienniel event played by four-man amateur squads from twenty-nine different countries. He accepted, in large part because the competition would be held at St. Andrews, and after a twenty-two-year absence he longed to see the place again, realizing it might be his last opportunity. Shortly afterward he received a telegram from the town's clerk asking if while he was there Bob wouldn't mind accepting an award naming him a Freeman of St. Andrews. Assuming this was something along the lines of the many ceremonial awards extended to him during this period of his life, he accepted.

When Bob, Mary, and two of their children arrived in St. Andrews on October 3, he soon realized that being offered the title of Freedom of the City and the Royal Burgh meant a great deal more than another key to the city from another Chamber of Commerce. The town was in effect granting him genuine citizenship, the first and only time they had extended that honor to an American since 1759. The only previous recipient: Dr. Benjamin Franklin.

As the day of the ceremony approached, Bob struggled to provide the town's officials with a copy of the speech he intended to give. The enormity of the occasion had dawned on him; he couldn't find the words to express his feelings and was loath to commit himself to something on paper when he preferred to speak from the heart. A reunion with his old Scottish caddie Jack McIntyre—who wept at the sight of Bob—helped him articulate what he hoped to express, and he trusted that the appropriate sentiments would come to him in the moment.

Thursday afternoon, October 9, a gray, desolate day, nearly two thousand people packed Younger Graduation Hall on the campus of St. Andrews University, including the officials and contestants from the international golf competition. Bob's family and various dignitaries took their seats on a platform behind a lectern flanked by two tables. Bob and the town's mayor, or provost, Robert Leonard, entered from the wings and took seats at the two tables. The meeting was called to order, and a prayer offered by the university's chaplain, Reverend Rankin. The town clerk then read the contents of the citation from a hand-inked scroll. Wearing the splendid ermine-trimmed crimson robe of his office, Provost Leonard spoke briefly about the great traditions of golf in his city and the enduring bond that had formed between its citizens and Bobby Jones during his previous visits.

Among the ancient rights of citizenship accorded by the ceremony were free license to catch rabbits, the right to dry his washing on the Old Course, and to take divots whenever he pleased. Leonard concluded by saying that Bob "is free to feel at home in St. Andrews as truly as in his own home of Atlanta. One of our own number, officially now, as he has been so long unofficially."

Provost Leonard placed the scroll in a small, exquisite silver casket adorned with the seal of the city and placed it on the table where Bob was seated to the right of the lectern. Bob signed the Honour Roll, which made his citizenship official, and the crowd gave him three rousing cheers and sang "For He's a Jolly Good Fellow." Then the mayor put a warm hand on Bob's shoulder, smiled, and said, "Now, Bob, the ordeal is yours."

No one expected what happened next. Bob rose from his seat, without canes, refusing assistance of any kind, and shuffled the eight feet to the lectern, the first steps he'd taken unaided in years. He realized during those few moments that he had "no need for the notes in my pocket. I knew that I would have no difficulty finding things to say to the people of St. Andrews."

"The provost has given me permission," he began, "to tell you that lacking a middle initial of his own, he will in future be known as Robert T. Leonard. I consider that the greatest triumph I have ever won in Scotland."

That raised a laugh, and relaxed both Bob and his audience. He spoke at length of his first visit to St. Andrews, in 1921, and the youthful errors in judgment and temperament that led to his disqualifying himself from the third round of the Open competition at the eleventh hole. He talked of how his bewilderment at the Old Course had led to curiosity and finally wisdom as he discovered her secrets. "The more I studied the Old Course, the more I loved it, and the more I loved it, the more I studied it—so that I came to feel that it was for me the most favorable meeting ground for an important contest."

He spoke of his astonishment at the warmth and approval he had received from the people of the town when he returned six years later and won the

Open, and three years after that when his victory at the Amateur started him on the road to the Grand Slam. He recalled the exquisite miniature replica of the British Amateur Championship Trophy that his fellow members of the R&A had mailed to him in Atlanta, bearing an inscription "which at this point I could not trust myself to repeat. . . . It has remained my prized possession." He described his first return visit to St. Andrews in 1926, how the presence of the huge crowd that spontaneously turned out to see him inspired him "to play the best golf I had played for four years, and certainly never since." In each instance it had been the respect and affection he felt from the people of the town that meant so much more to him than trophies or medals or championships.

"And now I have this. I could take out of my life everything but my experiences at St. Andrews and I'd still have a rich full life."

He spoke of friendship and expressed with a full heart and his precise lawyer's language exactly how much that overused expression meant to him. The spiritual clarity of his emotions rose to meet the eloquence of his words, and in his steady gaze and warm, measured baritone Bob reflected back to his audience the love he felt from them.

When I say that I am your friend, I have pledged to you the ultimate in loyalty and devotion. In some respects friendship may even transcend love, for in true friendship there is no place for jealousy. When I say that you are my friends, it is possible that I may be imposing upon you a greater burden than you are willing to assume. But when you have made me aware on many occasions that you have a kindly feeling toward me, and when you have honored me by every means at your command, then when I call you my friend, I am at once affirming my high regard and affection for you and declaring my complete faith in you and trust in the sincerity of your expressions. And so my fellow citizens of St. Andrews, it is with this appreciation of the full sense of the word that I salute you as my friends.

Friendship should be the great note of this world golf meeting, because not only people, but nations need friends. Let us hope that this meeting will sow seeds which will germinate and grow into important friendships among nations later on.

I just want to say to you this is the finest thing that has ever happened to me. Whereas that little cup was first in my heart, now this occasion at St. Andrews will take first place always. I like to think about it this way that, now I officially have the right to feel at home in St. Andrews as much as I, in fact, have always done.

Thunderous applause, then the room fell silent, the air hushed with gravity. Everyone stood to sing "God Save the Queen." Bob was escorted down the stairs to the center aisle, where an electric golf cart sat waiting for him. He climbed on board, and as the cart drove slowly up the aisle toward the exit, someone with a bright tenor voice broke spontaneously into a lilting old Scottish folk song called "Will Ye No' Come Back Again." Within moments, every other voice in that hall who knew the words had joined in. They reached out to touch Bob and his family as he passed. This was a true valedictory, the sort of tribute seldom given or received while the person being honored still lives, made possible only if that person has moved past longing and pride and illusions of the self into the rarest wisdom.

The golf writer Herbert Warren Wind was in the audience that afternoon. He reported that after he and his friends left the hall, ten full minutes passed before any of them were even able to speak.

Bob later called it the most emotional experience of his entire life.

Bob Jones had long ago exhibited a genius for the game of golf. The road of life is littered with broken dreams and squandered talent, but he had mastered his own brash unruly nature and honored the brilliant gift he had been given with uncommon discipline and faith. Anyone can fall short, and most stumble, but the truth is that the consequences of success are often harder to live with. "Hero" has become the most overworked word in the world of sports, and people are justifiably cynical about that breed of "heroes" these days, It's all too easy to mistake remarkable physical ability for uncommon personal character, a more trying test that most young athletes, steeped in self-interest and short on experience, aren't remotely prepared to meet.

Bob Jones is and always will be the greatest exception to that rule. His record in his sport cannot and never will be equaled, but it was the way in which he went about realizing his abilities that matters even more, because he stood for something rare and true, without trying to or saying so in speeches and empty gestures. He never talked about the meaning of what he had accomplished, he simply lived it, and in so doing left others with a far more meaningful path to follow. That's why his dedicated pursuit of the excellence that was born in him still holds the power to inspire. Some may discount his legacy by saying he only played a game, but what he achieved remains in its own right as powerful and permanent an expression of the human longing for perfection as any poem or song or painting. Greatness is rare and a solemn responsibility, and because he offered himself in service to his talent with a strong mind, a committed heart, and every ounce of strength in his being, he deserves a lasting place in our memory.

He had another great talent, and perhaps a genius, for friendship. Away from the golf course his virtues were quiet ones that he felt no compulsion to exaggerate or advertise: loving son, devoted husband and father, diligent and disciplined worker, loyal and generous friend. You have only to read the countless statements left by gifted writers like Pop Keeler, Grantland Rice, and Al Laney, who loved him like a brother, or the hundreds of other people whose lives he touched, who without exception felt honored to have known him, basked in his affection, benefited from his wise counsel, and shared his warm, embracing humor. These are hard qualities to quantify, unless you've been fortunate enough to experience them; they are in and of the present moment, where Bob lived his life. It was his presence alone, they all said, that gave you such a wonderful feeling. Alistair Cooke, who knew him only as an older, infirm man, explained by saying that Bob radiated simple goodness without a smidgen of piety. His modesty wasn't an act and there was nothing false about it; it was a genuine expression of his character, so out of the ordinary in the famous of our contemporary world that it seems unimaginable. Nor did he hold himself in such high regard that he felt contempt for the often rude and intrusive admiration of strangers that always came his way, even when it pained or inconvenienced him beyond what few people would have been able to bear. When athletes finally came along who surpassed some of his records, and to whom he was constantly compared, instead of retreating to the fortress of his past he extended a hand to them and helped them any way he could; and like so many of the men he played against in his own time, Arnold Palmer and Jack Nicklaus became his close and devoted friends.

This was who he was. A man who did such wondrous things, he had the world at his feet, but kept his feet on the ground. A man who always behaved decently, treating both the proud and the poor with unfailing courtesy and abiding respect. A man who gave hope to a country at its darkest hour, and asked for nothing in return. A man who stayed true to his principles, and kept his dignity when he could have auctioned it off for any price he named. He was no plaster saint, but he was a man's man; he smoked and drank, sometimes to excess, and was very much at home in the rowdy enclave of the locker room, but he stayed faithful to the one woman he loved throughout his life. Bouquets of hotel room keys were tossed his way during the bright shining years of his youth; there's no shred of evidence that he listened to any of those sirens' songs. He was a socially conservative gentleman from the Deep South, born in the Victorian age, who lived to see men walk on the moon. In an era of bewildering upheaval and change, he remained resolutely fair in his treatment of individuals, black or white; no one who knew him ever recalled a single racist epithet passing his lips. As early as the late 1920s, over the protest of many, Bob helped promote Woodrow Bryant, an African-American caddie and club maker, to the position of assistant professional at East Lake, where Bryant remained employed for the next fifty years. It's easy to judge any man's actions retroactively when viewed through a contemporary lens, but it's as futile an exercise for reaching a fair conclusion as is arguing how athletes from a different era would stand up against those playing today.

When in the second half of his life the countless blessings he'd received turned into a spiraling nightmare of pain, suffering and diminishment, he found the strength not only to endure but to triumph; nothing said more about the way he lived his life than the way in which he took his leave from it. Bob Jones lived for twenty-three years with that dreadful disease, but not meekly; he railed against and despaired at the relentless cruelty it wielded on him and never asked for pity. He soldiered on, and by the end it had stripped him of everything but the diamond sharpness of his mind. In a gesture that revealed more about those around them than they would have wanted to admit, in 1968 Bob was removed from the telecasts of the Masters for fear his appearance would upset viewers and advertisers. He spent his last few years bedridden, helpless and paralyzed; in many ways this was a fate worse than death. Near the end he weighed less than ninety pounds, his once powerful hands reduced to useless claws. Betrayed by his failing body, Bob found a form of grace as he made his peace with these hideous indignities because he knew that the hardest lesson learned during his playing days applied equally to matters of life and death: this was his fate, it had all been written in the Book, and he accepted it. For everything he had given to his game, the game gave him back this lasting gift—the strength to bear his trials—and called it even.

Bob converted to his wife's Catholic faith during his final days. Some thought he had done it to please Mary; others said he came to it of his own accord. Whatever the reason, by all accounts it seemed to give him comfort. Bob died at home, peacefully, in his sleep, on December 18, 1971. His funeral was brief and private, for family members only, as he had requested. There would be no parades now, no "great fuss." He'd had more than his share while he was alive. Modest to the end, he was laid to rest in Atlanta's Oakland Cemetery beneath a simple headstone bearing only his name and the dates of his birth and death. His beloved Mary would join him there only four years later.

The flags at East Lake, Augusta, and St. Andrews, and a thousand other places, were lowered to half-mast.

For decades Clifford Roberts had tried to build a statue of Bob at Augusta National, but Bob always rejected the idea. His instinct was correct: his essence can't readily be captured in an image of marble or bronze, because it was his life lived among the people whom he loved that made him who he was, not numbers on a scorecard or trophies on a shelf. If you want to catch a glimpse of his spirit, sit down by the water at East Lake on a cool April morning and remember a small fragile boy testing himself against the world's toughest game on this old hard ground and never yielding. Walk the fairways some afternoon at Augusta during Masters week, far away from the crowds and the tumult, when the setting sun filters pure golden light through starbursts of azalea, and feel the divine blueprint of a masterful mind creating beauty and order out of chaos. Stroll out to the Eden at St. Andrews on a gray, windswept eve during a long summer's twilight, near the hole they now call "Bobby Jones," and look back at that ancient arena where men first practiced to pit their hearts and souls against nature in this supreme and impossible game. Stand on a first tee, or confront a bad patch in life, anywhere in the world, and then ask yourself: Do I in this moment have what it's going to take to face the troubles this earth has set in front of me?

You'll find him there.

Bob, at the Masters.

*I remember a farmer who knew nothing about golf,
but who happened to watch Bobby playing one morning on
a suburban course near London. He did not know
who Bobby Jones was, but was so fascinated
by the rhythm of his swing that he
suddenly turned to a journalist I knew and said:
"This man is the greatest golfer in the world."*

— BERNARD DARWIN

ACKNOWLEDGMENTS

I am indebted to Sidney L. Matthew, without whose guidance and unfailing generosity this book could not have been written. If he were the only man alive who had been touched by Mr. Jones there would be no cause for concern that his memory will ever be forgotten. At the start of this journey Dr. Catherine Lewis at the Atlanta History Center, home of the largest exhibition on Bobby Jones, and her husband, John Companiotte, provided me with a map and perfect directions, and for their assistance I am most grateful. Tom Williams, formerly of the USGA, helped enormously with the research, and Rand Jerris, a friend and valued counselor still very much with the USGA, led me to him. Many thanks to Doug Stark, Patty Moran, and Shannon Doody at the USGA Library for their great patience and assistance.

A special thanks to Bill Stitt, Bob Bowers, and John Capers at Merion, Joe Ford at Augusta National, Dr. Lloyd Pearson at Interlachen, and two extraordinary gentlemen in Atlanta who represent a great living link to Mr. Jones, Charlie Yates and Tommy Barnes.

I wish to thank all the professionals in the golf world who extended a hand to this effort: Rick Burton and Chad Parker at East Lake Golf Club; Jock

Olson and William Kidd Jr. at Interlachen; Mike Schultz at Hazeltine; Scott Nye at Merion; Matt Massei at Pinehurst; Brian Morrison at Olympia Fields; Rick Anderson and Kevin Clark at the Atlanta Athletic Club; Bob Linn, Doug Hoffort, Marianne Huning, Chris Powel, Patrick Boyd, and Jeff Brockman at MountainGate. A very special thanks to a man I'm privileged to call my friend, Eddie Merrins of Bel-Air.

In the publishing world, love and gratitude to my friend and literary agent, Ed Victor, first, last, and always. At Hyperion, many thanks for their continued faith and partnership to Bob Miller, Will Schwalbe, Jane Comins, Christine Ragasa, and my wonderful editor, Gretchen Young. I am most grateful for the help of George Peper and Kevin Cook, and the continued friendship and support of Gaetan Burrus, Ian Chapman, Francis Esminard, Bob Oberneir, Jack Romanos, Bill Shinker, Will Sieghart, Ron Weir, and Peter Workman.

I am especially grateful for my long friendship with David Steinberg. Thanks also to John Walsh at ESPN; Dick Cook, Nina Jacobson, and Jason Reed at Disney; Leslie Moonves, Mary Murphy, Jason Sacca, and Jim Axelrod at CBS; and Sandi Mendelson and Judy Hilsinger. Thanks for a hundred different reasons to Steven Altman, Mark Andrew, Scott Baker, Larry Brezner, Jeff Freilich, Peter and Connie Goetz, Adam Krentzman, Steven Kulczycki, Martin Leren, Pat Miles, John O'Hurley, Susie Putnam, Doug Richardson, Martin Spencer, Jerry Stein, Stuart Stevens, Scott Turow, Sonny and June Van Dusen, Bruce Vinokour, Alan Wertheimer, Harley Williams, and Michael Zinberg.

One of the great joys of writing *The Grand Slam* has been the number of new friends it has brought into my life; chief among them, and many thanks to, Ric Kayne, Bill Paxton, Brad Faxon, Todd Field, Billy Andrade, Charley Norris, Selwyn Hirson, Mack Clapp, Mike Kaiser, Frank Bredice, and Tom Yellin. Continued and undying gratitude to J. Louis Newell, Bob Donovan, and all my friends at the Francis Ouimet Scholarship Fund: Denny Goodrich, Dick Connelly, Bill Foley, Anne Marie Tobin, and Denny Kelly among them.

My son, Travis, was born as I began writing this book. To him, my wife, Lynn, my parents, brother, sister, nephews, and brother-in-law, thank you for your love during this journey, and for teaching me the meaning of family.

A NOTE ON THE WRITING

To avoid confusion I have used the modern terms for all the golf clubs in this story; irons and woods were not generally referred to by numbers until after Bob produced matched sets with Spalding in the 1930s. All of the dialogue in this book is directly quoted from source material, chiefly the accounts left to us by Pop Keeler, Bob Jones, Grantland Rice, Walter Hagen, Chick Evans, Bernard Darwin, Al Laney, and Francis Ouimet.

Bob with the Grand Slam trophies.

INDEX

Keeler, Oscar Bane "Pop" (*continued*)
  Jones's interviews with, 276–77, 368
  Jones's retirement and, 411–12, 445–46
  at Jones's wedding, 216
  knee infection suffered by, 86
  Maiden and, 165, 295
  marriage of, 286, 289–90, 291
  on radio shows, 449
  retirement of, 446, 465–66
  Southern Amateur and, 51
  train trestle fire and, 416
  U.S. Amateur and, 104, 107, 108, 157–59,
    217–21, 234, 235, 280, 281, 298, 301
  U.S. Amateur of 1930 and, 424, 425, 427,
    431, 433, 434, 436, 437, 440, 441
  U.S. Open and, 152, 153, 165, 167, 168, 169,
    170, 228, 230, 231, 288, 289, 307, 309,
    311, 324, 325–26, 327
  U.S. Open of 1923 and, 186, 187, 189–95,
    197–203, 205–6
  U.S. Open of 1926 and, 269–71, 273, 275, 276
  U.S. Open of 1930 and, 391–93, 395, 400,
    401, 403, 407, 410–12
  Walker and, 214, 215
  Walker Cup teams and, 247–59, 261–65,
    267–69, 343–45
Keiser, Herman, 459
Kerensky, Alexander, 89
Kidd, Willie, 389, 396, 400
Kirkwood, Joe, 187, 188, 190, 209, 256, 369
Knepper, Rudy, 218–19

Lacey, Charles, 399, 404
Laney, Al, xi, 110–12, 133, 136–37, 189–90,
    261–63, 321, 322, 359, 464–65, 472
Lannin, Joe, 138
Lardner, Ring, 68, 69
Lauder, Harry, 342
Legg, Harry, 299, 300, 389
Lenin, Vladimir, 89
Leonard, Robert, 468, 469
Lido, 226–27
Life of Christ (Papini), 206, 215
lightning, xiii–xv, 327, 337, 419, 465
Lindbergh, Charles, 287, 297, 299
Little, William Lawson, 331
Lloyd, Harold, 94, 182
Lloyd George, David, 117
Lockhart, Gordon, 457
Lowell, William, 188
Lowery, Eddie, 96, 298, 299
Lusitania, 54–55
Lytham & St. Anne's Golf Club, 258–65

McAuliffe, Eleanor McIntosh, *see* Keeler,
    Eleanor McAuliffe
McAuliffe, Mack and Jack, 286
McCarthy, Maurice, 299, 429, 432, 453
McDermott, Johnny, 109, 213, 215

Macdonald, Charles Blair, xi, 6, 7, 8, 65, 154,
    171, 226
MacFarlane, Willie, x, 228, 229–32, 332, 390
Macfie, Allan, 371
McIntyre, Jack, 252, 258, 262, 264, 291, 345,
    380, 468
MacKenzie, Alister, 226–27, 331–32, 350,
    454–55
Mackenzie, Roland, 255, 259, 300, 342, 344
McLean, Edward, 151
McLeod, Freddie, 153
McMahon, Tommy, 289
Maiden, Jimmy, 10, 19, 21, 22, 185
Maiden, Stewart "Kiltie," x, 5, 10–11, 15, 21, 22,
    24–27, 42, 50, 52, 77, 84, 103, 104, 107,
    147, 154–55, 165, 230, 276, 283, 298, 301,
    386
  British Open of 1927 and, 290, 291, 294
  Carnoustie trip of, 294–95
  death of, 463–64
  Jones's son and, 458
  at Jones's wedding, 216
  Keeler and, 165, 295
  at U.S. Open of 1922, 165, 167, 168, 170
  at U.S. Open of 1923, 185, 200, 201, 203, 205
Malone, John, 121, 215
Malone, Mamie, 121, 215
Malone, Mary Rice, *see* Jones, Mary Malone
Mann, Willie, 5, 15, 26
Man o' War, 182
Marshall, George, 449
Marshall, Thomas Riley, 116
Marston, Max, 207, 220, 423
Martin, Dickie, 113, 115
Marx Brothers, 239
Massachusetts State Amateur Championship,
    43, 64
Massy, Arnaud, 146
Masters Tournament, 37, 341, 455–56, 457, 459,
    462, 467, 473, 474, 476
Mata Hari, 88–89
Matthew, Sidney, 148
Meador, Frank, Jr., 19, 20, 23
Medinah Country Club, 9
Mehlhorn, William "Wild Bill," x, 167, 213,
    214, 259, 270, 271, 272, 288, 390
Melville, Herman, 75
Mencken, H. L., 238, 317
Merion Cricket Club:
  U.S. Amateur of 1916 at, 48, 63–64, 66–77,
    83, 85, 104, 132
  U.S. Amateur of 1924 at, 207, 217–21, 223
  U.S. Amateur of 1930 at, 314, 411, 412, *414*,
    420–21, 443–44
Minikahda Country Club:
  U.S. Amateur of 1927 at, 282, 295–304, 437
  U.S. Open of 1916 at, 59, 60–61, 76, 110,
    207, 295, 410
Mitchell, Abe, ix, 259, 260, 287

PHOTO CREDITS